G 2951 LEME

# All the Same
# The Words
# Don't Go Away

**Essays on Authors,
Heroes, Aesthetics, and
Stage Adaptations from
the Russian Tradition**

Caryl
Emerson

STUDIES IN RUSSIAN AND SLAVIC | ARS ROSSIKA
LITERATURES, CULTURES AND HISTORY

Series Editor: Lazar Fleishman | Series Editor: *David Bethea*
(Stanford Universtity) | (University of Wisconsin — Madison
 | and Oxford University)

ACADEMIC
STUDIES
PRESS

# All the Same The Words Don't Go Away

Essays on Authors,
Heroes, Aesthetics, and
Stage Adaptations from
the Russian Tradition

Caryl
Emerson

Boston
2011

Library of Congress Cataloging-in-Publication Data

Emerson, Caryl.
All the same the words don't go away : essays on authors, heroes,
aesthetics, and stage adaptations from the Russian tradition / Caryl
Emerson.
p. cm. -- (Studies in Russian and Slavic literatures, cultures and
history)
Includes bibliographical references and index.
ISBN 978-1-934843-81-9 (hardback)
1. Russian literature--History and criticism. 2. Russian
literature--Adaptations--History and criticism. I. Title.
PG2951.E46 2011
891.709--dc22
          2010047494

ISBN 978-1-934843-81-9 (hardback)

Book design by Ivan Grave
On the cover: Saskia Ozols Eubanks, *St. Isaac's Cathedral After the Storm*. Oil on Panel, 2010
(a fragment).

Published by Academic Studies Press in 2011
28 Montfern Avenue
Brighton, MA 02135, USA
press@academicstudiespress.com
www.academicstudiespress.com

*For Sophia*
(Wisdom)

# CONTENTS

Preface . . . . . . . . . . . . . . . . . . . . . . . . . . . . . xi

Great Art Should Slow Us Down: "Participative Thinking" in the World
and as the World of Caryl Emerson. *By David Bethea* . . . . . . . . . . xiii

## I   ON MIKHAIL BAKHTIN
### (Dialogue, Carnival, the Bakhtin Wars)

1. Polyphony and the Carnivalesque: Introducing the Terms . . . . . . 3
   Polyphony, Dialogism, Dostoevsky (1997) . . . . . . . . . . . . . 3
   Carnival: Open-Ended Bodies and Anachronistic Histories (1997) . . . . . 30

2. The Early Philosophical Essays . . . . . . . . . . . . . . . . . 42
   Bakhtin at 100: Looking Back at the Very Early Years (1995) . . . . . . . 42

3. Coming to Terms with Carnival . . . . . . . . . . . . . . . . . 53
   Coming to Terms with Bakhtin's Carnival: Ancient, Modern,
   sub Specie Aeternitatis (2002) . . . . . . . . . . . . . . . . . . 53

4. Gasparov and Bakhtin . . . . . . . . . . . . . . . . . . . . . 74
   Twenty-Five Years Later: Gasparov on Bakhtin (2006) . . . . . . . . . 74

## II   ON THE MASTER WORKERS
### (Pushkin, Dostoevsky, Tolstoy)

5. Four Pushkin Biographies . . . . . . . . . . . . . . . . . . . 99
   Our Everything (2004) . . . . . . . . . . . . . . . . . . . . . 99

6. Pushkin's Tatiana . . . . . . . . . . . . . . . . . . . . . . . 132
   Tatiana (1995) . . . . . . . . . . . . . . . . . . . . . . . . 133
   Postscript to "Tatiana":
   the Reaction from Tambovsk, Pskov, Novosibirsk (1997) . . . . . . . . 154

7. Pushkin's Boris Godunov . . . . . . . . . . . . . . . . . . . . . . 162

Boris Godunov: Tragedy, Comedy, Carnival,
and History on Stage (2006) . . . . . . . . . . . . . . . . . . . . 163

Postscript on Pushkin's Boris Godunov (2010) . . . . . . . . . . 189

8. George Steiner on Tolstoy or Dostoevsky . . . . . . . . . . . . . 192

Tolstoy and Dostoevsky: Seductions of the Old Criticism (1994) . . . . . . 192

9. Tolstoy and Dostoevsky on Evil-Doing . . . . . . . . . . . . . 215

Dostoevsky versus Tolstoy on Evil-Doers
and the Art of the Novel (2001) . . . . . . . . . . . . . . . . . . 215

Postscript to "Tolstoy and Dostoevsky on Evil-Doing" (2010) . . . . . . . 222

10. Kundera on Not Liking Dostoevsky . . . . . . . . . . . . . . . 223

Milan Kundera on Not Liking Dostoevsky (2002) . . . . . . . . . 223

11. Parini on Tolstoy, with a Postscript on Tolstoy, Shakespeare,
and the Performing Arts . . . . . . . . . . . . . . . . . . . . . . 235

Review of Jay Parini's The Last Station:
A Novel of Tolstoy's Last Year (1990) . . . . . . . . . . . . . . . 235

Postscript to Parini and Hoffman, 2010:
Some Thoughts on Tolstoy in the Performance Mode,
with a Digression on Tolstoy and Shakespeare (2010) . . . . . . . . . . 240

12. Chekhov and the Annas . . . . . . . . . . . . . . . . . . . . . 249

Chekhov and the Annas (1997) . . . . . . . . . . . . . . . . . . 249


III MUSICALIZING THE LITERARY CLASSICS
(Musorgsky, Tchaikovsky, Shostakovich, Prokofiev)

13. Foreword to Richard Taruskin's Essays on Musorgsky . . . . . . . . 263

Excerpts from the Foreword to Richard Taruskin,
Musorgsky: Eight Essays and an Epilogue (1993) . . . . . . . . . . 263

14. From "Boris Godunov" to "Khovanshchina" . . . . . . . . . . . 269

Musorgsky's Libretti on Historical Themes:
From the Two Borises to Khovanshchina (1988) . . . . . . . . . . 269

15. Tumanov on Maria Olenina-d'Alheim . . . . . . . . . . . . . . 301

Review of Alexander Tumanov's
The Life and Artistry of Maria Olenina-d'Alheim (2002) . . . . . . . . 299

16. Tchaikovsky's Tatiana . . . . . . . . . . . . . . . . . . . . . . 304

Tchaikovsky's Tatiana (1997) . . . . . . . . . . . . . . . . . . . 304

Tchaikovsky's Eugene Onegin: the Women and their Worlds (2001) . . . . . 308

17. Little Operas to Pushkin's Little Tragedies . . . . . . . . . . . . 313

Little Tragedies, Little Operas (2003) . . . . . . . . . . . . . . . 313

18. Playbill to Prokofiev's "War and Peace" at the Met . . . . . . . . . 337

The Endurance of War, the Deceptions of Peace:
Prokofiev's Operatic Masterpiece (2002) . . . . . . . . . . . . . 337

19. Shostakovich's "Lady Macbeth of Mtsensk" . . . . . . . . . . . 342

"Shostakovich and the Russian Literary Tradition" (2004) . . . . . . . . 342

20. Princeton University's Boris Godunov . . . . . . . . . . . . . . . 362

Editor's Introduction:
Princeton's *Boris Godunov*, 1936/2007 (2007) . . . . . . . . . . . . 363

Editor's Postscript to Actors' Testimonials (2007) . . . . . . . . . . 369

Afterword: The Fate of the Jubilee Pushkin
on the Stalinist Musical-Dramatic Stage (2007) . . . . . . . . . . . 372

21. "Eugene Onegin" on the Stalinist Stage . . . . . . . . . . . . . 378

Sigizmund Krzhizhanovsky (1887–1950)
Bio-bibliographical sketch (2010) . . . . . . . . . . . . . . . . . . . 379

The Krzhizhanovsky-Prokofiev Collaboration on *Eugene Onegin*,
1936 (A Lesser-Known Casualty of the Pushkin Death Jubilee) (2008) . . . 391


In Conclusion . . . . . . . . . . . . . . . . . . . . . . . . . . . 416

Index . . . . . . . . . . . . . . . . . . . . . . . . . . . . . 418

# PREFACE

The articles, reviews, and excerpts from monographs gathered together in this book are drawn from twenty-five years of activity in the field. Such a winnowing is always instructive for the author, for it reveals a contour of interests that is often obscured as we tack from topic to topic. This tacking — which in retrospect becomes our "academic career" — responds in part to inner intellectual prompts but just as often to outside accident. Such accidents include a chance commission to read or to review another's work; a passionate if not professional avocation (in my case, singing); the research interests of a respected professor in graduate school (Michael Holquist's invitation to me, a clueless Ph.D. candidate fed up with the abstract cunning of French structuralism, to co-translate some essays on the history and theory of the novel by a just deceased and little known Russian thinker, Mikhail Bakhtin, in 1975); a buried archival document uncovered and shared by a generous colleague (how I happened upon Krzhizhanovsky in 2007, through Simon Morrison's work on Prokofiev). A trickier problem than this "view from within" is how to organize one's work from without, so it might prove useful and coherent to others while remaining open-ended.

To that end the material here has been arranged in three parts. First comes Bakhtin, my enduring critical inspiration; then the three great 19th century master workers who have been constant companions: Pushkin, Dostoevsky, and Tolstoy. The third part is devoted to "musicalized" classics. There my attention has shifted from nineteenth-century "native" opera (most stubbornly *Boris Godunov*, from the dissertation onward) to twentieth-century experimental stage works and, recently, to musically enhanced drama and the challenge of performed, as opposed to silently privately consumed, verbal art. All entries have been excerpted and lightly edited for this edition, provided with headnotes, and several have substantial "postscripts." With the exception of occasional corrections in the footnotes, the reprinted entries have not been updated to reflect more recent thoughts or publications — which would have been to risk wholesale rewriting. Two pieces were written for this volume: one on Tolstoy and Shakespeare (the fruit of this Tolstoy Centennial Year) and another on the focus of my recent research, Sigizmund Krzhizhanovsky. Overall I was astonished to discover how stable — or perhaps how crimped — my interests and aesthetic priorities have been over this past quarter-century, and how persistent are the patterns I detect in widely disparate cultural material. Whether this is the good news or the bad is difficult to say.

The title of this collection is double-voiced. The fact that "words don't go away" pays tribute to two happy accidents. First is my fascination with literary personality in danger of losing its depth, thoughtfulness and privacy to the immediacy of a "moving set" — to melody, harmony, rhythm, external gesture — and how such flattening-out can be, and has been, averted. Second is the fact that up to now in the humanities, the scholarly medium for a discussion of synthesizing artworks has remained the narrated word rather than visual, spatial, or musical expression. A dance, a mime, a portrait, a piece of sculpture, a sequence or pattern of projected lights, a soundtrack or interweave of melodic themes are all wonderfully rich signifying systems capable of precise communication, but they are far more difficult to master and to mount than a book of essays. So far, mainstream debates in aesthetics, even as regards technical aspects, remain mired in the realm of the word. And that means: having talked my way in to these fabulous multi-mediated worlds, I can still talk my way out.

Deep thanks are due to the editors and staff of Academic Studies Press (Lazar Fleishman, Igor Nemirovsky, Kira Nemirovsky, Sara Libby Robinson and Sharona Vedol) for encouraging me to compile this book and then expertly seeing it through; to David Bethea for providing an Introduction that startled me with its generous dialogic refinement of my often inchoate intent (including his inadvertent tribute to the book's dedicatee); to Ivan Eubanks for his programming, proofing, and indexing skills; to Saskia Ozols Eubanks, who painted St. Isaac's dome for the dust jacket and to Ivan Grave who incorporated it into the brocade of his cover design; and to my family, especially my husband Ivan Zaknic, for their apparently endless patience with my apparently unfinalizable projects. Fellowships from the Guggenheim Foundation and the American Council of Learned Societies funded my exploratory work on Krzhizhanovsky in 2009–10; it was around the edges of that huge project that the collection of essays here gradually coalesced. This volume is dedicated to my grandniece and goddaughter Sophia Budny, born in October 2009, to whom words have not yet come — much less gone away — in hopes that the book as such will still be a recognizable artifact in her time.

*Caryl Emerson*
November 2010

# GREAT ART SHOULD SLOW US DOWN: "PARTICIPATIVE THINKING" IN THE WORLD AND AS THE WORLD OF CARYL EMERSON

## David Bethea

"The words won't go away." Would it were that simple. Perhaps they don't just go away, in the sense that they are still being written and that they are out there, somewhere, circulating. But do they stick any longer? That is the question. Is the circulating a fruitless spinning, the rainbow top we get on our macs when something is hung up and the electronic gears can't seem to mesh with the other side? Or is it a way, as we go about our lives and search for meaning, to send a message in a bottle to the future — one that we hope will be read? It is of course both, hence the double-voicedness in the title. It is not only that other art forms, more performance-based and typically visually arresting, are crowding out the verbal in dialogues about aesthetics: the taut yet graceful balletic body that coils and extends through musical prompt; the cutting and juxtaposing of moving images that creates story in film; the all-the-world's-a-stage of the theater, where the footlights seem magically to propel the talking and gesturing and orchestrated activity on one side of the invisible divide through to the other side; and the song, now slimming down to chatter-like recitative or fattening out to full-blown aria, that is acted out of the opera. How can words on a page compete any longer with the synaesthetic sensory bombardment of these and other like modes? How can they be read and absorbed against the counterveiling pressures of ever greater speed and the glibness of the sound-bite?

Well, they can't, except in one essential way, which is also why they won't go away. They are the carriers of ideas. Not ideas as Wikipedia entries, chunks of freely edited semantic material, but ideas as intellectual duets, or better, elaborate dance routines where different bodies and spirits touch in unanticipated places and learn about each other, trying to keep the movement going in an innerly synchronized direction, a direction that takes in enough of the past and present to anticipate the future. Ideas that impart not only new information, which in and of itself can be sterile, but information *plus energy*, which in this new and enhanced configuration has been deeply and irresistibly eroticized. And by eroticized I do not mean determined by sexual motifs and traces. Rather I mean suffused with a kind of mental life force that is necessary for our species' survival. It is this version of ideas for which Caryl Emerson was born. They are her trademark, her special brand.

In the remarks to follow I do my best not to write hagiography, which on the one hand is bound to make the subject uncomfortable, and on the other does not do justice to the intellectual substance of her many achievements. What I attempt to do instead is make some generalizations about how CE's approach to ideas works and then apply those overarching comments to her more specific areas of interest and expertise: 1) Bakhtinian thought as internalized worldview and as something more than postmodern situational ethics and aesthetics; 2) the way the classics of Russia's literary Golden Age (Pushkin, Dostoevsky, Tolstoy, Chekhov) still speak to us today, but very much from within their specific "voice zones"; and 3) the issues raised by artistic "transposition" (a specific term CE uses to describe rendering the product of one art form/mode, say Pushkin's Shakespearean historical tragedy *Boris Godunov*, into another, say Musorgsky's opera of the same name), especially with regard to how a verbal artifact undergoes change as it enters musically or theatrically aestheticized space.

I begin with an example from Vladimir Solov'ev, a thinker (moral philosopher) congenial both to Bakhtin and to CE. Just as CE claims that her subject "lived by ideas,"[1] so too, I hope to show, does CE. In his remarkable article on Darwin entitled "Beauty in Nature" [Krasota v prirode, 1889], Solov'ev discusses different examples of beauty and ugliness in the natural world against the background of *On the Origin of Species* (1859). A diamond is beautiful in his reading because it brings two elements together and transforms, or transfigures [*preobrazhaet*], them into a third:

> The beauty of a diamond, which is in no way inherent in its material substance (as that matter is precisely the same thing as we would find in an ugly piece of coal), depends, apparently, on the play of light rays on its facets. . . . This means that the beauty, which belongs neither to the material body of the diamond, nor to the light ray refracted in it, is the product of

---

[1] When citing from Caryl Emerson's essays in the present volume I will give the title of the chapter and the page number: "The Early Philosophical Essays," 52.

both of them in their interaction [*v ikh vzaimodeistvii*]. The play of light, retained and transformed by that body, covers over completely the latter's crudely material appearance, and while the dark matter of the carbon is present here, as it is in the coal, it is so only in the form of a bearer of another, luminescent origin, which reveals in this play of colors its proper content. . . . In this unmerged and undivided [Solov'ev's signature *nesliiannyi i nerazdel'nyi* — DMB] union of matter and light both preserve their natures, neither one nor the other is visible alone, but rather there is visible a single light-bearing matter and a single incarnated light — enlightened coal and a stone rainbow.[2]

Note that for Solov'ev it is not the rock per se or the light per se, but what grows out of the one being suffused by the other into a third, that catches his attention. The matter and the light "mutually penetrate each other [*vzaimno pronikaiut drug druga*] in a kind of ideal balance."[3] This ideal-balance aspect, neither static nor outside time/history, is the essential ingredient in Solov'ev's three-part thinking; it serves the "Sophianic" role of revealing how the separate parts, through their emergent form and function, elide to produce, as it were, "enlightened matter." In the realm of ethics Solov'ev calls this love; in the realm of aesthetics, beauty; in the realm of ideas, truth. In another example that fully acknowledges Darwin's magnificent achievement but departs from the naturalist on aesthetic grounds (Darwin was also enraptured by the beauty in nature, but over the years came to believe that beauty had no connection to a higher intelligence), Solov'ev argues that the nightingale's song[4] cannot be explained exclusively from origins: yes, there is a utilitarian impulse (mating) that coexists in the material result, but there is also the recognition that *the biological need is transformed along the way into something of genuine aesthetic value*, and that thing of beauty can and should be distinguished from a tomcat's caterwauling from a rooftop. The one is the love song *that the female chooses*, the other the sound of the sexual impulse in all its naked desperation. In this respect the philosopher will not allow something of natural beauty to be flattened out into the sex drive; he recognizes that drive as a starting point, but he refuses to rely on it as an explanation of the thing in and of itself. An explanation from

---

2    V. S. Solov'ev, *Filosofiia iskusstva i literaturnaia kritika* (Moscow: Iskusstvo, 1991), 37–38.

3    Ibid.

4    By analyzing the parts-to-whole ensemble of the *solov'inaia pesnia* Solov'ev, as much a poet as a philosopher, could be punning on his own name.

origins is not the same as an explanation from ontological fact, from what the thing, in and of itself, is now: "The question '*What is* a known object?' never corresponds to the question '*From what* or whence *came* this object?'"[5] There is something in that integrating third element that cannot be fully illuminated by establishing where it came from. Its growth, evolution, in time and space makes of it something more than the urge to be born or to be fed. That's why Solov'ev himself was constantly hovering between Sophia as the material world in its current realization and Sophia as that same world in its future potential. She is *both/and*.

With this aside we can now circle back to CE's unique role as scholarly interlocutor (in Russian, *sobesednik*) and thinker. The clamp here is gender: Solov'ev's Sophia is a female principle (there can be exceptions) and CE's way of entering a dialogue partakes of that same principle. I would even go so far as to say that it, that principle as CE has practiced it, is "wise" in the way Solov'ev imagined. How can one make such a claim? First, because CE is an intellectual facilitator (an "in-between" consciousness) of the highest order. Her verbal incarnation is the response: "the only thing that can make us whole is a response,"[6] she repeats after Bakhtin in her piece on his early philosophical essays. As a personality in words she relates to others' ideas in such a way as to make those ideas come alive and, in the process, morph into unexpected "thirds." She is not afraid to serve an idea because it is the idea, not the individual carrier, that matters most (Bakhtin's so-called impersonality and his indifference to individual fate). As she wrestles with Bakhtin's original use of polyphony in the Dostoevsky book she both points out the ideational nexus giving birth to the term (the Russian Silver Age) and provides ample space to those critics (Kariakin[7]) who argue, often persuasively, that creating *hero-ideas* who are on equal speaking terms not only with each other but their author seems to ignore important aspects of authorial design, including the shaping of beginnings and ends (Bakhtin was a "middle"-obsessed thinker), the internalized logic behind the fates of individual heroes, the plots (Bakhtin was also not plot-oriented) that appear to lead in certain directions for certain reasons. She takes the "material" of Bakhtin's idea (polyphony), shines the light of other's objections on that material, and as a result comes up with the "diamond" of why polyphony

---

[5]   Solov'ev, *Filosofiia iskusstva*, 46.

[6]   "The Early Philosophical Essays," 46.

[7]   See discussion in "Polyphony and the Carnivalesque: Introducing the Terms," 7–8.

is still necessary to understand a great author's poetics and how it can still work in spite of what we know.

> Bakhtin was fascinated with scientistic models. He had come to maturity in an era fascinated by numerical manipulation and classification: series, sets, groups, the emergence of sociology as a profession. Numbers lent themselves to grids and structures. And much like Wittgenstein at a slightly later time, Bakhtin was concerned to preserve the principle of relationalism without endorsing system-based structuralism (and why indeed should relationships, to be valid, organize themselves into a system?).[8]

This is a really brilliant move for the reason that it takes us to an entirely different "third" that is based on Bakhtin and his critics but is a step further and, I would argue, a step into the future, that is, a step that opens things up beyond us. The dialogism and polyphony of Bakhtin's starting point are attempts, in a post-Einsteinian universe, to preserve the integrity of the relational—the "answerability" of the I-thou relationship—in a context where everything could become, and for many has now become, purely relative, as in purely situational, ephemeral, fungible. I would add only that Sophia is somewhere in this focus on the relational as opposed to the relative.

The perfect balance that Solov'ev looked for in worldly Sophianic incarnations comes through in CE's writings as a keen simultaneous awareness of how the ethical and the aesthetic, having shed any idealistic residue, combine not as essences but as productive tensions, parts striving to be, but never actually becoming, wholes. In terms of style and substance, CE is an indefatigable intellectual cross trainer. Translations from one language to another, one thought system to another, one historical context to another, that are elegant, precise, painstakingly nuanced. Beauty that focuses on the future more than the past, that is "assigned" [*zadan*] and not "given" [*dan*],[9] that works on itself and builds off its imperfections and mistakes more than it rhapsodizes about perfect physical bodies or symmetrical form—fruit whose fate, despite its captivating presence/present, is to become ripe, overripe, and then to fall. CE's different discussions of Bakhtinian carnival is a good example of this homeostatic tension. First, she explains why carnival has been such a fertile concept for the academic left over the previous half

---

8    Ibid., 27.
9    "The Early Philosophical Essays," 46.

century, inspiring inter alia Paris 1968, British postcolonial theory, Latin American literary practice, and continental and American feminist thought. "Carnival space," "holiday time," "rejuvenating laughter," and the "grotesque body" come together to produce a heady brew that "requires no special effort" to affirm.[10] So here again we see CE, in between Bakhtin and his western acolytes, moving in to set the record straight: with one leg amputated and no stranger to pain and infirmity (his chronic osteomyelitis), Bakhtin was anything but carnivalesque and fixated on the "lower bodily stratum" in his personal behavior; he had to defend his dissertation (the Rabelais book) at home against charges of "ideological depravity" and, yes, as he explained at the defense, he understood that he had dehistoricized the French writer and overstated the medieval worldview (which was already becoming infected by renaissance values) by boiling it down into essentialized binaries (official vs. unofficial culture, common people vs. privileged classes, public square vs. private space, etc.).[11]

But it is not only the what of Bakhtin's revolutionary understanding of carnival, including its exaggerations and oversimplifications, that interests CE, although she is as historically accurate as possible in laying out his positions. Equally if not more important is the why, for here is where the dialogue opens again and creates another third. Bakhtin was aware of what he was doing, but more than writing scholarship (cf. the divide between philology and philosophy, Mikhail Gasparov and Bakhtin, that is the subject of another of CE's essays) he was writing the life of ideas, trying "to catch existence in the process of becoming,"[12] and in this instance overstatements were necessary to punch out his points. Laughter has to be "fearless"—an attitude relevant not only to Rabelais's time, but to Bakhtin's as well. To be sure, "Bakhtin functions more as a mythographer than as a literary scholar and social historian. Perhaps mythography suited Bakhtin's intent."[13] As long as we call things by their right names and take a responsible position in between, we can remain true to Bakhtin's post-Kantian answerability imperative. For Bakhtin as well as for CE, "meaning must always *grow*."[14] There is no fear of overheated talking cures

---

10    "Polyphony and the Carnivalesque: Introducing the Terms," 31–32.
11    See discussion in ibid., 31–38.
12    Cited ibid., 36.
13    Ibid., 38.
14    "Coming to Terms with Carnival," 60.

or of professors enamored with the sound of their own voices because the interlocutor is listening to the other, "signing" for his actions.

> Our cognitive and creative forces are fueled not by reflections but by answerability, that is, by interaction between different, only temporarily consummated selves. . . . In his [Bakhtin's] understanding, our psyches are constructed to be curious about difference, not hostile to it or frightened by it. What marks "true love experience," then, is nothing necessarily erotic or possessive — and certainly nothing neurotic or compulsive — but rather a cognitive quality, a concentration of attention that enriches the beloved over time with extraordinary individuated responses.[15]

This same attitude and angle of vision apply to those CE calls the "master workers," the classics of Russian literature's Golden Age. Lest the reader forget, the scholarly industries surrounding these figures are truly massive, yet CE, through decades of hard work and an appetite for learning and absorbing others' thoughts that is seemingly inexhaustible, has made herself at home in this welter of primary and secondary sources. Even when engaging the most poetic of writers, Alexander Pushkin, CE finds new and heuristically challenging ways to open closed structures and reground the artist's (and human being's) urge to transcendence. The poet's Tatiana may be a muse figure or a "standing wave"[16] of beautifully untapped potential; she may also be something the hero Onegin *dreams* in order to prod him back to life and change from his overdetermined Byronic role-playing. This latter reading is certainly provocative, and CE knows it. In the spirit of dialogic fair play, much like her inclusion of Bakhtin critics in her pieces on polyphony and carnival, CE goes on in a postscript to cite the horrified Russian response to her assault on the Tatiana cult, which she presented as nothing more than a hypothesis. Maybe there was something in her presentation that seemed flippant, not sufficiently respectful (Russians, and not only Russians, have been falling in love with the Tatiana of chapter eight from the beginning), too comfortable with the democratic play of ideas. On the other hand, to call CE's argument a product of the "idle trivialized consciousness of the West,"[17] as the offended Tambov professor does, is a gross misrepresentation, which needs to be rebutted, and which CE calmly rebuts. Elsewhere she

---

15   "The Early Philosophical Essays," 50.
16   "Pushkin's Tatiana," 142.
17   Ibid., 155.

demonstrates with exemplary close readings how Chekhov's different "Annas" (from the stories "A Calamity" [Neschast'e], "Anna Round the Neck" [Anna na shee], and "Lady with a Pet Dog" [Dama s sobachkoi]) take the potential fate of their Tolstoyan namesake into prosaic post-affair territory: what does it mean if we avoid the suicidal grand gesture and continue to live out our messy, mistake-ridden, yet still *answerable* lives.

> Chekhov, so great a master at the malleable and the tender in human relations, opens Tolstoy's novel up to new confusions and compassions. Konstantin Levin might not have been so lucky. Anna's terrible denouement might be avoided. There will be a price, of course, for doing so, for suicide is an elegant one-way gesture and splendid closure; but that too is part of Chekhov's re-novelization [Bakhtin's concept — DMB]. Chekhov and Tolstoy had different ideas about closing things down.[18]

There are moments in CE's studies of the classics that are such crystal clear distillations of her way of thinking and being and are at the same time such gems of vigorous scholarly recuperation transformed into abiding insight that one has to hope they will take their place among the future highlights of the tradition (if there is a tradition). In an earlier article not included in this collection ("'The Queen of Spades' and the Open End"),[19] CE comes at Pushkin's famous problematic text in a novel (in various senses) way. Structuralist commentators and New Critic types have been attempting for years to find *the key* to this tale about gambling through numerological code-cracking and ingenious word and root play (paronomasia). Why does Germann choose the wrong card, the queen instead of the intended ace? Guilt, fantastic intrusion of a revenant, verisimilar powder that causes cards to stick together? In effect, suggests CE, the critics are searching for the secret that will unlock the magic box of the story just as the hero Germann is searching for the three cards that will win him his fortune at faro. But the true gambler, the one who takes risks and doesn't try at every turn to hedge his bets, works with *pieces of codes*, hunches about this combination or that combination. The true gambler will take a chance on love (Liza) and not use the other in a cunning game to get at the countess and her supposed secret. Although Pushkin was a poet (and gambler!) to

---

18    "Chekhov and the Annas," 252.

19    Caryl Emerson, "'The Queen of Spades' and the Open End," in *Puškin Today*, ed. David M. Bethea (Bloomington: Indiana University Press, 1993), 31–37.

his bones, this reading seems much closer to what he was striving for in his story (and in his life-art relations) and for that reason deserves a robust life now and in the future. It is not the tidy closedness of the elegant structuralist reading, nor is it the complete openness of an anything-goes indeterminacy; it is that relational in-between that we sense is a striving in the right direction.

Another perfect pitch moment of "participative thinking" [*uchastnoe myshlenie*],[20] where one senses strongly both CE's voice zone and the felt reality of her interlocutor, involves drawing the notion of evil in Dostoevsky and Tolstoy through the prism of J. M. Coetzee's novel *Elizabeth Costello*. Here again, the ability to pose the questions in this way, with this stunning cast of characters and their mental worlds understood so deeply and broadly, is uniquely CE's:

> Where Dostoevsky and Tolstoy would agree is that great art should slow us down. It should take up time and make us think. Both would insist that the cooption of art by the marketplace, by the corporate values of speed, power, consumerism, instant gratification and instant depletion leading to more consumption, is an obscenity and a disaster. To adjust art to the historyless pace and corporate values of commercial life in hopes of making it "relevant" is to eviscerate it. Art cannot turn back the clock, of course, but it must provide an alternative to the clocks that happen to be ticking today, together with their limited understanding of life. All art (and especially art of the great novel) is time intensive; it does not come ready-made, it is a striving. For all their different routes to this truth, both Dostoevsky and Tolstoy would agree that human beings are not built to benefit from immediate pleasures, cognitive or physical. What we need is the sense that the universe contains values or truths that must be searched for.[21]

Powerful words, essential words, words that express the cognitive tough love that CE practices as she tries to bring her readers into alignment with a world once inhabited, and hopefully still inhabited, by giants like Dostoevsky and Tolstoy.

CE's final broad area of interest involves the conceptual and aesthetic challenges related to adapting literary texts to other art forms. This interest

---

20 The term goes back to Bakhtin's early writings. See discussion in "The Early Philosophical Essays," 45.

21 "Tolstoy and Dostoevsky on Evil-Doing," 221.

began three decades ago with her first book[22] and the historiography (Karamzin's *History of the Russian State*)/historical drama (Pushkin's *Boris Godunov*)/opera (Musorgsky's *Boris Godunov*) axis. In recent decades it has exploded to encompass theater as well as opera. Among the figures and works engaged by CE in the essays collected here are Tchaikovsky (Pushkin's *Eugene Onegin*), Dargomyzhshky (Pushkin's *Stone Guest*), Rimsky-Korsakov (Pushkin's *Mozart and Salieri*), Cui (Pushkin's *A Feast in Time of Plague*), Rachmaninoff (Pushkin's *The Covetous Knight*), Prokofiev/Krzhizhanovsky (Pushkin's *Eugene Onegin*), Meyerhold/Prokofiev (Pushkin's *Boris Godunov*), Shostakovich (Leskov's *Lady Macbeth of the Mtsensk District*). Even when the originary text is historical and not strictly literary, as in Musorgsky's *Khovanshchina*, there is still the question of authenticity, versimilitude. "How," asks CE, "does one embed a historical event in artistic form so that the product is both true to history and true to art?"[23]

These essays that bring together CE's comparative expertises as literature, music, and theater scholar are some of the most intellectually daring ever undertaken by an American humanities professor, much less a Slavist or Russianist. CE's ability to mediate among discourses and to eschew the precious without dumbing down or slipping into generality is breath-taking. We see this vividly in "Little Tragedies, Little Operas," where the *kuchkisty* (the members of the Balakirev Circle or the "Mighty Handful"/ *Moguchaia kuchka*: Milii Balakirev, Modest Musorgsky, Alexander Borodin, Nikolai Rimsky-Korsakov, Cesar Cui) take up the challenge of composing operas whose libretti are true to the words of Pushkin's Little Tragedies. This radical (as in anti-conservatory) orthodoxy can backfire, however, when fidelity to one form creates a sense of rigidity and ploddingness in the other. Transposition is precisely that: not a literal translation from one form/genre/ mode to another (impossible), but a "positing over," a "placing again" that captures the essence, the spirit, of the one and resituates it in the other.

> Their [the *kuchkists*' — DMB] opponenets in the Turgenev-Tchaikovsky camp, also worshipers of Pushkin, were not persuaded by these efforts. To them, this clarion call to "be true to the source text" was worse than misplaced fidelity; it was mistaken identity, a failure to understand

---

22    Caryl Emerson, *Boris Godunov: Transpositions of a Russian Theme* (Bloomington: Indiana UP, 1986).
23    "From 'Boris Godunov' to 'Khovanshchina'," 284.

fundamental rules of musical genre and the musician's role in creating a synthetic work of art. If a play or any other complex literary narrative "goes into music" without resistance and without adjustment, it could only suggest that the original was imperfect or inadequate, in need of a supplement. An "accurate" musical hybrid would not be homage to Pushkin, but quite the opposite.[24]

Likewise, in the conceptually adventuresome *Khovanshchina* piece CE demonstrates how Musorgsky by this stage of his career had evolved away from his understanding of historical time in his two *Boris*'s and moved toward something in this unfinished masterwork much more baffling for the contemporary viewer to appreciate: the *Endzeit* of the Old Believers. There is still a versimilitude of sorts, but it does not equate to being unconditionally faithful to historical character (the different Old Believer-inspired revolts during the late seventeenth century are here telescoped and intermixed), to historical language (archaisms surface when phrases from documents are cited or certain characters speak, but other than that the language is contemporary to that of the audience), or to historical music (the native folksongs or church-style chants do not actually reflect seventeenth-century harmonies or musical forms). The verisimilitude that matters in the opera is, again, somewhere *between history and art* (what is true to both but can't be expressed wholly in one mode or the other): the idea that the Old Believers "have given up this world" and that their function "is to *stop time*."[25] This obviously changes the way we process the roles of characters like Marfa and Dosifei. These latter aren't simply representatives of a murky obscurantism being satirized by the populist and progressive Musorgsky (the standard Soviet take); rather they are witness to a terrifying world, presumably one the composer is now attempting to embody in all seriousness, whose inhabitants "are eternally alert, but ... can hear or desire nothing new."[26]

In this third category (artistic transposition) of CE's many remarkable achievements two stand out as exceptional and as worthy examples, if not of closure (*zamknutost'*, which really does not exist either in Bakhtin's or in CE's worlds), then of momentary completion (*zavershenie*, or a positive topping-off).[27] The first is her intense involvement with the premiering of

---

24   "Little Operas to Pushkin's Little Tragedies," 320.
25   "From 'Boris Godunov' to 'Khovanshchina'," 291.
26   Ibid., 297.
27   See "Polyphony and the Carnivalesque: Introducing the Terms," 39.

a "concept": Princeton's April 2007 production of the uncensored original 1825 version of Pushkin's *Boris Godunov*. The event was termed a "concept" and not a revival or restoration precisely because nothing about this play had ever been completed as originally planned. In this version, for starters, the work had twenty-five scenes, not twenty-two, and Pushkin called it a *komediia* [comedy], which changes a great deal. By the same token, the 1937 attempt to stage this *Boris*, at the height of the Stalinist purges, with the brilliant Meyerhold feverishly rehearsing and the recently repatriated Prokofiev providing a score, had remained, for obvious dark historical reasons, unfinished. A perfect event for Bakhtinian loopholes, backward glances and dialogues that refuse to close down! That this massive undertaking involved the close and complex collaboration of faculty, student actors, and various campus units; that news of it attracted major media attention, with performances selling out; and that the production itself, with its set design featuring illuminated "bungee cords" (what the actors did with this refashioned surgical tubing as they were speaking their lines reflected their emotions and moved the plot along), was powerfully innovative — all this speaks to the degree to which CE has taken her interest in living ideas out into our century's version of the public square. To read the testimonials and exuberant post-mortems by the student actors, who were themselves caught up in the quest for authenticity and whether finding ingenious ways to change costume or possessing the stage presence to adapt to the unforseen entered energetically into this fanciful modernist "reconstruction" of what had never before been performed, there emerges the definite sense that high culture can still be stunningly alive, that it need not be brought low to be brought out.

Last but not least is CE's current restoration project involving the "ethnically Polish, Ukrainian-born Russophone prosewriter-playwright Sigizmund Krzhizhanovsky (1887–1950)."[28] The multi-faceted, long neglected Krzhizhanovsky seems tailor-made as a career-capping focus for CE. First and most obvious, Krzhizhanovsky was involved, however precariously, in another Pushkin centennial undertaking, this one a stage adaptation of *Eugene Onegin*, commissioned by Tairov's Moscow Chamber Theater, and replete with a Prokofiev score composed for the occasion. Once again CE and her Princeton colleagues and students will try, this time

---

[28]   "Princeton University's *Boris Godunov*," 376.

in February 2012, to bring to life what Stalin, his cultural commissars, and — truth be told — the Pushkin purists thought should be permanently put to sleep. The conceptual issues surrounding this transposition will be as challenging, if not more so, than those raised by the 2007 *Boris* production. In bringing Pushkin's novel-in-verse to stage, for example, Krzhizhanovsky considered making the sorts of changes — removing the work's intrusive narrator, interlarding the action with fairytale and elegiac snippets from elsewhere in Pushkin's oeuvre, and most importantly and vividly, presenting Tatiana's pivotal wintertime dream in her own voice and from her own view — that go to the heart of the transposition process. In other words, the writer-thinker was attempting not to clone Pushkin's work but to create something on stage equivalent to it. And because so many of Krzhizhanovsky's most cherished ideas seem uncannily to hark back (presumably unconsciously) to notions of Bakhtinian dialogue, there appears to be a kind of happy homecoming to this new venturing out.

CE is finding substantial grist for her ever-active intellectual mill both in the still untranslated contents of Krzhizhanovsky's *Collected Works* (in five volumes, 2001–06), which she is duly bringing into the Anglophone orbit, as well as in her subject's Moscow archive. These writings include studies "on drama…original comedies, stage and radio-show adaptations, pantomimes, war-time libretti, feuilletons of Moscow in history and under seige, essays on theater (both as philosophy and technical craft), and interpretations of classic English repertory, especially Shakespeare and George Bernard Shaw."[29] Most telling, in this sprawling body of work, which is not new but can now be experienced as such, CE meets an array of personified ideas and viewpoints whose words, not going away, sound strangely familiar: "His [Krzhizhanovsky's] hero everywhere was the *idea* [*mysl'*] trapped in the brain. This idea, or individualized thought, has one task: to survive and grow by searching out the freest possible carrier, the person or plot that would least obstruct or obscure it on its journey."[30] We are back to the primacy of the idea (the intellectual genetic code, as it were) and the ephemerality of the carrier (provided the latter is free and able to take its cargo to new open spaces). There is even, one might say, a carnivalesque quality to this new dialogic partner: polymorphous, always shifting and evolving figuratively if not literally, unwilling or unable to play by the rules, given to construct

---

[29]  "*Eugene Onegin* on the Stalinist Stage," 378
[30]  Ibid., 379.

original thought groups around famous kindred interlocutors (Rabelais →
Shakespeare, Swift), driven by a wacky spatial poetics where sounds are
constantly being squeezed through narrow apertures to find their way out
(cf., again, Rabelais and the "lower bodily stratum"). But whereas Bakhtin
reprised a public square-space designed to produce carnivalesque inversions
to official culture, Krzhizhanovsky turns his attention to the dream-space
of the theater and to the everpresentness of performance. Meaning must
always *grow*. If there is an important difference between Bakhtin and
Krzhizhanovsky as thinkers, however, it is that the latter is in his way more
"aristocratic," more a proponent of the idea in its own right. By the same
token, he feels less obligated *to respond*.

Let us hope, then, as CE proceeds to immerse herself in the living
envelope of ideas that is Sigizmund Krzhizhanovsky, that the words don't
go away. May her dialogues with the artistically and metaphysically acute
find a new generation of readers as eager to engage with, and learn from, her
special brand of luminous answerability as we have been. Great art should
slow us down. So should the essays in this volume.

──────── I ────────

# ON MIKHAIL BAKHTIN

## Dialogue, Carnival,
## the Bakhtin Wars

1. *Polyphony and the Carnivalesque: Introducing the Terms* (1997)

2. *The Early Philosophical Essays* (1995)

3. *Coming to Terms with Carnival* (2002)

4. *Gasparov and Bakhtin* (2005)

# 1

# POLYPHONY AND THE CARNIVALESQUE: INTRODUCING THE TERMS

The First Hundred Years of Mikhail Bakhtin *(Princeton University Press, 1997) was my attempt to contextualize, for an American audience, some of the more accessible aspects of the Russian recuperation of Bakhtin. The following two excerpts, taken from chapters 3 and 4, summarize two of the most controversial ideas in the Bakhtin canon: the polyphonic novel and carnival. Each may be considered an extreme — and thus instructive — case of dialogism: one of the word, the other of the body.*

*When this centennial book was conceived in the mid-1990s, the backlash against the "cult of Bakhtin" was at its height. Since that time, the meticulous research of a handful of scholars, the editors of Bakhtin's Collected Works in Moscow and also, outside of Russia, Craig Brandist, Ken Hirschkop, Vadim Liapunov, Brian Poole and Galin Tihanov, documented Bakhtin's uncredited sources and intellectual inspirations, providing them with appropriate context. As the impatient "decrowning" phase was replaced by a more sober assessment, Bakhtin gradually moved into the category of world classic, the position he now holds in the second decade of the 21st century.*

Opening segment from chapter 3 of *The First Hundred Years of Mikhail Bakhtin*:

## POLYPHONY, DIALOGISM, DOSTOEVSKY
## (1997)

Let us recall the basic theses of Bakhtin's book on Dostoevsky. It begins with a familiar Formalist complaint: that literary scholars, dazzled by Dostoevsky's contributions to theology, moral philosophy, psychology and Russian nationalism, have failed to appreciate his even greater contribution to *literary* art. This oversight Bakhtin intends to correct — with, however, a concept of "literariness" that most Formalist critics would have found highly suspect. Whereas the Russian Formalists preferred to examine hard-edged mechanical or impersonal devices such as defamiliarization, retardation, parody, the "stringing" of events and step-wise construction in an author's literary texts, Bakhtin focuses almost entirely on a single (and decisively soft) "device": human consciousness.

In order to examine degrees of consciousness in the aesthetic realm, Dostoevsky created (or perhaps discovered) polyphony. According to Bakhtin, this idea was so radical that it caused a genuine paradigm shift, a "Copernican revolution," in the history of the novel. In the more "Ptolemaic" worldview that preceded it, an author sits at the center of things like Jehovah, passing out bits of consciousness piecemeal to the characters taking shape under the authorial pen, just enough to each person so that the cast of characters could obediently act out its predetermined roles. But Dostoevsky, Bakhtin intimates, endorsed a more "New Testament" model of authorship, one based on unresolvable paradoxes and parables rather than on certainties handed down as law. As in Christian parables, the rewards might appear unjust and the ends unclear, but the method increases the chances that both author and hero will genuinely learn from the process of defining one another. Incarnation — which is delimitation — always means increased vulnerability. When polyphonic authors "come down to earth" and address their creations not vertically but horizontally, they are designing their characters to know, potentially, as much as authors know. Such authors frequently craft a hero of whom they say: "he has to do that, but I do not know why."

To strengthen this reciprocal relation, Bakhtin claims, Dostoevsky designs as the hero of his novels not a human being destined to carry out a sequence of events — that is, not a carrier of some pre-planned "plot" — but rather an *idea-hero*, an idea that uses the hero as its carrier in order to realize its potential as an idea in the world. The goal then becomes to free up the hero from "plot," in both the sinister and humdrum sense of that word: from all those epic-like storylines that still clung to the novel with their routinized, and thus "imprisoned," outcomes, and also from events in ordinary, necessity-driven, benumbing everyday life. For events — as the biographies of both Bakhtin and Dostoevsky attest — rarely made you free. Bakhtin all but suggests that we leave this pleasant illusion to Count Leo Tolstoy (one of the few great writers against whom Bakhtin actively polemicized), an aristocrat to the manor born who loved life's delightful round of rituals, could afford to lose himself in it, developed an anguish of guilt about it, and came so powerfully to distrust language, that surrogate for action. Instead of unreliable events, Dostoevsky invites his heroes and readers to experience the richer, more open-ended discriminations and proliferations of the uttered word, in a context where all parties are designed to talk back.

To be sure, in choosing to structure works in this way, the polyphonic author is still authoring heroes and still "writing in" their stories. But by valuing, above all, an open discussion of unresolvable questions, such an author writes them into a realm of maximal freedom.

Polyphony brings further benefits. Once the grip between hero and plot is loosened, and once a dialogue of ideas (rather than a mass of improbable exotic adventures) becomes the common denominator between author, hero, and reader, more space opens up for the reader. Readers can participate actively in the narrative — which is to say, non-vicariously, on an equal plane, with the same equipment. A novel of ideas is less readily escapist or voyeuristic than other types of novels because its most exciting ingredient is thought, and there, willingly or no, we are all equal communicants. (Or as Bakhtin seems to be suggesting, no matter how crippled, constrained or impoverished our lives or bodies may be, we can all always listen in and contribute a response; in this resides Bakhtin's rough democracy.) In terms of their potential to communicate on shared ground, ideas are simply richer than experiences. Dostoevsky's working notebooks testify to his continual surprise at the turns his novels were required to take, in order to accommodate the unexpected growth in ideas that were carried — and tested verbally — by his characters.

According to Bakhtin, the polyphonic hero was Dostoevsky's first great contribution to the art of the novel. His second contribution was to a theory of language. Inside every word, Bakhtin maintained, there is a struggle for meaning, and authors can adopt various attitudes toward this struggle. They can choose to cap or muffle the dialogue, discouraging all outside responses to it, and thus employ the word *monologically*. Or they can emphasize the word's so-called "double-voicedness," by exaggerating one side (as in stylization); or by pitting two or more voices against one another while rooting for one side (as in parody); or, in a special, highly subtle category Bakhtin calls "active double-voiced words," an author can work the debates inside a word so that the parodied side does not take the abuse lying down but rather fights back, resists, tries to subvert that which is subverting it. Dostoevsky was exceptionally skilled at portraying this final, crafty type of word.

These two innovations — the "fully-weighted hero" who signifies alongside his creator, and the "dialogic word within a polyphonic design" — make up the theoretical core of the book on Dostoevsky. Bakhtin specifically declines to deal with the actions of Dostoevsky's heroes — all those scandals, rumored rapes, suicides, murders, instances of child abuse, as well as the sacramental moments of conversion and transfiguration. He also refuses to discuss the specific (and often quite unsavory) content of Dostoevsky's ideas, full of paradoxical wisdom and extravagant generosity but also no stranger to sadism, Russian chauvinism, reactionary politics and psychic cruelty. Bakhtin sticks to formal matters. "Miracle, mystery, and authority" — the three keys that will unlock the world, according to Ivan Karamazov's Grand Inquisitor — get no attention at all in Bakhtin's book on Dostoevsky.

Curiously, we do not know if this elegant formal exegesis is in fact the book that Bakhtin really wanted to write. Near the end of his life, he confessed to his close friend and disciple Sergei Bocharov that in his work on Dostoevsky he had been unable to "speak out directly about the most important questions...the philosophical questions that tormented Dostoevsky his whole life, the existence of God. In the book I was forced to prevaricate, to dodge back and forth continually. I had to hold back all the time. The moment a thought got going, I had to break it off."[1] But however Aesopian and self-censored the text might be in its two editions (1929 and 1963), Bakhtin made his peace with what had survived. Unlike Tolstoy, he was no utopian. When asked at the end of his life if the Good would triumph, he answered: "Of course, not."[2]

For Western readers, the idea of polyphony was at first simply an enigma. How can created characters "create" themselves? Does not the polyphonic author abdicate responsibility for the finished whole of a literary work? As a literary strategy, polyphony was conflated with dialogism, heteroglossia, voice-zones, chronotopic analysis — all those now-fashionable catchwords that Bakhtin had devised only later, in the 1930s, to apply to novels in general, not to the prior (and much more restricted) subset of polyphonic novels. But then there appeared on the scene, in Russia and in the West, critics of polyphony and of its later offspring, "dialogism" — who did not like them at all. Not for themselves, not as metaphors for human freedom, and not as insights into the workings of Dostoevsky's novelistic masterpieces.

---

[1]   S. G. Bocharov, "Ob odnom razgovore i vokrug nego," *Novoe literaturnoe obozrenie* 2 (1993): 70–89, esp. 71–72; English translation (flawed) by Stephen Blackwell, ed. Vadim Liapunov, "Conversations with Bakhtin," *PMLA* 109, no. 5 (October 1994): 1009–1024, esp. 1012.

[2]   G. Pomerants, "'Dvoinye mysli' u Dostoevskogo" [1975]. *Otkrytost' bezdne: Vstrechi s Dostoevskim* (Moscow: Rosspen, 2003), 173.

## Can polyphony exist? If so, does it apply?

The first complaints against Bakhtin's image of Dostoevsky concerned quite simply its appropriateness to its subject. Were polyphony and double-voicedness in fact part of Dostoevsky's design? Did the novelist intend the sort of openness for his plots and autonomy for his heroes that Bakhtin claims? There seems to be a strong "authority principle" in Dostoevsky — and especially in his final novel, *The Brothers Karamazov* — that pointedly resists the decentering impulse.[3] I sample here only one critic's case. In 1989, Yuri Kariakin, Dostoevsky scholar and political gadfly of Solzhenitsyn's generation, published a 600-page book entitled *Dostoevsky and the Brink of the Twenty-first Century*, in which he took his good friend Mikhail Mikhailovich gently to task.[4] Polyphony is a faulty hypothesis, Kariakin argues, because it concentrates solely on verbal dialogue and its current of ideas, tending to ignore the effect of fully-embodied scenes. (Dostoevsky was a great master at imagining the scene; and it is in this sense, we might add in support of Kariakin, that Dostoevsky is a "dramatist" — not in the trivial literal sense that his novels can be reduced or adapted to stage or screen, which has proved a far riskier enterprise.) Words come and go, taking pleasure in their own eloquence and ambiguities. But Kariakin insists that in his major scenes, Dostoevsky always included a silent "finger pointing at the truth." The "double-voiced word" [*dvugolosoe slovo*], which Bakhtin recommends as an interpretive unit for the novel, should thus be replaced by a "triple-voiced word" [*trekhgolosoe slovo*], with the word's third voice assigned permanently to Dostoevsky as author and, in this special moral sense, stage director. For Bakhtin is wrong, Kariakin contends, when he suggests that self-consciousness is the hero of Dostoevsky's novels. Self-deception is the hero — and all that polyphonic obfuscation, those thought experiments and the endless proliferation of alternatives, all those compulsive story-tellers and chatterers, are designed by their author not to provide the major heroes with invigorating, open-ended options but rather to thicken and

---

3   For the classic Russian argument, see V. E. Vetlovskaia, *Poetika romana "Brat'ia Karamazovy"* (Leningrad: Nauka, 1977); for a pioneering attempt to use Bakhtin as an aid in interpreting that novel's structures of faith and authority, see Nina Perlina, *Varieties of Poetic Utterance: Quotation in The Brothers Karamazov* (Lanham, MD: University Press of America, 1985).

4   Yuri Kariakin, *Dostoevskii i kanun XXI veka* (Moscow: Sovetskii pisatel', 1989), 649. The "triple-voiced word" is discussed on pp. 26–30; the case against consciousness and for self-deception as the "hero" of Dostoevsky's novels on pp. 69–72.

darken the texture of the work, to increase the obstacles and to test the heroes on their conflicted way to the truth.[5]

Kariakin's reservations on the structural plane are one type of complaint against polyphony. Other skeptical readers have applied the acid test to which every strong critic must submit, namely: are the feelings and reactions we experience when reading Bakhtin on Dostoevsky at all compatible with our feelings upon reading Dostoevsky himself?[6] At issue here are not merely morally repugnant plots or themes. In *Problems of Dostoevsky's Poetics*, we repeat, Bakhtin deliberately excluded considerations of ethical content, limiting himself to the workings of language. He remained consistently formalist in his reluctance to pass judgment on the ideology and virtue of Dostoevsky's plots. But remarkably, given its focus on the word, Bakhtin's book also does not address any ethical or metaphysical problems in the formal realm of language. Consider, for example, his treatment of *Notes from Underground*. The Underground, where consciousness is everything and where words never stick to deeds, is a deconstructor's paradise by postmodernist criteria. As we know, Dostoevsky considered it a wholly godless place; he intended its chatter to be read not simply as misguided or futile but as demonic, and he lays bare its dynamics with ice-cold satire.[7] Bakhtin does acknowledge that "underground" discourse is dead-ended, a *perpetuum mobile* and vicious circle. But ultimately that grim voided place represents for him a fundamentally positive principle, even if taken in this instance to unfortunate extreme: the virtue of "unfinalizability." For the logic of the Underground guarantees all speakers who reside there the right to postpone the final verdict — and to deliver a supplementary word on themselves that others do not, and in principle cannot, know.

---

5    For a more comprehensive discussion of *Dostoevsky and the Brink of the 21st Century* and the reservations it raises about Bakhtin's reading of the novelist, see Caryl Emerson, "The Kariakin Phenomenon," *Common Knowledge* 5, no. 1 (Spring 1996): 161–78, esp. 166–69, 173–75.

6    For two preliminary surveys, see Caryl Emerson, "Problems of Baxtin's Poetics," *Slavic and East European Journal* 32, no. 4 (Winter 1988): 503–25; and Caryl Emerson, "Word and Image in Dostoevsky's Worlds: Robert Louis Jackson on Readings That Bakhtin Could Not Do," in *Freedom and Responsibility in Russian Literature: Essays in Honor of Robert Louis Jackson*, eds. Elizabeth Cheresh Allen and Gary Saul Morson (Evanston: Northwestern University Press and Yale Center for International and Area Studies, 1995), 245–65.

7    The best account of the ideology of *Notes from Underground* remains that by Joseph Frank, in ch. 21 of his *Dostoevsky: The Stir of Liberation, 1860–65* (Princeton: Princeton University Press, 1986), 310–37. In a lengthy footnote (p. 346), Frank notes his reservations about Bakhtin.

The Underground viewed not as trap but as "aperture" is only one peculiarity of reading Dostoevsky through a Bakhtinian lens. Other critics have noted that Bakhtin's passion for the horizontally-cast dialogic word often comes at the expense of Dostoevsky's more vertical gestures, those leaps into iconic or transfigured time-space that provide the great novels with their crowning moments of personal conversion or collective Apocalypse.[8] Bakhtin has little sense of the sublime. With equal fastidiousness he avoids absolute bliss and absolute horror. He never mentions Dostoevsky's quasi-fictionalized prison memoirs *Notes from the House of the Dead*, for example, nor does he make reference to that gallery of tortured and silenced children that are so crucial a part of Dostoevsky's symbolic universe. Part of the problem, surely, is that those silenced victims cannot, or do not, talk (although they can be talked about); and left solely with the ugly, silent material aftermath of a violent event — a corpse, a suicide, an atrocity that leaves us speechless — Bakhtin as a reader of Dostoevsky's world seems somewhat at a loss. What is strange here, we should note, is not Bakhtin's unwillingness to be mired down (as so many have been) in Dostoevsky's cruel, crowd-pleasing gothic plots; such plots, after all, were the conventional and thus almost invisible raw material of the nineteenth-century urban novel. More significant is the fact that Bakhtin also has almost nothing to say about the centrally important, affirmative, "godly" dialogues — if they happen to be wordless. Among these crucial mute scenes are Raskolnikov and Sonya on the banks of the Siberian river in the Epilogue of *Crime and Punishment*; Prince Myshkin's meaningless babble as he embraces a silent Rogozhin over Nastasya Filippovna's corpse at the end of *The Idiot*; and — most famously — Christ kissing the Grand Inquisitor after having listened, in silence, to that brilliant monologic harangue.[9] In Bakhtin's readings, it seems, only the interaction of one verbal utterance with another verbal utterance can be adequate to the most subtle and multilayered communication. By definition, this interaction opens up new potentials. The possibility that verbal dialogue might actually drain away

---

[8]   See, for example, David M. Bethea, *The Shape of the Apocalypse in Modern Russian Fiction* (Princeton: Princeton University Press, 1989), esp. "*The Idiot*: Historicism Arrives at the Station," 103–04; and Malcolm V. Jones, *Dostoyevsky after Bakhtin: Readings in Dostoevsky's Fantastic Realism* (Cambridge: Cambridge University Press, 1990).

[9]   Bakhtin did make these suggestive jottings late in life, however, in a passage devoted to Dostoevsky: "The unuttered truth in Dostoevsky (Christ's kiss). The problem of silence. Irony as a special kind of substitute for silence." See "From Notes Made in 1970–71," in *Speech Genres and Other Late Essays*, eds. Caryl Emerson and Michael Holquist, trans. Vern W. McGee (Austin: University of Texas Press, 1986), 148. Henceforth *SpG 86*.

value, or flatten out a subtlety, or be so subject to terror and constraint that it depreciates into outright fraud, is not for Bakhtin a theoretically serious issue. On principle, he seems reluctant to project a human being so evil, weak, indifferent or exhausted that he or she can no longer listen to, or author, a useful word.

Let us now move into even more critical and suspicious corners of the Bakhtin industry. On the occasion of the thirtieth anniversary of *Problems of Dostoevsky's Poetics*, the editorial board of the Belarus Bakhtin journal *Dialog. Karnaval. Khronotop* distributed questionnaires to two dozen eminent scholars, soliciting their opinions on the role of the book and its author in the history of Russian thought. Returns began to appear in 1994.[10] Although the proper jubilee praises were sung, several of the scholars polled were clearly irritated at Bakhtin's single-minded pursuit of polyphony in every corner and at any cost. Polyphony was judged inadequate to Dostoevsky's complexity not only for the old reason — that the voice of the author must always be firmer and more primary than that of the created heroes — but for newly legitimated religious reasons as well. As one contributor put the issue bluntly, "the authoritativeness of the author's word...relies on the authority of Christian truths, whose conscious transmitter and preacher Dostoevsky was" (7–8). Unlike the uglier ideologies of the modern period, we are told, religious faith "could not be a monologism." Georgii Fridlender pursued the Christian line further. He classified the Dostoevsky book alongside works by Vyacheslav Ivanov and Nicolas Berdiaev as a prime text in Russian Orthodox "personalism" (14) — although he added that Bakhtin was perhaps too marked by the binary oppositions fashionable in his era, which lent his work a structural elegance but also a certain rigidity. By so stubbornly insisting on polyphony, "Bakhtin, paradoxical as it seems, was extremely monologic and didactic" (15). The genre theorist Vladimir Zakharov was least accommodating of all. Bakhtin "wanted to think freely in a totalitarian society" and yet was destined to work out his major ideas in resistance to Stalinist oppression. Under those conditions, Bakhtin came up with some brilliant formulations — but whatever he did not wish to think about, no matter how central to literary scholarship (Zakharov has in mind his own area of research, the Dostoevskian narrator), he simply ignored. "Without this resistance [to Stalinism], however, he would scarcely have

---

10  "Anketa «DKKh»," *Dialog. Karnival. Khronotop* 1 (1994): 5–15. Page references given in text. Henceforth this Bakhtin journal will be referenced in notes as *DKKh* + volume # and year.

been so original a philosopher.... May the Bakhtinians not be offended by what I say," Zakharov concluded, "but in many respects, Bakhtin already belongs to history" (9).

Zakharov's verdict, although addressed to a local forum of specialists, cannot be wholly dismissed. At the Bakhtin Centennial Conference in 1995, not a single paper, by Russians or non-Russians, was devoted exclusively to Bakhtin on Dostoevsky. This did not seem to distress his followers. Many defended Bakhtin's admittedly lopsided reading of the great novelist as simply "illustrative" of something more important — the way Freud, say, had used the literary image of Oedipus to illustrate his powerful hypotheses about the human psyche. Thus, it was felt, Bakhtin should not be subject to potshots from literary specialists. His book had become a classic of criticism, wedded to his personality, and Bakhtin (like any grounded personality) sees certain things as central, other things as peripheral. The precepts of his book had long been considered as magisterial, as grandfatherly and uncontroversial as, say, those of Wayne Booth, Warren and Wellek, Northrop Frye or Frank Kermode.

But let us push the critique further. For there is a group of critics, in Russia and in the West, who find Bakhtin's whole model of polyphony not only untrue to Dostoevsky's primary intentions as a novelist and a thinker, but also inconsistent and somewhat dishonest on its own terms — for psychological and linguistic reasons as well as for ethical ones. These critics are developing an argument that was made forcefully a decade ago by Aaron Fogel, in a fine book on Joseph Conrad entitled *Coercion to Speak*.[11] Fogel's point — which overlaps with Leo Tolstoy's — is that dialogue, as Bakhtin invokes it, is not the normal human relation at all. Most human speech, Fogel argues, is forced, awkward, or under constraint. Although dialogue, when it does occur, can at times be a blessing and a relief, the task of making it happen between two people is difficult, dangerous, and (here is the scary, non-Bakhtinian part) often made worse when we try, against all odds and against the interests of the participants, to "talk things out." Conrad was master of this truth. However Bakhtin might package it, Fogel argues, clearly much of the time, for a large number of human problems, dialogue is not a "talking cure."

---

[11]   Aaron Fogel, *Coercion to Speak: Conrad's Poetics of Dialogue* (Cambridge, MA: Harvard University Press, 1985).

## Unsympathetic case studies and suspicious close readings

In 1994, a postmodernist work of literary criticism was published in St. Petersburg titled *Anti-Bakhtin, or the Best Book about Vladimir Nabokov*.[12] Overall the book is impulsive and derivative (we quoted from it briefly in Chapter One, as exemplary of the crasser sides of the Bakhtin backlash) but its author, Vadim Linetsky, does remark tellingly upon one vulnerable area in a dialogic poetics. Linetsky protests that Bakhtin, in his essay "Discourse in the Novel," "reacts rather skeptically to dialogue in the traditional understanding of the word." By "traditional" Linetsky appears to mean all those situations where people simply talk back and forth in good faith — in order to exchange information, give one another cues, reveal their immediate desires, clarify one another's intentions, in short, try to tell the truth as each party understands it at that moment — and thereby resolve, sooner or later, on a course of real action. Linetsky observes that Bakhtin considers such ordinary, practical verbal exchanges to be rather flat and monologic, dismissing them as conceptually trivial and restricting their role to a "compositional" or merely "plot-related" function in the work. Bakhtin does so, Linetsky suggests, because he does not really value practical real-life distance between one person and another — even though all genuinely embodied dialogic exchange must be based on it. Distance is a prerequisite for the effective working of all addressed words, codes, controls and social hierarchies, however; real distance is required for any "materialization of power" in real life. Without a good intuitive sense of these parameters, none of us would ever open our mouths. And, we might add — as an old-fashioned gloss to Linetsky's faintly postmodernist casting of this problem in terms of power — this distance between one person and another is also what enables independence, privacy, and genuine acts of giving, just as it makes inevitable both human loneliness and longing.

Linetsky's reservation could be expanded. As we shall see in Chapter Five, Bakhtin builds both his ethics and his aesthetics around the virtues of "outsideness." But one suspects that Bakhtin would prefer us to be not wholly outside, not all that distant from each other: we should hover around a shared boundary, different but not *that* different, curious about others but not threatened by them, speaking not (of course) the very same language but *enough* the same language so as to insure that others hear us and incline

---

[12]  Vadim Linetskii, *"Anti-Bakhtin" — Luchshaia kniga o Vladimire Nabokove* (Sankt-Peterburg: tipografiia im. Kotliakova, 1994), 84–85.

toward us. Or, as Bakhtin put the matter with disarming simplicity near the end of his life, "the more demarcation the better, but benevolent demarcation, without border disputes."[13] This scenario is indeed inspirational: boundaries between people are to multiply, and yet all lethal disputes are to wither away. But the dynamics here apply to only a tiny fraction of the heroes in Dostoevsky's novels — and not, I wager, to the ones who excite us and strike us as the most deeply human, the ones whose maniacal inner workings we would expect a literary critic to elucidate. Further: these trapped maniacal heroes, more often than not, do not thirst after any fancy double-voiced dialogism, which can create for them only more doubts and confounding options. From within their own unhappy unstable worlds, these heroes simply want to believe in something. They crave to be understood, and they want to be loved.

An unsettling critique of Bakhtin's image of Dostoevsky can indeed be mounted along these lines. One place to ground it would be in Bakhtin's earliest philosophical writings, where he addresses the difference between *ethical* and *aesthetic* terrain in a work of art.[14] An event becomes "aesthetic," in Bakhtin's world, if there is an outside consciousness looking in on the event and embracing it, able to bestow upon the scenario a sense of the "whole." Such an external (and thus aesthetic) position is available to spectators watching, to readers reading, and to an author "shaping." But from within the artwork, that is, from the perspective of the created character who is undergoing a particular pleasure or torment, events are of course experienced as partial, unshaped, cognitively open, ethically irreversible, as matters not of art but of life and death. The hero — or at least the hero in a realistic novel, always Bakhtin's genre of choice — does not feel his own life to be a fiction. Let us apply this early distinction to some scenarios from the Dostoevsky book. It will help us glimpse the mechanism by which Bakhtin, working with such often desperate texts, arrives at his dialogic optimism.

Take, for example, death. Bakhtin turned to the topic often in his writings, and usually in a spirit of benevolent gratitude: death is aesthetic closure, that point where creative memory can begin, the best means for

---

13    "From Notes Made in 1970–71," in *SpG 86*, 137.

14    See the opening segments of "The Problem of the Author's Relationship to the Hero" and "The Spatial Form of the Hero": Mikhail Bakhtin, "Author and Hero in Aesthetic Activity," in *Art and Answerability: Early Philosophical Essays by M. M. Bakhtin*, eds. Michael Holquist and Vadim Liapunov, trans. Vadim Liapunov (Austin: University of Texas Press, 1990), 4–16; 31–46; 73–75.

making a gift of my whole self to another. As one Polish scholar has summed up this position, Bakhtin devised not a neo- but a "post-humanistic vision of man": if neohumanism takes the individual personality as its reckoning point and thus regrets its passing, Bakhtin, with his insistence that an "I" comes to exist only on the border between itself and someone else, provides us with a model of death that is neither an insult to consciousness nor a blessing to it but, as an event, simply irrelevant. Only that which exists *in itself* can die.[15] Thus the grimmer aspects of death — its abyss of silence, non-negotiability, unanswerability, aloneness — that so terrified other Russian writer-philosophers (say, Leo Tolstoy, to whose anxieties Bakhtin seems singularly immune) appear to have persuaded Bakhtin that the whole procedure, being so wordless and so unavailable to my own dying consciousness (*my* death can exist only for others, not for me), is not worth taking seriously.

This elegant resolution of the problem of our mortality — again recalling the Hellenistic philosophers — was graciously bestowed by Bakhtin on his own hero and scholarly subject, Dostoevsky. In his 1961 notes for the revision of *Problems of Dostoevsky's Poetics*, Bakhtin remarks that death hardly signifies at all for the great polyphonic novelist. In support of this claim and in contrast to Tolstoy, he points to the fact that "Dostoevsky never depicts death from within [the dying person];" death is an event solely for another, as yet living consciousness, and thus it "finalizes nothing" in the larger realm of the spirit. And why, indeed, should we fear extinction if, as Bakhtin put the matter movingly: "Personality does not die. Death is a departure.... The person has departed, having spoken his word, but the word itself remains in the open-ended dialogue.... Organic death, that is, the death of the body, did not interest Dostoevsky."[16]

Perhaps it did not. But, one might object, surely the death of the body interests Dostoevsky's *characters*. And death obsesses precisely those characters who reside in the novels that Bakhtin skirts most widely: the totally ignored *Notes from the House of the Dead*; the novel *Devils*, with its brutal arbitrary murders and its travestied Nativity scene (the mother and "illegitimate" son of Shatov's beloved family, who die almost as

---

[15] Dr. J. Wizinska, "Post-humanistic Vision of Man in the Philosophy of M. Bakhtin," in *Yazyk i tekst: Ontologiia i refleksiia* [Proceedings from a Conference on philosophy and culture held in St. Petersburg, 17–21 1992] (Sankt Peterburg: Eidos, 1992), 320–22.

[16] "Toward a Reworking of the Dostoevsky Book," in *Problems of Dostoevsky's Poetics*, ed. and trans. Caryl Emerson (Minneapolis: University of Minnesota Press, 1984), 290, 300. Henceforth *PDP*.

an afterthought in the wake of his murder); *The Idiot*, with its horrifying incoherence over Nastasya Filippovna's dead body in the final scene; and Dostoevsky's harrowing deathside monologue "*Krotkaia*" [The Meek One], which unfolds — which could only unfold — over a corpse. In fact, the only death-story that Bakhtin reads in any fullness is the tiny throwaway tale "Bobok," a menippean satire about obscene graveyard conversations carried on by the dead who refuse to die or fall silent. Bakhtin's less sympathetic critics see something disturbing in this pattern of omissions. Is the man so committed to unfinalizable dialogue, to the good we can do others if only we remain outside them and talking to them, that he is indifferent to the physical and ethical world as experienced by Dostoevsky's heroes, to its innerness and breaking points? For surely Dostoevsky, as author, did not intend his absorbed and captivated readers to react to the crisis-laden plots of his novels with bland hope or benign resignation, relegating those ultimate life-and-death questions to some ephemeral dialogue-in-the-sky; he was counting on horror. Some epiphanic vision or shock of revelation must precede a conversion. The unfinalizability is only in Bakhtin.

Death, then, is similar to aesthetic wholeness in that it, too, is the product of a dialogic situation. It also requires an outsider, or a *socium*, to bestow it. In Bakhtin's exegesis, this bestowal is simply not felt as murder. In fact, Bakhtin is as curiously untroubled by dying as he is by the possibility that outsideness will turn alien or hostile — although the best students of Dostoevsky routinely have found those two anxieties central. Gary Saul Morson, for one, has argued cogently that for Dostoevsky, an astute student of the fundamentally *social* vices, the state of being "external to" and in social relation put one at great moral risk.[17] As the novels demonstrate, we are indeed indispensable to one another — but for reasons that give no cause for rejoicing. Sociality is scandal space, the site of voyeurism. ("In Dostoevsky's novels," Morson writes, "suffering, shame, torture and death usually take place before a crowd of spectators who indulge in the quintessential social act of gaping. In Dostoevsky, the first sign of our essential sociality is that we are all voyeurs.... Nobody had a deeper sense of the social as an arena of gratuitous cruelty.") Reacting to this truth, several American scholars are now supplementing Bakhtin's "aesthetic" interpretations of Dostoevsky with darker ethical correctives that work with more than just words.

---

[17]    Gary Saul Morson, "Misanthropology," *New Literary History* 27, no. 1 (Winter 1996): 57–72, esp. 62, 71.

Among the thinkers most usefully invoked is Emmanuel Levinas and his philosophy of human obligation arising from eye-to-eye contact with a living, suffering — even if wholly silent — face.[18]

Must a Dostoevskian "idea-person" be at core a *talking* person? Most critics who are unsympathetic to Bakhtin are made uneasy by this question. Consider Raskolnikov. Words come out of his mouth — but what might well be taking place at such moments is not a response to another but a lunatic inner monologue that has been (for lack of genuine empathy, interest, or lived experience on Raskolnikov's part) simply embellished and exacerbated by other people's utterances. For the most powerful instinct in Raskolnikov, considered as a human being and not just as a repository for words or ideas, is always to stop talking with "real others" as soon as possible, to detach the words uttered by those others from the experience or the truth that had given rise to them in their own contexts, and to start using those words to rewrite the world according to his own prior and fixed notions of it. Dostoevsky, by all the indices we have, was acutely aware of this dynamic — and he might have intended his gifted but appallingly self-absorbed Raskolnikov to be perceived, if anything, as monologic because of it. After all, Raskolnikov was created after the Underground Man and is a refinement upon his type. Unlike that earlier, more overtly grotesque and thus far less threatening image, however, Raskolnikov has high intelligence, beauty, boldness, the ability to act. But he shares with his predecessor an inability to listen.

Among those who might have agreed with this hypothesis is the eminent literary scholar and Bakhtin's slightly younger contemporary, Lydia Ginzburg. One of Russia's best readers of Proust, Herzen and Tolstoy, Ginzburg was drawn to explicate literary worlds that were as hospitable to the Tolstoyan hero as Bakhtin's world was structured to wall that type of hero out. Central to the Tolstoyan world was the concept of "conversation"

---

18  See Leslie Johnson, "The Face of the Other in *Idiot*," *Slavic Review* 50, no. 4 (Winter 1991): 867–78; and Val Vinokurov's trenchant critique and expansion from a Levinasian perspective in his "Dostoevsky's Deaths: Towards a Post-Bakhtinian Reading of *Demons*" [unpubl. ms., 1996]. Vinokurov writes of Myshkin: "The Prince is simply profligate toward the face, and thus unable to live with the politics, the agony and violence of choosing between faces that justice demands when I and the other are not alone in the world. His departure is Christ's failure on earth. Leslie Johnson is too ready to fill in the blank of Dostoevsky's doubts by insisting so wholeheartedly on Myshkin's potential. The world does not fail Myshkin. The world <u>cannot fail</u>. Only the individual can fail against the resistance of the world. He can also, unlike Myshkin, succeed."

[*razgovor*], an uncomfortable, stressed, easily embarrassed form, rarely honest or articulate in its adult social manifestations and driven by impulses (vanity, lust, ambition) far more raw than pure ideas. Ginzburg is not sympathetic to Bakhtin's notion that Dostoevsky's characters, being "idea-persons" in pursuit of higher concepts, are thereby less selfish. "Tolstoy discovered the first principles of shared spiritual experience as it relates to the contemporary person, and this person is not even aware that he conceives of himself in Tolstoyan terms, that in fact he has no other choice," she writes in her 1960s book *On Psychological Prose*. "To be sure, this character finds it more *interesting* to conceive of himself in Dostoevskian terms, since doing so allows him to focus attention on himself."[19] Ginzburg and other non-Bakhtinians would see polyphony as a rapid, profound, and profoundly selfish internalization of relationships — a removal of human relations from the realm of responsible outer actions (or *inter*-actions) because that space involves commitment to unpredictable or unmanageable Others, into the safer realm of inner words and domesticated verbal images of the other. For a reciprocal act of communication is brought about not merely by thinking of another, nor by carrying on a mental conversation with another at one's own leisure and convenience.

Bakhtin suggests that polyphony in a novel serves to put the unfinalizable idea on trial. But in ethical life, an *un*finalized thing cannot be tested or put on trial. Trials follow completed deeds; they have verdicts, sentences, punishments. People are acquitted, locked up, shot. In benign contrast to the real courtroom trial, ideas in inner dialogue always have loopholes and a chance to be re-uttered. Bakhtin, it is true, intends the comparison between Dostoevsky's novel and polyphony as "a graphic analogy, nothing more" (*PDP*, 22). But the term polyphony, which Bakhtin often employs alongside another musical metaphor, "counterpoint," is surely meant to evoke, at a minimum, the image (or sonority) of a multiply harmonized texture composed of discrete, interwoven strands, receptive and inviting to others. As we have seen, skeptics would sooner call it a soliloquy of the isolated, narcissistic self. Furthermore, it is a soliloquy that, by its very dynamics and the doors it shuts behind itself, beckons

---

[19]    Lydia Ginzburg, *On Psychological Prose*, trans. and ed. Judson Rosengrant (Princeton: Princeton University Press, 1991), 243. Translation somewhat adjusted. It seems plausible that this somewhat arch retort is Ginzburg's response to Bakhtin's remark, in *Problems of Dostoevsky's Poetics*, that "all of Dostoevsky's major characters, as people of an idea, are absolutely unselfish, insofar as the idea has really taken control of the deepest core of their personality" (*PDP*, 87).

the speaker toward violence and murder. The revisionists insist that Dostoevsky, who was not at all naive about the difficulties of honest dialogue, would concur. What Dostoevsky was parodying, Bakhtin took for authentic coin.

According to the revisionist critics, then, such polyphonic manipulation of ethical choice — rendering it reversible and always "inner" — cannot be the major mechanism at work in Dostoevsky's novels. It cannot, because Dostoevsky is himself a discriminating moralist who arranges matters in his fiction so that major heroes are run not by ideas, as Bakhtin claims, but by *doubt*. These heroes do not wish to be polyphonically "free" of ultimate commitment. Rather the opposite is true: they want desperately to believe, and they cannot. They examine options in order to be rid of them, to move forward into the deed, not merely for the pleasure of elaborating more options. About passionate desire and passionate doubt — the predominant fuel of real, elusive, needful people, who change over time — Bakhtin, in the opinion of these critics, hasn't a clue.

Is this critique just? Again, it depends — quite literally — upon one's point of view. For what Vadim Linetsky, Yuri Kariakin, Lidia Ginzburg, and others who take Bakhtin seriously but with a severely critical eye have done in their analyses of polyphony is to consider a given experience or event in Dostoevsky's texts not "externally" — as a reader, philosopher, scholarly critic — but from the simple trapped perspective of the created hero, whose freestanding interests Bakhtin claims to champion. The method has merit, I might add, because ordinary untutored readers of novels (the audience for whom Dostoevsky actually wrote) identify in this way instinctively; it is one of the great pleasures of the genre. Put yourself in the hero's place. The first thing you will insist upon is that consciousness alone does not make a biography. My plot, after all, is my life. I do not want to be liberated from it. And least of all do I wish to be liberated by an author who values only my verbal residue and my trail of coherent ideas, not my decisions, unspeakable losses and irreversible events. Dialogic communication, if it aspires to an ethical position, must mean more than simply "Leave me alone to think about what you just said."

The non-Bakhtinians insist that Dostoevsky was fully aware of the solipsism in any "dialogue of ideas" that only pretends to fulfill a communicative function. For true dialogue is measured by many criteria — precision of expression, proper timing, impact on the listener, subsequent modification of behavior — and makes use of various instruments, of which words are only one. (In 1996, one practicing psychotherapist in the New Russia concluded an essay on Bakhtin and family counseling with a section whose title was surely inspired by Christ's response to the Grand Inquisitor: "Silence as the heights of dialogue."[20]) No reader would dispute that novelistic worlds must be reached *through* words; the novel is a verbal form. But once we are inside that world, arguably the real power of the genre is in the interpersonal space, the scene called forth, the entire complex that we (along with the characters) see and feel, not only what we hear, speak and think. Therefore these critics do not agree with Bakhtin when he states, in a passage written just prior to revising the Dostoevsky book, that "language and the word are almost everything in human life."[21] They sympathize, rather, with Alexei Kirillov, the monomaniacal, weirdly inarticulate nihilist in Dostoevsky's *The Devils* and one of that novel's few attractive, kindly and honest figures, when he says to his would-be murderer in the final conversation before his suicide: "All my life, I did not want it to be *only words*. This is why I lived, because I kept on not wanting it. And now, too, every day, I want it *not to be words*."[22]

Curiously, some centennial rethinkings of Bakhtin's Dostoevsky book endorse this polemic against logos-centric dialogism — but in an effort to redeem, rather than to undermine, Bakhtin's interpretation of Dostoevsky. In a 1995 paper, the Moscow philosopher Natalia Bonetskaia defended Bakhtin's second edition, and particularly its massive menippean satire insert, as a belated discovery on Bakhtin's part that the 1929 study was indeed inadequate to the darker sides of his subject.[23] The rosy, sentimental-Romantic view of reciprocal dialogue that governs the 1929 original version was simply too partial a picture to be allowed to stand, she argues; Bakhtin eventually wanted to "get at more than merely the poetics" (30). He felt

---

20   T. A. Florenskaia, "Slovo i molchanie v dialoge," *DKKh* 1 (1996): 49–62, esp. "Molchanie kak vershina dialoga," 60–62. Remarking on the unexpected ability of therapists to sense quickly the sort of language that will penetrate the most recalcitrant subject and have an effect, she then notes that dialogue requires not verbal language per se but only an act in which one's "dominant orientation is toward the interlocutor;" only under conditions of "the most intimate spiritual closeness" is silence between two people, "understanding without words," possible.

21   "The Problem of the Text in Linguistics, Philology, and the Human Sciences: An Experiment in Philosophical Analysis" [1959–61] in *SpG 86*, 118.

22   Fyodor Dostoevsky, *Demons*, trans. Richard Pevear and Larissa Volokhonsky (New York: Knopf, 1995), Part Three, II ("A Toilsome Night"), 615.

23   N. K. Bonetskaia, "K sopostavleniiu dvukh redaktsii knigi M. Bakhtina o Dostoevskom," *Bakhtinskie chteniia*, vyp. I, Materialy Mezhdunarodnoi nauchnoi konferentsii, Vitebsk, 3–6 July 1995 (Vitebsk, Belarus: 1996).

obliged to address the real pathos and perverse intonation of Dostoevsky's world. And what, Bonetskaia asked, could be more hysterical, chaotic, hellish, anti-dialogic than the spirit of carnival? If dialogue is "personality, reason, freedom, the realm of meanings, the light of consciousness and perhaps of Logos," then carnival is the existential void, the appearance of Dionysian chaos, a darkening of reason and the triumph of the elemental unconscious, "the night of human nature" (28). As shall become clear in the following chapter, such a reading — although ingeniously motivating the move from the first to second edition of the Dostoevsky book — requires a demonic view of carnival that Bakhtin's own demonstrably passionate attachment to the concept very poorly accommodates.

Can a balance on dialogue be achieved between the Bakhtin idolaters and the demolitionists? By judging Bakhtin's account of Dostoevsky negligent in this matter of responsible relationships with real others in real time, the anti-Bakhtinians raise substantial questions about the ethical center of his entire enterprise. Does dialogism affirm self and other, or efface both sides? Scholars at work on Bakhtin's Silver Age context have hinted at links between his thought and Solovievian and Symbolist experiments of the Russian Decadent period — which were, after all, not that distant from the young Bakhtin in Petrograd. Leading poets of the pre-war period were experimenting with non-consummated marriage, homoerotic utopias, metaphysical equivalents of family, and extravagant projects for transcending death. Under the influence of Platonic philosophy, they advertised a wide variety of self-absorbed, autonomous, sterile structures for intimate love.[24] Can it be said that Bakhtin's self-other paradigms belong to that company?

Let us turn to Bakhtin's own self-evaluation. In 1961, he summed up Dostoevsky's major innovations in the art of the novel with the following three postulates.[25] First, Dostoevsky is credited with structuring a "new image of a human being that is not finalized by anything (not even death)" — to which Bakhtin adds, with his characteristically inspirational stoicism, that such a human image is unfinalizable because "its meaning cannot be resolved or abolished by reality (to kill does not mean to refute)." Second, Bakhtin claims that Dostoevsky devised a way to represent,

---

[24]   For an excellent discussion, see Olga Matich, "The Symbolist Meaning of Love: Theory and Practice," in *Creating Life: The Aesthetic Utopia of Russian Modernism*, eds. Irina Paperno and Joan Delaney Grossman (Stanford: Stanford University Press, 1994), 24–50.

[25]   "Toward a Reworking of the Dostoevsky Book [1961]," in *PDP*, 184.

through words, the "self-developing idea, inseparable from personality." And third, Bakhtin honors Dostoevsky as the writer who discovered dialogue "as a special form of interaction among autonomous and equally signifying consciousnesses." How much of this three-part assessment is still intact?

The first and third "discoveries" have come under sustained attack. The most articulate opponents of Bakhtin today argue that Dostoevsky did indeed believe that "to kill was to refute" — and to neglect the importance of all the killing that goes on in his novels is simply to misread the novels. They have also argued that interaction within those novelistic worlds does not take place among "autonomous and equally signifying" voices: it takes place between mortal bodies. And the interaction there is either deadly political and manifestly unequal, as when Raskolnikov murders an old woman with an axe and Pyotr Verkhovensky stalks Kirillov with a gun, or — if we are dealing with polyphonic dialogue rather than with murder — the interaction, more often than not, is narcissistic, isolating, and indifferent to the real world (to death in the first instance, but also to any vulnerability or desire coming from, or directed toward, a needful other). Dostoevsky saw this misuse of language and parodied it. He was far more attuned to the healing effects of non-verbal communication — silence, icons, genuflections, visual images — than he was to the alleged beneficent effect of words. And thus, as regards the second achievement credited by Bakhtin to Dostoevsky, the "self-developing idea" fused to personality and freed from the distractions and humiliating constraints of plot: this has seemed to many readers more a recipe for monologue than for dialogue. I have my idea, you have yours, and we will feed them to each other without listening to each other until each of our ideas has ripened and the novel is over.

This critique has been taken — unjustly but provocatively — to an even more sinister extreme by one group of Russian postmodernists, the Conceptualists. They see something suspicious and evasive in the obsession with "dialogue" and "naming" that marks so many Russian philosophers, in whose ranks they now enroll Bakhtin.[26] In theory, they say, Bakhtin

---

[26] Speaking of Dostoevsky, the Conceptualist artist Ilya Kabakov has remarked that the incessant chatter which fills the novels does not "test an idea" at all; those endless debates succeed only in drawing in and implicating the reader to such an extent that "the thread is lost," the chains of debates grow to "monstrous length," and all parties forget what is at stake. Il'ia Kabakov, *Zhizn' mukh / Das Leben der Fliegen* (Kölnischer Kunstverein, n. d.), 128.

might have believed that "to exist [authentically] means to communicate dialogically," but in practice this dialogic utopia ends up as a "neurosis of incessant talk" that pretends to provide options for real people trapped in real places but in fact makes it altogether too easy and attractive for us to separate words from any ordinary real-life referents. Conceptualists claim there is a venerable Russian tradition of putting words in circulation for their own sake — and its genealogy reads like an honor roll of Russian literature. The starting point is Nikolai Gogol, whose genius created unprecedentedly palpable reality out of waxy masses of words and sounds not moored to any object. The brooding talkers and dreamers of Dostoevsky and his devoted servant Bakhtin are two intermediary steps. The proud inheritor, they insist, is Stalinist Russia. As their chronicler Mikhail Epstein has noted, the autonomy of the uttered word in Russia did not further the interests of civil liberty or freedom. Instead, it lent a sort of voodoo authenticity to fantasy constructs, including those fantasies that could inflict a great deal of public harm; "it was the hidden assumption of the Soviet system, after all, to give the status of absolute reality to its own ideological pronouncements."[27]

The psychoanalytic critic Aleksandr Etkind provides a concrete example. "Let us imagine Soviet interrogators, contemporaries of Vygotsky and Bakhtin," he writes in his 1996 collection of essays on the intellectual life of Russia's Silver Age titled *Sodom and Psyche*. "What they needed was the fact of an accused person's confession, because the other extra-verbal reality did not exist. Whether or not the accused was lying, slandering himself, doing it under threat or in order to bring an intolerable torture to an end — all that was unimportant, because something other than words was required in their account: feelings, acts, situations....In the Soviet person, there is nothing that is not expressed in words. Except for words,

---

[27] Epstein has thus argued the Conceptualist case *contra* Bakhtin, drawing on one of their prominent practitioners, Ilya Kabakov: "For Bakhtin, the dialogic relationship is the only genuine mode of human existence: addressing the other through language. For Kabakov, this obsession with dialogue bears witness to the lack of any relationship between words and a corresponding reality... Kabakov sees this inclination for verbosity as a symptom of Russia's fear of emptiness and the implicit realization of its ubiquity... For Bakhtin, to exist authentically means to communicate dialogically, which allows us to interpret Bakhtin himself as a utopian thinker seeking an ultimate transcendence of human loneliness, alienation and objectification. Kabakov advances a postmodern perspective on this dialogical utopia, revealing the illusory character of a paradise of communication..." Mikhail Epstein, "The Philosophical Implications of Russian Conceptualism," paper delivered at AAASS (Washington DC), October 1995.

nothing exists."[28] Thus do the Conceptualist critics and their ideological allies wish to destalinize Russia by fighting against the proliferation of ecstatic, indestructible, floating words and ideas, the sort of words that during the Communist period almost boasted of their independence from the world as it really was. Such words, precisely because of their immortality, are exempt from judgment and can be irresponsible, promiscuous, lie-bearing. Thus the Conceptualists build up and smash images, analyze museums and bombsites, compile lengthy treatises documenting the Life of the Housefly. Far more ethical than to work with the ever renegotiable poetic word, they argue, is to acknowledge a perishable world full of mortal, destructible, fully ordinary and thus precious events and things.

We have now come full circle. The polyphonic Bakhtin, freedom-fighter and champion of the individual voice, has become solipsistic Bakhtin, Stalinist fellow-traveler. This is surely a monstrous and untrue trajectory. We now return, as we close down this first problematic reassessment of the legacy, to a defense of Bakhtin — who remains, after all has been rethought and reargued, one of the most powerful thinkers of our century.

### "The Torments of Dialogue": in defense of Bakhtin

In a 1994 issue of *Filosofskie nauki*, to honor the upcoming centennial, the literary scholar and philosopher P. S. Gurevich published a lengthy (and rather negative) review of leading American Dostoevsky scholarship under the title *"Muki dialoga"* — the torments of dialogue.[29] He deems much Western work that draws on Bakhtin to be rather primitive, in part because it "ignores the polyphonic nature of polyphony itself" and too often endorses some monologic slice of an idea that is then allowed to regiment and dictate the whole. The polyphonic principle should not be viewed as simply one more method for analyzing artistic practices, Gurevich concludes.

───────────

[28]  Aleksandr Etkind, *Sodom i Psikheia: Ocherki intellektual'noi istorii Serebrianogo veka* (Moscow: ITs-Garant, 1996), 296.

[29]  P. S. Gurevich, "K 100-letiiu so dnia rozhdeniia M. M. Bakhtina: Muki dialoga," in *Filosofskie nauki* 4–6 (1994): 15–31. The scholars discussed are R. L. Cox [*Between Earth and Heaven: Shakespeare, Dostoevsky and the Meaning of Christian Tragedy*]; Robert Belknap [*The Structure of "The Brothers Karamazov"*]; Gary Saul Morson [*The Boundaries of Genre: Dostoevsky's "Diary of a Writer" and the Traditions of Literary Utopia*]; Joseph Frank [*Dostoevsky: The Years of Ordeal, 1850–1859*]; and Robert Louis Jackson [*The Art of Dostoevsky: Deliriums and Nocturnes*]. Further page references in text.

"Dialogue, polyphonism are passwords to a new cultural paradigm — which, with difficulty and through all the sluggishness, monologism and torments of communication, is cutting itself a path" (31). This sense of dialogue's great difficulty, the enormous pressure and precision required to carry it out honestly, is a useful preface to any understanding of Bakhtin's central concept. For the Conceptualists are wrong about Bakhtin and words. Although Bakhtin was certainly pro-language — he was, after all, a philosopher of language, that was the subject of his research — he did not share any of the transfigurational attitudes toward the word endorsed by Symbolists, avant-garde Futurists, and later by the state-sponsored Socialist Realists. He did not believe that one could subdue nature through words; he was no proponent of the theosophist doctrine that "naming could control the unknown" or that knowledge of the verbal sign permits one to manipulate reality. The sentiments underlying Andrei Bely's essay "The Magic of Words," with its invocation of a *zvukovaia taina* or a "secret to the very sound of things," were wholly foreign to Bakhtin. He steered clear of the theurgist, incantational, mystagogical or occult aspects of language, so in vogue during his youth. And of course, he had scant sympathy for the Symbolist and Futurist concept of time as millenarian, where empirical speech matters less than hieratic speech prophecy. In sum, for a Russian literary critic, Bakhtin was almost a pragmatic realist, remarkably phlegmatic about the ability of literary consciousness to transform the world. His logos-centrism, such as it was, differed profoundly from that of his contemporaries. He was ambitious for the word in another way.

Let us suspend those reservations about Bakhtin's reading of Dostoevsky, then, and consider one attempt to examine this "new cultural paradigm" at its root. In an essay published in the 1991 volume *M. M. Bakhtin and Philosophical Culture of the Twentieth Century*, Boris Egorov relates dialogism to the revolution in scientific thought preceding and following the Great War.[30] During that decade, he reminds us, the positivism, linearity and "singularity" of nineteenth-century thinking across a wide number of fields (philosophy, political economy, biology and the natural sciences) gave way to new pluralist and multi-perspectival models inspired by Einsteinian thought (15). More strictly scientific fields made this transition with remarkable speed — and, Egorov notes, Bakhtin was determined that literary consciousness not fall

---

[30]    B. F. Egorov, "Dialogizm M. M. Bakhtina na fone nauchnoi mysli 1920-kh godov," in *M. M. Bakhtin i filosofskaia kul'tura XX veka*, ed. K. G. Isupov (St. Petersburg: Obrazovanie, 1991), 1:7–16. Further page references in text.

behind. The young, intellectually precocious Bakhtin was passionate about a global coordination of paradigm shifts; a humanist, he poorly concealed his competition with the exact sciences.

Bakhtin's determination to connect the principles underlying modern physics with the principles animating human culture reflected the maximalist, unifying aspirations of Russian thought in general, to which Bakhtin was in no sense immune. Such ambitions are always alluring and always dangerous, Egorov remarks. For natural science is obliged to reckon neither with memory nor with faith — and in any event cannot afford to legitimate itself through such factors — whereas human culture (and especially culture as understood in the religious circles that Bakhtin frequented throughout the 1920s) cannot afford to ignore them. Such postulates as "universal relativity, dialogic ambivalence, the instability or transitoriness of all sensations and concepts," if moved mechanically from science into the humanities, could result in a destruction of "the very bases of human culture: the durability of traditions, ethical commandments and prohibitions, and other so-called 'eternal' categories" (15). Principles of relativity and ambivalence function differently among human beings than among particles of the universe. During a scientific revolution of such magnitude, only religious faith, with its *a priori* ideals and monologic dogma, "could offer a substantial counterweight to all the varieties of subjectivism and relativism" that would otherwise spin out of control. Bakhtin, a believer, presumed this counterweight to be in place. Religious consciousness would provide the proper discipline for dialogic relations occurring under the newly "relativized" conditions. But as Soviet history unfolded, cultural professionals in Bolshevik Russia (beginning with the atheistic formalists) were increasingly incapable of preserving, and soon even of perceiving, this anchor of Bakhtin's thought.

How might Egorov's remarks help us to modify the severe judgment on Bakhtin's polyphonic image of Dostoevsky? Linetsky and Ginzburg are wrong, I believe, when they suggest that Bakhtin does not appreciate ordinary dialogue, dialogue "in the traditional sense of the term." There is every indication that Bakhtin follows Dostoevsky in his reverence for such crystalline moments, which are awarded to innocent children, to beloved elders, and to the state of prayer. (Just such a dialogic moment descends upon Raskolnikov when, after Marmeladov's death, he asks Sonya's stepsister Polina to love him and pray for "thy servant Rodion.") If the hero of a novel functions not solely as a character acting out an uncomplicated plot function, however, but also as an *idea-person* [*ideia-*

*chelovek*, a "person born of the idea"[31] — that is, when a person is run by living concepts rather than by biology, a detective plot, or grace — then such ordinary, declamatory, preciously wonderful dialogues are extremely difficult to conduct. Such is the natural logic, or pressure, of polyphonic design. Sonya Marmeladova, almost wholly silent and rarely in control of her words, stands on the threshold between inner and outer acts. By contemplating her iconic image, Raskolnikov is driven forcibly over that threshold back into real-life communication (to confession and public trial) — not out of guilt, for he never acknowledges his guilt, but out of weariness and loneliness, as the only relief possible from the cacophony of unfinalized inner dialogue. Read Bakhtin carefully, and you will see that nowhere does he suggest that dialogue between real people necessarily brings truth, beauty, happiness or honesty. It brings only concretization (and even that is temporary), and the possibility of change, of some forward movement. Under optimal conditions, dialogue provides options. But there can still be mutual deception, mountains of lies exchanged, pressing desires unanswered or unregistered, gratuitous cruelty administered on terrain to which only the intimate beloved has access. By having a real other respond to me, I am spared one thing only: the worst cumulative effects of my own echo-chamber of words.

This being the case, one could argue that Kariakin, too, is only partially correct when he regrets the absence of a "finger pointing toward the truth" in Bakhtin's polyphony. For an ethical trajectory could be seen as inherent from the start in this spiraling alternation between polyphonic internalization of dialogue followed by escape from its unbearable torments. Moral growth might even be inevitable in novels of the sort Dostoevsky designed, where the chief crime is not murder, not even psychic cruelty, but the drive for excessive autonomy and the human failing that fuels this drive, which is spiritual pride. If (so this argument goes) I proudly internalize all dialogue so as "not to depend" on another's personality, or body, or service, or idea — I will *never* be at peace again. Inner dialogue will give me no rest. Not because

---

31  See *PDP*, Ch. 3, "The Idea in Dostoevsky": "It is not the idea in itself that is the 'hero of Dostoevsky's works,' as Engelhardt has claimed, but rather the *person born of that idea*. It again must be emphasized that the hero in Dostoevsky is a person of the idea: this is not a character, not a temperament, not a social or psychological type; such externalized and finalized images of persons cannot of course be combined with the image of a <u>fully valid</u> idea. It would be absurd, for example, even to attempt to combine Raskolnikov's idea, which we understand and <u>feel</u> (according to Dostoevsky an idea can and must not only be understood, but also "felt") with his finalized character..." (85).

I feel guilty, repentant, or even interested in another person's point of view (Raskolnikov was none of those things, even at the end) but because only external others, in responding to me, can check the monstrous growth of my own view on things, can concretize my thoughts long enough for me to get outside of them, assess them, and thus stand a chance to tame or modify them. Since no major Dostoevskian personality can survive a state of hyperactive inner dialogue for long, either suicide, or some form of religious conversion out of that solitary vortex, is unavoidable.

In sum: critics of dialogism and polyphony are correct that Bakhtin underestimates (as Dostoevsky never does) the sheer viciousness of the criminal imagination. True, Bakhtin was thoroughly familiar with bodily pain, not surprised by cruelty and not offended by death. He can also be faulted, it seems, for a lack of interest in the negative emotions and venial sins that, for many readers, constitute the core attraction of Dostoevsky's plots: lechery, lying, jealousy, greed, perversion and violence. To Mikhail Gasparov's complaint that Bakhtin too quickly encourages us to "expropriate others' words" and turn them to our own selfish use, Bakhtin would nod sadly in agreement: indeed, there is no reason why this process of appropriation need be virtuous, happy, healthy, or just — but it is universal. Although unimpressed by many of the stimulants natural to novels, about the inescapability of dialogue and the cost that dialogue exacts, Bakhtin is not naive.

Let us now sum up the fate of polyphony. Bakhtin was fascinated with scientistic models. He had come to maturity in an era entralled by numerical manipulation and classification: series, sets, groups, the emergence of sociology as a profession. Numbers lent themselves to grids and structures. And much like Wittgenstein at a slightly later time, Bakhtin was concerned to preserve the principle of relationalism without endorsing system-based structuralism (and why indeed should relationships, to be valid, organize themselves into a system?). Still, as the best Bakhtin scholars now acknowledge, a pure and unalloyed polyphony challenges not just systematic thought but also the very integrity of the personalities it pulls in.[32] Bakhtin himself returned to the ambiguities of the method

---

[32] Russian philosophers have thoroughly explored the shortcomings of the dialogic model and the danger of taking Bakhtin's ideal of polyphony too literally. As Liudmila Gogotishvili paraphrased the familiar complaint in her 1992 essay on the problem of Bakhtin's "evaluative relativism": "If speech belongs in turn first to me, then to the other, then to us, then to some third, and there is no superior possessor of meaning who might cap this uncoordinated clamor of voices with its own centralizing word, then

a half-century after he had coined the concept, in this note: "The pecularities of polyphony. The lack of finalization of the polyphonic dialogue...These dialogues are conducted by unfinalized individual personalities and not by psychological subjects. The somewhat unembodied quality of these personalities (disinterested surplus)."[33] Disinterested, perhaps even "somewhat unembodied," the "unfinalized individual personalities" who engage in polyphonic dialogue constitute a wondrous population: secure, full of the virtues, free of humiliating dependencies. It is not easy to see ourselves in it. And from our outsiderly perspective, therefore, we must confirm that as a reader of literary and real-life scenes there are certain things Bakhtin cannot do.

First. As a rule, Bakhtin does not do beginnings and ends. He largely does middles. Wholly committed to process and to the dynamics of response, Bakhtin concerns himself much less with how something *starts* (a personality, a responsibility) or how it might be brought to an effective, well-shaped end. This neglect of genesis and overall indifference to closure left a profound trace on his thought, imparting to his literary readings their strange, aerated, often fragmentary character. The passion for the ongoing middle of a text also separates him profoundly from his subject Dostoevsky, perhaps

---

it follows that the meaning of speech in Bakhtin's scheme of things loses all its objective features. If there is no direct word, that is, no word issuing forth from a stable 'I' or 'we' and confidently addressed to its object, it means that linguistic form cannot have any truth-significance at all. As a matter of principle, such a word cannot contain in itself the truth of the world" (145). Gogotishvili then answers this complaint. The error here, she advises, is the old one of assuming that people are like things, that they can attach themselves to values with no work or risk, and that a truth need be singular or eternal. Acknowledging any sort of a "we" where one can rest — and such first-person-plurals usually come to us in the form of genres — requires a great deal of individual effort (147). Gogotishvili notes four axes for registering meaning in an utterance — one's speech center, point of view, focus of attention, and the range of the self's participation in the world. Along all of them, in genres as small as an exclamation and as lengthy as a novel — *absolute polyphony* is impossible (152). Nor is it desirable. But polyphonic aspirations are not for that reason fraudulent, reductive, or self-serving. Polyphony is a generator. It generates boundaries, which are required to keep individual voices vulnerable and distinct from one another. For "the absence of a unified and singular direct word is not the absence of an idea or a rejection of higher values, but precisely the contrary: the fact that every speech manner is highlighted and conditioned by others is what protects the cultured word from barbarism" (172). L. Gogotishvili, "Filosofiia iazyka M. M. Bakhtina i problema tsennostnogo reliativizma," in *M.M. Bakhtin kak filosof*, eds.L. Gogotishvili and P. S. Gurevich (Moscow: Nauka, 1992), 142–74.

[33] "From Notes Made in 1970–71," *SpG 86*, 151.

the nineteenth century's greatest prose poet of original sin, Revelation, and Apocalypse.[34]

Second, Bakhtin cannot hear a fully self-confident monologue anywhere. As he matured, he became increasingly adamant on this point. In his view, even language deliberately employed "monologically" — in ultimatums, categorical farewells, suicide notes, military commands — in fact wants to be answered; it wants to be taken as only the penultimate word, and the person who utters such bits of monologic speech is always hoping that the person who hears it will care enough (against all odds and linguistic cues) to answer back. Within such heightened fields of expectation, a failure to respond is itself a response, giving rise to its own fully-voiced anguish. As long as we are alive, we have no right to pull out on another person who addresses us in need — and no right, apparently, to be left alone. No single moment is *ever* wholly authoritative or closed for Bakhtin. Even dying, it turns out, is no guarantee of an escape from dialogue.

Third, somewhat like Dostoevsky's Idiot Prince Myshkin — and very unlike Dostoevsky himself — Bakhtin was temperamentally unfit for polemics. He would not condemn or exclude. All memoir accounts of Bakhtin emphasize this aspect of his mature personality: whether due to tolerance, languor, aristocratic disdain, commitment to dialogue, carnival optimism, Christian meekness, or simply fatigue, chronic illness and pain — there was, as one Jubilee memoirist put it, a sort of "lightness," *legkost'*, to Bakhtin's person that made it absolutely impossible for him to take a firm or final stand on a question, to impose rigid constraints, or to endorse any form of violence.[35] This "lightness" has proved a serious obstacle to politicizing his thought. It also shaped his understanding of polyphony in Dostoevsky.

---

[34]  Without a doubt, beginnings and ends fascinated the novelist. To be fascinated does not mean to understand their causes, however. See, for example, these lines from Dostoevsky's essay "Two Suicides": "We know only the daily flow of the things we see, and this only on the surface; but the ends and the beginnings are things that, for human beings, still lie in the realm of the fantastic." October 1976 entry in Fyodor Dostoevsky, *A Writer's Diary*, trans. Kenneth Lantz (Evanston: Northwestern University Press, 1993), 1:651. Although Bakhtin remarked on several occasions that faith in a "miracle" [*chudo*] was both necessary and proper in life, he was far less willing than Dostoevsky to theorize about "fantastical" or mystical material.

[35]  Sergei Averintsev, "V stikhii 'bol'shogo vremeni,'" *Literaturnaia gazeta* 15, no. 45 (November 1995): 6.

$\asymp$

*This excerpt on carnival from Chapter 4 of* The First Hundred Years of Mikhail
Bakhtin *(Princeton University Press, 1997) also reflects an awareness — and wariness —
of the Bakhtin boom, which was launched in the West during the late 1960s around this
malleable, inflammable, and poorly-translated concept. It interpolates several pages from
Chapter 2 describing Bakhtin's dissertation defense. The whole of this section is briefer
than the polyphony discussion, since my appreciation of the carnival principle (which
remains for me a confusion and a challenge) was updated five years later; that essay from
2002 is excerpted later in this section.*

---

Opening and closing segments from chapter 4 (plus a section from chapter 2)
of *The First Hundred Years of Mikhail Bakhtin*:

## CARNIVAL: OPEN-ENDED BODIES AND ANACHRONISTIC HISTORIES (1997)

"M. Bakhtin possessed a genuinely philosophical gift for broadening out problems."[36] With this sentence, E. Yu. Savinova opens her 1991 essay entitled "Carnivalization and the Wholeness of Culture" — and as evidence of this breadth, she brings forward the fact that Bakhtin's "research into the writings of Rabelais resulted in the discovery of a completely new layer of culture in the Middle Ages and the Renaissance, which, in turn, altered the entire picture of the development of human culture." Savinova overstates the case, but in spirit she is correct. Of all Bakhtin's ideas, "the problem of carnival" has proved the broadest, most appealing, most accessible, and most readily translatable into cultures and times distant from its original inspiration.

---

[36]   E. Yu. Savinova, "Karnavalizatsiia i tselostnost' kul'tury," in *M. M. Bakhtin i filosofskaia kul'tura XX veka*, ed. K. G. Isupov (St. Petersburg: Obrazovanie, 1991), 1:61–66, esp. 61.

This ready translatability has been both a handicap and a boon. The handicaps are those that a skeptic detects in Bakhtinian dialogue as well: a somewhat facile solution to human aloneness; an indifference to compulsion and violence; naïve utopianism (in this case of the body rather than the word); a certain sentimentalism; a dismissal of history. But the boons brought to scholarship by the idea of Bakhtinian carnival have also been very real. Three years after the Rabelais book was published, an enthusiastic review article by a Soviet Sinologist appeared in the professional journal *Narody Azii i Afriki* [Peoples of Asia and Africa] titled, simply, "Reading Bakhtin."[37] The body of the article is devoted to the role played in Chinese culture by holidays, festive processions, and folk wisdom in anecdotes about Confucius. Its author credits Bakhtin with providing her with the scholarly precedent. Such irreverent celebratory rituals are under-researched in a field like Sinology, she notes, which has been dominated for so long by the study of the region's powerful, serious, duty-laden religions. Reading Bakhtin's book on a French writer opened up rich possibilities for her study of China; in fact, "the 'popular laughing carnival culture' that Bakhtin discovered makes available a new, fruitful elaboration of the two-cultures problem in every national culture" (106). Like Freud's fantasy of a single family romance that unfolds in each human psyche without exception, Bakhtin's carnival idea has the thrill of a cultural and biological universal.

As a communication model, carnival dynamics has much to recommend it. The suspension of everyday anxieties during "holiday time" and "carnival space" — the specific locus being the grotesque body, vulnerable yet superbly shame-free — rids both me and my most proximate neighbor of the excessive self-consciousness that keeps each of us lonely, our words insipid, our spontaneous gestures of outreach in check. (Remarkably, Bakhtin — a chain smoker and tea addict — attends almost not at all to the chemical side of carnival, that is, to intoxication, addiction, or drunkenness, although any practical understanding of holiday bawdiness or vulgarity is unthinkable without it.[38]) For the carnival self is not a wholly conscious entity. Its ideal

---

37    L. D. Pozdneyeva, "Chitaia M. Bakhtina," *Narody Azii i Afriki* 2 (1968): 94–106. Further page references in text.

38    The issue has received sensible attention in the West; see Marty Roth, "Carnival, Creativity, and the Sublimation of Drunkenness," *Mosaic* 30, no. 2 (June 1997): 1–18. Exploring the ancient linkage of intoxication with creativity and its reflection in "the Dionysian esthetic of Nietzsche and the carnival esthetics of Bakhtin," Roth notes that although carnival is unthinkable without drink and drugs, "mood-altering substances are left out of the mix that produces the Bakhtinian carnival, with the result that

is the open-ended and irregular body, which has no need for visions of symmetrical beauty, feats of self-discipline, or personalized acts of genuine intimacy. If the products of the mind (words, verbal dialogue, polyphonic maneuvers) are fastidiously individualizing and take a great deal of work to get right, then an imperfect body, by contrast, is something each of us possesses by definition — indeed, almost by default. However we might age, we will, in the natural order of things, have more of such a body, not less. To affirm it, therefore, requires no special effort; in fact, to affirm it is an enormous relief.

It follows that entry into the world and worldview of carnival costs ridiculously little. Even without any special accent on the grotesque, we would all probably agree that much of our basic physiology — located in what Bakhtin calls the "lower bodily stratum" — is identical, involuntary, and non-negotiable. Its processes and appetites can thus be said to constitute (in a metaphor popular with postmodern critics) a common "language," native to all humans. And yet, as Bakhtin describes it in his book on Rabelais, the common language of bodies is of a certain highly convenient sort. Whereas verbal languages must be learned, internalized, teased out of the mind — and even then, they can be easily "misspoken" at the level of form as well as intent — the body (and even more, the grotesque body) cannot misstep or make a mistake. It is by definition already out of step; and in any case a *faux pas* would not be noticed or remembered. The carnival body is available to all without discrimination.[39] Its energy and material structures are displayed, as

---

Bakhtin and his commentators cannot offer any explanation for that festive institution beyond itself" (1). Bakhtin might answer that one such explanation was famine. On the mystique of a good cigarette for Bakhtin, see Galina Ponomareva's remark that the first question Bakhtin asked her during their initial meeting was whether or not she smoked; answering in the negative, she relates, "at that moment I discovered how important it was for him — I wouldn't want to say it was a sacred ritual, but still — this communion while smoking, even if at times a wordless communion." Visitors could easily "sniff their way" to the Bakhtins' smoke-saturated apartment in Saransk and Moscow. G. B. Ponomareva, "Vyskazannoe i nevyskazannoe... (Vospominaniia o M. M. Bakhtine)," *Dialog. Karnaval. Khronotop* 3 (1995): 59–77, esp. 61. [Henceforth *DKKh*.] See also the (by now apocryphal) comment made by Bakhtin to one of his undergraduate advisees in Saransk, who "always saw him sitting at his desk... and uninterruptedly smoking: as soon as one cigarette was finished he immediately lit up another. A cup of strong tea. 'For some it is harmful to smoke,' [Bakhtin] often remarked; 'for others it is necessary to smoke.'" Yu. D. Ryskin, "Moi vospominaniia o M. M. Bakhtine," in *M. M. Bakhtin v zerkalo kritiki*, ed. T. G. Yurchenko (Moscow: Labirint, 1995), 111–13, esp. 112.

39   See Mikhail Bakhtin, *Rabelais and His World*, trans. Hélène Iswolsky (Bloomington: Indiana University Press, 1984), esp. ch. 5, "The Grotesque Image of the Body." One unfortunate mistranslation in this uninspired but serviceable English version is the

it were, on an exoskeleton, turned toward the outside world in a frank and welcoming way. Such communal "baseness," the vigor of *le bas corporel*, is the foundation of Bakhtin's carnival logic. It can be fueled by denunciation and aggressive rhetoric but is apparently tainted by neither; its laughter, even when defiant, is rejuvenating. Since the grotesque body costs nothing to keep up, does not care if it wears out, has neither vanity nor fear of pain, cannot be self-sufficient, and is always "a body in the act of becoming," it is guaranteed to triumph over classical form, institutional oppression, and individual death.

The optimism of all this is dazzling. The spirit of carnival grows out of Bakhtin's larger concept of *smekhovaia kul'tura*, a "culture of laughter," and the idea has proved irresistible. Although sensed as potentially subversive, unlike so many subversions elaborated by intellectuals it is not elitist (for we are working here — literally — with the lowest common human denominators). It promises a sort of freedom, even though the structures that grant this freedom are perceived as fixed and monolithic. Carnival and its corollary values moved with astonishing speed to inspire Paris 1968, British postcolonial theory, Latin American literature, continental and American feminist thought. The Rabelais book became a bestseller. On Russian soil, however, Bakhtin's carnival idea had a difficult and suspicious reception from the start, indeed, from the very day of Bakhtin's protracted and controversial dissertation defense.

Bakhtin's formal education had been interrupted by the chaos of civil war and by poor health; since childhood he had suffered from chronic osteomyelitis. After 1938, following the amputation of his right leg, Bakhtin's health improved. Two years later, in 1940, hoping to increase his qualifications for steady employment by possession of an advanced degree, Bakhtin submitted his study "Rabelais in the History of Realism" to the Gorky Institute of World Literature as a dissertation (although he never liked to refer to his book as such). The War intervened; he defended formally only in 1946, on the brink of a new wave of High-Stalinist xenophobia. Notwithstanding a divided vote slightly in his favor, he was eventually certified — in 1951, after a five-year delay — with the lesser academic degree of *kandidat* rather than *doktor nauk*. Before the dissertation could be approved and filed in public libraries,

---

rendering of *chrevo*, (Russian for the "belly/womb" or generalized region of digestive and generative functions, not of excrement per se), as "bowels": cf. p. 317, where the grotesque body, forever outgrowing and transgressing itself, allots an essential role to "those parts ... in which it conceives a new second body: *chrevo i fall* [the belly/womb and phallus]" (not, as Iswolsky has it, "the bowels and the phallus").

however, Bakhtin was required to cleanse and reorient those portions of the text that made his work, in the opinion of the Higher Accrediting Commission, "crudely physiological," bawdy, and "ideologically depraved."[40] The book that was published in Russian in 1965 and subsequently translated into the languages of the world was based on this shortened, sanitized version of the dissertation. The full stenographic transcription of Bakhtin's 1946 defense was published only in 1993.[41]

This transcript of the Ph.D. defense provides a fascinating glimpse into the dynamics of Stalin-era academic life. In a procedure that was far from routine for those years, independently-minded colleagues within the university took a bold stand in defense of their wayward candidate. Almost all the major arguments *pro* and *contra* carnival, the grotesque body, and cultures of laughter that we meet in the 1960s and 1970s were first broached during Bakhtin's dissertation defense twenty years earlier — in which context Bakhtin himself had a chance (indeed, an obligation) to respond and defend his hypotheses. This is precious information, because the septuagenarian Bakhtin of the 1960s and 70s rarely bothered to rebut criticism (or to court praise) when his works finally began to appear in print. He considered himself either above, or to the side of, such dialogue. Thus his required response, at age fifty, to his *opponenty* (the formal examiners at his defense) is one of the few sustained self-reflections we have by Bakhtin on his own work. What major objections were raised to *Rabelais in the History of Realism* in 1946, and how did Bakhtin justify his work in light of them?

---

[40]  The phrase here is "ideologicheski porochnoi" (guilty of an ideological sin). See the memoir by Bakhtin's enthusiastic supporter E. M. Evnina, who, as a junior scholar during these years, was required to "remove from the manuscript of her own book on Rabelais all citations and references to Mikhail Mikhailovich's dissertation." The Higher Accrediting Commission (VAK) criticized Bakhtin's scholarly work as "Freudian," "pseudoscientific," "formalistic," and, to the extent that the original submission contained a chapter on this great Russian writer, disrespectful to the genius of Gogol. See "Iz vospominanii E. M. Evninoi," appendix 3, *DKKh* 2–3 (1993): 114–17, esp. 117.

[41]  See "Stenogramma zasedaniia uchenogo soveta instituta mirovoi literatury im. A. M. Gor'kogo: zashchita dissertatsii tov. Bakhtinym na temu 'Rable v istorii realizma' 15 noiabria 1946 g.," annotated by N. A. Pan'kov, *DKKh* 2–3 (1993): 55–119. In addition, the issue includes a lengthy background essay by Pan'kov (29–54) as well as four appendices: the text of Bakhtin's formal dissertation prospectus or "tesizy;" a conversation with the literary scholar Valery Kirpotkin; a memoir on the fate of Bakhtin's dissertation after the defense by a fellow Rabelais scholar, E. M. Evnina, who was banned from citing it; and a brief statement (1944) in favor of Bakhtin's monograph by the eminent Formalist critic Boris Tomashevsky.

In many respects, Bakhtin's thesis was ingeniously appropriate for its time and place. Many clichés of communism are realized in it: carnival, after all, could easily be linked with the "common people," the collective body, and a buoyant disregard for individual death. Carnival had the additional advantage of being pro-materialist, anti-Church, disruptive of fixed order, and vaguely "revolutionary," both on its own terms and vis-à-vis more humanistic Western readings of Rabelais. Although prim, oppressive Stalinist culture had long since ceased to live by those destabilizing Bolshevik slogans, as verbal tags they could still embarrass and deflect hostile attacks. One Comrade Teriaeva, an examiner of few scholarly qualifications but with rigid Stalinist convictions and a good nose for treason,[42] accused Bakhtin of failing to reflect in his dissertation (submitted in 1940) the spirit of Zhdanov's 1946 proclamation on party-mindedness in literature. She also condemned his work for resembling more "private research" full of "superfluous references to Saturnalia and phallic cults" than an objective study of class antagonisms. Bakhtin responded in his final statement — with what must have been profound weariness — that his study dealt with one of the world's most revolutionary writers, that he saw no reason to write "what had already been written and spoken," that Comrade Teriaeva apparently wanted him simply to repeat "what she had already studied," and that "I, as a scholar, can be a revolutionary as well... I solved the problem [of Rabelais] in a revolutionary way."[43]

There were also responsible objections raised at the defense, however, by those who appreciated fully the value and originality of Bakhtin's work. Where is the spiritually serious side of humanism? Why is the great realist François Rabelais (whose role as author, artist, and cleric is scarcely discussed) cast backward into the Middle Ages and not forward, progressively, into the Renaissance? On what basis can the dissertator claim that mediaeval carnival or carnival laughter is so carefree and eternally "cheerful"? Why such simplistic binary thinking, which presumes that grotesque realism is solely the property of the masses — when in fact all strata of society

---

[42]  For a brief and exasperated professional biography of Mariia Prokofievna Teriaeva, see N. A. Pan'kov, "'Ot khoda etogo dela zavisit vse dal'neishee ...' (Zashchita dissertatsii M. M. Bakhtina kak real'noe sobytie, vysokaia drama i nauchnaia komediia)," in *DKKh* 2–3 (1993): 29–54, esp. 47–48. To this "Iago in skirts," literary toady and spy, specialist on "Stendhal and bourgeois realism"and thoroughly Stalinist persona, Pan'kov would "like to devote an entire sarcastic-annihilating diatribe."

[43]  Bakhtin's summary statement [zakliuchitel'noe slovo], "Stenogramma zasedaniia..," 98–99. Further pages references given in text.

(even those Bakhtin excoriates as "official") can be shown to have indulged delightedly in it? And for that matter, why do the commoners in Bakhtin's account only laugh and cavort, when in history they clearly broke their backs with work, suffered, and thirsted to believe? The entire hypothesis of "reduced carnivalization" in subsequent literary epochs struck some examiners as an artificial construct. Can one really leap unproblematically from Rabelaisian folkloric fantasy to Gogol's ambivalent humor or to Dostoevsky's tragic vision?

In his final statement, Bakhtin addressed these reservations, although in no sense apologetically. His kindly, aristocratic demeanor — tolerant of others because indifferent to their opinions — glimmers beneath the transcript. "I am an obsessed innovator," he admitted. "Obsessed innovators are very rarely understood." He was deeply gratified, therefore, for the support he had received and grateful for a chance to respond to objections. Yes, in his thesis (far too short for the task he had in mind) perhaps he had exaggerated and simplified cultural traditions as well as historical conditions. "I did not present Rabelais in the atmosphere of the French Renaissance. This is true. I did not do so, because in that area so much has already been done, and I would have addressed you here as a mere compiler. And why is that necessary, when those materials are available to everyone?...To repeat [what is known] is to beat down an open door" (94). In any future monograph, he assured his examiners, he would balance the record with attention to Rabelais the humanist. But as he had testified in his opening statement, the gothic and the grotesque had fared so poorly in literary scholarship — methodologically always partial to forms of "prepared and completed existence" — that in his study he had resolved to "catch existence in the process of becoming" (56) and to consider the epoch solely from that "unofficial," as yet uncoalesced point of view. As regards laughter, Bakhtin hastened to assure his audience: "I do not in the least mean to imply that mediaeval laughter is cheerful, carefree and joyous laughter" (97). In carnival, laughter and death are intertwined; death and pain are everywhere and are grimly real, only death never has the final word. "Laughter is a weapon, like fists and sticks." But unlike those latter two weapons, which can be wielded effectively in anger and in dread, laughter must be absolutely fearless; for precisely this reason it is progressive, pointed forward toward the Renaissance. "Laughter liberates us from fear, and this work of laughter...is an indispensable prerequisite for Renaissance consciousness. In order to look at the world soberly, I must cease to be afraid. In this, laughter played a most serious role"(98). No, Rabelaisian realism is not degraded, dirty, or an insult to consciousness; it is a forerunner of all objective critical consciousness. Of course the common people do not only laugh; they have many lives. "But this is the life that interested me, it is deeply progressive and revolutionary.... Excuse me if I have not satisfied you with my answers, I am so exhausted, and it shows" (100).

Despite these assurances at the defense, Bakhtin did not alter the text of his dissertation in a "more balanced," humanistic direction before seeking a publisher. In fact, his first attempt to publish was in 1940, soon after he submitted the text to the Gorky Institute. In 1944 he tried a second time to publish the text, also unsuccessfully, although there survives from that period a long set of notes, published for the first time in 1992 under the title "Additions and Revisions to *Rabelais*," indicating the scope of Bakhtin's ambitions for the larger project.[44] Projected chapters were to deal with official (that is, bad) versus unofficial (good) seriousness; with carnival as a universal theory of "limbic" images; with carnivalized aspects of *Hamlet*, *King Lear*, *Macbeth* and presumably other Shakespearean drama; and there is some loose speculation on the relation of carnival to nicknames and gesture. Regretfully, little of this plan was realized. The sanitized version required by the dissertation committee became the canonical text (apparently Bakhtin's 1940 Ur-*Rabelais* has disappeared).[45] For twenty-five years these quasi-public presentations, resubmissions, rumors of reader reports and memoirs from the audience entered public memory. Apocryphal and carnivalized stories began to circulate, such as the (unconfirmed) account by one eyewitness at the doctoral defense that "at the culminating moment, Bakhtin shouted at his opponents: 'Obscurantists! Obscurantists!' — and furiously banged his crutches on the floor."[46] In a word, by the time the typescript finally saw the light of day, it had accumulated an entire shadow history of legends.

As we know from Bakhtin's personal correspondence with Leonid Pinsky, Shakespeare scholar and fellow political exile, as late as 1960 Bakhtin considered his work on Rabelais and the history of laughter, however "cleansed," still unpublishable.[47] By the early 1960s, however,

---

[44] M. M. Bakhtin, "Dopolneniia i izmeneniia k 'Rable'" [dated 18/VI/44], prepared for publication by L. S. Melikhova, first published in *Voprosy filosofii* 1 (1992): 134–64.

[45] Pan'kov, "'Ot khoda etogo dela...,'" in *DKKh* 2–3 (1993): 40.

[46] The eyewitness was B. I. Purishchev; the anecdote was related to Pan'kov by Iu. M. Kagan, Matvei Kagan's daughter. See Pan'kov, "'Ot knoda etogo dela...'" 42.

[47] See Bakhtin's letter to Pinsky, 26 November 1960: "As regards my work on Rabelais, I am not counting on any possibility of its publication. What is more, it was finished twenty years ago and a great deal no longer satisfies me." "Pis'ma M. M. Bakhtina k L. E. Pinskomu," ed. N. A. Pan'kov, in *DKKh* 2 (1994): 57.

conditions had changed. After perilous delays, the Dostoevsky book had appeared in a revised edition. But Dostoevsky, for all his ideological unruliness, was nevertheless Russian and canonical; Rabelais was Western and (in Bakhtin's reading) indecent. Carnival laughter on the public square might be indeed "revolutionary" and "of the masses"—points stressed repeatedly by Bakhtin during his dissertation defense—but it was also a good deal more dangerous and potentially anarchic than the dialogic word in the novel, a genre designed for solitary individual consumption. It remains the most disputed image in the Bakhtin canon.

By the early 1990s, the problems with Bakhtin's carnival concept had been thoroughly aired by detractors and enthusiasts alike. No one doubted that Bakhtin's image was a utopian construct. Cultural historians from both East and West had persistently pointed out that real-life carnival rituals—while perhaps great drunken fun for the short term—were not necessarily cheerful or carefree. In its function as society's safety valve, a scheduled event that domesticated conflict by temporarily sanctioning victimization, medieval carnival in practice was frequently more repressive than liberating. Bakhtin's reluctance to highlight the crucial role of violence and scapegoating during carnival baffled many of his readers. And then there was the stiff binary nature of Bakhtin's social history, which presents such a strange image of popular appetites and upper-class taste. Since Bakhtin analyzes Rabelais's novel not primarily as an authored piece of literature but through the lens of preliterate (and arguably multinational) folklore, he tends to dehistoricize the text; in its pages, French medieval society appears rigidly and artificially stratified. Bakhtin functions more as a mythographer than as a literary scholar or social historian. Perhaps mythography even suited Bakhtin's intent. By supplementing his schematicized, quasi-historical picture of Rabelais's France with timeless folk images, Bakhtin could provide his immediate Soviet audience with thinly disguised psychological universals that were relevant to any (and most persuasively, to his own) time.

These reservations about Bakhtin's *Rabelais* were summed up from a Russian perspective by Aleksandr Pan'kov in his centennial study *The Key and Clue to M. Bakhtin*.[48] According to Pan'kov, Bakhtin's most repudiated value—traces of which could be found at the negative pole of every Bakhtinian binary—was *ofitsioz*, "officialese or official culture," the world as it looks when approved and controlled from a single sociopolitical center.

---

[48]   Aleksandr Pan'kov, *Razgadka M. Bakhtina* (Moscow: Informatik, 1995), 157–73. Further references in text.

Inside that center was stasis and silence, a moral void; the further one was from the center, the more talk, activity, variety and interest. Repelled from his earliest years by *ofitsioz* wherever it was found, Bakhtin "strove to extract from medieval ideology itself the principle of cultural two-worldness [*dvoemirie*]; he subjected living material to a typological cleansing...and at times the material clearly resisted" (168). Bakhtin's "body of the people" lost all historical or literary reality, becoming directly mythological and populist (but in the nineteenth-century Russian, rather than medieval French, sense of that word). The folk or *narod* was invested with a Romantic "metaphysical vital value"; and although presented as wholly spontaneous, self-absorbed, unself-reflecting, this folk also functioned for Bakhtin, in Hegelian fashion, as a progressive mechanism that could move history (171). With this romanticized "people" fixed in place, official culture could be reinterpreted negatively as an "artificial construction, genetically 'alien,'" an imposition and a burden. Bakhtin's social history unfolded in a quasi-fictional realm that "at times began to recall the Wall between 'city' and 'nature' in Zamyatin's [dystopian] novel *We*" (171–72).

§

In closing, we might turn to a thoughtful centennial essay by I. N. Fridman, "Carnival in Isolation."[49] Fridman attaches carnival in a complex weave to its apparent opposite, polyphony — and more generally, to the "I-thou" relation that Bakhtin celebrates in his dialogism. But he imparts a darker cast to the whole, tying it more tightly to the pressures of Soviet ideology. He interprets both polyphony and carnival in light of the major realignments in Bakhtin's thought at the end of the 1920s. The dynamics of polyphony, he suggests, reflect Bakhtin's waning ideal hopes for what openness alone could do to keep creativity and consciousness alive. The quality of "completion" [*zavershenie*] — previously valued as full of grace, lovingly bestowed, pragmatically necessary in order that personality function properly and that a work of art emerge in our disorderly world — is reinterpreted as "closure" or "enclosedness" [*zamknutost'*]. It becomes a destructive force that

---

[49]   I. N. Fridman, "Karnaval v odinochku," *Voprosy filosofii* 12 (1994): 79–98. Further page references in text. A similar thesis is suggested in Gary Saul Morson and Caryl Emerson, *Mikhail Bakhtin: Creation of a Prosaics* (Stanford: Stanford University Press, 1990), Part One, chapter 2.

behaves like "a robber on the high road," stealing up on us and attacking from behind (85). This shift from benignly beneficial to criminalized closure strikes Fridman as fatal, not just for Bakhtinian aesthetics but for any aesthetics; for in his view, once the aesthetic pleasure of catharsis has been exiled from the work of art, the boundary between life's processes and art's products cannot be sustained. According to Bakhtin's new understanding, ideas and forms (along with their human carriers) do not naturally desire consummation or resolution. Thus heroes, readers and authors are never taken down off the rack. The instability and psychic distress that accumulates in such a model eventually triggers the move from polyphony to carnival. For if the polyphonic image is "a 'world symposium' headed by an insane Chairman whose sole concern is that dialogue never end" (86) — Fridman's unkind paraphrase — then the only way Bakhtin can avoid this travestied extreme is to wrap the whole dialogic process in an anaesthetizing utopian envelope. Within that envelope, the "second life" of the mind in dialogue is like the laughing holiday, deeply authentic, perhaps, but suspended in both space and time.

According to Fridman, Bakhtinian polyphony and Bakhtinian carnival are equally utopian constructs. If Bakhtin's Dostoevsky book creates out of that author's world a personalist utopia of speaking minds, then the Rabelais book is its mirror opposite, a collective or *rodovoe* [clan-based] utopia of communing bodies (86). The two are connected, Fridman suggests, in the huge, new fourth chapter on genre in *Problems of Dostoevsky's Poetics*, added to the 1963 revision of the 1929 original book, through Bakhtin's eccentric concept of "genre memory" (87). This "memory of the genre" is really a sort of "ancestral or fore-memory" [*pra-pamiat'*], which combines elements of a collective preconscious with prerogatives of the conscious individual. Its one determining characteristic is that it seems to remember only what everyone else forgets. Bakhtin avoids the acknowledged classics in the art of the novel "like a danger zone"; and when he invokes genuine carnival forms, he lets it be known that any attempt to incorporate them into literature must reduce and distort them almost beyond recognition. For this reason, Fridman is reluctant to call Bakhtin an aesthetician at all. "The subject of Bakhtin's aesthetic theory," he writes, "its authentic substrate, are the peripheral zones lying on the threshold, on the border that divides art from pre- or supra-art, anything but art itself... [both the dialogic novel and the model of carnival] provide a definition of art — but only in the specific Bakhtinian sense of 'delineating the limits' of something, and even so, not from within but from 'without'" (88).

Fridman's comments lead us to the edge of that most fraught area in which Bakhtin has been rethought: *vnenakhodimost'*, exotopy or "outsideness." The term refers both to the cardinal value Bakhtin placed on external perspective, as well as to Bakhtin's own multiple identity as literary scholar, culturologist and ethical philosopher, an outsider to all established disciplines and native to none. With their competing methodologies and different validating logics, are these various professions eroded when combined in his person? And if so, is this a blessing or a misfortune? For however we might sympathize with Bakhtin's antipathy toward "official thinking" [*ofitsial'shchina, ofitsioz*], there is much to recommend professionalism. An internal consistency of argument, an obligation to assess what others have seen and registered, a consensus over basic terms, an agreement as to what constitutes a misuse of evidence, the modest placement of oneself within an established language: in the best of worlds, these are virtues that professional insidership can foster. And even in the worst of worlds, which arguably was the Soviet Union circa 1930–1950, the cohesiveness of intellectual tradition and a sense of shared texts was what had kept Russian philological scholarship alive.

Bakhtin, however, did not seek to be an insider to things. In places he rivals Leo Tolstoy in his reluctance to join, endorse or build upon (with any degree of appreciation) a definition that precedes his own. And in matters of art, as it was for Tolstoy so it was, to some extent, for Bakhtin: art is not primarily a matter of pleasure, beauty, perfect proportion or disinterested play but the site of other, more essential tasks: self-identity, communicative exchange, moral growth. Beauty and aesthetic pleasure might even be said to get in the way. But then we might ask: does form in itself possess adequate resources to survive the pressures that Bakhtin applies to it? The role that form plays in other paradigms of the creative process is occupied in Bakhtin's scheme by an assortment of more vulnerable and porous matter: chronotopes, speech genres, voice zones, loopholes, participatory outsideness, aesthetic love. Can Bakhtin's mature aesthetic, derived from Kant, from the theory of relativity, from biofeedback models and the example of Christ, steeped in Goethe and Schelling, ever achieve the minimum disinterestedness, attention to details and to wholes, and respect for stable form that we have come to expect from a theory of art?

# 2

# THE EARLY PHILOSOPHICAL ESSAYS

*The following review essay, reprinted with minor adjustments from* The Russian Review, *vol. 54, number 1 (January 1995), celebrates that moment in the Bakhtin Industry when the impact of his earlier, philosophically abstract work became available in English. Research on these early texts, believed by Bakhtin to be lost and published for the most part posthumously, made possible a responsible investigation of Bakhtin's intellectual origins in the largely German traditions of Romantic philosophy, Kantianism, and phenomenology.*

REVIEW ESSAY

## BAKHTIN AT 100:
## LOOKING BACK AT THE VERY EARLY YEARS
## (1995)

Bakhtin, M. M. *Toward a Philosophy of the Act.* Translation and Notes by Vadim Liapunov. Edited by Vadim Liapunov and Michael Holquist (Austin: University of Texas Press, 1993).

"... Aesthetic activity as well is powerless to take possession of that moment of Being which is constituted by the transitiveness and open event-ness of Being." Thus begins this little book under review, Bakhtin's maiden essay (ca. 1919–22), and a less grateful opening sentence by a famous literary critic can scarcely be imagined. Vadim Liapunov has accomplished the same minor miracle with this early, unfinished and unreworked seventy-page fragment — which appears to be part of the introduction to a far vaster project of Bakhtin's, never finished and first published in Russian in 1986 as *K filosofii postupka* — that he accomplished in 1990 with its lengthier sequel, "Author and Hero in Aesthetic Activity."[1] With this publication, almost all of

---

[1]    Michael Holquist and Vadim Liapunov, eds., *Art and Answerability: Early Philosophical Essays by M. M. Bakhtin*, trans. and notes by Vadim Liapunov, supplement translated

Bakhtin's extant writings have been moved into English.[2] What sort of a work is this, and why should people who value Bakhtin's later, more accessible ideas of polyphony, dialogism and carnival make the effort to read it?

We should make the effort, I believe, for two reasons. First, Bakhtin was published in Russian and translated into Western languages "inside out," with the middle-period writings rising meteorically to fame while the earliest and latest texts were still unavailable, in some cases their existence unsuspected. A major thinker deserves to be known in his genesis. Second, the complex concept of an answerable architectonic self — as opposed to the more straightforward, familiar dialogic and carnivalistic selves of the later writings — is first developed by Bakhtin in these early manuscripts; he returned with increasing frequency to the model in his mature years. In his notes from 1970–71, Bakhtin called this study of comparative selfhoods "philosophical anthropology." He incessantly reformulated its major concerns: "the nature of one's image of oneself," the degree of "self-sensation and self-awareness" in this image, and the role the other must play to keep this image from collapsing into the sterile duplications of a "person at the mirror," a tempting but fraudulent condition permitting a single consciousness to finalize its own image. For half a century, Bakhtin recruited major primary creators — Dostoevsky, Goethe, Rabelais — to help him interrogate this cluster of problems.

Bakhtin's early period is an enigma. For several years now, the journal *Chelovek* has been running partial transcripts of interviews conducted by a Soviet Mayakovsky scholar in 1973–74 with the aged Bakhtin.[3] Recounting

---

   by Kenneth Brostrom (Austin: University of Texas Press, 1990). [Henceforth *Art and Answerability*.] The dating of these early manuscripts is disputed; Brian Poole has argued that internal evidence suggests they might have been written as late as 1926, when Bakhtin first acquainted himself with the work of Max Scheler.

2   The Russian edition of the *Collected Works of Bakhtin*, currently being compiled in St. Petersburg under the general editorship of Sergei Bocharov, will contain some texts not yet published in the West. Of these the most important are several hundred additional pages of the manuscript on the Bildungsroman and on Goethe (researched by the Canadian scholar in Marburg, Brian Poole), and comments on Shakespearean drama, Dante, Heine and Goethe from Bakhtin's dissertation on Rabelaisian carnival that were not included in the 1975 book on Rabelais (this material was first published in *Voprosy filosofii*, 1992, no. 1).

3   The interviews were conducted over seventeen hours in 1973–74 by the Mayakovskii scholar V. D. Duvakin. Three installments, which take Bakhtin's life up to the mid-1920s, appeared as "Razgovory s Bakhtinym," in *Chelovek*, 1993, no. 4:136–53, no. 5:131–43, and no. 4–6:158–73. In 1996, the interviews were published in paperback as *Besedy V. D. Duvakina s M. M. Bakhtinym* (Moscow: Izdatel'stvaia gruppa Progress, 1996), and then retitled (to highlight the most famous party) and reissued in 2002 as *M. M. Bakhtin: Besedy s V. D. Duvakinym* (Moscow: Soglasie, 2002).

his youth, Bakhtin claims he had always wanted to be a moral philosopher, a *"myslitel'"* [thinker]; literary scholarship was for him a safe refuge from politics during those years when others were being harassed, organized, recruited. He insists that as a young college student in Petrograd he had been "absolutely apolitical." He lamented not only the October Revolution but the prior February abdication as well, predicting that it would end badly and "extremely;" he went to no political meetings, profoundly distrusted the Provisional Government under Kerensky, and continued to sit in libraries and read books. The image of a learned, apolitical, urbane, witty, fastidious and aristocratic young Bakhtin that emerges from these memoirs is in some tension, of course, with the mass-oriented Bakhtin popular in Western radical circles. But it meshes well with the philosophical core being vigorously restored to Bakhtin's thought in Russia today, in conference volumes, special Bakhtin journals, and notably the 1992 volume by the Russian Academy of Sciences, *M. M. Bakhtin kak filosof*— the latter containing essays on Bakhtin's Christianity, on his refutation of ethical relativism, and detailed notes by Lev Pumpiansky on Bakhtin's lectures from the mid-1920s on religious philosophy, Bergson, and Kant's *Critique of Pure Reason*. Deeply influenced by the neo-Kantian Marburg School and perhaps by the fin-de-siècle spirit of Nietzsche and Vladimir Soloviev, Bakhtin began his own life of the mind by posing very large questions, among them the "contemporary crisis of philosophy."

As Michael Holquist points out in his excellent, overly brief introduction to this volume, Bakhtin turned not so much to the neo-Kantians as to Kant himself. That great corpus of writings both attracted and repelled. What appealed about Kant, and what would become recurring motifs in Bakhtin's own thought, was Kant's unbending insistence on moral criteria for human behavior, his inclusion of time and space as participants in — not mere parameters for — our human understanding, and his head-on confrontation with the crucial question: How much can our reason know apart from lived experience? What alienated Bakhtin was the readiness with which Kant sought to avoid ethical relativism by positing the general or universal case. Relativism, Bakhtin was convinced, could be avoided at less cost. And hence he cast his inquiry as a philosophy not of a transcendent categorical "as if" or moral imperative, but of "the concrete step taken," *postupok*, the individual act.

In brief, and bringing down to far cruder earth the abstract Germanic lexicon employed by the young and erudite Bakhtin, the argument of the essay is this. A crisis in philosophy occurs when the realm of "culture" — that is, accumulated events, congealed content, human accomplishment that can exist autonomously, without immediate authors attached to it — is severed from the realm of "life" (actions personally committed by us). Whereas life feels shapeless and open, cultural content lends itself to arrangement in terms of norms and inner necessity. It feels good — indeed, fatally good — to lose ourselves in these structures (as Bakhtin puts it, we feel most sure of ourselves, most lucid and at home, where we are not actually present); but we should be cautious, he warns, because precisely in such abstract realms are we the most "determined, predetermined, bygone, finished" (9). In fact there are no moral, or creative, or psychical norms. There is no general theoretical "ought" at all, but only the obligation of the individual moral subject. Genuine subjects must do more than merely discipline themselves to obey a fixed standard, for nothing is easier for a strong will than to posit its own law and then follow it — or, alternatively, to assign success and/or failure to already completed acts in their "theoretical transcription" (26–27). An ethical subject must engage in the riskier, more humbling, present-tense practice of "participative" thinking [*uchastnoe myshlenie*]. This entails active empathizing: an entering-in to the other's position followed not by an identification with that other (in Bakhtin's world, any duplication or fusion is always sterile) but by a return to one's own position, the only place from which I can understand my own unique "ought" in its relationship to another.

To acknowledge this need for interpenetration and constant oscillation between self and other is not, however, to embrace Henri Bergson's solution, then much in vogue, which holds that we are largely "vital force" and unfixable "flow" (Bakhtin sees both these qualities as hopelessly theoretical). Nor is it to endorse relativism; quite the contrary. It is to insist on something infinitely more difficult than either: uninterrupted choice-making in the moral sphere and a willingness to answer for all one's acts in time, as one does them, which will result in a dynamic, "architectonically" whole personality. The self here is uniquely situated, non-generalizable, risk-taking and judging. Like all Bakhtin's constructs, it is post-Einsteinian: its consciousness is situated in a world that knows relativity. But this world also knows truth. And to invoke a defense often mounted on behalf of the American pragmatists, there is a massive difference between relativism and relativity. Relativism can work to invalidate moral judgment. In a universe governed by relativity (or better, relationalism), however, precisely because there are no single fixed points, moral judgment — and one's subsequent personal responsibility for moral judgments over time — is all the more indispensable. It is from this position that Bakhtin elaborates his own revision of Kant.

We might simplify Bakhtin's Kantian quest in this way: To escape being a mere random occurrence in life, to what sort of continuity do I aspire?

"A philosophy of life can only be a moral philosophy," Bakhtin writes; "a life that has fallen away from answerability cannot have a philosophy; it is, in its very principle, fortuitous and incapable of being rooted" (56). As a principle, this is easy and gratifying to endorse. But to what precisely are we answerable? Must there exist a normative ethical model against which I measure my act — or might there be other continuities and types of rootedness? To these questions Bakhtin insists that we answer not to any theoretical imperative or law, but only to our own unique "act-taking I." But how does an "I" cohere?

This problem fascinated the young Bakhtin. The coherence of culture, he intimates, takes care of itself (here Americans can only wonder at the awesome, identity-bestowing hold of Russian culture on its own communicants); one recognizes culture as such by its qualities of inter-relatedness and cohesiveness. What, then, makes a human whole possible, since persons must participate in so many fragmented things and are subject to so many pressures beyond their control? Here Bakhtin resists the easy intuitivist explanation so popular with his generation and devises in its place a cautiously interactive model that we can now recognize as a rudimentary, preverbal form of dialogue.

The basic components of this model, in Bakhtin's German-inflected Russian categories, are *dan* and *zadan*, "what is given" and "what is posited." Life presents us with "givens" [*dannost'*]: formless disasters, undeserved illnesses, mindless revolution, unexpected good luck. In lived experience, as a rule, we do not come upon already existent unities or wholes. What makes us whole — Bakhtin might even say, the only thing that can make us whole — is a response. It is rarely within our power to initiate and guarantee wholes in the world at large (at least in no world that Bakhtin ever knew), but it is always within our power to initiate a whole in ourselves through our own responsive act.

This apparently straightforward solution to identity is difficult to grasp, however, because our patterns of thought have been shaped by a false duality between transient and permanent, or between what Bakhtin calls the "once-occurrent" and the true. A performed act always has a sort of unity to it; that is, integrated reasons for its occurrence can be found. But it only happens once. Unhappily, Bakhtin notes, we have grown accustomed to associating the truth of an event with what is repeatable, constant, and universal in it, whereas in fact the opposite obtains: only the once-occurrent is fully true. "In this sense," Bakhtin writes, "the very word unity [*edinstvo*] should be discarded as overly theoretized;" key to understanding is "not unity but uniqueness" [*edinstvennost'*] (37). Abstract logic will not help us grasp this uniqueness or once-occurrent unity. But we do have a marvelously flexible tool at our disposal for this purpose, which is language. As Bakhtin notes in this early intimation of dialogism, words — with all their inevitable "fullness" — are ideally suited for "participative" modes of being. It is through words that the material of the world is most easily transformed from a state of givenness to a state of "positedness," *zadannost'*, awaiting a task. Bakhtin intimates further that only projections and tasks, that is, only what is posited for future solution rather than given in the past — can be talked about. Mere givenness, ready-made and always already there, is too coincident with itself and thus too indifferent, too inert, to require from us a conversation. In fact it cannot really be cognized at all, for cognition itself, Bakhtin insists, is a questing relationship among diverse consciousnesses.

The implications of this position (not, of course, wholly original with Bakhtin) are immense. In the second half of *Toward a Philosophy of the Act*, Bakhtin elaborates loosely on them — and while reading this difficult little book it might help to keep steadily in mind the main target of his concern. It is always the split between culture and life, and how to bridge that gap so that both sides are obligated. Merely to bring form and content together is insufficient. What is needed to achieve the proper clamp between culture and life is an attitudinal orientation that Bakhtin calls intonation or tone. "Emotional-volitional tone" is no passive vehicle; it is not something added to an utterance after the content has already been shaped. Nor is it mere reflex, a "passive psychic reaction." It is an external manifestation of the energy connecting that which is given (the world I wake up to; "culture in general" from which I receive my forms) with that which is not yet given, that which is "yet to be determined" or formed (that is, my life). My choice of "intonation" works on me in such a way that I cannot, however much I might desire it, lose myself in an act; on the contrary, I am forced to find myself in it. Tone permeates my act as soon as I "experience an experience as mine" (36).

"In all of Being I experience only myself — my unique self — as an I," Bakhtin writes (41). The motif of "mine," "my uniqueness," my own "uniquely obligated self" (also referred to as "once-occurrent Being as event" or my "nonalibi in Being" [40]) is a leitmotif throughout the essay. Such an egocentric focus might seem odd to readers familiar with the more famous, dialogic, other-directed Bakhtinian categories, where a self-confident first person singular, if it survives at all, is something of an embarrassment. For is not the "I" made up of many voices and various perspectives, is it not always conditioned by the needs of an Other, is not the whole idea of "mine" too reductive, solipsistic, static, monologic? Not at all — and why it is not is of crucial importance in grasping the dialogism to come.

Bakhtin, it could be said, began his philosophical career worrying about too little "I" in the world, not too much. He held that until an "I" could generate and answer for its own whole truth — that is, until it is willing to "undersign" or "put its signature on" an act — it is in no condition to interact with others. Perhaps surprisingly, Bakhtin insists that the unity (or, as he would prefer to put it, the uniqueness) that makes up my identity has little to do with the content of the acts I sign (truths or lies, goods or evils, inner consistency or flagrant contradiction), and everything to do with my acknowledging them as mine. My personality, he writes, is a "unity of answerability, not a constancy in content" (39). Several startling and — dare I say it? — refreshing things flow from this assumption.

First, Bakhtin is more or less indifferent to questions of justice, victimization, and such political-ethical questions as "Who is to blame?", "Do we get what we deserve?", "Why did this happen to me?", or "How can I express my rights, recover my rights, or enforce my rights in my struggle against an uncomprehending world?" The supremely apolitical Bakhtin, a philosophical stoic, is uninterested in self-pity and suspicious of those legalistic sorts of empowerment. He is concerned solely with one crucial aspect of an act: once it has happened to me, am I willing to sign it? My signature on an act, note, does not mean that I caused it or that I approve of it; it means only that I acknowledge it as an existing fact and that I will not withdraw into fantasy, denial, or utopia in the face of it. I agree to participate in it. Recall the eternal Russian question *"Chto delat'?"* [What Is To Be Done?], which has been answered over the years with such stiffneckery and whimsicality by Nikolai Chernyshevskii, Vasily Rozanov and Vladimir Lenin. To this question Bakhtin would say: Until a given, unique, unrepeatable "I" signs an act, nothing can be done — not for justice, nor for victims, nor for the whole huge world of the "non-I." Consciousness can move forward only in this answerable manner, because "I exist in a world of inescapable actuality, not of contingent possibility" (44). Here is Bakhtin before he arrived at the word-with-a-loophole and before the indestructible jesters of carnival began relativizing all values and laughing at death.

Second, Bakhtin insists on a pragmatic, concrete, nontransferable, hands-on criterion for obligation. This too is in subtle counterpoint with traditional Russian cultural values of collectivism, maximalism, communal sacrifice and poetic transcendence. "It is not the content of an obligation that obligates me, but my signature below it," Bakhtin writes (38); in fact, the more fastidiously we unify content in terms of a theory, "the poorer and more universal is the actual uniqueness" of that content (39). Thus my integrity and continuity are guaranteed not by stringing together a series of consciously chosen, compatible units of content — that human beings should be so fortunate to have that choice in their everyday lives — but by a string of personal signatures. Whatever I sign, I must work with; if I make a habit of refusing to sign, for whatever reason, I forfeit identity.

Categorical imperatives follow, but they are not Kant's. Since I am irreplaceable, I have irreplaceable potential and am obliged to act to "actualize my uniqueness" (41). Not to do so is to abdicate, to wish to be in another's place, or (worst of all) to attempt to live from an abstract, nonexistent time and place — in Bakhtin's parlance, to become a pretender. No question about it, irreplaceability and uniqueness guarantee anguish and doubt. There is something piercingly lonely about the entire model. But as compensation I can be assured that no initiative I take toward actualization can ever be entirely arbitrary; my act is always "unindifferent." Here Bakhtin stresses one easily misunderstood point. To live "from within myself and from my own unique place" does not mean to live *for* myself, that is, it is not, in the crude sense of the word, "selfish" (48–49, 60). Thinkers (and in this context, somewhat unjustly, Bakhtin mentions Nietzsche) who misconstrue this distinction might strive to free the self from the constraints of uniqueness. Since, however, meaningful freedom never happens all at once but is brought on incrementally, through repeated signatures and commitments, such liberators are left with "the absurdity of contemporary Dionysianism" (49).

Wonderful local insights abound in Bakhtin's essay, but three are especially telling: how his model deals with envy, politics, and love. Envy first. Since every unity is a uniqueness, and since our time-and-place at any moment is nontransferable, envy of another person is an ontological impossibility. After all, no one but I can do my specific "signed" task, and no one but the other can do the other's task. An envious orientation is simply an ignorant one. (This thought won't help us get through a bad day, but on a good day it can inspire us and save a great deal of time.) Or take his comments on politics, so unnervingly Russian. Similar to many of the Slavophiles, to Leo Tolstoy, and more recently to Alexander Solzhenitsyn, Bakhtin is suspicious of organized political activity and unimpressed by the benefits it might bring. Politics is always and on principle hostile to ethics. Persuasive moral scenarios contain two or three persons; as soon as you can no longer see or talk eye-to-eye with someone, as soon as you start thinking like a class-action suit, your effectiveness in the cosmos becomes less, not more. According to Bakhtin, "political answerability" and representational procedures, even the most benign, are fraught with distancing, depersonalization, ritualization — and can lead to unmanageable pride ("One has to develop humility to the point of participating in person and being answerable in person" [52]).

Safer and more satisfying than politics is Bakhtin's theory of love. It is, among other things, a lovely revisionist reading of the routine Christian adage that we should "love our neighbor as ourselves." This is difficult to do, Bakhtin intimates, not because we are innately selfish but because technically I cannot love my own self; I lack the categories for it. (The best I can do is fantasize some hypothetical other who might smile back at me and love me: this is the awful temptation of the mirror.) Our cognitive and creative forces are fueled not by reflections but by answerability, that is, by interaction between different, only temporarily consummated selves. During this interaction we do confer form on one another — in fact, such consummation is a gift we continually bestow upon other selves because each of us craves and deserves definition — but as long as the other is alive, we can never finalize his content or personality once and for all. Thus loving my neighbor as myself is not only poor advice (as if self-love were ever a model for anything); such activity is, strictly speaking, impossible. We should love our neighbor as our neighbor, as something distinct from us and only imperfectly translatable into our own terms.

The implication here is that before anything can be loved, boundaries must be confirmed and respected — for I can "answer" only across a boundary. For Bakhtin, the more of these boundaries and differentiations, the better. In his understanding, our psyches are constructed to be curious about difference, not hostile to it or frightened by it. What marks a "true love experience," then, is nothing necessarily erotic or possessive — and certainly nothing neurotic or compulsive — but rather a cognitive quality, a concentration of attention that enriches the beloved over time with extraordinarily individuated responses. "Lovelessness, indifference, will never be able to generate sufficient power to slow down and linger intently over an object, to hold and sculpt every detail and particular in it" (64). For this reason, Bakhtin concludes, only love can "see" the world with sufficient subtlety to be aesthetically productive. Appropriately, *Toward a Philosophy of the Act* breaks off on a lengthy "architectonic" analysis of self-other constructs in Pushkin's 1830 love lyric, "Razluka" [Parting].

Why, then, should we read this dense and difficult little book? The availability of Bakhtin's early ethical writings in English makes possible a rapprochement between Western images of Bakhtin (still quite beholden to, even bedazzled by, carnival and by refractive, open-ended dialogue) and the freshly de-ideologized, de-maximalized apolitical Bakhtin currently in the ascendancy in post-Communist Russia. Intellectuals over there, painfully sensitized to the dangers of politicized culture and ethical relativism, have paid much more attention than have we to Bakhtin's early philosophical texts. Not surprisingly, many post-Communist thinkers find in the idea of "architectonics" a very productive model. In contrast to the benign, generous, permeable, reversible give-and-take model of the dialogic self, and also in contrast to the transitory, wordless, ever-leaking one-dimensional carnivalistic self (really more a collective body than a self proper), the complexly responsible, ego-oriented and integrated architectonic self is exactly what is needed in our postmodernist, post-Communist times. Of all Bakhtin's "selves," it is this earliest self that is most concerned about individuation and answering for itself among others. While not yet fully dialogic itself, it is in training for the challenges and pitfalls of dialogue. Initiation into dialogue, it would seem, requires disciplined preparatory work. Not fidelity to a set of inherited rules, nor mere instincts and intuitions of love, nor vague intimations of a faceless wholeness will suffice.

To translate and package this complex philosophical fragment demands a high quality of professionalism. Vadim Liapunov (whose reputation as a leading scholar of the early texts is high in Russian Bakhtin circles) does an exemplary job with the scholarly apparatus of *Toward a Philosophy of the Act*. He provides not just the necessary references — thirty pages of notes — but also the etymology, largely German, of Bakhtin's most important terms: their genesis, ambivalences, and where the curious Anglophone lay philosopher might repair for more information. In the process, Liapunov reconstructs the history of Bakhtin's intellectual debts and reading habits, a task that Bakhtin himself — always supremely the servant of ideas and not of his own curriculum vitae — never bothered publicly to do. He simply read things, thought them through from his special perspective, and wrote down his reactions. For as Bakhtin remarked magisterially in his 1924 essay assessing formalist approaches to literature (the only substantial early piece actually prepared by its author for publication): "We have freed our study from the superfluous ballast of citations and references, for they lack any direct methodological significance in studies of a nonhistorical nature, while in a compressed work of a systematic nature they are entirely superfluous. For the qualified reader, they are unnecessary; for the unqualified, useless."[4]

---

[4]  "The Problem of Content, Material, and Form in Verbal Art," trans. Kenneth Brostrom, in *Art and Answerability*, 257.

The point is well taken. But times have changed, we are almost all unqualified, and in any event the major sources for Bakhtin's scholarly activity, given his international fame and high visibility, have become a matter of importance in their own right. Such bibliographical research is all the more imperative because biographical documents for the early period are relatively few. It is likely that Bakhtin never graduated formally from Petrograd University. He was something of a loner, a nonjoiner. If we are to believe his reminiscences fifty years after the fact, his most passionate learning experiences took place not in classrooms but in irregular study circles, one of which, "Omphalos," he recalled as a mix of the satiric spirit of Swift and the tomfoolery and irrepressible creativity of the youthful Pushkin's Arzamas. But Bakhtin censured even "the culture of circles"—which, he remarked, was too often dominated by "typical Russian chatter, chatter, with no serious scholarly papers at all."[5] Bakhtin wrote few letters. There were no children; apart from his wife, the adult Bakhtin had no intimate family. He left no extended memoirs. He remained cordial but formal with his colleagues, correct with his students, and he would never have turned his own personal life, so marked by the insecurity and casual tragedies of his era, into a reference point for any special understanding. His career pattern was decidedly peculiar. He lived by ideas.

In his editions of the early manuscripts, then, Vadim Liapunov has done Bakhtin the great service of taking him absolutely on his own terms. They provide nothing less than a proto-biography of Bakhtin's ideas. As such, Liapunov's work is a labor of love, the sort of love that "slows down and lingers intently" on its subject—and I believe that Bakhtin, for all his cavalier attitude toward the survival of his own written word, would have been astonished and grateful for it. *Toward a Philosophy of the Act* was transcribed fifty years after the writing, from water-damaged school notepads, barely legible and on the verge of disintegration, extracted from a lumber room in Saransk. The Russian publication of the text, and then this superb English edition, are yet another act that stands to bring Bakhtin the sort of "answerable" immortality that he believed only the word could bring.

---

5    "Razgovory s Bakhtinym," *Chelovek*, no. 5 (1993): 132–34, 141. The "circle" under censure was Vol'fil, the "Free Philosophical Association," whose sessions Bakhtin occasionally attended but at which he declined to deliver papers, dissatisfied with its "rhetorical eloquence, mostly of the liberal sort but also of a mystical, idealistic character."

# 3

# COMING TO TERMS WITH CARNIVAL

*The essay excerpted below originally appeared in* Bakhtin and the Classics *(Northwestern University Press, 2002: 5–26), edited by R. Bracht Branham. Branham is a specialist in Roman satire, especially Petronius, and a pioneering Bakhtin enthusiast within a discipline that initially received Bakhtin's incursions into its scholarly realm with some skepticism.*

## COMING TO TERMS WITH BAKHTIN'S CARNIVAL: ANCIENT, MODERN, SUB SPECIE AETERNITATIS (2002)

Protean carnival has long held center stage in debates over Bakhtin's legacy. In the postcommunist period alone, Russian readings present us with a remarkable spectrum. Some critics see Bakhtin's enthusiasm for carnival as Christian, godly, Eucharistic, inspired by the reverence for transfigured matter that is characteristic of the Eastern Orthodox Church. Others, equally visionary, have come to see carnival as sinister energy — demonic, violent, nihilistic, indifferent to individual pain and death, and thus in its essence and its effects Stalinist. Still others have classified carnival as a form of play: either the dangerous, disobedient sort of playfulness that strategically opposes itself to centralized power, or the more stupefied sort of foolishness that emerges in a population already traumatized by terror. A more sober group of scholars has investigated the carnival worldview in a neutral, hermeneutic way, as part of the academic study of folklore or theories of literary evolution.

These are all worthy, if incompatible, readings. But Bakhtin's legacy in this realm deserves more than a mere catalogue. Carnival logic is too organically prominent in Bakhtin, too omnipresent as that which stitches together his religious and secular concerns.[1] Coming to terms with carnival and its place in Bakhtin's philosophy would also benefit his current image in literary studies. It would help discipline the cult and trim back those ideas that now have the force of sanctified truth (for example, the canonical authority of Bakhtinian carnival for all types of "magic realism" in Latin American cultures); it might also help us to separate fact from fiction in Bakhtin's biography, so strewn with the heroic grotesque of rumor and legend that one is tempted to dismiss the life itself as hopelessly carnivalized. Happily, a mass of archival material, in Bakhtin's own hand and by the hands of students and friends, has been published in the last ten years. The intellectual sources of Bakhtin's theories are being filled in by scholars and sleuths.[2] Much of this testimony is contradictory, however, and even seems calculated to mystify. As Ken Hirschkop put the matter in his 1999 monograph *Mikhail Bakhtin: An Aesthetic for Democracy*: "For a long time, we knew very little about Bakhtin's life. Thanks to the efforts of post-glasnost Bakhtin scholarship, we now know even less."[3]

In one area, however, there is no dispute: Bakhtin was devoted to the carnival idea throughout his life. He associated it not only with the medieval feast and the public square but with a more general spiritual freedom, the loss of fetters that can accompany chance events or a lifting of deadlines and

---

[1]    For a pioneering discussion that documents, with great philological precision, Bakhtin's integration of profane and spiritual matters through carnival imagery during the Stalinist years, see Alexandar Mihailovic, *Corporeal Words: Mikhail Bakhtin's Theology of Discourse* (Evanston: Northwestern University Press, 1997), chaps. 4–6.

[2]    Not all of this sleuthing is complimentary to Bakhtin. See, for example, Brian Poole, who has demonstrated that Bakhtin incorporated verbatim (moved into Russian without credit) long stretches of Ernst Cassirer's published work on the medieval and Renaissance worldview; responsibility for this act, however, could lie with typists, editors, or simply the lack of non-Cyrillic typewriters. ("Bakhtin and Cassirer: The Philosophical Origins of Bakhtin's Carnival Messianism," in *"Bakhtin/'Bakhtin':* Studies in the Archive and Beyond," ed. Peter Hitchcock, special issue, *South Atlantic Quarterly* 97, no. 3–4 (summer/fall, 1998): 537–78, esp. 540–47).

[3]    See Hirschkop, *Mikhail Bakhtin: An Aesthetic for Democracy* (Oxford: Oxford University Press,1999), 111. In his chapter "Bakhtin Myths and Bakhtin History," Hirschkop points out falsifications in biographical fact (Bakhtin compiled a c.v. for himself that borrowed events from his brother's life); unsubstantiated legends about completed typescripts sent to publishing houses and subsequently destroyed in bomb raids or serenely smoked away as cigarette papers; an awesome reputation for erudition, which on inspection is wholly based on German plot digests. Hirschkop is harsher on credulous Bakhtin scholars who have accepted colorful rumor as fact than he is on Bakhtin himself, precarious survivor in a myth-laden, poorly provisioned, high-risk era (112–15).

quotas (the Russian root *prazd-*, as in *prazdnik* [free day or holiday], means celebratory and festive as well as unscheduled, empty, idle, in vain, "useless"). As he matured, Bakhtin linked carnival increasingly with gratitude. During the war years at Petrograd University, he and his brother ran a mock study circle, "Omphalos" [Navel], whose members took pride in being "jesters from scholarship."[4] Near the end of his life, Bakhtin frequently remarked on the "purely carnivalesque good fortune" of his fate — a political exile who survived Stalinism and spent his final years in a well-equipped hospital through the intervention of Andropov's daughter, one of his devoted students. This essay speculates on what it means to *see* and to feel life in a carnival way. It also investigates several paradoxes in Bakhtin's attitude toward the comic, suggests how contemporary genre theorists and philosophers of laughter might provide a context for Bakhtin's sacralized carnival idea, and wonders out loud whether such a spread of sensitivities and concerns can ever be reduced to an ethics.

### Carnival, a defense

It has seemed to many that the dynamics of carnival contradict the responsible and individualizing impulses of dialogue. Bakhtin himself saw no fatal contradiction. At no point did he consider the carnival mode necessarily disrespectful of personal freedom or indifferent to real history. Quite the contrary: he loaded an enormous number of virtues onto carnival space and time. Carnival-type laughter dissipates fear, encourages free inquiry, and is thus a route to knowledge. Laughing on the public square is radically democratic: there are no entry requirements, nothing has to be learned or earned. But in an odd twist, laughter — especially when incongruous or unexpected — can also be elitist. As with the early Christians who laughed while being fed to the lions, under certain conditions it takes fantastical discipline, spiritual courage, and a degree of self-confidence that approaches arrogance to be able to laugh. Bakhtin, like Freud in his fragment "Humor," surely sensed that ridiculing oneself — that is, "laughing down" the coward in

---

4  See *Besedy V. D. Duvakina s M. M. Bakhtinym* [*Conversations of V. D. Duvakin with M. M. Bakhtin*], 50–56; for Bakhtin's reference to "jesters from scholarship [or "science"]," 52. The word for "jesters" in the phrase here [*shuty*, pronounced *shooty*] is not the word for "simpleton" [*durak*] or "holy fool" [*yurodivyi*], each of which has specific resonances, respectively folkloric and spiritual. A *shut* is a civilized, mannered, even witty and learned "court" fool (such as we find in Shakespeare).

oneself — can preempt (or usurp) another's unfriendly response. As such, self-ridicule is a resoundingly healthy gesture, a profound form of self-affirmation and even of self-praise.

In a curious way, then, laughter can enable us and empower us, but not as contemporary theorists of power assume. Carnival laughter, which is based on modesty, inclusivity, and a sense of our relative smallness and transitoriness in the world of others (or in God's world), is a rebuttal of power-based etiologies. In Bakhtin's use of it, laughter alters personal attitudes; it does not change the givens of material existence. It facilitates what Epicurus held to be the proper limit of our pleasure, namely the removal of pain, understood both as physical discomfort and mental anxiety. Despite all the demonstrated meanness of satire and all the potential for hurt in parody, Bakhtin insisted that the central moment of true laughter was this sudden, often incongruous shedding or emptying-out of a negative burden, and thus a moment of relief and joy. Among the archival fragments published in the first volume to appear of Bakhtin's *Collected Works* (volume 5, the writings of the 1940s-1960s), we find a brief critical reference to *Le rire*, Henri Bergson's 1899 study of laughter : "Bergson's entire theory knows only the negative side of laughter," Bakhtin writes. "[But] laughter is a corrective measure; the comic is what does not have to be."[5]

The carnival spirit, then, is not only democratic, aristocratic, a carrier of knowledge, an agent for self-correction and a guarantor of slack and of relief;

---

[5]    "Smekh — eto mera ispravlenii; komicheskoe — eto nedolzhnoe" ("K voprosam teorii romana, k voprosam teorii smekha" ["Toward a theory of the novel and of laughter"], in "O Mayakovskom" ["On Mayakovsky"], in M. M. Bakhtin, *Sobranie sochinenii*, S. G. Bocharov i L. A. Gogotoshvili (Moscow: Russkie slovari, 1996), 5:50. [Henceforth *Bakhtin 1996.*] As the copious annotations to this jotting make clear, Bergson's theory of the comic is grim: laughter is uniquely human in that it is marked by an absence of feeling ("laughter has no greater foe than emotion") and by the stance of a disinterested spectator. But it is also naturally social ("laughter appears to stand in need of an echo"). *What* we laugh at, Bergson surmises, is always rigidity, inelasticity, the body reproducing itself blindly, repeating itself, or otherwise acting like a machine; and there are verbal equivalents of these gymnastics as well (i.e., wit). Although we might initially sympathize with the target of our laughter, our dominant impulse is to humiliate: "By laughter, society avenges itself for the liberties taken with it. It would fail in its object if it bore the stamp of sympathy or kindness... It has no time to look where it hits. Laughter punishes certain failings somewhat as disease punishes certain forms of excess, striking down some who are innocent and sparing some who are guilty, aiming at a general result and incapable of dealing separately with each individual case." See Henri Bergson, "Laughter" [*Le rire*, 1899], in *Comedy. "An Essay on Comedy" by George Meredith, "Laughter" by Henri Bergson*, ed. Wylie Sypher (Baltimore: Johns Hopkins University Press, 1959), 61–190, esp. 61–75, 185–88.

it is also healthy. Since it laughs down the bad, and since it contains no well-developed categories of memory, it does not look backward for its answers, as do most psychoanalytic therapies (this fact alone would explain, at least to a Bakhtinian mind, their mediocre rates of cure). Carnival laughter is simply not equipped to look for scapegoats or to glorify old wounds. It is not designed to keep us endlessly in analysis. What is more, although carnival is group-oriented and strenuously interpersonal, in contrast to many archaic primal cures there is no trace in it of that impersonal, violent, maniacal element associated with a Nietzschean reading of Dionysian rituals. Carnival laughter does not complain, nor will it embarrass us in public or private. And since it does not remember, it has nothing to forgive.

Finally: throughout his writings, Bakhtin hints that laughter serves as a precious means for deflating the genuinely corrosive emotions: regret, envy, disappointment, anger. As far as we can tell, Bakhtin was not especially alert to the benefits a given culture might reap from the results of *collective* anger, or envy, or disgust — such benefits, say, as political reform, cleanup campaigns against public corruption, or revolutionary social change. Such responses he tended to denigrate as satire, "one-sided" and thus uncreative: a merely instrumental response to the world. Bakhtin was a personalist. In addition he was something of a phenomenologist. He knew that anger and envy hinder perception. Obstruction of vision is a serious handicap, for, like his early mentor Kant, what Bakhtin values above all is clarity of perception, so essential to the scope and calibration of intellect. One theme that runs through all Bakhtin's writings is the immense difficulty of seeing ourselves soberly, from the outside, as another person might see us — a person for whom we are peripheral, no more than a temporary convenience or a passing stimulus. In a rueful insight appended to some notes toward an essay (never written) on Gustave Flaubert, jotted down in 1944, Bakhtin wrote: "Everything gets in the way of a person having a good look back at his own self."[6] Precisely laughter will help us to get this "good look," since it promotes modesty and scales down pretensions to authority. In his personal behavior Bakhtin, chronically in pain, was a Stoic; in his values, this admirer of Diogenes and Menippus was most certainly a Cynic.

---

[6]    "Vsyo prepiatstvuet tomu, chtoby chelovek mog oglianut'sia na sebia samogo." "O Flobere" ["On Flaubert" in *Bakhtin 1996*: 130–37, esp. 137]. The Flaubert fragment ends on this sentence. These notes by Bakhtin were found clipped together with a bibliography (and further commentary in another's hand), all of which suggests that Bakhtin projected a book on Flaubert during the Savelevo years.

To the disgusted, angry, or disillusioned person he would recommend either silence — or laughter.

Bakhtin respected dialogue, but doubtless felt not everyone in his immediate environment deserved it. And if the interlocutors on hand did not measure up, then it was no less real to hold dialogues with Socrates, Dostoevsky, or Rabelais: personalities far less dead and far more available for responsible exchange. Under stress, in public situations, when answers are expected, the words we utter explicate things and tie us down. Laughter, however, does not need to explain; it is at home in the realm of what "does not have to be." A laugh is responsive — but preserves the privacy and multiple meanings of the response; while loosening up a definition it does not insist on any specific replacement terms. It cannot so insist, because laughter, as a reflex of muscles and lungs, is in principle dynamic, thus destructive of fixed states. One cannot engage in this activity for long or at the same level of intensity without appearing (and perhaps even becoming) hysterical or possessed. It works in bursts. And since a burst of laughter — like a burst of shame — is a bridge to a new state or perception, it is always transitory.[7]

Thus laughter is a wonderful human resource. It is important to stress, however, that the virtues Bakhtin sees in carnival laughter are in no sense unique to his vision. They are the mainstream arguments routinely made by literary theorists and psychologists who would rescue the comedic genres from the millennia of neglect they have suffered through Aristotle's casual dismissal, at least in his extant texts, of all that is "non-tragic." Of the three basic theories about why we laugh — because we feel superior (the view of Plato and Aristotle), because we are struck by an incongruity (the

---

[7]    In his 1996 contribution to the philosophy of laughter, Leonid Karasev argues that the opposite of laughing is not seriousness or weeping but rather a sense of *shame* (Leonid Karasev, *Filosofiia smekha* [Moscow, 1996: "Shame is the reverse side of laughter, its symbolic inner seam" [67].) Laughter should not be opposed to seriousness or weeping, because those can go on forever; they make sense in prolongation and can even become "institutions." Neither laughing nor shame build lasting structures; both are instantaneous emotive explosions that sweep over us like little miracles, altering our moods radically. Although it is true that laughter optimally opens us up to new potential whereas shame (not to be confused with its more durable intellectual counterpart, guilt) makes us cringe and closes us down, both laughter and shame are borderline states: responsive, transitory, transfiguring. If a burst of laughter brings relief and the bond of benevolent communion, then a moment of shame is the moment of acknowledgment of one's own participation in evil. "Authentic laughter," Karasev writes (very much in the spirit of Bakhtin), "is born at the juncture of Good and Evil, as Good's answer to Evil: a good-intentioned response to Evil's opening line [*"blagoi otvet na repliku zla"*] (60)."

view of Kant, Kierkegaard, Schopenhauer, Bergson), and because we seek relief (Freud's psycho-physiological explanations)[8] — Bakhtin would have endorsed the second and sympathized, probably, with the third. Where he departs from these classic theorists and contributes an intonation of his own is in his emphasis on the sanity, goodness, and normalcy of a self that is split and "alienated" by laughter. Laughter not only makes me feel good (and bonds me with other laughers); it is also the most reliable means at my disposal for insuring that I remain "non-coincident with myself."[9] This bifurcation is not pathological, Bakhtin insists, nor the stuff of trauma; it is the most ordinary move in the world. When I look back (or over) at my own self, it is only natural that *what* I see — the noble shadow cast by Hegel's self-alienated Subjective Spirit — will appear to me as "someone else." Such self-alienation, celebrated with gusto in the essay "Epic and Novel," caused Bakhtin no anguish. He saw in it an endless potential for rejuvenation and an exciting new understanding of wholeness. But his attachment to the carnival idea, rich in distancings, is nevertheless paradoxical within the context of his thought as a whole.

### Several paradoxes

First, Bakhtin is committed to laughter — as physiological, psychological, and sociological truth — but in general, he is not a rigorous student of the passions. (The closest we can come to placing him in a "school" is probably alongside David Hume and Adam Smith, who also held that communication is pleasurable and sympathetic co-experience a craving of human nature.) Sentiments other than pity and love are hardly ever invoked in Bakhtin's

---

8     Peter L. Berger, *Redeeming Laughter: The Comic Dimension of Human Experience* (Berlin: Walter de Gruyter, 1997), part 2, 99–173, divides up the terrain somewhat differently, between laughter as "diversion" (benign humor), as "consolation" (tragicomedy), as "intellect" (wit), as "weapon" (satire), and then the special psychological benefits of folly and redemptive transcendence.

9     See Bakhtin, "Author and Hero in Aesthetic Activity," in *Art and Answerability. Early Philosophical Essays by M. M. Bakhtin*, eds. Michael Holquist and Vadim Liapunov, trans. Vadim Liapunov (Austin: University of Texas Press), 126–27: "What is the basis of my inner confidence? What straightens my back, lifts my head, and directs my gaze forward? Once again, it is my being present to myself as someone yet-to-be-that is what supports my pride and self-satisfaction...The form of my life from within is conditioned by my rightful folly or insanity of *not coinciding* — of not coinciding *in principle* — with me myself as a given."

writings. Much less are the passions examined, ranked, or sequenced. Again like his mentors Hegel and Kant, Bakhtin believed that human understanding of a culturally valuable sort — and the survival of culture was the highest priority for philosophers of the Marburg school — is not mystically emotive or untranscribable. Understanding is knowable, conscious, and cognitive. But unlike his august predecessors Hegel and Kant, Bakhtin never systematically discussed the relation between comic, tragic, and sublime passions, between laughter and tragedy, or between comedy and ethical duty. And so our first paradox: laughter and the comedic are reflexes of the well-tuned mind and body that the highly cerebral, morally astute Bakhtin embraces and places at the center of his carnival scenarios. But what sort of knowledge can they offer, and are there any duties that come with the terrain?

Once we raise the specter of "duty," another paradox follows. The carnival experience is defined as humanizing, consoling, wisdom-bearing. But try as we might, it is difficult to picture for long a laughing carnival face. Does carnival *have* a face? Does that face have eyes? If it does, then those eyes don't make eye-contact. It's the mouth and cheeks that matter, a sort of buttocks promoted to above the neck. Eye contact is heavy with obligation. Human eyes that gaze out but do not respond are reptilian eyes; the effect of their stare is far more frightening than the rudeness of turning away the face. But Bakhtin's carnival laughter is so (literally) effaced that it appears unattached to individual bodies with histories or memories of their own. What does the carnival body want? It is not political or greedy; it does not covet material goods (it has neither home nor storage space). Least of all is it mean-spirited, superior to others, aggressive or satirical, even when it is the featured hero of those sadomasochistic passages in Rabelais. What is more, Bakhtin hints at something precious about "carnival experience" that we can no longer appreciate — something an earlier historical epoch was able to grasp but that modern humanity no longer can. We have now arrived at a further paradox, which feels like an inconsistency in Bakhtin's sense of history.

In general, Bakhtin was an optimist about the growth and differentiation of human consciousness over time. If we take as normative his essay on the chronotope and his drafts for a study of the bildungsroman, we see how profoundly Bakhtin believed that over time, meaning must always *grow*. As literature matures, the consciousness and initiative of its heroes are ever more individuated and personally "voiced": slowly, the disjointed moments, interchangeable fates, and blind chance of a Greek romance give way to metamorphosis and then to genuine agency, culminating in the fully distinct and answerable personalities created by Goethe and Dostoevsky. One of

Bakhtin's most thoughtful critics, Graham Pechey, has even suggested that Bakhtin, after putting forth several successive and provisional "candidates for immortality" in his work (the personality, the common people), ultimately cast *meaning itself* in the role of major hero.[10] "The story of meaning," Pechey writes, "is, like much of Bakhtin's own story, a tale of exile which is often the richer in outcome for the length of its duration." Truth wanders and accumulates; no matter where we start or end our journey, the longer we take to get there, the more of value we will have to say. Ideas, as they age, are not purified or reduced to a single point. Duration itself is a virtue. In Pechey's view, this cumulative, unregulated, unsystematized concept of historicity—what Bakhtin calls "Great Time"—reflects a faith in the "eternity of semantic potential."

The faith that Bakhtin professed in the anti-entropic growth of meaning Pechey calls "the epistemological sublime." Such a sublime state of affairs might be said to characterize an entire subset of literary genres, all of which feature a mode of laughing self-awareness that insists on seeing the world as chaos. This is chaos not so much in the negative, stressful sense of that word as in the positive sense that the term enjoys in classical Chinese philosophy, where it indicates not the absence of order but the sum of all orders. Chaos thus understood is a field that can always accept *one more variable* and not be violated by it.[11] Such a chaotic mode of being, I believe, can house much that is essential to Bakhtin's carnival idea. In the Western tradition, we glimpse

---

[10]   Graham Pechey, "Eternity and Modernity: Bakhtin and the Epistemological Sublime," *Theoria* 81–82 (October 1993): 61–85, esp. 62, 63. The "eternity of potential" that Pechey posits for Bakhtin is saved from the dangers of relativism and abstract metaphysics by its insistence on the *"positional* absolute." That absolute, Pechey argues, is one of the few fixed points in Bakhtin's profoundly non-Platonic world.

[11]   In a paper that has not, to my knowledge, been followed up in Western Bakhtinistics, James H. VanderMey argues for a connection between Chinese thought and Bakhtin's patently non-Platonic system of values. "A changeless principle of Being behind it all is the cosmogonic vision that lies at the base of Western mythologies," he writes. "Chaos, linked with changeableness, contingency and relativity, then becomes the evil absence of order. The relationships between particulars become uninteresting and even threatening to the developed logocentric order. Bakhtin's architectonic project cuts against the grain of Western logocentrism... [In the classical Chinese tradition,] chaos is not the absence of any order; it is the sum of all orders—the plenitude, the field upon which particular events emerge. Chaos is not bad, empty, or separate... What Chinese thought can add to the Bakhtinian project is its experience in thinking in terms of difference, 'eventness' and harmony, rather than in terms of identity, being and Truth." James VanderMey, "Languages as Multiple Guiding Ways: Some Chinese Resources for Critical Practice." Paper delivered at a panel devoted to "Institutional Bakhtins" at "Aesthetics and Ideologies: An Interdisciplinary Conference," Michigan State University, 6–8 October 1994.

such a worldview at work in Diogenes and Menippus. Closer to our own time — and to philosophers dear to Bakhtin's heart — it is the *Kunstchaos* of the German Romantics, especially Friedrich Schlegel, who strove to elevate the genre of the fragment into a genuine art form. The chaotic-comedic principle is also germane to Hegel's discussion of the aesthetic shape of history, in which, catharsis-like, "comedy functions as a clearinghouse at the end of a particular civilizational course."[12] Only with the tragic mask removed can we finally take a good look back at our own self.

If, however, laughter and the comic are so indispensable to Bakhtin, and if the steady growth of meaning over time is a central preoccupation of his philosophy, one cannot help but notice that carnival laughter is radically unlike other historically developing entities in Bakhtin's cosmos. To this general growth pattern of good things, laughter is the major exception. Looked at over historical time, laughter has gotten thinner and worse. It is "reduced," collapsed into satire, moved from day to night, from Eros to Thanatos, from the public square to the smutty closet. Elsewhere in Bakhtin's scenarios, the future is favored over the past, the forward-looking open novel preferred to the closed-down epic. But here in the realm of carnival there is nostalgia and regret. The past of human laughter is rich — and irretrievable. How might we explain this grim vision?

Several hypotheses are possible. Gary Saul Morson has suggested that political cunning might have played a role. According to Morson, Bakhtin celebrates an anarchic, Dionysian vision of carnival in his study of Rabelais but ignores the more documentable influence of Attic comedy because, in the Stalinist 1930s, Bakhtin himself was playing the role of Aristophanes. He too was a cultural conservative in a Saturnine state corrupted by mob rule, and that fact had to be masked.[13] Another explanation, hinted at earlier in this essay, might lie in the relationship between laughter, privacy, and modesty. During the Stalinist years, when lyrics were being routinely politicized and epics (even opera libretti) sovietized, it could well have seemed to Bakhtin that only laughter of the most primal, unmediated sort stood a chance of

---

12   Bainard Cowan, "Dante, Hegel, and the Comedy of History," in *The Terrain of Comedy*, ed. Louise Cowan (Dallas: The Dallas Institute of Humanities and Culture, 1984), 89–109, esp. 101. See also the excellent discussion of Hegel's connection to a comedic or carnival vision by Galin Tihanov, *The Master and the Slave: Lukacs, Bakhtin, and the Ideas of Their Time* (Oxford: Oxford University Press, 2000), ch. 9 ("Hegel and Rabelais").

13   Comment by Gary Saul Morson to a paper by Anthony Edwards, "Historicizing the Popular Grotesque: Aristophanes and Bakhtin's *Rabelais and His World*," delivered at "Bakhtin and the Classics" conference, Emory University, 26–28 March 1998.

resisting the distortions of "progressive" (read: Hegelian) historical treatment. Some have even suggested that carnival was part of a larger archaic protest on Bakhtin's part against industrialization and modernization. From what we can tell, Bakhtin did not particularly welcome industrialized society, whether communist *or* capitalist.[14] Imperfectly or partially realized, modernization meant economic inequality. And when successfully realized, it smoothed out difference, stuffed people with ready-made things, taught you to swallow and hoard what you earned, harnessed you to the golden calf, and killed carnival.

Against that philistine model, Bakhtin would advise us to cultivate the ability to put ourselves in many different places — rapidly, sequentially, and at will. We should struggle against the tendency to affirm our own "I" as a fixed center of anything, and withhold from the experience of that "I" anything like a final word. I must accomplish a Copernican revolution on my own self — but not by denying my self or discrediting its experience. To do so would simply turn me into a voided space, a "pretender." Rather, the route I must take to reorient my "I" is the route Dostoevsky took to achieve his Copernican Revolution in the polyphonic novel. We must *multiply* the perspectives of the "I" by moving it continually outside of itself, insisting

---

14    See Craig Brandist, "Bakhtin, Cassirer and Symbolic Forms," in *Radical Philosophy* 85 (1997): 20–27. In Brandist's view, Bakhtin was inspired in his "historicizing" shift from Kant to Hegel by Cassirer's *Philosophy of Symbolic Forms*. Cassirer endorsed Hegel's faith in the forward motion of human thought but replaced Hegel's rigid logic with a more open-ended dialectic fueled by the "law" of symbolism, which everywhere works toward freeing us from the authoritative power of myth. Brandist argues that Bakhtin picks up on this opposition between the liberating multi-voiced symbol and myth's petty tyranny. "Myth" thus becomes a universal stand-in for the dead past, the inert epic, the single-voiced — and thus impoverished — lyric. Bakhtin's novel-centric, lyrophobic and epic-phobic essays of the 1930s all attest handsomely to this conversion. But Brandist has also claimed, in a roundtable discussion of Bakhtin's Rabelais project, that Bakhtin was not immune to the appeal of a more sociopolitical sort of myth: Russian nineteenth-century populism (entry in *Dialog. Karnaval. Khronotop* 1 (1997): 24–27). Like Bakhtin, Russian populists were influenced by German Romanticism and invested heavily in the mystique of "the people" — uncomplicated in its needs, unstratified in its social organization, utopian in its virtues. At this point Brandist makes a fertile remark that can bridge the two eras, prerevolutionary and postrevolutionary, and help locate Bakhtin in his own time. The Russian populists (unlike the more urban-minded Marxists) put their faith in the peasant commune; its ethos of collective responsibility and routine redistribution of wealth defined Russia's future as distinct from the crumbling, consumer-oriented West. Populists distrusted "primary capital accumulation." Bakhtin, in this respect a populist "fellow traveler," transferred the traditional distrust of populists under the old regime to the new-regime *Stalinist* "capital accumulation project," achieved at an entirely new scale of alienation and violence.

that it look back at its losses and gains from an outside position. And this must be done joyfully, gratefully, with the awareness that all these athletic maneuvers will never change the material givens of the world.

Conceived in this way, and invoking the religious imagery that permeates many of Bakhtin's most intimate scenarios, a carnival attitude can bring to a person the same benefits that gazing at an icon can bring to a soul in distress. A believer turns toward an icon in a needful state, when the spirit requires new ways out. This reverent gesture is not a denial of the world, nor is it seriously intended as a substitute for the world. Least of all is it the "bad gaze" of contemporary literary theory, which is supposed to reify, objectify, rigidify, and thus insult the thing it looks at. Contemplating an icon can console and transfigure the one on the outside, because the holy image is not believed to be merely an object. It contains in itself dialogic energy — which is to say, the icon is gazing back. (The two parties look *into* each other, not *at*.) A properly reciprocal reading of iconic space, like a proper orientation of the body during carnival, requires that we dislocate ourselves from single-point perspective. I must free myself from the prejudice that my body is at some focal center of the universe, poised along a visual corridor, ready to "walk into" the painting on my own terms. In short, I must be liberated from the thought that the comfortable perspective on things from *my* body is the only perspective that is real.

To be sure, if measured against the realistic optics of a photograph or a Renaissance portrait, Christian Orthodox icons do contain "inconsistencies." The flat, inverted planes of an icon offer the viewer a set of internally irreconcilable, "unrealistic" perspectives.[15] Visual paradox aids us in our struggle against the despair of entrapment; gazing along those strange incompatible planes, our repertory of responses (exits or paths forward) is enriched. It is possible that on some level Bakhtin — a devout Orthodox believer — hoped that carnival would function as an icon in just this sense. Of course, the *incarnations* of carnival are governed by an aesthetics wholly

---

[15] Charles Lock, an astute student of Bakhtin and Orthodox thought, has carried this icon analogy further. Renaissance perspective itself, Lock affirms, is a modern development that protects what is "inside the frame" from crude and uninvited contact. The subject in perspectival art, for all its roundedness and realism, is disembodied and safe — because inside the frame, Lock writes, "the optical becomes supreme, and the senses are valued insofar as they operate over distances (7)." See Charles Lock, "Iconic Space and the Materiality of the Sign," *Religion and the Arts* 1, no. 4 (Winter 1997): 6–22. Compare this comfortable distance with the carnival body, which celebrates almost every organ except the eyes; it relishes being inside, on top, underneath all at once, and it breaks the frame down.

opposite to that of Eastern Orthodox religious art: ample three-dimensional volumes that are forbidden in the Orthodox sanctuary, folds of flesh in place of the ascetic and serenely seeing eye, scuffles and curses (albeit always cheerful) on the public square instead of contemplation and stasis. But the spiritual harvest is comparable. We become more agile. Bakhtin understood carnival metaphysically as a "moment of transfer" from one mood to the next: an organ, as it were, for the production of our own freedom of response. In this sense only can we speak of Bakhtin's modernism. Twentieth-century modernist icons such as Picasso's Cubist guitars, with their flexible mapping and overlapping of space, provide the sort of visual freedom that the carnival vision also holds out. Since carnival is surplus-oriented [*izbytochnyi*], it always generates more ways in, and more unexpected ways out, than one needs. Thus such art can never be fully efficient, utilitarian, representational, or accountable in a strictly economic sense.

The above argument is yet another reason why Bakhtin might have been so drawn to Dostoevsky. The great Russian novelist argued in much the same way against the economic materialists and nihilists of his own 1860s. If I am to be free — Dostoevsky wrote a propos of the radical journalists who boasted of valuing boots over Shakespeare and cabbage soup over the Sistine Madonna — what I need in my life is an unreachable *ideal*, not some balance sheet.[16] An ideal will always grow alongside us, whereas a balance sheet breathes death. It also explains why Dostoevsky and Bakhtin, living out their lives in a materialist age, were so interested in miracles (sacred and profane), those moments where the absolutely unaccountable occurs. Several fine studies have been carried out recently on the theme of Bakhtin and the "apophatic tradition": the ideal of *not* naming a thing, not counting or accounting for it, resisting any attempt to limit it through frames or definitions.[17] At its extreme point, apophatic practice approaches the ideal of a kenotic emptying-out. Such kenosis leaves the spirit nourished but the

---

[16]  See Fyodor Dostoevsky, "Mr. —bov and the Question of Art" [1861], in *Dostoevsky's Occasional Writings* (Evanston: Northwestern University Press, 1963 / repr. 1997), 126: "How, indeed, is one to determine clearly and incontestably what one has to do in order to approach the ideal of all our desires and of all that mankind desires and strives for? One can make a guess, one can invent, conjecture, study, dream and calculate, but it is impossible to calculate every future step of the whole as one does a calendar."

[17]  See Randall Poole, "The Apophatic Bakhtin," in *Bakhtin and Religion: A Feeling for Faith*, eds. Paul J. Contino and Susan M. Felch (Evanston: Northwestern University Press, 2001), 151–75, and K. G. Isupov, "Apofatika Bakhtina," *Dialog. Karnaval. Khronotop* 3 (1997): 19–31. Poole makes the case from the secular perspective of intellectual history; Isupov, from mystical theosophy.

body — and the future — unencumbered. Key for Bakhtin, it appears, was the freedom to be found in plenitude without accumulation.

Plenitude that does not pile up: such is the logic of carnival abundance. It comes, goes, does not stick, should not stick: it is useful only as a lubricant for the spirit. One can see, in Rabelais's novel, how all those outrageous carnival catalogues — for example, that menu of codpieces and arse swipes for Gargantua that we get in the opening chapters — are hilarious precisely because they provide us with superfluous abundance, a parody of both epic heroism and utilitarian bookkeeping. Here is your list (since you require a list), but all it proves is that the richness of the material world is inexhaustible and not to be contained within it. Carnival writing takes the archaic genre of the catalogue and the inventory and makes it joyous and fertile. And this, Bakhtin insists, is what all true novels do.

### Larger contexts

Let me now attempt to put Bakhtin's spiritualized tasks for carnival into broader perspective. As we suggested earlier, the virtues that Bakhtin bestows on carnival laughter — fearlessness, flexibility, survival, ambivalence, mental and psychological relief — are the routine ones celebrated by philosophers of laughter and apologists for the comedic. To focus Bakhtin's contribution, let us consider the most famous European classic that raises the comedic to serious religious heights. We then close on a concern that lies deep at the core of Bakhtin's thought, at the intersection of his most precious genres and modes: how a carnival approach to the world is inherently a theory of creativity.

That world text is Dante's *Divine Comedy*. Bakhtin devotes only a few provocative paragraphs to this masterwork, where he associates its structure with the vertically constrained unfreedom of the medieval worldview in tense contradiction with real time.[18] But his lead has been taken up by others. In the

---

[18] See "Forms of Time and Chronotope in the Novel," in *The Dialogic Imagination: Four Essays by M. M. Bakhtin*, trans. Caryl Emerson and Michael Holquist (Austin: University of Texas Press, 1981), 158. The extraordinary tension that pervades all Dante's world, Bakhtin writes, is "the result of a struggle between living historical time and the extratemporal other-worldly ideal. The vertical, as it were, compresses within itself the horizontal, which powerfully thrusts itself forward. There is a contradiction, an antagonism between the form-generating principle of the whole and the historical and temporal form of its separate parts. The form of the whole wins out." Further down this page in the first edition, an inexplicable translation error reverses Bakhtin's

1970s, genre theorists from the Dallas Institute of Humanities and Culture began to read Dante's cosmos through a Bakhtinian lens. Major essays from this school are collected in an anthology edited by Louise Cowan, *The Terrain of Comedy* (1984). To organize her project Cowan devises an equivalent of Bakhtin's chronotope, but without his egregious privileging of the novel. She distributes human affects and strivings equitably among the four major genres, or as she prefers, "terrains," of lyric, tragic, comedic, and epic.[19] For her and her students, the most complexly interesting of these terrains is the one closest to Bakhtin's carnival chronotope: comedy. The work of this group, especially as it pertains to Dante's *Divine Comedy*, suggests a possible common denominator among disparate comedic affects and passions.

Indeed, only a cosmos as large as Dante's, and ultimately as redeemable from the perspective of the mortal who travels through it, could encompass all the benefits that comedy is supposed to provide while spending so much time, as it were, "down below." The terrain of comedy, Cowan affirms, is always "the realm of hope in a fallen world." It is a place toward which we can be guided, even if the Inferno is our first and most protracted exhibit. Cowan and her colleagues spend some time on this topographical progression upward, with special attention to the types of heroes we can expect at each level: infernal, purgatorial, paradisal. In brief, the argument is this.

---

meaning. The final paragraph before the section break on p. 158 should read: "But there were frequent attempts to resolve, so to speak, historical contradictions 'along the vertical,' attempts...to deny temporal divisions and linkages (from this point of view, all essentials can exist simultaneously), attempts to lay open the world as a cross-section of pure simultaneity and co-existence ..." The erroneously interpolated phrase "There are no" conveyed the opposite of Bakhtin's intent. This passage on Dante is important because it suggests (correctly, in my view) that Dostoevsky's polyphony was of Dante's sort: not only "melodic" or developmental / individuated in time, as is dialogue (the profane or sublunary plot), but also "harmonic" — sacred, vertical, aligned with fixed and permanent value.

[19]   See Louise Cowan, ed., *The Terrain of Comedy* (Dallas: Dallas Institute of Humanities and Culture, 1984), 1–18, "Introduction." Reaccented in terms of its time-space and expanded somewhat in its implications for temporality, Cowan's genre cycle (ibid. 9) has the following parameters. The *lyric* is immediately present, emotional, chamber-sized, the realm of "consummation and love." *Tragedy* is less compact, a matter of families rather than lovers: as the realm of suffering, loss, fragmentation, tragic time "looks backward" for its meaning and pain. *Epic* is larger still; it is the realm of struggle, of building, restoring, or founding the just city; and in this duty-driven mode, epic heroes travel the world, confident of their success because the privileged time of epic (in contrast to tragedy) is the future, the *end* of the quest. Further page references in text are to this "Introduction."

The realm of *infernal comedy* is populated with rogues, tricksters, deceivers, cynical minds in tough vigorous bodies. Wickedness is omnipresent and naturally multiplies. So much evil cannot be defeated by frontal attack, which would be suicidal; it can only be outwitted. In infernal comedy, the only resistance possible is "deception and delay," deceiving the deceivers and delaying the final word. The next tier, *purgatorial comedy,* offers another cast of characters and plots. What reigns here is not malicious or aggressive evil but incompetence and weakness, bad luck or confused souls; sufficient against these vices are the gentler, more common delaying tactics of confusion, suspension, interruption, "waiting to see." Although time is capable of healing things, it rarely does so in a wholly coherent way. The world of purgatorial comedy is not all of one piece — and that, surely, is part of its comedic effect, part of the reason it survives. It contains pockets of rest and restoration, marked off as if by magic from the stressful politics of the everyday world. (Consider the Forest of Arden in Shakespeare's *As You Like It*, where merely crossing the boundary assures transfiguration.) In such gardens and forests, deception is again present, but only in its soft, "loverly" variant, as comic doublings and disguise. Sweet are the uses of its adversity. Such deception is never deployed to hurt or punish people but only to make things more bearable, to make the world smile and laugh, to help events (that is, marriages) work out.

What about Paradise? If Purgatory requires some cunning and initiative on the part of its residents, *paradisal comedy* is comedic precisely because we are lifted to this level not by our own efforts and receive there more than we deserve. The god of comedy is nowhere a jealous god. Thus the theme of deception and disguise — which in infernal comedy is straight-out cheating and lying, and in purgatorial comedy is lighthearted cross-dressing — is at this ultimate paradisal level associated with divine grace, magic, and art. In connection with this highest realm, Louise Cowan makes a wonderful observation permeated with Bakhtinian intonations. The comedic terrain, Cowan writes, is always about "the hope...of being loved" (15). For this reason, "not revelation...but *receptivity* leads to its summit."

Let us now walk through Dante's landscape in a literary thought experiment, populating Cowan's behavioral grid with texts from Bakhtin's Russia and Russian literature. First, the Inferno. This lowest tier of comedy helps us to grasp how Bakhtin could laugh at Stalinism while neither dismissing nor trivializing its evil. The Terror of the 1930s and 40s was beyond individual response. In an infernal realm, justice and virtue, if pursued too rigidly, are positive handicaps. Naïvete will perish. To survive not only physically but also in some sense morally — that is, to avoid being forced to compromise or betray others — the appropriate tools are masks, duplicity, and multiplicity. If one must perform a distasteful public act in order to stay alive (as Bakhtin had to do in the early 1950s, in his capacity as Chair of the Department of World Literature at Saransk State Teachers College, prefacing each of his official presentations with a hymn of praise to Stalin), then make sure there is no concrete addressee who might be hurt by it. Make sure that everyone in that hellish landscape understands that words of this sort are merely phatic, not genuine utterances. For there is one prime, rock-bottom value respected in comedy of every type (and in Bakhtin's carnival as well): that *not everyone perish*, that someone to whom we have made a difference be left alive. Only if that remains true do our scattered selves have a chance to survive in the minds of others.

Is purgatorial comedy also a haven for Bakhtin's carnival vision? I believe it is: in five centuries of amoral self-serving picaros, all those Sancho Panzas whom Bakhtin always prefers to the Don Quixotes. Anton Chekhov most likely intended his plays as "comedies" in the purgatorial sense. Failure in them is rarely due to malice, and more often caused by an inability to connect, by bad timing, cowardice and weariness. And then there are the petty adventurers and pretenders of Bakhtin's beloved Nikolai Gogol. As a rule, Gogol specialists are not enthusiastic about Bakhtin's "carnivalization" of their writer's weird, demon-ridden landscapes. They consider Bakhtin too quick to lighten up the situation, to romanticize the effects of Gogol's grotesque, to see folk humor, punning wordplay and spiritual receptivity where in fact there is nothing but blank voided space.[20] But such benevolent readings are characteristic of Bakhtin. He reads Dostoevsky through the same optimistic filter. A blank space for Bakhtin is not a void but only a temporarily *cleared* space, a space that is waiting for new meaning to flow in along newly available perspectives — which is, indeed, the message of purgatorial comedy. All is not yet over. It might be neither fair nor fun, but dying is no longer an option. So work off one sin at a time and keep

---

[20] For this "lightened-up" interpretation of Gogol, see Bakhtin, M. M. "The Art of the Word and the Culture of Folk Humor (Rabelais and Gogol)," in *Semiotics and Structuralism: Readings from the Soviet Union*, eds. Henryk Baran and A. J. Hollander (White Plains NY: International Art and Sciences Press, 1976), 284–96. Bakhtin's dissertation discussed Gogol in some detail. Exemplary of scholarly skepticism toward Bakhtin's Gogol is the essay "Karnaval i ego okrestnosti" by Yurii Mann, dean of Soviet-Russian Gogol studies, which concludes: "The forms of comedism [in Gogol] which we have touched on here not only interact with the carnival tradition, but also resist that tradition and cast it off — at times rather strenuously" (*Voprosy literatury* 1, 1995: 154–82): 181.

your aspirations small: only then can entropy be reversed. By definition, all sinners are on an upward path.

The highest realm, paradisal comedy, is also a crucial part of Bakhtin's carnival mode. Perhaps it is not so much a part, however, as it is a *moment*, because Paradise (like the Inferno) does not know developmental time. Thus this highest domain can explain, as no other locus can, carnival's most ecstatic flashpoints, those moments that Bakhtin unabashedly calls "miraculous." Here belong the mass of "interpenetration" metaphors that have been traced throughout the text of *Rabelais and His World*, with their theological resonances of divine intercession.[21] Here also belong the best moments of Dostoevsky's Idiot, Prince Myshkin. Myshkin is that pure comedic marker: he does not "fit." But for all his awkwardness and outsideness, and for all the confusion and pain caused by his oddly charismatic person, Bakhtin insists that the atmosphere around Myshkin is bright and joyous, a "carnival heaven."[22] What is possible in paradisal comedy is not permitted in realms farther down—and one index of this special status of Paradise is the vexed relationship between comedy and memory.

Infernal comedy—or "carnival hell," as Bakhtin calls it— knows the wrong sort of memory. It is static, obsessive, stuck on itself, like the carnival hell of Nastasya Filippovna in *The Idiot* or Anna Karenina in her final moments, giving herself up to the punitive downward slide. Purgatorial comedy, in contrast, is time-sensitive, developmental, always potentially creative, and thus knows the right sort of memory. This is Konstantin Levin (to continue from Tolstoy's novel) deciding to live and not to die when he realizes, quite by accident at the end of the book, that even sinners can be trusted to make the right choices and invest in the good. Paradisal comedy, of course, is already at a height beyond earthly right and wrong. Thus it can transcend personal memory, even the tragic memory of an unjust death. Here, of course, belongs the glorious and transfiguring scene at the end of Dostoevsky's final novel, Alyosha Karamazov at the Stone, rallying a group of enthusiastic young disciples who have gathered for the funeral of their

---

[21] See Mihailovic, *Corporeal Words*, esp. chap. 5, "Carnival and Embodiment in *Rabelais and His World*," esp. 149–55. For a darker Protestant interpretation of Bakhtin's religious imagery, with an excellent discussion of Bakhtin's distinction between "bad" (official) and "good" (open, tragic, pathos-producing, unofficial) types of seriousness, see Ruth Coates, *Christianity in Bakhtin: God and the Exiled Author* (Cambridge: Cambridge University Press, 1998): chap. 7, "Christian Motifs in Bakhtin's Carnival Writings."

[22] Bakhtin makes this comment about Myshkin's carnival heaven, alongside one on Nastasya Filippovna's "carnival hell," in *Problems of Dostoevsky's Poetics*, 173–74.

prematurely departed friend. The Stone serves both as a gravestone and as a pulpit.[23]

One final word on this three-tiered Dantean model, which has just been filled up with literature from farther east. A thesis prominent in the Dallas School's concept of the comedic and explaining its phenomenal variety is that the genre of comedy always presumes abundance.[24] Comedy is backed up with a mass of things, acts, and words. These words or things can be truths or lies, precious artifacts or simply junk; it doesn't much matter, because comedy rejoices in sheer diversity and species survival, regardless of local outcome. Comedy is optimistic, again, *not* because it denies the existence of evil or trivializes it — comedy takes evil very seriously — but because it thinks it can engulf evil, outwit it, swamp it with a mass of things, dilute it, and thus terminally confuse it. The comedic outlook thoroughly rejects the Platonic idea that true things don't change. On the contrary, true things *must* change, and change constantly, otherwise evil (which is far more single-minded and humorless) will seek out the good and put it to death. If tragedy clears the stage, kills everyone off, and finds out the truth (consider Oedipus), then comedy, in contrast, clutters the stage, impregnates everything, and resolves nothing. Just this sort of clutter, energy, and lack of resolution constitutes Bakhtin's trademark landscape.

In comedy, and in Bakhtin's carnival as I have stripped it to its essential energies here, life must be kept going at any cost. The *continuity* of life — the proliferation of options, the filling-up of every possible niche, the menippean

---

[23]  I was guided toward these speculations on memory by Will R. Russ, Princeton Class of 1999, whose ambitious senior thesis, "A Preacher, a Prophet, and the Struggle to Solve Life: The Literary and Philosophical Visions of L. N. Tolstoy's *Anna Karenina* and F. M. Dostoevsky's *The Brothers Karamazov*" (1999), also applies the Dallas critics (of whom his father is one) to the classics of Russian literature.

[24]  For this cluster of ideas I am indebted to Robert S. Dupree, "The Copious Inventory of Comedy," in Cowan, ed., *The Terrain of Comedy*, 163–94. Dupree opens on Bakhtin's complaint that literary criticism has been hobbled by the "skimpy and impoverished" examples of comic literature available during the last three centuries. He does not consider this bias of Bakhtin's against the present state of the laughing arts to be paradoxical. He thinks that the modern world of comedy is indeed "shrunken," and goes on to explain why Bakhtin is correct. The essence of comedy, he maintains, is not to be sought in Aristotelian categories of character, plot, spectacle, song, idea — all devised for tragedy — and not in any objective indices of productivity, but in a more raw, unreworked dimension: in simple *copia*, in the presumption of plenitude and abundance. Great eras of comedy sense immense and optimistic security in a world thus provisioned. But nowadays, Dupree concludes, "we fear the comic inventory as such as we do tragic self-knowledge" (190). One reason we do, surely, is that "comedy is not about knowledge, but about change" (169–70).

refusal to die because the experiment is still going on — must be valued over the logic of life. It is this conviction that sits at the comedic core of Dostoevsky and is tested in each of his great novels. I would even suggest that this rather crude criterion is what keeps Shakespeare's two darkest "problem comedies," *Measure for Measure* and *All's Well That Ends Well*, within the realm of comedy. Although injustice in those dramas is everywhere and the lives of major heroes are saved quite by accident, by the final scene, barely, through all sorts of incongruous, seemingly arbitrary and imperious moves, marriages and impregnations *do* occur — which is the dramatist's shorthand for assuring us that not everyone is dead.

For comedy to happen, then, final endings must be put off, or diluted, or — in the lighter, delightful varieties of the genre — whimsically fly-by-night in their coming about. This, again, resembles Hegel's view of comedy: a universal solvent that does not renounce the real world but significantly does not award that world any permanence.[25] In comedy, as in Bakhtin's carnival of Great Time, duration in itself matters, because at no point is a whole ever fully confirmed. Since nothing is fated in past *or* future, an accident or a miracle can change things at any moment. Heroes who take themselves and their acts with high seriousness — the types of heroes that flourish in lyric, epic, tragedy and determine the plots of those genres — are rare in comedy. If they do appear, they strike us as inflated, self-absorbed, of limited vision, and are immediately parodied. To work properly, both carnival and comedy need modesty, fertility, diversity, and slack: that is, they need a great deal of space to get lost in or hide away in, a rich and cluttered environment, and lots of time to change. Here, in closing, we return to the questions posed at the opening of this essay.

Bakhtin is an ethical philosopher. Are there any *duties* that come with comedic or carnival terrain? The type of laughter that Bakhtin appears to have valued most is *not* rooted in the verbal (that is, not satire, wit, wordplay, or the genius of Aristophanes, who goes almost unnoticed in Bakhtin's world). It does not manifest itself in fixed structures or narratives. It will not tell you what is good and what is evil. It is an attitude, a flexibility of the spirit. What are its obligations? They reduce, I believe, to one: wherever we find ourselves, our duty is to *add* options to the terrain, not to subtract them. Since I always remain free to set a new goal for myself as long as I remain alive, nothing ever *has* to fail — and every event is always not yet over.[26]

---

[25]  See Bainard Cowan's illuminating discussion (n. 12), 99–103.

[26]  Vladimir Turbin, in a posthumously published essay on Bakhtin and Dostoevsky, speculated along these lines on the relationship between life and art. "Metaphors

One of the gains of the recent debates over carnival is that this omnibus concept already has to answer less often for the big things: mass political rallies on the public square, the wholesale redemption of souls, their hopeless demonization. Carnival is beginning to be seen more as a personal outlook (literally, how I choose to look out on the world), an inner form of truth. And indeed, this is precisely how Bakhtin referred to festive laughter in his book on Rabelais, a book which, in its original version as a dissertation, employed the word "carnival" sparingly, if at all.[27] This turn toward the hopeful, the humorous, the flexible, and the multitude of the small might help explain Bakhtin's lack of sympathy for the epic, as well as his relative indifference to formal problems that arise in more unified, sculpted poetics. The mission of comedy everywhere is to spread out, de-center, focus on whatever parts of the world can grow, and thus restore the natural order of things. What interested Bakhtin — who himself lost so much throughout his material life — was the survival of the field, its eventual repopulation and plenitude.

Carnival laughter, therefore, does not break forth because we feel superior, and it is not merely a response to incongruity or the body's need for relief. It is the energy that permits us to procreate in the broadest sense, to create. Arthur Koestler had just this idea in mind in his study *The Act of Creation*, a book that Bakhtin would have found deeply compatible.[28] A burst of laughter, Koestler argues, is genetically akin to a burst of discovery and a burst of inspiration. All three are *Aha!* experiences that do not just release or rid us of things — although they are indeed experienced by us as a release of pressure; just as crucially they feed us cognitively, and in highly efficient ways. To laugh when we get a joke and to smile when we have solved a problem afford us much the same pleasure. Thus the minimum triad for humanness, Koestler suggests, is the sage, the artist, and the jester. Those who cannot laugh will have trouble knowing and creating. This point of faith is not everyone's idea of salvation, but for Bakhtin it was the sublime.

———————

accompany each of us sinners," he wrote, "[metaphors] that place each of us on that boundary beyond which life turns into art. Every person is potentially artistic, artificed. But what is important is that this possibility not be realized until the very end of our days — and may God preserve us from attempts to realize it prematurely" (Turbin 1997: 156). Carnival as a worldview and laughter as a strategy keep us from becoming, once and for all, the metaphors we cling to.

27 Vitaly Makhlin, personal communication, 17 February 2000. Bakhtin's dissertation as submitted in the 1940s has not been published.

28 Arthur Koestler, *The Act of Creation* (London: Hutchinson, 1964), 27–28.

# 4

# GASPAROV AND BAKHTIN

*The essay here, back-translated from the Russian with some cuts and restorations for an Anglophone readership, first appeared in the journal* Voprosy literatury *[Questions of Literature] 2 (March-April 2006): 4–40. A reworked version appears as "In Honor of Mikhail Gasparov's Quarter-Century of Not Liking Bakhtin: Pro and Contra," in* Poetics, Self, Place: Essays in Honor of Anna Lisa Crone. *Catherine O'Neill, Nicole Boudreau, and Sarah Krive, eds. (Slavica, 2007): 26–49.*

    *Mikhail Gasparov (1935–2005), Russia's great verse scholar, classical philologist, public intellectual, and for two decades Bakhtin's best known, most ardent detractor, managed to read the final draft before his untimely death in Moscow on November 7, 2005. In a personal communication in early October, very gravely ill, Gasparov graciously thanked me for "opening up new perspectives" on his disagreements with Bakhtin; confessed that "about New Historicism he had read little and without interest," that he was "ignorant of music" [v muzyke ya neuch] and thus intrigued by my paraphrase of Aleksandr Makhov (a Russian musicologist who has detected a sacred aspect to Bakhtin's use of the word polyphony), and that the alternation in approaches to philology between "the rational and the irrational" was probably dependent upon cyclical shifts in artistic taste. Picking up on a comment at the end of my essay he also apologized, in a way that could only make me cringe, for "being occupied with his own image-making."*

    *The essay appeared in* Voprosy literatury *with this headnote:*

    *"At the beginning of September, the Russian and English versions of this essay were sent to M. L. Gasparov. Already home and recovering from the medical treatment that turned out to be his last, Mikhail Leonovich was so kind as to read the text and respond to it at the beginning of October, making several small corrections concerning the ancient term 'serio-comical.' With his usual gallantry he only requested that I soften 'several of the eulogistic expressions about me' (which I did not), in this way letting me know that he was satisfied with how I had presented his position, and with the essay overall. Relying on this evidence, I dedicate the essay to his memory."*

## TWENTY-FIVE YEARS LATER: GASPAROV ON BAKHTIN (2006)

During the past quarter century, much has changed in the Bakhtin industry—but some things have remained the same. One of those unchanging things is Mikhail Gasparov's attitude toward Mikhail Bakhtin.

Among American Slavists, Mikhail Leonovich enjoys a very high reputation: as a world-class scholar, an academic with an irrepressible sense of humor, a memoirist both astute and droll, and (although he would probably resist this designation) as a clear-thinking, commonsensical philosopher of the humanities. Out of the many scholars, critics, and cranks who have raised objections to Mikhail Bakhtin during his rediscovery and boom, M. L. has been Bakhtin's most principled opponent. By "principled" I mean: when Gasparov speaks out against an academic practice or a scholarly worldview, it is because he opposes to it a set of principles equally consistent, logical, value-laden and non-arbitrary. There has been a tendency among Bakhtin scholars to dismiss this criticism or to ignore it. I believe this is a mistake.

The present essay attempts to put the tension between Bakhtinians and Gasparovites into some context and intercultural perspective. Gasparov's opening statement appeared in 1979: "M. M. Bakhtin in Russian Culture of the 20th century," in a Tartu School publication.[1] His most recent update was a talk delivered in Moscow in November 2004: "The History of Literature as Creativity and as Research: The Case of Bakhtin."[2] In the intervening quarter-century, variations on these two position papers are echoed in Gasparov's copious memoirs and writings on the humanities. It must be emphasized that the "dialogue" between these two scholars is of a special type. Since it was begun posthumously, one party (Bakhtin) has never been able to explain itself or answer back. Bakhtin's followers and disciples, often with intonations of impatience and protectiveness, have done so in his name. Only in the past decade has a team of highly-qualified intellectual historians (most of them in Moscow or in Manchester, England, and many associated with the Bakhtin Centre in Sheffield) begun to piece together what that name might have been

---

[1] See M. L. Gasparov, "M. M. Bakhtin v russkoi kul'ture XX v." [1979] in M. L. Gasparov, *Izbrannye trudy* (Moscow, 1997), 2:494–96. For a history of the "Gasparovite" position on Bakhtin, see the commentary (507–10) to the reprint of Gasparov's 1979 essay in K. G. Isupov, ed., *Mikhail Bakhtin: Pro et Contra* (St. Petersburg: Izdatel'stvo Russkogo Khristianskogo Gumanitarnogo Instituta, 2002), 2:33–36. References to this essay in the text made to the Isupov edition. English translation by Ann Shukman: Mikhail Gasparov, "M. M. Bakhtin in Russian Culture of the Twentieth Century," repr. in *Critical Essays on Mikhail Bakhtin*, ed. Caryl Emerson (G. K. Hall, 1999), 83–85.

[2] M. L. Gasparov, "Istoriia literatury kak tvorchestvo i issledovanie: Sluchai Bakhtina" [The History of literature as creativity and as research: the case of Bakhtin]. Materialy Mezhdunarodnoi nauchnoi konferentsii 10–11 noiabria 2004 goda, *Russkaia literatura XX–XXI vekov: problemy teorii i metodologii izucheniia*. Moskovskii gosudarstvennyi universitet im. M. V. Lomonosova, filologicheskii fakul'tet. The essay is reprinted in *Word, Music, History. A Festschrift for Caryl Emerson* (Stanford: Stanford Slavic Studies #29–30, 2005), 1:23–31.

for itself, that is, for Bakhtin and his close associates, in their own time.[3] What is more, although the disagreement separating Bakhtin and Gasparov has become wider and wordier over the years, it has not necessarily become wiser. In the 1970s, Gasparov grouped Bakhtin together with the Petrograd Formalists as a "man of the Twenties" who shared the appeal as well as the weaknesses of other radical methodologies of that era. Overall, the tone of that early judgment was more insightful, measured and temperate than the recent complaints.

Gasparov has a potent defense. He would say that Bakhtinian truisms have so triumphed on the world market, and have caused so much more damage to humanities scholarship than anyone could have been predicted in 1979, that dissenting voices (of which his is the most famous) must be even more outspoken and vigilant. Gasparov is a methodological conservative and a bookish man, but with a high-profile publicistic side, unintimidated by theoretical vogue. To celebrate his seventieth birthday in 2005, the journal *Novoe literaturnoe obozrenie* devoted a forum to his accomplishments in various genres (scholarly, aphoristic, memoiristic), praising Gasparov as an "academician-heretic."[4] It was no surprise that this heretic-philologist of the old school was among the first to detect potential problems in Bakhtin as theorist and in the pattern of Bakhtin reception in the West. The brute surface of Bakhtin's ideas and images, grafted on to neo-Marxism, French neo-Freudianism, and the power-scenarios of Michel Foucault, had produced a philosophy of "transgressive words in a subversive body" that was enthusiastically embraced on European and American campuses in the politically radical 1960s and '70s. Bakhtin would have been astonished at this evolution of his message. Gasparov was appalled. There is some irony in the fact that the criticism Gasparov makes in his 1979 essay — his presumption

---

3    Among the most active scholars are Craig Brandist, Ken Hirschkop, David Shepherd and Galin Tihanov. For two excellent recent reconstructions in English of Bahktin's sources and contexts, see Craig Brandist, *The Bakhtin Circle: Philosophy, Culture and Politics* (London: Pluto Press, 2002), and Craig Brandist, David Shepherd & Galin Tihanov, eds., *The Bakhtin Circle: In the Master's Absence* (Manchester UK: Manchester University Press, 2004).

4    "M. L. Gasparovu — 70 let," in *Novoe literaturnoe obozrenie* 73 (2005): 150–81, followed by a selection of eight essays "Vokrug Gasparova." [Henceforth, *Novoe literaturnoe obozrenie* will be abbreviated *NLO*.] Many tributes are anecdotal or testimonial, but among the most insightful is the "anti-jubilee offering" by three editors Aleksandr Dmitriev, Il'ia Kukulin, and Mariia Maiofis, "Zanimatel'nyi M. L. Gasparov: akademik-eretik ("Antiiubileinoe prinoshenie" redaktsii "NLO")": 170–78. They point out that M. L.'s vibrant, eccentric voice had grown up inside the Soviet-era academy and had been rewarded by its institutions, but he was not entirely of that academy — and enjoyed being the outside jester to any pomp or pretension.

that Bakhtin can be classified together with the radical Formalists in a single camp, with a collective set of methodological sins — fits into this Western perspective. Russian theory has routinely appealed to Western academics because it was sensed as exotic, dynamic, disruptive, "revolutionary."

Thus did Mikhail Leonovich take up his post as gadfly, speaking his truth to the tyrannies of critical fashion. Over the past quarter-century, the methodological divide between Bakhtinians and Gasparovites has become so well focused that it can now function as a threshold across which the costs and rewards of various approaches to knowledge in the humanities might be compared. What is philology? What is scholarship [or science: *nauka*]? What is the status of a surviving cultural trace (a book, fragment, legend, artifact) and are there reasonable limits to the stories that the critic can weave, in his own name, around this trace? What does it mean to "make contact with" another culture, especially one distant in time, space, language, and place? Can consciousness be captured by the word, and later retrieved from the word, in such a way that it effectively lives forever? Or are these claims merely one more chapter in the fanciful history of Russian philosophy's quest to abolish death? Answers to these questions vary widely. On balance, we can say that Bakhtin has served Gasparov well. Through a Bakhtinian lens, M. L. has been able to test and refine his own deeply-held convictions, not only regarding philology and scholarship but also in respect to ontology, creativity, morality, intimacy, addressivity [*obrashchennost'*], and — to apply an important distinction in Russian religious thought to the humanities — philological sobriety [*trezvost'*] versus philosophical pridefulness [*prelest'*]. Although the humanities are not an exact science and our paradigms do not undergo scientific revolutions, most of us would agree that the terms and metaphors we employ can blunt and corrupt us. Is Gasparov correct in suggesting that we, as humanist scholars, have been blunted and led astray by Bakhtin's priorities?

My own feeling is that Mikhail Gasparov is a healthy corrective to Bakhtin Studies: to its moments of excess, hyperbole, and facile application. In an unexpected way, M. L. has even been Bakhtin's ally, warning us against the egocentrism natural to the creative and critical arts and urging a distance between ourselves and our objects of study. Both Bakhtin and Gasparov argue that "being outside looking in" is a more reliable starting point for knowledge than "being inside looking out." By making academic modesty his trademark, Gasparov reminds us of the more strictly service duties of literary scholarship — obligations alien to many Romantic-era and Postmodernist critics. But I could not ignore the fact that every Russian Bakhtin scholar whom I consulted on this matter, all of the highest calibre, expressed extreme disapproval of Gasparov's behavior vis-à-vis Bakhtin. Puzzled, I re-examined Gasparov for areas where Bakhtin might have been misrepresented. And indeed: there were identifiable moments.

This lack of acceptance began with Gasparov's secular and ironizing commitment to a "distrust toward the word" [nedoverie k slovu].[5] Back in 1979, Gasparov had claimed that such distrust was necessary in order to "train us away from the spiritual egocentrism" so natural to humanistic inquiry and urge us toward a healthy objective ontology and from there to a sober philology. In Gasparov's view, the morality of philology lies precisely in its insistence on the virtues of objectivity and distance. For him, to respect distance means to realize that the written artifact I am now analyzing was not addressed to me, does not speak my language, is indifferent to my values, and should not be interpreted in light of my needs. In contrast, Bakhtin was less interested in the relationship between subject and artifact. His concern was always with the relationship between subjects. For him, distance is mandatory because "I" cannot know myself, only the Other can hope to know me. Thus Gasparov and Bakhtin both value "outsideness," but they put it to different purpose. In his objections to Bakhtin, Gasparov contributes to an ancient and venerable tradition. In his misrepresentations of Bakhtin, he is more original. This essay considers only two of Gasparov's objections and suggests possible rebuttals to them. The first objection is conceptual: Gasparov's non-acceptance of dialogue and its sister concept polyphony as useful or truthful tools for literary analysis. The second is methodological, and focuses on Bakhtin's love for the menippea — a preference that Gasparov takes as exemplary of Bakhtin's willingness to generalize a big theory out of rumors and shreds.

### Author and hero in academic activity, according to Gasparov: the distorting masks of dialogue

Gasparov would reject outright the notion that his relationship with Bakhtin is a dialogue. He finds that idea as foolish and misleading as the kindred fantasy that fictional creatures can "converse" on their own initiative with

---

5    "Philology," Gasparov writes in his essay "Filologiia kak nravstvennost'," must "begin not with trust but with distrust of the word," for "it is natural to trust only the words of our own language." Philology is obliged to resist the temptation to reduce everything genuinely alien to something we can trust (that is, something we can talk to or converse with). M. L. Gasparov, "Filologiia kak nravstvennost'," the final entry in a forum on the Tasks of Philology in Literaturnoe obozrenie 10 (1979): 26–27, esp. 27.

one another, or (as purportedly happens in polyphony) with their creator-author. All this talk of dialogue is delusionary, Gasparov would insist, because Bakhtin and his world are dead. Philology, which began as the study of ancient vanished cultures and languages, understands this fact and has adjusted its ambitions to the modest tasks of recuperation and transcription. A philologist does not refer to "conversation between the ages."

This part of Gasparov's argument has ancient credentials. The idea that dialogic form, and especially dialogue preserved in written form, is no more than a fraudulent reflection of life and thus cannot be revivified, finds its canonical expression at the end of the *Phaedrus*. In that Platonic dialogue, Socrates insists that words fixed in writing are dead, helpless to defend themselves before later audiences, and without any rights as regards their future addressees. Although these graphic representations "seem to talk to you as though they were intelligent," they will always resemble more an image painted on the wall than a true living conversation; "if you ask them anything about what they say, from a desire to be instructed, they go on telling you the same thing forever."[6] Socrates suggests that writing and reading, characterized as they are by phonic silence and bodily absence, can only enfeeble or efface the genuine other. And if the other is flattened and made mute by the written word, then only the all-powerful, present-tense "I" of the currently alive reader is competent to move in and supply all voices for all sides of the dialogue.

Gasparov has been applying the acerbic skepticism of the *Phaedrus* to literary criticism for many years. Humanists mislead themselves about their "intimate relations" with their objects of study, he remarks. The fact that we work with the traces of deceased human consciousness, and not with inanimate objects or lower forms of life, should make us more cautious in our methods, not less. In a polemical jotting titled "Pseudo-philosophical note," Gasparov insists that "the zoologist relates more intimately to his frogs and worms that we do [to our human subjects]."[7] This is wholly proper. Human consciousness does not lend itself to scrutiny like the tendon of an amphibian under a microscope. It requires more delicacy, more awe and respect. "The most everyday experience tells us that between myself and my most intimate friend there lies a massive block of mutual misunderstanding,"

---

6    "Phaedrus," in *Plato: The Collected Dialogues*, ed. Edith Hamilton and Huntingdon Cairns (Princeton: Princeton University Press, 1961), 521.

7    "Primechanie psevdofilosofskoe [iz diskussii na temu 'filosofiia filologii')" in M. Gasparov, *Zapisi i vypiski* (Moscow: Novoe literaturnoe obozrenie, 2000), 100–102, esp. 101.

Gasparov writes; "after that can one even entertain the thought that we understand Pushkin? It is said that between a philologist and his object of study a dialogue takes place: what this really means is that one interlocutor is silent and the other devises answers to questions he himself has posed. On what grounds does he devise those answers? This is the question that must be answered, if the philologist is a person of science" (101).

This argument is reiterated, less patiently, in 2004. To see or hear "dialogue" and "otherness" on the printed page is simply an illusion. Or perhaps it is something worse: a "solipsistic, egocentric self-affirmation" that masquerades as two autonomous consciousnesses. Voices and words fixed in a text do *not* change or respond on their own. Rather it is we the readers who are growing, speaking, and evoling over time. Thus it only "seems to us that the text-interlocutor before us is changing," Gasparov insists. "The text is but a mirror reflecting our own changing face. Bakhtin gazes at his own 'I' in the mirror, and he imagines that it is Thou." Such egocentrism in a researcher—or in any reader—can only distort and repress surviving traces of real others, especially when attention is focused on the process [*stanovlenie*] rather than the product [*proizvedenie*] of creative activity. Gasparov's conclusion is that the sober procedure of philology, for all that it is accused of "necrophilia," in fact "respects the other more."

Such epistemological modesty is Gasparov's starting point and the source of his distinctive comic tone. Communication between people is far more difficult than we would like to believe. Bakhtin makes it appear easy and pleasant. The result can only be a profound misreading of where my self ends and another's self begins. On this score, Gasparov turns out to be a skeptical and shrewd thinker of the Tolstoyan school.[8] We flatter ourselves when we find a "trace" and think it is talking to us, Gasparov argues. We lack the discipline even to listen to fully-embodied others in our very presence. As he remarked in his 1995 essay "Criticism as an End in Itself": "even when living people converse, we often hear not a dialogue but two chopped-up

---

[8]  Not coincidentally, such penetrating scholars of Tolstoy as Lydia Ginzburg (also a skeptic concerning Bakhtin's pan-dialogism) have long been making Gasparov's argument. It is Tolstoy, not Dostoevsky, who grasps fully the difficulty of socially contingent verbal communication, she insists; in Tolstoyan "conversations," more often awkward and failed than honest and eloquent, we recognize the dilemma of our expressive self. See Lydia Ginzburg, *On Psychological Prose* [1971 rev. 1977], trans. Judson Rosengrant (Princeton: Princeton University Press, 1991), 243: "To be sure, he [the contemporary human being] finds it more *interesting* to conceive of himself in Dostoevskian terms, since doing so allows him to focus his attention on his own self."

monologues....One could talk with a stone with equal success and imagine the stone's answers to one's questions. Few people talk to stones nowadays, at least not publicly, but every energetic person talks with Baudelaire or Racine precisely as with a stone..."[9]

Bakhtin might have countered this line of argument. Were he competent to conduct dialogue on Gasparov's terms (that is, if he were not bio-chemically dead), he would probably remark that his opponent, in his screed against dialogue, greatly inflates the power and single-voiced unity of any given living "I." My self is not an unconditioned absolute, and it is nowhere near as potent as Gasparov assumes. It cannot colonize others with impunity. Likewise, it cannot be reduced to a flat, reflected, bounded image (as Bakhtin excellently understood: for he, too, was an astute student of mirrors and a severe critic of all forms of duplicative sympathy). Mirrors are very poor metaphors. Voice belongs to another category of representation. No subject, however privileged in time and space, possesses a sufficiently high degree of power, integrity, or control to *initiate* a voice. Realizing a written dialogue, in Bakhtin's view, is not to assign it a voice but to respond to an already-hybrid voice. This voice-complex is already *in* the word. Coming across that word, I will always find more richness in it than its author-transcriber put there. Analogously, I will always find something different from the meaning that I alone could have invested in that word, had I myself uttered it. From this Bakhtinian perspective, the other is not only preserved by means of written embodiment but can even be enhanced, liberated, and returned to fuller consciousness. It is this conviction that motivates Bakhtin's choice of the novel — the world's first art form designed to be silently written and silently consumed — as the most freedom-bearing of all genres. Sergei Bocharov had this defense in mind when he offered his rebuttal to Gasparov in 1995: a past culture cannot be approached as a dead and foreign language.[10]

For all the energy put in on both sides, the distance between Gasparov and Bakhtin here cannot easily be bridged. Their core assumptions, unverifiable in themselves, are too different, touching on the most vital of our human intuitions about interpersonal relations. When literary scholars begin to talk in terms of dialogue, they become, for Gasparov, "philosophers" — and in the context of professional literary study, this is not a compliment. Consider the opening lines of Gasparov's 2004 "Case of Bakhtin":

---

9     M. L. Gasparov, "Kritika kak samotsel'," in *NLO* 6 (1993–94): 6–9. esp. 8–9.
10    Sergei Bocharov, "Sobytie bytiia: O Mikhaile Mikhailoviche Bakhtine," in *Novyi mir* 11 (1995): 211–21, esp. 212.

M. M. Bakhtin was a philosopher. However, he is also considered a philologist — because two of his books are written about Dostoevsky and Rabelais.
This has been the cause of many misunderstandings. In culture there are
creative areas and research areas. Creativity complicates the picture of the
world, introducing into it new values. Research simplifies the picture of
the world, systematizing old values and putting them in order. Philosophy
is a creative area, as is literature. But philology is a research area. Bakhtin
should be valued highly as a creator — but there is no reason to attribute
to him the achievements of a researcher. A philosopher in the role of
a philologist remains a creative temperament, but manifests this trait in
a highly unusual manner. He creates new literature as a philosopher creates
a new system.

For this reason, Gasparov notes, "philosophers" (and Russian "philosophizing")
are at special risk when they attempt to research the world. They enjoy
constructing systems. But in their systems-building, they are too often
motivated not by curiosity about the world but by anxiety, personal will,
and — most dangerously, because most admirable in its own right — creativity.
Whenever scholars are seized by a vision of themselves as creative centers,
they become vulnerable to a dual seduction. First, they will take from the past
only what satisfies their own need. And second, they will deny the reality of
death — in the belief that they, from their present-tense position, can extract
a "living word" from a past literary trace, permitting all of us to live forever.

Very early in his Bakhtin-watching activity, Gasparov must have feared
that this rediscovered luminary on the Russian horizon would tempt the
literary scholar to commit just such cognitive and ontological blasphemy.
In urging readers to be creators or co-creators, Bakhtin (together with his
contemporaries, the Petrograd Formalists) were promoting aggressively
interventionist habits of reading. The very word "dialogue" invites these
habits, Gasparov argues in his 1979 essay. When a reader enters into
dialogue, he has a choice: either he "fits himself to the context of the thing,
or fits the thing into his own context.... Dialogue is a struggle. Who will
give in?" (34). In this struggle, it is always easier and more pleasant to fit
the alien thing to us rather than to fit ourselves to it. Gasparov admits that
the psychological reasons for doing so are very compelling. *We* have needs,
whereas the thing (the inert text) does not.

To be sure, Gasparov's binary model — either I fit in to the text, or the
text fits in to me — might strike some as a bullying set of options, a *kto-
kogo* relationship [who beats up on whom?] transferred to the plane of
literary dynamics. In its very structure, it implies a vertical power relation of

mastery for one side, submission for the other. For Gasparov, however, that imbalance is its virtue and an index of its honesty. Gasparov trusts traces of words more readily than he trusts their present-day carriers. Traces are disinterested. Always the professor and professional, Gasparov opposes any methodology that grants excessive interpretive rights to readers, for such methods cannot be standardized and cannot be taught. They are a trap. In the equalizing Bolshevik 1920s, Gasparov suggests, literary opportunism of this sort — making a work of art useful to *my* identity, my creativity, the wakefulness of my perception — was part of the anarchic and self-affirming spirit of the epoch. For very different reasons, this "present-tense self" was indulged by Formalists, Marxists, and Bakhtin in his neo-Idealist mode. In 1979, however, Gasparov was more generous than he was later to become, acknowledging that Bakhtin (unlike the posthumous industry that grew up around his word) was fully aware of this opportunism.[11]

What, then, is the mission of the philological self? Gasparov is a magnificent generator of definitions, aphorisms, and glossaries. His *Zapisi i vypiski* [Notes and jottings][12] from 2000 contains an idiosyncratic thesaurus of concepts, quotations, and trenchant observations to rival Ambrose Bierce's *Devil's Dictionary*. But nowhere in his writings on the humanities does Gasparov define precisely and without irony what he considers to be appropriate motivation for literary study. The researcher's disinterested curiosity? Archeological investigation and recuperation for its own sake? The positivist dream of an answer to fill every blank, a history that "adds up"? A personal training course in modesty and discipline? If research is indeed destined to "simplify the world," generalization must occur at some level. What principles should govern it? Gasparov does not elaborate; the history of culture is a self-evident objective value.

---

[11]   As Gasparov wrote in 1979: Bakhtin's followers "made a research program out of his program for creativity. And these are things which are in principle opposed: the point of creativity is to transform an object, whereas the point of research is not to deform it ... Just as Bakhtin called on his contemporaries to take only what they thought necessary for themselves, so now his new adherents take from his writings only what they think is necessary for them. But it is always best when this is done consciously, as Bakhtin himself did." Cited from Isupov, ed., 35; in Shukman translation (n. 1), p. 85, translation adjusted.

[12]   M. L. Gasparov, *Zapisi i vypiski* (Moscow: Novoe literaturnoe obozrenie, 2000). The book is assembled as a "thesaurus" containing several hundred pages of alphabetically arranged fragments and quotations (both correctly cited and hilariously distorted) "*Ot A do Ia*" [From A to Z], interspersed with parables, cameo memoirs, short critical essays, letters, and bits of verse.

Gasparov would emphasize, however, that the suspicious stance of philologists toward philosophers is *not* because philologists believe that the verbal trace, the recorded or transcribed word, is incommunicative. The opposite is the case. Philologists revere the recuperated word. It carries precious information. For an historian of verse such as himself, most precious and authentic would be information contained in the form: patterns, rhythms, alliterations, rhymes, phonetic and semantic structures. These forms gain in sublimity and significance as they repeat, refract, and interrelate. For Gasparov, the life of the word is located in such dynamics — and this life is vital. But he would insist that no grounds exist for assuming that a word uttered or deployed by a person in the past can be *resurrected* or "spoken with," as if it were a sort of ghost or spore of consciousness. Nor can it give birth polyphonically to new persons, words, or forms. Gasparov suspects the Bakhtinians of making that mystical argument. His argument, therefore, is with the living.

In closing this section, we might note that the Gasparov-Bakhtin controversy has echoes in the American academy. On one side are the positivist, book- and print-bound scholars, "old historicists" who insist that the past belongs to the past and we must serve it on its own terms, through its intact masterpieces, because our predecessors did not produce their work with our values in mind (a position we might call "Gasparovism").[13] On the other side are their contextual, postmodernist successors, most colorfully the "New Historicists," who insist that the past is available to us not only as a written text but also as a resonating field. This past is a source of information but also of wonder; when we enter this field, like Prospero on his isolated isle, we (or our obedient spirits) can activate it. The unique magic of literature is, as Stephen Greenblatt has claimed, its "uncanny ability of seeming to be written ... 'for us.'"[14]

To the extent that Bakhtin and Greenblatt are both "anti-Gasparovites," they are a strange pair: of different generations, specializations, theoretical interests, passions, and temperaments. Gasparov, however, would see the similarities in a trice. He would find it fully correct that Greenblatt mentions Bakhtin as one of the "powerful intellectual encounters" influencing his

---

[13]   Since the past belongs to itself and not to us, there is no reason why it should want to enter into dialogue with us. See M. L. Gasparov, "Kritika kak samotsel'," in *NLO* 6 (1993–94): 6–9, esp. 8: "Nothing has been created or adapted for me in this world ... every step of ours on this earth persuades us of that."

[14]   Stephen Greenblatt, "What Is the History of Literature?", *Critical Inquiry* 23.3 (Spring 1997): 460–481, esp. 481.

work.[15] The trajectories of these two academic stars in American intellectual culture are to some extent parallel. Greenblatt was also a cult figure during the 1970s and '80s. His imprecise but enticing New Historicism (like Bakhtin's imprecise and enticing "dialogism" and "carnival") was everywhere in the air. Both were credited with providing, in the wake of the dessicating rigors of a dominant impersonal structuralism, a new methodology for connecting context to text, a new model for relating parts to wholes, a new and more alive definition of the cultural artifact, and a sense of history liberated from strict linear causality. The scholarly style of each ingeniously combined eccentric micro-readings with bold mega-generalizations. What is more (and what would especially disturb Gasparov), each approach promises a fabulously creative role for the critic, albeit hidden beneath a self-effacing non-theoretical mask. For the mature and seasoned scholar this could be exciting; for the apprentice graduate student, disastrous.

Consider the confession that opens Greenblatt's 1988 essay launching the New Historicism: "I began with the desire to speak with the dead."[16] He is disarmingly honest about the status of these "dialogues" he wishes to pursue and the polyphonic "resonances" he hopes to detect — or to construct:

> This desire is a familiar, if unvoiced, motive in literary studies, a motive organized, professionalized, buried beneath thick layers of bureaucratic decorum: literature professors are salaried, middle-class shamans. If I never believed that the dead could hear me, and if I knew that the dead could not speak, I was none the less certain that I could re-create a conversation with

---

[15]   In the 1960s and 70s, Russian theory was overwhelmingly viewed abroad as liberating and radicalizing. In the Introduction to his collected essays, *Learning to Curse: Essays in Early Modern Culture* (New York and London: Routledge, 1990), Stephen Greenblatt mentions several "powerful intellectual encounters" that helped shape his new approach to literary study: the Marxist Raymond Williams at Cambridge, Michel Foucault at Berkeley, but also the work of "Mikhail Bakhtin, Kenneth Burke, Michel de Certeau" (3). It would seem that early Russian formalists also played a role, with their combination of objective estrangement and sentimental concern for the intimately subjective. "I could not endure the compulsive estrangement of my life, as if it belonged to someone else," Greenblatt confesses, "but I could perhaps understand the uncanny otherness of my own voice. . . . I am committed to the project of making strange what has become familiar" (8).

[16]   Stephen Greenblatt, "The Circulation of Social Energy," Chapter One of *Shakespearean Negotiations. The Circulation of Social Energy in Renaissance England* (Berkeley CA: University of California Press, 1988), 1–20, esp. 1. Gasparov would agree absolutely with Greenblatt on the realness of the desire. But rather than justify one's method thereby, Gasparov would expect the scholar to resist the temptation.

them. Even when I came to understand that in my most intense moments of straining to listen all I could hear was my own voice, even then I did not abandon my desire. It was true that I could hear only my own voice, but my own voice was the voice of the dead, for the dead had contrived to leave textual traces of themselves, and those traces make themselves heard in the voices of the living.

Greenblatt's confession can be read as an eloquent summary of Gasparov's complaints against the literary profession today, many of which he lays — justly or unjustly — at Bakhtin's door. These include the scholar as "shaman," whose deep psychological desire to practice magic somehow justifies his indulgence in it, his assumption that the dead can speak through his voice and with his voice. There is also the scholar as confessant, who fights against a fantasy but then, with an attractive display of candor, gives in to it, begging the reader's pardon. And mostly, there is the confusion of scholarly research with private needs and personal therapy (Renaissance self-fashioning is primarily the self-fashioning of the critic). Circulation, negotiation, exchange, contingency, "resonance": all are inspired by the same heady possibility that every body can become an agent and leave a trace whose energies might be released by later critics. Gasparov would consider the "Case of Greenblatt" saturated with the neo-Romantic, quasi-mystical spirit of Bakhtinian readings. Precisely these aims and procedures of New Historicism are the profligate hopes of dialogue and (on the strictly literary plane) of polyphony.

### Author and hero in academic activity, II: polyphony, simultaneity, and sacred form

Critics of novelistic polyphony have long been bothered by its "faith-based" dynamic. How can a literary device lay claim to that moment in real life we call a "quickening of consciousness"? To be sure, polyphonic design serves a peculiar sort of creativity. Its endpoint is not a "creation" (a creature, an artifact) but other speaking personalities, that is, creatures which are designed in turn to create. Since they are verbal artifacts, what they create is more words, that is, the same material out of which they themselves were made. In order to ring true, conversation between such "creating creatures" must foster a sense of spontaneity and freedom. Students of more fixed literary forms have not been persuaded. But increasingly sober definitions of polyphony are being put forth — and if shown to reflect Bakhtin's intent, they might provide a more disciplined sense of "polyphonic form" that would pacify even the Gasparovite skeptics.

One pioneer in this regard has been Michael Holquist. In his explorations of Bakhtin and organicism, he advocates something more than a linear, alternating or oscillating model of dialogic and polyphonic relations. Holquist argues that Bakhtin's central theoretical concern, exemplified by his abiding interest in organic as opposed to mechanical unities, is *simultaneity*, the condition of continual feedback and "same-time-ness" among the varied phenomena necessary to life.[17] Life-sustaining relations do not unfold or communicate "in a row" (such rows are merely our hobbled format for transcribing spoken dialogue) but rather co-exist on a field, the way voices and intonations co-exist within an uttered word, continually auto-adjusting and self-monitoring. Visualized as the meshing of many responsive variables, polyphonic design is not a sequence but a ground of being. Like any successful organism, it must grow — but never autonomously, and never in directions wholly unconditioned.

This alertness to the constraints operable in effective polyphony has received unexpected support from the history of music criticism. In his 2005 essay "The 'music' of the word: from the history of a certain fiction," Aleksandr Makhov examines the lengthy, two-way tradition of terminological borrowings between music and verbal-art critics, coming to rest on Bakhtin's polyphony.[18] Bakhtin has been criticized for his choice of this musical term, Makhov notes: it appears to confuse words with sounds and to rely parasitically on another artistic medium. But these objections are misguided. First, the term polyphony (like the concept of sonata form) originated in the teaching of Rhetoric and was borrowed by medieval music theorists from philological criticism. Bakhtin was not burglarizing the term but returning it to its original literary home. And second, polyphony has been isolated, wrongly but in most cases innocently by a secular readership, from the other two values that Bakhtin enters into the Dostoevsky book during the same discussion: simultaneity [*odnovremennost'* or "at-one-timeness"] and eternity [*vechnost'*]. These two supplementary terms are in some tension

---

17　See, as an opening statement, Michael Holquist, *Dialogism: Bakhtin and His World* (London and New York: Routledge, 1990), 18–20, "The fundamental role of simultaneity," and also Michael Holquist, "Bakhtin and the Task of Philology: an Essay for Vadim," in *In Other Words: Studies to Honor Vadim Liapunov*, Blackwell, Finke, Perlina and Vernikov, eds. Indiana Slavic Studies vol. 11 (2000), 55–67, esp. 56.

18　Aleksandr Makhov, "'Muzyka' slova: iz istorii odnoi fiktsii," *Voprosy literatury* (September-October 2005): 101–123, especially 119–23.

with dialogue, which, for most of us, suggests something more this-worldly, linear, responsive, contingent, open-ended, a servant of freedom — at least to the extent that it welcomes an eruption of the unexpected along a temporal continuum. But neither simultaneity nor eternity is in any tension at all with medieval polyphonic music.

In its historical context, Makhov points out, sacred polyphony was a musical equivalent to *allegory* — that is, to the mystical simultaneity of Old-Testament events and their purported New Testament analogues. Such a semantic palimpsest does not generate or confirm the new: that is the noble task of dialogism in novels. Rather, its purpose is to enrich the reality of the old with new instantiations. Music (which tolerates repetition and duplication far more graciously than does the word) is ideally suited for this project. Verbal realizations of allegorical narrative — its "plot" — are inevitably limited by the fact that the words, to bear their message in an intelligible way, must occur one after the other. Only in musical polyphony can simultaneity become an uncompromised reality, a hetero-voicedness [*raznoglasie*] where the voices, no matter how abundant and particularized, never crowd one another out nor fail to contribute their part to the tonality of the whole. A tiny slice of time can communicate a manifold number of relationships.

Music, then, commands resources — or perhaps better, resonances — beyond the semantic parameters of the spoken utterance. Musical polyphony creates not only a multi-layered sound-space but also a multi-layered meaning-space: powerfully fueled, compressed, contrapuntal, standing still while also moving toward a future already in place, inducing in us hope and faith. The paradigm that Makhov offers is Bach's Passions, where key sacred events are compacted and overlapped with no loss of suspense or dramatic power. Knowing what must happen and what has already happened, we are still on the edge of our seats. To be sure, this space is teleological and static. There is nothing unfinalizable or open-ended about it. But it would explain those radiant moments in Dostoevsky — unique to that writer in the modern period — where eternal questions are *simultaneously* posed, tested to the death, found to be helpless in altering the real course of events, yet nevertheless transcendently resolved: Raskolnikov at Sonia's knees in the Epilogue to *Crime and Punishment*, the Elder Zosima's advice to the desperate peasant woman who has lost her last remaining child; Alyosha Karamazov at Ilyushechka's funeral and his speech to the boys at the Stone.

We cannot know whether Bakhtin had in mind the potentials of sacred medieval polyphony. Musical genres do not play a large role in his thought and there is no genealogy of the idea in his notebooks. Most Bakhtin scholars assume his precedent to have been more strictly literary, dissonant, and modern[19] — and indeed, one prong of the multi-voiced word might answer that intent. A hint of Makhov's sacred scenario, however, can be found in the final pages of the Dostoevsky book (in both its 1929 original and the 1963 revision):

> At the level of his religious-utopian worldview Dostoevsky carries dialogue into eternity, conceiving of it as eternal co-rejoicing, co-admiration, concord. At the level of the novel, it is presented as the unfinalizability of dialogue, although originally as dialogue's bad infinity.[20]

Here we glimpse those two tiers of human existence that Makhov's vision of polyphony accommodates. The lower level of experience is dialogic: freely developing, unfinalized, open, unpredetermined, unstable — and thus, while radiant with personality, potentially tragic. The upper level is stable, true, eternal, "polyphonic" in a more fixed and sacred sense: the realm of joyful reconciliation.

If we take seriously Makhov's hypothesis, then, the phrase "polyphonic dialogue" is something of an oxymoron and deserves a sober reassessment. Dialogue in the sequential, linear, open-ended sense is certainly present in Dostoevsky's novels, and just as certainly leads to tragedy and pain. Such verbal dialogue must be laid out in a linear way. A novel, after all, is not a libretto. The conventional novel has no means for registering "ensemble talk" — the simultaneous singing or uttering of multiple messages and voice-lines with the expectation that the listener or reader will process the episode minute by minute as a single unified texture. But for that very reason, perhaps the concept of polyphony should not be fused with the dialogic idea, nor be defined merely as one extreme case of it. Dialogue

---

[19]  The most recent hypothesis on Bakhtin's source for polyphony, Brian Poole's, is incompatible with Makhov's. Poole has traced Bakhtin's source to German philosophical criticism, namely to the 19th-c. German novelist and critic Otto Ludwig, as cited in a 1923 study by the genre theorist Ernst Hirt. The relevant phrase *polyphonischer dialog* occurs in Ernst Hirt, *Das Formgesetz der epischen, dramatischen und lyrischen Dichtung*, although it is used there largely to explicate Shakespearean drama. See Brian Poole, "From phenomenology to dialogue: Max Scheler's phenomenological tradition and Mikhail Bakhtin's development from 'Toward a philosophy of the act' to his study of Dostoevsky," in Ken Hirschkop and David Shepherd, eds., *Bakhtin and Cultural Theory*, rev. and exp. 2nd edition (Manchester: Manchester University Press, 2001), 109–35, esp. 119; 131 n43.

[20]  Mikhail Bakhtin, *Problems of Dostoevsky's Poetics*, trans. Caryl Emerson (Minneapolis: University of Minnesota Press, 1984), 252. Translation adjusted.

and polyphony might be two different, separate moves. If—as Makhov suggests—polyphony began as a dream of rhetoric, the dream that the world's apparent contradictions and heterogeneity could be expressed on one plane simultaneously, distinctly, yet still harmoniously, as a cosmic moment when the Music of the Spheres reinforces the Music of the Soul, then we have, in all its glorious fullness, the teaching of the Elder Zosima in pure trans-musical form. And, we might add, whatever Bakhtin's intentions as a literary critic and whatever we wish to make of Bakhtin's professed Christianity, this medieval polyphonic vision is surely a crucial aspect of Dostoevsky's mature message. What else is his vision of Christian reconciliation: with one another, with reality, with the Truth? Dostoevsky loved that triune vision. But he found it terribly difficult to embody successfully—perhaps because words always fell short, and words were the sole tools of his trade.

What does Makhov's rehabilitation of Bakhtinian polyphony have to offer secular skeptics like Gasparov? Very little, to be sure, of religious inspiration. The Gasparovite critique does not consider spiritual consolation a proper concern of philological scholarship. (For the first time in 2004, Gasparov added to his Bakhtinophobe commentary some overt remarks about the Deity and the unfortunate, misplaced interest in Him that suffuses Bakhtin's literary philosophizing.[21]) But Makhov's commentary does address another vulnerable area in the literary wing of Bakhtin studies, and here Gasparov might find unexpected nourishment. Most critics of Bakhtin would agree that the customary interpretations of "dialogism" in Dostoevsky minimize or enfeeble the novelist's unitizing, transcendent message. Bakhtin is not especially good at accounting for Dostoevsky's epiphanies, spiritualized wholes, or intimations of Great Time. As an analytic tool, the "dialogized word" is far more successful with the concrete exchanges of Small Time. However, through Makhov's conceptual envelope for polyphony, we might accept Dostoevsky's great novels (and his own faith system also) as two-tiered: dialogic on the secular plane and simultaneously sacred-polyphonic on a higher plane.[22] The lower dialogic perspective is contingent, evolving,

---

[21] "What Bakhtin wanted most of all was to talk about the transcendental, i. e. about God (about that God who is present as a Third above all human dialogues), but in general it is impossible to speak adequately about God in a human language, even independent of Soviet censorship conditions. About God one can only speak paradoxically."

[22] It is of some interest for our enquiry into a more disciplined polyphony that Milan Kundera, a novelist with no love for Dostoevsky's themes but with a great love for (and training in) music, defines his own novelistic ideal, in the section on "Melody" in his "Improvisation in Homage to Stravinsky" from *Testaments Betrayed*, as contrapuntal

tormented, continually open to doubt, "real." The upper polyphonic structure is as controlled, non-contingent, exquisitely balanced and spatially ever-present as a poem. And, of course, it is no less real. How could Mikhail Gasparov remain indifferent to the poet-musician who composed this complex fabric, or to a philosopher-critic who had glimpsed its design?

### Author and hero in academic reality, III: menippea, Rabelais, and the disputed move from a cultural artifact to an artistic whole

Gasparov's 2004 "Case of Bakhtin" included several new charges against the defendant, in addition to that casual remark about God. Among the most damning pertains to the genre of menippea, "a new, previously unheard-of literature [so Gasparov tells us] whose program Bakhtin composed." Note he says *composed* [*sochinil*], not discovered or researched. As a classicist trained at the sources, Gasparov is troubled by Bakhtin's habit of selecting the most minuscule data-base of surviving fragments upon which to construct the most extravagant generalizations on literary history and the human condition. For how does Bakhtin procede? His first step is to apply a very broad genre definition to a very small body of documents. Gasparov cites the enormous range of "basic characteristics" that Bakhtin, in the new Chapter Four of his revised Dostoevsky book, attributes to menippean satire: fourteen traits overall, ranging from "the comic" to "the everyday" to "adventure" to "the fantastic" to "the quest," "the test," "the threshold," and "moral-psychological experimentation."[23] The presence of any one of these traits qualifies a work for the genre. What narrative anywhere in the world would be excluded? Since almost every conceivable plot can be made to fit some part of this

---

and polyphonic, somewhat as Makhov invokes the procedure here. Kundera's exemplary genre is the twelfth century polyphonic chant. What he loves about this ancient form is its "embrace of two melodies belonging to two different eras," one individually inspired, daring and transitory, the other sublimely archaic, clarifying, and eternal. See Milan Kundera, *Testaments Betrayed: An Essay in Nine Parts*, trans. from the French by Linda Ascher (New York: HarperCollins, 1995), 72. Earlier, in his study *The Art of the Novel*, Kundera had introduced concepts of novelistic counterpoint and polyphonic form, emphasizing how crucial to novelistic construction are the simultaneity and heterogeneity of multiply *unfulfilled* polyphonic lines: on this plane characters need not meet, converse, or affirm one another, because "the novel is the realm of play and of hypotheses" (his beloved example is Hermann Broch's *Sleepwalkers*, although Dostoevsky is also granted mastery: "He is a great thinker only as a novelist"). See Milan Kundera, *The Art of the Novel*, trans. Linda Ascher (New York: Grove Press, 1988), 73, 78.

23    Bakhtin, *Problems of Dostoevsky's Poetics*, 114–19.

definition, for this "philosopher in the role of a philologist" a second step is indispensable: to select for analysis those texts, or fragments of texts, that "please Bakhtin personally, that he considers good and important."

Gasparov acknowledges the necessity of working with fragments. Literary history of the ancient period is a fragmentary science. However, this fact of the profession should impose greater caution and discipline on the philologist's imagination, not less. Thanks to Bakhtin — the exemplary creative philosopher falsely taken for a philologist — precisely the opposite has occurred with the menippea. In this distortion of our Greek and Latin heritage, Bakhtin lays bare his method and gives himself away. Why does he ignore the great canonized works of ancient literature, for example, the comedies of Aristophanes? Because, says Gasparov, the greatness and integrity of these finished works of art are felt by him as an impediment: "because Aristophanes is too politicized, too single-mindedly satirical, too non-chaotic, but ultimately because he exists — as a text, and not as a conjecture [domysel]." An integral, fixed text constructed by an individual genius imposes its own structures and its own truths, which humble its readers and restrict their free creative response. Since philosophers prefer to develop their own thoughts rather than analyze the objective data of the outside world, they naturally feel liberated by working with tiny fragments, which function not as aesthetic wholes but as isolated stimulants to their own fantasy and will.

Gasparov hints that such priorities also account for the strangely non-philological qualities of Bakhtin's study of Rabelais. Where in that book is Rabelais as author, where is the integrity of his novels, why is there so much "cultural environment" — public squares and folk rituals — and so little attention to literary style or overarching Christian symbolism? If, as some have suggested, Bakhtin tends to evaluate the folk ritual of French peasant life in Rabelais's novels through the binary norms and taboos of Russian folk culture, it is because such intercultural, inter-epoch moves are easy and pleasant with so loose a methodology. Valuing the fragment over the whole, the energetic anecdote over the unitary vision, is common to Bakhtin's study of Dostoevsky (in part), of Rabelais (in greater part), and wholly of his remarks on the menippea. And the pseudo-scholarly results, Gasparov insists, are the fruits of ethical philosophizing, for which the most important thing "is not the system but the process."

Gasparov is troubled further by the fact that the "serio-comical" menippea as a genre was hardly known to European literary history — even to those who supposedly practiced it. "But this fact is often forgotten, because it is not historians but theorists of literature who use Bakhtin's ideas in their research." Bakhtin has name recognition; for the impatient theorist his word is authoritative, not the facts of literary history. He provides simple, satisfying categories that urge even apprentice scholars toward unwarranted intellectual boldness. Here Gasparov's charge resembles that mounted by American scholars against New Historicist methods.[24] It also recalls reservations raised by American historians of Russian medieval culture against the mesmerizing binary paradigms popularized by the Lotman-Uspensky school.[25]

## In conclusion:
### *The paradoxical glories of the Russian critical tradition*

One paradox implicit in the present essay is that as personalities, Gasparov and Bakhtin share so much. Both are classicists, polyglots, bookworms, men of deep personal modesty, devoted more to library pursuits than to social causes, reluctant to put their private phobias or intimate struggles on public

---

[24]   These complaints begin with the priority given to "cultural fields" over individual artworks, and to the "environment" over the individual author. Bakhtinian turns of phrase (as reflected in that earliest bestselling volume of essays in English, *The Dialogic Imagination*) occur repeatedly in the anti-New Historicist critiques — invariably negatively inflected. Dialogue, loosely defined, is one of the master metaphors for a research method based on "circulation and exchange." The New Historicism considers the old historicism "monological," Edward Pechter remarks (1987); "Greenblatt prefers to see literary and cultural knowledge as parts of the same interpretive enterprise, as inter-animating each other" (293). But "the flow here is markedly one-way, from the cultural to the literary text, and the effect again is to privilege the cultural text as the stable and determining point of reference" (293). Earlier, that center was presumed to be the author. Now it is the field — a domain filled not with persons but with "power" and "discourse" (296). Fields and their "cultural texts" cannot be stable in the way that authored artworks are. They do not have determination and intention. Thus the stable center becomes the contemporary critic. Edward Pechter, "The New Historicism and Its Discontents: Politicizing Renaissance Drama," *PMLA* 102, no. 3 (May 1987): 292–303.

[25]   See the pioneering volume edited by Samuel H. Baron and Nancy Shields Kollmann, *Religion and Culture in Early Modern Russia and Ukraine* (De Kalb: Northern Illinois University Press, 1997), Editors' Introduction ("Religion and Cultural Studies in Russia, Then and Now," 3–16). For a tactful cautionary word on using cultural semioticians (identified loosely as "structuralists") as a source for historical thinking, see also the essay by David A. Frick, "Misrepresentations, Misunderstandings, and Silences: Problems of Seventeenth-century Ruthenian and Muscovite Cultural History" (149–68, esp. 152–54).

display. A brilliant memoirist, Gasparov writing in that genre nevertheless cultivates a cool, wry, ironic persona; Bakhtin, as we know, expressed no interest in writing his memoirs at all.[26] Both scholars avoid sentimental confession as a means of bonding with their readers. But they have come to exemplify two profoundly different academic worlds. What is the ultimate verdict on Gasparov's "Case of Bakhtin"?

That verdict is still out. Technically, the disagreement might be less over Bakhtin the thinker than over philosophy — or over the appropriate ways to think. For Gasparov, a discipline is known by its fruits. Philosophy is creative imagination, and philology (the path of the scholar) must be more recuperative, restorative, more formal and positivist. Bakhtin had another vision. His thought was speculative, ethical, of cosmic reach, and colored by German Romantic Idealism (in the Bolshevik 1920s, it was not Freud or Marx but Friedrich Schelling that he discussed lovingly for weeks on end with his close friends Lev Pumpianskii and Maria Yudina).[27] The early German Idealists, of course, were no strangers to system nor to academic life; the modern humanities research university began in Jena and Berlin. But the fruits by which the Romantic philosophers are now known also cannot easily be fit into our academic disciplines. To the dedicated scholars now excavating the original contexts of Bakhtin's work, it seems that Bakhtin was neither a conventional philosopher nor a traditional philologist. He was an intermediate type of thinker, concerned — in the words of one sympathetic student of his thought — with "that new point of intersection between the problem-field of philosophy and of the humanities" at the turn of the twentieth century, an intersection that led to "the displacement, at the end of the 1910s, of any firmly-established concept of boundaries between science, philosophy, and religion."[28]

Gasparov, too, admits of many types of philology and himself practices more than one type of criticism. In a brief paper delivered in 2002 entitled

---

[26]  See M. M. Bakhtin, *Besedy s Duvakinym* (Moscow: Soglasie, 2002), "Shestaia beseda," 295: "D: 'So you do not intend to write your reminiscences [*vospominaniia*]?' B: 'I absolutely do not intend to do so.'"

[27]  "I loved him [Schelling] very much and knew him through and through and from the bottom up," Bakhtin remarked. When Duvakin tried to prompt Bakhtin with Soviet-approved literary Romantics like Hoffmann, Bakhtin tactfully returned to the philosophical, idealizing writers "with a religious inclination," such as Novalis, who formed the core of his discussions (always on German texts in the original) with the Schellingist Maria Yudina. *Besedy s Duvakinym*, "Shestaia beseda," 271–273.

[28]  See Irina Popova, "O granitsakh literaturovedeniia i filosofii v rabotakh M. M. Bakhtina," in *Russkaia teoriia 1920–1930-e gody* (Moscow: RGGU, 2004), 103–114, esp. 107.

"How to Write a History of Literature," he gave his blessing to several different varieties of research: histories of forms, readerships, translations, reception.[29] Each type is valid, Gasparov writes, with one proviso: that it serve to "systematize our knowledge." And for those that do not? "As regards a history of literature undertaken not as a means for systematizing our knowledge but as a means of our spiritual self-affirmation — let there be as many such histories as one likes," he concludes (146). They live "from fad to fad." Such accounts will always be written. Born of the needs of the present, they will die with the present. They are not part of the philological record. Gasparov suggests that it is good practice for a scholar (and here we sense the imprint of his beloved Moscow formalist-folklorist B. I. Yarkho) to look even *at the present* with the eyes of the past — for "in fairytales, living water has its proper effect only after [we have encountered water that is] dead" (146).

Bakhtin was far less offended by histories that move "from fad to fad," because key for him was not a positivistic inventory of knowledge for its own sake, but the fact of movement itself. Bakhtin was also not particularly concerned, as a theorist, with the boundary between life and death. For that reason he tended to look at the past with the eyes of the present, or more precisely, through the potentials of the present. It was difficult, Bakhtin believed, to kill something off completely; not death but animation was the natural state of the world, and the spoken word was simply the best carrier of this principle. This essentially religious worldview probably cannot be packaged as philology. What appeals about Gasparov is his resolute and skeptical secularism; what dismays such thinkers about Bakhtin is his willingness to entertain the more spiritual side of the humanities. Gasparov's scholarly activity aims to save the text from careless or biased readers. Bakhtin, in contrast, sees the literary text from the very beginning as so gloriously multi-voiced, multi-centered and multifaceted that it is in no danger of being destroyed by any single reading or misreading. This conviction is central to Bakhtin's carnival spirit.

Over many years, Gasparov has cultivated a highly attractive, highly public persona, full of wit and the self-deprecating charm of understated performance. His memoirs and "jottings" are academic bestsellers. How this came to pass mystifies and delights his fans, even those not competent to appreciate his technical scholarly achievements in a dozen languages.

---

[29]  Originally a presentation at the 2002 Tynianov Readings, this short sketch was published a year later as M. L. Gasparov, "Kak pisat' istoriiu literatury," *NLO* 59 (2003): 142–46.

"Mikhail Leonovich Gasparov endeavored throughout his entire life to eclipse himself behind his heroes and his texts," writes Yurii Leving in a special 2005 forum devoted to Gasparov's seventieth birthday, "but despite his exemplary scholarly modesty, he has not been successful: a style has emerged."[30] Bakhtin, in his time, was also a professor held in high esteem. But he was not a person of aphorisms or witticisms. All his wisdom passed through the texts he read, which he considered sufficient to ground his personality. With Bakhtin, so little is known of his doubts, raptures, and dead ends. Whereas Gasparov has been an active shaper of his own person and thus a participant in his own mythologization, Bakhtin had far less opportunity, and far less energy, for this task. They were heroes of different times.

---

[30] Yurii Leving, "Pro captu lectoris: Fakul'tet nuzhnykh veshchei M. L. Gasparova," in *NLO* 73 (2005): 155–62, esp. 155.

# ON THE MASTER WORKERS

### Pushkin, Dostoevsky, Tolstoy

5. *Four Pushkin Biographies (2005)*

6. *Pushkin's Tatiana (1995)*

7. *Pushkin's Boris Godunov (2006)*

8. *George Steiner on Tolstoy or Dostoevsky (1994)*

9. *Tolstoy and Dostoevsky on Evil-doing (2004)*

10. *Kundera on Not Liking Dostoevsky (2002)*

11. *Parini on Tolstoy (1990 / 2010), with a Postscript on Tolstoy, Shakespeare and the Performing Arts*

12. *Chekhov and the Annas (1997)*

# 5

# FOUR PUSHKIN BIOGRAPHIES

*The title of this review essay on four biographies of Alexander Pushkin (Slavic and East European Journal, vol. 48: 1 (2004): 77–97) refers to one of the most sacred clichés or "winged words" of Russian culture: "Pushkin is our everything"* [Pushkin — nashe vsyo].

*The phrase is attributed to the literary and theater critic Apollon Grigoriev (1822–64), who, in his 1859 survey of Russian literature since Pushkin's death, wrote: "Pushkin is our everything. Pushkin is the representative of all that is spiritual in us, all that is peculiar to us, he is that which remains spiritual and peculiar to us after all collisions with other and foreign worlds." A sentiment like this is a sitting duck for parody — and has been parodied since the moment of its utterance. But the essay below, which reviews four items from the cosmic fallout of the Pushkin Bicentennial of 1999, was conceived in a reverent spirit. If not absolutely everything, he is nevertheless infinite.*

## OUR EVERYTHING
## (2004)

T. J. Binyon, *Pushkin: A Biography*. London; HarperCollins, 2002, USA imprint New York: Alfred A. Knopf, 2003, xxix + 731 pp.

I. Surat and S. Bocharov. *Pushkin. Kratkii ocherk zhizni i tvorchestva*. Moscow: Iazyki slavianskoi kul'tury, 2002. 220 pp.

Ariadna Tyrkova-Vil'iams. *Zhizn' Pushkina*. Tom pervyi 1799–1824 [1929]; Tom vtoroi 1824–1837 [1948]. Rep. in series "Zhizn' zamechatel'nykh liudei." Moscow: Molodaia gvardiia, 2002. Vol. 1: 468 pp.; vol. 2: 504 pp.

Feliks Raskol'nikov. *Stat'i o russkoi literature, Part I: Pushkin*. Moscow: Vagrius, 2002.

Now that the Jubilee harvest has been gathered in, inventory for a new century of "my Pushkins" can begin. Each of the biographical projects under review here — one by a British academic, another by a pair of professional Russian Pushkinists in Moscow, and two by émigrés of widely dissimilar generation and calling — has its own angle of vision on Pushkin: the Life.

T. J. Binyon's enthralling narrative, with magisterial self-confidence, gives us the daily behavior of the outer man as it might appear to an observer distanced in time, place, and cultural perspective. With good reason has his achievement been called Tolstoyan in its scope and mercilessness. The "brief sketch" by Irina Surat and Sergei Bocharov announces itself as an "experimental book" in the opposite direction, an attempt to provide the "inner biography of an artist" as might be grasped "in a single glance." In her youth, Ariadna Tyrkova-Williams (b. St. Petersburg 1869, d. USA 1962) was a classmate and friend of Nadezhda Krupskaya, Lenin's wife. She became a Kadet activist, married a British journalist and emigrated, began working on her biography of Pushkin in London during the 1920s, and published the second volume only in 1948, when she was nearly eighty. Of the many scholarly and nostalgic tributes to the poet from the Russian diaspora, hers is the longest and perhaps the least known. Feliks Raskolnikov departs from the strictly biographical task, although a primary aim of his revisionist *Essays on Russian Literature* is to call into question today's methodologies for integrating the life with the works. Taken together, these four books not only bring Pushkin to life in a fascinating set of parallel stories, but can serve as object lessons in biographical recuperation — the most rewarding and risk-laden form of history practiced in the humanities.

## I. The outer man (Pushkin through T. J. Binyon)

The 10 June 2003 issue of the *Guardian* ran a notice by John Ezard titled: "Crime writer's Pushkin steals £30,000 prize." Binyon was a dark horse. Betting had been far higher on the six other bestsellers competing for the Samuel Johnson award, Britain's most generous. In that notice we also learn that Binyon is crime reviewer for the *London Evening Standard*, as well as author of two criminal mysteries and a study of the role of the detective in fiction. A university don and Slavist with teaching experience at Leeds and Oxford, he came to this bicentennial commission handsomely equipped in nineteenth-century social history and the Russian classics. Is there something about a crime writer's approach to Pushkin's life that might help explain this impressive success?

We might first note that Binyon is the British biographer of another nation's preeminent poet. He is creating the life story for an audience that knows the poet and his wonder-working words only at second hand. Under those conditions, what might be the relevant devices of a good detective?

Come to the evidence with an open mind. Trust that the material world leaves traces. Stick to public documents in their proper order (the volume is prefaced by detailed genealogies and maps). Don't tell too much at once; attend to the contrary detail and to those obstacles that delay the easy end. Write vibrantly and without sentimentality. Assume a readership that values a rapid pace and cultivates a retentive memory capable of detecting a web of subtexts under every given fact. One nice design detail is the integration of dozens of Pushkin's line-sketches from his albums and notebooks — and this proximity of the poet's hand lends an energy to Binyon's narrative that recalls Khrzhanovsky's animated film from 1987, *Liubimoe moe vremia (po risunkam Pushkina)*, where sketches start to gallop, lines of script wrap themselves around trees to resemble birch bark, and Pushkin's handwriting comes to life before our eyes.[1] Such is Binyon's explicit target: the immediately available, visible outer man. To this end he peels back Jubilee encrustations, leaving the Pushkin Industry to the critics — and for this reason, he explains, "literary analysis has been eschewed" (xxix). Coherence and justification are not to be achieved through retrospection or myth, but must emerge linearly out of a chronological sequence, aided by the detective's eye for details in their original context. Later contexts and interpretive webs are overall off limits. On those rare occasions when Binyon engages a biographical piety (as with the encounter between Pushkin and the corpse of Griboyedov in the summer of 1829, described as a real event in *Journey to Arzrum* but demonstrably fictional), he corrects the facts neutrally in the text while noting the Russians' passionate adherence to the legend in a gloss (300).

These occasional exceptions to a biography "strapped to its subject's back" are themselves of interest. They all work to deflate the preening critic and enhance the multivalence of the artwork in its own time. When, for example, Binyon hops forward to Valery Briusov's 1909 essay on "The Bronze Horseman," this departure from his own stated procedures was most likely prompted by Briusov's essay itself, which discredits scholarly presumptions to decode the poem (436–37). Binyon's own discussion of the competing schools of "Queen of Spades" criticism — realistic and supernatural — appears similarly motivated; the two explanations coexist in perfect paradox, he

---

[1]    "A marvelous technique for replicating the creative process," writes Stephanie Sandler in her fine analysis of this whimsical and captivating film. See Stephanie Sandler, *Commemorating Pushkin: Russia's Myth of a National Poet* (Stanford: Stanford University Press, 2004), 156–67, esp. 160.

claims, "the literary equivalent of one of those prints by Escher that conflates two mutually contradictory perspectives" (445–46).

Nevertheless, for the literary biographer "eschewing the critical industry" is arguably more defensible than eschewing discussion of the literary works themselves. Early reviews reproached Binyon on this score. James Wood closes his highly laudatory essay in the *London Review of Books* (February 20, 2003) with the caveat that the biography's "only fault is its lack of extended literary criticism"; Clive James, in a dazzling irreverent review in the *Times Literary Supplement* (September 27, 2002), remarks pointedly that Binyon "has declined to make a priority of crying up the poetry's uniqueness." The charge is unfair. True, Binyon takes for granted that Pushkin is the greatest poet in the Russian language, anchored there as Shakespeare is in our English. The formal perfection of the poetry is rarely addressed, and as a rule the plots are not retold. But Binyon's blank verse equivalents to the lyrics are clean and austere. There are some stunning life-contextualizations that cause the lyrics to jump off the page. For example, the rumor of Nikolai Turgenev's deportation to England in 1826 is adduced as a stimulus behind Pushkin's lyric about the sea as enabler of man's three-fold fate, to be "tyrant, traitor, or prisoner" (228); the sudden juxtaposition of the poet's madcap life with an inspired rendering of "The Prophet" (245) jolts the reader into realizing that Pushkin's mission is far more than meets the eye. The Belkin Tales especially receive succinct and insightful appreciation (384–85). By "eschewing literary analysis" Binyon need not be implying a disdain for the products of literary genius. But he is reluctant to enter that edifice of insiderly professional debate that relies on itself for its excitement, dissociated from the processes of primary creation. Binyon insists on returning Pushkin's works to their own time. No insulation, no props. So earnest is Binyon in this task that he would even strip away the myth that did accrue to poetry during the Romantic period, and to this immensely charismatic poet during his lifetime.

Up through 1825, Binyon segments Pushkin's life in the conventional ways: Ancestry and Childhood, the Lycée, St. Petersburg, the Caucasus and Crimea, Kishinev, Odessa, then Mikhailovskoe. Everywhere, emphasis is on movement. For the final decade, another organizing rubric applies: settling down. The years 1826–29 (Chapter 10) are titled — prematurely, it might seem — "In Search of a Wife." That chapter is followed by others marked by an equivalent intimacy, which reflect a circling down to home, hearth, grave: "Courtship," "Married Life," "The Tired Slave," "A Sea of Troubles," "The Final Chapter." The wife might be the Muse, but poetry itself is unable to save

Pushkin in this fatal arc. The impression provided by the Table of Contents is of a powerful bellows, with the restless Pushkin first seeking freedom on the road or in changes of residence and then increasingly propelled inward, toward the final apartment on the Moika. What is absent from this trajectory is any mystique attending to the mission of a poet.

How to portray the poetic gift in its genesis and concreteness is a complex problem for a biographer, and Binyon has clearly thought hard about it. First, there are all the constraints of a relatively undramatic medium: a poet chewing at the tip of a quill pen is simply not as interesting to watch, hour after hour, as an architect realizing a building, Van Gogh over one of his canvases, or Mozart conducting *Le nozze di Figaro*. Second, consistent with his commitment to the outer man, Binyon respects Pushkin's privacy. The works do get written, but somehow at the edge of the picture, out of that excess of energy made available when the poet's body is temporarily or involuntarily stilled. The young poet, we read, got down to serious writing only when bedridden; venereal disease was the "wet-nurse" of *Ruslan and Liudmila* (90). The infuriating constraints that brought about the first Boldino autumn are given their due, with a useful inventory of the physical property on this distant estate and a chilling account of the cholera epidemic in Russia and Europe (338–45) — but Binyon will not linger on the divine creative miracle of that season. The occasional glimpse of Pushkin composing verse is registered (like almost everything else in this biography) as an outsider would look in on it, a person for whom the scene is bizarre in the extreme. Early one morning in Kishinev, Ivan Liprandi caught his friend Pushkin in the act of creation. The poet was unclothed, cross-legged on the couch, beating time, surrounded by little scraps of paper, which he then gleefully gathered up as soon as he realized he was being watched (145–46). This dervish-like image is of one piece with the poet-in-exile who appears in mixed company in transparent muslin trousers, no underlinen, and who challenges a casual acquaintance to a duel over the type of dance a provincial orchestra should play.

As we move through Binyon's book, an image of the poet comes together that is both more dissolute, and more miraculous, than we could have imagined. How, when did he manage to do it? Exasperated beyond all measure by Pushkin's swaggering bawdiness and by his readiness to call out even his close friends on some trivial pretext, Karamzin, Zhukovsky, and Vyazemsky emerge as bulwarks of sobriety and sane common sense. Tsar Nicholas himself intervened more than once on Pushkin's behalf against Faddei Bulgarin, urging the poet to ignore slanders cast at him, but Pushkin wouldn't hear of it. Even in a society where brilliant irregularities were celebrated, poetic genius revered, and a bourgeois work week unheard of, Pushkin's public self tried the limits of patience. Such was the daily behavior of the outer man. If the life of Pushkin's class and social set was all there was to how Russia was run — uninterrupted balls, receptions, dinners, duels, campaigns, card tables and love trysts — then Pushkin's world would have struck us as one huge masquerade along lines soon to be immortalized by the Marquis de Custine. But Binyon thickens the picture at crucial points, singling out institutions necessary to Pushkin economically and (in the broad sense) conceptually. These include censorship and police surveillance, literary publishing and marketing, foreign policy (especially the Polish uprising and the wars against the Ottomans), and the *modus operandi* of an aristocratic, serf-owning economy (debts and mortgages). Binyon's command of detail here is breathtaking, as is his deftly timed deployment of it.

Take, for example, debts. Binyon keeps a close eye on Pushkin's finances, and we are privy to the poet's account-keeping during those years when he cared deeply about his ability to provide. In early 1831, with his wedding imminent, on the debit side there were 24,800 rubles lost at cards (Pushkin insisted on paying these debts in full, even to cardsharps [337]); on the credit side, a hopeful 10,000 rubles for the publication of *Boris Godunov* and another 38,000 rubles from a 37-year mortgage taken out on 200 souls from Kistenevo, a village wondrously discovered to be unencumbered (353). By 1833 the picture was much grimmer. With his wife's expenses at court, a growing family, the large number of domestics desired by both husband and wife, and continuing gambling losses, Pushkin was obliged to weigh the liabilities and benefits of taking over the Boldino property in his own name (460ff). Half of its income went to pay interest on the debt. His wastrel father and idle brother had to be supported on the remainder. Pushkin, the sole creator of capital in the family, is revealed here as a strict, shrewd, no-nonsense manager of property, human as well as immobile. Ownership of Boldino would be worth the risk only if he could turn over to the government the sluggards and troublemakers among his serfs as a "recruit quittance," that is, as credit toward the draft quota. But despite his publishing ventures, the Tsar's bail-outs, and his modest subsidy as Historian Laureate, Pushkin could not make ends meet. This state of affairs severely strained his sense of honor.

In Pushkin's life, honor and its burdens accumulate gradually. At first, the poet acted like everyone else (his parents, his peers). He spent freely. He relished confrontation and public display. He took for granted his right to cuckold other men — even Count Mikhail Vorontsov, his immediate superior — while expressing horror that such a thing might happen to him. Attached as a civil servant to the Ministry of Foreign Affairs during his southern exile, he rejected the idea that any work should be asked of him at all: in Kishinev in 1821, to be sure, he was assigned one translation (137), but at a later point in his "service," when asked to gather information on locust damage in the field, he was enraged at the presumption on his time and autonomy (183). Pushkin appears at peace with his entitlements, if not with his fate.

With time, however, the poet's sense of honorable behavior became more nuanced and complex. At these delicate moments, Binyon reveals himself a master at narrative perspective. At times he reinforces Pushkin's worldview, causing us to wince alongside the poet trapped in his own white lie — as during the fiasco with the faked aneurysm in 1825, or the *Gabrieliad* incident in 1828 (where Pushkin denied authorship of the blasphemous poem to the investigating officials but felt obliged to reveal it to the tsar, resulting in deep personal humiliation, "which immeasurably strengthened Nicholas's hold over him" [282–83]). At other times Binyon's voice reflects the routine expectations of society or of the imperial bureaucracy. Thus we learn that in 1824 the locust epidemic was a serious matter; civil servants of higher rank than Pushkin had been given similar tasks; the poet was provided with money for expenses at three times the going rate, and even so he did not return the balance. By such mobility of perspective, Binyon creates an illusion of objectivity that does not exclude deep compassion. From the outside, Pushkin's reactions to events appear erratic, inconsistent, often uncoordinated. We see the poet dazzled by the image of the Emperor, dazzled by the greatness of Russia against the whining of the Poles, but in 1829, back from Arzrum, he refuses to produce the expected ode on the Turkish campaign — just as in 1826 he had refused to produce the reactionary pap on national education that Benckendorf believed was the government's due for having pardoned the poet (254). Through these vacillating gestures of resistance and compliance, the outline of a minimal acceptable honor slowly comes into focus.

The painful culmination of this balancing act comes with Pushkin's attempted resignation from imperial service in 1834, which Binyon reconstructs in excruciating detail (449–56). Once again the privacy of the poet's intimate correspondence has been violated. Pushkin writes in his diary, paraphrasing Lomonosov: "I will be a subject and even a slave, but not a chattel [*kholop*] or a jester [*shut*]." He submits his resignation to Benckendorf. Tsar Nicholas replies that he keeps no one in his service against his will, but that he would of course deny further access to the archives. The entire episode horrifies Zhukovsky, who browbeats Pushkin into withdrawing his resignation. Pushkin rethinks, sends a second letter with an apology, then a third letter confirming it. But the true revelation comes later. Zhukovsky, consummate courtier who is privy to all these missives, continues to be appalled: "You are out of your mind," he writes Pushkin; "you should order yourself a flogging to return you to your senses, don't you understand the Sovereign is grieved, he considers this to be ingratitude." Pushkin is puzzled. Like a self-respecting man, he asks Zhukovsky: "but how is this a crime or an ingratitude, when for the sake of the future of my family, personal circumstances, my peace of mind, I wish to retire to the country?" Zhukovsky (one senses through Binyon's cool prose) is at his wits' end. Does Pushkin really not get it? Must it be spelled out? What the poet has to do is grovel, for groveling is what will assuage the tsar's grief. But Pushkin does get it. It is precisely a chattel and a jester that the Sovereign desires as interlocutor, not a loyal servitor or (in Pushkin's fantasy-ideal) a great poet collaborating with a great tsar. And scandalously for Zhukovsky, Pushkin's sense of honor required that he have some say about how he would serve. But the parade grounds, ballrooms, and bureaucratic suites of Nicholas I's Russia were not the site for such relations. When the widowed Natalie insisted, to the Emperor's keen displeasure, that Pushkin be buried in his black frock coat and not his court uniform (631), she paid her fallen husband the most honorable final rites.

In the dynamics of this bungled resignation, I felt the beginning of the end for the poet. That line between subject/slave (acceptable to one's honor) and chattel/jester (unacceptable) could not be sustained. Perhaps Binyon would disagree, but from this point on in the story there seemed to be an upsurge of compassion for the Pushkins, which earlier had been in very short supply. Binyon is kind to and supportive of Natalia Nikolaevna. He presents her as a helpmeet as well as a trophy wife, a conscientious mother and good household manager, a woman with a head for finances — but whose extravagant tastes, alas, were shared fully by her husband. Although not immune to flattery, she did not lead her suitors on. D'Anthes disgusts Binyon (who nevertheless allots him a full and fascinating biography). He is weak, sentimental, frivolous, a darling of the court, a stalker and blackmailer (556–61). Husband and wife both do their best against such a phenomenon, but they are poorly equipped. Part of Binyon's closing strategy is to stress the normalcy of the final month (mid-December 1836 to mid-January 1837). The Pushkin melodrama has peaked; society is already talking of other things. All the more compelling, then, is the shock of that final furious challenge. When no one was looking, the unspeakable subtext erupted and suddenly became the text — and then the hero was dead, the crime hopelessly diffused.

Binyon's achievement is immense. Its limitations are intentional and self-imposed. But some reservations might still be raised. At times, Binyon goes too far to make Pushkin seem bad — or rather, to reduce him to his immediate impulses and perceived indignities. That the poet's appetites and exhibitionism might have been at least partly adopted for show is not seriously entertained. On the epigram war with Bulgarin, where both parties aim decidedly below the belt, Binyon remarks: "On reflection he [Pushkin] might have considered that it was neither edifying nor profitable" (319). Of course Pushkin did consider and reflect deeply on the issue. In an unpublished dialogue drafted in 1830, he gently mocks writers (that is, himself) who mistake an epigram for a refutation or an insolent exchange of wit for genuine criticism.[2] But since Binyon has resolved to be true to the public image and public record of the poet, Pushkin's more moderate (and profoundly wise) private meditations are not given their due weight.

Then Binyon strikes me as borderline naïve about Pushkin's marriage and family life. Pushkin was certainly ambivalent about settling down, up until the final moment, and there is evidence that a part of him even wanted to be refused. He probably surprised himself with the ardor he felt for the novel roles of husband and father. But Binyon underestimates, I believe, the poet's astonishing power to remake himself for his own sake once a decision had been taken. "As with many men, the experience of fatherhood had a profound effect on Pushkin," Binyon writes (447), citing as evidence Pushkin's delightful, pious closing phrases in his letters to his wife, which bless her and the children and urge her toward more frequent prayer. Such a man, Binyon adds, would not take lessons in pure atheism or pen the *Gabrieliad* with a wholly clear conscience. About that it's hard to say; but the important point about Pushkin's marvelous letters to his wife seems to lie elsewhere. As Brian Horowitz has persuasively argued, the poet's spiritual self-fashioning in the early 1830s involved not only very hard work over a prose style, but also over a new identity for the professional writer (a

---

[2]   The dialogue was jotted down in 1830 in response to articles appearing in the journal *Galatea*. Pushkin's two interlocutors discuss the state of Russian criticism. 'A' remarks that "Pushkin even replies to his critics in epigrams. What more can you ask?" To which 'B' replies: "But satire is not criticism — an epigram is not a refutation. I am working for the good of literature, not simply for my own personal satisfaction."

sober, hardworking *pater familias* and domestic provider).[3] Pushkin's letters home not only display him in that newly-fashioned role, but seem designed to induce his wife to "adopt the value system inherent in this new image." Reading his letters (as she did not read his poems), Natalia Nikolaevna would be educated in the virtues of domestic tranquility and the inviolate privacy of the hearth. This is not to suggest that Pushkin was deficient in love for his wife and children. But it is to suggest that when Pushkin changed, it was primarily in a literary-poetic direction, to increase his arsenal of creative resources — and those, as he well knew, were trans-historical and immortal. The family became an essential supporting muse. It was to prove more productive of mature spiritual growth than his earlier models of seducer, prophet in the wilderness, rebellious genius, or wandering Byronic poet. Since Binyon sticks so close to the marrow of the present and resists any move toward mythologization, Pushkin's efforts at *zhiznetvorchestvo* — at creating one's life as a work of art and for the sake of art — can only be a minor theme.

Finally, there is Binyon's overall ethical intonation. Does he approve of the story he tells? He would like this question not to matter. His strategy is to let the "facts speak for themselves." But a fact has many faces and a documentary is never innocent. If the compiler declines to intercede for the historical subject, even the most objective documents can easily default to value systems operative in the reader's own present. Consider one easily quantifiable theme running throughout the biography: financial indebtedness. Binyon presents the sums straightforwardly. Yet he does not go out of his way to explain that a gentleman's indebtedness meant something different in the 1820s and 1830s than in successive bourgeois eras more familiar to us. Within certain limits the more debts a man could carry, the better his word of honor was considered to be. Binyon is no sociologist. He simply describes, which risks conflating moral reflexes natural to us today with those native to Pushkin's time. In the mode of great detective writing, a sense of the present is kept vibrantly alive throughout. To an unprecedented extent we feel that we know and can touch the vulnerable man. But the costs of this palpability are real. To achieve a shared present, Binyon, for all the brilliance of his period detail, is prone to transpose Pushkin forward into our time rather than attune us backward, to the socio-ethical realities of the Romantic era.

---

[3]   Brian Horowitz, "A. S. Pushkin's Self-Projection in the 1830s: 'Letters to His Wife'," in *Pushkin Review / Pushkinskii vestnik* 3 (2000): 65–80. Subsequent quotation on p. 66.

## II. The inner man (Pushkin through Surat / Bocharov)

If Binyon presents us with the social imprint of the outer man, then the strategy of Irina Surat and Sergei Bocharov is its polar opposite. They begin with the internal — and the eternal. Their volume, we learn, is the result of an encyclopedia entry that outgrew its genre boundaries (7). Traces of the original rubric remain in the opening and closing lines: "PUSHKIN Aleksandr Sergeevich [26.5 (6.6) 1799, Moscow — 29.1 (10.2) 1837, Petersburg] — poet. Father — Sergei Lvovich"; then, two hundred pages later, "on 29 January at 2:45 p.m. he passed away." Unlike Binyon, who provides an Epilogue on the fate of Pushkin's writings, wife, children, and nemesis D'Anthes, Surat/ Bocharov remain strictly within the consciousness of their subject. There is something thrilling about this encyclopedia frame. It lends an authoritative dryness to the famous profile, yet celebrates (as encyclopedias are designed to do) the canonized, memorialized status of the subject.

Everywhere the authors display exceptional tact. Where Binyon gives us Pushkin at his most provocative, relishing scandals and even setting them up, Surat/Bocharov are non-committal and nonjudgmental. Their verb of choice for outrageous situations is *oslozhniat'sia*. Awkward, inconstant moments in the poet's life are moments that have "become complicated." When the liberationist rhetoric of Pushkin's early poems or his apparent sympathy for the insurrectional Greeks appears to contradict the pride that Pushkin takes in imperial bayonets aimed against the freedom-loving tribes of the Caucasus, resolution is matter-of-fact: "Thus was born and gradually matured in Pushkin's consciousness a complex collision between empire and freedom" (33). Such inconsistencies are not presented as irresponsible; they are conceptually and morally productive. They trigger in Pushkin a deeper appreciation of history, and especially of the paradoxical Peter the Great, both autocrat-tyrant and revolutionary. The seduction of Elizaveta Vorontsova in Odessa is evaluated first for the splendid love lyrics and graphics it produces (a half-dozen poems and over thirty sketches); only then do we read that the love affair "complicated Pushkin's personal and service relationship with her husband" (40). Nothing about the rumor of Vorontsova's swarthy infant daughter perhaps being Pushkin's child; and nothing about Count Vorontsov's indifference to his wife's infidelity, which freed the General for his own mistresses and greatly irritated Pushkin, a man at home with scandal but who despised being patronized against his will (Binyon 177–78).

What is "experimental" about this reverent co-authored biography is at first obscure, but soon becomes clear. Details of the outer life that others see are to be measured solely by their inner literary fruit. If the most serviceable verb is "to become complicated," then a favored modifier throughout is *dushevnyi*, that untranslatable space between the spirit and the conscious mind where all creativity begins. What happens to Pushkin "on the outside" is of interest, of course, and will work to simplify or complicate his life, but the fulcrum around which all value revolves is the poet's own inner sense of his genius and his concomitant obligation to generate the poetic word. Relations between external event and the internal imperative to create are two-way and reciprocal. The poet writes "Vol'nost'" at a time when his own political convictions are not fixed ("at that moment, Pushkin simply didn't have any" [20–21]); the ideas it contains are the banal, clichéd formulas of the French Enlightenment. But these familiar sentiments prove freshly dangerous because "Pushkin was above all a poet, and from his pen political ideas received such public poetic strength as the radical minds that had given birth to them could only dream of" (20). It is the arousing power of poetry, not of politics, that makes for revolution. Thus Pushkin the poet is exiled and put under surveillance, not for any radical sympathies or madcap deeds (indiscretions that in Binyon have pride of place) but precisely, exclusively, for his words. This dialectic between word and deed is laid out in the prefatory note "from the Authors": "A poet is a special creature, he does not live like everyone else. He doubles his life with his word, he encloses it in the word, and the word becomes his fate" (7–8).

It is no surprise that the authors take seriously Pushkin's 1819 encounter with the German fortune-teller in Petersburg — not because her precaution was accurate (such privileged speech is hard to disconfirm), but because Pushkin all his life believed in it. By the spring of 1835, he had even come to feel that the "moment for fulfilling the prophecy was drawing nigh" (191). But one's fate, *sud'ba*, must be understood in Pushkin's sense, which was that of the ancient Greeks. *Sud'ba* is not superstition, not providence, not an end-point. It is a dynamic. To know your fate is not to fall passive before it; constant struggle is required to realize your fate in the proper, honorable way. Chance occurrences continually clutter the path. Pushkin "did not live like everyone else" in part because he grasped the shape of this struggle. At the beginning of his southern exile, Pushkin already "had begun to see the outline of his fate" (24) — and was devising means for surviving it and turning its unfreedom into creativity.

Scattered along this trajectory are many deft capsule readings of individual works. *Ruslan and Liudmila* startled its first readership as a "humorously modernized image of Ancient Rus'," in which pious motifs were profanely lowered (21); *The Gypsies* bore a trace of the poet's skeptical encounter with Rousseau (43–45). Much is made of Pushkin's curiosity, beginning in 1826, toward sacred texts from exotic, non-Russian cultures. Glinting through the narrative are moments of keen insight on the psychology of the lyric and the ironized prose consciousness of *Evgeny Onegin*, recalling Surat's impressive cycle of Pushkin studies from the 1990s and Bocharov's preeminence as a disciple of Bakhtin. But it is as an experimental "sketch of the life" that this biography is most distinctive. The authors divide it into three segments: Lycée-Mikhailovskoe (1811–1826), Mikhailovskoe-Boldino (1826–1830), and "The Thirties." Each segment ends on a spiritual threshold requiring the poet to define himself anew, in a more risk-laden way. This new definition is then tested, stripped of its illusions, and embodied in poetic masterpieces. Up through 1826, the life is governed by the poem "Prorok" (71). The threshold achieved is the confluence of two contradictory Decembrist themes: the gallows (for his friends) and mercy (for himself). The middle section opens on Pushkin's audience with Tsar Nicholas, a "pivotal moment in his biography" (74) because the highest authority, it now seemed, sought his advice and ideas: to his role of prophet Pushkin has added *sovetnik tsaria*, "councilor to the tsar." The rapturous autumn of 1826 marks the end of his rebellious youth. But unhappily, it was not the hoped-for beginning of an imperial service worthy of his genius.

By 1830 Pushkin had resolved to redirect his energies. His bachelor life, his *Onegin*, his love lyrics and on-the-road verse now give way to a pursuit of stability and the family hearth, reflected in a turn to the Russian past, to prose, and to a "poetry of reality" and thought (123). This new sobriety burdens the poet with new obligations: to prophet and would-be advisor to power is added the poet as witness to history. Pushkin's travels in Pugachev country, his interviews with survivors of the rebellion, and his impulsive attempt to participate in military action during the Arzrum campaign are all testimony to the ambitions of this new voice. Among the fascinating details of this self-fashioning trajectory are the works that Pushkin chose *not* to create, in keeping with his sense of his fate. In 1824–25 he wrote an elegy to André Chenier and not (as everyone expected he would) to Lord Byron (55); in 1836 he confirmed his earlier refusal to produce an ode on Russian military victory by transforming his Arzrum travel notes into a wryly deflated reminiscence (186–88).

To be sure, this conventional tripartite division of the life obscures some works. The 1825 *Boris Godunov*, for example, composed six years before the poet's prescribed turn to history, risks being read more for its innovative dramatic form than for its superbly well-informed historical grasp of that pivotal reign. But on one point, Surat/Bocharov are refreshingly post-Soviet. Throughout the 1830s, their Pushkin doggedly pursues ways to serve the Emperor with honor. He stubbornly nourishes his desire to see in Nicholas I the reforming potential of Peter the Great. Only with the second Boldino autumn, 1833, does disillusionment (or revelation) descend irreversibly, as evidenced by the endings of *Angelo* and *The Captain's Daughter*: their fairy-tale resolutions come to pass solely through arbitrary acts of mercy, not through honest dealings under law (151). The justice awarded Pyotr Grinev — "a simple man in very complicated circumstances out of which he emerges with honor, again and again" (175–76) — is available to him because he is as fearless, faithful, and truthful as a folklore hero. But his survival is an accident and a miracle.

Such utopian motifs are as far as Surat/Bocharov will go in documenting Pushkin's growing entrapment and despair. But even despair, we are given to believe, registers on Pushkin differently than on ordinary people. Professional humiliation leads to an inner resignation that is also harnessed to the muse, giving rise to the apocalyptic, pagan, and Christian themes in the final poems. Although Pushkin hoped that his journal *Sovremennik* would permit him service with honor (and an income as well), still, he resolutely went forward to realize his fate; during the final two years, "dramatic outer conditions [...] were complicated by an acute need for inner self-orientation in premonition of the end" (193). Debts mount, sales of his works are poor, harassment intensifies, but these disasters are presented very abstractly; whatever responsibility the extravagant Pushkin might bear for them is morally invisible.

The biography postpones until the last possible moment any mention of D'Anthes. If Binyon's Pushkin tumbles toward his end, Surat/Bocharov's prophet-poet sees it, prepares for it, is fueled creatively by it, and awaits the trials that D'Anthes (an arbitrary carrier of fate) will place in his path. A more serious omen than this trivial officer of the Guard is the fruitless autumn of 1835, which deeply depressed the poet, and the lyrics on madness. Surat/Bocharov pay scant attention to the marriage, its joys or its anguish. Whereas Binyon makes Pushkin's quest for a wife a focal point from 1826 on, there is almost no comment here on this huge shift in the poet's daily life and responsibilities — beyond the *dom/penaty*/hearth theme in the poetry. Only two of the couple's four children are graced with a birth notice. Thirteen pages before the end (207), D'Anthes makes his appearance, but his pursuit of Natalia Nikolaevna is diluted immediately with three other unnecessary duels that Pushkin provoked in the early winter of 1837. Tucked in after a detailed discussion of the Stone Island cycle is another mention of the Frenchman renewing his suit (215). But an integrated view of the final months is ventured only on the penultimate page.

Surat/Bocharov would like to dismantle the myth of Pushkin's overreaction to the fatal anonymous letter. The poet, they insist, knew what was at stake. His increasingly inflammatory responses to this provocation were necessary "to affirm publicly the truth about himself and his family life, to preserve his name unsullied, which, he knew, already belonged to history" (218). His fury was "an act of full liberation from society" (218), a declaration of independence from all that had not answered to his high hopes for the calling of a poet. But it was more: "The inner starting point of the final duel was the contrast between the intrigues, the floods of slander and filth inundating the Pushkin home, and the image of authentic existence toward which he had been striving during the final years" (219). By this point in the biography, everything has become inner. What the outside world happens to see has little status as evidence. If Binyon's Pushkin in his final months is a bit of a bore and a laughingstock, a gifted man harassed out of his mind but too stubborn to follow the sensible advice of his friends, then Surat/Bocharov's is a tragic hero, for whom every life-move had been an investment and for whom pursuit of "authentic existence" is dissociated from personal behavior. No significant thing, it would seem, is ever Pushkin's fault. Both versions of the life must agree, of course, on the peerless courage and stoicism of the final two days.

How do these two profoundly dissimilar biographies measure against one another? Surat/Bocharov is firmly in the Russian (and Romantic) tradition of maximal reverence toward the poet, not only as a privileged consciousness but also as a human being set apart, exempt from judgment, who acts as he does in order to write what he must write. Within that tradition, these two authors represent a specifically "Moscow" methodology, more spiritual and speculative than the textologists of St. Petersburg's *Pushkinskii Dom*.[4] One palpable predecessor for Surat/Bocharov's project is Yury Lotman's graceful biographical classic from 1981 (although their co-authored image is far less athletic than his). Lotman too presents the poet as a sort of alchemist who intuitively turns

---

[4]  For an excellent discussion of these two Russian schools (and of foundational Pushkinistics in general), see David M. Bethea, "Introduction: Of Pushkin and Pushkinists," in *The Pushkin Handbook*, ed. David M. Bethea (Madison: University of Wisconsin Press, 2005), xvii–xlii.

every misfortune into precious metal. In contrast to this Russian model, Binyon, following a more secular and demystified Western pattern, gives us a Realistic — or perhaps an acidic and satiric eighteenth-century — picture of the poet on the ground, a person who must answer for his deeds like everyone else. In this profane tradition, "real" often means ugly, low, the comedy of life viewed close-up. As a result, the same facts feel utterly different in the two biographies. When Surat and Bocharov remark that Pushkin's lyrics affirm a "cult of immediate sensual pleasures" [kul't siiuminutnykh naslazhdenii] (18), it sounds more like a philosophical position than an appetite. Binyon simply shows us a vital man grabbing for what he loves.

But here is the remarkable thing. Binyon's Pushkin — so full of lust, rage, hunger, error, curiosity, a profligate in life — seems somehow happier and more real than the Russians' image. In Surat/Bocharov, Pushkin's life is one long taking-on of obligations and burdens: prophet, councilor, witness to history, martyr. The poet desires to do and to be all this, of course, but we sense in this image little zest for the actual experience of living. Pushkin looks around, sees an inadequate world, sighs, and sets to work. Emblematic is the end of the 1820s, when Pushkin seriously begins to tackle prose. "The shaping of Russian prose," we read, "turned up on his creative path as a national task"; and "this obligation too he took upon himself" (97). Readers will differ, but to my ear this constant undertone of martyred duty muffles the most precious ingredients in Pushkin's life. With Binyon — and forget that he does not analyze the poems — we are on the edge of our seats, always wondering when this madcap will find the time to create his masterpieces; with Surat/Bocharov, never. Read in tandem with Binyon, the Russian way stands out in sharp relief. While appreciating playful enthusiasts such as their own Andrei Sinyavsky, Russian academics will most likely continue to find their comfort in biographical modes more hagiographical than the Tolstoyan-style razoblachenie, "expose and embarrass the subject," that wins prizes in the West.

### III. The perishable things of Pushkin's world (Tyrkova-Williams and thick description)

The third volume under review — longer than both the preceding books combined — adopts a composite methodology, both romantic and naturalistic. Its author was an amateur. In the Herzen and D. S. Mirsky mode of Russian émigrés in London, Ariadna Tyrkova-Williams was as political as both but far less enamored of the socialist experiment. She embarked on her Pushkin biography in the early 1920s, in part to recuperate what she knew was lost forever. This sense of absolute loss dictated her special type of nostalgia: precise, thick, objective, unsentimental. The appearance in 1929 of Volume 1 of *Zhizn' Pushkina* (covering 1799–1824) was met with polite silence from professional émigré Pushkinists such as Vladislav Khodasevich and Modest Gofman; both volumes, however, were eventually well received in the general press as *narodnaia biografiia*, a "popular/people's/national biography" of the poet. Its reprinting in the late 1990s and then in 2002 in the series "The Life of Remarkable People," with a lengthy introduction about the author, marks the welcome return of a prominent anti-Bolshevik to post-Communist Russian culture.

"For me the biography of Pushkin is a school, and a revelation, and relaxation, and an inexhaustible resource of the Russian spirit," Tyrkova-Williams wrote to her son Arkady in Paris in April 1927. "I began to think about it in January 1918, at a time of pitch-black grief and despair. Many years have passed since that time, and I have succeeded in doing little. But if I succeed, it will be a genuine 'white deed.' A source of faith in Russia."[5] By then she was 57 years old and settled permanently in England. Little in her tempestuous prior life would seem to explain this passion. Ariadna Tyrkova was born into an ancient Novgorod merchant family in 1869 and raised, with her six siblings, in the radical-intelligentsial spirit of the 1860s. Her brother Arkady was exiled to Siberia in 1881 in connection with the assassination of Tsar Alexander II; young Dina, just into her teens, was expelled from the *gimnaziia* (where she had befriended Nadezhda Krupskaya). In 1888 Ariadna enrolled in the Higher Course for Women and married a maritime engineer. In the mid 1890s — divorced, with two children to support — she began working as a journalist under a male pseudonym for various provincial newspapers in Yaroslavl and Ekaterinoslav, providing feuilletons, reviews, news summaries, and fictional sketches. Her first literary skills, then, were acquired in the Chekhovian manner, as a livelihood and not as a leisurely aesthetic pursuit. Key to her writing was a keen eye for detail, setting, and a talent for evoking sympathy with the well-focused human scene.

---

5   Oleg Mikhailov, "'Dva chuvstva divno blizki nam...' (Ob A. V. Tyrkova-Vil'iams)," in Ariadna Tyrkova-Vil'iams, *Zhizn' Pushkina* (Moscow: Molodaia gvardiia, 2002), 1:7–26, esp. 21. The biographical summary given here is indebted to Mikhailov's account and also to Alexandra Smith, who, in person and in her writings, introduced me to this unusual émigré project. See Aleksandra Smit, "Formirovanie literaturnogo kanona v knige Ariadny Tyrkovoi-Vil'iams 'Zhizn' Pushkina,'" in *Pushkinskie chteniia v Tartu* 2 (Tartu: Tartuskii universitet, 2000): 267–81.

By the turn of the century, Tyrkova was known to the leading revolutionary activists (as she later remarked, "the three founders of Russian Marxism were married to my school friends" (10)). Influenced by Gorky, Artsybashev, Andreyev, and Briusov, her own politics grew more radical. In the first revolutionary period (1903–05) she was twice arrested; faced with a two-and-a-half year prison term, she decided to flee abroad. In Stuttgart she met the Englishman Harold Williams, left-leaning correspondent for the *Times*, who became her life's companion. In Geneva, visiting her friend Krupskaya, she first encountered Lenin (who made an intensely negative impression). More significantly, she met Peter Struve, from whom she received her first systematic political education. Tyrkova's career as a Constitutional Democrat began. Rising quickly in the party, she led the Kadets in the State Duma, 1906–07, and by 1912–13 was covering Duma events for various Petersburg papers. As editor of *Russkaya molva*, she recruited Aleksandr Blok for her columns. She and Williams hosted literary evenings in their large Petersburg apartment where, she recalled, "everyone was there but Mayakovsky" (15).

A half-century later she remembered this stressful, hopeful period between the Vyborg Manifesto and Kerensky's brief regime as one uninterrupted attempt to shore up the illusion of a potentially liberal Russia. Throughout 1916, Tyrkova-Williams represented the Kadet Party (loyal to the government and the war effort) in the Petrograd City Duma. In January 1918 she spent some time in the Rumyantsev Museum in Moscow, acquainting herself with Pushkin's manuscripts. This glimpse would become precious to her later, when, as an émigrée in London, she would have access to scholarship from both the exile community and the Soviet Union — but by then, Soviet interpretations of the manuscripts were ideologically constrained. Tyrkova never disdained the fine textological work produced by official Soviet-era Pushkinists in the 1920s-40s, but also never ceased to plead for the full publication of all extant manuscripts — the prime necessary resource, she insisted, for any literary biographer.[6] By March 1918, threatened with arrest, Tyrkova moved with her husband to England.

---

[6]   See the author's Preface to Volume 1 (1928): "Up to the present day neither the private publishing houses, nor the Academy of Sciences, nor Pushkinskii Dom have published the whole of Pushkin in all its completeness. In Russia, despite all catastrophes and shocks, a cult of Pushkin has been created and continues to grow. Pushkiniana is immense. But no one has published everything from his hand, all that was written, rewritten, marked up, crossed out, struck out... not knowing all the variants, how can one investigate the birth and movement of the verses? His poetry and his character, his work on a manuscript and his work on himself [...] are so fused that it is impossible to dissociate them" (30).

Attempts to raise an anti-Bolshevik alarm on British soil were not successful. In October 1919, Tyrkova returned to Rostov-on-the-Don (then held by Denikin's Whites) and soon after to Kharkov, for a Kadet congress (the party's last). Narrowly escaping by ship from Novorossiisk, she made it back to England; miraculously, her mother and children were also safely evacuated. Beginning in 1922, the Williams home in London became a haven for visiting Russians of the first emigration (their guests included Remizov, Bunin, Zaitsev, Tsvetaeva). In this cultured environment, in her early fifties, surrounded by family and by her own admission at the happiest, most secure time of her life, Tyrkova began writing her biography of Pushkin. She was fortunate in her resources. The British Museum was nearby, as was the London Library with its Ostafiev archive and Russophile director. The first volume of *Zhizn' Pushkina* was completed in 1928. In that year Harold Williams died, and his widow interrupted her Pushkin labors to write his biography. Only in 1935, at age 67, did she return to her Russian subject — whom she had left stranded, she wrote her son Arkady, in the wilderness of Darial. Volume 2 was finished in time for the Jubilee year 1937. Tyrkova brought the manuscript with her to Paris (where Volume 1 had been published) in May 1940. The timing could not have been worse. Paris fell. Throughout the occupation, Tyrkova and her son were trapped in the south of France, in wretched quarters near Grenoble. In 1948 Volume 2 finally appeared. Soon after, Tyrkova and Arkady emigrated to the United States, where she died in 1962, in her ninety-third year.

What are we to make of this 950-page project, written by a contemporary of Chekhov's over a period of thirty years, which is only finding its readership now, in the early twenty-first century? Tyrkova-Williams was better equipped for the task than it might at first appear. Unlike many academic Pushkinists in her native country, she had practical political experience — and of the answerable, parliamentary sort. She was not repelled by the prospect of important people, even poets, cooperating with state power, nor by the need for pragmatic compromise. She was also an experienced journalist with an ear for alien voices and an excellent sense of place. Her biography of Pushkin, while not thickly or precisely footnoted, is saturated with excerpts from memoirs, letters, and popular legend, always apt if at times vaguely tagged ("Annenkov," "Pushchin," "Rasskaz Ia. N. Tolstogo"). For all its bibliographical casualness, this is not a biographical novel. As the third of our texts under review, it adds an ambitious new dimension.

Binyon emphasizes how Pushkin looked and sounded to others; Surat/Bocharov, how Pushkin looked and sounded to himself. Tyrkova-Williams attends primarily to how the world looked and sounded to Pushkin — and why his reactions to that world were reasonable, given those impressions and pressures. For a vital component of émigré recuperation projects was to capture a disappearing world, not only to register a poet's alchemy on that world. Tyrkova works by thick description. The confirmation of facts or the correction of errors in earlier accounts — a telltale impulse separating the academic professional from the amateur — is not her purpose; her ideal reader is the common one, perhaps a newspaper audience, curious, naïve, a person who can be drawn in with startling indicators of a world positively different than our own. On those rare occasions when she does engage the Pushkin Industry, it serves her larger vision of the poet as a political liberal. One such moment is her lengthy interpretive gloss on the *shut / tut* controversy (p. 38 of the 1826 Mikhailovskoe Notebook #2368, embellished with gallows and five hanging bodies). Should we decipher Pushkin's handwriting here as "and like a fool [*shut*] I could have been …" or "I too could have been there [*tut*]"? Tyrkova insists on *shut*, relying on her examination of the manuscripts in 1918 (2: 136–37). But she enters this quarrel at all, it seems, largely because scholars in Stalinist Russia were now obliged to confirm the opposite as regards Pushkin's revolutionary Decembrist sympathies.

As we have seen, building a scene from the bottom up is also Binyon's way. But since his goal is to demystify the poet and free his image from its pious straightjacket, his details tend to debunk and abrade. Tyrkova rarely moves against the Pushkin Cult in that aggressive way. On the contrary, she is more prone to interrupt her realistic inventory with a passage of high Romantic pathos — reminding us of the East-West biographical divide, and locating her hybrid émigré narrative squarely between Binyon and the Surat/ Bocharov model. A case in point is Chapter 3 (1: 66–78), introducing the Lycée years. First the school is placed in an all-European perspective (its advanced pedagogy from La Harpe, its unprecedented exclusion of corporal punishment), then a Russian one (only eight years earlier, it had been decreed that foreign as well as native professors throughout the Empire conduct their classes in Russian; thus a technical lexicon was still lacking for many classroom subjects). Details of the inauguration ceremony, the architecture of the school, the changing color scheme for student uniforms, the approved diet and drinking code, the daily schedule (from 6:00 a.m. to 10 p.m. with an unusually high number of breaks for *progulki* [nature walks]), and the multifaceted curriculum are followed by a catalogue of personnel (directors and professors). Finally we meet the Lycéeists themselves: a gifted, rowdy bunch of boys with a high sense of entitlement. At their core, but not yet in the spotlight, is twelve-year-old Pushkin — getting on with some teachers, not with others, and finding the strict daily routine a relief from the disordered household he had left behind. (Habits formed here would prove durable: early morning work time remained the poet's practice until the end.) But then suddenly this glittering reconstruction fast-forwards to the fully grown myth, worthy of Surat/Bocharov and laying bare the larger rationale for Tyrkova's fine-grained contextualization: "And most important: not suspecting that among them there was one chosen by the gods, that their Lycée life was lit up by the light of his genius, that thanks to Pushkin all details, trifles, foolishness of that entering class would be preserved in the memory of Russian people for many long years, and would become the special mark of Russian history" (69). She's right, of course. Would she have bothered to track down all that colorful and meticulous detail if Pushkin had not emerged from it?

These occasional ecstatic inserts, interrupting and justifying a narrative otherwise glued to its own time, release Tyrkova-Williams from the need to pass judgment on individual actions. A sense of causality and responsibility emerges that is quite distinct from that achieved in the other two biographies. First, like a feuilletonist or *ocherkist*, Tyrkova sketches in the world; only then (so the logic of this genre goes) might a reader later hope to approximate what felt normal for a biographical subject of that world. The strategy is apparent from the opening chapters, "The Past" and "Sashka" (1:32–63). Information is given initially in visual images, textures, sounds. "Pushkin was born [...] on the threshold of two centuries," begins the biography. "Around his cradle stood people in powdered wigs" (32). These eighteenth-century wigs then become the minor instance, the civilized anomaly in a Moscow where cockfights and fisticuffs are standard street entertainment, where physical danger is everywhere the norm, where twenty-five miles from the city the untamed frontier already begins and the larger estate-owners routinely arm a portion of their serfs (out of rivalry or boredom, these serf militias would often do battle with one another), where domestic violence is wholly unmarked (fathers whipped their grown sons). Only after this general background picture has been sketched in do we learn that "Pushkin's family was too enlightened for the savage practices of serfdom," preferring the "freedom-loving French spirit." But this spirit too requires qualification. "The Pushkins were insufficiently serious to have matured into humanism, but they were Voltaireans, which introduced a certain restraint into their gentry habits" (35). Tyrkova-Williams, a well-traveled *intelligentka*-journalist from the provinces who was born only three decades after Pushkin's death, surely knew what sort of behavior could be expected of such generations in such environments.

In between these two poles — Moscow the violent village, and Voltaire — Pushkin's childhood unfolds. The same fused extremes are noted in his ancestry: *Gannibalovshchina*, patriarchal rage, coexists with a 400-volume library that its owner hauled intact all over Russia. Pushkin's mother, "La Belle Creole" with her yellow palms, is the capricious female variant: pampered, lacquered, exhausted by pregnancies (eight children, of whom five died in infancy), impossible to please. Maternal grandmother and beloved nurse provide whatever nurturing there is, and an introduction to Russian history as well (Maria Alekseyevna's small property of Zakharovo once belonged to Boris Godunov). But Tyrkova never fails to point out where, in the cracks of parental virtue, seeds of their elder son's calling might have taken root. Nadezhda Osipovna knew the social value of a smooth French exterior and made certain her two surviving sons acquired it. Father and uncle were of course inadequate mentors, but their best was still not a bad place to start for a precocious child with a keen memory. Little Sashka absorbed their wicked wit, skill at repartee, drawing-room theatricals and bawdy humor that would pass without warning into morose pouting or rage. When rage struck (the elder Pushkins were known to slap their children in front of guests), there was always the refuge of the library. "All in all," Tyrkova concludes, "Pushkin was not an unhappy child" (60). He was not guided, but also he was not stifled, and this very porousness allowed him considerable rein. In salon and library, he learned a great deal that should have been hidden. And when he left for the Lycée, he did not look back.

Tyrkova's placid texture and cool explanatory tone recalls more Turgenev or Chekhov than it does hagiography or Tolstoy. Undergirding it is the assumption that people, and especially extraordinary people, are not heroes as much as survivors and optimizers of circumstance. Their life-strivings and potentials take shape around what feels possible, comfortable, normal, worth trying out within those circumstances. Thus must Tyrkova spend so many pages setting up palpable surroundings. She employs the same technique with every new space Pushkin enters: the Caucasus and Crimea (1:345ff), Kishinev (1:288ff), Mikhailovskoe (2:89ff). First she sketches its history, then its flora and fauna, its roads and restaurants, its local entertainments and curiosities. This technique brings her close to Binyon — except Binyon tends to fill in human stories; Tyrkova-Williams emphasizes geographical and institutional ones. Pushkin's world is set in motion as a confluence of environmental conditions. Neither fate nor willfulness has a defining role. It becomes as difficult to reproach Pushkin as to deify him.

Take, for example, Karamzin and Zhukovsky. Binyon presents both as wise counselors, respecting Pushkin's gift but reprimanding the man. Surat and Bocharov admire these two courtiers as adorers of poetry. Tyrkova is less impressed. Although she quotes Zhukovsky's letter to Pushkin of November 1824 ("To all that has happened to you and that you have brought on yourself, I have one answer: Poetry [...]"), she shrugs off its stoic eloquence, noting only that Zhukovsky "did not hurry to answer the poet's desperate letters" (2:13). In Chapter 13, titled "*Tverdyi Karamzin*" [tough-minded / firm Karamzin], she acknowledges that the historian was intensely irritated by Pushkin's "wild living, mocking tone, Voltaireanism" (1:184) but also that the older man was dry and severe with the poet, "did not like him, and did not trust his moral authenticity" (1:233). Tyrkova sees nothing irregular in Pushkin's affair with Eliza Vorontsova. In her chapter "David and Goliath" (1:416–26), we learn of General Vorontsov's hypocrisies and disrespect for Pushkin, the impudence of Alexander Raevsky (who dared to court Eliza as well), and then the dastardly final blow: Vorontsov actually assigned Pushkin an official task (the infamous inspection tour of locust damage, Chapter 35, "*Sarancha*").

These locusts are a useful focal point. In Binyon, we recall, this incident is narrated in a bureaucratic voice zone (181–82): a reprimand is in order, for an absolutely idle salaried official was shirking his duties. Binyon dismisses as disingenuous and less than honest the letter that the "horror-struck" Pushkin wrote in his own defense to the Odessa official Kaznacheyev, in which he defends his trade as a full-time poet and explains his salary-for-no-work as compensation for being denied access to the book markets of the capitals. Binyon insists that this was fantasy: however unjust his exile, at that point in his life Pushkin had never dreamed he could live by his pen. His first royalties (for *The Fountain of Bakhchisarai*) had arrived only the previous March and had taken him quite by surprise. And after receiving that bonanza, Pushkin "became even more outrageous in his behaviour" (179). Tyrkova-Williams, not averse to a retrospective view at threshold moments, contextualizes the event quite differently. Pushkin's honorarium was the first such paid to any Russian writer, and it "opened a new epoch in Russian literature; [this was] a triumph for all writers, for the entire intelligentsia just being born," whose task it was to create a self-respecting "industry of the mind" (1:387). She interprets the letter that Pushkin was obliged to write to Kaznacheyev as a historically symbolic act, "one stage in the agonizing, years-long correspondence of a great poet with bureaucrats who did not understand that poets too serve the Motherland and the state" (1:448). This struggle becomes emblematic of the crippled state of Russian civic society. Indeed, the highest compliment Tyrkova can pay a government official is to call him a "humanist," that is, a person who instinctively protects individuality and creativity from the caprice of power. (General I. N. Inzov, Pushkin's indulgent supervisor in Kishinev, is described as one such "typical Russian humanist of the eighteenth century" [1:289]). There are moments when even Alexander I seems to qualify for the epithet. Tyrkova speculates that the tsar's heart must have thrilled— albeit illicitly—when he heard the dangerous ideas of his own youth, inevitably proclaimed during that era in stiff rhetorical French, take harmonious wing in Russian for the first time in "Vol'nost'," an ode composed by a poet scarcely graduated from the school bench (1:221).

No biography of Pushkin can forego discussion of "Poet and Tsar." Tyrkova's chapter under that title (2, ch. 9) focuses on Pushkin's premiere audience with Nicholas I in September 1826, a much-mythologized event. She is remarkably even-handed. Among her repeating motifs is that the time-honored Russian standoff between literary words and state power has been miscast; the line of hostilities should be drawn not between "Poet and Tsar" but between "Poet and Bureaucrat" [poet i chinovnik]. Although Tyrkova resembles our other biographers in her attention to Pushkin's quest for service with honor, her angle of vision is far more subtly adapted to the expectations and circumstances governing all major players, not just Pushkin, and she sympathetically reflects what would feel normal for each. In this quest, it turns out, poet and tsar are equally powerful, needy, anxious, and flawed.

Tyrkova presents Pushkin before 1820 as an almost unqualified winner. In verse-making he was the awe of the capitals. In lovemaking he was a "born Don Juan" (1:186), the envy of his far handsomer friends. In pride of nation, he was at one with his class and his era: serious Shishkovian and comic Arzamassian each loved Russia in his own way, and the "authentic patriotism" of both was never in doubt (1:119). But if love of country was taken for granted by Pushkin's generation, *service* to one's country, including a personal identity achieved through the daily fulfillment of duties, was a more stressed matter.

Service had not been the norm in the childhood of the poet. Both parents "had spent their entire lives in *prazdnost'* [unfettered freedom, holiday time, "dutylessness"], with no concept of the conditions required for work" (2:11). The structured life of the Lycée provided a wondrous counter-model. But Tyrkova suggests that Pushkin did not seriously consider the problem of service until the first year of his southern exile, while traveling with the Raevsky family. He was discomfited, unable to press his suit with Maria Raevskaya, and embarrassed by a lack of funds. In a chapter intriguingly titled "*Robkii Pushkin*" (1, ch. 20), Tyrkova traces the poet's timidity to his intimacy with that glittering family of military servitors. *Shtatskii Pushkin*, Pushkin the Civilian, is a major theme throughout Volume 1. The stage is set in the opening pages, where the Alexandrian epoch is described as an era when everybody fought all the time, "east, west, north [...], in jest, in mischief, in swashbuckling, in duels, and sometimes simply in brawls" (1:34). "Civilian Pushkin lived among military men," Tyrkova writes (1:296–97); "[he ...] completely shared the conviction of his military friends that one's honor must be defended with a weapon in one's hands." With no contradiction, then, the poet could admire a "defense of honor" by rebel Greeks against the Turks, by Russian bayonets in the Caucasus, and — in his own personal life — by those unnecessarily provoked duels in Kishinev. The common denominator in each instance was not freedom, but honor. Belligerency was a primary ingredient in friendship, courtship, and service. "At the beginning of the nineteenth century," she assures us, "military service was not an external duty but a matter of conscience and honor" (361).

For this reason, civilian Pushkin — proud, even morbidly proud, of his ancestors in the service nobility — was uncertain how to define his role. It would not be by assessing locust damage, of that he was sure. But neither would he produce celebratory odes on demand. If poetry was his trade [*remeslo*], then it too could produce wealth, self-sufficiency, and conditions that enabled honor. But financial autonomy gained by honorable employment was only one aspect of Pushkin's mature understanding of service. The other was his concept of *izbranniki sud'by*, "those chosen by fate" (the title of Chapter 27 in Volume 1) — a category, it appears, that could apply to a tsar, a rebel, and a poet. Chosen tsar and chosen poet obligate one another mutually. For all that the initial audience between them was "staged with Napoleonic theatricality" (2:142), Nicholas I and Pushkin are treated here with equivalent respect. Each was eager to impress the other, each needed the other, and each had to struggle to approach the other with an open mind (1:143). Tyrkova's willingness to see matters also from the tsar's point of view — to defend his imperial sense of honor as well as the poet's — is unusual for Pushkin biographies. The sympathy begins with her account of the Decembrist debacle (Chapter 7, "*Rokovoi den'*" [2:107–19]). It ends 300 pages later, with her impassioned defense of Nicholas I against the slanderous "legend" of his seduction and conquest of Natalia Nikolaevna, an insinuation leveled by P. E. Shchegolev in 1911 and reprinted in Bolshevik Russia in 1928 (2:462–67).[7] Such open-minded sobriety complements Tyrkova's humanistic liberalism in other areas, imparting to her biography an intonation neither native nor émigré.

Tyrkova devotes some time to the Decembrist Uprising, explicitly basing her account on a memoir that Tsar Nicholas I wrote for his children in 1835. The misunderstandings and anguish of that day are given largely in his royal zone. We learn of his rigid upbringing, his ignorance of his brother Konstantin's renunciation of the throne, his utter unpreparedness to rule, his desire to do his duty while not knowing in what it consisted, his awareness of his own unpopularity among the soldiers, officers, and at court (and thus his reliance on his loyal friend Benckendorf during those awful hours of the interregnum). Finally she considers Nicholas's valiant but vain efforts to prevent bloodshed. The tsar-elect had lists of suspects and could have moved with preemptive arrests. Why did he not do so? Harsher measures undertaken sooner would have averted the catastrophe, Tyrkova insists, especially since the conspirators themselves had lost hope in the success of their enterprise by the night before (she considers Prince Trubetskoi's failure to turn up on the Square an act of great courage [2:111]). Nicholas hesitated, she argues, because he admired these men, acknowledged their sense of honor [chestnost'], and was horrified at their fantastically unreal plan. She notes that after the disaster of the Crimean War had exposed the corruption and incompetence of the Russian army, Nicholas, by then close to death, said bitterly: "My friends the Decembrists would never have done this" (2:118).

All in all, Tyrkova rather takes Tsar Nicholas's side — and invisibly allies Pushkin with it. The "soft-hearted dreamer" Ryleyev (who was present on the Square, and executed) and the sober, commonsensical Pushkin (who was absent, and spared) are grouped together. "Had they managed before the uprising to share their mental experience, perhaps they could have restrained the conspirators from an armed demonstration" (2:102). This reading of events is certainly not the conventional "Poet versus Tsar." It cannot surprise us, however, coming from an exiled Constitutional Democrat turned Pushkin

---

[7]    Together with the *shut* / *tut* controversy in Mikhailovskoe Notebook #2368, this flare-up of anger at unjustified slander of the Romanov dynasty constitutes Tyrkova's major corrective incursion into 20th-century academic Pushkin scholarship. Shchegolev's "Duel and Death of Pushkin" is a well-documented study, she notes, except for this one sensationalist rumor — present in innuendo, dependent upon unreliable French sources, and designed to portray the Russian tsar as some "Asiatic monster" (2:463, author's note).

biographer, disillusioned with the Decembrist Myth that had polarized one hundred years of subsequent Russian politics.

Ten more years of wary relations between Russia's premier soldier and her premier civilian poet is half of the story left to tell in Volume 2. Tyrkova interweaves three factors, each with an anti-Bolshevik, anti-bureaucratic edge. First comes Pushkin's post-Decembrist loyalty to the imperial principle and the monarchical system, blunted (both then and now) because his friends insisted on seeing in him the pre-exile firebrand. That reality, she insists, was no more. Then there is the poet's idealization of Nicholas I, not wholly without cause. After September 1826, Pushkin enjoyed no more audiences with the tsar until the time of his marriage, when the two men began to meet very cordially in Tsarskoe Selo; "[d]uring those five years, Pushkin's feelings toward the tsar had not changed, and if anything had strengthened" (2:318). Finally, there is the irritant of mindless censorship, and Pushkin's ignorance (willful or naive) regarding the constant surveillance to which he was subjected by Benckendorf's network of spies. Tyrkova makes much of the fact — an accident of those terrible days of the 1825 interregnum — that this Chief of Gendarmes, a "limited and desiccated careerist," ignorant and suspicious of all enlightenment, was one of the few men whom Nicholas trusted (2:215–16). Pushkin was so good-natured, so patient and self-respecting that he never suspected the extent of the constraints under which he labored. Each time some random caprice came to light (an intercepted letter, a slanderous accusation), he was startled and enraged anew. By the time he bolted for Arzrum, he probably suspected the truth.

As a weaver of contexts and circumstance, Tyrkova-Williams shows us Pushkin striving to realize his fate in the proper way. But others have their fates too — and the role of chance events in these multiple unfoldings is left open. Driving with his second, Danzas, to the site of the duel, relaxed, in good humor, at last on his way to defend his honor with a weapon in his hand, Pushkin jokingly noted that they were taking a roundabout path. "Danzas had deliberately chosen a well-peopled route, hoping that someone would notice them and stop them," Tyrkova writes (2:485). "Benckendorf could not have been unaware of the duel underway. The entire city was talking about it, including the tsar. How many times the gendarmes had prevented duels. This time they did nothing." The final act of this drama between poetry and bureaucracy was fought not over Pushkin's body but over his unpublished papers, which Benckendorf wished to seal up but which Zhukovsky insisted be inventoried under his supervision (2:502–3). The tsar's benign consent is part of that posthumous struggle as well. Only at the very end, as the dead genius is being slipped into his grave attended more by gendarmes than by family or friends, does Tyrkova allow Nicholas I, from whom the poet had expected so much, to reveal his hand. "The tsar had no authentic respect or friendly feeling for the slain man," she concludes (2:499). When Prince Paskevich-Erivansky remarked that he regretted the loss of the writer Pushkin at a time when his talent had just matured "but as a man he was no good [*durnoi*]," the Emperor answered: "Your opinion about Pushkin I share absolutely." For all its delicate balancing, then, the theme of "Poet and Tsar" ends as in Tsvetaeva's 1931 poem of the same name: in the "otherworldly hall of the tsars," the marble statue of Nicholas I is nothing more than a "pitiable gendarme of Pushkin fame."

The other half of the story that Tyrkova tells in Volume 2 is Pushkin's quest for the right woman. The transitory muse gradually gives way to the gentle ideal of Tatiana and then to the necessary wife. Women writers who love Pushkin and take up the task of recreating the poet's life are a fraught category, not free of a certain possessiveness, in part because of the magisterial twentieth-century accomplishments of Tsvetaeva and Akhmatova in this realm. As a biographer, Tyrkova-Williams is a product of the nineteenth century, and she enjoys certain benefits by being no poet herself. Chernyshevskian traces of an *intelligentka*'s view of women's rights and appetites — where women too are agents, able to calculate their own best interests — suffuse her image of Pushkin in his successive roles of Don Juan, bridegroom, and husband. Two points are made repeatedly. First, that physically Pushkin was extremely undistinguished: short, fat-lipped, kinky-haired, "just like a monkey" (the candid opinion of the gypsy singer Tania, 2:159–60). And second, that women found Pushkin irresistibly attractive, from his adolescent years to the day of his death, and responded rapturously to his overtures. Women were the hungry ones. Pushkin was fussy, even though he always had more than enough.

Tyrkova opens Chapter 11, "*Baryshni*" [Young Ladies] with the remark that "many people who are highly susceptible to falling in love require a single great feeling. Pushkin was one" (2:168). Unlike Binyon, who presents Pushkin's libido as goatishly indiscriminate, and unlike Surat/Bocharov, who present it largely as a prompt for magnificent love lyrics, Tyrkova offers us a disciplined, fully rational quest on the poet's part to lose control and be bound to a fated love. Sophie Pushkina, Ekaterina Ushakova, Annette Olenina, all these trial runs were quickly forgotten and caused the poet little grief. Part Three of Volume 2, titled "In Pursuit of Happiness (1829–1833)," begins with the long-awaited moment when Pushkin, now smitten by Tasha Goncharova, realized, with relief and dread, that he was no longer free. His behavior as a bridegroom was bizarre. And "there was something strange, wrong, non-Pushkinian about this marriage, in this striving to attain the hand of a girl who had done nothing to indicate that she loved him, or that she found him attractive" (2: 264). Once the step was taken, however, and Pushkin had adjusted his muscular organism to the pressures of the new regime, he was ecstatic. Tyrkova notes that Tasha Goncharova became Pushkin's wife to the buzz of much skeptical gossip. She was sloppy, disorderly, tasteless in her attire; "*Moskovshchina* was reflected in her rather noticeably" (2:305). How could this untutored girl become the consort of a great poet? But "Natalia Nikolaevna had good reserves of inborn female intuition" (307); she knew how to adjust. In fact she learned household management rather well. The couple became known as superb, if extravagant, hosts. It was this pliability, combined with the indispensable absolute beauty, that made her precisely the sort of woman to whom Pushkin desired to lose his freedom.

Chapter 20, "*Zhenatyi Pushkin*," goes further than the other biographies in defending the integrity of the wife. If Binyon tends toward the sentimental, positing a powerful but involuntary change in the poet after he experienced marriage and especially fatherhood, Tyrkova insists that Pushkin consciously constructed the gilded cage of his home life. Friends were astonished at his happiness. Natalia Nikolaevna had always been indifferent to the poetry, but "it is possible that Pushkin, especially at the beginning, found a reassuring charm in the fact that for Nathalie he was simply a husband and not a famous poet" (2:308). Nathalie was a skilled embroiderer — it was her one "domestic skill" — but "she soon gave it up, in order to devote herself fully to that which her husband considered her true calling: the entertainments of high society" (2:331). Her jealousy too "delighted him and consoled his male vanity" (316). Of the couple's four children Tyrkova speaks little; their names and birth dates are provided in one brief paragraph (2:342). Her focus is everywhere on the passionate bond between husband and wife, presented as deeply satisfying both physically and spiritually. If there is foolishness on one side and Pygmalion on the other, Tyrkova does not speculate about it.

By 1834 these two themes, the tsar's court and the necessary wife, were dangerously interwoven. Several events are highlighted as fatal: the insult of *kammerjunker* rank, the insult of the intercepted letter, the strain of settling the two older Goncharov sisters in the Pushkin household (a move the poet tried to prevent). Having molded his wife into the perfect temptation, he now had to shoulder the risk and the cost. But the cage was too transparent and the strands tying him to power too compromised. Tyrkova (like Binyon) considers the attempt of a beleaguered Pushkin to resign from service in 1834 a "reasonable request." But she also understands the tsar's fury [*"Tsar' razgnevalsia"*], quoting his regal word that archival access was granted only "to people enjoying the special trust of the authorities" (2:379). Pushkin's desire to withdraw from the world—from that world—for the sake of his work, family and sanity was not only a suspension of service; it was a betrayal of trust.

These two massive vulnerabilities of Pushkin, his wife and his Emperor, receive a parallel reassessment in Tyrkova's final chapters. In 1825–26, the new tsar was treated sympathetically, as the carrier of a valid point of view on Russian society and personal honor that Pushkin largely shared. Pushkin nurtured this ideal throughout the 1820s, fretting at bureaucratic caprice and stupidity but careful to separate this unpleasantness from the Sovereign's name. But as the end nears, and even more so after the end, Tsar Nicholas emerges in his true colors: an unworthy object of hope. Likewise, Pushkin's passionate devotion to his wife (and to his self-fashioned ideal of a wife) is supported by Tyrkova enthusiastically as long as the poet himself considers it a challenge and is able to cope. But by Part Five of Volume 2, titled "The Predictions Come True (1836–1837)," Pushkin can no longer cope. Accordingly, Tyrkova's tone toward Natalia Nikolaevna changes abruptly. She ceases to consider whether this wife was what the poet wanted her to be, and the narrative takes on the carping "mean-to-Nathalie" tone that is routine in accounts of Pushkin's life.

To sample but a single page (2:446). "She was drunk on her own beauty, it turned her empty little head," Tyrkova writes; poetry readings in her presence never bothered her because, as she was proud to announce, "All the same I don't listen." She continued to call Pushkin and his friends by the condescending term *sochinitel'* [something like "hack writer"] rather than writers or poets; and "no one has preserved for posterity a single one of her witticisms, not a single apt remark" (2:446). D'Anthes was not her only suitor, and toward all of them she acted the same: laughing, posing, wounding her husband. "This frivolous, empty woman filled her life not with love, but with a play with others' feelings." At this point it crosses the reader's mind that Tyrkova is reacting to Pushkin's wife as would a radical *intelligentka* of Chernyshevsky's generation, for whom seriousness of purpose and the ability to carry through on a feeling were virtues more to be prized than spousal fidelity. Natalia Nikolaevna, it now seems, was too trivial and dishonest even to consummate her own flirtations. At home she still graced the hearth, laying her lily-like head on her husband's knee, but "it was enough for her to don a ball gown and she was transformed from an affectionate wife into a frivolous coquette" (2:473). Thus does the wife emerge in her true colors: an object unworthy of love. Hope, trust, love: of all this the poet was stealthily deprived. Only honor remained wholly under his own control, and the duel was its instrument.

§

What might we learn from these three different Lives of the Poet? Binyon's biography was a major breakthrough: the most ambitious, thorough, irreverent and best written page-turner on Pushkin's life that we are likely to have in English for some time. Surat/Bocharov was less a pioneering effort than a culmination: an immensely stretched-out elegy in prose, composed in the reverent, abstract and uncritical spirit of Russian tributes to their great poets. The two volumes of Tyrkova-Williams, appropriately for an expatriate Russian writing in London, fit in between these two extremes, longer than the former but as compassionate as the latter, beholden to no special pieties but the one that also held Nabokov fast: an émigré's love for an unrecuperable past. We are left with several interesting questions. Which is the more reasonable portrait to attempt: the outer or the inner man? Must the history of a private life, in order to qualify as demythologized and "real," be reduced by the biographer to *byt* — that is, to a record of everyday observable habits and pleasurable or stressful routines? Grigory Vinokur discussed these issues in his 1927 study "Biography and Culture," drawing heavily on Pushkin's life.[8] The terms "inner" and "outer" are of course hopeless when each is taken alone, he writes (34); biography, as "the history of a private life," must assume that one is conditioned by the other. Pushkinists of the "Did Pushkin smoke?" persuasion, who limit themselves to "counting the number of bottles drunk up or the property gambled away," have only themselves to blame when "their Pushkin comes out not Pushkin, but Nozdryov" (22). At the other pole, biographers of the "spiritual life" err in their willful self-serving application of psychology, which (Vinokur cautions) "apparently enjoys unlimited and absolute rights in this region,

---

8    G. O. Vinokur, "Biografiia i kul'tura" [1926, published 1927], in *Biografiia i kul'tura / Russkoe stsenicheskoe proiznoshenie* (Moscow: Russkie slovari, 1997), 17–88. Page numbers in the text.

where we make bold to enter with our own goals" (23). Most desirable is a synthesis of the two, which Vinokur would seek in "concrete psychology." In such a method, "biography is not so much a problem as a source" (26). To re-create a personality [*lichnost'*] in its own time, the most difficult task facing the biographer is to define the filter, that is, the optimal procedures for the selection of material.

Over the subsequent two decades, Vinokur, one of the great Soviet-era Pushkin scholars, had ample opportunity to experience within the Stalinist literary establishment the anxiety that can attend a correct selection of material. In 1927, the political imperative was not yet decisive. On the far side of Communism, however, the politically conditioned aspects of canonized biography have once again become a point of contention. Here Feliks Raskolnikov's work on Pushkin can serve as instructive closure.

### IV. Post-communist sobriety (a coda on Feliks Raskolnikov)

Part One of *Stat'i o russkoi literature* (2002), titled "Pushkin," contains seven essays written between 1987 and 2002. The topics range from close readings ("Arion," *Boris Godunov*, *Pir vo vremia chumy*, "Pikovaya dama," and *Skazka o zolotom petushke*) to topics of more thematic sweep ("The criminal in Pushkin as a tragic figure"). These discussions contain bold, at times eccentric, almost always provocative interpretations of individual works. But as a coda to this review of Pushkin biographies, it is Raskolnikov's three-page "Introduction" justifying his volume (9–11) that is most immediately relevant. In it he suggests that a critic's "selection of material" is not innocent in either direction: the works are always stitched into the life, and life-values are inevitably extracted from the works.

The time of his book's writing coincides with a historical arc stretching from perestroika to the present day. During that period the Communist system of controls weakened, collapsed, was overwhelmed by a chaotic multiplicity of alien or previously suppressed methodologies, and then literary study attempted to cleanse itself. Raskolnikov, in emigration since 1979 and for many years a professor at Michigan State University, has been chronicling this process from a distance for two decades. All the essays collected in his book (which discuss, in addition to Pushkin, texts by Lermontov, Gogol, Chekhov, Esenin, Pilnyak, Gorky, and Sholokhov) are unified by one task: to counter the hasty and overwrought post-Soviet correctives to Communist clichés with further correctives from a more dispassionate Western-outsiderly perspective. Himself a methodological conservative, Raskolnikov is concerned to stabilize Pushkin's life and snatch it back from the backlash.

His argument is straightforward. Pushkin's mature period (1830–36) is the phase of the poet's life least honestly analyzed by Soviet scholars. Obliged to exaggerate his "revolutionary" support of the Decembrists, to muffle his move toward enlightened conservatism, and to ignore his spiritual evolution, these researchers piled up authoritative but isolated life-facts and literary facts that did not illuminate one another. Taboo themes were left to Western Pushkinists or Russian religious scholars writing in the diaspora — and for the most part were treated subjectively, at times impressionistically. After 1991, this mandate for an atheistic, politically radical Pushkin dissolved and the opposite extreme was indulged. Veteran Pushkinists such as Georgy Lesskis and Valentin Nepomniashchy began to argue that Russian Orthodox Christianity and the messianic, ascetic ideal (with its resistance to rationalism, hedonism, commercialism, and Western-style individualism) lay at the core of all Pushkin's creativity. This corrective was valuable, Raskolnikov affirms. But a profligate Christianization of all the texts was clearly also unbalanced. The erotic, life-affirming Pushkin as closet ascetic has as much basis in fact as the Party-approved image of Pushkin, proto-Bolshevik. "Having focused their attentions exclusively on religious motifs in the works of Pushkin, they now 'ideologized' and simplified him, although differently than the Soviet literary scholars had done" (11). And so Feliks Raskolnikov moves steadily through the corpus, seeking an objective (ideally a golden) mean between the theses of Communist-era unfreedom and post-Communist reflexes against that unfreedom.

Comparativist biographical and literary scholarship received powerful impetus from the Pushkin Bicentennial. We can expect successive waves of such counter-correctives in future years. Inevitably, as Pushkin's receding world becomes ever more illegible, as the Russian tradition of scrutinizing its literature for clues to "what it means to be Russian" gives way to more global pursuits, and as poets cease to be front-line martyrs for the political folly of the day, we will look back on the Pushkin Myth that flourished for two centuries as a primary literary fact. Whether exposé, reverent tribute, or thick description will best serve to keep the poet alive in his native medium is a question for later generations and ever-wider readerships.

# 6

# PUSHKIN'S TATIANA

*This essay first appeared in an anthology edited by Sona Stephan Hoisington, A Plot of Her Own. The Female Protagonist in Russian Literature (Evanston: Northwestern University Press, 1995): 6–20. Delivered in a compressed Russian version in 1995 at a conference at Moscow State University honoring the Centenary of V. V. Vinogradov and published in its Proceedings (Vestnik Moskovskogo universiteta, seriia 9, Filologiia [no. 6, 1995]: 31–47), it caused a minor fracas. Its reprinting in the Bulletin of Tambov University (Vestnik Tambovskogo universiteta, vol. 3–4, 1996: 36–46) added still more fuel to that fracas. The Tambov "Tatiana" stimulated such negative commentary from the pen of one local professor, who so completely failed to grasp my praise of Pushkin's heroine and fixated with such baffling earnestness on the essay's trivial remarks on sexual subtexts, that I ventured to submit a lengthy and unnecessarily confrontational "open letter" in defense of the piece. The editors graciously agreed to print it a year later, together with a final riposte from the offended professor (Vestnik Tambovskogo universiteta, vol. 4, 1997: 69–77).*

*Late in 1996 the essay received a probing, more open-minded review, delivered at a Pushkin conference in Pskov by a scholar from Novosibirsk State Pedagogical Institute. He suggested a "Nabokovian" source for my hypothesis, which interested me greatly, and also assigned pride of place for revisionist interpretations of the Russian classics not to a decadent, triumphant West eager to pervert Russia's sacred values, as had the Tambov professor, but to Russia's own critical tradition, especially Tynianov and the Formalists.*

*The negative Russian reaction to this essay was only partially due to the protective reflexes of the Tatiana cult. The piece could easily be read as enhancing that myth, not as debunking it. Nor can we wholly blame the raw post-communist 1990s — when, as censorship dissolved, Russian academics witnessed their Russian classics being subjected to all manner of slick, cavalier exploitation by Western critical theorists and irreverent outsiders (although that too played a role). The lesson to be learned from the acrimonious fallout of "Tatiana," I believe, was my inattentiveness to the grating, flippant sound of my hypothesis against the traditions of Russian philological scholarship. In the English original, my scenario for Chapter Eight of Eugene Onegin is cast as a "musing" conversation of the critic with herself; a speculation, a parallel world and simultaneously a shadow-reality mirroring the creative process. It does not exclude or discredit other readings. In the Russian version, this tentative intonation was greatly weakened; the essay (I realized too late) sounded preachy and polemical. Some Russian academic circles, tolerating playfulness from artists like Nabokov or Sinyavsky, found whimsical relations toward beloved subject matter disrespectful from a "foreign scholar." The fracas amounted to little in the end. But it was indicative of the clash between our two "Pushkin industries" (old versus new, hagiographic versus irreverent) after the Wall came down. Excerpts of this Tatiana aftermath are translated here as a postscript to the essay.*

*It could also be that my argument is simply wrong. Re-reading the essay now after fifteen years, it strikes me as naïve in its treatment of Romantic convention. But that Tatiana is the miracle of poetic tension and that Pushkin meant this as moral reality: that idea I stand behind. In retrospect, the comedy with Tambov illustrates avant la lettre Mikhail Gasparov's case against Bakhtinian readings, in which everyone (author, hero, reader, critic) is equally alive, eager to talk, and trustworthy. Such a literary thought experiment, Gasparov believed, was sooner bad philosophy than useful philology.*

# TATIANA
## (1995)

> "[Tatiana], as is well known, besides being Onegin's ill-starred partner and the cold-blooded wife of the general, was Pushkin's personal Muse.... I even think that's the reason she didn't start anything up with Onegin and remained true to her unloved husband, so she'd have more free time to read and reread Pushkin and to languish over him."
>
> — Abram Tertz [Andrei Sinyavsky],
> *Strolls with Pushkin*

> "Простите мне, я так люблю / Татьяну милую мою." [Forgive me: I so love my precious Tatiana.]
>
> — The narrator, *Eugene Onegin*,
> chap. 4, xxiv

The heroine of Pushkin's *Evgenii Onegin* carries the most famous, deceptively complex female name in all of Russian literature. Paradoxes abound in her image, which is to varying degrees derivative, impulsive, naïve, renunciatory, passive, majestically disciplined and inexplicably faithful. Starting with the narrator who tells her story and ending with many successive generations of critics, almost everyone who touches this image falls in love with it — or with its unrealized potential. It could be argued that Tatiana and her exquisitely "withheld" personal fate functioned as the single, most richly inspirational source for Russian literary heroines well into the present century.

This essay grew out of my bewilderment over the Tatiana cult. What has made this collage of female attributes — sentimental, vulnerable, stubborn, largely silent — so resilient and irresistible? Tatiana's energies and virtues have been enormously inflated, by detractors as well as devotees. In one of the earliest portraits, Vissarion Belinsky, smitten by Tatiana but resisting the fate that Pushkin provides for her, lamented that she could not break free into her own autonomous life.[1] Dostoevsky, pursuing the other extreme in his Pushkin Speech of 1880, elevated that fate to the level of hagiography by crediting Tatiana with every possible civic and metaphysical virtue, eventually investing her marital fidelity with the cosmic dimensions of Ivan Karamazov's challenge to an unjust universe.[2] And then there is the troublesome denigration of Evgeny that usually attends the exaltation of Tatiana. He is made "superfluous" not only to his own life and times but also to the novel that bears his name; his honest and honorable actions vis-à-vis the rural maiden who thrust herself inopportunely upon him are read as mental cruelty, frivolity, even depravity.[3] (Here, Tchaikovsky's wonderfully nuanced 1879 reworking of the novel into opera — "lyrical scenes" that probably should have been titled Tatiana — must figure as a crucial phase in the maturation of the cult.) To be sure, some eminent Pushkin scholars (Gukovsky, Bondi, Slonimsky, and Makogonenko in the Soviet period) have attempted a rehabilitation of Evgeny. This move is often linked, however, with an extra-textual and politically motivated hypothesis cobbled together from hints in the fragmentary chapter 10: since Evgeny was "becoming a Decembrist," he deserved Tatiana's support and the reader's sympathy.[4]

Perhaps more serious than these facts of reception or transposition is the disjointed image of Tatiana within the text itself. There are some

---

1    For Belinsky on Tatiana, see V. G. Belinskii, *"Evgenii Onegin" A. S. Pushkina* (Moscow: GosIzdKhudLit, 1957), esp. 59–84 (Stat'ia 9-ia).

2    Dostoevsky proclaimed in his Pushkin Speech (1880): "Perhaps Pushkin would have done better had he called his poem by Tatiana's name and not by Onegin's. She utters the truth of the poem." Fyodor Dostoevsky, "Pushkin," in *Russian Views of Pushkin's "Eugene Onegin,"* ed. and trans. Sona Hoisington (Bloomington: Indiana University Press, 1988), 56–67, esp. 59.

3    Interestingly, it is Belinsky in his Eighth Article on Pushkin (1844) who defends Onegin against the incipient Tatiana cult. "The heart has its own laws," Belinsky writes, "Therefore, Onegin had a perfect right, without fearing the stern judgment of the critics, not to fall in love with the girl Tatyana and to fall in love with the woman. In neither case did he act morally or immorally . . . There is nothing dreamy or fantastic about Onegin. He could be happy or unhappy only in reality and through reality." See Vissarion Belinsky, "*Eugene Onegin*: An Encyclopedia of Russian Life," *Russian Views of Pushkin's "Eugene Onegin,"* 34, 40.

4    For a survey of the ebbs and flows in Tatiana's critical image (as of the early 1970s), see Geraldine Kelley, "The Characterization of Tat'jana in Puškin's 'Evgenij Onegin'" (Ph.D. dissertation, University of Wisconsin-Madison, 1976), esp. part 1.

obvious stumbling blocks: for example, that Tatiana is assembled from imported sentimentalist scraps and yet, on the strength of one folklore-laden nightmare and a love of winter, represents the "Russian soul"; or that the moments of Tatiana's most profound transformation are concealed from us by the garrulous and possessive narrator. But there are also more radical discontinuities. Foremost among them is the hectoring, sententious and holier-than-thou tone that Tatiana adopts in her final rebuke to Evgeny in chapter 8: a lecture, as I shall suggest below, that Tatiana in all likelihood could never have delivered to Onegin in the form that Pushkin transcribes it.[5] In this essay I suggest an alternative reading of Tatiana's role in the novel, one that acknowledges her extraordinary vigor and potency but makes it more aesthetic than moral, and—here's the blasphemous, counter-cultic rub—that sees this potency as largely Evgeny's achievement.

### Falling in love with Tatiana, four hypotheses

All three creators in the novel (Pushkin, the narrator, and Evgeny in his capacity as title role) sooner or later come to love Tatiana, each for his own reasons. Although the courtships of these respective suitors are carried out on different planes and often overlap, the following motivations for Eros can be distinguished. First there is the "forbidden fruit" argument, largely associated, I would argue, with Evgeny's sphere. The narrator does not doubt

---

[5]   Among those critics who have found unpersuasive the final meeting between the love-struck Onegin and Princess Tatiana, three will have special relevance for my reading: Nabokov, Little, and Gregg (see below). I lay aside Viktor Shklovsky's famous claim that the narrator's primary stance toward Tatiana throughout the novel—and in fact his stance toward plot in general—is parodic. Two factors suggest caution: (1) Tatiana (like all Pushkin's heroines after the mid-1820s) is smarter than the plots in which she finds herself and does not need the heavy hand of outside commentary to help her outgrow her setting; and (2) the early polemical Shklovsky tends to see parody everywhere; for him the work often serves to legitimate the device and not the other way around. See Viktor Shklovskij, "Pushkin and Sterne: *Eugene Onegin*" [1923], in *Twentieth-Century Russian Literary Criticism*, ed. Victor Erlich (New Haven: Yale University Press, 1975), 63–80. Shklovskian parody has corroded both hero and heroine. Consider a brief essay marking the 1937 Pushkin Jubilee by the émigré scholar Pyotr Bitsilli, who asserts that Tatiana, before and after, never understood Onegin, cast unfair aspersions on him at the end, and in fact "*killed* Onegin, turned him from a living human being into a 'laboratory animal,' a 'type'—and what she did with him, others have done with her" ("Smert' Evgeniia i Tatiana," *Sovremennye zapiski* 44 [Paris, 1937]: 413–16).

its power, over the hero and over people in general, as he tells us in the famous lines from chapter 8, xxvii:

Что вам дано, то не влечет,
Вас непрестанно змий зовет
К себе, к таинственному древу;
Запретный плод вам подавай,
А без того вам рай не рай.

[What's given to you does not entice,
The serpent calls you incessantly
To himself, to the mysterious tree;
The forbidden fruit must be offered you,
Without it, paradise does not seem paradise.]

We must remember who is offering this wisdom. Being deeply in love with Tatiana himself, the narrator has his own reasons for discounting the possibility of anything like genuine growth or spiritual commitment on the part of his rival Onegin — whose sudden passion for Tatiana he would prefer to fob off as perverse. But even so, we must admit that the forbiddenness of the Tatiana-Onegin bond always lent it enormous erotic energy. He likes her now because she is off limits; in the provinces she had been in the palm of his hand and so, in Byronic fashion, he had yawned and turned away. The portrait of Onegin back from his travels (8, xii–xiii) suggests that right up until the end of the novel, the pattern of his life — transitory stimulation and restlessness followed by renewed anesthetization — has not altered. Only illicit love will effect that change. Interestingly, both parties share this economy; Onegin's distanced unavailability had earlier fueled Tatiana's passion as well. As she put it in her fateful letter, she might have been satisfied with casual social contact but Onegin, being "*neliudim*" [unsociable], could be reached only in this covert, confessional, maximally risk-laden, epistolary way. The letter prematurely formalizes the terms, celebrates her helplessness, and heats up the terrain.

The dynamics of Tatiana's life remain in this covert zone. Richard Gregg has done a persuasive reading of her dream along these lines, interpreting its "phallic shapes," "priapic creatures" and shuddering, violent denouement as punishment self-imposed by Tatiana for her illicit desire.[6] "It becomes

---

6    Richard A. Gregg, "Tat'yana's Two Dreams: The Unwanted Spouse and the Demonic Lover," *Slavonic and East European Review* 48 (1970): 492–505, esp. 502.

clear," he writes, "why Ol'ga first breaks in on the would-be lovers; for her shallow, conventional, and well-advertised love differs from Tat'yana's deep, clandestine passion for the 'demonic' Onegin" (502). Both nanny and mother had been married off without love, the sister is en route to being married off without obstacle; neither of these options is, for the likes of Onegin or Tatiana, "paradise." They are destined to experience something deeper. «Погибнешь, милая», the narrator predicts, «но прежде / Ты в ослепительной надежде / Блаженство темное зовешь...» [You shall perish, my dear, but first in blinding hope you will summon forth dark bliss] (3, xv). The prophecy is only a half-truth. That Tatiana does not perish, as do the ill-fated sentimental heroines Julie, Clarissa, and Delphine upon whom she modeled her life, is an issue to which we will return. For now, suffice it to note that throughout the novel, erotic interest between Tatiana and Evgeny is propelled forward by the clandestine and forbidden.

There is a second argument for falling in love with Tatiana, one associated with Pushkin as author. The 1820s, the decade of *Evgenii Onegin*, inclined Pushkin increasingly toward prose, toward national history, toward genealogy and family — and aggravated his anxieties over social status and rank. Compulsively attractive here for the mature Pushkin is the image of the married Tatiana as *kniaginia* [princess] and the chilling, elevating epithets she gains in this context: *Pokoina. Vol'na. Ravnodushna. Smela. Nepristupnaia boginia roskoshnoi, tsarstvennoi Nevy* [Calm. Unconstrained. Indifferent. Bold. Inaccessible goddess of the luxuriant, regal Neva] (8, xxii–xxvii). It has been argued that placing Tatiana in *very* high society — so high that coquetry, a primary medium for the bachelor Pushkin, had no place at all («его не терпит высший свет» [highest society does not tolerate it] 8, xxxi) — was an act of wish fulfillment on Pushkin's part. Negotiating in 1829 to become a bridegroom himself, Pushkin desired to believe what was certainly contrary to his own high success at seducing other men's wives: that female constancy in marriage was possible.[7] And then there was the poet's own social ambition. Douglas Clayton, one of Pushkin's best close readers, has suggested that the married Tatiana's graceful persona and accomplished social skills were a surrogate for her creator's personal fantasies. "Pushkin,

---

[7] For a discussion of the evolving status of marriage as the novel progresses — from the site of open ridicule to the site of potential honor — see Leonore Scheffler, *Das erotische Sujet in Puškins Dichtung* (University of Tübingen, 1967), chap. 3, "Tat'jana Larina," 178–200. "Marriage is spoken of pejoratively in the first six chapters," Scheffler notes. "Only after the sixth chapter does the accent change... In the eighth book the subject is silently closed... [There,] Pushkin's initial irony about Tatiana is missing entirely" (194).

the marginalized, the invalidated, the heretic…was metamorphosed into the heroine — not the hero — of his poem," he writes. "Her acceptance at court, her brilliance, her tenderness, passion, and conviction — all these were the qualities Pushkin sought for himself."[8]

Even without the poet's envy of his own heroine's fate, however, Tatiana as princess is a powerful external success. By the novel's end she has mastered what salon society of the early nineteenth century valued most of all: the ability to adapt oneself effortlessly to any appropriate role in the interest of social harmony. It is in this sense that William Mills Todd considers Tatiana's "cultural maturation" complete once she has become the hostess of a highly regarded Petersburg salon — which was, he reminds us, "the highest form of creativity open to a woman at this time," and one that enabled her to impose "what her age considered an aesthetic order upon reality."[9]

Aesthetic considerations lead us to a third argument for falling in love with Tatiana, perhaps the most profound, this time identified with the narrator's persona. Unlike his friend Onegin, the narrator is a poet. But unlike the poet Pushkin, whose stylized image he represents, the narrator can be garrulous, inefficient, sentimental. As befits a "novelist" (even a novelist writing in verse), the narrator might be understood as embodying some aspects of Pushkin at the turn of the decade, a poet on the brink of turning to prose, since the novel, as we know from Pushkin's famous quip to Bestuzhev, requires above all *boltovnia* [chatter]. The unity of this narrator's voice throughout the nine years of *Onegin*'s genesis is problematic.[10] On one point, however, the narrator is unflaggingly constant, and that is his love of Tatiana. From her initial introduction onward, she is revered as something untranslatable, as a quality that cannot be completely transmitted, as that which inspires us but that eludes precise description. The narrator refers to this elusive presence as his Muse. We first hear of this Muse — who grants a voice to the poet only after the storm of love has passed — at the end

---

8    J. Douglas Clayton, "Towards a Feminist Reading of *Evgenii Onegin*," *Canadian Slavonic Papers* 29 (1987): 255–65, esp. 261. See also Clayton's *Ice and Flame: Aleksandr Pushkin's "Eugene Onegin"* (Toronto: University of Toronto Press, 1985), chap. 1, "Criticism of *Eugene Onegin*" (7–71, esp. 57), for a sociobiographical Soviet explanation of the mature Tatiana that combines both spousal and aristocratic motifs.

9    William Mills Todd III, *Fiction and Society in the Age of Pushkin: Ideology, Institutions, and Narrative* (Cambridge, MA: Harvard University Press, 1986), 129 [in chap. 3 on *Eugene Onegin*]; see also chap. 1, "A Russian Ideology."

10    See J. Thomas Shaw, "The Problem of Unity of Author-Narrator's Stance in Puškin's *Evgenij Onegin*," *Russian Language Journal* 35 (1980): 25–42.

of chapter 1. At the beginning of chapter 8 she is personified, identified with a chronological sequence of Pushkin's literary heroines, and finally "presented" to Petersburg society in a gesture coterminous with Tatiana's coming-of-age in the salon. How does the narrator present Tatiana as both beloved subject and Muse?

We first meet Tatiana in chapter 2. One of the more remarkable aspects of her opening portrait, surely, is how little of it there is. In her initial description, negatives abound: «Ни красотой сестрой своей, / Ни свежестью ее румяной / Не привекла б она очей» [Neither with her sister's beauty nor rosy freshness would she attract anyone's eye] (2, xxv). Unlike the heroines of her sentimental novels, and unlike Olga, Lensky, and Onegin in Pushkin's novel, Tatiana is endowed by the narrator with no precise physical attributes: no colors, clothes, supporting equipment, musical or domestic activities (we *assume* she is dark because her sister is blonde). From early childhood on, Tatiana's prime characteristic has been a detachment from her surroundings. She had not snuggled up to father or mother; she had not frolicked with the other children; she had not played with dolls or shown interest in news or fashion. She has deep feelings; but in contrast to the heroines of her favorite books, she is not in the habit of using these feelings to manipulate the behavior of others. She does not swoon or faint, weep in public, pray noisily, or interact commodiously with the world.[11] Tatiana, we might say, attaches to the inside and not to the outside of things.

This "insideness" and inaccessability continue to characterize Tatiana even at her most exposed moments, and for this we must thank her jealous mentor and most passionate protector, the narrator. He filters out large parts of her life, keeps them for himself, and gives them to us only in translation. Tatiana's love letter to Onegin is originally in French but we only see its cooled-down Russian version (whereas Onegin's letter, by contrast, is immediately in the public domain — for who cares, here it is, "*toch'-v-toch*'" [word for word]). After Tatiana moves from country to city and becomes a princess, we sense she has become some marvelous thing. But the narrator cannot find Russian words to describe her: she is "comme il faut," "not *vulgar*" (8, xiv, xv), and these foreign words convey not so much a physical image as

---

[11]  For a discussion of Tatiana's reduced "portraiture" and her patterns of detachment and non-interaction, see Kelley, part 1, "Narrated Characterization," esp. 27–57. Also significant, I believe, is the haunting quasi-representational sketch of a kneeling female figure (front or back? clothed or nude?) on an 1824 rough draft of Tatiana's letter to Onegin (reproduced in Clayton, *Ice and Flame*, 137).

a mode of behavior, a sense of ever present appropriateness, of not doing anything awkwardly or wrong. Like the veil draped over the face of a harem favorite, they conceal from casual passers-by the essential positive thing. For this the narrator disingenuously apologizes: «Не знаю, как перевести...Не могу» [I don't how how to translate it...I can't].

Indeed, he must not translate her. Tatiana sits by the window, waits, watches, and perceives; the narrator only rarely makes us privy to her thoughts. I would argue that he cannot do so, for Tatiana is poetic inspiration — which, according to Pushkin's own inspired definition, is neither an ecstatic outpouring of feeling nor a fixed accomplishment but something more intimate, private, disciplined, and creative: a cognitive receptivity of the mind to potentials. Or as the poet drily put it: inspiration is a "disposition of the soul to the most lively reception of impressions and thus to a rapid grasp of concepts that facilitate explaining them."[12] Tatiana takes in, understands and orders impressions, but (except for the single very large instance of her passionate letter) *does not spend*. And thus the fourth hypothesis: that as readers we love Tatiana because she represents the energy (and knowledge) captured in a certain sort of poetry.

### *Tatiana as synaesthesis*

"It is the essential privilege of beauty," Santayana writes, "to so synthesize and bring to a focus the various impulses of the self, so to suspend them to a single image, that a great peace falls upon that perturbed kingdom."[13] The Tatiana of chapter 8 has just such an effect on the boisterous tempo and restless variety of *Evgenii Onegin* — if not on its aroused and bewildered hero — and it is her unexpectedly abrupt departure that brings the novel to an end. How might we understand Tatiana's spiritual economy? Admittedly the heroine of a novel, she is also and crucially a heroine in *verse*; and as such

---

12  Pushkin is responding here (in unpublished draft) to an 1824 article in *Mnemozina* by his friend Vilgelm Kyukhelbeker, in which the author declared "strength, freedom and inspiration" essential to all true poetry and identified inspiration with ecstasy [*vostorg*]; Pushkin disagreed. See Carl R Proffer, ed. and trans., *The Critical Prose of Alexander Pushkin* (Bloomington: Indiana University Press, 1969), 52.

13  George Santayana, *The Sense of Beauty* (New York, 1896), 235–36, as cited in William K. Wimsatt and Cleanth Brooks, *Literary Criticism, A Short History* (Chicago: University of Chicago Press, 1957), 2:618–19, in the chapter "I. A. Richards: A Poetics of Tension," an excellent survey and critique of Richards's aesthetic positions.

she is more, I suggest, than the mere sum of her personality and plot. She is also an aesthetics.

The Romantic period knew various Dionysian theories of poetry: as emotive release, as madness, as divine spontaneity. But there were countervailing views as well, which understood poetry either as that residuum following the moment of rapture (Wordsworth's celebrated formula, a "spontaneous overflow of feelings recollected in tranquillity," shared by Pushkin's narrator in *Onegin*) or, more conservatively, as something akin to passion under constraint, to a "pattern of resolved stresses." With his strong neoclassical inclinations, Pushkin certainly would have been attracted to such a "poetics of tension." In more recent times, the thinker who has given most elegant expression to this aesthetic is the English analytical critic and poet I. A. Richards.

In Richards's view there are two fundamentally different types of poems, based on the two ways in which impulses may be organized: by inclusion (synaesthesis) or by exclusion.[14] The most powerful and stable poems — the ones least vulnerable to disruption though irony — belong to the former synaesthetic category; that is, they sustain a maximally large number of opposed, heterogeneous impulses in meticulous balance. Associations then form between "stable poises," which enable and constitute memory.[15] Such verbal art is profoundly enabling, but in a special, aesthetically disinterested, almost architectural way. We begin to see "all around" things, in larger and more serene context, for "the less any one particular interest is indispensable, the more detached our attitude becomes...One thing only perhaps is certain; what happens is the exact opposite to a deadlock, for compared to the experience of great poetry every other state of mind is one of bafflement" (Richards, *Principles,* 252).

---

[14]  I. A. Richards, *Principles of Literary Criticism* (New York: Harcourt, Brace and World, 1925), chap. 32, "The Imagination," 239–53, esp. 249–52. Richards's comments on the relative value of emotions (of lesser import) and attitudes (of greater) for any given experience recall Pushkin's distinction between ecstasy and genuine inspiration: "It is not the intensity of the conscious experience, its thrill, its pleasure or its poignancy which gives it value," Richards writes, "but the organization of its impulses for freedom and fullness of life. There are plenty of ecstatic instants which are valueless" (132).

[15]  "Imagine," Richards writes in chap. 14, "an energy system of prodigious complexity and extreme delicacy of organization which has an indefinitely large number of stable poises. Imagine it thrown from one poise to another with great facility, each poise being the resultant of all the energies of the system...Such a system would exhibit the phenomenon of memory: but it would keep no records though appearing to do so. The appearance would be due merely to the extreme accuracy and sensitiveness of the system and the delicacy of its balances" (104).

It could be argued that Tatiana functions at the end of the novel as a tension-filled, painstakingly balanced, stable and harrowingly lucid synaesthetic poem. Can such an analogy help us understand her ultimately dazzling effect on Onegin, the inveterate prosaicist who comes to read her most passionately? Several obvious factors mark her as a synaesthetic Muse: her autonomy and detachment from her immediate surroundings, her literariness, the tenacity of her memory, the vivid inwardness of her imagination. (In an intriguing supplementary analogy from acoustics, Tatiana and the type of poetic tension she represents might be seen as a "standing wave," a complex resolution of internal antagonisms occurring within a closed air column or along a plucked or vibrating string that only incidentally, and as part of its own inner task, radiates energy in the form of music to the outside world.)[16] After the initial "pluck" or impact of Evgeny, Tatiana's tensions in matters of love are essentially self-generated, independent of further outside event. This self-absorption and stasis is crucial to the stability of her image.

Much work has been done, for example, on the specific textual links between Tatiana and the heroines she adores: Rousseau's Julie, Richardson's Clarissa.[17] But we should note that Pushkin's love-smitten heroine employs these borrowed motifs in her letter quite without cause. As one chronicler of Tatiana's fate has sensibly remarked, Rousseau's Julie appeals to St. Preux's honor in trying to fend off his amorous advances, but "Tat'jana is not in need of defense from Onegin's passions."[18] Onegin has given her no real-life grounds

---

[16]  A transverse standing wave develops between two fixed nodes when a direct wave, the result of a shock, pluck, or other impact, comes to be superimposed in one direction upon its reflection going the other way. Within this column, troughs and crests pulsating at regular intervals generate a complex matrix of fundamentals, partials, and harmonics. Curiously productive in this acoustic analogy is the degree of inner concentration required to resolve these antagonisms, and the fact that a byproduct of this resolution is an exquisite "radiation" of sound — much more complex than can be appreciated by our hearing apparatus, which distorts and orders the escaping aural energy to serve its own, rather primitive "communicative" purpose. The wave itself, wholly occupied by its internal economy, is indifferent to any music-making effect it might have on the air outside. I thank my father, David Geppert (Theory Department of the Eastman School of Music, now retired), for this suggestive analogy with Tatiana's aesthetics.

[17]  See Leon Stilman, "Problemy literaturnykh žanrov i tradicij v 'Evgenii Onegine' Puškina," in *American Contributions to the Fourth International Congress of Slavists* (The Hague: Mouton, 1958), 321–67; Michael R. Katz, "Love and Marriage in Pushkin's *Evgeny Onegin*," in *Oxford Slavonic Papers*, ed. J. L. I. Fennell and I. P. Foote, n.s., 17 (Oxford: Clarendon Press, 1984), 77–89; and Stanley Mitchell, "Tatiana's Reading," *Forum for Modern Language Studies* 4 (1968): 1–21.

[18]  See Kelley, "Narrated Characterization," 129–30.

for considering him, even potentially, a *"kovarnyi iskusitel'"* [treacherous tempter].[19] If anyone tempts in this novel, it is Tatiana herself: as she well knows, she is the one who oversteps the bounds and presents this near stranger with premature options (guardian angel, seducer).[20] Such an understanding of Tatiana's autonomous, already wholly formed love, for which she takes full and anguished responsibility, lends support to John Garrard's point that in the famous triad of Tatiana's literary prototypes — "Clarissa, Julia, Delphine" (3, xi) — the "Yuliia" in question is not Rousseau's sentimental and lachrymose Julie but rather the "Donna Julia" of canto 1 of Byron's *Don Juan*.[21] Donna Julia is an emotionally experienced woman, deeply marked by her passionate and ill-fated love for the immature Juan. After the scandal is discovered and she has been immured in a convent, she writes him a stunning letter of love and renunciation that the poor adolescent boy can hardly comprehend.

Let us pursue this Byronic subtext. "Man's love is of his life a thing apart, / 'Tis woman's whole existence.../ And so farewell—forgive me, love me—no, / That word is idle now, but let it go" (canto 1, 194–95): these famous lines from Donna Julia's letter to Don Juan do indeed suggest the same intoxicating mix of active passion, resignation, surrender, memory of the past and reconciliation with the present that so resonates in Tatiana's final high-minded scene with Onegin.[22] But viewed from within the economy of

---

[19] In Tatiana's defense I cite Richard Gregg, who was generous enough to give this essay a compassionate reading containing this insight: "One could argue that Onegin is for Tatiana a *kovarnyi iskusitel'* in the same way that a shot of bourbon is for an alcoholic. The liquor is, ethically speaking, innocent. But it treacherously tempts all the same."

[20] There have been attempts to soften Onegin's "rejection" of Tatiana's ill-timed suit, for example by Ludolf Muller in "Tat'janas Traum": the snowy landscape is read as Tatiana's lonely, internal pre-love state; the accommodating bear as sexuality (the "dark drive of love" that will release her from loneliness); Onegin himself as the one human figure who can tame the frightening ogres that inhabit the hut of potential erotic life; but "the marriage is not consummated. A lack of interest on Onegin's part is not to blame: we saw that in the depth of his being he indeed loves her, and that a longer, well-intentioned neighborly contact could have awakened this seed of love within him." See Ludolf Muller, "Tat'janas Traum," *Der Welt der Slaven* 7 (1962): 387–94, esp. 393.

[21] John Garrard, "Corresponding Heroines in *Don Juan* and *Yevgeny Onegin*" [1993], unpublished ms. Garrard notes that Amedée Pichot's French prose translation of *Don Juan* softened Byron's sarcasm and helped move the focus of the text to Julia; he also notes that the episode of Julia's letter is one of the very few patches of Byron's text free of corrosive narrative irony (a tone Pushkin disliked, and that his own narrator completely drops in chapter 8).

[22] Stephanie Sandler has provided the best reading of chapter 8 and of the entire novel as a "text of renunciation and a text of continuing attraction." See her *Distant Pleasures: Alexander Pushkin and the Writing of Exile* (Stanford: Stanford University Press, 1989), esp. 207.

a synaesthetic poem, one that balances opposing tensions but does not spend, this is renunciation only in a special sense. It must not be understood wholly as sacrifice or personal loss. Tatiana herself does not indulge in explanations, as Byron does for his Donna Julia and as Tatiana's sentimentalist predecessors most assuredly would have done. She does not motivate or justify her action beyond her one efficient statement to Evgeny, and the frame surrounding her final monologue is stripped of almost all narrative commentary. She simply departs. And just as we must not read Tatiana backward to those over-determined eighteenth-century heroines, so must we resist reading her forward. It is a mistake, I submit, to see in Tatiana a realistic heroine out of Turgenev or Tolstoy, a woman with a strictly biographical fate and fully psychologized significance.

Some highly unorthodox implications will be eased out of this idea at the end of this essay; but now to return to the mature Tatiana as Muse. I suggest that she be appreciated not as tragic heroine or renunciatory object but as a special sort of dynamic poetic principle, authoritative because of its lucidity, its ability to maintain all its parts intact under pressure, and its willingness not to spend impulsively merely to resolve the external, overtly manifest plot. This reading shares some terrain with the intriguing hypothesis put forth by the great Soviet developmental psychologist Lev Vygotsky, whose chapter 10 of his youthful treatise *The Psychology of Art* contains a provocative reading of *Evgenii Onegin*.[23] Because, Vygotsky argues, we are predisposed to assume static protagonists in this tightly spinning verse tale, Pushkin easily confounds us with his misleading symmetries. All the loves, love letters, and parallel confrontations that so neatly mirror one another distract us from the possibility that both hero and heroine have genuinely matured by the end of the novel. Vygotsky takes seriously the dozen or so questions that crowd into stanzas vii and viii of chapter 8: "Is it really Onegin? Could it be him? Is he the same or has he changed? What's he like now? Do you recognize him? Yes and no..." (ellipsis in original). These questions matter, Vygotsky intimates, because real inner change is never perfectly transcribable

---

[23]   L. S. Vygotskii, *Psikhologiia iskusstva* [1925] (Moscow: Iskusstvo, 1968), 282–88: in English, Lev Semenovich Vygotsky, *The Psychology of Art* (Cambridge, MA: MIT Press, 1971), 222–28. In chapter 9, "Art as Catharsis," Vygotsky expresses dissatisfaction with most explanations of aesthetic response because they ignore a theory of the imagination and a theory of real-life emotions — two components that always interact in our response to art, which is why artistic effect is so much more than an "illusion." Such theories are difficult to come by, he admits, because critics (unlike his sort of psychologist) work at the level of analysis; they have no direct access to primary artistic synthesis.

on the outside. In the first half of the novel, so taken up with descriptions of Onegin's cluttered, thing-packed life, the narrator does indeed give the illusion of biographical transcribability — but that is because on both sides, love begins as an artificed construct. Onegin is defined as "the sort of person who cannot be the victim of a tragic love," Tatiana as the maiden who falls in love with a fabrication of her own devising and thus must perish. But then, Vygotsky argues, "Pushkin develops the story against the grain of the material." He introduces genuine drama — which, unlike the expected, fixed outcomes of sentimentalism or tragedy, is always open. According to Vygotsky, the greatest art always prepares us for this sort of catharsis. What we see in great dramatic art is only one provisional resolution; and the more lucid and lighthearted this resolution is, the more it bespeaks a plurality of other possible resolutions swarming underneath. Vygotsky claims that Pushkin's poetry always contains at least two contradictory feelings; when these opposing impulses collide, we experience aesthetic delight.[24]

## The ending: perhaps it didn't happen?

The final portion of this essay will be undertaken in Vygotsky's developmental spirit. Throughout *Evgenii Onegin*, the narrator sings the praises of the perfectly calibrated and predictable life: «Блажен, кто смолоду был молод / Блажен, кто вовремя созрел» [Blessed is he who is young in his youth / Blessed is he who matures at the right time] (8, x). The advice is apt, for the plot of the novel is one massive demonstration of the unblissful effects of ill-timed growth and missed opportunity. But juxtaposed to this value is a corollary that celebrates open, uncertain process: the magic crystal and the "free novel" only dimly discerned in it. These two values are best focused in the conflict between Onegin's letter to Tatiana and her excruciatingly delayed response, which brings him to her feet.

Tatiana in that final encounter is perfect control and passionate constraint. Whatever she means, she will not spend that meaning in the present tense of the novel; when she leaves, she carries that energy poised within her. In contrast, surely one of the more discrediting aspects of Onegin's lovesick letter is that he now spends extravagantly. He has

---

[24]  In his final book, Yuri Lotman discusses Pushkin's concept of inspiration precisely in terms of such collisions: see his *Kul'tura i vzryv* [Culture and explosion] (Moscow: Gnozis, 1992), 35–43, and especially the book's final chapter, "The Phenomenon of Art."

collapsed entirely into the present, which must hold the promise of her presence, «Я утром должен быть уверен / Что с вами днем увижусь я» [In the morning I must be assured that I will see you later in the day]. Evgeny now imagines his life desperately closed down. As if recalling the narrator's warning — «Но жалок тот, кто все предвидит» [Pitiable is he who foresees everything] (4, li) — Onegin opens his letter to Tatiana on a hopeless note: «Предвижу все» [I foresee everything] (8, xxxii). We recall how he had facilely predicted disaster for marriage in his initial remonstration with Tatiana over her letter; now he sees the grim side of just such an approach to life, so unavailable for surprise or renewal. It is not that Onegin is dishonest. Quite the contrary: as several critics have noted and as I remarked above, in his own letter to Tatiana, Onegin is more conscientious at recalling their shared past than is Tatiana in her reconstruction of events during their final accounting. Onegin is honest enough; his problem is that he has lost all control over time, all sense of time's richness and unpredictability, and he is thus unable to displace or contain himself. At just this point the narrator pulls out abruptly, without having sealed the plot with a marriage or a death (as Pushkin's friends complained), with Tatiana fully contained and Onegin wholly vulnerable. Such elegant reversals and symmetries have encouraged some astute Pushkinists to see in *Onegin* a variant of the Echo and Narcissus myth.[25] But if process-narratives and Pushkin's own capriciously parodic practice urge us to anything, it would be to distrust the absolute illusion of the mirror. Is there any way that this poetically symmetrical ending might be opened up into the hopeful, linear type of narrative, kaleidoscopically complicated and strewn with potentials, that the "magic crystal" of this novel appears to value so highly?

In response to that question, let us pursue an alternative reading of chapter 8. Taking our cue from its opening digression (also a belated introduction), this final chapter will be about the Muse, and how the poet-narrator glimpsed her image — radiant, volatile, caressing, *sauvage* — at crucial moments in his life. Apprehensively, the narrator now brings his Muse for the first time «на светский раут» [into high society] (8, vi). But in her ultimate embodiment she is no cause for apprehension; respectful of

---

25  See Riccardo Picchio, "Dante and J. Malfilâtre as Literary Sources of Tat'jana's Erotic Dream (Notes on the Third Chapter of Puškin's *Evgenij Onegin*)," in *Alexander Puškin: A Symposium on the 175th Anniversary of his Birth*, ed. Andrej Kodjak and Kiril Taranovsky (New York: New York University Press, 1976), 42–55; and more recently Marina Woronzoff (Yale University), "The Tale of Echo and Narcissus, Retold: Pushkin's Tatjana and Eugene," paper delivered at AATSEEL Annual Meeting, Toronto, December 1993.

hierarchy and order, she has mastered the decorum of the salon and works flawlessly within it.[26] The Muse is Tatiana, and this is her final enabling transfiguration.

And Onegin? He has always been more aggressively stubborn and contrary, yawning where he should applaud, foreseeing everything, opposing himself to poets. Having suffered this extraordinary, inexplicable onset of love, he is at first totally without mechanisms for processing its effects. But the sequence of his reawakening is worth noting. Whereas before he had reflected his own exquisite image in various mirrors, reacted trivially to events, attended little or not at all to memory, and distracted himself at life's various feasts, now his past begins to align itself in answerable patterns and thus to haunt him. His attempts to confess this inner shift to Tatiana are rebuffed. As a man who had always preferred the fashionable closed forms of disillusionment and despair, how convenient it would be to act out the romantic hero who can spend recklessly, throw himself at his beloved's mercy and be done with it; then he might return to that familiar state where, once again, events begin boisterously, end tediously, and life holds no secrets because always «хандра ждала его на страже» [spleen lay in wait for him] (2, liv). But if Tatiana as provincial maiden was susceptible to such Byronic posturing, Tatiana as mature, creative Muse is indifferent to this indulgence. She now contains her energy like a standing wave, composed and resonant, and is no longer needful of outside provocation. Onegin seeks signs of confusion, compassion, some trace of tears on her face, but detects nothing: «Их нет, их нет!» [There aren't any, aren't any!] (8, xxxiii). Eerily, Onegin begins to "tune himself" to Tatiana, to duplicate her trajectory in the novel. He withdraws, grows pale, begins to read obsessively. But he cannot keep her at bay; in her realm — a realm that absorbs and reworks rather than reflects — memory is born; Evgeny's past begins to intrude, he is forced to come to terms with the trivial and violent acts of his youth; and as backdrop to this birth of a responsible biography, between the lines of his reading

---

26 Here one might supplement Yuri Lotman's gloss on chapter 8, VII, 1–4, in which he appears almost to apologize for Tatiana's tolerance of the "structured order and mix of ranks and ages" in the aristocratic salon (in Iu. M. Lotman, *Roman A. S. Pushkina "Evgenii Onegin": Kommentarii* [Leningrad: Prosveshchenie, 1980], 346–49). Lotman assures his readers that such an "affirmative assessment of high society" from a heroine representing Russian national virtues indeed rings oddly in a novel that contains so much social satire. But if we assume, as in my reading Pushkin invites us to do, that Tatiana is the spirit not of Russian virtues but of poetry, then nothing could be more appropriate for this hybrid novel-in-verse than admiration for "structured order and mixed rank."

he sees a country house, «И у окна / Сидит *она*...и все она!» [And at the window she sits...always she!] (8, xxxvii).

Against the grain of most readings of the final chapter, I suggest that at this point in the novel all real interaction between the hero and heroine ends. To be sure; Evgeny «не сделался поэтом, / Не умер, не сошел с ума» [did not become a poet, did not die, did not go out of his mind] (8, xxxix). But the winter was not an easy one. Unable to settle accounts with the past or project a future because of the unforgiving needs of his present, driven to despair by Tatiana's nonresponsiveness and stimulated by a season of indiscriminate reading, Onegin commits the only act that can bring about a permanent present tense in his life: he *fantasizes* his final visit. The strangeness of that sudden visitation has long been noted by critics.[27] The speed with which Evgeny moves through the city toward his beloved; the uncanny absence of any domestics at the door or in the halls of the Prince's house; the extraordinary ease with which Evgeny gains access to Tatiana's boudoir—all this has been interpreted variously as dreamlike activity, fairy-tale logic, or the narrator's gentle irony. Indeed, hints of dream space prefigure Evgeny's infatuation. In chapter 8, immediately after his glimpse of Princess Tatiana, he thinks: "That girl...or is it a dream?" (xxx; ellipsis in original); and later, Evgeny's "sleep [*son*] is disturbed by fantasies [*mechtoi*] now melancholy, now charming" (xxi).[28] But as we approach the final decisive tête-à-tête, we come upon many more fantastical and fantasizing details that signify a more substantial phase change, not only in the hero but in the larger narration as well.

The first thirty-five stanzas of chapter 8, and especially the elegiac, quasi-autobiographical digression on the Muse that opens the chapter, are almost

---

27  See, for example, T. E. Little: "Onegin's journey through Petersburg has a dreamlike quality about it... [His] entry into Tatyana's house resembles the entry of a fairy tale prince into an enchanted castle. He meets no servants; the house appears to be empty." T. E. Little, "Pushkin's Tatyana and Onegin: A Study in Irony," *New Zealand Slavonic Journal*, no. 1 (1975): 19–28, esp. 21.

28  In his survey of dreams in Pushkin, Michael Katz notes the "proliferation of dreams and dreamers in *Eugene Onegin*," concluding that Tatyana reconciles herself to the results of her choice and station whereas "Onegin remains a slave to his dreams [*mechty*] and is completely unable to accept the realities of life. Therefore she must reject him." See Michael R. Katz, "Dreams in Pushkin," *California Slavic Studies* 2 (Berkeley and Los Angeles: University of California Press, 1980), 71–103, esp. 92 and 99. In my reading, Tatyana is indeed reconciled to her fate, or perhaps even embraces it—but it is precisely Onegin's realization of this irreversible fact that triggers in him his ultimate *mechta* or fantasy-dream of their final intimate scene.

entirely free of the narrator's ironic, undercutting banter. Now that tone is back, jostling Onegin, *"moi neispravlennyi chudak"* [my unreformed eccentric] and making asides to the reader at his expense: «Куда. . . / стремит Онегин? Вы заране угадали; точно так» [You've already guessed / where Onegin is rushing; precisely] (8, xxxix–xl). At an ominously rapid pace, the narrative begins to resemble *erlebte Rede* or inner speech: "He was hurrying to her, to his Tatiana" [*k svoei Tat'iane*] — since when is she "his"? Only in the reality of his own longing. Unseen by anyone, he slips into her private rooms; it is, after all, a mental journey that he has now been rehearsing for months. But two conditions must obtain before the creative inner fantasy can begin to unfold in earnest. First, Onegin must reassure himself that Tatiana cares for him, that she spends the same obsessive time over his image that he has spent over hers, that she weeps (albeit in private) and that there are traces of "confusion, compassion and tears" on her face. Second, he must be persuaded that time is reversible.

The second condition is held in suspension: Is princess Tatiana in fact still the *"prezhniaia Tania"* [former Tania] of earlier years, and can that image be recovered? Until the very end of the scene, the reader is not allowed to know. The first condition, however, is easy to imagine and is immediately supplied. It is the stock-in-trade device of the beloved woman accidentally discovered, alone, *"neubrana,"* *"bledna"* [not yet made up, pale], shedding tears over passionate letters sent her by her repentant lover. (Pushkin will use this device to lovely comic effect in *"Baryshnia-krest'ianka"* [The Young Lady-Peasant], the last and most festive of his *Belkin Tales*.) Tatiana does not cast Evgeny away, but neither does she urge him on; she is as impassive as a shade. In this intense and static scene, what does Evgeny seek? He is still no poet; he will not be granted a poetic Muse. But Tatiana is available to him, I suggest, as inner conscience, and it is this voice that is internalized in him and matures in her presence.

Interpretations of Tatiana as Onegin's "fatum," as "the tangible expression of the weight of his conscience," are not new in the literature on this final scene.[29] But such readings assume that the Tatiana of this scene is real; it is only Evgeny's conscience and the quality of his love that might be fraudulent. I argue the opposite case here: that precisely because Evgeny's love and suffering are real, because there has been this genuine, inexplicable change in him brought about by — who knows? — the passage of time, or the onset of true love, Tatiana does not need to be physically present. She can

---

[29]     See, for example, Clayton, *Ice and Flame*, 112.

be conjured up, which is, after all, the proper ontological state for an ethical Muse. Nowhere in his drafts or variants for chapter 8 does Pushkin suggest that such was his intention. But we do know that Pushkin worried over the ending of his novel and experimented with various means for deepening the reader's knowledge of the hero, including a travel diary and a salon album, both ultimately abandoned. As Leslie O'Bell chronicles the novel's composition: "It was the *razvjazka* or resolution that came hard...The Journey and the Album, like the sequence in Onegin's Library, were both devices for the self-revelation of the hero."[30] I suggest here that Tatiana's crowning lecture to Onegin can be read in precisely this way, as a "self-revelation of the hero."

Astute readers have long expressed dissatisfaction with this final encounter. Vladimir Nabokov, arguing against the mass of "passionately patriotic eulogies of Tatiana's virtue," insists that her altruistic rejection of Onegin is simply a cliché of French, English, and German romantic novels; what is more, "her answer to Onegin does not at all ring with such dignified finality as commentators have supposed it to do."[31] More radically, T. E. Little urges us to take the entire love relation between Tatiana and Onegin as ironic from the start: Tatiana's silence might well be due neither to moral strength nor clandestine pining but simply to indifference or disgust. The ending scenario, where "sentimental heroine meets a reconstructed Byronic hero," is simply "a typical Pushkinian jest" in which Tatiana mercilessly teases her victim.[32] Richard Gregg, turning from the form to the content of Tatiana's final monologue, finds in it a dozen inaccuracies, or, more kindly, subjectively emotional opinions on Tatiana's part that unfairly slander Evgeny.[33] Such

---

[30] Leslie O'Bell, "Through the Magic Crystal to *Eugene Onegin*," in *Puškin Today*, ed. David M. Bethea (Bloomington: Indiana University Press, 1993), 152–70, esp. 164–65.

[31] Aleksandr Pushkin, *Eugene Onegin*, trans. Vladimir Nabokov, vol. 2 [Commentary and Index]' part 2 (Princeton: Princeton University Press, 1975), 241.

[32] T. E. Little, "Pushkin's Tatyana and Onegin: A Study in Irony," 19–28.

[33] See Richard Gregg, "Rhetoric in Tat'jana's Last Speech: The Camouflage that Reveals," *Slavic and East European Journal* 25 (1981): 1–12, esp. 1 and 6. Although mightily bothered by this speech, Gregg does not draw my radical conclusions. He restricts himself to ascribing Tatiana's indiscretions to rhetorical devices and an emotional loss of control, asking "to what extent do her remarks square with the facts?" while noting that "sincerity is, after all, no guarantee of veracity," and to asserting that although "Tat'jana cannot lie" (why not? Is Gregg under influence of the cult?), "in one crucial area of her experience she is an exceedingly unreliable witness." Kindly reacting to a draft version of this essay, Gregg responded thus to this inquiry of mine: "EMERSON: 'Is Gregg under the influence of the cult?' GREGG: 'Yup.'"

verdicts are justly motivated by a sense that something is awry in this final scene. But to my mind they unjustly trivialize both parties — and especially the hero.

Gregg is certainly correct that Tatiana's memory is faulty and her tone with Evgeny gratingly abrupt. I would go further: her tone is almost male, as if this painful but necessary denouement had to begin with Evgeny addressing a portion of his own self. In my scenario, of course, he is. (Tatiana refers to him throughout as "Onegin," the way men do to one another, the way Evgeny did with Lensky). In fact, much of what she says to him makes better sense if understood self-referentially, as confession. Tatiana rejects Onegin — just as his inner self, now more sensitively attuned and responsible to its own past, knows that she must. If Tatiana now remembers "only severity" [odnu surovost'] in Onegin's reaction to her letter and reproaches him for his "cold glance" and "sermon," we know that this misrepresents his actual tone and tenderness on that day. Under present conditions, however, Onegin quite forgivably desires to punish himself for having let something pass him by then that is now so utterly indispensable to him. Onegin also knows in his heart (and thus Tatiana makes the point to him explicitly and repeatedly) that at crucial moments in their unsynchronized courtship he had indeed acted honorably, given what he was and what he knew about himself at the time.

Tatiana's final speech is peculiar in other ways. Measured against the one anguished and hopelessly smitten letter of Evgeny's we are shown in the text, Tatiana's response is capricious, harsh, and explicit in ways that would appear unseemly for a woman of her tact and station. Although Evgeny does indeed have erotic designs on her person, Tatiana gives him very little quarter (that is, for a woman in love, as she claims she is); she insinuates that he loves her now primarily because she is rich, noble, close to the court, married to a battle-scarred older man of princely rank, and that this love could only serve to bring shame upon her and "scandalously alluring fame" [soblaznitel'naia chest'] to him. Again, where such aggressive candor might seem inappropriate from the tactful, superbly disciplined Tatiana (even if temporarily reverted to her more innocent rural self), Evgeny, freshly burdened with a conscience about his past, could easily have had such shameful suspicions about *himself*, and might wish to exacerbate them in a punitive gesture of self-castigation. One of the final monologue's most oft-quoted lines — «и счастье было так возможно, так близко» [and happiness was so possible, so close] (8, xlvii) — is, logically speaking, only something that Evgeny could say. In that now-distant time, lest we forget, it was only for him, who held all the male rights to initiative in these matters, that "happiness was close and possible." From the very first line of her desperate love letter, Tatiana had been always in a state of risk, shame, and premature intimacy. In Tatiana's final speech, however, love is no longer the primary value. Gone is that simple Byronic sentiment, the pivot of every woman's "whole existence." The recurring themes now are those male virtues so precious to Pushkin himself: *upriamstvo* [stubbornness], *gordost'* [pride], *chest'* [honor].

When Tatiana rises and leaves the room, Evgeny feels "kak budto gromom porazhen" [as if struck by thunder]. Usual readings of this denouement admit of irony, of Evgeny's shock at Tatiana's moral excellence, at her self-control, at the sound of her husband's approach and the painful ridiculousness of his position. In the present fantasized context, however, the thunderbolt could be one of realization and internal growth. No wonder Evgeny is impressed at her speech. It belongs to him, to his own better self, to his conscience (the Muse now speaking from within, available for inspiration and moral orientation). Evgeny is still no poet, in the sense that Lensky and the narrator are poets. But the ideal inner companion that Tatiana had become for him could serve many purposes.

And here we might speculate on the end of *Onegin* in the context of Pushkin's own creative biography. By 1829 Pushkin himself had begun to investigate other, more prosaically grounded muses. These included the muse of prose, of history, perhaps of his own imminent marriage. Common to all — and here we should recall the second condition that Onegin longed for in his fantasy with Tatiana, the one that was not granted him — is the realization that time is irreversible. The hero of reversible time had been the chameleon-like "salon pretender" of the mid-1820s, epitomized by the flexible, carefree Dmitry Samozvanets, an adventurer whose many masks were all equally authentic and for whom the search for a "real self" would have been utterly inappropriate. Eventually, this "reversible" pretender would be replaced in Pushkin's creative imagination by the infinitely more serious one-way pretendership of Pugachev, for whom risks were high and historical responsibility was real.

*Evgenii Onegin* presages this shift. When Tatiana walks out, Evgeny is left with an irreversibly needful self that feels the weight of events in time. On one level, perhaps, the General's clanking spurs on the threshold presage scandal, duel, dishonor. But that scenario was tediously familiar, the old masks. Here was something new: both Onegin and the reader look up with that sinking, anguished feeling that comes upon us when we are caught "in the act" — in the middle of a necessary, deeply private, partly illicit conversation with a beloved and loving voice, whose intimations of truth about ourselves we have only begun to summon up the courage to confront.

Whither Tatiana? Contrary to the teachings of Belinsky (with whom the critical history of *Evgenii Onegin* began, and under whose brooding person much of it remains), and contrary to the childhood passion of the precocious Marina Tsvetaeva, so taken with that "unlove scene on the bench,"[34] we cannot worry about Tatiana's fate. Muses do not have fates in that sense. Even to put that question to the text is a modal impropriety. *Evgenii Onegin* is neither a sentimental eighteenth-century novel nor a realistic novel of the Tolstoyan or Dostoevskian sort.[35] Rather it belongs, as one critic aptly placed it, in a group of two together with *Dead Souls*: a one-time-only novelistic experiment in form and genre by a genius in a transitional period.[36] For as the Formalist critics repeatedly remark, this is a novel in verse, and the verse component constantly deforms both the shape of the work and the personalities that mature within the work.[37]

Here we might heed one of America's most seasoned Pushkin scholars, Thomas Shaw, who warns: Do not overemphasize the prosiness of Pushkin's novel. Although the hero does not become a producer of poems, "actually, the entire novel suggests the importance of being poetic. Perhaps the basic underlying question of the novel is not simply the stages of development, but how a poet (or the poetic in man) can develop to maturity and remain, or once more become, poetic."[38] With these priorities in mind, the eponymous hero still remains the hero. Tatiana is best appreciated as a *verse presence*

---

[34] See Tsvetaeva's ruminations on Tatiana's fate in *My Pushkin*: "A bench. On the bench, Tatiana. Then Onegin arrives, but he does not sit down; rather she gets up. Both stand. And only he speaks, all the time, for a long time, and she doesn't say a word. And here I understand that...this is love ...My first love scene was an unlove scene: he didn't love (that I understood), for that reason he did not sit down, she loved, for that reason she stood up, not for a minute were they together, they did nothing together, they did everything in reverse. He spoke, she was silent, he didn't love, she loved, he left, she remained...Tatiana sits on that bench forever." Marina Tsvetaeva, "Moi Pushkin," in her *Izbrannaia proza v dvukh tomakh* (New York: Russica, 1979), 2:249–302, esp. 260–61.

[35] See Yury Lotman, "The Transformation of the Tradition Generated by *Onegin* in the Subsequent History of the Russian Novel" [1975], in *Russian Views of Pushkin's "Eugene Onegin,"* 169–77.

[36] Simon Franklin, "Novels without End: Notes on 'Eugene Onegin' and 'Dead Souls'," *Modern Language Review* 79 (1984): 372–83, esp. 372.

[37] See especially Yury Tynyanov, "On the Composition of *Eugene Onegin*," in *Russian Views of Pushkin's "Eugene Onegin,"* 71–90.

[38] Shaw sees three "phases" in the narrator's stance (youthful perceptivity, disenchantment, mature re-enchantment), and locates Onegin in an arrested second phase, ripe for re-enchantment — although, of course, Onegin remains no poet. J. Thomas Shaw, "The Problem of Unity of Author-Narrator's Stance in Puškin's *Evgenij Onegin*," 25–42, esp. 35.

in the work, a highly condensed moral muse. She is there to enable what Shaw calls Evgeny's "mature re-enchantment," an inner process that, once having begun, releases him from the need to be narrated from without. In this reading, *Evgenii Onegin* is a finished work, over when it is over and complete as it stands. With its mixed sense of gratitude, nostalgia, and absolute irreversibility, the final leave-taking of the poet-narrator resembles Tatiana's abrupt departure several stanzas earlier, which had brought Evgeny to his senses. The truncated end is thus another well-constructed illusion, designed to launch the now matured and newly sobered hero across an unimagined threshold where we cannot follow him. In the final stanzas, Pushkin dismisses his readers with the same congenial, leisurely open-endedness that he invests in Onegin's unknown future. And it is Tatiana's very poeticity, I would suggest, that enabled this emergence of a genuinely *novelistic* hero. May we all part on such self-respecting terms with our creations.

## POSTSCRIPT TO "TATIANA": THE REACTION FROM TAMBOVSK, PSKOV, NOVOSIBIRSK (1997)

*S. B. Prokudin, «"Евгений Онегин" неисчерпаем...(Ответ американскому профессору Кэрол Эмерсон» ["Eugene Onegin" is inexhaustible..."A Reply to American professor Kerol Emerson]," Bulletin of Tambov University [Vestnik Tambovskogo universiteta] 3–4, 1996: 47–52.) Excerpts, beginning with the opening paragraphs:*

The well-known American Slavist Kerol Emerson is irritated by Pushkin's Tatiana. She calls the attitude toward her a cult, and poses this question: "What, pray, makes this sentimental mix of naïveté, stubbornness and dimly outlined female qualities so persistent and irresistible?" And she proposes another variant, her own, for reading Tatiana's role in the novel. I will say outright that in my view, this "new" variant, which is emphasized assertively by the scholar but rigged one-sidedly, speaks to K. Emerson's concern to 'say something unfailingly new, unfailingly strange, something never before heard or seen by anyone' (Gogol). In her opinion, there are three creators of the novel: Pushkin, the narrator, and the narrator's friend Onegin. All three are in love with Tatiana, and the reason for this infatuation is the same — Eros, appearing because it is 'forbidden fruit.'

You will agree that from the point of view of a Russian reader, the proposed approach is a very peculiar one for grasping the secrets of Pushkin's novel, but it is customary for the idle trivialized consciousness of the West [*osuetevsheyesia soznanie Zapada*]. [...] [Pushkin's] novel opens up an 'abyss of space': a tragic struggle of good with evil, pangs of conscience, the drama of guilt." But for K. Emerson everything reduces to the illicit love between Tatiana and Onegin, which carries colossal erotic energy. She is not afraid to muddy crystal-clear depths. [...]

K. Emerson sympathetically cites the idea of the Canadian Slavist Douglas Clayton, who proposes that the aristocratism and elegance of the married Tatiana and her success in high society is in essence only a continuation of the fantasy that Tatiana's creator holds about himself. Clayton writes: 'Pushkin, the marginalized, the invalidated, the heretic (?! — S. P.)...was metamorphosed into the heroine — not the hero — of his poem. Her acceptance at court, her brilliance, her tenderness, passion, and conviction — all these were qualities Pushkin sought for himself.' Here, for the first time dropped into the consciousness of the reader, is the idea of Tatiana's transparency; she is denied any independence from the author, she ceases to be a person acting according to the logic of her own character. And this, as we shall see, is the main goal of K. Emerson, who does not reckon with the fact we are dealing here with a realist novel, where the basic concern of its author is 'the truth of passions, the verisimilitude of feelings [...]'.

K. Emerson and other penetrating readers who think along her lines do not like Tatiana; they are irritated by her Russian soul, precisely by her soul. There's no doubt about it: an entire broad collection of impressionistic inspirations are utilized in order to convince the reader: Tatiana is not real, this is only an abstract fleshless image, a woman without a biographical fate, without a psychologically motivated character. [...]

Tatiana is drawn by Pushkin solely as a positive character. She does not succumb to the idol of idle vanity. '*Otdana*' ['given away', cf. Tatiana's parting words to Onegin: «Но я другому отдана; / Я буду век ему верна» (But I am given to another / and shall be faithful to him forever)] does not mean subjection to human will, Tatiana is not a victim of this will, there is no despondent submissiveness in her. She is consciously fulfilling the 'will of heaven'. Tatiana's final monologue takes up 77 lines of verse. In

21 of those lines she speaks as an 'I'. The heroine of the novel was raised in the [Russian] Orthodox spirit of wise humility [*smirennomudrie*], kindness, tolerance. In her we find the author's own idea of the 'self-respect' of the Russian person, of fidelity to oneself, to one's national essence. [...]

And finally: it is impossible to exhaust the text of *Onegin*, because everything created 'belongs to an order of eternally living and moving phenomena; each epoch pronounces its own judgment on them, but always leaves it to a subsequent epoch to say something new and more true' (Belinsky). Yes, but we add, with one condition: try not to distort a precious value, even if only someone else's.

§

*In response I wrote an intemperate letter — too intemperate, I now feel — which was published a year later together with Prokudin's counter-response* (Vestnik Tambovskogo universiteta 4 [1997]: 70–77). *Excerpts of my letter translated into English below:*

«Открытое письмо С. Б. Прокудину» [An open letter to S. B. Prokudin] (19 May, 1997)

Much-esteemed Prof. Prokudin:

It was gratifying to learn that my article evoked such a lively and ardent response from your side. I won't hide the fact that your answer also did not leave me altogether indifferent. [...] In its tone and emotional charge, your answer resembles a huge counter-slogan. [24 *points of rebuttal follow, of which 4 are reproduced here.*]

3) What does the phrase 'idle trivialized consciousness of the West' mean in the context of a scholarly polemic? I wouldn't wish to identify my own understanding of Tatiana with an entire geopolitical region or cultural tradition.

4) It is difficult to argue against the fact that Eros is a reason for being in love. It's as much a truism as hunger being a reason for appetite. That's how people are created, and that is how Pushkin, in the half-jesting lines I cite, writes about it. In any event, 'forbidden fruit' is named by me as only one of the reasons that Onegin's passion might have been awakened.

7) On Onegin as 'heretic' [in Douglas Clayton's phrase]. Here the translation is at fault, and the mistake is mine. The English word *heretic* is more polysemantic [than the Russian *eretik*]. It can refer not only to a blasphemer against true faith, but to a person who thinks in a dangerously untraditional manner, holding unorthodox ideas in the broadest sense, not only religious.

8) As regards the genre of EO: all that we know for absolute fact about the genre of 'EO' is that it is a novel in verse, and only a few critical schools consider it 100% realistic. Any critic has the right to reckon with that designation, or to ignore it. For Pushkin, the very concept of Realism did not exist. He proceeded from other criteria for organizing his creative work. What concerned Pushkin was verisimilitude and the boundaries of 'thingness' in poetry, its relationship to the ideal, and here he formulated his own special approach: 'true Romanticism' [*istinnyi romantizm*]. But to state that Pushkin pondered the question of Realism as such — that is to run ahead and err against the truth."

§

In his counter-response, Professor Prokudin reiterated that Tatyana without a palpable, flesh-and-blood "biographical fate" was unacceptable; that Dmitry Pisarev, 19th-century radical critic and debunker of Pushkin, had also criticized Tatiana as "sentimental and naïve" and now we have an attempt to "hammer that point home completely" [*okonchatel'no utaldychit'*]; that it mystified him why "the speed with which a man in love hurries to a beloved woman should remind critics of descriptions of dreams or the logic of fairy-tales"; and that other "critical schools" might say what they please but he knew for a fact that "Russian Pushkin Studies considers Pushkin's novel realistic."

§

Meanwhile the essay was also receiving feedback of a more productive sort, such as the following by Yuri N. Chumakov (Novosibirsk State Pedagogical University), delivered in Pskov and published in *Vokrug Pushkina*, "Materials of the International Pushkin Conference (1–4 October, 1996, Pskov)" (The Pushkin Museum at Mikhailovskoe / Pskov State Pedagogical Institute):

[Citations from "Tatiana" are back-translated from the often imprecise Russian version]

## "«Евгений Онегин» в современном прочтении (по поводу статьи Caryl Emerson «Татьяна»"" ["Eugene Onegin" in a contemporary reading (à propos of Caryl Emerson's article "Tatiana")]

The growing popularity of *Eugene Onegin* in world culture indubitably flatters Russian national feeling. However, under these conditions it is easy to imagine interpretations that do not share our own prejudices...the American Slavist K. Emerson has come out with a hypothesis according to which the final meeting of the heroes in Petersburg took place in Onegin's imagination. This radical re-interpretation — by no means impartial, but professional and dexterous — cannot leave any reader of Pushkin's novel in verse indifferent, since a new point of view on a classic episode fundamentally changes the whole picture of events and customary evaluations. Without attempting a detailed survey of K. Emerson's article, we intend here to lay out our provisional impression.

The emotional charge of K. Emerson's essay is contained in its negative attitude toward any presumption of superiority of Tatyana over Onegin. She is irritated by the 'inexhaustible list of virtues' in Pushkin's heroine; she does not agree with Dostoevsky, who 'elevated Tatyana's fate to the level of hagiography, highly valuing her everyday and spiritual qualities and ultimately raising her spousal fidelity to cosmic proportions' [ . . . ]. Here K. Emerson is absolutely correct, since Dostoevsky, in his providential speech, interpreted the novel above and beyond the text, inserting into it categories of positive and negative hero convenient for the undemanding reader but mocked by Pushkin himself. Naturally she is 'bothered by the degradation of Onegin, which is usually accompanied by an ecstatic attitude toward Tatyana,' polemically announcing that '... this fascination, attractiveness and spiritual growth I dare to associate with the personality of Onegin, and not Tatyana.' This does not mean, however, an inversion of Dostoevsky's construct. Tatyana continues to fulfill the highest role in the text, since, in connection with the Author's love of her, 'she is equated not with a person, a woman, but with poetic inspiration itself.' Thus Tatyana does not cease to be the heroine of the novel, but at the same time her 'image in the work signifies much more than a simple linking of her character and the novel's plot. She is aesthetics itself.' Being a 'dynamic poetic principle' — that is, to some extent doubling the function of the Author — Tatyana does not want 'to spend herself impulsively merely to resolve the activity of the external plot.' Partly for that reason does she 'so splendidly restrain and control herself' during the final meeting. But that's not all. K. Emerson sees the novel as something as 'complex and unpredictable as a kaleidoscope, abounding in thousands of potentials.' In this connection she proposes an 'absolutely untraditional means for reading the eighth chapter.'

The essence of the reading is that Tatyana, in that chapter, is a Muse — but not only the muse of the Author, which means the muse of everything we have read so far, but also the muse of Onegin, whom she inspires, and 'he only gradually becomes worthy of her.' Love begins to shape Onegin, but Tatiana does not allow him to explain himself to her, does not answer his letters, and 'under the influence of her image, as a symbol of the beginning of his new life and the appearance of a feeling of responsibility, memory is born.' In despair from loneliness, sunk in visions of the past, thirsting for Tatiana's presence, Onegin 'imagines his final visit with her. The words of her monologue are a conversation 'between "two" men — between Onegin and his inner "I".' As a result, and 'in contrast to the abstraction and "verse-like quality" of Tatiana, Onegin is a dynamic novelistic figure, the hero of a "free novel," who must bear responsibility for his behavior in time.' Thus the plot finds closure, untraditionally and in a fully sublime manner. Simultaneously, the very thing that irritated K. Emerson is removed from the novel: the literal meaning of Tatiana's 'crowning lecture'.

Some grounds exist for suspecting a direct source for K. Emerson's idea. This is the suggestive parallel with V. Nabokov's *Lolita*, or more precisely, not so much with the novel itself as with one of its recent interpretations. A. A. Dolinin has managed to decode the double nature of the text of *Lolita*, where the main hero Humbert-Humbert speaks at length about his sinful attraction to the 'nymphet' and then composes, without demarcating the borders between 'confession' and 'novel,' the entire remaining history — with Lolita's letter, his meeting with her married and pregnant, and the murder of Clair Quilty. Of Nabokov's hero it is noted that 'his exit beyond the boundaries of his own "I", his leap from egoism to love,' in addition to the fact that 'passing over to another plane of existence, G. G. [H-H] acquires something akin to creative force'[39]... this entire process K. Emerson sees in Onegin of Chapter Eight, with his imaginary visit to Tatiana accompanied by references to Nabokov's commentary regarding the final meeting of Pushkin's heroes. One might even suggest that Nabokov's work over the translation and commentary to *Eugene*

---

[39] A. A. Dolinin, "'Dvoinoe vremia' u Nabokova (ot *Dara* k *Lolite*)," in *Puti i mirazhi russkoi kul'tury* (St. Peterburg: Severo-Zapad, 1994), 310, 311.

*Onegin*, parallel to *Lolita*, somehow influenced its conceptual structure, and as a result *Lolita* already shed light on little-noticed features of the poetics of Pushkin's novel.

There is nothing surprising about a retrospective illumination of the poetics and intertextuality of *Eugene Onegin*. Interpretations of the novel have always arisen supported by poetics that relate to more recent texts. Yu. N. Tynianov was able to write about the 'movement of verbal masses' after A. Bely's experiment in 'First Meeting,'[40] and even Dostoevsky interpreted Pushkin's heroes proceeding from the realistic and didactic presumptions of his own later epoch. K. Emerson's scenario can be linked with all this in complete seriousness; one must clarify, however, whether it is simply being inserted into the poetics of *Onegin*, or if it fundamentally modifies the novel's structural dependencies and conclusions on the plane of meaning. My thoughts on this will of necessity be brief.

Broadly applicable throughout the multi-planed structures of *Eugene Onegin* is the principle of penetrability/nonpenetrability. Even if we demarcate the boundaries of, say, Tatiana's Dream, this does not alter the diffusion of the dream throughout the entire novel. But most often boundaries are not noticeable, especially between outer and inner worlds. It was the same in Zhukovsky: a waking state passes over seamlessly into Svetlana's dream. In *Onegin*, the authorial 'I' remains unified even in incompatible spaces. The same is the case with the episodic townswoman (ch. 6), who is both a person in the novel and a reader of that same novel. Boundaries are often blurred between narrative and poetic plots, between their real and potential lines of development. K. Emerson's assumption about the inner event of the final encounter corresponds fully to the poetics of *Onegin*. Also correct are the comments concerning the well-known 'dream quality' of Chapter Eight. In general, K. Emerson's tendency toward an immanent-poetic, rather than a socio-cultural, analysis of the text is very much in the spirit of our present day.

But diverse consequences inevitably follow if we transfer the final encounter of the heroes to the inner world of Onegin. The compositional balance that resulted when two real meetings frame two imagined ones (Tatiana's dream and her visit to the hero's estate), now inclines more toward the dream state. Consequently, even the heroes lose the unity of their worlds, insofar

---

[40] See Chumakov, Yu. N. "'Pervoe svidanie' A. Belogo v rusle oneginskoi traditsii," in *Zhanrovo-stilevoe edinstvo khudozhestvennogo proizvedeniia* (Novosibirsk: Myzhvuz. Sb. Nauch. Gr., 1989), 117–118.

as Tatiana, functioning primarily as Muse, is pulled into the author's world, and thus her participation in the narrative plot fades. It seems to me that in the Eighth chapter Pushkin manages to balance all three hypostases of Tatiana: Princess N, Muse, and 'poor Tanya.' In our view, to emphasize unduly the various grounds for loving the heroine on the part of Pushkin, Narrator, and Onegin is to 'pilfer' the united authorial 'I,' woven together out of heterogeneous structures, and even slightly to blur the principle of immanence — since 'Pushkin' [as Author] is located beyond the space of the novel. I leave to one side all those objections which, it goes without saying, will arise from partisans of the traditional perception of *Eugene Onegin*. [ . . . ]"

One final postscript is in order. In 1999, Olga Peters Hasty (Princeton University) published her *Pushkin's Tatiana* (University of Wisconsin Press), the first book-length study of this heroine in any language. In chapter 6, Hasty eloquently extends the debates around Tatiana's image to hint at a new appreciation of Pushkin's novel-in-verse:

> That love be consummated is a novelistic expectation. *Eugene Onegin* is a defense of poetry — a genre, as Pushkin demonstrates, into which the novel can be absorbed. Pushkin leaves his hero and heroine not locked in embrace, but free to come into their own and to savor that moment of opening that Eugene ever feared and that Tatiana ever courted but believed to be lost. . . . Surely this is the happiest of all endings.[41]

---

[41] Olga Peters Hasty, *Pushkin's Tatiana* (Madison: University of Wisconsin Press, 1999), 211. Among the issues Hasty examines in exquisite detail are relationships between inner growth, love, and reading, and the psychological movement of the heroine's two pivotal experiences, the Letter and the Dream. "Tatiana," Hasty has remarked, "is the Russians' Mona Lisa."

# 7

# PUSHKIN'S *BORIS GODUNOV*

*A chance encounter with Musorgsky's opera* Boris Godunov *as a teenager was the beginning of a love affair with Pushkin's 1825 history play, and with the composer of its most famous operatic transposition, that has lasted to the present day. It worked itself out through a dissertation, a book, several decades of delivering lecture-recitals on the Russian "realistic" art song (Dargomyzhsky and Musorgsky), and in 2006 culminated on a fascinating production of the play planned by Vsevolod Meyerhold, with music by Sergei Prokofiev, for the 1937 ("Stalinist") Pushkin Jubilee. That production (along with much else in the first year of the Great Terror) never made it to opening night.*

*It was my good fortune, in 2007, to co-manage at Princeton University a "re-invention" of this aborted 1936 production of Pushkin's drama (see Chapter 20). The central textbook for that all-campus project, acquainting Princeton's director and cast with the author, period, history, and play, was a recent volume by Chester Dunning (with contributions from myself and two Russian Pushkinists):* The Uncensored Boris Godunov: The Case for Pushkin's Original "Comedy" *(Madison: University of Wisconsin Press, 2006). The volume as a whole defended the unpublished 1825 version of the play and Pushkin's excellence as an historian (not only as a playwright) during the mid-1820s. Dunning's book also contained a new acting English translation of the 1825 play by Antony Wood. The excerpt below, from my chapter 5, continues the debate around Bakhtin's carnival, suggests the genre of a "tragicomedy of history," and revises an idea about the working of time already sounding at the end of "Tatiana": if indeed there can be reversible and irreversible heroes in a history play, then Pushkin creates his Pretender as the former, his Tsar Boris as the latter.*

*Pushkin adored the stage, but he was not a man of the theater. He had no practical experience working with scenes, sets, or players, and never benefited from the feedback of rehearsals or live performance. He wrote plays with the dramatic imagination of a poet. Following the 2006 entry below on Boris Godunov, a postscript from the pen of just such a "theater person," Sigizmund Krzhizhanovsky (1887–1950), will tie Pushkin's play into my current research project on unrealized works for the Stalinist stage.*

# *BORIS GODUNOV:* TRAGEDY, COMEDY, CARNIVAL, AND HISTORY ON STAGE (2006)

> "In the usual sense of the word, there is no meaning to comedy. Meaning is what comedy plays with."[1]

[...] Among the ancient distinctions between the lofty epic-tragic genres and the lowly comic ones is that epic and tragedy must bear responsibility: for founding a city, for realizing justice, for finding out enough about the world to assign cause and blame. It is emblematic of comedy that its characters do not shoulder these burdens. Comic heroes in all genres (Falstaff, Sancho Panza, Master Elbow, the Good Soldier Švejk) have the right to be inept as historical agents, indifferent to destiny, addicted to simple pleasures, cynical toward the workings of justice. Is it then possible, in a drama that strives for a responsible representation of historical events, to combine tragic and comic worlds in a trustworthy way? For Pushkin, the comic had tasks to perform more serious than topical satire, that is, than the humiliation of a pompous public figure or a pretentious ideology. Nor was comic activity a mere temporary distraction from a tragic denouement — what is often called "comic relief," a dramatic device handled skillfully by Shakespeare in his tragedies or problem comedies (*Hamlet, Macbeth, King Lear, Measure for Measure*) and in the delightfully comic-erotic scenes in his chronicle and history plays. Pushkin understood such relief, as well as the verbal wit essential to it, designing entire scenes in its spirit. But on balance, comic behavior in Pushkin is not especially therapeutic, neither for stage heroes nor for their audience. Comedic behavior becomes an historical agent.

The idea was radical. There were few precedents for "historically significant" comedic episodes on the nineteenth-century stage. A telling illustration can be found in the genesis of the opera *Boris Godunov*, some three decades after Pushkin's death. In July 1870, in between his two versions of *Boris*, Musorgsky played a portion of his newly-composed "scenes with peasants" to a musical gathering at Vladimir Stasov's estate, Pargolovo. It is

---

[1]    Robert I. Williams, *Comic Practice / Comic Response* (Newark, DE: University of Delaware Press, 1993), 55.

unclear from Musorgsky's account precisely which scenes were performed, but most likely they included the opening mass chorus in the courtyard of Novodevichy Monastery. The composer's shockingly "Shakespearean" choral dramaturgy was surely in evidence: a stylized mass song or choral lament punctuated by cynical, individualized voices in self-ironizing counterpoint. The effect must have been comic. But at the same time these peasants were passing irreverent judgment on power-makers in the Muscovite state, as occurs in Pushkin's equivalent scene. Such judgments were a potential historical force. That evening, Musorgsky communicated to Rimsky-Korsakov his bemused concern over the reception of those scenes. "I've been at Pargolovo twice and yesterday I played my *pranks* [*shalosti*] before a large audience," he wrote. "As regards the peasants in *Boris*, some found them to be *bouffe* (!), while others saw tragedy."[2] The exclamation mark is significant. Commoners crowded into a public square could have two meanings: they were either trivially festive (that is, festive without historical consequence) or else emblematic of the fixed fate of a people or a nation, carriers of the distanced wisdom of a Greek tragic chorus. It was impermissible not to be told which convention applied. Musorgsky was well aware that he had given mixed signals, and that only tragedy carried with it the weight of historical respect. In historical drama, or in historical music-drama, a *serious* mixing of tragedy and comedy — for purposes more profound than comic relief or satire — could only create ambiguity about a nation's destiny and the power of its heroes to shape that destiny.

In addition to genre confusion, there were more practical problems. Throughout the nineteenth century, tragedy and comedy each had its own sphere of concerns, its own linguistic registers and stylistic norms. The internal architecture of the imperial theaters in the Russian Romantic period was not conducive to a flexible combination of these two modes. If ancient tragedy had been designed for an arena stage or theater-in-the-round, and neoclassical tragedy — the special target of Pushkin's impatience — for the flat, deep box of the proscenium stage, then *Boris Godunov* was surely conceived in the spirit of the Elizabethan thrust or apron stage, with its several levels jutting exuberantly into audience space, making possible overlapping scenes of action and corners of intimacy. As we know from Pushkin's disgruntled commentary, he did not consider the neoclassical imperial theaters of 1826 properly equipped to mount a dramatic spectacle

---

[2]   Musorgsky to Nikolai Rimsky-Korsakov, 23 July 1870; see Jay Leyda and Sergei Bertensson, *The Musorgsky Reader* (New York: Da Capo Press, 1970), 148.

such as *Boris*.[3] The popular stage could perhaps do it justice — but *Boris* was not vaudeville, operetta, or farce. It was *thoughtful* comedy, yet with the rapid pacing, simultaneous exits and entrances, radical refocusings of audience attention, and fluid linkage of scenes that are the trademarks of Pushkin as dramatist. For comedy is not only a genre. It is a terrain, a tempo, a youthful world view for processing events and responses to events that is intrinsically hostile to pomposity and heroic self-absorption, traits associated with old age. The comic spirit tends to ridicule any slowness in gesture or articulation. From early adolescence on, Pushkin felt very much at home in this world. For him, comedy cut across genre or period. Whereas he took constant potshots at neoclassical tragedy, he was enthusiastic about neoclassical verse comedy throughout his life. Among his earliest playwriting efforts at the Lycée was a five-act comedy.[4]

In recent times, literary-critical minds of the first order, such as Andrei Siniavsky in his *Strolls with Pushkin*, have made the comedic lightness, swiftness, and decentering of Pushkin's texts illustrative of all the values most precious to the poet: chance, gratitude, generosity, superstition, and a joyous surrender to fate.[5] Indeed, the comedic is so pervasive in Pushkin that it is difficult to assemble a comprehensive list of the devices employed. L. I. Vol'pert opens her 1979 essay on Pushkin and eighteenth-century

---

3   See his draft article on *Boris Godunov* written in 1828 (intended for, but not sent to, the editor of *Moskovskii vestnik*): "Firmly believing that the obsolete forms of our theatre demand reform, I ordered my Tragedy according to the system of our Father Shakespeare..." Pushkin then provocatively lists his departures from neoclassical unities and formulas. In Tatiana A. Wolff, *Pushkin on Literature* (Evanston: Northwestern University Press, 1998), 220–23, esp. 221.

4   A. D. Illichevskii to P. N. Fuss, 16 January 1816: "Pushkin is now writing a comedy in 5 acts, under the title 'The Philosopher.' The plan is rather successful and the beginning, that is, the first act which so far is all that is written, promises something good; as regards the verses — what's there to say — and such an abundance of witty words! God only grant him patience and perseverance, which are rare qualities in young writers ..." Cited in V. Veresaev, *Pushkin v zhizni*, 2 vv, 6th ed. (Moscow: Sovetskii pisatel', 1936), 1:81.

5   "The calculating man in Pushkin's works is a despot, a rebel. Aleko. The usurper Boris Godunov. The petty thief Hermann. The calculating man, having calculated everything, stumbles and falls, never understanding why, because he is always dissatisfied (grumbles at fate). Pushkin relates in dozens of variations how opponents of fate are brought to their knees... There is something providential in Pushkin's consonances: his discourse, which has scattered in different directions without a backward glance, suddenly notices in amazement that it is surrounded, locked up by an agreement between fate and freedom." Abram Tertz (Andrei Sinyavsky), *Strolls with Pushkin*, trans. Catharine Theimer Nepomnyashchy and Slava I. Yastremsky (New Haven: Yale University Press, 1993), 65–66.

French comedy with this disclaimer: "To elucidate the meaning and place of the comedic genres in Pushkin's creative evolution is an important, as yet unresolved problem in our literary scholarship. Insufficient study of this question can be explained by the situation, at first glance paradoxical, that Pushkin wrote no single finished comedy, but his entire creative output is permeated by a vivid comedic quality."[6]

Pushkin did finish one full-length work in 1825 that he called a comedy. But the critical tradition has been more comfortable working with the later canonical text, analyzing it under an alternative label, a "Romantic [which is to say, *not* neoclassical] tragedy." Pushkin himself defended his play most often in this negative way, in terms of what it was not, stressing the originality and excitement made possible by a violation of the classical unities. For him, true Romanticism always involved an element of surprise, usually achieved by juxtaposing diverse perspectives at unexpected angles. A tragedy subjected to a "Romantic" impulse would make legitimate a looser plot, freer in form (as in Shakespeare's tragedies), more attentive to real dialogue and individualized psychology. For those relatively few scholars who have taken the evolution of the play's hybrid genre seriously, tragedy routinely ends up in the defining and definitive position. But some have lingered more thoughtfully over the problem. A recent example is J. Douglas Clayton in his 2004 monograph, *Dimitry's Shade: A Reading of Alexander Pushkin's "Boris Godunov."*

Clayton notes that Pushkin's sense of the comedic was shared by three landmark plays that defined the genre during his lifetime: Shakhovskoi's *The Waters of Lipetsk*, Griboedov's *Woe from Wit*, and Gogol's *Inspector General*.[7] In all three (as well as in the later, great comedies by Turgenev and Chekhov), the Western model for comedy is subverted. Love triangles are lopsided and unpredictable, stage action does not end with marriage for the young couple, old age is not universally ridiculed before new youthful life, and stasis (or a moment of shock) can substitute for the usual sexual consummation. "Russian

---

[6]   L. I. Vol'pert, "Pushkin i frantsuzskaia komediia XVIII v.," in *Pushkin: Issledovanie i materialy* 9 (1979): 168–87, esp. 168.

[7]   J. Douglas Clayton, *Dimitry's Shade: A Reading of Alexander Pushkin's "Boris Godunov"* (Evanston: Northwestern University Press, 2004), ch. 2, "*Boris Godunov* and the Theatre," 31–32. Clayton's chapter contains an excellent discussion of Pushkin's interest in contemporary French debates over neoclassical versus Romantic drama (triggered by August von Schlegel's controversial writings on the subject) as well as a context for Pushkin's many abandoned prefaces to *Boris* in the "theatrical" or "dramatic manifesto," a polemical genre inspired by Victor Hugo (35–37). More problematic, however, is the larger thesis of Clayton's book: that by 1825, Pushkin's social and religious convictions were already conservative, and that this ideology is reflected in the play.

comedies are very serious, 'dark' comedies, but it is precisely this generic innovation that distinguishes them within the world tradition," Clayton argues (32). He acknowledges "a shift in Pushkin's own perception of the work from when he completed it in Mikhailovskoe to when he finally received permission to print it," seeing in the playwright's increasing reference to his play as tragedy an assimilation to "Shakespeare's tradition" (45). These adjustments included shedding the blatant archaisms, reducing the unwieldy medieval title (in Shakespeare, the comic situational marker) to the eponymous hero's name, as is the practice in Shakespeare's tragedies and historical dramas, and recasting the play uniformly in unrhymed iambic pentameter — or eliminating those scenes that did not fit that meter (45–46). All the same, many vital scenes in Pushkin's play remain as much Racinian as Shakespearean. Clayton concludes that the canonical *Boris* is on balance tragedic, not comedic, albeit a tragedy subjected to a potent Romantic-Shakespearean corrective.

There is a third and minor "genre option" for the play that does take the comedic very seriously indeed. It entered twentieth-century Pushkin scholarship in the wake of the world-wide explosion of critical interest in Bakhtin and carnival. One side effect of the carnival boom has been to refocus attention on the initial version of Pushkin's play. Can this new vision compete with the romantic and the tragic in accounting for the richness of Pushkin's *Komediia*?

## *"Boris Godunov" as carnival: pro and contra*

In the preceding chapter, Sergei Fomichev embraces both the enthusiasms and the vulnerabilities of the carnival thesis. The 1825 *Komediia*, he argues, is set in a "laughing world," the realm of the carnivalesque. For the carnival critic, the energy that Andrei Siniavsky sensed in Pushkin's individual persona — his lightness, brightness, speed, the weightless ethers of poetry against pedantry and self-pity — is manifest in certain institutions of Russian medieval culture itself. To accomplish his reading, Fomichev relies on the hypotheses of the eminent medieval scholars and folklorists Dmitry Likhachev and Alexander Panchenko: their *"The World of Laughter" in Old Russia* (1976) and its expanded sequel with Natalia Ponyrko, *Laughter in Old Russia* (1984).[8] Inspired by Bakhtin's brilliant readings of sixteenth-century French public-square culture

---

[8]  D. S. Likhachev. A. M. Panchenko. *"Smekhovoi mir" Drevnei Rusi* (1976); D. S. Likhachev, A. M. Panchenko, and N. V. Ponyrko, *Smekh v drevnei Rusi* (1984). Subsequent page references are to the more recent volume, abbreviated *Smekh*.

in the novels of François Rabelais, this distinguished team sought — and found — equivalently robust, progressive cultural forms in the Russian late middle ages. Central among these are the irreverent *skomorokh* or wandering minstrel, banned by the Orthodox Church for levity and promiscuous music-making; the *yurodivyi* or holy fool, whose public scandals are analyzed here less as feats of personal humility than as provocative social spectacle (with bold political overtones); and the *lubok* or comic-strip woodcut, so expressive of the common people's anxiety and resilience in the face of catastrophic social change. The ambivalent — or black — humor of such formidable pre-Petrine personalities as Ivan the Terrible and Archpriest Avvakum is shrewdly dissected. The two volumes were a scholarly sensation. Carnival, it seemed, had come home.

It was soon realized, however, that the Likhachev-Panchenko thesis, for all its initial Bakhtinian impulse, had little in common with the utopian mix of Western habitats and Slavic folklore that constitutes Bakhtin's carnival study of Rabelais. The Rabelaisian "laughing world" is intensely personalistic. Organic, fearless, affirmative toward the asymmetrical and grotesque body, this world is invested by Bakhtin with incarnational, Eucharistic virtues. In contrast, the Likhachev-Panchenko model displays far more structural constraint — and far fewer opportunities for epiphany or unexpected spiritual gain. (In general, official late-Soviet-era proponents of a medieval "laughing world" reflect their materialist upbringing by muffling the religious intonations of their subject matter, its redemptive and ecstatic sides, in a reflex that would have been unacceptable to both Pushkin and Bakhtin — and unthinkable to Rabelais.) The Likhachev-Panchenko thesis is supra-personal in focus and semiotic in an elegant binary way. It presents the medieval Russian worldview as strictly dualistic.

"The universe is divided into a world that is real, organized, a world of culture — and a world that is not real, not organized, negative, a world of anti-culture," Likhachev writes in his opening chapter. "In the first world, there is prosperity and an ordered regularity to its sign system; in the second, beggary, famine, drunkenness, and the complete confusion of all meanings" (*Smekh*, 13). Residents of the second world do not have stable positions in it. They cannot, because this second world — called variously an "antiworld," an "outer / infernal world" [*mir kromeshnyi*], and a "world turned inside out" [*iznanochnyi mir*] — is not in itself real; it is a fabrication, a semiotic inversion. Its primary function is to remind people of its opposite: "the tavern replaces a church, the prison courtyard replaces a monastery, drunkenness replaces ascetic feats. All signs mean something opposite to what they mean in the 'normal' world." As in Shakespearean festive comedy, the very fact of doubling or mirroring (the idea of an anti-world) is itself sensed as comic.

This bipolar model of the world, which distributes medieval Russian culture neatly (if rather too schematically) between sacred and demonic, is a curious mix of freedom and unfreedom, of optimism and despair. Evil in it is not radical or permanent, but transitory. The laughter of medieval texts is heard as intelligent, liberating, healthy, a carrier of strength. "Laughter was directed not at others," Likhachev insists, repeating a deeply Bakhtinian precept about carnival, "but at oneself and at the situation being created within the work itself" (*Smekh*, 11). Everywhere emphasized in the 1984 book is the rebellious and cleansing potential of laughing forms. Likhachev's chapter on "Laughter as Worldview" highlights the "Rebellion [*bunt*] of the outer world," whereas Panchenko's chapter on "Laughter as Spectacle" ends with "Holy Foolishness as social protest."

Since subversion and destabilization are as indispensable to post-modernist rhetoric as they were to reigning communist doctrine, the Likhachev-Panchenko paradigm caught on in a powerful way, both East and West. Among Russian classics, Pushkin's *Boris Godunov* proved especially attractive. Panchenko cites appreciatively Pushkin's remark that "drama was born on the popular square" (*Smekh*, 84). Note is made of the play's memorable medieval images: a holy fool, a poet-*skomorokh*, and an ambitious evil monk (the latter two figures occurring only in the 1825 original). All are rebels. Of Nikolka the Iron Cap we read: "In Pushkin, the holy fool insulted by children is the bold and unpunished denouncer of the child-murderer Boris Godunov. If the *narod* in Pushkin's drama is silent, then the holy fool speaks for it — and speaks fearlessly" (*Smekh*, 116). Carnival protest and carnival courage are universal, but every culture embodies this energy in its own way. Thus is Belinsky's socially progressive reading of Pushkin's *narod bezmolvstvuet,* not only as nemesis but as political optimism, echoed 150 years later by Soviet medievalists, part of a recurring effort to integrate Russian national history into the European fabric.

The Likhachev-Panchenko picture of a laughing, carnival-spirited Russian Middle Ages did not go uncontested. The most powerful resistance came from a source that might at first seem surprising, Yury Lotman and the cultural semioticians of the Tartu School. Surprising, because much in the Likhachev model must have struck Lotman's group of pioneering theorists as quite correct: the binary nature of Russian traditional culture and the semiotic inflexibility of its worlds. Where the Tartu scholars had reservations was with the nature of medieval laughter and the benevolent, transient "irreality" of the infernal world. In an important review article in *Voprosy literatury* (1977), Lotman and his colleague Boris Uspensky respectfully laid out their objections to the Likhachev team.[9] They were disconcerted by the fact that the corpus of evidence was largely literary, in a culture where written records were scanty and distorted by taboo. They insisted that Bakhtin's glorification of ambivalent, open, participatory laughter in Rabelais — laughter that conquered fear and suspended human judgment by creating a sort of "purgatorial" space between two timeless absolutes — was not translatable into medieval Russian culture, which (as the Likhachev-Panchenko model itself suggested) distributed itself unambiguously between the sacred and the demonic. The public square was as much a place of tortures and executions as of festivities (as several scenes in Pushkin's *Boris Godunov* attest). On this square, laughter was not perceived as liberating; it was blasphemy, the guffaw of Satan. Thus one could not say that for the medieval Russian subject, to laugh more meant to fear less. Such a confluence of attitudes could have occurred only late in the seventeenth century, under the influence of Western texts and practices. In traditional Muscovite consciousness, the behavior of holy fools was neither magic (a contractual relationship, reliable and comforting), nor was it comic or incipiently democratic; it was strange and specular, meant to strike terror or awe in the audience. In a cautionary footnote, Lotman and Uspensky warn against the faddish or mechanical extension of Bakhtin's ideas "into areas where their very application should be a subject of special investigation" (51).

Literary criticism routinely inherits the backwaters and tidal residue of theories that utilize the professional language of more strictly monitored disciplines. The debate over carnival has been no exception. Long after sociologists had grown suspicious of it and historians had pointed out its inappropriateness to documented experience, Bakhtin's carnival paradigm, as an interpretive tool for literary humanists, retained its popularity. Certain fictional texts were especially favored. Since Bakhtin had cited a scene from *Boris Godunov* in the final pages of the Rabelais book, the carnival resonance

---

[9]    Iu. Lotman and B. Uspenskii, "Novye aspekty izucheniia kul'tury Drevnei Rusi", *Voprosy literatury* 3 (1977): 148–66, esp. xxx. A translation (not wholly reliable) by N. F. C. Owen can be found in Ann Shukman, ed., *Ju. M. Lotman, B. A. Uspenskij: The Semiotics of Russian Culture* (Ann Arbor: Michigan Slavic Contributions No. 11, 1984), 36–52. Page references in the text are to the English translation.

of those jester-monks, holy fools, and public-square crowds was easy to sustain. Any attempt to account for all the play's components under this rubric, however, confronts serious obstacles.

Exemplary of the difficulty is Sergei Fomichev's essay on Pushkin's "Komediia" from the mid-1990s, included in his *Prazdnik zhizni. Etiudy o Pushkine* (1995). There, decades of uncertainty about the proportion of tragic to comic in Pushkin's play eventually came to rest on a noncommittal mean.[10] Freed from the ideological formulas of the communist era, Fomichev makes many astute observations. He notes the unruly abundance of characters and the diversity of literary forms in the 1825 version (its excess of heroes, its disregard for well-rounded dramatic episodes, the predominance of prose in the comic patches and the odd metrical choice for the "Evil Monk" scene). He resists any "heroic" Belinskian reading of the *narod*, citing all those places where the crowd, whether massed on stage or merely cohering in the imagination of its leaders, is shown to be undisciplined, ungrateful, and capricious in its political judgment (96–97). Citing Likhachev on "cultures of laughter," he remarks on the difficulty experienced by stage directors who try to bestow on these crowds anything like an historically leading role; the *narod*'s laughter sooner "returns the world to its original chaotic state" (97). Laughter, Fomichev claims, is the background noise [*smekhovoi fon*] for the entire play. It is healthy in a Bakhtinian sense: modest, decentering, indifferent to power. Although the people mock authority, they are wise enough to want none of it for themselves. "In Pushkin's drama it is the *narod* that embodies in itself this chaos, this Time of Trouble, this instinctive resistance to system," Fomichev writes (98). "In those instances when it is forced to subordinate itself to this system, it turns its laughter on itself." Into this anarchic and cheerfully self-deprecating context, Fomichev fits the two competing political figures, Boris and Dmitry. Tsar Boris is "genuinely tragic, strong, willful, sworn to the highest power but in violation of the moral law...overcome by torments of conscience and tragic guilt;" fate subjects him to a cleansing catharsis (100–101). Dmitry, on the other hand, serves the comedic principle. As an emanation or specter from the anti-world, he has no tragic task. The carnival *narod* — which is also without a task — is intuitively predisposed to elect this carnival king, an "historical phantom."

---

[10]  "Komediia o velikoi bede Moskovskomu Gosudarstvu, o tsare Borise i o Grishke Otrep'eve," in S. A. Fomichev, *Prazdnik zhizni. Etiudy o Pushkine* (St. Petersburg: Nauka, 1995), 82–107. Further page references in the text.

Through this lens, the politics between tsar, people, and pretender is primarily symbolic. Fomichev values the person of Tsar Boris but largely as tragic misfit and antihero. When he touches upon real history and real historical attitudes in the play, he treats them as potent but transitory metaphors, local color within a larger "comic instrumentation" (95). In keeping with most prior scholarship on the play, Fomichev cares less about history than Pushkin did. "'Long live Dimitrii Ivanovich!'" Fomichev writes (95). "Could Pushkin have treated such a scene seriously? Of course not." Because the purpose of the present volume is to argue for the integrity of the initial version, as well as for the seriousness of Pushkin as historian and the accuracy of his vision, such dismissals must be scrutinized carefully. Are Fomichev's two readings (from 1995, and then the essay in this volume) too swayed by the carnival mystique? Or, to pose the question more broadly: perhaps carnival is not the best way to make sense out of the comedic element in this play?

There are, it seems, at least three areas where carnival readings of *Boris Godunov* fall short of accounting for the whole. First, a poetics of literary carnival—inspired by Bakhtin's reading of Rabelais—does not possess a sophisticated, well-elaborated model of language. Communication during carnival, which can indeed be joyous and intense, takes place not as much through words as through body gestures, most of them related to the "lower bodily stratum" and involving orifices other than the eyes and the mouth. What utterances there are tend to be short expletives, always tautly expressive and preferably obscene. This is dialogue, certainly, but not the complex verbal dialogue that deserves analysis in the work of a great poet. For this reason, carnival readings of *Boris Godunov* tend to ground themselves in its larger worldview, in crude energetic movements capped with some verbal device: a mildly shocking epithet, a comic ditty, a perfectly timed insult. Some critics (following Bakhtin's methodology with Rabelais) ignore altogether the stylistic particulars of the text. But surely the most overtly comic scenes in *Boris Godunov*, as in Shakespeare's plays, involve a graphic blend of both physical vitality *and* verbal wit: the three languages speaking past each other in the hilarious "mercenary" scene with Captains Margeret and Rosen, "A Plain near Novgorod-Seversky," or, several scenes later, "Sevsk," where a Prisoner and a Pole exchange insults that are partly words, partly a threatening fist. Such comic routine, backed up with vigorous physical gesture, is authentic carnival—but linguistically it can exist in the play only as moments, not as the norm. The norm is narrative poetry, at a level both fluid and philosophical. As Grigory Vinokur observed in his classic essay on Pushkin's language, the remarkable accomplishment of *Boris Godunov* as stage drama is that "the poet in Pushkin constantly triumphs over the stylizer"; archaic written sources are transformed into "concrete lyrical language" made up of utterances that living people, listening to one another, could actually exchange at normal tempo, within a sixteenth-century worldview that had the feel of Pushkin's verse-line.[11] Such a deployment of language is fully compatible with comedy. But it is not an essential part of the carnival world; in fact, it can even be an obstacle to it.

A second and related shortcoming of carnival readings is that they cannot deal satisfactorily with guilt. Carnival is not weighed down by the burden of memory, which is so essential for conscience; the fact that the present tense is sufficient for carnival is a major source of its strength and resilience. But what, then, is to be done with Tsar Boris? There is a respected, well-researched line in *Boris* scholarship which holds that the unfortunate tsar was not responsible for the death of Dmitry of Uglich — and certain contemporaries of Pushkin, most insistently the historian Mikhail Pogodin, encouraged the poet to rethink his own "Karamzinian" assumptions on this score. If Tsar Boris had not ordered Dmitry's death nor indeed even wished it, he was nevertheless a beneficiary of that tragic event and this fact alone could generate guilt. However one disputes the historical options here, the "stain" on Boris's conscience and the agony it causes him (in both versions of the play) cannot be simply brushed away. Too much that matters flows from it. Those critics who identify the guilt of the tsar as the play's governing principle invariably turn the work into a full-scale tragedy, albeit of a special spiritualized sort. Olga Arans, for example, has read *Boris Godunov* as a "Christian tragedy" in which Pushkin investigates a startlingly new idea, the crime in thought, as an alternative to the classical, externally committed crime in deed. [12] Such a transgression entails radically new modes of verification and punishment. Boris-centered readings like this, which take seriously the capacity of drama to narrate a story without defaulting to a single moralizing voice, are also not the whole of Pushkin's truth. But they are an inseparable part of it — and the lessons they teach are elevated, not carnivalistically debased.

---

11    G. O. Vinokur, "Iazyk 'Borisa Godunova'," in "Kommentarii [k *Borisu Godunovu*]," in *Polnoe sobranie sochinenii A. S. Pushkina*, vol. 7 (Dramaticheskie proizvedeniia: 385–505) (Moscow: IAN SSSR, 1935): 350–87, esp. 368, 373.

12    O. P. Aranovskaia [Olga Arans], "O vine Borisa Godunova v tragedii Pushkina," *Vestnik russkogo khristianskogo dvizheniia*, no. 143 (1984, iv): 128–56.

These two caveats prepare us for the most serious problem with carnival as an interpretive lens for Pushkin's drama. Carnival — and even more, "carnival laughter" — cannot be made historical. It too much resembles play, that is, human behavior outside the sphere of necessity and utility that liberates activity from consequence. In his essay "Bakhtin, Laughter, and Christian Culture," Sergei Averintsev intimates that Bakhtin's utopia of laughter can only be poor authority for any historically grounded project.[13] Even if one assumes that the medieval *narod* was driven by laughter (and here we have a choice between the open-optimistic Likhachev-Panchenko thesis and the demonic-pessimistic Lotman-Uspensky), Averintsev reminds us that in the Bakhtinian model laughter is transcendental, "not laughter as an empirical, concrete, palpable given, but as the hypostatized and highly idealized essence of laughter..." (84). Averintsev speaks as a cultural historian, for whom Bakhtin's formulations about laughing cultures are elevated "to such heights of abstract universality that raising the question of verification becomes, in itself, impossible" (84). The problem to which Averintsev refers is one that conscientious Western historians of early modern Russia began to address forcefully in the 1990s. They were dismayed at the tendency of some experts in the social sciences, whose research area was Russia, to take the findings of the literary-spiritual mythographers as straight historical fact, defaulting (as one of their members has put it) to *The Brothers Karamazov* for their theology and to structuralism or semiotics for the manageable polar opposition.[14]

Carnival, anti-world, and the world-turned-inside-out offer a certain elegance of form, as do all binary theories. But *historical* drama as Pushkin understood it was obliged to achieve its symmetry by uncovering more complex mandates. In matters of state interest, Pushkin was a keen believer in historical necessity. In his annotations to the first book of the *Annals* of Tacitus, for example, made for the most part during 1825, Pushkin defends

---

[13]  Sergei Averintsev, "Bakhtin, Laughter, and Christian Culture" [1988], in Susan M. Felch and Paul J. Contino, eds., *Bakhtin and Religion: A Feeling for Faith* (Evanston: Northwestern University Press, 2001), 79–95. Further page references in the text.

[14]  See the pioneering volume edited by Samuel H. Baron and Nancy Shields Kollman, *Religion and Culture in Early Modern Russia and Ukraine* (De Kalb: Northern Illinois University Press, 1997), Editor's Introduction: "Religion and Cultural Studies in Russia, Then and Now," 3–16. For a tactful cautionary word on the cultural semioticians as a source for historical thinking, identified loosely as "structuralists," see also in the same volume David A. Frick, "Misrepresentations, Misunderstandings, and Silences," 149–68, esp. 152–54.

(against the sardonic tone of the historian) the political murder of the young Agrippa Postumus by the Roman Emperor Tiberius — because Tiberius was a skilled statesman and because the Empire benefited for two decades from the deed. Pushkin's mood during the *Boris* year, as he outgrew the moralizing approach to history appropriate to Tacitus or Karamzin, is reflected in these annotations. The poet surely pondered the parallels between that Roman succession crisis in the year 14 and the reign of Boris Godunov (the same duplicitous reluctance to take the crown; and eventually even a False Agrippa). Pushkin's "Machiavellian" position here has been variously interpreted by scholars.[15] But however it is read, a carnival view of history along Bakhtin's lines cannot accommodate such a vision of state or political necessity. Indeed, carnival is the loophole out of such necessity.

Thus we return, on the far side of the carnival divide, to the larger question of comedy and tragedy. Like most comedies, the 1825 *Boris* is attentive to attractions and stresses among non-heroic persons in the social and domestic domain. But it has the potential and the intent of becoming something more: the representation of a historical period. Its comedic core is not just social, but highly politicized. Given Russia's politics during the 1590s–1610s, in the devastated wake of Ivan the Terrible, no part of its plot could culminate in a return to Nature or "a restoration of the natural order" after the usual fashion of festive comedies — that is, by retreating to gardens and forests. (The one nature-laden garden scene in *Boris*, the Pretender's tryst with Maryna, is a parody of such boy-gets-girl culminations.) Nor can it default to those other comedic genre markers: the frivolous, the funny, the private, the low-born, the "happy end." History, and especially national history during a Time of Troubles, is manifestly serious, in the public eye, and full of unhappy ends.

Pushkin did not make light of that national history, nor could he have wished to do so. As Fomichev points out in chapter 4, the earliest plans for a Boris play from November 1824 contained almost no comic elements; the comedic entered the text in stages, as (among much else) a congenial way

---

15   For an excellent survey by a classicist, see G. W. Bowersock, "The Roman Emperor as Russian Tsar: Tacitus and Pushkin," *Proceedings of the American Philosophical Society* 143, no. 1 (March 1999): 130–47. On the difficult question of Pushkin's punitive attitude toward Boris Godunov, so out of keeping with his sympathy toward Tiberius, see B. G. Reizov, "Pushkin, Tatsit, i 'Boris Godunov'," in *Iz istorii evropeiskoi literatury* (Leningrad: LGU, 1970), 66–82, esp. 72–73. In defining the poet's sense of historical necessity, Reizov concludes that Pushkin punishes Boris Godunov not out of moral considerations but because he *fails;* his reign devolves into terror and bloodshed, so his criminal deed cannot be condoned.

of handling causality and time. Pushkin desired to present history not as a reconstruction from a later period — the temporal privileging common to neoclassical tragedy and epic — but as a slice of experience sufficient unto itself, acting only on the rumors it knows, free of "hints and allusions" to subsequent events. As he wrote testily in an unsent letter to the editors of *Moskovskii vestnik* several years later, "Thanks to the French, we cannot understand that a dramatist can fully renounce his own line of thought in order to transfer completely into the period he is describing."[16] Against the end-driven plot and the epic perspective, Pushkin sensed something comedic in the very workings of history when it was viewed "close up," in its own time. It is this possibility — the parallel dynamics of comedy and history, when a piece of the past is honestly represented in its own present — that Pushkin explores in his play, not the *escape* from history that comedy (and even more, its subset carnival) traditionally presumes and exploits.

### *Comedic and tragic expectations —*
### *and how a history play might cope with them*

[...] If distance and awe are necessary to the effects of tragedy, then unpretentiousness, incongruity, and spontaneous response are keys to comedy. Its natural medium is not pity and terror, but laughter. Here, however, we confront a comedic paradox that must have thrilled the neoclassically inclined Pushkin. Comedy is indeed fertile, fast-paced, abundantly "overflowing" when measured against tragedy. But equally important is comedy's insistence on symmetry and proportionality. However hopeless the muddle in the middle, however often all hell breaks loose, the ending must restore the decorum and order appropriate to the social class or dominant worldview of the dramatic personages on stage. As life is reconciled with its imperfections, the original hierarchies are restored and reaffirmed. It is often remarked that the final moments of the 1825 *Boris Godunov* are intuitively symmetrical in this way.

In the opening scenes, members of the nobility conspire darkly while the commoners, herded together and commanded to cheer by Shchelkalov from the Main Porch of the Granovitaia Palace, obediently (and cynically) hail the aspirant to the throne, whoever it may be. At the end, this time in a murderous conspiracy, Mosalsky, also from a Kremlin palace porch, commands the crowd

---

[16] "On Boris Godunov" [possible draft preface to the play, written 1828], in Wolff, *Pushkin*, 223.

to welcome Dmitry Ivanovich with a cheer—which it obediently does. Such symmetrical behavior is comedic. But it would be a mistake to play the final cheer as manipulated or forced. At the beginning of the play, fixed precisely in Moscow, February 20, 1598, the people are reacting to what they know at that time and in that place: that the powerful Regent, the boyar Boris, is angling for the throne. He has long been at the helm, and they take his ascension as a given, merely wondering (as Prince Shuisky himself wonders in the bracketing scenes) how to adjust to this fact with the least pain and the maximum profit to themselves. The end is different. What the people now know (and all they know in 1605) is that Tsar Boris has been a tyrant for six years. Everything they have heard about Tsarevich Dmitry, whether triumphantly emerged from hiding or miraculously resurrected, promises a change for the better. Their cheer is not necessarily elicited from under the knout; it is open-ended, hopeful, and (as Pushkin was aware) historically accurate. Seen from within its own present and true to the rules of comedy, Dmitry's "return" to the throne of Moscow would restore the violated hierarchy and reaffirm the proper order of things. The *narod* was capable of both cynical acquiescence and genuine faith in a returning warrior prince. Those options were the energetic ones that the young Pushkin coded into his *komediia* in 1825. It was symmetry with a difference, because in fact history does not repeat. Each moment of the present generates its own potential. Only later, at the turn of the decade and into the 1830s, do we find a grimmer verdict on popular energy, in the omitted chapter from Pushkin's novel about Pugachev, *The Captain's Daughter*: "May the Lord save us from another such senseless and ruthless Russian rebellion!"[17]

These ruminations on comedic shapes in history suggest the possibility of a second hybrid form. Historical tragedy is familiar; but can there be *historical comedy?* If so, what might it look and sound like? It is no accident that Herbert Lindenberger's well-known study of historical drama, which sets out to explore the "characteristic shapes" that describe "relationships between drama and reality," divides its material into conspiracy, tyrant, and martyr plays: three manifestly somber, tragic categories.[18] Tragedy fits history more comfortably. To test the comedic-history hypothesis, one would have to take a piece of tragic history (say, Karamzin's account of the

---

[17] "Omitted chapter from 'The Captain's Daughter'" [1835–36], Appendix A in Paul Debreczeny, ed. *Alexander Pushkin: Complete Prose Fiction* (Stanford: Stanford UP, 1983), 450.

[18] Herbert Lindenberger, *Historical Drama: The Relationship of Literature to Reality* (Chicago: University of Chicago Press, 1975), xi and ch. 2: "History and the Structure of Dramatic Action."

Fall of Boris) and recast it so as to reduce the distance, demote the language, focus on the present moment, refrain from prophetic authorial asides, allow intimate access to the loftiest heroes not only in their eloquent moments but also in their morbidly embarrassed ones. Conspirators, tyrants, and martyrs should be made to look a bit ridiculous, so the audience will laugh with relief. Most importantly, the playwright must make it seem as if chance events really mattered, perhaps even made all the difference. Making history comic is exhilarating — but there are immediate practical difficulties with it. In politically controlled cultures that care about art (and nineteenth-century Russia was one such culture), a canonized historical plot treated comedically could quickly become disrespectful, even subversive. The lightness and "presentness" of comedy can threaten teleological explanations in general, by questioning whether today's suffering and sacrifice can in fact be justified in the name of some future glory "waiting in the wings." Unlike tragedy, comedy does not trust wings. The future does not yet exist, no destined events yet fill it, and thus glory (or any other fate) cannot passively *wait*. Instead, comedy puts its trust in happy coincidence and in the boundless inventiveness and resilience of human beings flourishing in the now.

The strongest argument for *Boris Godunov* as historical comedy is probably Pushkin's belief in the potency of chance. His conviction that "chance is a tool of providence" sits squarely at the center of his paradoxical theory of history. A faith in the fortuitousness of events can coexist easily with all types of disaster and failure, as well as with the buoyancy that marks Pushkin's historical fiction, but it cannot be squared with the workings of neoclassical tragedy, or with most historical tragedy as it was practiced in Pushkin's era. That a momentous sequence of events "might have been otherwise" — Pushkin's favorite thought experiment — is not a truth that the winning side likes to hear. Chance and laughter are supposed to govern only lesser fates. For good reason, comedy on stage (vaudeville and "bouffe") was conventionally associated with the follies of non-historical private life, that is, with the weaknesses that *unite* us. In contrast, tragedy depends for its sublime communicative moment on the ideologies that divide us, that elevate a cause and make it worth dying for. Or worthwhile slaying others.

### Tragedies and comedies of history

[ ... ] A comedy of history, then, will do what comedic drama does best: make relationships modifiable in the present by relying on coincidence and chance.

But what happens then to memory and conscience? To the pastness of the historical event and its autonomy in its own time? And to the fact (lying at the core of all tragedy) that the awful event has happened, is now over, and its consequences must be lived with and paid for? Pushkin was well aware of the challenge in combining history and drama on stage — a different order of challenge than his exercise in combining history and fictional prose (*The Captain's Daughter*), or history and verse (*Poltava*). In those hybrid genres, reception is more private, representation less embodied. But drama is public performance. It was diminished, Pushkin felt, when the playwright inhabits his text like a lyric poet, distributing universalized bits of himself (however fascinating) to his characters; this bad habit he saw in Byron's plays.[19] "What is necessary to a dramatist?" he asked in a jotting of 1830. "A philosophy, impartiality, the political acumen of an historian, insight, a lively imagination. No prejudices or preconceived ideas. *Freedom*."[20] What, then, was necessary to the historian?

In her thoughtful study of Pushkin's methods as historian, Svetlana Evdokimova suggests that for the poet-playwright, history and poetry are a complementarity. Each has its own "multiple perspectives and autonomous truths" that are not subject to any easy synthesis of oppositions.[21] "Pushkin does not privilege one kind of writing over the other. Neither poet nor historian, according to Pushkin, can portray the way things really happened. [...] The reconstruction of the whole truth requires the omniscience that neither the artist nor the historian can achieve" (27–28). What rings true in this statement is its grasp of what we might call Pushkin's epistemological modesty, his willingness to discriminate between what can and cannot be known. Just because some future point of view, arbitrarily selected and conveniently frozen in place, happens to know how one open-ended moment of the past was eventually resolved implies no special wisdom. The honest playwright must renounce all such privilege for his own arbitrarily selected time of writing as well. But by the same token, Pushkin tolerated no collapse into historical nihilism. Although art on historical themes must not contradict known facts, it is still obliged to coordinate those themes

---

19   See Pushkin's draft commentary "On Byron's Plays," 1827, in Wolff, *Pushkin*, 209. Pushkin acknowledges that Byron himself understood this weakness in his dramatic writing and strove to overcome it.

20   "Notes on Popular Drama and on M. P. Pogodin's *Marfa Posadnitsa*" [1830, unpublished review], in Wolff, *Pushkin*, 264.

21   Svetlana Evdokimova, *Pushkin's Historical Imagination* (New Haven: Yale University Press, 1999), 14. Further page references given in the text.

and reflect them in an ordered way, if not in a mirror then in that beloved poetic image from the final stanzas of *Evgenii Onegin*, a magic crystal or kaleidoscope. Historical events are like random fallings of chips during the turn of a kaleidoscopic wheel. Viewed through the funnel of art, these fallen chips are refracted and juxtaposed as patterned domains. The historical poet is this crystalline lens; he cannot intervene, but he must discern the pattern. Pushkin felt keenly the obligation of poets to embed the known within the unknown in a humble manner, so that the boundaries of each are respected. It was the absence of such humility that caused him to chafe against the excessively dogmatic skepticism of Voltaire, and that might have prompted his surprisingly harsh criticism of the unfortunate Alexander Radishchev.[22]

Much of what we know from Pushkin about his own genre experiments was elicited by his disappointment in others' reception of his work. Most likely the poet would have considered historical tragedy — assuming that it aimed to be true to history at all — a poor vehicle for portraying historical knowledge in an acceptably "modest" way. But a comedy of history would also not be sufficient to his purpose. Through his historical personages and sets, Pushkin raised concrete social issues that he meant to be taken seriously, even if no historical documentation underlay their presentation on stage: the details and placements of the battle scenes; Afanasy Pushkin drinking mead at Shuisky's house and talking drunkenly and seditiously about serfdom; Tsar Boris speaking privately with Basmanov about abolishing *mestnichestvo*.[23] Pimen, too, was "not my invention," Pushkin noted in that same open letter to *Moskovskii vestnik* from 1828. "In him I drew together those characteristics of our ancient chronicles which captivated me: the innocence of soul, the disarming humility, the almost child-like quality which is at the same time combined with wisdom, the pious devotion to the Divine Right of the Tsar" (222). Not every scene in *Boris Godunov* can be speeded up to a comic briskness. Some moments are clearly designed to be riveting, lofty, tragedic: Pimen's monologue, the Patriarch's lengthy recitation of the miracle at Uglich to the Tsar's Council, the dying Boris's farewell to his son. A thoroughly comic

---

[22] See Pushkin's 1836 review of *Journey from St. Petersburg to Moscow*, intended (but not approved) for his journal *Sovremennik* ("Alexander Radishchev," in Wolff, *Pushkin*, 390–91).

[23] It was Faddei Bulgarin's use of this last detail, among others, in his own historical novel *Dimitrii Samozvanets* that triggered Pushkin's accusations of plagiarism. Bulgarin (or his research assistant) could not have come upon this historical reality himself, Pushkin realized, for "All these are dramatic fictions and not traditions handed down by history." Pushkin notes this fact with irritation in his "Refutations to Criticism," a private list of complaints compiled in 1830. See Wolff, *Pushkin*, 254.

presentation would probably have struck Pushkin as unbalanced, for balance requires a juxtaposition of different modes. More likely, Pushkin's goal was neither historical tragedy nor historical comedy, but some intermediate construct, something approaching a tragicomedy of history.

## Tragicomedy and the real

The term "tragicomedy" or "tragedo-comedy" was known in Pushkin's era. "Mungrell Tragy-comedie" had been deplored in England as early as the 1580s, and Shakespeare was often accused of writing in this motley form, especially his later plays. Formal treatises on the genre were familiar in Italy from at least the early seventeenth century and in Russia from the early eighteenth.[24] Its identifying marks include the interspersing of comic scenes throughout what is otherwise a tragedy, a display of elevated protagonists in domestic or private settings, and an ending designed to evoke muted audience response: not punitive toward individuals, not cathartic through pity and terror, but also not set up for the happy marriage. Rather than resolve in either direction, the end is compassionately suspended, sympathetic to the ambivalent, often compromised situation in which all parties find themselves. (Giovanni Guarini, the most important Renaissance apologist for tragicomedy, stressed the social advantages of such a moderate ending; by avoiding extremes, it educated the spectators away from either "excessive tragic melancholy or comic relaxation."[25]) In such endings — neither closed through the attainment of full knowledge, nor happy through romantic consummation or military victory — we would seem to approach the effect of Pushkin's original cheer on behalf of the Pretender Dmitry.

Pushkin's library contains no theoretical works on this mixed genre. But the fondness Pushkin repeatedly expressed for Pierre Corneille, and especially for his innovative tragedy *Le Cid* (1636, initially called a tragicomedy), suggests that he admired precisely the French playwright's attempt to create a "third type" of drama, one bold enough to abandon the straightjacket of neoclassical

---

[24] The phrase "mungrell Tragy-comedie" belongs to Sir Philip Sidney. For two good introductions to the complexities of the genre, see David L. Hirst, *Tragicomedy* (London and New York: Methuen, 1984) and Nancy Klein Maguire, ed., *Renaissance Tragicomedy: Explorations in Genre and Politics*. The Italian playwright, librettist and theorist Giovanni Battista Guarini (1538–1612) published his *Compendio della Poesia Tragicomica* in 1601.

[25] See R. I. M. (Robert I. Montgomery), entry on "Tragicomedy," *The New Princeton Encyclopedia of Poetry and Poetics* (1993), 1302. Defenders of tragicomedy tend to be suspicious of Aristotle's claim that tragic catharsis in fact settles the passions rather than inflames them.

tragedy, leave uncertain the fate of the lovers, and yet not sacrifice highborn heroes, nobility, or lofty tone.[26] Tragicomedy (like Pushkin's own transitional label, "Romantic tragedy") encourages its audience to think in terms of the resilience of parts over the finality of ends, even when those parts are arranged in an orderly or symmetrical way. Like comedy proper, tragicomedy strives to restore balance to the represented world, but — and here we speak to the core of Pushkin as an historian — it holds open the possibility that there are other routes to balance than strong, definitive closure, whether of grief or of joy. Thus tragicomedy has a perpetually "modern" feel, something we sense acutely when Pushkin's treatment of history is measured against the later, and more conservative, playwrights in Russia's Age of Kukolnik.

"In its modern context it signals the final breakdown of the classical separation of high and low styles," writes John Orr in his *Tragicomedy and Contemporary Culture*. It is "a drama which is short, frail, explosive and bewildering. It balances comic repetition against tragic downfall," often calling into question "the conventions of the theatre itself."[27] Beckett, Pinter, Genet, and Shepard all share with Pushkin this eclectic spirit of the tragicomedic genres, and all those modern playwrights exercised influence on twentieth-century productions of *Boris Godunov*. But tragicomedy alone is not enough. We now arrive at our final genre refinement. A tragicomedy *of history* would seem to face further challenges, especially when the playwright is concerned about how to register historical experience in an accurate, responsible way.

This subgenre, a tragicomedy of history, has been treated in recent decades by such accomplished critics as Paul Hernadi.[28] He observes that dramatizations of history in the tragicomedic mode have been especially abundant in the immediate aftermath of times of trouble (the post-World

---

[26]    *Le Cid* was the cause of a bitter literary debate in 1637, when it was attacked by Scudery for its bad versification and violation of the unities; the French Academy had to step in and mediate (see Hirst, *Tragicomedy*, ch. 4, "French seventeenth-century tragicomedy," 48). Pushkin certainly knew of these debates. In his passing comments on *Le Cid* he expresses sympathy for the liberties taken by Corneille: "Voyez comme Corneille a bravement mené Le Cid. Ha, vous voulez la regle des 24 heures?" (draft letter to N. N. Raevsky, July 1825, repeated in a draft preface to *Boris Godunov* in 1830, in Wolff, *Pushkin*, 155, 247); or in his 1828 comments on *Boris Godunov*, "Note that in Corneille you do not find allusions" (Wolff, *Pushkin*, 223). Corneille thus escapes criticism that Pushkin directs freely at Racine and Molière.

[27]    John Orr, *Tragicomedy and Contemporary Culture: Play and Performance from Beckett to Shepard* (London: Macmillan, 1991), 1.

[28]    Paul Hernadi, *Interpreting Events: Tragicomedies of History on the Modern Stage* (Ithaca: Cornell UP, 1985). Further page references in the text.

War I and II worlds). But his discussion, like John Orr's cited above, opens on a type of nay-saying that would sooner usurp than supplement the tasks of the historian. "In part no doubt as a backlash against nineteenth-and twentieth-century efforts to turn historiography into an objective and predictive or even quantifiable science," Hernadi writes, "some of the best historical plays of the last decades *conspicuously fictionalize history*" (10). Hernadi sets us up well to appreciate the complexities of Pushkin's genre-mixing experiment. Pushkin's 1825 play was as eclectic and radical for its time as any post-catastrophe modernist experiment. But it was written in an era, the 1820s, that challenged its historians on other ground. In Western Europe as well as in the Russian empire, historical writing had only recently parted company with the belletristic. Karamzin himself began as a poet who, in his twilight years, trained in the archives in order to turn the stories of the Russian past into a patriotically edifying bestseller.[29] The historiographical "efforts" toward scientificity that concern Hernadi had not yet happened. No schools preached historical truth as objective or quantifiable. But history as *prediction*, an idea anchored in the figural Christian tradition, was, during Pushkin's time, practiced in several genres. Pushkin's immediate source, Karamzin's Sentimentalist narrative, partook of such a tone at its loftiest moments, seeing in the Fall of Boris an "apostrophe to the future."

Pushkin was dissatisfied with the models of both historical writing and dramatic writing available to him in the 1820s. To combine the two in something like a tragicomedy of history would require not only a balance between repetition and linear collapse, and not only a mixing of high and low styles, but above all, discipline about the workings of time. How might a poet who wished *not* to "conspicuously fictionalize history" achieve a balance between the claims of patterning and the openness of chance? The poet in Pushkin saw patterns everywhere, and relished working within a strict formal economy. But as an historian, he was suspicious of any patterning that might serve to close time down. For time serves the past and the future differently. A past event can always be understood after the fact as a combination of realized plans and unexpected accident. But whatever pattern eventually emerges from this mix of calculation and chance must not be imposed

---

[29]   In the Preface to his *History of the Russian State*, Karamzin specifically instructed the "simple citizen" to read history: it would "reconcile him with the imperfections of the visible order of things... [and] console him during state disasters, giving witness to the fact that similar events had happened earlier, events that were even worse ..." From "Predislovie (K "Istorii gosudarstva Rossiiskogo")" in N. M. Karamzin, *Predaniia vekov* (Moscow: Pravda, 1987), 31.

upon the future — which remains open to shocks wholly unforeseen. This is the meaning (or one of the meanings) of Pushkin's famous remark in 1830 apropos of the French historian Guizot that "the human mind is not a prophet, but a conjecturer . . . it cannot foresee chance — that powerful and instantaneous instrument of Providence."

As Evdokimova glosses these lines, Pushkin's problem with French Romanticist historiography was its obsession with system, and precisely systems presuming to predict (53–54). In her reading of Pushkin's view, such systems-thinking might work with European history, which was (or liked to believe it was) rational and progressive. But not with Russian history. Russia, explains Evdokimova, "demonstrated anything but progressive development." Because of the wide scope allowed its tyrants, its high degree of political centralization, and the rigid but still erratic and arbitrary nature of its governance, the principle of chance was far more potent in Russia and chance events more lethal. Like belief in gambling, a belief in chance has acute behavioral consequences. Lengthy preparation and sensible planning seem superfluous; attention is forced on the absolute present. What sort of historical causality could be traced in societies such as this? "Pushkin," Evdokimova writes, "was incessantly preoccupied with the role chance plays in history and the way it should be incorporated in accounts of the past" (55). If we follow Evdokimova, to expect laws or regularities to function in a state such as Russia was to fictionalize its history. Again, balances or patterns might emerge after the fact; with his keen poet's eye, Pushkin glimpsed them amidst the most awful chaos, in the Time of Troubles and later in Pugachev's Rebellion. And indeed, Pushkin's historical eye did spy the pattern out. As Chester Dunning has eloquently argued, *Boris Godunov* was incomplete; Pushkin intended a comedic arc for his historical panorama, of which the Boris play was only the first part. His plan was "to produce a trilogy dramatizing the Time of Troubles from beginning to end — that is, from the election of Boris Godunov in 1598 to the election of Mikhail Romanov in 1613."[30] The second play would cover the rise and violent fall, in one year, of the "Pretender" Tsar Dmitry I; the third, of Tsar Vasily Shuisky. It is possible that in form and spirit this tripartite *Comedy*, had Pushkin's bitter experience with *Boris* not dissuaded him from writing more, "might have ultimately fused with *Henry VIII* and patriotic pageant history plays" (79). Chance enabled events to work out, but the pattern was clear only at the end.

---

[30] Chester Dunning, "The Exiled Poet-Historian and the Creation of His Comedy," in *The Uncensored Boris Godunov*, 77–78.

Why must we wait until the end? In his fragment "On Tragedy," written while at work over his *komediia*, Pushkin remarked on the lack of verisimilitude in all dramatic genres, in tragedy especially. He lamented the artificial impediment imposed by the classical unities and insisted that such strict constraints on time, space, and character could not gratify a serious audience; "Interest," he remarked archly, "is also a unity." And in the final line he noted enigmatically: "*smeshenie rodov kom. trag. — napriazhenie*" [a mixing of the genres of comic and tragic — a tension].[31] The plan, it would appear, was to provide his Romantic tragedy with the necessary tension (plot and character interest) by an admixture of the comic. How might "tragicomedic" potentials have equipped Pushkin to be a better historian?

First, tragicomedy vastly increases the repertory and subtlety of audience response. In place of the old dichotomy — stage heroes who, as Paul Hernadi puts it, are either "tragically hardened and consummated" or "comically softened and preserved" (46) — a whole spectrum becomes available that approaches the complexity of reactions we encounter in real experience, lived history. "Besides laughing (comedy) and weeping (tragedy) and besides gaze (romance) and frown (satire)," Hernadi writes, "I see tragicomedy as capable of also integrating various combinations and degrees of cheer (festivity), sob (melodrama), jeer (farce), and throb (mystery)" (46). All those emotions are evoked in *Boris Godunov*, and especially acutely in its 1825 original. Second, when fate and prediction are downplayed, the more unsentimental, Machiavellian aspects of Muscovite politics can be revealed in all their wit, eloquence, and savagery — that vein of Ivan the Terrible, so well developed in the latter years of the reign of Tsar Boris. "Neither legitimacy nor sin is accorded much importance by Machiavelli," Monika Greenleaf notes in her discussion of this dimension of *Boris Godunov*. "Pushkin's insights into the workings of realpolitik and political imposture in his own time suggested a demystified, and at the same time appropriately Renaissance, outlook on the strange careers of three of Russia's sixteenth-century tsars."[32]

---

31  "Draft note on tragedy," in Wolff, *Pushkin*, 130, translation corrected. Wolff incorrectly renders the Russian *Interes — edinstvo*, as "Interest is All."

32  Monika Greenleaf, *Pushkin and Romantic Fashion: Fragment, Elegy, Orient, Irony* (Stanford: Stanford University Press, 1994), 177. Greenleaf observes that Pushkin had "nothing but contempt" for the popular Romantic reading of "the allegedly Shakespearean tragicomedy," which "had become the vehicle for Romantic revolutionary heroes transforming their nations' destinies — often an unsubtle form of political allegory masquerading as history"(160). This was to misuse both drama and historical perspective.

Finally there is the question of love. In a conventional tragedy, love is usually half the problem (the other half being politics or war); in most historical tragedy, there is a romantic subplot requiring the young lovers at some point to chose between private Eros and public (or political) Duty. Prompted perhaps by Voltaire, Pushkin was intrigued by the possibility of getting rid of this subplot altogether.[33] ("A tragedy without love appealed to my imagination," he wrote to Nicholas Raevsky in 1829, preparing to send him a copy of the play.[34] To deprive a tragedy of its viable romantic subplot was a bold idea. But almost more outrageous for the time would be a *comedy* without love, which Pushkin, in 1825, strove to produce. In the *Komediia*, the scene "Maryna's Dressing Room" — struck out in 1830 — contained historically true information about the Pretender as well as a comic routine between mistress and maid recalling the sassy *soubrette* of French neoclassical comedy. There was, however, this all-telling difference: Ruzia the maid (along with other flirtatious and savvy Poles) is trying to inject a little romance into the situation, while Maryna, purportedly the romantic lead, steadfastly repudiates it. Maryna Mniszech is composed entirely of politics and military glory. Pushkin was fascinated by her ambitious historical persona and wished to return to her in later compositions. For in her violation of erotic-dramatic expectations — canonical as regards the female side — he might well have seen the core of a new type of plot. Tragedies have romantic subplots; comedies are resolved by romantic union. Pushkin, combining the two genres, permits true love to dissipate.

An enormous semantic space is opened up by this excision of love. A tragicomedy without love? What's left to talk about? Surely Pushkin would say (again echoing Voltaire), everything important to history: politics, conscience, loyalty, paternal responsibility, good governance, the suffering of the people, serfdom, civil war. These topics could be raised with less bombast and more seriousness in the open-ended comedic forms, which Pushkin was always careful not to reduce to parody. In his 1830 survey of Russian drama (in connection with Pogodin's historical play *Marfa Posadnitsa*) he remarked: "Let us note that high comedy [*vysokaia komediia*]

---

[33] For a persuasive discussion, see Brian James Baer, "Between Public and Private: Re-Figuring Politics in Pushkin's *Boris Godunov*," *Pushkin Review / Pushkinskii vestnik* 2 (1999): 25–44. Baer argues that Voltaire recommended merely omitting the romantic subplot from tragedy, whereas Pushkin, more boldly, proceeded to "lay it bare," exposing it as false and forcing it to serve political ends.

[34] Pushkin to Nikolai Raevsky the Younger, 30 June or 30 July 1829; see *The Letters of Alexander Pushkin*, trans. and ed. J. Thomas Shaw (Madison: U of Wisconsin P, 1967), 365.

is not based solely on laughter, but on development of character, and that it often approaches tragedy."[35]

We might speculate, then, that in composing *Boris Godunov*, Pushkin was driven by the same delight in genre-mixing and code-switching that had been a trademark of his work since *Ruslan and Liudmila*. Part of the respect (often misplaced) that Pushkin bore toward his readers was the assumption that they would recognize the forms he started with, appreciate the work he had put in to alter those forms, and tolerate being in a state of "genre insecurity" — creative tension — for the duration of the work. Such tension, he must have hoped, could only heighten their interest and (when patterns became manifest) aesthetic pleasure. Was *Evgenii Onegin* a verse narrative or a novel? "The Queen of Spades" a supernatural gothic tale or a realistic spoof of one? The "Little Tragedies" really tragedies or just the lopped-off fifth acts of tragedies? "Poltava" a history or a romance? "The Bronze Horseman" an ode to Peter the Great or a prosaic lament for the martyred little man? *Boris Godunov* a historical tragedy, historical comedy, or tragicomedy of history? In the case of this last masterpiece, experiencing the play correctly meant experiencing history correctly. In 1825, much was at stake for both these new aspects of Pushkin's professional development, now that the poet believed he had fully matured as a writer, and could create.

---

[35] "Notes on popular drama and on M. P. Pogodin's *"Marfa Posadnitsa,"* in Wolff, *Pushkin*, 265.

One of the unexpected benefits of Princeton's production of the Meyerhold-Prokofiev *Boris Godunov in 2007 was my introduction to Sigizmund Krzhizhanovsky, a Russian modernist and philosopher of theater who, in 1936, adapted* Eugene Onegin *(also with Prokofiev's music) for Alexander Tairov's Moscow Chamber Theater. A year later, Krzhizhanovsky's essay "Russkaia istoricheskaia p'esa" [The Russian History Play], appeared in* Teatr 7 *(1937): 35–42. Thematically related to a sister essay Krzhizhanovsky had composed on Shakespeare's chronicle plays (1935, publ. 1936), it includes interesting comments on the national history play of Pushkin's time — comments that in places were borderline double-voiced and not entirely party-minded.*

*This essay was not among those selected for reprinting in Krzhizhanovsky's* Collected Works *(2001–2010). It was published in 1937 with substantial cuts. We cannot know for sure (as we cannot know with Pushkin's play itself) whether these cuts were the pre-print revisions of the author or deletions by an editor / censor. The segments below are translated from the full archival typescript, dated 1937 and held in the Krzhizhanovsky fond of RGALI (Russian State Archive of Literature and Art) in Moscow, f. 2280, op. 1, ed. khr. 51.*

*The first segment, the cautionary colorful opening of the typescript, was deleted from the printed version and is here set off by brackets. The second segment, which did see the light of day, deals with the theatrical pre-history of the Russian history play (in Pushkin and Shakespeare, inevitably these were war plays). It is worth noting that Musorgsky's 1874 opera, for all its "realism," bloats the love interest, ends on a stylized pageant-like "invasion," but sets none of Pushkin's battles. In contrast, Prokofiev's incidental music for the 1936 production confirms the Marina / Dmitry courtship as the poisonous, unredeemed "battle between the sexes" that Pushkin intended, and provides frightening, comically cacophonous battle music for the play's several crucial war scenes (both Russians against Poles throughout the second half, and civil insurrection at the end).*

*In Krzhizhanovsky's view, there was never anything decorative or sentimental about Pushkin. He had written a real history play in the sense of a Shakespearean chronicle, with risk and bloodshed at the center of it. His observations mesh with Vsevolod Meyerhold's: the central pulse of* Boris Godunov *is real war, not true love. Further, Krzhizhanovsky suggests that the first professional theater constructed in 18th-century Moscow was unpopular because public war pageants had provided spectators with the same thrills, but for free — and in the freedom of the streets. Why pay money to go inside and be trapped in a seat? Krzhizhanovsky was an amateur historian of Moscow, his beloved adopted city, and his capsule commentary on the early theaters sounds far more like the Godunovs' Kremlin than any Petersburg space Pushkin might have frequented.*

# POSTSCRIPT ON PUSHKIN'S *BORIS GODUNOV*
## (2010)

"The Russian History Play" [two sections relevant to Pushkin's *Boris Godunov*]

### S. Krzhizhanovsky

[In order to write a history of one's country, one must have them: both a country and a history. It is also necessary to love one's past, to be able to study the good even from within the most evil facts of bygone times. And finally, it is necessary to know the history of one's country, to gather material fully — for only then can thought visually encompass the events that pass by it, row upon row, in a history play.

A fairly good book exists describing the rise of the 'feeling for nature' in art. But up to now there has been no research into a 'feeling for history.' Such a feeling arrives relatively late, in bursts, intensifying at certain times and then dying down. A history play must be felt as very *necessary*, it must serve the everyday thoughts of a person — only then will it enter into repertory. [ ... ]

Slonimsky, in his work on Pushkin's *Boris Godunov*, speaks of the 'dim, diffuse [*rasplyvchatyi*] genre of historical representations'. [36] It is indeed extremely difficult to indicate precisely the "from-what-point and towards-what-point" of the history play. If we compare the growth of historical events with the growth of a tree, then we see that the tree can be sliced either lengthwise along the fiber, along the lines of growth, or across, as a cross section to reveal a butt-end. One can provide, for example, the reign of Peter I without moving away from his inkpot and blotting equipment, so that the number of phenomena equals the number of decrees; but it is also possible to take the theme in cross-section, showing how Peter's words flow out in all directions and wander through the immeasurable expanse of the country, how they fare in it and are assimilated. Shakespeare, for example, during his first period writing historical chronicles, proceeded lengthwise through time, creating his history almost exclusively out of historical personages;

---

[36] In the typescript the Slonimsky quote is not identified. It comes from A. A. Slonimskii, "Boris Godunov i dramaturgiia 20-kh godov," in Boris Godunov *A. S. Pushkina*, ed. K. N. Derzhavin (Leningrad: Gosudarstvennyi Akademicheskii Teatr Dramy, 1936), 43–77, a recently published and widely cited collection of scholarly articles on Pushkin's *Boris Godunov*. Slonimsky's context concerning the 1820s began: "Tragedy was crowded out by neighboring genres. A diffuse genre of historical representations was replacing it..." (p. 49).

then he introduces Falstaff and his companions, and this "Falstaffian background" [Engels], which somewhat slows down the action, introduces everyday life, cutting cross-wise through events, a slice of time. One more step — and history itself would be transformed into a simple theatrical backdrop, a stage set against which certain events just happen to take place. And precisely this fatal step was taken by almost all Russian dramatists. In so doing, they took their plays — which still looked like history plays on the surface — beyond the boundaries of history.]

[Krzhizhanovsky then mentions two playwrights who did not succumb to this fatal step: Alexander Ostrovsky in the second half of the century, Pushkin in the first.]

§

From the published essay in *Teatr* 7 (1937): 35–36.

The first viewers of the first Russian spectacles were considerably better acquainted with the histories told in the Old Testament than they were with facts of their own history. Thus the first performances made use of such subjects as Judith and Holofernes, Mordecai and Esther.

But during the reign of Peter I, suddenly, under the din of drums and blare of trumpets, history invaded the theater. These were the triumphant visual spectacles, usually mounted on the occasion of a just-sustained victory. Directly from the theater of military operations the battle passed into the ordinary theater — of course, in its special holiday representation. By crowds crammed tightly in the street ships on wheels sailed by, carts full of people in their own and the enemy's uniforms, people who were firing into the air or striking with sabers. Mythological figures took part too, such as Mars, Bellona [Roman goddess of war]. Thus, in 1702, there passed through the streets of Moscow a lively theatricalized battle "The Taking of Oreshok," accompanied by verse doggerel in which it was said that Peter "subdued the Swedes painfully, avenged himself sufficiently."

Then an attempt was made to move some of the same themes inside a theater building. At the very beginning of the eighteenth century, on Red Square, the first pay-for-admission theater was built. But Muscovites, willingly gazing on the festive triumphant processions for free, weren't all that keen to visit these evening performances lit up only by torches, and what is more, to pay money for it. They would have to return home by night-time streets, barricaded at the crossroads by turnpikes. True, a theater ticket served as a pass, but all the same, a journey from the theater homeward on one's own was a dangerous business, and the theater soon closed for want of spectators.

The first attempts to create a Russian national history play are connected specifically with the names of Sumarokov, Kniazhnin and Ozerov. All these authors, under the powerful influence of the metaphysical worldviews and pseudoclassical aesthetics of Boileau, shared a common flaw, which seriously got in the way of their success: they did not believe that history could be interesting *in and of itself*, and thus they colored it and decorated it, sweetened it up as if it were a bitter pill. [...] And meanwhile, a young twenty-four-year old poet, in silence and incarcerated in his small Pskov estate, was preparing an authentic creation in the realm of his native history.

# GEORGE STEINER
# ON TOLSTOY OR DOSTOEVSKY

*The essay below is tribute to a classic in Russian literary criticism written in the "Old Style," a little battered but still robust: "Tolstoy and Dostoevsky: Seductions of the Old Criticism" [a retrospective essay on George Steiner's* Tolstoy or Dostoevsky *(1959)], in* Reading George Steiner, *ed. by Ronald A. Sharp and Nathan A. Scott, Jr. (Baltimore: Johns Hopkins University Press, 1994), 74–98.*

*In this essay too, one feels the Gasparov-Bakhtin divide between "philosophers and philologists." As in the fracas over "Tatiana," there are traces of Russian versus Western ways of reading the classics. In editing this essay for republication, I expanded somewhat on Steiner's contribution to the Tolstoy-versus-Shakespeare wars. Those wars (with a focus on the part played by George Bernard Shaw during the last six years of Tolstoy's life) were a major scholarly preoccupation of mine during the Tolstoy Centenary year, 2010.*

## TOLSTOY AND DOSTOEVSKY:
## SEDUCTIONS OF THE OLD CRITICISM
## (1994)

A Tribute to George Steiner

George Steiner wrote his major contribution to Russian literary studies, *Tolstoy or Dostoevsky: An Essay in the Old Criticism*, in the late 1950s.[1] At the time, academic critics in the West felt much closer to nineteenth-century Russian culture than to any literary product of that forbidding and well-sealed monolith, the Soviet state — even though, paradoxically, our regnant

---

[1]    The book was first published in 1959. All citations for this essay are taken from George Steiner, *Tolstoy or Dostoevsky: An Essay in the Old Criticism* (New York: Dutton, 1971). Page numbers are included in parentheses in the text.

New Criticism recalled in many particulars the spirit of Russian Formalism from the Soviet 1920s. Now over thirty years old, *Tolstoy or Dostoevsky* still renders useful service to those two great Russian novelists. But the book casts unexpected light on our own current critical debates as well.

Steiner opens his essay with a defense of his "old" critical approach. Its primary purpose, he tells us, is to serve the text "subjectively." Thus its starting point must be a positive, almost an electrical, contact between an artwork of genius and its admiring and energized reader. In Steiner's words, "when the work of art invades our consciousness, something within us catches flame. What we do thereafter is to refine and make articulate the original leap of recognition" (45). This quasi-mystical mission — which only Steiner's great erudition and good taste could bring down to earth in our suspicious, secular age — is then pointedly contrasted with the spirit of the New Criticism; "Quizzical, captious, immensely aware of its philosophic ancestry and complex instruments, it often comes to bury rather than to praise" (4). In retrospect Steiner is perhaps too harsh on the New Critics, whose captiousness is but a minnow to the leviathan of later postmodernist burials of the world's great literature. Still, he sees ample evidence of a falling away from earlier, more radiant modes of reading. The unhappy vogue of "objective criticism," he claims, has made us uncertain of our great books and suspicious of tradition. "We grow wary of our inheritance," he writes. "We have become relativists" (4).

Why relativism in one's literary relations should be a sin or a shame is not spelled out, but Steiner's basic position is clear: he defends the literary canon and the reader's unmediated primary contact with it. As *Real Presences* indicates, this commitment has not changed. But what, precisely, is primary contact? It does not have to mean immersion in the native language of the literary text (in his dealings with Tolstoy and Dostoevsky, Steiner apologizes for his ignorance of Russian, although it hampers him little in the texts he discusses); nor does it mandate a meticulous, insider's knowledge of the political or cultural background of every world-class text. Primary contact, for Steiner, is both more modest and more risk-laden. It requires from the reader less an intellectual than an *aesthetic* commitment, a willingness to "tune oneself" to the artwork and thus to become part of the text's glorious problem rather than its solution. In short, we come into primary contact when, one way or another, we fall in love with a piece of art and are moved to expand on its value in ways that expose our own vulnerabilities before it. "Literary criticism should arise out of a debt of love," Steiner writes (3). From this primary love relation, apparently, there are no merely scientific or "secondary" ways out.

In our current climate of interrogating texts and their authors, all this sounds very, very old. But what takes us by surprise, in rereading *Tolstoy or Dostoevsky*, is its high degree of theoretical sophistication. The number of potent critical ideas that Steiner eases directly out of primary texts (and it goes without saying that Russian scholarship has a vast "secondary" industry on each of these novelists, but Steiner is not, and cannot be, indebted to it) is exhilarating. His resulting thesis is so intelligently cobbled together from the bottom up, out of the wide-ranging and integral worldviews of the novels themselves, that it easily survives the language barrier and the passage of time. To reconstruct and extend that thirty-year-old thesis, with an eye to some intervening critical developments, will be the major task of this essay.

§

Steiner's thesis, anchored firmly in the ancient world, can be summed up in a topic sentence. Tolstoy's art revives the traditions of Homeric epic, whereas Dostoevsky's art reenacts, in novelistic garb, Greek tragic drama. One is immediately struck, of course, by the derivative nature of the whole dichotomy — by its apparent indifference to the manifest "novelness" of the novel, which has been justly celebrated as the most non-Aristotelian of genres. Many have argued that the novel's messiness and potential indeterminacy were precisely what appealed to these two Russian innovators in the genre. This intractable failure of the great Russian novel to fit into a classical poetics led the twentieth century's greatest student of Dostoevsky, Mikhail Bakhtin, to posit the novel as a genre that is in principle *opposed* to both epic and drama. This dialogue between Bakhtin and Steiner, so suggestive and full of intricate complementarity, shall be pursued at the end of the essay. Let us first turn first to the general lineaments of Steiner's juxtaposition of Tolstoy and Dostoevsky.

Chapter One sets the scene by marking similarities. Both novelists wrote immensely long books. But, Steiner notes, the length of these books was of a different order than the length, say, of *Clarissa* or *Ulysses*; for those latter authors, length was an invitation to elegant and precise mapping, to tying down, whereas for Dostoevsky and Tolstoy, "plenitude was an essential freedom" (14). Freedom and plenitude: out of these two ideas Steiner constructs his larger contribution to the history of the novel. Much ink has been spilt on comparisons between the "European" and "Russian" novel, Steiner remarks. But the more interesting and valid comparison is between the European novel, on the one hand, and on the other the Russian and the American novel — two generic strands fused, as it were, at the still half-savage periphery of Europe's sphere of influence. Steiner explains his typology. The European novel, he argues, arose as a private genre that was secular, rational, social. Its task was the successful portrayal of everyday life. But the genre was plagued from the start with a question of legitimacy: could the prosaic and quotidian ever attain to the "high seriousness" expected of great art? The grand novels of the Romantic period were spared the full implications of that question, because Dickens, Hugo, Stendhal could abandon the familiar plots of classical antiquity and draw, for inspiration and grandeur, on the heroic (but still contemporary and local) events of the 1810s-40s, on the Napoleonic theme and its aftermath. The problem became more serious in the second half of the century, Steiner notes, when the mainstream European novel — tacking to and fro in search of a new word — confronted the pervasive, leveling "bourgeoisification" of everyday life. As a genre devoted to secular readings of ordinary experience, its predictable endpoint was Zola's desiccating naturalism and Flaubert's *catalogue manqué*.

According to Steiner, this "dilemma of realism" was felt less acutely at the periphery of the novel's reach. "The masters of the American and the Russian manner appear to gather something of their fierce intensity from the outer darkness," he writes, "from the decayed matter of folklore, melodrama, and religious life" (30). Melville and Hawthorne are the American States' Dostoevsky: writers on an untamed frontier, creating their narratives in isolation, plagued by crises of faith in their pre-Enlightenment societies, and radically insecure in the face of Europe's complacent cultural superiority. Russian and American novelists had no trouble filling their novels with "high seriousness" and at the same time claiming "exceptionalist" status. Having established the special compatibility of these two quasi-civilized European outposts, Steiner then returns to the classics — and shows how the Russian novel became the salvation of that profoundly civilized legacy.

Steiner's book falls into two parts, each with its own thesis and demonstration: Tolstoy as Homeric bard, Dostoevsky as tragic dramatist. For a critic such as Steiner, uninterested in such hypotheses as the death of the author or the impossibility of authorial intention, the first thesis is the easier to document. Tolstoy himself desired to be compared with Homer. Indeed, we sense intuitively that Tolstoy's novels have some kinship with epic: in their immensity, seriousness, spaciousness, in the serene confidence of their narrative voice. But certain other parallels have been neglected, Steiner claims. The most crucial of these are Tolstoy's specific structural imitations of Homeric epic, and the concordance between Tolstoy's epic manner and his anarchic Christianity (which Steiner will later bring unnervingly close to paganism, to an anthropomorphic "theology without God" [266]). In a leisurely and learned manner Steiner constantly weaves scenes from the *Odyssey* and *Iliad* into his own paraphrases of Tolstoyan plot and doctrine. A welcome byproduct of these subtle penetrations is Steiner's continual reassurance that Tolstoy's novels are not unworked "slices of life," not the fluid puddings or baggy monsters that Henry James christened them, for no one would deny an epic poem the status of real (not naively realistic) art. If the great Russian novel little resembled its European counterpart, it was not because Russian novelists had no interest in craft; it was because the craft of these Russians was unreadable in the context of the Romantic or naturalistic Continental novel (49–58).

Classicists might balk at Steiner's bold, homogenizing definition of the "epic vision." But, as Steiner gradually sculpts this vision to fit his thesis about Russian writers, Tolstoy's novels take on an integrity—both artistic and theoretical—that their bulk and their sprawl of detail usually defy. Invoking as foil and counterexample the negated, manipulative world of *Madame Bovary*, which stuns us with its cold and perfect distance, Steiner dwells on the deeply epic reflexes of Tolstoyan novelistic prose: the sensuous, dynamic, personal energy that physical objects continually absorb from their human context, keeping them warm ("The sword is always seen as part of the striking arm" [51]). Epic is also sensed in the frequent elevation of tiny realistic detail to a matter of passionate significance, and in the utter lack of sentimentality about death or individual tragedy ("War and mortality cry havoc in the Homeric and Tolstoyan worlds, but the centre holds.... 'Keep your eyes steadfastly to the light,' says Tolstoy, 'this is how things are'" [78, 77]).

Of great and disorienting importance in the Tolstoyan vision is the effective absence of God. Steiner devotes part of chapter four to this seeming paradox: a deeply religious thinker who constructs his Christian theology without the Church, and his Christ without a heavenly Father.[2] A partial answer might be found, again, in the Homeric model. Tolstoy is a pagan,

---

[2]  In his discussion of Tolstoy's religious beliefs, Steiner presciently notes what later specialists have amply documented, that despite Tolstoy's much-advertised "conversion" of 1881–82, continuity rather than break was the norm: "Actually, most of the ideas and beliefs expounded by the later Tolstoy appear in his earliest writings and the live substance of his morality was plainly discernible during the years of apprenticeship" (242). For a comprehensive exposition of this continuity thesis, see Richard F. Gustafson, *Leo Tolstoy: Resident and Stranger* (Princeton: Princeton University Press, 1986).

Steiner insists, of the most sophisticated and ethically responsible sort. Within such a world view, neither confession as a sacrament nor faith in a miracle-working savior can remedy human error; error is righted only through something akin to stoic resolve, changing one's life as a result of painful contemplation or movements of an isolated conscience. We should not be misled by the superficial frivolity of the Greek gods and their irresponsible antics on and off Mount Olympus. The continuum of Homer's world — its ultra-heroism for human beings and its semi-divinity for gods — suggests precisely the sort of leveling of the secular and the divine that we would expect from the author of a treatise entitled *The Kingdom of God Is within You.*

Steiner is alert, of course, to those aspects of the epic that do not match up with Tolstoyan values. He notes, for example, that the ethic of Tolstoy is profoundly antiheroic (80) and that his later pacifist self would never have approved (although it always deeply understood) the epic lust of the battlefield. However, the world views of Tolstoy and the epic do share one vital quasi-religious dimension: "The humanity of the gods signifies that reality — the controlling pivot of man's experience — is immanent in the natural world" (267).

Throughout Steiner's argument, the novel appears to be the tenor of the metaphor, cast in a passive or imitative holding pattern, while the epic is the more active defining vehicle. But in one final comparison, Steiner makes an impressive contribution precisely to understanding the novel as a genre. This is his discussion, in chapter Two, of the "double and triple plot structure" of epics and of Tolstoyan narratives. Steiner does not probe the formal implications of this structure for Tolstoy's larger ethical vision — for that one must repair to Gary Saul Morson's splendid monograph on *War and Peace*[3] — but he does make numerous acute observations that assist the reader in integrating this baffling mega-narrative.

Steiner acknowledges that multiple plot structure in the epic lends it narrative grandeur, scope, and disinterestedness. He also discerns that Tolstoy employs such multiplicity for very special purposes. (On the master list of talents Tolstoy commands as novelist, disinterestedness must rank rather low.) "Double vision" and double plots can be polemical, of course, in the overtly didactic sense: they can reinforce and generalize a particular instance (thus making it more authoritative), or they can ironize and

---

3    Gary Saul Morson. *Hidden in Plain View: Narrative and Creative Potentials in "War and Peace"* (Stanford: Stanford University Press, 1987).

undercut an instance, trivializing the original statement, as well as later parodic replays of it. Although Tolstoy is surely no stranger to this kind of didacticism, Steiner suggests a third possibility: that multiple vision, in the form of many blunt-edged and competing plot lines, can be deployed purely to thicken the texture of the work, "to suggest realness by making the design of a work dense, jagged, and complex" (98).

So far, no surprises. But Steiner then stresses that the purpose here is not to saturate the novel with *realia* for its own sake, nor to despise — in the name of some brute realism — the author's obligation to structure a coherent story. He points out, correctly, that Tolstoy's plots incorporate every bit as much artifice and coincidence as the jerrybuilt, crisis-driven adventure plots of Dostoevsky. However, the mesh of narrative strands in Tolstoy is so dense, and the degree of "humanization" that even the most episodic characters receive is so high and precise, that coincidence and artifice do not shock us. With that much living material, it seems only natural that a great deal of it will interact.

Steiner then speculates on the connection between this thickening of texture in Tolstoy's novels and the nature of Tolstoyan closure. The mass of meticulously tended plot lines and the open, often unresolved endings of the great novels prompt Steiner to regard length, complex plotting, and multiple vision as a "stringent test" for the "aliveness" of a character: "whether or not it can grow with time and preserve its coherent individuality in an altered setting" (104). In this insight — which will not be the last such curious overlay — we see the germ of the Steiner-Bakhtin debate. At base are their deeply incompatible notions of the potential of epic. For Bakhtin, the epic hero is defined as a closed and ready-made character who fits neatly into a prescribed plot with no slack or superfluity. Bakhtin's novelistic hero, by contrast, is a character in whom "there always remains an unrealized surplus of humanness, there always remains a need for the future and a place for this future must be found."[4] What Steiner does, then, is to graft on to his epic model a novelistic sensibility that undoes some of Bakhtin's most famous dichotomies. In the current theoretical climate that has turned so many Bakhtinian terms into banal mental reflexes, this revision is provocative. Through it, Steiner proves himself as strong a reader of Tolstoy as Bakhtin was a weak one.

---

4    Mikhail Bakhtin, "Epic and Novel," in *The Dialogic Imagination: Four Essays by M. M. Bakhtin*, ed. Michael Holquist, trans. Michael Holquist and Caryl Emerson (Austin: University of Texas Press. 1981), 37.

§

As a bridge to his second major theme, Dostoevsky as tragic dramatist, Steiner discusses Tolstoy and the drama — and specifically the most scandal-ridden corner of that topic, Tolstoy and Shakespeare. Tolstoy's vitriolic 1903 essay "On Shakespeare and on Drama" opens with a caricature of the plot of *King Lear*. It then condemns as unworthy of human intelligence all Elizabethan theatrical convention, judging Shakespearean language a tedious pomposity and the Bard an ungifted scribbler. The treatise has long been assigned to that category of eccentricity permitted great writers. Steiner, however, takes Tolstoy's essay more seriously. For one thing, it contains a lengthy passage praising Homer (for seriousness and detached narrative voice) at Shakespeare's expense; this broadside appeals to Steiner, for he sees in Tolstoy's gravitation toward epic, with its commitment to a "totality of objects," a lodestar of Tolstoyan aesthetics. Second, Steiner correctly stresses that Tolstoy's writings on drama are not the ravings of a man who rejected or misunderstood the stage. Tolstoy was an excellent and effective playwright. He rejects not drama itself, but only what he perceives as Shakespeare's inability to produce on stage the right sort of illusion.

Accordingly, Steiner deals with Tolstoy's rejection of Shakespeare in terms of "two different types of illusion." The first type is straightforwardly false (the seduction of Natasha at the opera in *War and Peace*); the second type Steiner refers to, unsatisfyingly, as "some undefined notion of 'true illusion'" (122). Steiner's argument would have benefited from consideration of a key text on aesthetics that Tolstoy wrote five years before the essay on Shakespeare. For the Tolstoyan paradox of a "true illusion" is not at all "undefined" but the bedrock at the base of Tolstoy's earlier treatise, the 1898 *What Is Art?*

What is Art, and why does Shakespeare fail at it? In his attempt to answer the question posed by his title, Tolstoy avoids the simple binary opposition "true-false." With his passion for inventories and lists, he constructs a much more interesting evaluative model of (at least) two axes. Along the first axis, an artwork can be true or counterfeit. If counterfeit, the art simply won't "take," that is, it will be deficient in aesthetic effect. If true, we enter more dangerous territory, for the artwork can be good (moral) or bad (immoral). According to Tolstoy, true art (presumably both moral and immoral) must satisfy three criteria: it must be lucid, sincere, and non-derivative ("particular," that is, the result of an emotion really experienced by the artist creating it). These three traits bring on the "infection" of the reader and/or spectator by the emotion the author underwent during the act of creation. The resultant communication — in essence an act of solidarity between artist (infector) and audience (infectee) — constitutes the mission and justification of art. But artists can have genuinely bad feelings, and people can be genuinely infected by bad art. This is one paradox of *What Is Art?*. Another is that Tolstoy never answers his own question. He does not even tell us how art is made, but only what it is supposed to do, its effect on the audience. As a superb practicing artist, Tolstoy knew that the work of creation was internal and inexplicable; he avoids discussing the craft required of the artist. Rather, he resolves the dilemma of counterfeit, immoral, but universally celebrated art by appealing to a dynamic as patho-somatic as the idea of infection itself, namely: mass "hypnosis," the baleful influence of fashionable critics and ugly vogue.

Here the problem of Shakespeare becomes acute. For Tolstoy insists that Shakespeare's plays are *both* counterfeit and bad. Counterfeit because derivative, at every point worse than their literary prototypes, poorly motivated, created by and for actors (that is not a compliment), and — unlike Homeric epic — the work of an insincere author who "does not believe in what he is saying." Tolstoy never made his peace with Shakespeare's skill at representing many different points of view, many different moral positions, with equal eloquence and persuasiveness. How can a playwright be sincere if he bestows upon all parties, even the evil and corrupted, the same loving form? But these "counterfeit" plays are also bad immoral art: tempting spectators with crooked or obscene plots, trivial ideas, deceptive language. Tolstoy is not the first serious voice in the international world of letters to raise objections against the Bard, of course. Criticism has been fulsome from Samuel Johnson (who also bristled at *King Lear*) through Pope, Voltaire, Orwell and Bernard Shaw. But arguably no world-class writer has ever allowed himself a condemnation of Shakespeare that is as selective, self-righteous, self-serving and breezily inaccurate, as Leo Tolstoy's. The sophisticated, thoroughly aesthetic Steiner is curiously forgiving of it, both in his *Tolstoy or Dostoevsky* from 1956 and — thirty years later — in his W. P. Ker Lecture "A Reading against Shakespeare." As Steiner put the case in that later lecture:

> Himself a supreme creator of animate form and a playwright of considerable power, Tolstoy found much of Shakespearean drama puerile in its sentiments, amoral in its fundamental worldview, rhetorically overblown and often insufferable to adult reason ... Much would be worth saying about Tolstoy's ascetic, puritanical realism; about his almost instinctive loathing

of 'make-believe'; about the secret, subconscious rage he may have felt in the face of Shakespeare's creation of Lear...Nevertheless, even after the inference of psychological motive and ideological myopia, there are points worth careful notice.[5]

Steiner does not detail those things "worth saying" about Tolstoy's prejudices as a reader of Shakespeare — perhaps because Steiner, like Tolstoy, is a strong critic. Strong critics all crave "careful notice" for their unorthodox opinions. Also, what Steiner appreciates in Tolstoy's treatise might be what Bernard Shaw also applauded, its rage against the *cult* of Shakespeare, adulation kept alive by cultural inertia. While others are too cowed to question literary reputation, Tolstoy confronts it head on. If Shakespearean drama is both counterfeit and bad (as Tolstoy has proved it is), how did "infection" occur? How did the entire European 19th century collapse into idolatry before this false playwright? Tolstoy's answer: that the popular press, helped by the mental sloth of the public, has perpetrated a hoax, an "epidemic suggestion" [*vnushenie*, lit. "infiltration"] concerning Shakespeare's writerly worth. People have fallen for it the way an unsuspecting subject falls helpless under hypnosis.[6] Tolstoy argues his case without humor. It is hard to imagine any iconoclast more dismissive of the legitimacy of an opinion differing from his own.

Steiner, perhaps out of strong-critic solidarity and perhaps out of a sense that the world at large is indeed a drugged place, will not call Tolstoy on this improbable explanation of Shakespeare's enduring fame. That Steiner does not do so is fascinating, given his anxiety over the encroaching "relativity" in literary relations, his insistence that we love our literary inheritance rather than suspiciously interrogate it, and his solidly old-fashioned defense of the canon in which Shakespeare has such pride of place. Yet Steiner must have sensed the punitive element in Tolstoy's essay, written not to explicate Shakespeare but to expose and discredit those who delight in him or learn from him. In his treatise, with full disclosure of the reasons why, Tolstoy focuses on the effect of art's

---

5    "A Reading against Shakespeare"(The W. P. Ker Lecture, 1986), repr. in George Steiner, *No Passion Spent. Essays 1978–1995* (New Haven: Yale University Press, 1996), 108–28, esp. 113.

6    As the argument appears in the first English-language edition of Tolstoy's essay: "There is only one explanation of this wondrous fame: it is one of those 'epidemic suggestions' to which people are constantly subject, startling in its deceitful influence and senselessness, such as faith in witches, the utility of torture for the discovery of the truth, the search for the elixir of life or the philosopher's stone, the passion for tulips that suddenly seized Holland ..." Leo Tolstoy, "Tolstoy on Shakespeare," transl. V. Tchertkoff (New York and London: Funk and Wagnalls, 1906), 97.

message on the audience. But he does so with utter disdain for the dramatic conventions that might govern the reactions of an audience—conventions that permit the art work to "speak" emotionally, authentically and without mediation to spectators in its own time. He is equally disdainful of all who might be curious to co-experience that unmediated reaction, and to learn its lessons, by reproducing those conventions at a later time.

A glance at Tolstoy's letters and diaries will document this insistent preoccupation with "counterfeit reception," understood by him as the unacceptable fact that others find real what he finds false. As Tolstoy wrote to Vladimir Stasov, a confederate in the Realist cause, in October 1903, the trouble with Shakespeare was not his aristocratism as much as "the perversion of aesthetic taste brought about by the praise of unartistic works." And then he continues: "Well, let them abuse me if they like. Perhaps you will too, but I had to express what has been cooped up in me for half a century. Forgive me."[7] As always, Tolstoy's transparency—his awareness of his own violently personal response to art and his readiness to assume full responsibility for his subjective views (that is, not to lob them off as scientific method)—coexists with his deep need to believe in common moral denominators and the possibility of human unity. There is much that Steiner might have mined in this passion of Tolstoy's to unmask Shakespearean drama on behalf of the world's aesthetic health.[8] But on this topic Steiner, strong critic, keeps his eyes perhaps too steadfastly to the light of his thesis about Tolstoy as the clear-seeing epic bard. Three decades later, the author of *Real Presences* would have in Tolstoy a perfect candidate for his "republic of primary things," that hypothetical city from which all non-creating critics are banished. But the nineteenth century's greatest creative Naysayer would have kept his distance.

§

If Tolstoy's understanding of the drama was ineluctably tied to a single voice with the authority of an epic narrator, then Dostoevsky represents for Steiner the opposite case: a novelist who looked to drama, and specifically to tragic drama, for both the structure and the spiritual focus of his novelistic world.

---

7     Leo Tolstoy to V. V. Stasov, 9 October 1903, *Tolstoy's Letters*, ed. and trans. R. F. Christian, 2 vols. (New York: Scribner's Sons, 1978), 2:633. Translation adjusted.

8     The thinness of Tolstoy's argument is clear in this crude form, but it is sobering to see how his idea (on the baleful influence of fashionable critics and vogue) has resurfaced in current politicized theories of literary value.

Steiner begins chapter three with a most useful account of the nineteenth-century eclipse of tragic form. Music, that darling of the Romantics, had accomplished less than had been hoped in the narrative arts; the stage had been captured by popular melodrama and vaudeville. The "tragic vision" was thus picked up and perfected by Melville and Dostoevsky.

What does genuine drama require? In approaching this question, Steiner is both helped and hobbled by his reluctance to attend to specific requirements (or, for that matter, even simple definitions) of the novel as a genre. The essence of drama, for Steiner, is concentration, compression, "moments": all affects piled into a mass confrontation, where it is imperative that "speech should move and motion speak" (163). In Steiner's view, however, this highly controlled and often stylized nature of drama does not in the least restrict its freedom of meaning, nor reduce it to cliché. This fact is of crucial importance for Steiner's next move, which is to attach to tragic drama, as a resolute genre attribute, what many critics (again, most famously Bakhtin) have considered the central achievement of the Dostoevskian polyphonic novel: the power to invest heroes and plots with genuinely free potential. As Steiner puts his thesis, "Dostoevsky, like all genuine dramatists, seemed to listen with an inward ear to the independent and unforeseeable dynamics of action... [Thus] the characters seem admirably free from their creator's will and our own previsions" (173).

For Steiner, then, the "law of composition" in a Dostoevskian novel is dramatic in the sense that it is "one of maximum energy, released over the smallest possible extent of space and time" (147). But this energy and compression are so volatile, so chemically unstable that the playwright cannot hope to do more than set up the scene and then stand back. Thus genuinely dramatic scenes always convey the sense that "things could be otherwise" (unlike, in Steiner's control case, the absolute determinedness of human action in the novels of Henry James). "The tightness, the high pitch of drama," Steiner writes, "are brought on by the interplay of ambiguous meanings, of partial ignorance with partial insight" (277). To be dramatic in Steiner's sense is not to be tied to specific unities, speech styles, or roles, but to be ever uncertain how the scene will end.

So much, then, for dramatic character in Dostoevsky, which is indeed saturated with polyphonic novelness. What about dramatic plot? At this point in chapter three, Steiner treats us to some European literary history (one of many such treats in the book) on a topic too often overlooked by Russianists. Steiner wishes to defend Dostoevsky's plots. These plots have taken a beating, both in their own and in our century—for their exaggerated pathos, their perversity, and for their apparent incompatibility with the sophisticated moral philosophy that Dostoevsky weaves around them in his novels. The extremism of these stories encourages critics (especially of the psychoanalytic persuasion) to seek in the personal psychology of their creator some abnormal pathological core. But Steiner advises us to read Dostoevsky the Creator against the background of *his* century, not our own. The 1950s readership dismisses much of Dostoevskian thematics as low culture, as kitsch, or (in an alternative coping mechanism) finds it so repellent that we prefer to analyze it as a matter of "private obsession" (201). But violence against children, seduction of virgins, murder over mysterious inheritances, and the related landscapes of eroticism, terror, and sadism were "the public material at hand" — that is, the set plots available to any European novelist, so familiar as to be almost invisible. This material was the indifferent, indeed the clichéd stock in trade of gothic melodrama and the grotesque. The fact that Dostoevsky considered the crude but complex conventions of these genres — which flooded the popular stage as well as the popular novel — to be acceptable material for high art provided him with a matchless opportunity. He could write bestsellers that compromised nothing in intellectual rigor; and he could resurrect tragic drama on the basis of forms that were already part of the reading public's most basic literacy, namely, the gothic romance.

Steiner argues this case with skill. What reservations one has about his thesis arise on different and prior ground, back at the point where the graft between drama and novel was originally joined. To take one example: in defense of his drama/novel analogy, Steiner notes at one point that "with each year, the list of dramatic adaptations of Dostoevskian novels grows longer. During the winter of 1956–57 alone, nine 'Dostoevsky plays' were being performed in Moscow" (141). What Steiner does *not* note — in addition to the fact that Dostoevsky's big novels, on page and stage, had been largely taboo in Russia between the Revolution and the death of Stalin — is that almost all the stage dramatizations of Dostoevsky's novels were bleached-out and bad. This badness is not due to any lack of talent on the part of the playwrights; Albert Camus's *Les Possédés*, a dramatization of Dostoevsky's massive novel-satire on revolutionary morality, *The Devils*, is clearly the work of an earnest, gifted writer.[9] It is simply that everything

---

[9]    In his "Preface" to the play, Camus reinforces much of the Steiner thesis: "For almost twenty years . . . I have visualized its characters on the stage. Besides having the stature of dramatic characters, they have the appropriate behavior, the explosions, the swift and disconcerting gait. Moreover, Dostoevsky uses another technique in his novels: he works through dialogues with few indications as to place and action . . . And yet I am well aware

"Dostoevskian" — except for the melodramatic, Gothic skeleton of the plot — disappears.

In itself this is no bad thing, of course: adaptations need not imitate their parent texts. But the derived text must have its own vision and succeed on its own new terms. In this regard the dramatizations of Dostoevsky — at least the ones with which I am familiar — fail more routinely and more miserably than do most such projects. This failure must at least partly be due to the temptation to extract that tragic-dramatic core that Steiner so clearly sees — to strip the novel of all that had obscured its originary scenic composition — and then to stop there. The inadequate result is instructive, for the difference between original and stage adaptation is a measure of the crucial non-coincidence between the private, innerly realized world of the novel (at least the novel of ideas) and the publicly performed world of drama. Dostoevsky may think through his plots as a dramatist, but he uses words, and his characters use words, as would a novelist. As Bakhtin has argued this case, "drama is by its very nature alien to genuine polyphony: drama may be multi-leveled, but it cannot contain *multiple worlds*; it permits only one, and not several, systems of measurement."[10]

Near the end of chapter four, Steiner gives us one of those bold and lapidary juxtapositions that are his trademark. In what he engagingly calls "a myth of criticism, a fancy through which to re-direct our imaginings," he proposes "to read the Legend of the Grand Inquisitor as an allegory of the confrontation between Dostoevsky and Tolstoy" (328). There is much to recommend the exercise. The Inquisitor's indictment of Christ as carrier of "all that is exceptional, vague and enigmatic" is indeed Tolstoy's problem with the New Testament — and Tolstoy would like to replace its heady visions and parables with "thorough, unhesitating common sense" (337). Steiner does not take up the obvious counter-argument, that the Inquisitor corrects Christ's work with the triad "miracle, mystery, authority" (which Tolstoy rejects out of hand), but never mind: in the tough old Cardinal there

---

of all that separates the play from that amazing novel. I merely tried to follow the book's undercurrent and to proceed as it does from satiric comedy to drama and then to tragedy. Both the original and the dramatic adaptation start from a certain realism and end up in tragic stylization." For an English version, see Albert Camus, *The Possessed: A Play*, trans. Justin O'Brien (New York: Vintage Books, 1960).

10  Mikhail Bakhtin, *Problems of Dostoevsky's Poetics*, trans. Caryl Emerson (Minneapolis: University of Minnesota Press, 1984): 34. Later Bakhtin expands on the implications for stage performance: double-voiced language of the sort we get in dialogic novels "is difficult to speak aloud, for loud and living intonation excessively monologizes discourse and cannot do justice to the other person's voice present in it" (198).

is not a drop of genuine humility or piety, and this is the point Steiner is resolved to make about that sophisticated pagan aristocrat, Leo Tolstoy. Dostoevsky, throughout his life passionately undecided about the nature of moral choice and deeply convinced that "no system of belief, however compelling, could confer immunity from guilt, doubt, or self-contempt,"[11] remained ever willing to take a chance on genuine mystery.

In the blunt contours of this Dostoevsky-Tolstoy comparison, Steiner is certainly correct. Many students of the two novelists have elaborated this difference before and since, but one eloquent variant on the thesis can serve us as summary. In 1929, Prince D. S. Mirsky, the great Russian literary historian and critic, then an émigré in England, observed that the problem of Tolstoy was indeed complicated—but, he added,

> I do not imply that he was a particularly complex character, there was no very great variety of ingredients to his personality. He cannot in this sense be compared to Rousseau, to Goethe, to Pushkin, or to Gogol. He was one of the most simply composed of great men...His mind was essentially dialectical, in the Hegelian sense...But unlike Hegel's system, Tolstoy's mind did not surmount the contradiction of "thesis" and "antithesis" by any synthesis. Instead of Hegel's "triads," Tolstoy was all arranged in a small number of irreducible and intensely hostile "dyads"... Dualism is the hallmark of the ethical man. The essence of ethics is a dualistic pattern, an irreducible opposition between right and wrong or good and evil. As soon as a third element is introduced, as soon as anything *one* is allowed to stand above good and evil, the ethical point of view is adulterated and ultimately lost.[12]

Perhaps here, through Mirsky's controversial judgment over Tolstoy, we can integrate the various contradictory genre traits that Steiner sees in his two great subjects. The Tolstoyan novel, for all its expansiveness and intricate multiplicity, is "unitary" in the way the Manichean universe is unitary. Thus its epic narrator, albeit often subtle in judgments of right and wrong, tends to keep the audience in awe of higher-order meanings and does not invite its new or uncontrolled synthesis. In contrast, the Dostoevskian novel—for all its compression and ideologically precise juxtapositions—continually

---

[11]   The phrase is Aileen Kelly's. See her excellent essay "Dostoevsky and the Divided Conscience," *Slavic Review* 47, no. 2 (Summer 1988): 239–60, esp. 239.

[12]   D. S. Mirsky, "Some Remarks on Tolstoy," *London Mercury* 20 (1929): 167–75, repr. in D. S. Mirsky: *Uncollected Writings on Russian Literature*, ed. G. S. Smith (Berkeley: Berkeley Slavic Specialities, 1989), 304.

gives rise to genuinely new confusions. In Steiner's terms, Dostoevsky's art is open-ended dramatic conflict, with only the most minimal interference from authorial stage directions.

§

How viable is Steiner's thesis today? What is the feel of this classic essay amid the comings and goings of current theory and criticism? What strikes us first about *Tolstoy or Dostoevsky* is how wonderfully it is written. For cadence and complex poetry of style, perhaps its only competition in Russian studies is the highly personal prose of Isaiah Berlin. It is a truism — and, like most truisms, largely true — that in this age of ideological criticism the plain art of writing well has become terribly debased. Ground down by the ugly and careless, it is easy to forget the power that a perfectly tuned sentence can have. Some of Steiner's formulations stop you in your tracks. "Both *The Death of Ivan Ilych* and *The Kreutzer Sonata* are masterpieces, but masterpieces of a singular order," he writes. "Their terrible intensity arises not out of a prevalence of imaginative vision but out of its narrowing; they possess, like the dwarf-like figures in the paintings of Bosch, the violent energies of compression" (283). Or on the urban landscape: "Dostoevsky moved with purposeful familiarity amid a labyrinth of tenements, garrets, railway yards, and tentacular suburbs... Tolstoy was most thoroughly at home in a city when it was being burnt down" (198).[13] Steiner has a special way with the lower animals. "Gania's house [in *The Idiot*] is one of those Dostoevskian towers of Babel from whose dank rooms an army of characters pours forth like dazzled bats" (159). And further: "D. H. Lawrence's dislike of the Dostoevskyan manner is notorious; he hated the strident, rat-like confinement of it" (208).

Closely related to this exquisite literacy is a trait that Steiner shares with Vladimir Nabokov in his pedagogic mode: an unembarrassed willingness to retell large amounts of plot and cite huge chunks of primary text. It is the sort of thing we always warn our undergraduates against: "Assume," we say, "that the person grading your paper will already know the plot." Now Steiner assumes that his readers will know a great deal — the depth, spread, and light touch of his allusions make that clear — but he nevertheless walks us,

---

[13]  One compromising side effect of Steiner's relentless pursuit of elegance, however, is a certain rhetorical imprecision: "railway yards" and "tentacular suburbs" are not really characteristic of Dostoevsky's cities, but rather of novels by Dickens or Zola set in Paris and London — or by an American novelist such as Theodore Dreiser.

episode by episode, through twenty pages each on *Anna Karenina*, *The Idiot*, and *The Possessed*, for what seems to be the sheer pleasure and love of it. "Just look at how good this is," he appears to be saying over and over — much in the spirit of Nabokov's lecture notes on Chekhov and Tolstoy, which often do little more than note and annotate the primary author's moves over a wide stretch of text. When Nabokov really dislikes an author, as he does Dostoevsky, we get scornful and rather abstract analysis.[14]

On one level this is doubtless a commonsense acknowledgment that readers can love a novel but still benefit from some rehearsal of the plot before being asked to follow an analysis of its more subtle moves. More importantly, however, plot summary seems to be Steiner's way of leaving his readers with a fuller taste of the primary text than of its secondary critical effluvia. When the critic himself is a gifted writer, this is not an easy task. Although Steiner, to be sure, is much more the mediator and literary tour guide than Nabokov, both seem to nurse a nostalgia for that "city of primary things" from which critics should be, and have been, banished.

A final observation might be made on Steiner's evaluation of his own contribution to learning with this book. At the end of chapter one, Steiner apologizes to the professionals in Russian literature: "I shall be approaching the Tolstoyan and Dostoevskyan texts by way of translation. This means that the work can be of no real use to scholars of Russian and to historians of Slavic languages and literature" (44). This is nonsense. If Steiner were analyzing poetry, or doing textological work and close reading for dialect or style, then of course; but the bulk of Dostoevsky's and Tolstoy's genius is eminently translatable. What is more, this body of work has been subject to at least as many constricting or superficial readings by native speakers and readers of Russian as by gifted outsiders. To assume that humanistic thought must always work with the grain of "original national languages" in order to make an authentic contribution to scholarship is to underestimate the power of ideas, the mission of prose, and the value of minds from various cultures working on one another.

Only occasionally does one sense the relative thinness of Steiner's feel for the Russian context: his strange rendering of *Notes from Underground* as *Letters from the Underworld*, for example, which suggests a classical

---

14 Compare, for example, Nabokov's admiring discussions of *Anna Karenina*, "The Death of Ivan Ilych," and "The Lady with the Little Dog" — all annotated plot summaries — with his vituperative putdown of Dostoevsky's banal plots and "neurotic" heroes. Vladimir Nabokov, *Lectures on Russian Literature* (New York: Harcourt Brace, 1981).

inspiration (Lucian's "Dialogues with the Dead") attractive for this volume but not relevant for Dostoevsky; and his habit of referring to adult women of good standing by their first names only ("Nastasya") rather than name and patronymic ("Nastasya Filippovna"). These intonations give a European sheen to these two titans that softens their Russianness. But overall, the benefits that Steiner's broadly cast net brings to Slavists far outweigh the occasional local misprision. Steiner's readings oblige Russian literature professionals to confront yet again a question that never seems to go away: How much in Russia's great writers is irreducibly Russian (as the writers themselves, caught in a massive identity crisis along with their nation, would like to claim), and how much overlaps and duplicates the experience of Western Europe? We recall Steiner's thesis in chapter one: the European novel knew itself, but the American and Russian novel was always — and often unhappily — in search of itself.

Two examples from Tolstoy. In the Russian field we have what is called a *tolstoyeved*: a specialist on Tolstoy or, in the Soviet academic context, a scholar who has spent the better part of a life ingesting every text and commentary in the ninety-volume Jubilee Edition. This person will have a thick cloud of references to back up the genesis of every one of the master's ideas. All contradictions have already been classified; Tolstoy has long been a product, and at times even a prisoner, of his own extensive self-documentation. So has the *tolstoyeved*. Steiner brings a different sort of ballast to the task — and, as it were, loosens the Tolstoyan text for a moment from the paper trail of its author's life.

Consider the First Epilogue to *War and Peace*. I was surprised that Steiner, with his independent and astute eye, reads these final domestic scenes in the irredeemably negative way common to readers in the West — for whom, Hollywood-like, any weight gain for the heroine is the beginning of the end. "Brightness falls from the air" (108), Steiner says. Natasha has become stout, stingy, untidy; Sonya is weary; the old Countess is senile. "The saddest metamorphosis is that of Pierre. With marriage to Natasha, he has suffered a sea-change into something neither rich nor strange" (109). "Tolstoy's iconoclasm is relentless," Steiner writes; "each character in turn is seen corroded" (109).

True, Steiner does see some small surviving light in the larger picture. The Epilogue can be read in two ways, he suggests. "In its corrosive account of the Rostov and Bezukhov marriages there is expressed Tolstoy's nearly pathological realism" (that is clearly the bad side); but there is also the good side, a formal loophole implicit in the very openness of the ending, which "proclaims the Tolstoyan conviction that a narrative form must endeavor to rival the infinity—literally, the unfinishedness—of actual experience" (112). Possible, yes, but unfocused and pale. Then Steiner hints, albeit without enthusiasm, at a potential third reading: that Tolstoy, although he records "with the hard irony of a poet" all of Natasha's "parsimony, untidiness, and querulous jealousy," nevertheless does enunciate through her person "essential Tolstoyan doctrines." Thus he probably intends us to applaud her "ferocious standards of monogamy and...utter absorption in the details of childbearing" (110). What is missing, however, from this grudging debt to redemptive family-making is any non-trivial attempt to respect, or to understand from within, the evolving world view of Tolstoy himself, a man as experienced in married life and parenthood as he was in words.

Why does this matter? Because anyone familiar with the long, subtle genesis of Tolstoy's views on families and on love will agree that the Epilogue provides us not with a "pathological realism" but with scenes of genuine prosaic bliss. In the late 1850s, in the final volume (*Youth*) of his childhood trilogy, Tolstoy outlined a three-part typology of love from which he henceforth never deviated. Types one and two—respectively, the "beautiful-romantic" and the "self-sacrificing" modes of loving—are mercilessly exposed as false and internally contradictory. Only type three, "active love," is genuinely worthy of the name, and its purpose is not to encourage in one's mate more of the "rich and strange" but rather to anticipate everyday necessities; to clarify, bind, and infiltrate the other life, to *serve the quotidian need*. Both Natasha and Marya accomplish this task splendidly in their married states. Unmarried, Natasha was irresistible, yes, but she was also unstable, too full of self and uncertain where to invest it, a type one (so, for different reasons, was her brother). Sonya was, and remains at the end of the novel, a sterile type two. The rhythms of family—which Tolstoy deeply understands but never idealizes nor presumes to be without cost—can only succeed with type-three lovers. Otherwise you will not have the energy to survive and multiply. In reading the Epilogue as negative and "corrosive," Steiner, the model pan-European, gives himself away. Courtly Renaissance moorings, the Distant Beloved, and conventional Tristan-and-Isolde reflexes in matters of love are precisely what Tolstoy has set out to refute with his scenes of everyday, and thus imperfect and real, human commitment.

Now for our second example. In his discussion (129–31) of Tolstoy as dramatist, Steiner devotes some time to his final play, that "colossal fragment" *The Light That Shines in the Darkness*. Steiner correctly reads the play—essentially a chunk of Tolstoy's own diaries cast in dramatic form— as an exercise in autobiography. Comparing Tolstoy with Molière, who is alleged to have "satirized his own infirmities in *Le Malade imaginaire*," Steiner asserts that "Tolstoy did something crueler: in his last, unfinished tragedy he held up to public ridicule and indictment his own most hallowed beliefs" (129). As Steiner interprets the play, its hero — the patriarch and pacifist Saryntsev — comes out the loser in almost every dramatized encounter with his family or ideological opponents. "With pitiless veracity Tolstoy shows the man's blindness, his egotism, and the ruthlessness which can inspire a prophet who believes himself entrusted with revelation..." Nowhere was Tolstoy more naked," Steiner concludes. "He presented the anti-Tolstoyan case with uncanny persuasiveness" (129).

Taken in the context of Tolstoy's other writings during his final decades, this reading of the play is quite astonishing. For however much we might wish to reassure ourselves, there is little indication that Tolstoy meant us to see Saryntsev, the light that shone in the darkness, as blind or ruthless. On the contrary, Saryntsev was making morally correct choices. The outer world — the outer darkness — would inevitably judge these acts in terms of the suffering they brought others, and thus call them blind or cruel. That cruelty, however, is the inescapable byproduct of ethically consistent behavior and must be borne. Such is the epic's dispassionate horizon, the relentless moral "dyad," not the compassion of novel or even of tragedy.

The dilemma here thus resembles the one surrounding Prince Myshkin in *The Idiot*: through his Christ-like goodness, the prince ruins every life he touches. How does Dostoevsky resolve this disagreeable truth? Steiner is very good on Myshkin in this regard: "The 'idiot' is love incarnate," Steiner writes, "but in him love itself is not made flesh:...Myshkin's 'crime' is the excess of compassion over love" (171). Such humility, alas, is not Tolstoy's. Tolstoy was unable to finish his final play, I suggest, not because he was embarrassed or stricken by the "pitiless veracity" of its hero's failure — but because Tolstoy, as playwright, had not yet found a way to make his point of view more irresistibly persuasive. Tolstoy was no advocate of the overly clever "problem play." Rather, he believed in the theater as a crucible for the right sort of "infection," one whose first task was to move human feelings. Mere outrageousness or run-of-the-mill unhappiness hardly mattered to the rightness of a moral position (witness Tolstoy's relish at the scandal over *The Kreutzer Sonata*, and his insistence that he stood behind its ideal of marital celibacy). Impartiality of the Shakespearean sort was corrupt. The unfinishedness of *The Light That Shines in the Darkness* can sooner be attributed to Tolstoy's frustration over the proper portrayal of his "positive hero" — the parallels with Dostoevsky's quest to portray a "perfect man" are intriguing — than to any special discomfort on the part of Tolstoy, who witnesses his own nakedness in a perfectly crafted self-parody.

In both these readings, Steiner reads and reacts as a sophisticated, culturally flexible European. Together with Joseph Frank, he is probably our most accomplished comparativist at work on Russian material. Inevitably, some of his balanced good sense and breadth rub off on his subject. For Slavists who read Tolstoy and Dostoevsky within these novelists' own more savage, insecure worlds, this can be an often startling corrective.

§

In conclusion let me return to the comparison, mentioned in the opening pages of this essay, between Steiner and Bakhtin. In Steiner's poetics, Tolstoy is at heart an epic writer and Dostoevsky a tragic dramatist. In Bakhtin's poetics, however, neither novelist by definition can be either of those things — because for him the essence of the novel lies, first, in transcending the stasis and impenetrable "absolute distance" of epic, and second, in surpassing the easy staged performability and "compositional dialogue" (almost always monologic) immanent to drama. For Steiner, the "epic" aspects of Tolstoy are revealed in a lack of sentimentality, in a passion for the pitiless effect of circumstances and things on human beings, and in a pagan insistence that all moral dilemmas must be resolved in *this* world — without recourse to the miracles, mysteries, and authorities of God. Aspects of Tolstoyan aesthetics that do not fit the Homeric model (Tolstoy's rejection of heroism, for example) Steiner does not hide, but also he does not elaborate. And well he might not, because to a very large extent Tolstoy's militant anti-heroism is what makes the Tolstoyan novel what it is.

The case is more complex with the analogy between Dostoevsky and tragic drama. At base the problem is Steiner's rather uncomplicated notion of dialogue, which he sees as a continuum from its novelistic to its stage-drama poles. "It should be noted," Steiner remarks in his discussion of *The Idiot*, "that our difficulties in perceiving all the levels of action at a first reading [of this scene in the novel] are strictly comparable to the difficulties we experience when first hearing a complex piece of dramatic dialogue in the theater" (161). But they are not "strictly comparable" at all, if readers of the novel attend to the intricate layers and voice zones that permeate even the simplest narrative filler between slices of direct speech. Bakhtin's major concern — how words work in novels — is not Steiner's. That Steiner does not engage his texts at this level has little to do with the language barrier and much to do with the indwelling "unspeakability" of novelistic worlds (especially Dostoevsky's worlds), their potential to sound several voices at once, and thus their resistance to even the most subtle intonation on stage — which would embody one side of them too aggressively and thus flatten them out.

At several points, Steiner aligns Dostoevsky with the Aristotelian notions of dramatic catharsis (213) and a fusion of "'thought' with 'plot'" (228). Significantly, Bakhtin resists both these moves. "Tragic catharsis (in the Aristotelian sense) is not applicable to Dostoevsky," Bakhtin writes. "The catharsis that finalizes Dostoevsky's novels might be — of course inadequately and somewhat rationalistically — expressed this way: *nothing conclusive has yet taken place in the world, the ultimate word of the world and about the world has not yet been spoken, the world is open and free, everything is still in the future and will always be in the future.*"[15] Steiner admits the radical freedom of Dostoevsky's characters, their freedom both from "their creator's will and our own previsions." He senses the polyphony that Bakhtin makes explicit. But then he attaches it to the dramatic, not to the novelistic.

To conclude, then. In this refitting of Tolstoy and Dostoevsky back into epic and tragedy, that is, into the two genres most central to a classical poetics, we feel most palpably and literally the "oldness" of Steiner's Old Criticism. This sense of the richness of the old, its ever-present relevance, is surely one of the most liberating aspects of Steiner's book. For in contrast to so much in modern critical practice that reduces the past to a pale, always inadequate reflection of the values and politics of the present moment, Steiner starts with the assumption that all great literature is richer than any single subsequent time could possibly appreciate in full.

Again Bakhtin might be an appropriate guide to Steiner's larger intent. In 1970, near the end of his life, Bakhtin was invited by the editorial board of Russia's leading literary journal to comment on the future of Soviet literary studies. In his open letter Bakhtin wrote: "Authors and their contemporaries see, recognize and evaluate primarily that which is close to their own day. The author is a captive of his epoch, of his own present. Subsequent times liberate him from this captivity, and literary scholarship is called upon to assist in this liberation."[16] Now "liberation" is a fighting word. But in his

---

15    Bakhtin, *Problems of Dostoevsky's Poetics*, 165–66. Emphasis in original.

16    M. M. Bakhtin, "Reply to a Question from the *Novy Mir* Editorial Staff," in *Speech Genres and Other Late Essays*, trans. Vern W. McGee (Austin: University of Texas Press, 1986), 5.

letter Bakhtin intends the word in a sense quite contrary to the radical intent so commonly invested in it by activist critics. For Bakhtin, "liberation" meant a *suspicion* of the impulse to measure all of past culture by the social or political standards of the present day. Precisely that narrowing of vision makes an author—and a reader—a "captive of his or her own epoch." Releasing us from that captivity is the most important service that other times, past and future, can tender us; this is *what great novels are for*. Thus to "liberate authors from their epochs" is not to read them into contexts that are immediately relevant to us. In Bakhtin's world view, more likely the opposite obtains: to liberate authors is to make them as open as possible to as many times as possible.

This conviction lies at the base of Steiner's critical world view as well. In *Real Presences* he takes severely to task the hardcore pretensions of literary theory—starting with the "absolutely decisive failing" that occurs when theoretical approaches attempt more than linguistic description and classification, "when such approaches seek to formalize meaning."[17] In *Tolstoy and Dostoevsky*, the ancient past is revealed as a rich and surprising source for present insight. Or as Bakhtin put this point, musing on the paradox that going forward begins by looking back: "Dostoevsky has not yet become Dostoevsky, he is still becoming him."[18] More than anything, such faith qualifies George Steiner as a resident in his own republic of primary things.

---

[17] George Steiner, *Real Presences* (Chicago: University of Chicago Press, 1989), 81. Steiner defines literature (and art and music as well) as "the maximalization of semantic incommensurability in respect of the formal means of expression" (83).

[18] Mikhail Bakhtin, "Toward a Reworking of the Dostoevsky Book [1961]," in *Problems of Dostoevsky's Poetics*, 291.

# 9

# TOLSTOY AND DOSTOEVSKY
# ON EVIL-DOING

*In 2001, two Princeton seniors founded* Troubadour, *an annual undergraduate journal for creative writing that focused on travel, international encounters, and culture shocks with an uncomfortable ethical seam. Each issue had a theme: "Pirates," "Empire," "Resurrection." This brief conversation piece appeared in issue 4 (Winter 2004), devoted to "Evil-doers."*

*The essay has been slightly expanded and dedicated to Gary Saul Morson, whose foundational writings on the moral dimensions of Russian Realist-era prose over many years (now as familiar and necessary to our debates as any classic) constitute the gravitational field organizing my arguments.*

## DOSTOEVSKY VERSUS TOLSTOY ON EVIL-DOERS
## AND THE ART OF THE NOVEL
## (2001)

### *A Tribute to Gary Saul Morson*

Good topics rarely appeal to only one taker. Joseph Frank, emeritus professor at both Princeton and Stanford and the most celebrated biographer of Dostoevsky in the English-speaking world today, recently contributed an excellent essay to an issue of *Partisan Review* (volume LXX, 2.2003) titled "Dostoevsky and Evil." I came across it with a sinking heart, because at the time I was working on a *Troubadour* commission with the same cast of characters and concerns: the ethics of the Russian prose masters through J. M. Coetzee's latest novel, *Elizabeth Costello,* and specifically through its chapter (or Lesson) 6, "The Problem of Evil."

To be sure, it was a coincidence waiting to happen. Coetzee had just won a Nobel prize. He knows Russian and Russian literature well, and had written an earlier novel based on Dostoevsky's life. He was a good friend of Joseph Frank's. And he had a splendid angle on Russian literature. The great nineteenth-century Russian novel is notable for its reluctance to take seriously those staples of the European genre — money, career, sex, political ambition — and its admirers, of whom Coetzee is one, are not embarrassed to raise the "eternal questions" and give them to aging, exhausted characters to discuss. Elizabeth Costello, heroine of his new novel, is herself a successful novelist. She has moved in circles that witnessed the twentieth-century nightmares of which Dostoevsky was the uneasy prophet. But it occurred to me, while reading Frank's excellent discussion, that this was only half the classic Russian story. The other half, as so often proves to be the case, is Leo Tolstoy. This essay will begin with a summary of Costello's (or Coetzee's) argument and Frank's "Dostoevskian" response to it, and then pose a thought experiment. How might the mature Tolstoy have responded to them both? I end with some speculation on our contemporary species of armed corporate evil-doers, and how Dostoevsky and Tolstoy, each in his own way, would advocate a proactive role for art capable of addressing such evil-doing and retarding its growth.

Lesson 6 of Coetzee's novel has been widely debated. Elizabeth Costello delivers a public lecture in Amsterdam on the problem of evil, focusing on a recent historical novel about the Nazi period that includes graphic torture scenes. The torture is itself evil, of course, but Costello places the initial blame elsewhere: on the novelist who wrote the awful scene up, brought it to life, embellished it with words and thoughts, drew the reader in. "That is my thesis today," she concludes, "that certain things are not good to read *or to write*...I take seriously the forbiddenness of forbidden places." This sounds archaic, superstitious, an apology for censorship, and Costello tries to explain her position both to herself and to her disgruntled audience. It seems that she "no longer believes that storytelling is good in itself" and that "writing itself, as a form of moral adventurousness, has the potential to be dangerous." Costello is in her mid-sixties and very tired. That could be part of the answer. But the debate is of course far older, dating back at least to Plato's *Republic*: the familiar suspicion against fantasy and imagination (even in the service of truth) that can prompt a government to exile or silence its poets for the sake of public well-being. Costello, a writer and not a policeman, makes the even stronger case. She can no longer be sure that "writers who venture into the darker territories of the human psyche always return unscathed." Or as she generalizes on her profession, which is the artful use of words: it is by no means clear "whether the artist is quite the hero-explorer he pretends to be." Yes, of course the artist is free to explore, but Costello would hold the wordsmith accountable for all discoveries. Perhaps, she suggests, the western world's commitment to "unlimited and illimitable endeavor" should be re-examined.

Joseph Frank sees this scenario in *Elizabeth Costello* as the gift that it is, for anyone interested in writers like Dostoevsky. In his *Partisan Review* essay, Frank carries the topic exactly where a Russian author would carry it: "whether an author should be relieved of all responsibility for the effect created by his work." Frank does not soften that problem by the familiar dodge, that the damaging or obscene effects arise from mere fictions; he notes that Dostoevsky was routinely accused of obscenity in his "unflinching explorations of evil." Nor does he emphasize the forensic benefit of exposing real-life atrocities through narrative devices. Frank counterattacks on another plane. Dostoevsky's probings into evil are merciless, but not satanic. His strategy is to show us the abyss, and then show the tormented consciousness trying to get out of it. For who can predict the effect of a work of art? As readers, we command a far larger repertory of responses than mere duplication or mimicry. Exposed to these horrendous plots, generations of readers have been inspired, purified, uplifted, drawn into a love-ethic. If Elizabeth Costello is scandalized by novelistic episodes in which "there is no evidence of pity, only terror and even horror," this is not the use to which they are put by Dostoevsky. For him, the grisly detail serves the potential for transcendence. The whole picture unfolds in "parable space," beyond the realms of logic and justice; it is the Book of Job, not the kingdom of the righteous, that glints out from under the Petersburg slum. Evil-doing must be highlighted if it is to be stopped in its tracks by wonder and grace.

Frank is on to a gorgeous bit of Dostoevsky's texture, which perhaps is no longer legible in our time. The world is full of evil-doers; they are energetic and passionate, and they compete on equal terms with the Good. A novel that duplicates this competition on a symbolic plane — as all his great novels do — supplies the reader with a series of worst-case examples, followed by the harrowing testing of the sinner. While undergoing this test, the evil-doer comes to despise (or disdain, or grow disgusted with) his evil. For in Dostoevsky's experience, even the most hardened criminal, even those who insist upon the justice (and the justification) of their criminal acts, always acknowledge their guilt and thus their need for forgiveness. "I had a right to do it, but I am also guilty for having done it." It is the responsibility of the novelist to describe both the transgression and the repentance in such a way that the reader is drawn in to the horror, identifies with it (that is, can imagine having done it), and longs for an answer to it. After the crisis, even if the fictional hero does not survive, the reader should assemble in the afterglow of the novel's events a personal world where hope is less arbitrary and more securely grounded. Such, for Dostoevsky, was the Christian path. Without a doubt there are some very ugly, gratuitously sadistic moments while evil is being probed—and not only on the part of executioners. Dostoevsky makes everywhere explicit what Elizabeth Costello only hints at in her Amsterdam talk, that part of the "obscenity" of such writing is the role of the observer, whether inside the text watching or outside the text reading. Each of us has a voyeuristic appetite that Dostoevsky, with the instinct of a professional newspaper man, pulls up into the light. We want to "peek and see," to watch the axe come down or the flesh being flayed off, and this desire to be aroused while passively watching is almost worse than taking the risk of doing the evil oneself. The "scandal scene" is also a Dostoevskian signature: people crowding in at the site of others' disasters and humiliations.

Elizabeth Costello, at the end of her career as a writer, has come to disagree with this method of moral suasion. She would also disagree, I think, with Joseph Frank's defense of it in Dostoevsky's name. This is because Elizabeth Costello, in my reading of her life, is a Tolstoyan. On the question of evil-doing and how to limit it, these two great Russian novelists held very different views. In a Dostoevskian cosmos—and Frank appreciates this fully—we are roused to change through crisis. We live most fully while being tested *in extremis*, which leads to revelation. Big ugly shocks can trigger big beautiful conversions and turning-points, inside the novel and outside it. Thus both fictional heroes and readers sense an ethical imperative to experience more and more, deeper and more darkly. Dostoevsky (like his Raskolnikov and Ivan Karamazov) is driven by curiosity. To cease to probe the limits of things is to become philistine, complacent, spiritually inert. And for all that this curiosity might end in madness as readily as it ends in faith, we respect its fruit.

Leo Tolstoy found this logic profoundly flawed. It was his conviction that we live not by curiosity, but by habit. Axe murders, rape of children, patricide, the Nazi torture chamber that so agitated Elizabeth Costello—these melodramatic and extravagant crimes, according to Tolstoy, are not too horrific to contemplate, but too easy. Chances are small that in our everyday lives we will have to grapple with those dilemmas, so we can become armchair voyeurs: they won't affect my life, so while reading Dostoevsky I can indulge in merely theoretical pros and cons. Tolstoy was convinced that as a moral compass, ideology—"ideas"—were exceptionally unreliable; they could and would prostitute themselves to a bodily impulse or sensual need in the twinkle of an eye, and the slicker and sleeker the words backing up the idea, the more dangerous it was. True art, Tolstoy believed, infects us with a feeling, not with an idea. In building his novels, Tolstoy was as suspicious of "systems of ideas" as Dostoevsky was dependent on them. That is one reason why Dostoevsky's characters "stand for things" (Prince Myshkin for meekness, Ivan Karamazov for his challenge to God, Raskolnikov for the right to murder) and Tolstoy's do not: Pierre Bezukhov, Konstantin Levin, even Anna Karenina, these are not people with any idea to prove. Upon what, then, does Tolstoy depend?

He depends upon daily rituals and wholesome reflexes, which will generate good ideas in a human organism the way a repeated trip on foot will cut a path in the soft earth. Since in his view we learn not by crisis but by patterns of everyday life, Tolstoy came to believe that evil too can become a matter of habit. As Joseph Frank is one of our surest guides to Dostoevsky, so the most lucid insights into this Tolstoyan counterstance have been provided by Gary Saul Morson, whose writings in praise of "prosaics" I draw upon here.[1] Tolstoy's mature ethics, a variant of Christian anarchism, taught non-violent resistance to evil, pacifism, manual labor, purification of the body (no liquor, tobacco, stimulants, anaesthetizing agents): virtue from the bottom up in defiance of conventions and institutions. Tolstoy knew that most of us can avoid without difficulty the evil of killing our fathers, axing the pawnbroker down the street, or violating a girl of thirteen — all riveting plots, to be sure, real "news" with high market value — but it is far more difficult to avoid the everyday, non-criminalized failures: telling a white lie, being rude to your spouse, killing an animal for your plate and then lighting up a cigarette to help you forget that dead animal. (It is no accident that two Lessons in *Elizabeth Costello* discuss her militant vegetarianism.) For Tolstoy the aging writer, only what we meet in ordinary life is a true moral task — that is, non-voyeuristic because fully engaged and constantly a temptation. Since evil-doing begins with non-crisis situations, we have to train ourselves first of all in decent habits. We are not strong enough, or attentive enough, to fight each temptation consciously or on its own. As regards Elizabeth Costello and the rest of us in the writing trade, Gary Saul Morson might even go further, to suggest that for intellectuals and academics, reading and imagining is a primary reality, our biggest daily habit. So what we do with

---

[1]   For Morson's major works where this idea plays a guiding role, see his: *Hidden in Plain View: Narrative and Creative Potentials in "War and Peace"* (Stanford: Stanford University Press, 1987); *Narrative and Freedom: The Shadows of Time* (New Haven: Yale University Press, 1994); *"Anna Karenina" in Our Time: Seeing More Wisely* (New Haven: Yale University Press, 2007), and, with Caryl Emerson, *Mikhail Bakhtin: Creation of a Prosaics* (Stanford: Stanford University Press, 1990). Morson is not responsible, of course, for the uses to which I put his ideas here.

words (the amount of time we spend moving words around) must take on the contours, and the responsibilities, of an acted-out deed.

This is surely the great Dostoevsky-Tolstoy divide. It marks the movement of their novels and the effect they hoped these novels would have on their readers. Because our evils come about in small, even invisible steps, Dostoevsky's heroic pursuit of the extreme case and his particular sort of curiosity is to Tolstoy inadmissible. Give in to the temptation of an idea, push it through to the end, and you risk creating very bad appetites. Tolstoyans don't like to talk about censorship. They talk about infection or addiction, and of its opposite: self-discipline, self-limitation, and a careful monitoring of what it is that gives you pleasure or joy. Don't try it, you might like it — and then, the body being the powerful source of energy and automatization that it is, you might fall under its blind sway. To be in the grip of a bad habit is to lose control in a serious moral way. Seizing a weapon in a rage is merely a passing flare, it cannot define you. Your habits can, and do, define you. At this point it might be objected that Raskolnikov committed his axe murder in a trance, that he immediately realized it was an error, that in breaking out of his obsessive deadlock he was plunged into suffering and thereby came to moral consciousness. Tolstoy would grant that, of course: of *Crime and Punishment* he remarked that Raskolnikov committed the murder not on the day he shed the blood but while lying on his couch in his filthy garret, doing nothing about his life month after month, getting used to the idea. But Tolstoy would consider the entire test somewhat hyped up, sensationalized, not what we need. He would say, along with Elizabeth Costello: *don't go there, and if you see nowhere else to go, it is better not to write at all.*

Coetzee ends his novel on a thought experiment: Elizabeth Costello at the Gate. Before the Gatekeeper will let her in, she must "make a statement" about her belief. She responds that she is a writer, that it is not her profession to believe in things, that all she can do is an imitation of belief, and would that be sufficient? The Gatekeeper is not taken in by that, as Tolstoy would not be taken in. This final scene is too good to be given away, but to my mind it can be experienced as an immense battleground between Dostoevsky and Tolstoy: the desert expanses of eternity that Ivan Karamazov's Devil tempts us with, those writerly prerogatives of fantasy and free choice, brought up against Tolstoy's insistence that such pictures are mere aesthetic distractions, because what we believe is no more, no less, than how we have acted in the world. In the end we are not an idea; we are a fact.

In closing, a thought experiment of my own. How would the big-time evil-doers in America today be seen by Dostoevsky and Tolstoy?

In the final decade of his life, Dostoevsky became an imperialist—even a corporate imperialist—who preached the chosenness of the Russian people and the colonization of non-Christian peoples by the sword. But for all the smugness and ethnocentrism of that position, Dostoevsky was not a *commercial* imperialist: he was proud of Russia's poverty, the fact that her prophets wandered across the wild expanse of the continent in rags, for (as he put it in a public speech on Pushkin in 1880) "was not Christ born in a manger?" Dostoevsky's portraits of evil-doers are terrible, but the radiant confidence of his late, great Christ-like heroes—Alyosha Karamazov, the elder Zosima—outshine the sinners. Tolstoy, in contrast, lived the last third of his life as a pacifist and philosophical anarchist. He was devoted to the Good in its most minuscule manifestations. And yet Tolstoy, the great *netovshchik* or "naysayer" of the Russian land, affirmed very little of the life around him and saw evil-doing everywhere: not just in war, government, the organized Church, canonized works of Western art, but also in money, sex, meat, liquor, tobacco, railroads, modernization. Curiosity and energy Tolstoy retained until the end, but of ecstasy there is almost none.

Where Dostoevsky and Tolstoy would agree, however, is that great art should slow us down. It should take up our time and make us think. Both would insist that the cooption of art by the marketplace, by the corporate values of speed, power, consumerism, instant gratification and instant depletion leading to more consumption, is an obscenity and a disaster. To adjust art to the historyless pace and corporate values of commercial life in hopes of making it "relevant" is to eviscerate it. Art cannot turn back the clock, of course, but it must provide an alternative to the clocks that happen to be ticking today, together with their inevitably limited understanding of life. All art (and especially the art of the great novel) is time-intensive; it does not come ready-made, it is a striving. For all their very different routes to this truth, both Dostoevsky and Tolstoy would agree that human beings are not built to benefit from immediate pleasures, cognitive or physical. What we need is the sense that the universe contains values or truths that must be searched for. Overall, corporate or mass culture does not encourage such striving. Both Russian writers would thus regard with dismay the rhetoric and technology of modern Western life, which has so little use for duration. Fewer and fewer of our citizenry, they would observe, are inclined to make the effort to seek the elusive things. This state of affairs not only prompts us to do evil, when we can be stirred at all out of our voyeuristic condition to commit an act; it can close the door to repentance. For Tolstoy, this was the triumph of the animal side of the self. And it was Dostoevsky's definition of hell.

# POSTSCRIPT TO "TOLSTOY AND DOSTOEVSKY ON EVIL-DOING" (2010)

*Joseph Frank was kind enough to send this hypothesis (that Elizabeth Costello is a Tolstoyan) to J. M. Coetzee, who found it interesting but not quite on target. More importantly, he said, "Elizabeth Costello is old." It is, he suggested, a novel mostly about the horror and weariness of aging. This corrective too reminded me of Tolstoy: the number of stubborn, enfeebled, very old people we witness dying in their beds or disappearing into deep old age: Count Kirill Bezukhov, Prince Nikolai Bolkonsky, Father Sergius, the peasant Nikita from "Master and Man." To my mind, these descriptions are in every way more persuasive than Tolstoy's more sensational deaths in childbirth (Lise Bolkonskaya) or by a wasting—that is, morally-inflected—disease (Ivan Ilyich). If aging it is, then for Elizabeth Costello waiting at the dusty Gates, Tolstoy is also the substrate. Dostoevsky would seem too mercurial, too voluble and Shakespearean in these situations, too ready to give his heroes eloquent words and energy right up to the end.*

*In the July 2009 issue of* The Yale Review, *Victor Brombert published an essay, "J. M. Coetzee and the Scandal of Death," that also addressed this question of Elizabeth Costello, "surrogate witness and censor of Coetzee's own writings," turning away from evil while being also (as is every writer) a voyeur to it. Brombert is harsher on Costello—because, I believe, he too takes Coetzee to be a Dostoevskian, that is, a person highly tuned to the outer spectacle. But the sensitivities he notes are inner ones, that special texture of our organisms from within that is so much Tolstoy's home. "The body with its miseries is a steady presence in Coetzee's work," Brombert writes; "it represents from the outset a repellent reality." In support of this idea he cites* The Master of Petersburg, *Coetzee's novel about Dostoevsky seeking out knowledge of his stepson Pavel's final terrible moments. "The victim's awareness of dying [both the human animal, and any animal] is at the core of Coetzee's insistent imagining of what goes on in a consciousness during the second or split second before annihilation," Brombert concludes. Such moments constitute the "obscenity of death." Coetzee's fictive Dostoevsky was seeking the outside view, the tower from which his stepson had fallen to his death. But evil, in Tolstoy, is lonely—and always most visible from the inside. In loving others we can break its power over us, and dying is a release. If others choose to look on, so be it.*

# 10

# KUNDERA ON NOT LIKING DOSTOEVSKY

---

*This paper was delivered at the North American Dostoevsky Society panel at the annual convention of AATSEEL (American Association of the Teachers of Slavic and East European Languages), December 2002 in New York City. It is part of a larger curiosity about Dostoevsky-phobes and Dostoevsky-philes in Central European culture.*

*The positively smitten Czechs have provided some spectacular musical settings of the major prose, especially during periods when Soviet ideology discouraged representations of the metaphysical Dostoevsky on the Russian stage. Leading the list is Leoš Janáček's astonishing final opera* From the House of the Dead *(1927–28), libretto by the composer; another pioneering large-scale transposition was the 1928 opera* Bratři Karamazovi *by Otakar Jeremiáš (1892–1962), Czech Modernist composer of conservative tastes, with a prose libretto by Czech Symbolist dramatist Jaroslav Maria (1870–1942).*

*Novelists proved more resistant. Kundera combines a temperamental, Nabokov-like suspicion of the "mystical-intuitive Russian Way" with despair and disgust at the Soviet-led invasion of Prague in 1968, a turning-point in Czech relations with this big Slavic brother. Western indifference to that event, which confirmed the slide of Central Europe into "Eastern Europe" that had begun after World War II and prolonged its enslavement for another two decades, was in Kundera's mind akin to a Dostoevskian perversion enacted on a European culture.*

---

## MILAN KUNDERA ON NOT LIKING DOSTOEVSKY
## (2002)

Dostoevsky has had some distinguished detractors among master writers of the Slavic world who are part East, part West: Vladimir Nabokov, Joseph Conrad, Czesław Miłosz.[1] In Czech literary history, however, we can almost

---

[1]   See, for example, Conrad's *Under Western Eyes*, set in prerevolutionary Russia, a merciless revision of *Crime and Punishment* without a hint of redemption; Nabokov's "Dostoevski" lecture from his *Lectures on Russian Literature* ("Dostoevsky is not a great writer, but

speak of a *tradition* of dislike. Or better, a tradition of love-hate, a trajectory from adulation to distrust, with the greatest writers of the past hundred years participating in it. Dostoevsky's reception in the Czech lands was powerful and peculiar.

The reasons are geopolitical as well as temperamental. Nineteenth-century Czech writers often sought relief from their Germanizing Habsburg institutions by turning toward imperial Russia for a confirmation of their Slavic identity — only to realize that they felt their Westernness most acutely when confronted by that quasi-mystic and implacable Russian chauvinist, Dostoevsky. When Czech translations of the great novels began to appear in the 1880s, their impact was profound. The young Tomáš Masaryk, later Czechoslovakia's first President, considered *The Brothers Karamazov* the greatest book in the world. But as he matured, Masaryk became more critical. In the third volume of his monumental study *The Spirit of Russia*, Masaryk sees Dostoevsky as a Pan-Slav whose conflicted attitude toward the Far Abroad (that is, Western Europe) was as nothing compared to his straightforward hate for the Near Abroad, that is, for Poles and to a lesser extent Czechs, carriers of heretical Catholic and Protestant ideas.[2] (Masaryk dismisses Dostoevsky's attitude toward the Jews as a far less central, and less interesting, prejudice.) The Russian soul, Masaryk concluded, was a composite of the Russian God and the Russian Christ — and Dostoevsky was the imperialist prophet of all three.

Karel Čapek experienced a similar shift, although on more literary terrain. He deeply admired Dostoevsky's "psychological novel" — but became impatient with its overwrought gestures and intonations. "The hysterical

---

a rather mediocre one — with flashes of excellent humor, but, alas, with wastelands of literary platitudes in between ... I am very eager to debunk Dostoevski" [98]); and the entry on Dostoevsky in *Miłosz's ABC's* ("Undoubtedly a prophet. But also a dangerous teacher. [A book by me on Dostoevsky] would have to be a book based on mistrust, and one cannot do without trust" [99–102]).

2    Volumes 1 and 2 of *The Spirit of Russia* were completed in 1909–1912. The third volume, containing the theses on Dostoevsky, was left unfinished at the time of Masaryk's death in 1935, and published only in 1967. Relevant chapters are reprinted in a forum devoted to the Kundera-Dostoevsky debate in *Cross Currents: A Yearbook of Central European Culture* 5 (1986): 455–68. Concerning the Jewish question we read: "Dostoevsky avoids this issue, which is such an important one for Russia. Jews do not appear in his works as active characters; in the north he had no opportunity to study the Jews or their relations with Christians" (Masaryk then mentions briefly the Kovner correspondence and Dostoevsky's linking of Jewish bankers with socialism and the Anti-Christ).

world of Dostoevsky" is how Čapek referred to it in a letter to his fiancée, Olga Scheinpflugová, in 1934, as he was writing his own trilogy of short psychological novels — the first of which, *Hordubal*, is a dark Sub-Carpathian variation on *Crime and Punishment*. What is this Dostoevskian world? "Somebody commits some atrocity and then begins to beat his breast, and look, the moral order is preserved and the human soul saved."[3]

A half-century later, Milan Kundera expanded sympathetically upon Čapek's insight. His essay, written in French, appeared in *The New York Times Book Review* (January 6, 1985) and also as the Preface to "Jacques and his Master"— his whimsical dramatic replay of Diderot. The piece might have passed unnoticed amid the general East / Central European animus against things Russian, had not Joseph Brodsky responded to it two weeks later, also in the *Times*, in an outspoken piece titled "Why Milan Kundera is Wrong About Dostoevsky."[4]

In this paper, I will briefly outline the disagreement between these two writers, and then consider possible sources for Kundera's position.[5] My focus will be the concept of polyphony, a convenient meeting point for several reasons. Bakhtin is famous for applying that term to Dostoevsky, "creator of the polyphonic novel." Kundera, who intensely dislikes what goes on in Dostoevsky's novels, relies heavily on this same musical metaphor in his own theoretical treatise, a series of musings on the genre collected and published in French in 1986 as *The Art of the Novel*. A look at how Kundera as critic, and Bakhtin as critic, use the term "polyphony" can tell us something about the craftsmanship of both Dostoevsky and Kundera as novelists. And also, I believe, it tells us something about what gets on Czech nerves about their illustrious neighbor to the East.

To begin with Kundera's essay. By 1981 the novelist had lived almost a decade in France. He opens on a reminiscence: why he had refused, in

---

3   Letter of Čapek to his wife Olga, July 18, 1934, in *Sebrané spisi* (Praha: Český spisovatel, 1993), 23:258–59, esp. 259.

4   Kundera's "review," entitled "An Introduction to a Variation," is reprinted together with Joseph Brodsky's response (*The New York Times Book Review*, Feb. 19, 1985) in *Cross Currents* 5 (1986): 469–76 and 477–83.

5   Among such reasons we must entertain the possibility that Kundera is projecting on to Dostoevsky some of his own innerly perceived flaws, just as we are prone to cast out on to our enemy a distilled essence of ourselves. So, at least, thinks Gabriel Josipovici, who concludes his excellent review of *The Art of the Novel* with this thought: "In the end, it seems to me, Kundera's stance of ironic aloofness, that mixture of eroticism, cynicism and playfulness, is really only a variant on, and not a rejection of, Romantic lyricism." *Times Literary Supplement* (June 24–30, 1988): 696.

Prague 1968, to undertake a stage adaptation of *The Idiot*. "Even if I were starving," he writes, "I could not take on the job. Dostoevsky's universe of overblown gestures, murky depths, and aggressive sentimentality repelled me." He insisted that it wasn't because of the Russian tanks — after all, he still loved Chekhov. It wasn't even because he doubted the aesthetic merit of those fictional worlds. "What irritated me about Dostoevsky," Kundera wrote, "was the *climate* of his novels: a universe where everything turns into feeling; in other words, where feelings are promoted to the rank of value and truth." He was struck by the Dostoevskian resonances of those well-meaning Soviet soldiers who filled Czech roads with their military equipment and then asked him: *"Kak chuvstvuetes'?"* [which Kundera translates as: What are your feelings?]. Here was where he saw the special awfulness of Russian culture as distilled in Dostoevsky: "the elevation of sentiment to the rank of a value." Russia as a nation had fallen for the Christian commandment to love indiscriminately — and stern Judaic Law, in all its clarity, was lost. Christian Europe had sobered up on the Renaissance, but Russia went on loving and feeling, noisily, brutally, humorlessly, without the Western counterbalances of Reason and Doubt. Kundera goes on to praise two great Western novels that, in his view, care more about complexity of invention, thought, and wit than about feeling: Sterne's *Tristram Shandy* and Diderot's *Jacques le Fataliste*. "No novel worthy of the name," he concludes, "takes the world seriously."

Joseph Brodsky mounted his counterattack on two fronts. First, Kundera was wrong about Dostoevsky because his critique is fueled not by aesthetics but by his "sense of history." He has every right to be disgusted by the occupying Soviet troops. After such a misfortune, one must point a finger at something. But this does not give Kundera the right to assume that "feelings, elevated to criteria for truth" have some sort of geopolitical locus, lying "roughly in the direction of his pointed finger, from which both Dostoevsky and the tanks have come." It was the Frenchman Rousseau, after all, who had started the cult of sentiment, just as it was a Western idea, Marxist Communism, that stood behind those tanks. But Kundera is also wrong about Dostoevsky himself. Dostoevsky is not particularly about feelings. He is about good and evil. He might use emotions to get you to that topic, but this whole issue is not to be resolved along the East-West divide. That simplistic binary has become an embarrassment to both parties, and a mess. And finally, Brodsky remarks, the supremely creative moment is — for better or worse — more "felt" than "reasoned out." This is not because creativity is sentimental, but because a creative idea is valued more by the quality of the *response* it elicits than by any self-contained cognitive play. Dostoevsky reveals to us our "optimal parameters," our "spiritual maximum." And (Brodsky concludes) "the metaphysical man of Dostoevsky's novels is of greater value than Mr. Kundera's wounded rationalist, however modern and however common."

A great deal in Brodsky's measured response must have irritated the touchy, hyperbolic Kundera, who so prided himself on his small-nation nationalism. Several substantial issues cut close to the bone.[6] This little exchange in the *Times* between two exiles, the Frenchified Czech novelist and the Americanized Russian poet, even generated a modest secondary literature of its own. In 1993, Peter Petro published an essay titled "Apropos Dostoevsky: Brodsky, Kundera and the Definition of Europe," in which he intimates that Kundera protests altogether too much. For Dostoevsky is everywhere present in Kundera's fiction, Petro points out: from his comically debased variant on *Crime and Punishment*, *The Farewell Waltz*, through *The Joke* (where the Lucie episode recalls Myshkin's "Marie story" in *The Idiot*), to the multi-layered and multi-voiced structure of all his best novels. Petro insists that Kundera exploits Dostoevsky largely as a symbol, the "symbol of an unacceptable variant of European culture," but that a careful reading of his novels suggests that "Dostoevsky as a thinker and a master of the polyphonic novel is a major influence on Kundera's work."[7]

---

6   Such as: "Having lived for so long in Eastern Europe (Western Asia to some), it is only natural that Mr. Kundera should want to be more European than the Europeans themselves." And near the end of his response, Brodsky quotes Kundera's signature phrase about 1968: "In a small Western country I experienced the end of the West." To which Brodsky replies: "Sounds grand and tragic, but it's pure histrionics. Culture dies only for those who fail to master it, the way morality dies for a lecher. Western civilization and its culture . . . is based first of all on the principle of sacrifice . . . The Russian night that has descended on Czechoslovakia is no darker than it was when Jan Masaryk was thrown through a window by the agents of the Soviet Secret Service in 1948. It's Western culture that helped Mr. Kundera to survive that night, it's in that night he came to love Denis Diderot and Lawrence Sterne and to laugh their laughter. That laughter, however, was the privilege of free men, as were the sorrows of Dostoevsky." For a good discussion of Kundera's "small-nation chauvinism," see Peter Hruby, *Daydreams and Nightmares: Czech Communist and Ex-communist Literature (1917–1987)* (New York: Columbia University Press, 1990), ch. 11, "The Literary and Political Development of Milan Kundera," 231–49, esp. 244–45.

7   Peter Petro, "Apropos Dostoevsky: Brodsky, Kundera and the Definition of Europe," in *Literature and Politics in Central Europe: Studies in Honour of Marketa Goetz-Stankiewicz*, ed. Leslie Miller et al. (Columbia SC: Camden House, 1993), 76–90, esp. 81–83.

Petro is on to an important distinction. He does not develop it, but I will attempt to do so for the rest of this talk.[8] There is indeed an "intonation" in Dostoevsky — a complex of priorities and behaviors — that Kundera despises, which resembles what Čapek and Conrad despised. Kundera associates this "unacceptable variant of European culture" (that is, a texture that is too sentimental, exhibitionist and extremist) with Russians in general and with Dostoevskian characters in particular: how they talk, think, suffer, intrude upon others, and live out their values. Kundera's dislike for this intonational cluster is consistent throughout his career. Its core ingredients are found in that essay from 1981 to which Joseph Brodsky responded so forcefully, but they are present in various fictions as well, perhaps most fully in Kundera's sixth novel, the last he wrote in Czech, *Nesmrtelnost* [*Immortality*], published in 1990. Fully a half-dozen pages in chapters 9 through 16 are devoted to the narrator's musings about what is wrong with the Russians, as exemplified by Dostoevskian heroes and heroines.[9] First, and at the core of the problem for Kundera, is all that bad or non-existent sex. He admits that almost all great European love stories are stories of frustration and sublimation — but the Russians, he says, are far worse than the norm. Sublimation brings them no pleasure, no art, no wisdom, no confidence or potency, nothing but sentimentality, self-mutilation and hot air.

As it happens, Kundera is inaccurate in recalling the necessary plots. But whether this inaccuracy is due to his irritation at Dostoevsky's intonation, his general indifference to male-female relations not centered wholly on the pursuit of sensual pleasure, his scarcely concealed misogyny, or simply to his ignorance, is hard to say. It's even possible he is trying to make us laugh — as we laugh at a clever parody on a universally recognized, beloved original — but I'm not persuaded of that. Kundera as literary critic talks constantly about the need for laughter and caprice, but (unlike Dostoevsky himself) as a creative writer Kundera is rather necessity-driven and humorless. James Wood put it well in a recent review essay in *The New Republic*, when he called

---

[8]    Two details are interesting here in passing: first, in 1943, the émigré artist Mstislav Dobuzhinsky approached Vladimir Nabokov, on behalf of the composer Artur Vincent Lourié, as possible librettist for a musicalization of *The Idiot*, to which Nabokov declined absolutely, saying that "he could not abide Dostoevsky"; and second, the "feelings" defense is a strange one to apply to Dostoevsky, Russia's greatest novelist of ideas. It is more completely the case that Tolstoy based his theory of art on emotional reactions (of both characters and readers), saving all sober reasonable consciousness for himself.

[9]    Milan Kundera, *Immortality*, transl. from the Czech by Peter Kussi (New York: Perennial Classics, 1990), 196–212.

Kundera more a "didactician of the comic" than a genuine comic novelist.[10] For whatever reason, Kundera senses no playfulness or humor in Dostoevsky. Let me quote from those central chapters in *Immortality*:

> In his novel *The Idiot* [Kundera writes in Chapter 9], Dostoevsky let Nastasia Filipovna sleep with any merchant who came along, but when real passion was involved, namely when she found herself torn between Prince Myshkin and Rogozhin, their sexual organs dissolved in their three great hearts like lumps of sugar in three cups of tea. The love of Anna Karenina and Vronski ended with their first sexual encounter, after which it became nothing but a story of its own disintegration, and we hardly know why: had they made love so poorly? Or, on the contrary, had they made love so beautifully that the intensity of their pleasure released a sense of guilt? (197).

This is in many ways a pigheaded passage — Nastasia Filipovna is not promiscuous, that surely is part of the problem, and Anna's passionate physical love for Vronsky continues to grow precipitously throughout the novel, that surely is the problem — but be that as it may, the "great samovar of feeling" in which sex organs purportedly dissolve is only the beginning of the Russian tragedy according to Kundera. Since Russian literature can't "perform," it defaults to *feeling*. In chapter 11, Kundera returns to *The Idiot*, a novel with which he was apparently obsessed. Like hearing Dostoevsky on Pushkin in 1880, hearing Kundera on Dostoevsky in 1990 tells us almost nothing about the worldview of the writer under discussion, but a huge amount about the anxieties of the speaker:

> I said that Myshkin admired all women who suffered [Kundera writes], but I could also turn this statement around: from the moment some woman pleased him, he imagined her suffering. And because he was incapable of keeping his thoughts to himself, he immediately made this known to the woman. Besides, it was an outstanding method of seduction (what a pity that Myshkin did not know how to make better use of it!), for if we say to any woman "You have suffered a great deal," it is as if we celebrated her soul, stroked it, lifted it on high. Any woman is ready to tell you at such a moment, "Even though you still don't have my body, my soul already belongs to you!" (201).

---

10    James Wood, "Laughter and Forgetting" [A review of Kundera's *Ignorance*], *The New Republic* (December 23, 2002): 33–37. The phrase "didactician of the comic" appears in the opening sentence.

Kundera then concludes his chapter: "Under Myshkin's gaze the soul grows and grows, it resembles a giant mushroom as high as a five-story building, it resembles a hot-air balloon about to rise into the sky with its crew. We have reached a phenomenon that I call *hypertrophy of the soul.*" These mushrooms and hot-air balloons are indeed faintly funny, but two chapters later Kundera makes it clear that something morbidly serious is at stake. He is digressing about music, and the target of his ire at this point is the hyper-richness of such Late Romantic music as Gustav Mahler's, which taught man "the worship of his feelings and his feeling self." Sit in the concert hall, soak up the violinist's first two notes — and reason and aesthetic judgment are silenced. "Mere musical sound [Kundera writes] performs approximately the same effect upon us as Myshkin's gaze fixed upon a woman. Music: a pump for inflating the soul. Hypertrophic souls turned into huge balloons rise to the ceiling of the concert hall…" (204). Four chapters later, the final shoe drops. The hypertrophic air-ballooned soul is not only the weepy-eyed devotée of Mahler but also, we read, the soul of the 20-year-old youth who [Kundera writes] "joins the Communist Party…It begins with a festering, unsatisfied love for himself, a self he wants to mark with expressive features and then send…on to the great stage of history, under the gaze of thousands, and we know from the example of Myshkin and Nastasia Filipovna how such a keen gaze can make a soul grow, expand, get bigger and bigger until at last it rises to heaven like a beautiful, brightly-lit airship" (212).

Here's the sequence, then, familiar to us from as far back as poor Ludvik in *The Joke* but for which Prince Myshkin now seems to bear most of the blame. Bad sex leads to sentimentality, which must conceal its impotence under a cult of suffering; the resulting inflated, hypertrophic soul finds its satisfaction in bad music and revolutionary politics, which together degrade culture and destroy human dignity. This sequence is not wholly outrageous, of course — all of us who have been toiling in Russian literature for three decades or more have known days when this list seems pretty true, even if exaggerated and traced back to an unlikely starting point — but Kundera is in earnest. In the final section of this paper, I would like to fit the caricature of Dostoevskian worlds and intonations that we are given in *Immortality* (and elsewhere in Kundera's fiction) into the other half of Peter Petro's statement: his conclusion that "Dostoevsky as a thinker and a master of the polyphonic novel is a major influence on Kundera's work."

Petro is partly right. For all his disgust at Myshkin's Gaze and its attendant disasters, Kundera has always esteemed Dostoevsky as a novelist who could manipulate ideas and as a gifted architect of novelistic space. In *Testaments*

*Betrayed*, his 1993 volume of critical essays, Kundera remarks in several places on Dostoevsky's craftsmanship as a constructor of plot and a deviser of dramatic scenes.[11] But can we say that Kundera admired Dostoevsky as a "master of the polyphonic novel?" Here we run into problems, which are made more tenacious and interesting by the fact that Kundera defines his own work (and the work of novelists he admires) also as contrapuntal and polyphonic. To clarify the picture, we must forget all the meanings that Bakhtin attached to the term "polyphony" and that, for better or worse, now cling to Dostoevsky's novels like self-evident truths. Bakhtin intended the term loosely, suggestively, as a tribute to the presence of responsive, interactive, but autonomous personalities answering to (and for) one another within a novel. The term would never have been used in that imprecise way by Kundera. He was the son of a concert pianist and professor of music in Brno, and had received an excellent music education; to take a precise technical term and turn it into a cloudy metaphor was not his habit. *Testaments Betrayed* is distinguished by being as much about music as about literature, and its music commentary is of high quality. There are lengthy discussions of Janáček, Stravinsky, Schoenberg, and even a three-page essay on "Melody" that is, in effect, a love song to the 12th century polyphonic chant.

What Kundera loves about this chant is the "embrace of two melodies belonging two different eras… like reality and parable at once" (71–72). This type of polyphony contains a repeating, memorizable cantus firmus line in counterpoint with an improvised (unmemorizable) melismatic embellishment. One line is forever; the other line is inspired, new, and tansitory. The task of the medieval musician was to improvise (within a vocabulary of fourths and fifths) an open harmonic entity in the service of a stable, ancient, "sublimely archaic" truth. The beauty and consolation of parallel and free organum comes with its interweaving of disciplined, distanced intervals. In the Classical period, Kundera notes, the situation

---

[11]  Milan Kundera, *Testaments Betrayed: An Essay in Nine Parts*. Trans. from French by Linda Ascher (New York: HarperCollins, 1995). Discussing the freedom with which pre-19th century writers like Rabelais, Cervantes, Diderot and Sterne "improvised" their novels, Kundera notes admiringly Dostoevsky's seven books' worth of plans, motifs and plots for *The Demons*. "The more calculated the construction machinery," Kundera writes, "the more real and natural the characters. The prejudice against constructional thinking as a 'nonartistic' element that mutilates the 'living' quality of characters is just sentimental naivete from people who have never understood art" (18–19). Later, Kundera cites Dostoevsky, Walter Scott and Balzac as novelists who build their novels via scenes, producing texts that resemble "a very rich film script" (pp. 129–30).

changes: melody is cut up into manageable, repeatable, recombinable phrases, it heats up and is expected to "describe emotions"—already we see where this is leading—and the symphony orchestra enters the picture, thickening the texture and overwhelming the whole (73).

The clean, unencumbered experience of early polyphony remains an inspiration for Kundera in the writing of his own novels, and it is a touchstone for what he loves in others. In Part Four of his treatise *The Art of the Novel*, an interview titled "Dialogue on the Art of Composition," Kundera expands on his concept of novelistic counterpoint and polyphonic form. Only one segment of his sophisticated and suggestive discussion can be noted here: his eulogy to Hermann Broch's 1932 trilogy *The Sleepwalkers*, one of his favorite novels. There are three narratives with three different heroes from three different eras: 1888, 1903, and 1918. A mass of embedded genres and embedded nationalities—a Czech prostitute, an Austrian banker, an Alsatian scoundrel—are tied together by military history as well as by lengthy poetic and philosophical digressions, rather like the Austro-Hungarian Empire itself. Themes and motifs recur, but characters only occasionally intersect. Kundera especially admires the fact that *The Sleepwalkers* is made up of five "purposely heterogeneous lines," quite distinct in content, value systems, and style. Or as Kundera puts it: "Each of the five lines is magnificent in itself. Still, though they are handled simultaneously, in constant alternation (that is, with a clear 'polyphonic' intention), the lines do not come together, do not make an indivisible whole; in other words, the polyphonic intention remains artistically unfulfilled."[12]

When asked by the interviewer whether the application of polyphony to literature does not "set up demands a novel could never meet," Kundera is careful to explain just how difficult it is for the novelist-musician to succeed. Polyphony in music is the actual simultaneous sounding of fundamental, equally indispensable voices. Verbal narratives (excluding, of course, libretti that transcribe ensemble singing) cannot accomplish such a feat directly, because they are unilinear compositions. But the best novelists always try to break free of that constraint. As an example of one 19th-century master who tried, he brings forward Dostoevsky and his *Demons*. Dostoevsky packed three stories inside one box: an *ironic* novel of the love between Madame Stavrogina and Stepan Verkhovensky; a *romantic* novel of Nikolai Stavrogin and his amorous exploits, and a *political* novel of revolutionary intrigue. This

---

[12]    Milan Kundera, *The Art of the Novel*, trans. from the French by Linder Asher (New York: Grove Press, 1988), 73.

is indeed polyphony, Kundera admits, but Hermann Broch did it better and further, he wove in radically different genres as well: short story, reportage, poem, essay (74–75). The implication here, of course, is that the effect of the generic collage is experienced not by the characters (who are pushed around like bits of glass in glue) but only by the reader, who alone has the all-encompassing vision to appreciate that which the author has assembled. These genres must startle one another; the novelist's task is to wake the reader up to fresh perception. (It comes as no surprise that Shklovsky is mentioned here as a useful theorist of the novel [74]). Kundera claims that his own work is polyphonic in this modernist, audience-oriented way. His role model is the composer Leoš Janáček, idol of his youth and the most famous musical native son of Brno, Kundera's home town. Janáček's rule was: "Harsh juxtapositions instead of transitions, repetition instead of variation, and always head straight for the heart of things" (72).

Now, in closing, to bring in Bakhtin. I will also speculate on why these two types of novelistic polyphony, Bakhtin's and Kundera's, might contribute to Milan Kundera not liking Dostoevsky. To repeat, this dislike was not over Dostoevsky's treatment of ideas, which Kundera admired highly for its decentered, virtuosic polyphonic complexity.[13] The dislike appears to start with the effect of the "polyphonic method" on *personality*. For Kundera, who modeled himself as novelist on a medieval musician, personality should not be free to range freely on its own, surprising (as Bakhtin puts it) even its own maker. Polyphony is a function of plot. There are eternal repeating motifs and themes, and above those themes there is a singular author who weaves an unpredictably rich and original melody. This melody is not the arc or ebb and flow of individual passions — those hypertrophic hot-air balloons so offensive in *The Idiot*. In this sense, Kundera's position is Aristotelian: a satisfying artwork cannot be built on character, only on plot, and it is the author who determines the beginning, the middle, and the end. Kundera is a monologic polyphonist.

Bakhtin developed his concept of polyphony in resistance to the Aristotelian model, which, he felt, might work for the well-built tragedy but had little relevance to the novel, that vehicle of human freedom. It is not the well-shaped plot that runs the polyphonic novel, but open-ended

---

[13]   "Dostoevsky is a great thinker only as a novelist," he remarks later in *The Art of the Novel*. "In his characters he is able to create intellectual universes that are extraordinarily rich and original. People tend to find in his characters a projection of his ideas — Shatov, for instance. But Dostoevsky did his best to guard against that." (78).

human consciousness. To be sure, in bestowing polyphony on Dostoevsky's novels, Bakhtin downgraded (or as some would say, cavalierly dismissed) the importance of plot to this master prosewriter. And what happens when the author's grip on the plot is loosened, and individual personality is allowed to chart its own quest? What happens — Kundera would say — is what happens when the huge and arousing forces of the Romantic orchestra are let loose on an audience. Human beings lose control, they become sentimental, they bloat and float to the ceiling, they go to seed. Kundera doesn't trust personality unless it is harnessed to the author's plot. For him, the building block of Bakhtinian polyphony, the "idea-person" or *ideia-chelovek*, is an unreliable construct waiting to go wrong.

And this leads me to my final comparison. Even those who love Kundera (and I am cautiously among their number) acknowledge that he has a cruel and mechanical side, a side that enjoys looking in on humiliation (consider those tedious sex scenes, the worst parts of his novels, where the vacuous woman is always left hungry and humiliated, the man always potent and cogitating). With Dostoevsky, one feels that our appetite for voyeurism is being shamed and judged. With Kundera, it is being enjoyed. Or take the endings of Kundera's novels, often powerfully lyrical but almost always lonely: one mind resolving a mournful truth for itself, having cast off, or passed through, all other voices. In contrast to this disrespect toward the potential of purely human relations — including the most intimate dialogues one can imagine — Dostoevsky's cruelty scenes are completely technical, merely a means to move us toward a moral question. Joseph Brodsky is right. Dostoevsky's novels really aren't about feelings. They are about good and evil. At his best, Kundera has the courage to admit that his polyphony and counterpoint are not sufficient to take that problem on.

# 11

# PARINI ON TOLSTOY, WITH A POSTSCRIPT ON TOLSTOY, SHAKESPEARE, AND THE PERFORMING ARTS

*This review of Jay Parini's novel* The Last Station *appeared in one of the early issues of a newly founded forum in the Slavic field, the* Tolstoy Studies Journal (TSJ), *issue 3 (1990). Twenty years later, in preparation for the Tolstoy Centenary and also for Michael Hoffman's acclaimed film, I re-read the novel — and found it wonderfully good, better than my somewhat condescending and nit-picking commentary below. Excepting minor upgrades in grammar and some shifting of footnote material into the main text, the review is reprinted without change. But it is followed by a postscript where Hoffman's* The Last Station *(starring Christopher Plummer and Helen Mirren as the Tolstoy couple) is the starting point for further thoughts on the more general question of a "performed" and performing Tolstoy, one that includes adaptations of the novels, productions of Tolstoy's plays, and (inevitably) "productions" of the writer's life. While working through these paradoxes, I was enormously helped toward my hypothesis by Tolstoy's implacably hostile attitude toward Shakespeare.*

## REVIEW OF JAY PARINI'S *THE LAST STATION: A NOVEL OF TOLSTOY'S LAST YEAR* (1990)

Jay Parini. *The Last Station: A Novel of Tolstoy's Last Year.* New York: Henry Holt and Co., 1990. 290 pp.

Parini's novel is the sort of book that almost begs to be dismissed by professionals in the field. We know too much, and there is too much to know. Parini's task was too easy (that "Tolstoy's life is a novel" is a great truism). The real life characters themselves wrote up — indeed, over-wrote up — the events of that last year from every conceivable angle; and for potting around in this rich earth, the novel has already received too many wildly positive reviews. This first impulse to reject on our part would be a mistake. Jay Parini has done a very creditable job, achieving in his portrait of a deeply divided and estranged Yasnaya Polyana such moments of translucent paralysis that the reader must take a deep breath just to push on.

Parini's technique — surely the correct one to apply to a colony of graphomaniacs engaged in a war over diaries and memoirs — is to alternate chapters from the pen, or point of view, of the major participants. He surrounds Tolstoy with five distinct spheres of influence and commentary: Sofya Andreyevna, Dr. Makovitsky, Valentin Bulgakov, Vladimir Chertkov, and the youngest Tolstoy daughter and most ardent disciple, Sasha. These five persons are all to one extent or another "novelized," that is, although the events they relate in "their" chapters are documentable and familiar, Parini has filled them in, motivated them, added inner and outer dialogue. But there are two other types of chapter as well. The first type, entitled "J. P.," consists of Parini's own lyrics, which serve to suspend tensions for a page or two at critical points. The second, labeled "L. N.," are excerpts from Tolstoy's own writings (letters, diary entries, the final scene of "The Death of Ivan Ilyich"). Clearly these two initialed chapter-types belong to a special category of authoritative voice — to, as it were, real authors. Parini respects this difference between himself/Tolstoy and everybody else in the novel by inserting Tolstoy "whole" and on his own; in these lofty "L. N." chapters, Tolstoy's texts are reproduced without contextualization or commentary. Others at Yasnaya Polyana always risk Parini's intervention, but the sage is allowed to speak absolutely for himself. (A check of the Tolstoy letters and diaries quoted by Parini indicates for the most part unabbreviated, and — with one or two inexplicable exceptions[1] — accurate direct quotation.) Tolstoy, it seems, can create fictions, even fictions of himself, but he is not a victim of them.

---

[1]    The major "inaccuracy" occurs on Parini's p. 30, ch. 19 ("Chertkov"). Chertkov is recalling a treasured letter he had received from Tolstoy dated November 7, 1884, in which Tolstoy recalls his unfinished novel about Peter I. The explanation Tolstoy gives of Peter's evil deeds was that the tsar was "simply too busy" building ships, working the lathe, making proclamations. He recommends for Chertkov "a little more calm and idleness." Tolstoy writes (in R. F. Christian's translation): "It's a truism that idleness is the mother of vice; but not everyone knows that feverish, hasty activity is the handmaiden of discontent with oneself and especially with other people." This point is reversed in Parini's truncated version of the sentence, which reads: "It's a truism that idleness is the handmaiden of discontent with oneself and, in particular, with other people."

The error is unfortunate, for it not only reduces Tolstoy's good counsel to a banality but misses a chance to prefigure Tolstoy's mature doctrine of "non-doing" as a route to the avoidance of evil. It is, I believe, over-clever to assume that readers of Parini's novel would recognize this compression — or interpret it as a suppression of memory on the

No one senses the unfairness of this better than Sofya Andreyevna —
in my opinion the novel's finest, although by no means fairest, creation.
At one point she is trying to win Valentin Bulgakov to her side; she knows
she has nothing to win, and her bitterness and jealousies run so deep that
she could hardly work with her winnings if she made them. She begins by
praising the young secretary:

> "I think it surprises him that such a young man could be learned. When he
> was your age, he was whoring in the Caucauses."
> The dear boy cleverly ignored my derisory remarks about Lyovochka —
> a good sign. Tact is among the more socially useful forms of insincerity. It
> is noticeably lacking among my husband's associates. Lyovochka, of course,
> has never had to worry about not offending people. If you are Leo Tolstoy, you
> merely reveal the Truth (67).

In that paragraph there is so much anger, helplessness, wounded pride and
awareness — so much, in short, of Dostoevsky's Underground — that one
can only involuntarily admire her ability to survive at all. It is not the sort
of sympathy transmitted, say, by Louise Smoluchowski's spousal biography
*Lev & Sonya*.[2] We have moved far beyond that. With Sonya it is a matter of
animal desperation, and Parini has a poet's ear for patterns of entrapment
as an older woman might feel them: the fading of her body as an endpoint
for Tolstoy's interest, the exhaustion of over a dozen pregnancies, a morbid
weariness about the present interrupted by long stretches of absolute lyrical
recall of the past. Sonya's wandering memory gives the novel most of its
historical dimension. And the results are disastrous, because that sort of
remembering leads her into traps like "... I will triumph. Our love will
triumph." "Our love" is now solely her possession.

The other characters are also successful, but shallower. There is
the embittered and God-ridden Dushan Makovitsky; the translucently
inexperienced Valentin Bulgakov, a marvel of mental balance; Chertkov,
ungenerous and manipulative but — like so few of the others — utterly
attuned to Tolstoy's needs in the present; and ponderous Sasha, combining

---

part of the rigidly doctrinaire and unforgiving Chertkov, always ready to correct Tolstoy
into his own version of a "Tolstoyan."

There are also a few liberties in chronology that do not seem to be motivated by
any special novelistic intent. On Parini's p. 173 (ch. 25, "L. N."), the famous letter to
Sofya Andreyevna of 14 July 1910 is dated 14 <u>June</u>; likewise, some of the diary entries
are only approximately dated.

2    See the review of Smoluchkowski's 1987 book by Stephanie Sandler in *TSJ* 1 (1988).

her mother's tenacity with her father's intellectual stubbornness. The image of Tolstoy himself through these various lenses is quite fine, most of all for its being very old. Its closest competitor is the marvelous portrait that Vsevolod Meyerhold recalled in the mid-1930s to his theater company, in connection with their planned production of Pushkin's *Boris Godunov* and the sly, severely moral character of the monk Pimen. The octogenarian Tolstoy is key to Pimen, the great director mused. He described to his troupe his pilgrimage to Yasnaya Polyana some three decades earlier. Meyerhold had been in awe, gazing at a spot high on the door where the great man was bound to appear: "…at last the door opened and in came this little figure in a black overcoat and a yarmulke, a little man like this, and with teeny little steps he headed off somewhere, to go the bathroom or someplace. Tolstoy turned out to be a dried-up, little old man. I was speechless…"[3] Parini, too, is good with age. For all the patience, humility, and authority of Tolstoy's own writing in the "L. N." chapters, through others' eyes we see a frail, revered and very stubborn old person, one who cannot abide change in any ritual or personality except at his own initiative, and who deeply needs at all times a rapt audience. Chertkov with his Tolstoyan colony on call and Makovitsky with his endless pious note-taking understand and cater to this. That they are the least attractive characters in the novel must give us pause.

Here the underside of Parini's "authoritative" strategy is revealed. In giving Tolstoy's voice that uninterrupted and unmediated status in the novel, he suggests to the reader — or to this reader — that a steady diet of "confession in diary form" is a pretty poor way to grow if your goal is a Tolstoyan one. The well-known letter to Sofya Andreyevna from 14 June 1910 (which Parini reproduces as his ch. 25) makes this very clear. First there is the problem of love. "I have never stopped loving you," he writes, even though he then insists that all the possibilities for active love had disappeared (a half-century earlier, at work over the three-part typology of love in chapter 24 of *Youth*, Tolstoy would not have allowed himself to say this). Then there is the problem of private narrative itself. If you feel misrepresented, Tolstoy writes to his wife, "I shall happily take this opportunity to say, in my diary or in this letter, what my relations with you were really like, and what your life has been, as I have seen it." Sonya is right: in this format all her husband ever has to do is "reveal the Truth." Everyone else, in their chapters, must put up with messy dialogue on the spot.

---

[3]   See the rehearsal notes in Paul Schmidt, *Meyerhold at Work* (Austin: University of Texas Press, 1980), 120–21.

Parini is familiar with the translated primary documents of the period, a formidable body of writing to organize. What could we possibly add? The traces of life and thought left by the Tolstoy clan and their associates are so articulate, lucid and self-aware that one wonders how any later writer could improve on them — short of trimming, juxtaposing, in essence assembling a collage. There's an element of that in this book, although this fact should in no way detract from the creative achievement (the balance and the beautiful writing) of the novel.

A more serious criticism, however, is that Parini — with the great iconoclast and nay-sayer Leo Tolstoy as his subject — has written such a *conventional* novel. It succeeds in communicating and skillfully foreshadowing all those things that Tolstoy polemicized so passionately against, pointing to truths, or more often to paradoxes, that the reader must ponder in the most painful "one-way" contexts. But still it is a novel replete with scenes of sexual voyeurism, that *sine qua non* of the genre (the virgin Bulgakov being deflowered by green-eyed Masha at Telyatinki, a very boring story; Dr. Makovitsky recalling an act of oral sex with a Hungarian prostitute, his one experience with women; the initially subtle and then leaden intimations of lesbianism between Sasha and Varvara Mikhailovna). All these activities might well have gone on, but biographical novels leave a lot out and it would have been better if some of those descriptions had been, well, left out. They distract and coarsen the texture. Parini is so excellent with the traces of things, with those situations that require restraint and register tiny, terrible shifts of mood. He understands best how old and worn-out things keep on living, and even get miraculously revived (the old Tolstoy on the train, suddenly surrounded by a rapt audience, is one example). But perhaps the inclusion of the body in its young and spontaneously erotic forms is Parini's final challenge to Tolstoy — and to Tolstoy's disgust at novels that pander to the ready market for such scenes. If so, the strike is cruelly on target.

One might consider Parini's book in connection with the meditative Finale to George Eliot's *Middlemarch*. "Marriage, which has been the bourne of so many narratives, is still a great beginning," she writes. "It is still the beginning of the home epic — the gradual conquest or irremediable loss of that complete union which makes the advancing years a climax, and age the harvest of sweet memories in common." It is doubtless truer, as George Eliot sensed, to end a novel on old age than on happy weddings. And what about real life? Parini's novel shows us the Tolstoy family at work undermining both beginnings and ends, with the only way out an absolute reinvestment in the old man's written texts. If those texts weren't so extraordinary, it would be a bitter harvest.

## POSTSCRIPT TO PARINI AND HOFFMAN, 2010:
## SOME THOUGHTS ON TOLSTOY
## IN THE PERFORMANCE MODE, WITH A DIGRESSION
## ON TOLSTOY AND SHAKESPEARE
## (2010)

Hoffman's film adaptation of *The Last Station* was greeted rapturously. The all-star cast proved equal to its world-class subject matter. It's even likely that Tolstoy himself, with his instinct for showmanship and keen interest in the potential of cinema for the presentation and communication of feelings, would have sighed and stayed glued to the screen. For moving pictures, he said, were a wondrous thing. Although he figures among the world's greatest wordsmiths, Tolstoy never doubted that the truth of a situation was sooner in the movement of minds and bodies than in the words that so clumsily mimicked that movement. Tolstoy was not a cultist about language, and in his view, the ability to write bestowed upon a person no special virtue. Writing too well could even be a trap. This is perhaps the surest proof that Tolstoy was not — in the metric, metaphoric, and prophetic sense — a poet, but some other sort of creator.

*The Last Station* the Movie also received appreciative reviews from academics "inside the industry." To be sure, some did carp on what could only strike a Tolstoy specialist, a *tolstoyeved*, as grating errors or mistakes in judgment (along the lines of my corrective first footnote on Parini's novel in the 1990 review). In a recent discussion of the film, for example, Professor Michael Denner, editor of the *Tolstoy Studies Journal* and currently at work on a short biography of Tolstoy, identified some of these "minor factual flaws...more irritating than consequential": "Almost to a one, the pronunciation of estates and family names is butchered, and many of the Russian signs are misspelled. (Could the set designers really not find a single educated Russian to help out? The Russian director Andrei Konchalovsky, Nikita Mikhalkov's brother, is listed as a producer.) The estate in Saxony where the film was shot is far swankier than dowdy Yasnaya Polyana, and the huge train station where Tolstoy dies in the film is nothing like the shack where Tolstoy actually died."[4] Previous jointly-advised films of nineteenth-century classics (Martha and Ralph Fiennes's *Eugene Onegin* from 1999 comes to mind) suggest that such inflation in architecture, landscape, provincial elegance and other visual pomp might be the Russians looking

---

[4]   Michael Denner, "Stop Scribbling!" *Chteniya* (Spring 2010): 122.

back nostalgically to their aristocratic imperial age, exaggerating its elegance so as better to set off the shabby socialist century that followed. Or do people really think that Russia outside its cities (even today) has villages kept up like German or Swiss towns, with trimmed cemeteries and mowed lawns?

Denner noted the handsomeness and radiant bulk of the leading role. Christopher Plummer is a charismatic human being, as was his real-life subject — but, Denner remarks, "Tolstoy was a tiny man, more a restless electron than the dominating proton of Plummer's screen presence." To this I would add two things. First, "Sasha" (the youngest Tolstoy daughter, Alexandra Lvovna) was altogether too slender, too glamorous; the Tolstoy women were beetle-browed and fat, and in general the family, while extremely fertile, was not a handsome one. At some level this coarseness pleased Tolstoy. And second, Tolstoy's teeth. He had lost most of them by his late twenties. Tolstoy's diary records episodes of gazing glumly into the mirror at his rotting stubs. It was a delicate point. In the fiction, a sure sign that a man (even an unworthy man) is a serious rival is when he reveals a row of "strong, compact teeth," such as graced the mouth of Count Alexei Vronsky. Tolstoy so often seems to frown or pout in his photographs, especially in those many late, sternly prophetic portraits arranged by Chertkov — and toothlessness must have contributed. Tolstoy was not a humorless man; he loved pranks and responded with infectious delight to jokes. But Plummer's dazzling full-frontal octogenarian smile is not, and cannot be, Tolstoy.

Part of this biographical quibbling might just be the humanities professoriat wondering why the outside world so rarely knocks at its door to get things right (when it matters, as it does here; the real-life Count Tolstoy felt miserable about living in luxury, after all — and this movie makes it look like he really was). Part might be due to the principled disregard in English-speaking countries, and England especially, for any "foreign prejudices" in the pronunciation of other nations' sounds (Melancholy Jake-wess and Don Joo-en are canonical, but why the near certainty that every British production of a Chekhov play will put the incorrect stress on half of the names over two syllables?). Since these decisions are not matters of taste or interpretation but simply wrong, it is mystifying for those who know Russian why we English speakers go out of our way to make them. But Denner remarks on more serious liberties, which scandalize the wretched participants of the year 1910 even more than the facts warrant. Sofya Andreyevna had indeed faked a few suicide attempts that summer, and she was miserably, hopelessly jealous in a situation where that emotion was simply not effective. But she never fired a gun at Chertkov's portrait.

In reviewing Hoffman's adaptation, the general press divided its attention between what was stunning in the quasi-fictional film and what was stupefyingly unacceptable in the historical Tolstoy. A. N. Wilson, in the *Times Literary Supplement*, admires the landscape and the actors, but like Denner laments the fact that "Christopher Plummer is far too genial. (And far too handsome — could not the make-up people have shoved a blob of putty on to Plummer's fine nose?)"[5] About the geniality, Jay Parini, in a post-film interview, appears to agree.[6] It is unfortunate, however, that so few reviewers attend in any detail to Parini's novel or its relation to the film built off it. Wilson plays indirect tribute to that primary written source text — and to the fact that it was composed out of even more primary written texts — in his discussion of the singularly cruel letter that Tolstoy penned on May 13, 1909 and then filed away for his wife to read after he was gone. "The letter is a good example of how the Tolstoys by now conducted many of their deadliest assaults on one another in writing," Wilson notes shrewdly. "They did not want their disagreements to be things of the moment, or their marital rows to evaporate in the air. And one of the comically deft things about the Hoffman film is that in most scenes someone or another is keeping notes, or writing the conversations down. At several points Sofya bursts out in protest or tries to snatch the notebook from the copytaker's hand." Wilson is right, the scenes are both hilarious and unbearable. As Tolstoy pursues his quest for universal love and brotherhood, words are forever being tested and found wanting — but words, especially written-down words, remain the overwhelmingly authoritative medium of choice. And the more they hammer the cosmic ideal in place, the more they document its failure closer to home. "Having spent the first part of his creative life fashioning experience into story," Wilson remarks of the Master, "he spent the second half making his own life into a sort of grotesque parable."

---

[5]     A. N. Wilson, "Despite his faults: Two Cinematic Versions of Late, Great Tolstoy [The Kreutzer Sonata, The Last Station]," *Times Literary Supplement* (February 19, 2010): 17–18, esp. 18.

[6]     See "Interview with Jay Parini" conducted by William Nickell (author of *The Death of Tolstoy: Russia on the Eve, Astapovo Station, 1910* [Cornell University Press, 2010]) in *Tolstoy Studies Journal* XXI (2009): 67–73, esp. 73: "Christopher Plummer is a brilliant, classically trained actor, and he's the right age. And he's got a kind of gravitas and warmth. In fact I think he has a warmth in the film that I somehow doubt that Tolstoy had in real life. To be quite frank, increasingly when I look back at Tolstoy and read him I come to the conclusion that he was a real pill...I was left with the impression, having spent six months rereading Tolstoy last year, that the guy was a pill, and a fairly humorless pill."

This parable was acted out in Yasnaya Polyana — to an incalculably large audience. By his final decade, Tolstoy had become the world's most "imaged" literary celebrity, routinely spied on in the paths and bushes of his estate by reporters with new-fangled recording equipment, the technological miracles of the first media revolution. In the film, this sense of performing live to an instant and rapt international audience is superimposed on the scribbling note-takers of Tolstoy's inner circle. That world had literally become a stage, its men and women players. Perhaps to remind the movie-goer that Tolstoy wanted out of this world but also (like all great reformers and performers in possession of a precious script) wanted readers and spectators to watch him and listen to what he had to say, Wilson devotes a full half-column of his *TLS* review to Tolstoy's "notorious essay" on Shakespeare and on drama. This Elizabethan connection is my bridge from Hoffman's film to more general comments on Tolstoy and the proper stage performance.

One final review will set the scene. In his discussion in *The New Yorker* in December 2009, David Denby discusses *The Last Station* with insight and sympathy. The astonishing Helen Mirren is everywhere praised in this "most emotionally naked work of her movie career," where "she gives poetic form to the madness and the violence of commonplace jealously...letting her age show and still the most sexual actress onscreen." When her husband rises to the bait in the right ways, for a few minutes Sofya Andreyevna lives on; but he is easily her superior in self-control and articulation, so mostly she is undone. "Plummer, who is turning eighty himself, effortlessly suggests largeness of spirit even in foolish old age," Denby writes. "Like a great night at the theater, the two performing demons go at each other full tilt and produce scenes of Shakespearean affection, chagrin, and rage."[7] This is a fine focal point, given Tolstoy's disgust toward Shakespeare as a dramatist.

The best-known part of Tolstoy's polemic against the Bard is his travesty of the plot of *King Lear* that opens his 1903 screed "On Shakespeare and on Drama," later made famous by George Orwell's 1947 essay on it, "Lear, Tolstoy and the Fool."[8] But Tolstoy's dislike had begun decades before, long before

---

[7]   David Denby, "Love Hurts," *The New Yorker* (December 14, 2009): 96–98, esp. 96.

[8]   George Orwell, "Lear, Tolstoy and the Fool" (1947), in *Shooting an Elephant and Other Essays* (New York: Harcourt, Brace & World, 1950), 32–52. Prefiguring the tensions in Hoffman's film, Orwell suggests that Tolstoy's horror at *King Lear* was in part due to its autobiographical resonance (stubborn father, faithful daughter, the rest of the homestead a nest of plotters): "The subject of *Lear* is renunciation...The most impressive event in Tolstoy's life, as in Lear's, was a huge and gratuitous act of renunciation. Lear

that treatise and the family scandals of 1910. Other aspects of Shakespeare repelled Tolstoy more thoroughly than the senseless second-hand plots, of which he found *King Lear* a most sorry example. Tolstoy was an artist. And in his view, what qualified Shakespeare's dramaturgy most of all as "counterfeit art" was its unrelieved eloquence and constant striving for sensational verbal effects. Even when they should be struck dumb with horror, even when on the edge of murdering or strangling others, Shakespeare's characters keep talking, in an uninterrupted string of witty, profound statements. Tolstoy was especially offended by the culminating scene of *Othello*, a work that he otherwise considered one of the Bard's "least bad plays." "Othello's monologue over the sleeping Desdemona, about his desiring her when killed to look as she is alive, about his intending to love her even dead, and now wishing to smell her 'balmy breath,' etc., is utterly impossible. A man who is preparing for the murder of a beloved being does not utter such phrases..."[9]

This remark à propos of the jealous Moor is a good example of what prompted A. N. Wilson, in the paragraphs of his *TLS* review dealing with this inflammatory topic, to call Tolstoy's reading of Shakespeare "grotesquely wrong" (17). It is that, without a doubt. And the short defense, should one wish to mount it, is that Tolstoy did not accept the conventions of Renaissance staging or stage language, its metaphorical extravagance as well as its non-illusionist Choruses and prefatory bards.[10] What feels most wrong in Tolstoy's treatise on Shakespeare, however, is not its opinions, which Tolstoy is free to profess in his own name, but its contempt for others' opinions, its insistence that anyone who reacts otherwise to the English playwright is drugged, hypnotized, duped, in the blind grip of "epidemic suggestion" propagated by a self-serving press, not in his right mind, only pretending to like it. Such a tactic appears to come with the territory of the Tolstoyan personality, and no amount of assumed humility can bleach it out. Tolstoy denies others the dignity of their own reactions on behalf of his

---

renounces his throne but expects everyone to continue treating him as a king. Tolstoy, like Lear, acted on mistaken motives and failed to get the results he had hoped for" (43–45).

9    See "Tolstoy on Shakespeare," by Leo Tolstoy, translated by V. Tchertkoff and I. F. M., Followed by "Shakespeare's Attitude to the Working Classes" by Ernest Crosby and a Letter from G. Bernard Shaw (New York and London: Funk & Wagnalls Company, 1906). No rights reserved, 65–66. Translation slightly adjusted.

10   In his essay "Leo Tolstoy, Subverter of Shakespeare" [«Лев Толстой — ниспровергатель Шекспира»], Alexander Anikst notes correctly that if we turn everything Tolstoy rejects into a positive sign, we have a perfect recipe for Elizabethan theater. Aleksandr Anikst, "Lev Tolstoi — nisprovergatel' Shekspira," *Teatr* 11 (1960): 42–53.

commitment to brotherhood—his deep desire that every mind and body, once cleansed of pollutants, would think and feel as his did—and this vision was a linchpin of his life's work not soon to be dislodged. More genre-specific to his loathing of Shakespearean drama was his belief that lengthy moral self-presentation through words, monologues of inner self-searching, were not appropriate for the stage.

As Tolstoy told Teneromo [Isaak Fainerman] in an interview in 1907, such inward-gazing psychology was the task of novels, not drama. A theater audience would find it "boring, tedious, artificial" [«скучно, нудно, и неестественно»].[11] Thus Tolstoy was not interested in those words, or passages, in Shakespeare that paralleled his own moral searching or echoed his personal ethical stance on power, mortality, fidelity, war. Edmund in *King Lear* on not blaming astrology for our freely-chosen vices, Isabella on political power in *Measure for Measure*, Helena on stubborn active love in *All's Well that Ends Well*, Macbeth on human fate, the soldiers Williams and Bates on war (to their disguised sovereign on the eve of the Battle of Agincourt in *Henry V*, an episode reflected in *War and Peace*), Coriolanus on the vagaries of loyalty, Hubert in *King John* against the murder of princes, Prince Hamlet on fear of death: the content of these magnificent monologues is full of Tolstoyan wisdom, but Tolstoy refuses to register it. It is almost as if he did not hear them—or rather, did not read them, for his acquaintance with Shakespeare was largely through print. He attended live performances rarely, and only to persuade himself that the plays were as bad as he remembered them to be.

Without the psychological insights of the monologues, Shakespeare might indeed seem a sensationalist shell for the "animal in man," the purely *zhivotnoe*. But the ubiquitous lust and violence of Renaissance plots could not have been the only irritant for Tolstoy. As regards on-stage enactment of cruelty, Tolstoy's own play *The Power of Darkness*—in which a newborn child is methodically crushed to death over several minutes—rivals the tortures of *King Lear* or even the mutilations that stud a revenge tragedy like *Titus Andronicus*. (Tolstoy was aware of this vulnerability in his peasant drama and provided a less graphic variant for his fourth act; but he retained the murder taking place in story time). Apparently it is not the violence of the deed itself that is offensive to Tolstoy. Nor are words alone to blame. Tolstoy's non-acceptance of Shakespeare comes to a head over the relationship of words to deeds on stage, over what we might call Tolstoy's sense of the morality

---

[11]  I. Teneromo (1908), "L. N. Tolstoi o teatre" [1907], *Teatr i iskusstvo*, no. 34 (1908): 580–81.

of a performing genre. In certain situations, eloquence cannot go on. At a certain point, deeds must make us mute. Words cannot be allowed to "pretty up" a deed and make it compelling, whether for animalistic reasons or spiritually lofty ones. Matryona is evil in *The Power of Darkness* because she has a smooth, wise-sounding folk saying ready for every situation — just like a Shakespearean Fool, the target of Tolstoy's special scorn.[12] It doesn't matter whether the Fool speaks falsehoods or truths.

Tolstoy's most reliable righteous people are inarticulate: stutterers, bunglers, shy, ill-spoken, like Alyosha the Pot. That the upright old man Akim in *The Power of Darkness* is a stutterer was crucial to Tolstoy. As he wrote in March of 1887 to Pavel Svobodin, the actor in Petersburg's Aleksandriiskii theatre who would be playing Akim: "He speaks with a hesitation, and then suddenly phrases burst out, and then again a hesitation, and 'y'know'...As I see it, it's not necessary to mumble. He walks firmly enough...His motions — his movements — are punctilious; only nimble smooth speech God did not grant him." [«Говорит с запинкой, и вдруг вырываются фразы, и опять запинка и «тае»...Шамкать, мне кажется, не нужно. Ходит твердо;...Приемы — движения — истовые, только речи гладкой Бог не дал».][13] "Smooth speech" of the sort that "God did not give Akim" is the most stage-worthy vehicle for virtue. Perhaps if Shakespeare's jesters and fools were not so "smooth of speech," if they stuttered while walking firmly, they could also be for Tolstoy the vehicle of truth that they are for the rest of the world.

Let me close by returning to a point suggested at the beginning of this Postscript: that for Tolstoy as dramatist — and perhaps for Tolstoy in

---

[12]   One wonders whether Tolstoy's English simply could not grasp the Fool's subtleties — or if, on the contrary, subtlety itself was the problem. In "On Shakespeare and on Drama," Tolstoy expresses his irritation at Lear's "long and high-flown speeches" followed by his habit of summoning his Fool and eliciting his jokes, "notwithstanding the despair he has just manifested." The jokes themselves are not funny, Tolstoy insists, and "besides creating an unpleasant feeling similar to shame, the usual effect of unsuccessful witticisms, they are so drawn out as to be positively dull" (18). George Orwell picked up on this loathing for the Fool, put it in his title, and found it especially worthy of rebuttal: "Tolstoy sees no justification for the presence of the Fool," Orwell writes. [But] "the Fool is integral to the play. He acts not only as a sort of chorus, making the central situation clearer by commenting on it more intelligently than the other characters, but as a foil to Lear's frenzies. His jokes, riddles, and scraps of rhyme...are like a trickle of sanity running through the play." ("Lear, Tolstoy and the Fool," 40).

[13]   Tolstoy on 1887 March 5 to P. M. Svobodin [Kozienko], L. N. Tolstoi, *PSS* t. 64 *Pis'ma* (1953): 24.

general — the truth of a situation was to be found in minds and bodies, not in words. A spectacular application of this hypothesis was tried in a production of *The Realm of Darkness* in 2010, by the Arts Program at Eugene Lang College in New York City.[14] The entire production took place in a tiny interior space, with bleachers for the spectators lining two sides of the room and doors opening out left and right for the players. The crushing of Akulina's illegitimate baby under boards in the cellar was projected in black-and-white on a screen above the audience's head. By the Fifth Act, as Nikita is being driven wild by his own dissoluteness and acts of murder, the audience too begins to feel uncomfortably trapped. To the horror of his smooth-talking mother, Nikita confesses: first to Marinka, then to Akulina, finally to his father. When the police arrive to take Nikita away, father Akim, stuttering ecstatically, begs them to hold off: "God's work is being done, this is no time for your 'dictments...Speak, my child, don't be 'fraid o' people, God, God! He is here!" Nikita willingly submits to being tied up: "It was my idea, my doin'. Take me you know where."[15]

At that point and with that line, Tolstoy's play is over. But the production did not end. As soon as the final words were spoken, the dialogue (and the characters) ricocheted back to the beginning of Nikita's confession to Marinka. Then the final six or eight minutes of Act Five were replayed, perhaps a bit faster, but without change. Again we reached the end; again the action spun back to the critical moment, as if we were caught in a vortex — and the final confession rushed through us again, with an even greater degree of urgency. The audience on the bleachers had no idea when it would end, or how many repetitions it would take. Suddenly the roof opened up. Light poured in, on player and spectator alike. When finally the actors stopped on the final word, the moment of Nikita's full confession and Akim's ecstasy, still they did not release the play. They froze in place, and appeared ready to wait forever. We the spectators didn't know how to get out, or when to get out. Five minutes must have passed before someone looked at her watch and crept down off the bleachers for one of the side doors. Eventually the rest of the spectators picked their way down and out through the statues.

---

14   *The Realm of Darkness*, acting version derived from the Kantor-Tulchinsky translation. Designed and directed by Zishan Ugurlu, literary advisor Inessa Medzhibovskaya. La Mama Ellen Stewart Theater, New York City, March 4–7, 2010.

15   Leo Tolstoy, *The Realm of Darkness*, in *Plays: Volume Two, 1886–1889*. Translated by Marvin Kantor with Tanya Tulchinsky (Evanston: Northwestern University Press, 1996), 1–90, esp. 88–90.

It was a fabulous rendition of Tolstoy's drama, fully in the spirit of its author. It was also squarely in the tradition of Russian drama, where frozen, shocked, or silenced endings are a trademark of moral urgency: the tableau at the end of Gogol's *Government Inspector*, the abandoned holy fool and unresolved chord at the end of Musorgsky's *Boris Godunov*, the announcement of Treplev's suicide at the end of Chekhov's *Seagull*. In this production, Shakespeare's accessible stage and direct appeal to the audience were in full force — for call it what you will, *The Power of Darkness* rises to Shakespearean heights. But there was no fanfare, no verbal adornment. And, of course, no formula to release the audience from the show, or to separate out their world from the pleasant fantasy of a stage. We have (literally) heard all the words before and can now cast them off. Realms of darkness, we were given to believe in this production, will go on forever until the vortex is punctuated with light. And then each member of the audience crawls out alone. Hoffman's film of *The Last Station* is easier on those who watch. It is linear, the performers have a script, the public knows what to do: follow the coffin in a mass procession to the grass-covered grave. But that night downstairs at La Mama, Tolstoy was everywhere.

# 12

# CHEKHOV AND THE ANNAS

*This piece originally appeared in the festschrift* Life and Text. Essays in Honour of Geir Kjetsaa on the Occasion of his 60th Birthday, *edited by Erik Egeberg, Audun J. Mørch, and Ole Michael Selberg (Oslo 1997).*

## CHEKHOV AND THE ANNAS
## (1997)

— Отчего я не сплю по ночам?
— Не знаю, милая. А когда я не сплю по ночам, то закрываю глаза крепко-крепко, вот этак, и рисую себе Анну Каренину, как она ходит и как говорит...
"Невеста"

На этот раз Лаевскому больше всего не понравилась у Надежды Федоровны ее белая, открытая шея и завитушки волос на затылке, и он вспомнил, что Анне Карениной когда она разлюбила мужа, не нравились прежде всего его уши, и подумал: «Как это верно! как верно!»
"Дуэль"

"In *Anna Karenina* and *Evgeny Onegin* not a single question is solved, but they satisfy fully because questions are posed correctly."
Chekhov to Alexei Suvorin, 27 October 1888

How did Chekhov respond to *Anna Karenina*? Most scholarly attention has been devoted to Chekhov's struggle with Tolstoyanism. His early infatuation with Tolstoy's moral precepts was eventually followed by the "counter-stories": "Skučnaja istorija" [A Boring Story] as a more honest reflection of the dying process than "Smert' Ivana Il'iča" [The Death of Ivan Ilyich]; "Mužiki" [Peasants] as the non-sentimentalized picture of peasant life that the aging Tolstoy was reluctant to tell; "Palata No. 6" [Ward No. 6] as the real, ghastly result of non-violent resistance to active evil. Finally, in a number of letters after his return from Sakhalin peaking with the *Kreutzer Sonata* scandals, Chekhov emancipated himself from the Tolstoyan "hypnosis." The usual approach to this evidence has been to trace the struggle between a mature, maximally flexible Chekhov at the height of his powers — and the late, didactic, maximally inflexible Tolstoy, a great writer who had come to distrust many types of art deeply.[1]

This juxtaposition of two "contemporaries in person" (that is, meeting in the same time, although Chekhov was by three decades the younger man) is powerful, but inevitably skewed. My concern in this essay is to look at an earlier wedge of the relationship. For Chekhov also responded to a more tractable Tolstoy, Tolstoy *before* those polemics against art and sex had become so single-minded. This response took the form of a literary "reply" — not to a hardened ideology, but to a masterpiece that the younger writer deeply admired. In at least half-a-dozen stories, all from the 1880s-90s, Chekhov takes on the challenge of the Anna Plot. He recombines its couples, re-accents its themes, alters the timing of its events. Three of the most famous stories — "Dama s sobačkoj," "Anna na šee" and "O ljubvi" — have heroines named Anna. Repeatedly, crucial events take place on or near railway trains. Some involve "first balls" where one falls in and out of love, and others exploit that Tolstoyan moment when a freshly-unloved partner is suddenly seen in a new, less sympathetic way (Karenin's ears that so irritate Anna upon

---

[1] The affected years — when Chekhov acknowledged he was under Tolstoy's influence — were 1882 to 1894. During the initial period, Chekhov produced stories that were direct reflections of Tolstoyan ideology and, as art, rather weak ("Khorošie ljudi," "Niščij," "Kazak," "Pis'mo"); then, after transitional explorations of Tolstoyan ideology in practice (such as "Moja žizn'"), the famous renouncing letters: to Pleshcheev, 15 February 1894, about Tolstoy "out of sheer stubbornness... not taking the time to read two or three pamphlets written by specialists;" and to Suvorin, 27 March 1894, "Tolstoyan morality has ceased to touch me profoundly [it was not the precepts themselves that had affected me but] the way Tolstoy expressed himself, his immense common sense, and, no doubt, a sort of hypnosis. But now something inside me challenges it." For surveys in English see Beverly Hahn, *Chekhov: A Study of the Major Stories and Plays* (Cambridge: Cambridge University Press), ch. 7, "Chekhov and Tolstoy;" Sophie Laffitte, *Chekhov: 1860–1904* (New York: Charles Scribner's Sons, 1971), ch. 18, "Tolstoyan Interlude"; Ronald Hingley, *A Life of Anton Chekhov* (Oxford: Oxford University Press, 1989), ch. 11, "Melikhovo, 1892–97".

her return to Petersburg). All of the stories confront head on that complex of assumptions Tolstoy made about the sinfulness of sexuality — especially Anna's moment of physical "Fall" with Vronsky presented by Tolstoy as shame, nakedness, spiritual death and expulsion from the Garden of Eden.

One comment on methodology. We know that Chekhov sharpened his craftsmanship in the 1870s and 80s by writing a large number of literary parodies — of Gogol, Lermontov, Turgenev, as well as a host of lesser hack writers.[2] Parodies can be respectful, affectionate, dismissive, abusive, but whatever the intent, an author can embed references to an earlier authoritative plot in several ways. Easiest (and most comic) is to have fictional characters in distress make reference to the earlier canonized plot, hoping thereby to escape responsibility for their own shoddy intentions or behavior by identifying a famous prototype. Such, for example, is Laevsky's famous remark in "The Duel" about his mistress Nadezhda Fyodorovna's white neck and curls reminding him of Anna Karenina's distaste for her husband's ears; or, in "The Bride" [Nevesta], Nina Ivanovna's remark to her daughter Nadia that, during bouts of insomnia, she comforts herself by thinking how Anna Karenina walks and talks. More difficult, surely, is to sustain a retell of the prior narrative throughout the entire newly-authored plot, re-accenting it at multiple points and questioning the entire reasonable basis or moral integrity of that earlier world. In his Anna stories, I believe, Chekhov took on this larger task. But in addition to testing Tolstoy, these tales provide another service: they illustrate various ways by which prose writers can achieve a "realistic effect."

One route to realism is that of the 19th-century mega-novelist. This was the way of Dickens, Balzac, Trollope, George Eliot, Tolstoy: pile up detail, fill in the landscape, saturate the reader with author's commentary, narrator's insights, characters' perspectives or potentials. But working in the short form, Chekhov had no space or time for that. How might a realistic sense of breadth and multiple options — the sense of a genuinely open world — be realized in a compact form? Not wishing bulk, such writers could still achieve that "open effect" by eroding or undermining a stereotype. Chekhov could use *Anna Karenina* in this way because Tolstoy's famous novel, by the 1880s, had become an "infidelity stereotype." The briefest invocation of its story, via easily recognized motifs (black curls, squinting eyes, prominent ears, trains), could set the stage for an estrangement or a re-emphasis of the

---

[2]  See Karl D. Kramer, *The Chameleon and the Dream: The Image of Reality in Čexov's Fiction* (The Hague: Mouton, 1970), ch. II, "Literary Parodies," 28–48.

plot. This new, barely sketched-in world would then *suggest* options without having to prescribe them or exhaustively fill them in. Such a suggestion of alternative fates for a familiar, given set of character-relations could be seen as a re-novelization (in Bakhtin's sense) of Tolstoy's canonized plot — and thus, paradoxically, Chekhov's modest short-story variants could be seen to enact the "spirit of the novel" *on* a novel.

With this dynamic in mind, let us consider some stories. Each takes on one large, stubborn aspect of the mature Tolstoyan worldview. But it is Tolstoy mediated through a mid-career novel where that worldview is not yet ossified (as it will be for the narrator of *Resurrection*) — where it is still, as it were, softer cartilage, subject to the malleability and tenderness of competing interpretations. Chekhov, so great a master at the malleable and the tender in human relations, opens Tolstoy's novel up to new confusions and compassions. Konstantin Levin might not have been so lucky. Anna's terrible denouement might be avoided. There will be a price, of course, for doing so, for suicide is an elegant one-way gesture and splendid closure; but that too is part of Chekhov's re-novelization. Chekhov and Tolstoy had different ideas about closing things down.

The simplest and most lapidary re-write of the Anna plot, one could argue, is the 1886 story "Neščast'e" [A Calamity]. The story, told from the woman's point of view, is packed with trains, with flirtations around train stations, and features an unresponsive husband as well as a child who suddenly appears disappointingly graceless to the mother in the afterglow of an illicit preliminary tryst. The heroine, Sofya Petrovna, married and with a daughter, has been pursued for some time by the lawyer Ilyin. His helpless, humiliating passion for her eventually wears her down and simultaneously arouses her. By the end of the story she is driven to seek him out, driven by something "сильнее и стыда ее, и разума, и страха..." [stronger than shame, or reason, or fear]. That something is lust, and in this physiological sketch Dr. Chekhov arguably administers to Tolstoy a lesson in ordinary female sexuality and its strategies of fulfillment. Its counter-scene in the novel is Anna's "fall" with Vronsky, described melodramatically and morbidly, or perhaps the later Pozdnyshev's bizarre insistence that women instinctively dislike the carnal relation. To be sure, Sofya Petrovna is not proud of her behavior (to that extent the story unfolds under the star of Tolstoy); she is disgusted by her own duplicity, condemns herself for this frivolous behavior so injurious to her vanity, and is forced to acknowledge her ordinariness. Consummation of the affair with Ilyin, which lies just beyond the boundaries of the story, is not heroic, sacrificial, suicidal — all Anna Karenina motifs;

it is quite possible, Chekhov suggests, to consummate and to go on living, perhaps more honestly than before.

One subtext to the title "Neščast'e" might be Tolstoy's early work "Semejnoe sčast'e," also written by a man from a woman's perspective. But with this important inversion: Tolstoy's tale ends precisely where the family unit — with its disillusions, displacements and the obligations of parenting — claims total rights. Chekhov's story is not "семейное" at all, but rather a serious treatment of the one thing Tolstoy (who was endlessly interested in his own sexual behavior) so often manages to evade — female desire and all its embarrassing dynamics: seduction, shame, cowardice, curiosity, temporary resistance and ultimate acquiescence. In *Anna Karenina*, the train and its murderous potential had put a glorious, tragic stamp on the heroine's whole ruined life. In Chekhov's understated "Calamity," train imagery makes the heroine not demonic, tragic, operatic, but simply ordinary, like everyone else, precisely not a novelistic heroine. When Sofya Petrovna first hears, during her flirtation with Ilyin, the "сиплый...свист локомотива" [the hoarse whistle of the locomotive], it does not signify the high symmetrical poetry of *Anna Karenina*, where a fatal train accident early in the novel prefigures what a frantic Anna "knows she must do" at the end. In Chekhov, it remains the random sound of a "товарный поезд," a freight train. This whistle brings her to her senses; for it is, as Chekhov writes, the "extraneous, cold sound of everyday prose" [посторонний холодный звук обыденной прозы]. Chekhov's "Neščast'e" — and the title may or may not be ironic — is the story of a genuinely prosaic, not a poetic, consummation.

Is this a good or bad thing, Sofya Petrovna's "fall?" Chekhov does not pass judgment; Sofya does enough of that on herself. "Neščast'e" triggered widely disparate opinions in the Russian press. How wonderfully you are able to express love "in all its most subtle and sacred manifestations," Grigorovich wrote to Chekhov in December 1880; Bilibin, on the other hand, was moved to remark à propos of the story: "To hell with the whole poetic side of love!"[3] Our next re-write is very much in Bilibin's spirit, namely, the Anna plot in a totally cynical key.

That story, written in 1895, is one of Chekhov's darkest: "Anna na šee" [Anna Round the Neck]. Here too we have trains (the bride and groom first know each other physically in a couchette); here too we have a radiant heroine at her first ball, and the world of love contrasted with the world of grey

---

[3]  For these letters, see the commentary to the story in A. P. Chekhov, *Собрание сочинений в 12-и томах* (Moscow: 1961), 4:550–51.

officialdom. But the Anna Petrovna of the opening pages, married at 18 to pompous Modest Alexeich who is over twice her age, already resembles — on her wedding day — Tolstoy's Anna at the end of the novel, a woman in moral decline. Chekhov has chosen an intriguing starting point. For one of the fascinating, surely calculated lacunae in Tolstoy's very long *Anna Karenina* is its almost total silence on Anna as newlywed. What little we hear comes late in the novel and tucked into Alexei Karenin's story, already hopelessly alienated from the consciousness of the heroine. Whether or not the Karenin marriage was a "good" one when we meet it (and marriages can be good, self-respecting and self-sustaining, without being passionate) is still much debated. But how did it start out? We eventually learn that Anna Oblonskaya was beautiful but not a profitable match; that Karenin had visited her often enough to make a proposal the proper thing to do; but of the drive or curiosity of love, marital or extramarital, we are told nothing. In contrast to that shrouded pre-history, Chekhov's just-married Anya is all drive and curiosity. She flirts with Artynov straightaway at the railway station, coquettishly "screwing up her eyes" [прищурила глаза], whereas Anna Karenina, we recall, begins this practice only in her final months of self-deception. When Tolstoy's Anna Arkadievna acts this way, we sense tragedy, her need to screen out the truth. Chekhov's Anna Petrovna is incapable of tragedy. Except for the leitmotif of her alcoholic father and two pathetic brothers, all increasingly distanced from Anya's life and eventually forgotten, there are no victims in the story at all. Chekhov's fictional world is morally akin to Tolstoy's Petersburg, peopled entirely with Sappho Stolzes and Betsy Tverskaias. Indifferent to fidelity, to family, and to love, all parties are satisfied — including, of course, the betrayed husband, who uses his wife to rise in the service. There is more than a hint here of Russian high society during Pushkin's earlier, unabashedly licentious era, far more "French" and dry-eyed about sexual access and calculated liaisons. To be sure, Anna Petrovna's self-serving behavior is perhaps better justified than the empty-headed antics of Sappho Stolz. But that we can never know for sure, because Tolstoy was quite unable to tell any neutral stories from the perspective of the likes of Sappho — any more than he could have related Sofya Petrovna's "fall" in the Chekhovian manner of "Neščast'e," that is, from within that woman's own frustrated, hungry and fed-up zone. Chekhov specializes in just such "speech from within the zone."[4]

---

[4]     Writing in the afterglow of the great tendentious novelists, Chekhov was quite canny in his defense of this "objective" prerogative. For him, presenting characters in their own voice and value zone was not only efficient; it was also more authentically ethical. See

In "Anna Round the Neck," the lowest point in the heroine's marriage is reached right before her success at the ball. She is poor (although she had been married for the money), unfree, unloved. Chekhov tells us that Anna Petrovna's husband reminded her of all those oppressive authorities who, "with an insinuating and terrible force, moving in on her like a storm cloud or a locomotive, were ready to crush her" [как туча или локомотив, готовый задавить]. That is the Tolstoyan Anna's recurring bad dream, but this Anna will confront it and overcome it. The morning after the social triumph that insures her independence, she greets her husband with "подите прочь, болван!" [Out of my sight, you fool!]. And we learn that Anna Petrovna finally feels free: the "ancient terror before that force, which moved in on her and threatened to crush her, now seemed to her ridiculous" [казался ей смешным].

But is this really a triumph, is there no external reminder of the ethical dimension? In Tolstoy's novel the moral measurement is always family — and usually children. Anna's young son Seryozha feels awkward around Vronsky, not knowing Vronsky's role in the household but sensing his mother's passionate awareness of him; more importantly, Anna and Vronsky feel guilty around Seryozha, for he (Tolstoy tells us) is the compass showing them how far they have strayed off course. In Chekhov's tale, family is either shoved out of the picture altogether (her drunken father and anxious younger brothers, with their refrain, "Папочка, не надо..." [Papa, don't]), growing ever more faint, or else the idea of family and children is parodied grotesquely on the bodies of the married couple. The "Anna" that the wife becomes around Modest Alexeich's neck and the "little Vladimir" to which his Excellency is to stand godfather are state decorations. Chekhov is giving us a picture of the high-society world as it *should* run — according to the values of, say, Madame Vronskaia, who belongs wholly to that world and behaves obediently within it. As she sees her devastated son off to the wars, you recall, Madame Vronskaia remarks of Anna Karenina's suicide: "But why,

---

the letter to Alexei Suvorin (1 April 1890): "You upbraid me about objectivity, styling it indifference to good and evil, absence of ideals and ideas, etc. You would have me say, in depicting horse thieves, that stealing horses is an evil. But then, that has been known a long while, even without me. Let jurors judge them; for my business is only to show them as they are...Why, in order to depict horse thieves in seven hundred lines I must constantly speak and think as they do and feel in keeping with their spirit; otherwise, if I add a pinch of subjectivity, the images will become diffuse and the story will not be as compact as it behooves all short stories to be. When I write, I rely fully on the reader..." Cited from *Letters of Anton Chekhov*, selected and edited by Avrahm Yarmolinsky (New York: Viking, 1978), 133.

I ask you, all these desperate passions? Whatever you say, she was a bad woman: ruined herself and two splendid men." Chekhov's Anya will never have that sin on her conscience.

In our final two rewrites, the entrapment of the Chekhovian hero and heroine is presented with more redeeming moral features. While still incapable of big, tasteless, desperate action, the men and women involved in these plots do not entirely give up, nor do they give in; and thus the stories are among Chekhov's most haunting masterpieces. The first (and perhaps most famous of all the Anna tales) is the story of Anna Sergeyevna and Dmitri Gurov in "Dama s sobačkoj" [Lady with a Pet Dog]. Here too, we have our share of trains and theaters, but there is none of the clinical coldness of "Neščast'e" or "Anna na šee." "Dama s sobačkoj" is a genuine love story, one of the world's greatest, in which Chekhov mixes Tolstoyan prototypes, and at times Tolstoyan diction, to achieve a new perspective on adultery and responsibility.

The plot everyone knows. But what about the human material, if measured against Tolstoyan character-types? Gurov resembles a Vronsky, or perhaps an Oblonsky, and Anna Sergeyevna is a timid, inexperienced Kitty. But there is this important difference at the outset: neither Gurov nor Anna Sergeyevna are free (both have Karenin-like spouses). Also, neither expects nor is prepared for the abiding seriousness of their affair. One way to read this seriousness is to see the first two chapters — up to Anna Sergeyevna's departure, on a train, for home, and Gurov's plans to leave Yalta for Moscow soon after — as written in the voice zone of a young Vronsky or Oblonsky, from the light philandering perspective of an experienced male on "ты" [thou] with his girl while she is still on a tremulous "вы" [you] with him. Chapter 2 concludes one sort of infidelity plot, a "serial" structured to repeat, but not to grow more profound, with a new cast. But then comes the second half of the story. Chapters 3 and 4 witness real love that grows unexpectedly out of this stereotypical beginning — much as Anna and Vronsky's love had become creative, expansive, and "real" by the mid-parts of Tolstoy's novel. The dependencies are now mutual. Gurov tracks Anna Sergeyevna down in the city of S., after which she begins to come to Moscow. A rhythm is established that reflects a deep, and deepening, fidelity. The story ends on the word "начинается," beginning. This inconclusive ending is perhaps a type of tragedy, but with no tragic climax or closure — and its very stability becomes a moral achievement.

The key to the change worked on Tolstoy's worldview comes at the end of the story, with Gurov's meditations en route to the Slaviansky Bazaar where Anna is waiting. As he walks, he explains how thunder works to his daughter; in his thoughts he is elsewhere. His ruminations concern a human being's inevitably "double life," the fact that the way we act in the world is not what we are. Gurov concludes that this is a very good thing, for "каждое личное сосуществование держится на тайне" [every personal co-existence is sustained on a secret]. The whole binary tone of the passage, with its frequent repetitions of phrase, recalls Tolstoy's style — but the moral is purely Chekhovian. For Tolstoy, the secret could not be wholly sustained; sooner or later there would be an integration between inner and outer. The false life would have to be brought into line with the true life before a spiritual epiphany could occur (what Ivan Ilyich glimpses before death, or Konstantin Levin experiences at the end of the novel). The Tolstoyan self, in this resembling the Tolstoyan image of humanity, strives toward wholeness. Like poor Anna Karenina, that self wishes to "have it all" — lover, son, social respect, constant access to the beloved, unchanging and unaging beauty. When Anna cannot have it all, she self-destructs. The Chekhovian self is far more modestly constituted. Its credo is not self-perfection and self-completion but rather the lesson (dear to Turgenev as well) taught by those sea waves on the Oreanda beach: the "шум моря" [noise or humming of the sea], which displays an indifference to the life and death of each of us and thus holds out the promise of our salvation. In Tolstoy, indifference and compromise could never bring salvation. And thus the inadequate, makeshift, purely private and secret structures that sustain true love in "Dama s sobačkoj" could not, for Tolstoy, be an acceptable moral resolution.

The final entry in this pantheon of Anna rewrites is, to my mind, the deepest and most perfect: "O ljubvi" [About Love], the third story in Chekhov's 1898 "Malen'kaja trilogija." The story is Alyokhin's account of his unconsummated passion for Anna Alexeyevna, wife of his friend Luganovich. It is framed by his confession, years later, that his failure to consummate this love was probably a mistake. Allusions to Tolstoy's cast of characters are everywhere, but this cast is scrambled, differently matched up, ill-served by life's timing. The basic realignment is as follows. In "O ljubvi" a Levin and a Kitty fall in love — both decent, modest, proper people, committed to responsible behavior — but *after* she has married someone else. This is the plot that might well have happened in Tolstoy's novel if Tolstoy had not so conveniently taken Kitty out of circulation (ill from Vronsky's jilt of her, she was sent to a spa abroad) until his alter-ego and author's pet, Konstantin Levin, had time to recover from his pout over her rejection of him — if, that is, Kitty had married someone else before Levin could get back to her. Chekhov's Alyokhin carries many of Levin's traits and virtues (his patronymic is Konstantinovich): he is a loner, an intellectual turned farmer, an "educated man rushing about and working hard in the country." He falls in love with Luganovich's wife, and she with him. But, being neither Anna Kareninas nor Vronskys, not possessing that heroic initiating power that breaks through to its desired object regardless of cost — they continue, over several years, to "do the right thing," which is to do nothing.

Irritations and tensions increase, to their mutual distress. Alyokhin cannot speak of his love because of his code of honor (Levin's circle, after all, is not Vronsky's); Anna Alexeyevna cannot speak of love because, as Chekhov put it, "she would either have to lie, or tell the truth, and in her position both would be equally inappropriate and terrible." There is insufficient selfishness at work here to launch the Anna plot. What energy there is, is employed to fight against that plot, in the larger interest of kindness and prior commitments. Thus they are spared Anna's and Vronsky's terrible denouement. But "O ljubvi" still ends on a train scene — and it is for the reader to judge whether this scene is a victory or a defeat. In the coach, saying farewell, they finally confess their love. Relating the story years later, Alyokhin remembers this parting with bitter pain. "When you love," he concludes, "in your reasoning about that love you must proceed from something higher and more important than happiness or unhappiness, sin or virtue in their usual sense, or you must not reason at all."

"…Или не нужно рассуждать вовсе" [or you must not reason at all]: a more non-Tolstoyan maxim could hardly be imagined for a story about extra-marital love. What makes "O ljubvi" such a fine reworking of Tolstoy? Not only does its programmatic title evoke Tolstoy's own preemptory titles for his didactic essays — "O vojne," [On war], "O religii" [On religion] "Tak čto že nam delat'?" [What then must we do?], "Čto takoe iskusstvo?" [What is art?]; also, it challenges the whole crafty enterprise of Tolstoy as "prosaicist." For several years now, Gary Saul Morson has been elaborating on the prosaic values, virtues and plots in Tolstoy.[5] Tolstoy's prosaic heroes are the unheroic ones, Morson argues, the ones who live without melodrama, without fixed or noisy rules, but with strongly disciplined mental and moral habits. Bad things do happen to these heroes,

---

[5]     Two prime texts for Tolstoyan prosaics are Gary Saul Morson, *Hidden in Plain View: Narrative and Creative Potentials in "War and Peace"* (Stanford: Stanford University Press, 1987), esp. ch. 5 and 7; and Gary Saul Morson, "Prosaics and *Anna Karenina*," in *Tolstoy Studies Journal* I (1988): 1–12.

to be sure — Levin loses his Kitty in the first few chapters — but they suffer through misfortune in all the right, small ways, just as Anna Alexeyevna and Alyokhin do in "O ljubvi." They remain kind, they attend to particulars, they resist inflating their moods, they know how to take their pleasure in healthy distractions like hunting, farming, nursing the sick. And in Tolstoy's world — here is the point I wish to stress — good things come to them. Awkward, rebuffed Levin gets his Kitty, even though he had stupidly interrupted his initial courtship and fled Moscow, confusing all parties; that glorious moment comes when he enters the Oblonsky drawing room and realizes that Kitty (still free, fresh, flushed) is "waiting for him alone." This is a prosaicist's paradise, and Gary Saul Morson is certainly correct in saying that Tolstoy was drawn to it. In his fiction, Tolstoy plots this world carefully. He teases his Konstantin Levin and sets him back, but in the end, since Levin so completely embodies his author's most cherished values, Tolstoy sees to it that the good things come.

It took a very different sort of writer, one without Tolstoy's stubborn instinct for the moral shape of plots, to show the truly dark side of a virtuous prosaics. We have such a writer in Anton Chekhov, and — as I have tried to suggest — in Chekhov's various reworkings of the Anna Plot. Alyokhin and Anna Alexeyevna act like virtuous Levins and Kittys, and the good things do *not* come. This is not a question of Chekhov being a "pessimist" and Tolstoy a singer of nature, in whose works (more life-like than life itself) "things happen naturally." Nothing could have been easier, more prosaically normal, in Tolstoy's novel than to enact the "O ljubvi" plot: that is, to have Kitty — an attractive princess and prime marriage material — already recovered and married by the time Levin's hurt pride was healed. After all, if she fell in love with a Vronsky, she could easily fall for another man of his omnipresent sort. Tolstoy will not allow that to happen.

Chekhov, however, will allow it to happen — and this is what makes reading Chekhov so terribly real, and so very sad. Chekhov understood how virtuous prosaic living often turned out: a muddle, a mess, full of casual mistimings that become permanent tragedies, at times even denying people a decent memory by which to organize psychological material. For Tolstoy, prosaic values, "living right" minute by minute, simply *had* to work out — and he would fabricate all manner of authorial scaffolding to pair off the good folks and reward them. Even the unsung Dolly loves her ridiculous Oblonsky and continues to bear, nurse, raise, and bury his children throughout the novel, thus confirming her in her own best self until a passing comment from the author at the very end hints that she has finally, perhaps, had enough. Tolstoy might appear "realistic" and "non-romantic" in his focus on the small and decent gesture. But then Tolstoy makes certain that this gesture does not just get lost, or disintegrate, or pass unnoticed, or cause pain. That is Chekhov's terrain.[6] Chekhov is full of people who do their best — but this does not deter him from casting his heroes and heroines back onto more helpless, weaker, altogether less rewarded sides of themselves. As Chekhov outgrew Tolstoy throughout the 1890s, he re-created out of those satisfying Tolstoyan plots smaller and more compromised survivors. In so doing Chekhov does not satisfy us less; but he does lay out for us the parameters of his distinctive type of comedy, which baffled Tolstoy until the end.

---

[6]    Relevant here are the comments on Chekhov's use of the "idea" in the final chapter of A. P. Chudakov's still unsurpassed *Chekhov's Poetics*. Chudakov argues that the idea as such — say, love — is not dogmatically developed in Chekhov's aesthetics, whether within a single consciousness or spread out along an entire plot. Unlike Dostoevsky and Tolstoy, ideas do not become more true the more wholly they are carried to their extreme ("As a matter of principle his ideas are not developed to their fullest"). Rather, their "truth" is always concrete, punctuated with interruption and shaped by the palpable details of everyday living. What matters for Chekhov is not so much the idea in itself as the "field of its existence" that constrains and shapes it. This principle results in a special sort of modesty vis-à-vis ideological resolution in general and the private lives of the protagonists in particular. Chekhov need not command any higher synthesizing vision, nor does he necessarily have access to the inner private worlds of his heroes (what, for example, Gurov lives by in his secret life). Tolstoy would never relinquish that knowledge. See A. P. Chudakov, *Chekhov's Poetics*, trans. Edwina Jannie Cruise & Donald Dragt (Ann Arbor: Ardis, 1983), 191–216, esp. 192, 201.

# III

# MUSICALIZING
# THE LITERARY CLASSICS
## Musorgsky, Tchaikovsky,
## Shostakovich, Prokofiev

13. *Foreword to Richard Taruskin's* Essays on Musorgsky (1993)

14. *From* Boris Godunov *to* Khovanshchina (1988)

15. *Review of Tumanov on Maria Olenina-d'Alheim* (2002)

16. *Tchaikovsky's Tatiana* (1998)

17. *Little Operas to Pushkin's* Little Tragedies (2003)

18. *Playbill to Prokofiev's* War and Peace *at the Met* (2002)

19. *Shostakovich's* Lady Macbeth of Mtsensk (2004)

20. *Princeton University's* Boris Godunov (2007)

21. Eugene Onegin *and the Stalinist Stage* (2008)

# 13

# FOREWORD TO RICHARD TARUSKIN'S ESSAYS ON MUSORGSKY

---

*The entry below initially appeared in 1993, as a Foreword to a book of ground-breaking essays on Modest Musorgsky by Richard Taruskin (*Musorgsky: Eight Essays and an Epilogue *[Princeton: Princeton University Press, 1993]). At the time Taruskin was the foremost authority on Russian music in the Western world; by now (2010) he has become foremost in several other areas as well. To his writings and generous mentorship I owe my education in this Russian composer.*

---

## EXCERPTS FROM THE FOREWORD TO RICHARD TARUSKIN, *MUSORGSKY: EIGHT ESSAYS AND AN EPILOGUE* (1993)

In 1839, the year of Musorgsky's birth, the Marquis de Custine made a three-month journey through the Russian Empire. The travel account he published four years later, *La Russie en 1839*, became an international bestseller; to this day, fairly or no, it is read as a key to that country's most grimly persistent cultural traits.[1] Astolphe de Custine (1790–1857) was an aristocrat from a family ravaged by the French Revolution. Nevertheless, he came to view the Russian absolute autocracy (and the cunning, imitative, servile subjects it bred and fostered) as far more deceitful and potentially

---

[1] See the reprint edition of the first (anonymously translated) English version of 1843, The Marquis de Custine, *Empire of the Czar: A Journey through Eternal Russia* (New York: Anchor-Doubleday, 1989). Quotations in this essay occur on pp. 600, 109, and 206 respectively. George Kennan has called *La Russie en 1839* "not a very good book about Russia in 1839" but "an excellent book, probably in fact the best of books, about the Russia of Joseph Stalin" (George F. Kennan, *The Marquis de Custine and His Russia in 1839* [Princeton: Princeton University Press, 1971], 124).

dangerous than the more straightforward instability his family had known at home. As chief historical culprit Custine named Peter the Great, who, "paying no respect to time," had thrust Western forms so precipitously onto his barbaric homeland that organic maturation had become almost impossible.

And yet the Russian sense of time fascinated him. Contemplating the austerity and earnestness of Tsar Peter, Custine wrote:· "In Russia at that time, everything was sacrificed to the future; everyone was employed in building the palaces of their yet unborn masters...There is certainly a greatness of mind evidenced in this care which a chieftain and his people take for the power, and even the vanity, of the generations that are yet to come...It is a disinterested and poetical sentiment, far loftier than the respect which men and nations are accustomed to entertain for their ancestors."

The Marquis de Custine was unjust in many of his judgments, but on this point he was right. Imperial Russia — and especially its capital, St. Petersburg — was heavily mortgaged to future glory. This appetite was reflected in all the arts. In the 1840s and 1850s, sentimentally optimistic historical drama was extremely popular on the Russian stage; from the 1860s on, in a flush of patriotic feeling occasioned by the Great Reforms and later fed by emergent Pan-Slavism, Rimsky-Korsakov and many lesser talents were turning these dramas into historical operas inspired by both socially progressive and statist-expansionist historiography. Even that small band of gifted, contentious autodidacts making up the "New Russian School of Music" (the *Moguchaya kuchka* or "mighty little heap") was not immune to the call for a great and forward-looking Russia. The patriotic ideology of Serov's 1865 opera *Rogneda* had much in common with Glinka's founding text of thirty years before, *A Life for the Tsar*.

One member of the Nationalist School, however, remained consistently outside this understanding of empire and historical progress. Where other composers of his generation celebrated integration and grandeur, he was at his best breaking things down, isolating Russian leaders from the people they aspired to lead and denying historical effectiveness to both sides. He invited his audience to laugh as well as to weep at the broken parts; and his special talent, it seemed, was to juxtapose estranged social classes so that maximal confrontation produced minimal communication. Because his creative personality underwent major (but usually well-masked) shifts throughout his short life, the most painstaking scholarly energy and insider's knowledge is required to reconstruct the musical and extra-musical context for his works. It is this fully illuminated story that Richard Taruskin, in the path-breaking essays collected here, unfolds around Modest Musorgsky, Russia's greatest national composer.

Musorgsky's vision was neither populist nor imperial. He granted the people no special virtues. Nor was Musorgsky a Hegelian; he doubted that the passing of time in itself could assure to any nation victory. In 1872, several weeks into the gala celebrations marking the bicentennial of Peter the Great's birth, he wrote to Vladimir Stasov: "The power of the black earth will make itself manifest when you plow it to the very bottom... At the end of the seventeenth century they plowed Mother Russia with just *such* [alien] tools... And she, our beloved, received the various bureaucrats, who never gave her, the long-suffering one, time to collect herself and to think, '*Where are you pushing me?*'... '*We've gone forward*'—you lie. '*We haven't moved!*' Paper, books have gone forward—we *haven't moved*... The people groan, and so as not to groan they drink like the devil, and groan worse than ever: *haven't moved!*"[2]

Anyone familiar with Musorgsky scholarship will sense how embarrassing this piece of epistolary evidence could be for the received image of the composer, both in Russia and abroad. Musorgsky the *narodnik* or radical populist, Musorgsky the rebellious anti-establishment figure and singer of the Russian folk—these were obligatory epithets in the civic-minded 1860s and 1870s as well as during the Soviet era. Along with this political correctness came the image of Musorgsky as a latter-day holy fool: the tragic and seedy figure in Repin's famous portrait, an amateur of genius who was also, alas, an alcoholic, a man who in his lucid moments jotted down raw, unconsidered masterpieces—in short, a creator not in control of his own significance. At the base of both images is the same assumption: that Musorgsky remained, throughout his life, a contrary child. Thus the composer is not perceived as having developed through his own disciplined, consciously creative choice. He is explained as naively spontaneous or as politically "oppressed" — and everywhere he is seen as a man in opposition to the institutions and traditions that surrounded him, rarely an integral part of them. The most enduring virtue of Taruskin's work, perhaps, is its reconquest of a wider, healthier, more complexly intelligent image of Musorgsky. As a musician Musorgsky was indeed deficient in some areas

---

2    Letter from Musorgsky to Vladimir Stasov, 16/22 June 1872, in *The Musorgsky Reader: A Life of Modeste Petrovich Musorgsky in Letters and Documents*, ed. and trans. Jay Leyda and Sergei Bertensson (New York: Da Capo New York, 1970), 185–86.

of technique, and he was clearly a man of unappealing prejudices. He was also, however, a fastidious craftsman open to multiple influences, flexible on many occasions but equally distinguished by a principled stubbornness.

[...]

Taruskin opens his book not on the big known operas but on tiny, more peripheral matters: the dating of two versions of an early, relatively unfamiliar song ("Little Star"); the grounding of Musorgsky's unfinished experiment in realistic recitative, a setting of Gogol's *Marriage*, in the neoclassical mimetic theories of art of Georg Gottfried Gervinus; the composer's relationship with the then-celebrated, now-forgotten Alexander Serov. In so doing Taruskin liberates both his hero and his reader from the anachronistic temptations of a later fame and places Musorgsky back into the thick of the 1860s, where he was a minor and eccentric figure still very much in search of his own voice. Chapters 4 through 7, the book's inner core, give us the Musorgsky corpus we know best and love most, *Boris Godunov* and *Khovanshchina*. But beware: Taruskin's revisions of received wisdom are many and profound. Among the most significant are his insistence on the integrity and autonomy of the two authorial versions of *Boris*; his refusal to endorse the image of Musorgsky as martyr and its concomitant "myth of the malign directorate [that is, the Imperial Theaters]"; his uncovering of historiographical subtexts for the final Kromy scene in *Boris* that detach it ideologically from mass scenes in other contemporaneous operas; his account of the weirdly complex, counterintuitive origins of the folk songs in *Boris*, in particular the famous *Slava!*. Most provocative of all is a bold reading of *Khovanshchina* that, contrary to the reformist spirit of the sixties and despite its populist-sounding subtitle, defines this second historical opera as the precise opposite of a progressive "musical folk drama." Heretically and persuasively, Taruskin classifies *Khovanshchina* as an "aristocratic tragedy informed by pessimistic historiography." One wishes that the Marquis de Custine could have seen a performance of the opera thus construed; he would have rejoiced.

Chapter 8 on *Sorochintsy Fair* takes as its starting point the ambivalent moral and political message underlying Nikolai Gogol's contribution to Russian opera. Taruskin — again against the conventional grain — suggests that Gogol's Ukrainian tales, massively popular as sources for potential libretti, were permeated by the same retrograde, non-progressive, implicitly imperialist brand of folklore that came powerfully back into vogue in the

1860s through the efforts of opera composers such as Alexander Serov.[3] En route to *Sorochintsy Fair*, Musorgsky's talent evolved from extremist-realist recitative to so-called "rationally justified" melody of the *Khovanshchina* sort, where folk melody marked the identity not of persons but of groups and moods — in short, a return to the world of romantic *narodnost'*, folk nationalism. Did this conservative turn in Musorgsky's musical thinking bespeak a larger and less attractive conservatism in other realms? That question is addressed in the opening and closing chapters of the outer frame, where the politics of Modest Musorgsky are deftly pre- and post-figured.

This outer frame displays a satisfying structural symmetry. Taruskin's Introduction, "Who Speaks for Musorgsky?", focuses on what we might call, echoing the opera, "*Stasovshchina*," the *-shchina* suffix referring to distortions, however well-meant, brought on by the pervasive, possessive meddling of Vladimir Stasov both during and after the composer's life. Stasov's grim rectitude is contrasted with the more aristocratic and "decadent" intimacy that Musorgsky achieved with Count Arseny Golenishchev-Kutuzov, poet for several of Musorgsky's most inspired songs and later a high-ranking official at the imperial court. The tension between the composer's "aristocratic inclinations and *kuchkist* pose" is thus set up from the start, not to be resolved until the end of the eighth chapter.[4]

But does Taruskin resolve this tension? In the Epilogue, he notes with pleasure the fact that Musorgsky, whose jubilee decade (1981–89) loosely overlapped the *glasnost'* years, is now no longer routinely "Stasovized." To be sure, in the Russian context this has not meant that he was depoliticized, nor that his image was released to seek its own free-wheeling, contradictory stability. "So far from the proto-Soviet populist of old," Taruskin writes of this era that so eagerly dethroned precursors to communism, "he was now to be consecrated as the grim prophet of the Soviet tyranny." This inversion has occasioned some peculiar, quite fanciful inventions, most noticeably the Christianization of Musorgsky's operas and worldview. But in that, too, Taruskin sees the healthy first steps toward genuine cultural pluralism.

---

[3]    For more extensive development of Serov's pivotal role in Russian musical culture, see Taruskin's massive *Opera and Drama in Russia as Preached and Practiced in the 1860s* (Ann Arbor: UMI Research Press, 1981), especially chapters 2–4.

[4]    It is worth noting that the animus against Golenishchev-Kutuzov, and a defensive dismissal of his memoirs of Musorgsky, is still alive and well among Soviet trained musicologists, even those publishing in the West. See the intemperate preface in Alexandra Orlova, ed. and compiler, *Musorgsky Remembered* (Bloomington: Indiana University Press, 1991), x–xii.

Of course, Musorgsky's own artistic intent should be recuperated under conditions of optimal scholarly freedom. But those documented intentions need not constrain later competing interpretations of the work.

The Russian literary scholar Mikhail Bakhtin put this point well in his discussion of the artistic potential of great works. "Neither Shakespeare himself nor his contemporaries knew that 'great Shakespeare' whom we know now," Bakhtin wrote. "There is no possibility of squeezing our Shakespeare into the Elizabethan epoch...The author is captive of his epoch, of his own present. Subsequent times liberate him from this captivity."[5] Taruskin concurs: "The works are ours now, not Musorgsky's." And thus we have Taruskin's goal in this collection of essays, one he has vigorously pursued in other forums where questions of musical authenticity are debated: "to inform choice, not delimit it."

To return, in closing, to the Marquis de Custine. In 1839 he was negatively impressed by the imitativeness, regimentation, and frivolity of Russian efforts in the realm of culture. "The Russians have not yet reached the point of civilization at which there is real enjoyment of the arts," he wrote from St. Petersburg. "At present their enthusiasm on these subjects is pure vanity; it is a pretense, like their passion for classic architecture. Let these people look within themselves, let them listen to their primitive genius, and, if they have received from Heaven a perception of the beauties of art, they will give up copying, in order to produce what God and nature expect from them." Whatever complex image we eventually construct of Modest Musorgsky, he was indisputably a titan of that generation that the skeptical, keenly attuned Marquis de Custine so hoped would arrive, to reveal to Russia her own intensifying and protean self.

---

[5]   "Response to a Question from the *Novy Mir* Editorial Staff" [1970], in M. M. Bakhtin, *Speech Genres and Other Late Essays*, trans. Vern W. McGee (Austin: University of Texas Press, 1986), 4–5.

# 14

# FROM "BORIS GODUNOV" TO "KHOVANSHCHINA"

---

*The essay below, published in* Reading Opera, *eds. Arthur Groos and Roger Parker (Princeton: Princeton University Press, 1988), 235–67, was my pioneering attempt to move off* Boris Godunov *and on to Musorgsky's late, unfinished wonderwork* Khovanshchina, *a musical-historical drama differently constructed in almost all respects. It resulted in a sea-change of sympathy — which was rebalanced only by my reBorisification in 2007, brought about through contact with Prokofiev.*

---

## MUSORGSKY'S LIBRETTI ON HISTORICAL THEMES: FROM THE TWO *BORISES* TO *KHOVANSHCHINA* (1988)

Just over one hundred years ago — in February 1886 — an amateur music group in Petersburg staged the premiere performance of Musorgsky's *Khovanshchina*.[1] Both music and libretto in this production differed profoundly from the piano-vocal score that Musorgsky had left incomplete at the time of his death five years earlier. This in itself should occasion no surprise; re-doing Musorgsky's compositions is a minor industry. What is surprising is that *Khovanshchina* survived at all.

After Musorgsky's death, Rimsky-Korsakov spent two years on the manuscript, cutting some 800 bars of music and orchestrating, reharmonizing,

---

[1]   For an account of the premiere and a brief performance history, see M. Rakhmanova, "K 100-letiiu prem'ery 'Khovanshchiny'" [In Honor of the Centennial of the Premiere of *Khovanshchina*], *Sovetskaia muzyka*, 1986 (3), 88–96. *Sovetskaia muzyka* is cited hereafter as *SM*.

and shaping the score into a performance version.[2] The libretto passed the state literary censorship in September 1882, and Bessel published a full score the following year.[3] But in tsarist Russia, dramatic texts approved for print were then subject to another, more severe censorship for public performance.[4] When *Khovanshchina* came up for consideration, Russia was in a period of crisis and political reaction. Tsar Alexander II, liberator of the serfs, had been cut down by a terrorist's bomb in March 1881, the very month of Musorgsky's death. Literary advisory committees attached to the imperial theaters were understandably nervous about historical opera on political themes. "One radical opera by Musorgsky is enough," the Imperial Opera Committee reputedly said when *Khovanshchina* came to a vote, and was rejected, in 1883.[5] Rimsky-Korsakov resigned from the committee in protest. When the opera was finally brought to the amateur stage, its plot was unrecognizable. All reference to the Old Belief had disappeared (including the entire self-immolation scene at the end), and the religious dissenters had been replaced by a nondescript group of Muscovites vaguely politicking on behalf of Andrei Khovansky.[6] In an article marking the fifth anniversary of

---

[2] The most important cuts were: the wrecking of the Clerk's booth (Act 1); Golitsyn's reading of his mother's letter, the episode between Goiitsyn and the Lutheran pastor, and a substantial portion of Dosifei's dialogue (Act II); and the *streltsy*'s "Rumor Song" (Act III).

[3] The first edition of the Rimsky-Korsakov redaction of *Kbovanshchina*, published by Bessel in 1883, bears a censor-stamp dated 8 September 1882. The score contains plate numbers at the beginning of clearly detachable dramatic episodes, which suggests that Bessel contemplated marketing individual arias and choruses as sheet music. I thank Robert William Oldani for information on the 1883 score and its U.S. location (Boston Public Library).

[4] Robert Oldani, who is currently researching this stratification of censorship, has located no single statute that draws a distinction between the right to read a text and the right to perform it. But such secondary censorship indisputably existed. Three years after the *Khovanshchina* score was published, "theatrical censorship" made its presence keenly felt in the premiere performance. Konstantin Pobedonostsev, lay head of the Russian Orthodox Church and chief advisor to the Tsar, objected to the libretto's graphic portrayal of state persecution of religious dissenters, and that theme was "rewritten" in the performing version. For the problems Rimsky encountered in bringing *Khovanshchina* to the stage, see A. Gozenpud, "V bor'be za naslediia Musorgskogo" [Fighting for Musorgsky's Legacy], *SM* 1956 (3), 88–93. On Musorgsky's earlier experience with the censorship over *Boris*, see Oldani, "*Boris Godunov* and the Censor," *19th-century Music* 2 (1979): 245–53.

[5] See Gozenpud, 89, and V. V. Stasov, "Po povodu postanovki 'Khovanshchiny' (Pis'mo k redaktoru)" [Concerning the Production of *Khovanshchina* (A Letter to the Editor)] in V. V. Stasov, *Stat'i o muzyke* (Moscow, 1977), 3:277.

[6] For details of the changes in the premiere, see Rakhmanova (n. 1 above), 94, and Gozenpud, 88–89. Gozenpud relates that E. Feoktistov, Chief of the Main Bureau for

Musorgsky's death, Vladimir Stasov remarked bitterly: "Is it even thinkable that in Germany people would conceal and stubbornly forbid to be staged a still unperformed opera of Wagner's? But with us it's fully thinkable."[7]

One hundred years have passed, and Musorgsky's move from musical eccentric to mainstream classic is now well-researched territory. Centennial celebrations in the last decade have occasioned a new round of discussions in the Soviet press on Musorgsky's skills as a librettist and on his historical sensibilities. The present essay grows out of that recent literature, and out of my own dissatisfaction at attempts to yoke together Musorgsky's two major operas under a single continuous "philosophy of history." Several central questions remain unresolved. What changes occurred in Musorgsky's historical imagination as he moved from *Boris Godunov* to *Khovanshchina*? Is there continuum, or a conceptual break? The music of the two operas is plotted and distributed according to very different principles. Can the two libretti on historical themes be said to have an integrated poetics?

I will argue here that Musorgsky's mode of emplotting history did indeed evolve, but in a direction uncongenial both to the progressive Hegelians of Musorgsky's own era and to the ideology of his later Soviet interpreters. Within nineteenth-century Russian culture, this evolution is not so much linear as circular, a return to the source of Musorgsky's initial inspiration in historical drama, Pushkin's *Boris Godunov*. But this return is complex and indirect. Along the way, Musorgsky appears to have developed a vision of history quite radical for historical opera—even as he embodied that vision in increasingly conventional, Italianate operatic forms. We might open the argument with a review of Musorgsky's earlier experience as a prose dramatist.

*I*

Although Musorgsky was librettist for all his operas, his source material came in varying degrees of literary "preparedness." His first operatic experiment

---

Printed Materials and advisor to Pobedonostsev, exhorted Rimsky-Korsakov to remove the Old Believers from the opera and "turn them into people dissatisfied with something." "But dissatisfied with what?" Rimsky asked. "There's lots to choose from," Feoktistov answered. "Ultimately, I guess, Peter's reforms" (Gozenpud, 88). The time of the opera, of course, precedes Peter's reforms by at least a decade.

7  "Iz stat'i 'Pamiati Musorgskogo'" [From the article "In Musorgsky's Memory"], in Stasov, *Stat'i o muzyke*, III, 283. The article originally appeared in the journal *Istoricheskii vestnik* (March 1886): 644–56.

drew on a novel, Flaubert's *Salammbô*; his second was a word-for-word setting of a portion of Gogol's dramatic farce, *Marriage*. At the end of his life Musorgsky again returned to Gogol, this time to the Ukrainian tales, for "The Fair at Sorochintsy." All these projects were either abandoned or left incomplete. The two great operas for which Musorgsky is remembered, *Boris Godunov* and *Khovanshchina*, do not have prose fiction at their base but rather historical drama — or the naked historical document itself. Let us first consider *Boris*.

Out of Pushkin's *Boris Godunov* Musorgsky created two versions of an opera, one in 1869 and a revised version between 1872–1874. As Richard Taruskin has persuasively argued, these two operas are not variants of a single plan but two quite separately conceptualized wholes.[8] Musorgsky composed his initial 1869 version under the influence of a strict realist aesthetic, in which fidelity to the verbal text and the intonational patterns of Russian speech took precedence over musical form or development.[9] This first version nevertheless reflects a curious type of fidelity. The words that characters sing, and thus the sentiments they express at any given moment, are indeed those of Pushkin's characters realized in music. Since music slows down a text, however, Musorgsky was obliged (as are most librettists who adapt an existing stage drama) to cut and simplify the story drastically. This reduction in the number and complexity of scenes could only result in a very casual fidelity to the whole of the source. Pushkin's sense of the historical event, as well as his balancing of one scene against another that is so crucial for a poet, was inevitably lost.

The 1874 version of the opera has an equally complex relation to its source. After the Theater Directorate rejected the initial version, Musorgsky returned to Pushkin and created an entire new act out of the Polish scenes. The new

---

[8]    Richard Taruskin, "Musorgsky vs. Musorgsky: The Versions of *Boris Godunov*," in *19th-century Music* 8 (1984–85): 91–118 and 245–72. On Musorgsky's adaptation of Pushkin's text in the context of the musical aesthetics of the 1860s, see my *Boris Godunov: Transpositions of a Russian Theme* (Bloomington, IN: Indiana University Press, 1986), 142–206.

[9]    The libretto drew on only eight of Pushkin's twenty-five scenes, but those eight scenes follow Pushkin's text closely. Musorgsky either set the words almost verbatim, as in the Cell and Inn scenes, or he condensed and paraphrased — respecting, however, Pushkin's basic intent in plot and character. In one important respect only does the initial version differ from its literary source: the onstage prominence given to the title role. The opera favors scenes in which Tsar Boris either appears or is the immediate topic of conversation. Unlike Pushkin's drama, which minimizes Boris's grandeur, the 1869 opera magnifies the Tsar's sufferings and ends conventionally on the Tsar's death.

opera thus incorporated more of the larger shape of Pushkin's play. At the same time, Musorgsky revised both music and text of the previously composed scenes, in places radically altering the words and worldviews of Pushkin's characters. Their operatic counterparts became static and less subtle, their behavior more melodramatic, their musical line less declamatory.

To this conventionalization of the leading roles Musorgsky added an unconventional ending, the mass scene of popular rebellion in Kromy Forest. This scene is neither in Pushkin's play nor in the primary source for that play, Karamzin's *History of the Russian State*. The Kromy scene of the revised opera is without literary prototype; Musorgsky pieced it together from chants, folksongs, Jesuit hymns, episodes in Nikolai Kostomarov's popular history of the period, and previously composed procession music. The scene contains no extended recitative, and its sequence of events is essentially non-narrative. Musorgsky did not oblige himself in this instance to compose a plot. He was satisfied with musical tableaux that suggested a historical event but neither portrayed its logical progression nor created coherent, motivated dialogue among its participants.

The inspiration for the Kromy scene — as well as its appropriateness to the opera — has been widely debated.[10] In its openness and ambivalent ideology, this final scene recalls the ending that Pushkin had devised for his version of the story. At the close of Pushkin's play in its published version, a government official announces the death of Boris's widow and son and then orders the crowd to cheer the victorious pretender. The crowd does not respond: in what is perhaps the most famous stage direction in all Russian literature, «Народ безмолвствует» [The people are silent]. Not answering an official command is a special, dangerous, pregnant sort of silence that will not be allowed to continue indefinitely. Something of the same tense emptiness opens up at the end of the noisy and rhythmically compelling Kromy scene. Having created an expectation of robust sonic closure in the form of competing choruses, at the last minute the choruses are taken

---

[10] Several forums have appeared over the last two decades in the major Soviet music journal, *Sovetskaia muzyka*. The most important are: "K izucheniiu naslediia M. P. Musorgskogo: Stsena 'Pod Kromami' v dramaturgii *Borisa Godunova*" [Researching Musorgsky's Legacy: The Kromy Scene in the Dramaturgy of *Boris Godunov*], discussants Yu. Tiutin, E. Frid, B. Iarustovskii, A. Kandinskii, P. Aravin, in *SM*, 1970 (3), 90–114; A. Tsuker, "Narod pokornyi i narod buntuiushchii" [The People Submissive and Rebellious], *SM* 1972 (3), 105–109; I. Obraztsova, "K ponimaniiu narodnogo kharaktera v tvorchestve Musorgskogo" [Toward an Understanding of the People's Character in Musorgsky's Works], *SM* 1980 (9), 95–101. See also Emerson, *Boris Godunov*, 198–206.

away—leaving the stage empty except for a holy fool, who, hopping distractedly to center stage, sings of Russia's coming destruction as the curtain falls. Both play and revised version of the opera express at their final moments a sense that historical process is capricious and governed by chance or by silence. In both, the meaning of historical events is not to be found in the fate of the title role — who has long since departed the stage.

Thus Musorgsky in 1874 was both less and more faithful to his literary source. Although the words that characters sing and the operatic personalities that emerge depart significantly from their counterparts in Pushkin, it could be argued that the actual sense of historical process in the later opera is closer to the spirit of Pushkin's play than is the technically more "faithful" first version.

We might say, then, that Musorgsky's strategies for adapting his source in the two *Boris* libretti serves as a case study of problems we confront when considering a librettist's fidelity to sources — and to the larger whole of a historical event. Libretti based on literary texts will inevitably "leave something out." But the parts left in can be faithful to their source on several different planes. They can be true to the characters or true to the narration. When whole portions of spoken text are moved verbatim into the libretto, as Musorgsky chose to do in his first version of *Boris*, the first strategy obtains: the privileged fidelity is to the characters' integrity, the degree to which libretto personalities sound or behave like their literary prototypes. Their words and stories are of course condensed and simplified, minor figures disappear or are elided, but for the ones that survive, the librettist strives to respect their inner perspective on events and preserve their images intact.

The second strategy, more characteristic of Musorgsky's revised version of *Boris*, is founded less on fidelity to the words or characters than on the spirit or narrative structure of the source. By melodramatizing Tsar Boris, adding love interest, and interpolating a number of set songs into the score, Musorgsky made the body of his opera more suited (as he himself admitted) to the "grand stage."[11] But this operatic whole then reconnects with its source text on a higher, "historiographical" level. The new final scene in Kromy Forest moves the focus away from the title role and into the uncertainties of the

---

[11]    In a letter to Golenishchev-Kutuzov (15 August 1877), Musorgsky explained that a composer writing for the grand stage must project characters "in bold relief," true to their "dramatic inevitability." See M. P. Musorgskii, *Pis'ma k A. A. Golenishchevu-Kutuzovu*, ed. Yu. Keldysh (Moscow-Leningrad, 1939), 69; for a translation, see *The Musorgsky Reader*, ed. and trans. Jay Leyda and Sergei Bertensson (New York, 1970), 360.

nation's fate — just as Pushkin's play had done. With the exception of that final scene, however, both strategies for libretto genesis draw on a single literary source that embodies a unified aesthetic vision of a historical period.

## II

One year after the Kromy scene was composed and two years before *Boris* was premiered, Musorgsky began work on another opera. Its libretto strategy could be said to pick up where the Kromy scene left off. Like the final scene of *Boris*, *Khovanshchina* drew on no single literary source text; Musorgsky created the plot out of raw historical sources, from various authors bearing various ideologies. Thus the *Khovanshchina* libretto was not vulnerable to the charges brought against *Boris Godunov* — charges of infidelity to a source, disrespect for a canonized poet, distortion of a literary masterpiece. On the contrary, reviewers of the premiere scarcely mentioned the libretto. The fact that the opera's plot made little sense was not perceived as a weakness — and this is a good index of the conceptual distance separating *Khovanshchina* from the two *Boris* libretti. The angry reviews following the 1874 *Boris* premiere had been directed at least as much against the words as the music. The music was dissonant and declamatory enough to offend professional opera critics, and the libretto (in what was surely the worst of both worlds) was faulted for being both derivative of and unfaithful to its source. *Khovanshchina* reversed this impression. Its music was unexpectedly melodious; the opera rang with fanfares, folksongs, dances, choruses, and arioso-style lyrical monologues. A more conventional musical structure, in short, appeared to placate the demand for a rigorously motivated libretto. The problems *Khovanshchina* presents are of another sort altogether.

There is, first, the usual difficulty in ferreting out "authorial intention" from an opera unfinished, and unpublished, during its composer's lifetime. Secondly, there are the special problems that accompany any research into Musorgsky's later period: poor documentation, the composer's many evasive masks, and the personal tragedy of poverty and alcoholism. Lastly, there is the peculiar status of the libretto itself, which exists in several versions with and without its music. All these factors must become part of any interpretation of *Khovanshchina*.

*Boris Godunov* confuses us because it has two authorial versions; *Khovanshchina*, strictly speaking, has none. Musorgsky left only a piano-vocal score in manuscript, with completion dates for the separate episodes ranging from 1873 to 1880.[12] Select pieces from the opera had been orchestrated (and even performed) during his lifetime, but the whole was much too long for continuous performance and the finale had only been sketched. Rimsky-Korsakov's efforts to turn his friend's unfinished opera into a performable work have therefore not been castigated as have his wholesale recastings of *Boris* — which was, after all, a published and performed work. Some critics have even credited Rimsky with joint authorship of *Khovanshchina*.[13] But for that reason it has been all the more difficult to get at an "authoritative" — that is, single-authored — text. In the early 1930s Pavel Lamm "de-Rimskified" *Khovanshchina*, as he had *Boris*, on the basis of manuscript materials; Shostakovich re-orchestrated the Lamm piano-vocal score in the late 1950s.[14] But even when the Shostakovich orchestration is used in performance, Rimsky's cuts in the score and libretto are often retained — as indeed they were, by and large, in the Metropolitan Opera's 1985 production.[15] The

---

[12]  The sequence of composition (based on Musorgsky's own dating) suggests that the opera did not unfold as a chronological whole but was sketched, revised, and then "filled in." Approximate completion dates are: for Act I: 1873 (first half) and 1875 (final two episodes); for Act II: most episodes 1875–76; for Act III: 1873 (first half) and 1876 (second half); for Act IV: most of the Act in 1876 and two episodes in 1880; for Act V: most scenes sketched during 1873 and separate episodes dated 1876, 1878, 1879, 1880.

[13]  See V. Karatygin, "'Khovanshchina' i eia avtory" [*Khovanshchina* and Its Authors], in *Muzykal'nyi sovremennik* 5–6 (January-February 1917): 192–218. Karatygin surveys Rimsky's cuts, praising him for this most difficult task: "He not only healed the wounds, but did it in such a way that one gets the impression no operation ever took place" (194); "*Khovanshchina* has two authors, although only one spirit of genius" (218). Karatygin's article (which appeared in a journal edited by Andrei Rimsky-Korsakov, the composer's son) was itself highly polemical, an attempt to discredit the 1913 Diaghilev production of *Khovanshchina* mounted in Paris with the collaboration of Igor Stravinsky.

[14]  See V. I. Gurevich, "Shostakovich — redaktor 'Khovanshchiny'" [Shostakovich as the Editor of *Khovanshchina*], in *Muzyka i sovremennost'* 7 (Moscow, 1971): 29–68, and V. I. Gurevich, "Shostakovich v rabote nad 'Khovanshchinoi'" [Shostakovich at Work on *Khovanshchina*], in *Voprosy teorii i estetiki muzyki* 11 (Leningrad, 1972): 84–108. Less technical background can be found in Georgii Khubov's introductory essay to the 1963 Shostakovich score, "M. Musorgskii, *Khovanshchina*, partitura" (Moscow, 1963), 7–14.

[15]  The libretto made available for the Metropolitan Opera production is the English version by Christopher Hunt for the San Francisco Opera Company (1984). Its omissions and conflations are peculiar. Act I respects all of Rimsky's massive cuts in the manuscript; Act II omits the reading by Golitsyn of his mother's letter but inserts Dosifei's comments about his past life as Prince Myshetsky (an episode cut by Rimsky), and includes one exchange present in the piano-vocal manuscript that Musorgsky himself cut from his 1879 libretto; in Act III, the Susanna-Marfa confrontation is shortened as per Rimsky. A more complete version of the opera, with a startlingly full, multi-voiced first act, was produced at Covent Garden (1972) under Edward Downes.

sound might be closer to Musorgsky's, but the dramatic concept is still several editings away.

Compounding these textual problems is the general paucity of material on Musorgsky's final years. His working methods make it almost impossible to retrieve clear stages of creation "intact" from drafts. Apparently the scenic situation, verbal text, and musical characteristics occurred to him as a unified whole, and he constructed his plot in scenic blocks, by a sort of "free improvisation."[16] Our best sources for the genesis of the libretto are not drafts at all but Musorgsky's lengthy letters to Vladimir Stasov (who differed with the composer on the direction of the plot) and a "Notebook for Khovanshchina" that Musorgsky compiled in 1872. He eventually filled twenty pages of this little notebook with citations from seventeenth-century eyewitness accounts, historical documents, and excerpts from contemporary histories, either transcribed literally or paraphrased.[17] Whole chunks of this material — mostly documents dating from 1682 — were moved into the libretto almost intact: Shaklovity's denunciation, for example, and Sophia's love letter to Golitsyn.[18] Of the secondary sources cited in the Notebook (both eighteenth- and nineteenth-century), most are by authors whose allegiances were anti-Old Belief and pro-Peter. But Musorgsky did not passively absorb this framing ideology; his extracts favor historical personages speaking in their own voices. Often Musorgsky would lace these citations with his own commentary or rejoinders, so the entries could evolve into primitive dialogues.[19] From these quasi-dialogized fragments Musorgsky created his plot.

The shape of Musorgsky's intended dramatic whole has also been the subject of some controversy. The problem here centers neither on the confused state of the manuscript scores nor on Rimsky's reworkings, but on a document that turned up unexpectedly fifty years after Musorgsky's death. In 1931, Pavel Lamm had just reconstructed the original piano-vocal score of *Khovanshchina*

---

16    Ruzanna Shirinian, *Opernaia dramaturgiia Musorgskogo* (Moscow, 1981), 170–71.

17    The contents of this notebook have been thoroughly analyzed. For a title page and table of contents, see *The Musorgsky Reader* (n. 11 above), 195. For analysis see esp. Galina Bakaeva, *"Khovanshchina" M. Musorgskogo* (Kiev, 1976), ch. 1 and 2; Emilia Frid, *Proshedshee, nastoiashchee i budushchee v "Khovanshchine" Musorgskogo* [Past, Present, and Future in Musorgsky's *Khovanshchina*] (Leningrad, 1974), ch. 2, esp. 74–97; also Shirinian, 152–66.

18    For texts of the denunciation in the notebook and in the libretto, see Bakaeva, 51–52; for the texts of Sophia's letters to Golitsyn (in the source that Musorgsky most probably consulted), see Mikhail Semevskii, "Sovremennye portrety Sofii Alekseevny i V. V. Golitsyna," *Russkoe slovo* ([St. Petersburg], December 1859): 429–30.

19    See Bakaeva, 38.

from the surviving manuscripts. But no drafts of a libretto were extant in the Musorgsky archive, and none of Musorgsky's surviving letters mentions any such separate libretto-writing activity. Lamm assumed, correctly, that *Khovanshchina* had been composed without a pre-existing libretto. Then in 1932 a blue school notebook filled with Musorgsky's handwriting turned up in the Golenishchev-Kutuzov archive.[20] Kutuzov, a minor poet, had roomed with Musorgsky in 1874 and 1875, and had provided the words for Musorgsky's vocal cycles *Sunless* and *Songs and Dances of Death*. When Kutuzov left to get married, Musorgsky remained in correspondence with the poet, often consulting with him on matters of prosody.

The blue notebook in the Kutuzov archive contained an undated libretto of *Khovanshchina* written out entirely in prose. Compared with the manuscript piano-vocal score, this verbal text is much simplified and "accelerated"; four major dramatic episodes are cut.[21] Drawing on evidence provided by the publication dates of folksongs included in Act IV, the Soviet editor assigns the blue-notebook libretto to 1879 or 1880 — making it one of Musorgsky's last literary projects.[22] And here a paradox presents itself.

If the dating is correct, Musorgsky wrote out the libretto when the concept of the operatic whole had finally settled in him. He did not live to adjust the already-composed music of his piano-vocal score to this new verbal text. And yet this text now enjoys the status of an authoritative libretto among Soviet researchers, who presume, not unreasonably, that the blue notebook was to serve Musorgsky as a guide for his final revision and orchestration.[23] Its precise wording and division of scenes, however, are not those of the manuscript scores, nor are they those associated with the opera for most of

---

[20]  See M. P. Pekelis, "Musorgskii — pisatel' — dramaturg," in M. P. Musorgskii, *Literaturnoe nasledstvo / Literaturnye proizvedeniia* (Moscow, 1972), 31–34. The blue-notebook libretto (henceforth Pekelis) is reproduced in prose on 124–48, with departures from the piano-vocal manuscript indicated in notes.

[21]  The four cut or shortened episodes are: a dialogue between the Moscow folk and the Clerk in Act I; the episode between Golitsyn and the Lutheran pastor in Act II; an exchange between Marfa and Susanna, and between Dosifei and Susanna, in Act III and Act V, which is fragmentary in the piano-vocal score and in the blue-notebook libretto even more so. The blue-notebook libretto divides the text into six scenes [*kartiny*], with no markings for acts.

[22]  This dating must remain a hypothesis. In personal communications, both Robert Oldani and Richard Taruskin have expressed reservations about so late a date. Oldani points out, for example, that familiarity with folk songs among folk-oriented composers in the 1870s can scarcely be limited to published editions. To my knowledge, Soviet scholars have not offered any other grounds for the attribution of an 1879 date.

[23]  See Pekelis, 33, and Shirinian (n. 16 above), 172–73.

its performance history. Such a non-coincidence of texts cannot be easily remedied by any "restoration," because no complete or continuous music exists for this libretto. The editor has suggested that the unusual prose layout of the libretto (extending even to embedded folksongs and chants) was a deliberate attempt on Musorgsky's part to emphasize the purely dramatic concept of the opera, undistracted by the pull of musical form.[24] Kutuzov, in whose archive the notebook was found, was a writer of historical drama as well as a very decent poet; quite possibly Musorgsky sent him the libretto for his advice and recommendations. The presence of numerous "corrections" in red pencil indicate that this was most likely the case.[25]

The blue-notebook libretto thus has a peculiar legitimacy as an independent *literary* work, almost an artistic unity in its own right. However provisional in Musorgsky's mind, it probably represents his final — and thus arguably most advanced — dramatic concept of the opera.[26] Its rights to performance

---

[24]    Pekelis, 33.

[25]    Robert Oldani, in a personal communication, raises legitimate doubts about this interpretation. How do we know that the red-pencil corrections are Kutuzov's? And does the notebook's authority end there? Since many of Musorgsky's own cuts and compressions in the blue-notebook libretto are ones that Rimsky-Korsakov later adopted, is it not possible that Rimsky knew of this blue-notebook libretto and used it as a guide when preparing his own version of the opera? If so, Rimsky's reworking was much less arbitrary than it has appeared. One can only regret that Kutuzov's discussion of *Khovanshchina* in his *Reminiscences of Musorgsky* (written in the 1880s) is so brief. Kutuzov deals with the opera largely in musical terms, praising its wealth of song and lyricism, which pleases him "despite all the inconveniences presented by the plot, which is not only not an operatic subject but not even a dramatic one, and chosen for God knows what reason." See A. A. Golenishchev-Kutuzov, "Vospominaniia o M. P. Musorgskom," in *Muzykal'noe nasledstvo* (Moscow, 1935), 25.

[26]    Only in one respect must this hypothesis be qualified. The blue-notebook libretto ends with an apparently incomplete final act, primarily choral and containing none of the dialogue among principals (Marfa, Andrei, Dosifei) that was sketched in the piano-vocal manuscript. Pekelis (n. 20 above) states simply that "here the libretto comes to an end" (200). A. Vul'fson has researched the final scene, and has ascertained that the love duet between Marfa and Andrei was indisputably part of Musorgsky's plan (the scene was often sung in a solo version by Daria Leonova between 1878 and 1889), but after Musorgsky's death that manuscript was lost; Andrei's part was found in 1947). The absence of this love duet in the blue-notebook libretto "should not be awarded exaggerated significance," because clearly "the work was interrupted, not completed." See "K problemam tekstologii" [*Toward Problems of Textology*] SM, 1981 (3), 103–10, esp. 104. Both Vul'fson and Oldani point out that Musorgsky neither signed, dated, nor dedicated the blue-notebook libretto — a significant detail for a composer who habitually signed with a flourish his completed works, even his completed scenes and segments of works.

depend, of course, on the way one resolves the competing claims of words versus music in a given operatic text, and on one's approach to the general problems of co-authorship, dating, and multiple versions. With a textual history this uncertain, what constitutes an "authoritative production?" One in which music is devised to fit a coherent libretto, or one where words (or other transitions) are created to patch together all segments of surviving music?

Here students of the opera may simply make a choice. The 1879 blue-notebook libretto, except for its incomplete final scene, will serve as the basis for my comments on the "historical worldview" of *Khovanshchina*. That worldview has proved elusive. The best students of Musorgsky are routinely embarrassed by the opera's ideological implications, and several of their solutions are relevant to my own reading.

## III

The Soviet debate over *Khovanshchina* opened with the controversial thesis put forth by the Soviet musicologist Boris Asafiev in the 1930s.[27] Asafiev was concerned — as were many in the Stalinist era — to understand Musorgsky's move from the second version of *Boris* to *Khovanshchina* as linear and historically progressive. The difficulty came, of course, in deriving *Khovanshchina* from the Kromy Forest scene. In Kromy, the Russian masses on stage are inspired with a spirit of rebellion, a sense of freedom and free choice, even though they ultimately exercise it on behalf of a pretender. In *Khovanshchina*, apart from a few boastful drinking songs, there is no freedom at all. The mutinous troops in Act III instantly succumb when Prince Khovansky declines to lead them into battle against Peter's troops. Act IV ends with a pardoning of the mutineers, but only after they file meekly by with nooses round their necks, carrying their own execution blocks and axes. The famous last scene, where the Old Believers prefer to set fire to themselves rather than surrender to government troops and

---

[27] See "V rabote nad 'Khovanshchinoi'" [At Work on *Khovanshchina*], in B. V. Asafiev, *Izbrannye trudy* (Moscow, 1954), 3:160–67. Asafiev wrote the essay in 1931, in connection with his own efforts at orchestrating Musorgsky's piano-vocal manuscripts (Asafiev's score, if it exists, has not been published). During the war years Asafiev returned to the ideology of Musorgsky's opera with even more historical optimism; see "Russkii narod, russkie liudi" [The Russian Folk, the Russian People] (1944) in *Izbrannye trudy* (Moscow, 1955), 4:118.

the Anti-Christ, does indeed show resistance—but it is of a peculiarly passive and historically reactionary kind. Everywhere the people die, or are disarmed and humiliated. How can a plot of this texture qualify as "people's musical drama?" How can it be squared with "progressive" history? Asafiev's solution is to rethink the label Musorgsky devised for his opera, "people's musical drama" [«народная музыкальная драма»]. The composer notwith-standing, Asafiev declares, this is not a drama of the people but a drama of the *state* (166). One social class after another is isolated and rendered powerless; the libretto unfolds as stages in the dying of Old Muscovy. And the idea of Old Russia dying is itself progressive. This reading, of course, is a Soviet extension of statist historiography in the 1870s—best exemplified by the works of Sergei Soloviev, known to be among Musorgsky's sources for *Khovanshchina*.[28] In the organic, centralizing statist view, history might indeed cause pain to some groups of people; the course of history is ineluctable and unsentimental. But Peter the Great in the wings of *Khovanshchina* is ultimately more progressive than all the self-confident joyous delusions of the Kromy scene. Asafiev almost celebrates in *Khovanshchina* the collapse of popular resistance, seeing it as historically necessary for the growth and defense of the Russian state. Not surprisingly, this bold Stalinist reading of the opera has come under attack in recent, more liberal years.[29]

Two of these recent "revisionist" readings of *Khovanshchina* are of special interest. Both claim that Musorgsky did indeed have an artistic plan, and that the fate of the Russian people is at the center of it. But neither is political in Asafiev's vein. Both seek, rather, *aesthetic* precedents for Musorgsky's embodiment of history in opera, and both vaguely locate that precedent in Alexander Pushkin.

---

[28] See the letter from Musorgsky to Vladimir Stasov, 6 September 1873: "I am re-reading Soloviev, to become acquainted with the epoch" (*The Musorgsky Reader* [n. 11 above], 251). Internal evidence suggests that Musorgsky drew upon and modified ch. 3 ("Moskovskaia smuta 1682 goda") of Soloviev's *History of Russia from Ancient Times*, vol. XIII, which describes in detail several of the events in the opera (the execution of the Khovanskys, the cooperation between *streltsy* and Old Believers, the destruction of the "pillar" [*stolp*] on Red Square, etc.). See S. M. Soloviev, *Istoriia Rossii s drevneishikh vremen*, Book VII (vv. 13–14) (Moscow, 1962), 261–302.

[29] For a good example of a routine anti-Asafiev disclaimer, see S. Shlifshtein, "Otkuda zhe rassvet?" [So Where's the Dawn Coming From?], *SM* 1971 (12), 109–13. Later editors are quick to insist that Asafiev did not mean "state" in the Marxist-Leninist sense (as something, presumably, that should wither away), but "state" in the sense of a patriotic, defense-oriented unity of the whole people. See note 5 to "V rabote nad 'Khovanshchinoi,'" *Izbrannye trudy*, 318.

Galina Bakaeva's 1976 monograph on *Khovanshchina* is the more conventional.[30] She adopts Asafiev's basic dramatic scheme for the opera: the first two acts bring the forces of Old Muscovy on stage, and then each group is eliminated in an inevitable unfolding of historical necessity (57–61). But she stresses, as Asafiev did not, that Peter's troops — not to mention Peter himself — are forever invisible and offstage (189–91).[31] To the participants onstage, Peter I and his men are specters, and terrifying ones. Statist historians in the 1870s idealized Peter I and strove to see in their reigning Emancipator-Tsar, Alexander II, traces of Peter's vision and boldness. Musorgsky refused to make any gesture born of the present binding on the past. The personal histories of his characters are backward-looking, locked in time, and obsessively simple. Episodes do not combine dynamically to move action forward. From this Bakaeva concludes that Musorgsky "had decisively rejected the narrative principle in the dramaturgy of a libretto" (72).

The second monograph, Emilia Frid's 1974 study *Past, Present, and Future in Musorgsky's "Khovanshchina,"*[32] also targets mode of narration as a key to the opera's peculiar stasis, and refers us back to Pushkin. But Frid then speculates at length on this radically innovative dramaturgy. If Musorgsky's operatic *Boris* departs profoundly from the spirit of its Pushkinian source, then *Khovanshchina*, oddly, returns to it. Reminiscent of Pushkin's play, *Khovanshchina* is not organized narratively, not even linearly; it is more a vertical cut through compressed time. This cross-section branches out into various plot lines, each of which is extremely simple and relatively isolated from the others. And yet the action onstage strikes us as quite complex. This complexity is achieved, Frid argues, not by development and interaction among characters but by static episodes passing through one another — strata, as it were, that move across our

---

30   Bakaeva (see n. 17 above).

31   The exact location of Peter's trumpeters and troops (backstage, or moving onstage as the final scene draws to a close) differs in the stage directions of various versions. The blue-notebook libretto, skimpy in general with its stage directions, provides little help here, breaking off before the final episode. But Musorgsky could never have brought Peter the Great on stage, even had he wished to; censorship forbade any representation onstage of a ruler from the reigning house of Romanov. Musorgsky, it could be argued, was making a virtue out of necessity. But this does not invalidate Bakaeva's thesis that Peter's absence has ideological significance for the opera as a whole, however non-negotiable the matter was for a composer.

32   See n. 17 above.

field of vision at arbitrary points, without clear climaxes or well-marked ends (240–43).

This time-space structure has an inevitable effect on the relationship between personality and idea in the opera (279 — 91). Here Frid contrasts *Khovanshchina* with *Boris*. In *Boris*, the lofty tragic style is linked with one person: the Tsar himself. Other factors — fate, the people, history — take on weight through association with his theme. In *Khovanshchina*, by contrast, the tragedic style is not linked personally with any single character, nor with the moral gravity of any one person's particular sin. Rather this lofty style "unites all those who episodically become carriers of the general idea" (280).[33] Frid leaves the content of this idea strangely open; what interests her is the relationship between idea and personality as a formal problem. If *Boris Godunov* is dramatic opera built up out of guilt and personal choice, then *Khovanshchina*, in its basic contours, is an epic.

But, Frid hastens to add, this is not the epic music-drama of Wagner or the fairy-tale epic of Rimsky-Korsakov. Dramatic conflict in *Khovanshchina* is too decentered; the source of the conflict is never localized or concentrated (306–309). And more important still, *Khovanshchina* is too closely tied to actual historical events to be mythical or lyrical after the usual manner of such operas. The originality of *Khovanshchina*, Frid concludes, lies in its bizarre fusion of drama and epic, in which lyricism — conventionally the vehicle for private and fictional fates — serves to embody generalized extra-personal images, longings, and historically grounded philosophical ideas (310).

Frid's extended discussion is, in my view, the most convincing conceptualization to date of Musorgsky's "people's musical drama." But the energy she must expend to make the familiar categories of epic, drama, and lyric cohere in *Khovanshchina* suggests that the opera's identity might better be sought altogether outside such labels. I would like to offer another framework for viewing the opera — one that draws upon, but modifies as it extends, the insights of this recent Soviet scholarship.

---

[33] This thesis would explain — to take but one example — the apparent "inconsistency" in Shaklovity's character that routinely baffles opera-goers. How can this slippery bureaucrat, who concocts a false denunciation of the Khovanskys in Act 1 and cold-bloodedly murders Ivan Khovansky in Act IV, deliver in Act III a somber, heartfelt lament on the tragedy of Russia's violent history and internal feuding? Frid (284–85) argues that "character consistency" is not part of Musorgsky's plan. Shaklovity's aria is not his own: it is lyrical, Glinka-like, from nowhere to everywhere, a timeless patriotic sentiment that does not issue from Shaklovity's historical character but rather uses Shaklovity as *its* mouthpiece.

## *IV*

My own point of departure is a question that occupied Pushkin as he worked on his *Boris Godunov*: how does one embed a historical event in artistic form so that the product is both true to history and true to art? Musorgsky, I would argue, never lost his early *kuchkist* passion for verisimilitude in art. But he became more flexible and subtle about the areas where it might apply, and less hostile to conventional operatic techniques. The *Khovanshchina* libretto does not raise questions of fidelity to a literary source; the challenge here, rather, is to use contemporary resources — musical and metaphysical — to construct a text faithful to an era and evocative of its spirit.

Late seventeenth-century Muscovy knew several times simultaneously, each with its own spirit. There were old princely families like the Khovanskys, jealously guarding what remained of their independence. Supporting them, unreliably and erratically, were the *streltsy*, garrison troops in the capital. In the cities a new bureaucratic class of scribes and clerks peddled literacy for profit. And in the Kremlin, a partial Westernization had been achieved under Tsar Alexis, which was later extended by his daughter Sophia Alexeyevna, regent while Peter was a child. Sophia's favorite, Prince Vasily Golitsyn, embodied that tentative impulse to learn from Western culture that would become a compulsion of the court under Peter the Great. Finally there was a massive schism in the Russian Orthodox Church, precipitated by Tsar Alexis and his autocratic Patriarch, Nikon. Nikon had decreed some changes in Orthodox ritual and orthography, and a large vocal portion of the faithful (the so-called "True" or "Old" Believers) refused to cooperate. They interpreted the reforms as an indication that the past was no longer sacred, the End of the World was nigh, and the Antichrist, posing as Peter the First, was already abroad in the land.[34]

Among the various times and degrees of change represented by these social groups, "Old Believer time" has a special status. It is not merely another way of assessing what happens in the present, or debating what social class will inherit the future. It is millenarian, an end to *all* presents; in fact, it is an end to time itself, and thus inherently incompatible with other attitudes toward history. In a music-drama where Old Believers play a role, then, their understanding of time cannot really be integrated with the others. There are

---

[34]   See Michael Cherniavsky, "The Old Believers and the New Religion," *Slavic Review* 25 (1966): 1–39.

two options for Old Believer time: it must be rated as hierarchically superior or dismissed as superstition.

Soviet researchers, who have tended to apologize for Musorgsky's tenderness toward the schismatics, favor the latter option. Not surprisingly, they comb the sources for evidence that the composer was a materialist, a realist, and a progressive Hegelian in his understanding of historical process.[35] Dosifei is usually perceived as a fanatic — albeit an astute and noble one[36] — and Marfa as an experienced politician who predicts Golitsyn's fate not because she can read fortunes in a bowl of water but because she knows the workings of Sophia's court. The mystical and supernatural elements in the Old Belief, and in Musorgsky's own beliefs, are routinely passed over lightly or simply ignored.

My reading of the opera will pursue the first option: the possibility that Musorgsky took the Old Believer concept of time very seriously — indeed, that he structured his whole opera around it. In this view, Musorgsky created *Khovanshchina* with one particular verisimilitude in mind: he wished to be true to the world as the Old Believers saw it, and thus grants them the ultimate victory. This was a hugely ambitious spiritual experiment for the realist and materialist 1860s, to be matched only much later by Rimsky-Korsakov in his quasi-Symbolist 1905 opera *The Legend of the Invisible City of Kitezh and the Maiden Fevroniya*. To place *Khovanshchina* more firmly in its own history, however, we should first consider various other types of verisimilitude Musorgsky might have pursued. There are, it seems, at least four: fidelity to event, character, music, and language itself.

Verisimilitude can be registered, first, in the actual sequence of events, in historical chronology itself. Musorgsky chose to compress and rearrange events, combining elements from three *streltsy* revolts between 1682 and 1698. The bulk of the action, and most of the actual historical documents embedded in the libretto, date from 1682. That year was one of constant turmoil.[37] One tsar had just died; the ten-year-old Peter and his sixteen-year-

---

[35] See Bakaeva (n. 17 above), ch. 1, especially 36–40, 49, 139, and 188–202; Frid (n. 17 above), 156–63; M. Sokol'skii, "'Khovanshchina' v Bol'shom teatre" [*Khovanshchina* at the Bolshoi Theater], *SM* 1950 (6), 17–18.

[36] Aleksei Ogolevets's treatment of Dosifei is characteristic: "The image of a religious fanatic, a partisan of the past, is completely alien to us" (*Vokal'naia dramaturgiia Musorgskogo* [Moscow, 1966], 395, 249).

[37] See Robert O. Crummey, *The Old Believers and the World of Antichrist: The Vyg Community and the Russian State, 1694–1855* (Madison, WI: University of Wisconsin Press, 1970), ch. 3 ("Death by Fire").

old half-brother Ivan were elevated to the throne under the regency of their older sister Sophia. The *streltsy*, restless in the interregnum and recently brought under the protection of Ivan Khovansky, joined with militant Old Believers to demand a cancellation of the Church reforms. Sophia alternately placated and repressed this complex revolt. She beheaded one leading religious dissenter and initiated severe persecution of the Old Belief throughout the Empire. In the autumn of 1682 both Ivan Khovansky and his son Andrei were executed, but when the *streltsy* rose up in protest against these deaths the Regent did not dare to carry out mass reprisals. Fearful for her own position, she pardoned the troops (this is the source of the macabre pardon at the end of Act IV, attributed to Peter).

Tucked into this basic 1682 chronology are events from much later years. In 1689 Sophia herself attempted to lead the *streltsy* (then under the command of her appointee Shaklovity) against her half-brother Peter and thus to secure the throne in her own name. But Peter was by then grown up, or grown-up enough — and dangerous. This is the situation reflected at the end of Act III, where Khovansky (historically seven years dead) declines to lead the *streltsy* into battle because "times are different now: Tsar Peter is terrifying!" The 1689 rebellion failed; Shaklovity was executed, Sophia imprisoned in a convent, and Golitsyn, Sophia's lover, exiled to Siberia (the fulfillment in Act IV, scene 2 of Marfa's prophecy from Act II).

Final retribution against the *streltsy* did not come until 1698, when Peter I returned from his European tour to suppress a third rebellion. This historical event is the source for those mass gallows on Red Square that we see almost under construction in Act IV. But in history the pardon never came: Peter had 1,000 rebel troops tortured and put to death, and the surviving *streltsy* disbanded.

Retribution by Peter's state against the final rebellious group, the Old Believers, was necessarily more diffuse and inconclusive, since threat of death was not a serious deterrent. For millenarians it could be an enticement. Musorgsky's choice of a self-immolation scene to end *Khovanshchina* is especially appropriate for an opera set in the 1680s. Sophia's regency ushered in an authentic inquisition. An edict from 1684 established search-and-destroy missions against Old Believer communities, with orders to take the dissenters alive. The following decade witnessed an epidemic of mass suicides by communities intent on sacrificing the body so that the soul might be saved from the Antichrist: 2,700 burned to death in a chapel on the White Sea in 1687; several thousand perished in like manner on Lake Onega in 1688, another 1,500 in 1689.

As regards verisimilitude to event, then, Musorgsky selected from the historical record both real and representative "facts" to construct his plot. But he did not observe chronological accuracy. To a certain extent, this license with historical sequence freed him from the constraints and expectations of causality; events that cannot be linked in a chain of effects stand alone and appear fated to happen.

Verisimilitude with respect to historical character—our second category—is also observed only partially.[38] Some of the historical roles, such as Ivan Khovansky and Golitsyn, are given their "own lines" taken literally from documents written by their historical counterparts. Other characters appear to be amalgams of several historical figures—as is Dosifei, who combines features of the schismatic Prince Myshetsky, Nikita "Pustosviat" [the Bigot] beheaded by Sophia in 1682, and the most celebrated preacher of the Old Belief in Russian history, the Archpriest Avvakum.[39] Still other characters, including Shaklovity and Andrei Khovansky (the son), bear genuine historical names, but the events associated with them in the opera do not accord with the historical record. And a final category (including the Clerk, Marfa, Emma, and Susanna) has precedent as a social or historical type, but is modeled on no specific historical figure. So character, like event, is true to history only in crude outline, intermittently and with artistic embellishment.

Two more verisimilitudes remain to be considered. The first concerns embedded musical genres. *Khovanshchina* is significantly less declamatory than Musorgsky's earlier operas. The sinuous dances of Persian slave girls and female peasant choruses that amuse the orientalized satrap Ivan Khovansky in Act IV (distracting from and leading up to his murder) are as conventional an inserted ornament as in any eighteenth-century chamber opera—and in the brutal context of Muscovite politics, far more terrifying. Folksongs and church-style chants adorn and at times govern the musical texture. But these native genres do not, as a rule, embody seventeenth-century harmonies or musical forms.[40] Musorgsky's sources for folk music (both words and melodies) were contemporary anthologies—or songs making the rounds of the capital, as was the case with Marfa's famous song

---

38  For details on historical prototypes, see Bakaeva (n. 17 above), 29–47; Frid (n. 17 above), 127–85; Shirinian (n. 16 above), 202–22.
39  On sources for Dosifei, see Frid, 164–78.
40  See Vladimir Morosan, "Folk and Chant Elements in Musorgsky's Choral Writing," in *Musorgsky: In Memoriam, 1881–1981*, ed. Malcolm Hamrick Brown (Ann Arbor, Mich., 1982), 99–131.

in Act III.[41] His settings are closer to Western European harmony than to anything in the indigenous Russian tradition. Recent work on the Old Believer texts and choruses has shown that Musorgsky did not draw upon authentic liturgical texts, nor does he appear to have been familiar with ancient church chants.[42] In sum, the musical genres in *Khovanshchina*, like its chronology and its characters, are only partially, in this case impressionistically, true to their time and historical prototypes.

It remains to consider the verbal fabric of the libretto itself. Here the parameters of verisimilitude are complex. Musorgsky had constructed his earlier operas, *Marriage* and the first version of *Boris*, on the principle of fidelity to spoken Russian. This "speech" was adjusted, at times stylized, and enriched with signature motifs and embedded songs, but the uttered phrase still remained the intonational touchstone of the opera, that to which it was true. *Khovanshchina* presents a significantly different picture. Here, as one Soviet musicologist has put it, "the composer does not go from word to melody (as in *Boris*) but from melody to word, from a melodic generalization to a manifestation, in words, of the associative content of the melody."[43] If the rule for *Marriage* and *Boris* is singularity, the unique utterance unfolding through time, then the rule for *Khovanshchina* is repeatability, the single melodic unit that recurs obsessively behind many different words. Exemplary here is the opening "Dawn" motif and, of course, Marfa's love theme — which occurs ten times in the opera, always to different words and in different situations.

The stability of melody in *Khovanshchina* does not mean, however, that the settings ignore the intonation patterns of a prose text. Here as elsewhere, Musorgsky demonstrates an extraordinary ear: at least one student of the opera detects a different socio-linguistic rhythmic layer for each character.[44]

---

[41] See Frid (n. 17 above), 223. "Iskhodila mladen'ka," the most famous folksong melody associated with *Khovanshchina*, was by Musorgsky's time well known in musical circles. It was published in Vil'boa's folksong anthology in 1860, and Tchaikovsky included it in his own collection, *50 Folksongs Arranged for Piano Four-Hands* (Tchaikovsky also used the melody in his own "Groza" overture). Musorgsky apparently first heard the song from the actor and folklorist Gorbunov.

[42] See Morosan, 123–26. The opera as a whole contains only one Old Believer melody, sung in the final immolation scene, and even that is not a liturgical chant but a secular devotional song.

[43] Ogolevets, *Vokal'nala dramaturgiia Musorgskogo* (n. 36 above), 318. The subsequent comment on Marfa's musical line occurs on the same page.

[44] See Shirinian (n. 16 above), 173–74. Ivan Khovansky's language is ritualized, narrow in scope, with phrases that barely move (he has a "leitword" — "Spasi Bog!" — rather

But this linguistic differentiation is not that of the seventeenth century. Except in those places where actual documents from the 1680s are set to music almost intact—the denunciation, the pardon, and the personal letters—the language of the opera is contemporary with its composer, not with its events on stage. To create a sense of historical verisimilitude in language, Musorgsky saturated certain roles (especially the Old Believers) with archaisms. But he did not create the libretto wholly in the language of its depicted time.

We see, then, that language verisimilitude in *Khovanshchina* is as partial and artistically hybrid as are the other fidelities. It is this last linguistic category, however, that marks most clearly the space separating *Khovanshchina* from *Boris Godunov* as historical opera. The language in *Boris* (with the exception of several stylized portions in the parts of Pimen and Varlaam) is thoroughly modern; its source text, after all, was written in 1825 in keeping with a Romantic aesthetics. In the *Boris* operas, Musorgsky made no special effort to mark the cultural distance between his nineteenth-century present and the sixteenth-century Muscovy of Tsar Boris's time—as Pushkin, excepting the occasional colorful archaism, had not before him. The primary verisimilitude observed (in the first version especially, but in the second as well) was the truth of Russian intonation as spoken in Musorgsky's own era, amplified and embellished into melodic recitative. *Boris Godunov*, with its 300-year-old plot, presents itself on stage as something dynamic, dramatic, and contemporary.

The events depicted in *Khovanshchina* occur a half-century after the reign of Boris Godunov, on the brink of Russia's modern era. But the verbal fabric sounds immeasurably older; text, music, and theme combine to distance the opera from the audience's present. This distancing effect, as suggested earlier, has led some musicologists to classify *Khovanshchina* as an epic.[45] But the "epic essence" of *Khovanshchina* is more far-reaching than most

---

than a leitmotif); Andrei Khovansky's lexicon is full of poetic folk expressions, crudely parodied in his cynical pursuit of Emma; Golitsyn's language is "Europeanized," with fewer Russian roots, and his melodies more changeable; the Clerk sings a public-square language of comic self-abasement. Dosifei is master of many styles: to the Old Believers or in his lyrical monologues his speech is dominated by Church Slavonicisms, but to Marfa his language is lyrical and passionate. Marfa, too, has an extremely rich lexicon, although musically her part could be described as one sustained lament.

[45] See Frid (n. 17 above); also Shirinian, who prefers the category of "lyrical folk epic"— remarking on the unhurried pace of most scenes, the many digressions on Russia's fate, the solemn and predominantly trochaic meter of the text, and the lack of a sense of proportion among the opera's parts (166–87).

critics have suspected. The alternative framework for reading the libretto that I offer here alters the dramatic intent of the opera. Its legibility depends upon a fifth verisimilitude in addition to historical event, character, music, and language: fidelity to each character's inner vision of time.


*V*


*Khovanshchina*, I suggest, is not merely distanced from its audience, as are all epics. In addition, each character is distanced from every other character within the opera. Each major role lives in its own time, and that time is valuable primarily for what is past about it. The *streltsy* mourn their lost autonomy; Marfa mourns her lost Andrei and the memory of their love; Emma mourns her exiled fiancé and Andrei — obsessively — his lost Emma; old Khovansky mourns his loss of rank vis-à-vis the upstart princes at Sophia's court; and chief among those princes, Vasily Golitsyn, mourns the passing of his glory, both as Sophia's lover and as military commander. Nothing that is mourned in this opera ever returns, at least not on the plane of this world. For the characters within the opera, the future is as closed as epic plots are to later audiences. All true value remains in the past.

This might explain why Musorgsky routinely resisted Stasov's request to make the libretto more dramatic and give the characters more to do. Turn Marfa into Golitsyn's mistress, Stasov advised, put Marfa on trial for her illicit love, add the potential of passion to the characters' (and hence to the audience's) present.[46] In the end, Marfa remains a vehicle of memory, and the other characters are astonishing in their unwillingness (or inability) to learn from events on stage.

The crucial emblem uniting all these isolated, bereaved fates is the Old Belief. It surely is no accident that the only loving, communicative exchanges in the opera occur between Marfa and Dosifei — because they have given up this world. For them, time has genuinely stopped. History is already over. The passing of more time can only confirm what has already been decreed; it can introduce nothing new. As Dosifei gives us to understand at several points, the Old Believers (in their own lexicon, "True Believers") are not in Russia,

---

[46] See Stasov's letter to Musorgsky of 18 May 1876, in which he complains about the purposelessness of activity in the opera and the characters' strange, vacant interactions, the "jerkiness and external episodic quality of the whole" (*The Musorgsky Reader* [n. 11 above], 333–36).

but have lost Russia and are seeking her. Holy Russia is in another time and space altogether, in a static future that will, in the act of martyrdom, fuse with a sacred past. Then perfect memory will triumph over change, that curse of the present.

The hypothesis that Musorgsky structured his entire opera around "Old / True Believer time" requires some expansion. The opera's secular or profane plot is a single tissue of blind self-interest, lust, power-mongering, and murder. Only among the Old Believers does any genuine faith or love operate. Musorgsky copied into his *Khovanshchina* notebook more excerpts (fifteen) from the Archpriest Avvakum's autobiography than from any other single source, but none of these excerpts reflects the Archpriest's intolerant or aggressive side.[47] Baiting intolerance is not the province of the Old Belief in this opera. The Old Believers' function is to stop time. And here, it seems, is a productive way to understand Bakaeva's claim that in *Khovanshchina* Musorgsky rejects the "narrative principle." Old Believers appear whenever a stand-off debate, or self-doubt, or personal rivalry, begins — that is, whenever time threatens to change something, whenever drama invades the libretto.

Consider the general pattern of plot movement in the opera. At various points in Acts I, II, and III, the forces of Old Muscovy gather — and are deadlocked. Then Dosifei or Marfa comes onstage to disperse the tension: Marfa to save Emma from Andrei, Dosifei to save Emma from both Khovanskys. In the next scene, Dosifei arrives to separate Khovansky and

---

47   Frid (see n. 17 above), 164–69; Bakaeva (see n. 17 above), 29–38 and 59–60. Bakaeva considers the lexical borrowings from Avvakum's autobiography so benevolent and so uncharacteristic of the historical Archpriest that she doubts that Avvakum should be considered a prototype for Dosifei. See also A. Andreev, "Zametki o soderzhanii 'Khovanshchiny'" [Comments on the Contents of *Khovanshchina*], *SM*, 1981 (3), 99, where a case is made for Dosifei's different temperament: his is one of renunciation, whereas Avvakum is decidedly free of that "consciousness of chosen martyrdom" that Dosifei assumes and that so isolates the Old Believers in the opera. Toward the same end, Musorgsky made changes in the blue-notebook libretto that lessen Marfa's dramatic and accusatory function. Omitted from Act 1 (Scene 1 in the libretto) is an exchange where Marfa accuses Andrei of being false to his Orthodox oath "not to fall under the charm of the Lutheran faith, a snare of the Antichrist" (Pekelis [n. 20 above], 149); likewise, the scene with Marfa, Susanna, and Dosifei is considerably shortened in the final libretto version. In an earlier variant (151) Marfa defends herself vociferously against possible condemnation by a court of her fellow schismatics; in the 1879 text, Marfa ignores Susanna's ravings about court proceedings and concentrates on saving Susanna's soul — i.e. driving devils out of it (138–40). She is already transported far beyond any "legal" reality on a secular plane.

Golitsyn and then to offer protection to Marfa. But the deadlocks are not resolved, they are simply dissolved. Dosifei enters a scene and silences both sides. No one resists him, but no one is changed by him. The Old Believer element thus presents that odd spectacle of authority that is unquestioned but somehow is impotent to move action ahead in this world.

In the blue-notebook libretto, Dosifei appears in five of the six scenes, and his presence is much more prominent and paradoxical than in the versions of the opera familiar to us. In every appearance, Dosifei maximizes his authority with his immediate audience by sensing the tone that makes his presence most authoritative for them. With Marfa he is a loving father; with Susanna he drives out devils; with Golitsyn and Khovansky in Act II — a conversation severely cut and simplified by Rimsky — he teases the two men with his possible past identity as Prince Myshetsky.[48] All the squabbling factions are continually put to shame by the sophistication and dignity of Dosifei, but ultimately he owes his own moral stability to an abandonment of the social reality in which all the others live.[49]

Marfa and Dosifei, the only morally uncontaminated persons among the major heroes of *Khovanshchina*, live in "Old Believer time and space." As a genuinely apocalyptic structure, it cannot co-exist; given any credence

---

[48]  Dosifei seeds and then confirms rumors of his princely lineage as soon as his secular counterparts place any constraint on his authority. See the lengthy passage from the 1879 libretto, omitted by Rimsky, which reads in part:
DOSIFEI: Princes! Calm your rage.
GOLITSYN: Dosifei! I beg you to keep within your proper limits. You have forgotten that princes have their own way of doing things, it's not your way, my good man.
DOSIFEI: I've not forgotten, I have only to remember my own past. [...] a forgotten past, forever buried [...] My princely rights, which I myself cast aside [...] [The princes debate the rumor, and Khovansky then chides Dosifei for disavowing his rank.]
DOSIFEI: But let's drop this empty chatter, princes. We've gathered here to advise one another: let's begin, time will not wait. (Pekelis [n. 20 above], 136)

[49]  One recent Soviet commentator on Musorgsky has confronted this issue squarely. "Dramatic development in *Khovanshchina* is unusual in the extreme," she writes. "In the final analysis, the conflict between the departing 'old' and arriving 'new' is resolved by Musorgsky in accordance with historical truth. The old order perishes in the face of the new. But at the same time all the major heroes of the opera perish" (Elena Abyzova, *Modest Petrovich Musorgskii* [Moscow, 1985], 122–23). This understates the case. In a letter to Stasov in August 1873, Musorgsky describes the confrontation of the princes in Act II: his intent was to "expose this vile conference at Golitsyn's in its true light, where they're all grabbing at the throne and scepter, and probably Dosifei is the only one with a firmly fixed conviction" *(The Musorgsky Reader* [n. 11 above], 240). This is true — and the conviction firmly fixed in Dosifei is that the new order perishes in the face of the old — and the old will be forever.

at all in a work, it must dominate. The bleak strength of the Old Belief is compelling in the blue-notebook libretto, where the (admittedly incomplete) final immolation scene contains no Marfa and no Andrei. The only surviving hero is Dosifei, exhorting the true believers to sacrifice, as the shrouded chorus responds: "We have no fear, father, our promise before God is sacred and unalterable. [ ... ] The enemy of man, the prince of this world has come! Terrible are the fetters of the Antichrist!"[50]

In Soviet scholarship, the preferred image of Musorgsky as populist and progressive has tended to narrow the role of Old Belief. The schismatics are either cast as exotic and ornamental or — in an alternative move — presented as proto-revolutionaries, constrained by their religious prejudices to play a reactionary political role but nevertheless a genuine anti-government force. The centerpiece for the latter argument is always the hymn sung by Dosifei at the beginning of Act V: "We shall burn, but we shall not surrender" [*sgorim, a ne dadimsia!*] — a line which, in any case, is not in any of Musorgsky's manuscripts and which Rimsky-Korsakov apparently invented.[51] The effect of both "exotic" and "revolutionary" approaches to the Old Belief has been, in my view, to domesticate the radical, and radically disturbing, historical framework that Musorgsky offers in this opera. Its events cannot be incorporated into a comfortable historical continuum of future revolutions, or even of failed attempts at revolution. The representation of "apocalyptic time and space" has more unsettling implications for historical opera grounded in real events. Musorgsky tells the story from a point of view sympathetic to the one group that did not believe in a future. This permits him to be both realistic and otherworldly at once, and true to his desire to reflect the spirit of an age. That age presents no easy transition to our present.

One important index of meaning in any apocalyptic structure would be its frame, its sense of beginnings and ends. *Khovanshchina* begins with

---

50  See Pekelis (n. 20 above), 147–48. At the end of this brief scene, Pekelis adds: "A dialogue between Marfa and Andrei Khovansky was projected, as well as a scene with Dosifei and the schismatics." See also n. 26 above.

51  The line occurs in the 1883 Bessel (Rimsky) first edition, at the end of thirty measures of text and music wholly by Rimsky: "Brothers! Our cause is lost! Throughout Russia we are persecuted. Old man Khovansky is dead, Golitsyn is in exile, our hope Prince Andrei is hiding with us in the hermitage. And whose fault is it? The quarreling of the princes themselves [...] The time has come to suffer for the Orthodox Faith. [...] We shall burn, but we shall not surrender!" (Act V, scene 2, 189–90). Rimsky's text returns Dosifei vigorously to the political arena — in contrast to Musorgsky's versions, where Dosifei's final words are already abstract and liturgical, no longer of this world.

the beautiful, but ideologically ambiguous, prologue, "Dawn over Moscow River." But Musorgsky left the end of Act II,[52] and also the end of the opera, unfinished—leaving to later editors and arrangers the necessity of tying up the whole. This is a delicate task, for whatever is done to the final scene of an historical opera will generate a philosophy of history retroactively applicable to the rest of the work. Unfortunately, Musorgsky himself is an uncertain ally in this project, for he expressed his views on Russian history (and on the role of the schism within it) with characteristic eccentricity. His personal ideology has been intensely and inconclusively debated.[53]

Among those obliged to create endings for Musorgsky, Rimsky-Korsakov has been the most influential—and he chose a progressive statist solution. He completed Act II with a recapitulation of the "Dawn" theme, thus linking Peter's final edict to "arrest the Khovanskys" with this inspiring theme of a new dawn for Russia. Rimsky then further advanced Peter's cause by

---

[52] Apparently Musorgsky was experimenting with new ways to end his scenes, and had projected a vocal quintet to end Act II. An ensemble piece to climax the second act of an opera was "new," of course, only in the context of Musorgsky's evolution; it is a conventional ending structure, quite in keeping with the Romantic, lyric emphasis in *Khovanshchina*. Musorgsky's failure to compose the finale was probably due to the challenge of composing a grand quintet for the unusual combination of three basses, one tenor, and one mezzo.

[53] In the 1930s, as we have seen, Asafiev popularized the idea of the people as carrier of the statist principle. Scholarship in the 1940s advanced the thesis that the "Dawn" theme opening the opera (and recurring at various points in Rimsky's redaction) was intended to refer positively to the Petrine reforms and a new day for Russia (Asafiev, "Russkii narod, russkie liudi" [n. 27 above]). In the post-Stalinist period a cautious rethinking began. M. Sokol'sky suggested that the "Dawn" theme was not necessarily so optimistic; the true theme of *Khovanshchina* was not the people, but the *deception* of the people, who are forever misguided, caught off guard, and unable to rally in time ("Narod v 'Khovanshchine' Musorgskogo" [The Folk in Musorgsky's *Khovanshchina*], SM 1954 [12], 61–72). Recently A. Andreev has updated this idea, turning deception into parody: Musorgsky is giving us a parodied "Dawn" scene, he suggests, the ironic evocation of a fairy-tale to open an opera that then unfolds as one hideous disintegration after another (See "Zametki o soderzhanii 'Khovanshchiny,'" [cf. note 47 above], 95–99). In the 1970s, the Musorgsky specialist Shlifshtein decisively separated himself from the Asafiev thesis: the Petrine reforms were *not* progressive for the people, and Musorgsky was careful to idealize no special social class—preferring to be, as Pushkin had been before him, "as dispassionate as fate" ("Otkuda zhe rassvet" [see n. 29 above], 106–17). Frid (see n. 17 above) argues an ideologically neutral position: Musorgsky was sympathetic to social movements and ideas, she writes, but "he did not have a clear-cut *system* of opinions on social matters" (72). Less persuasive is M. Rakhmanova's attempt to link Musorgsky with the *pochvenniki* of the 1860s and their "progressive" understanding of the Schism: see her "Musorgskii i ego vremia," SM 1980 (9), 95–110, and 10 (1980), 109–15.

adding his own aggressive finale to the closing scene: as the hermitage burns, a trumpet fanfare by Peter's troops obliterates the Old Belivers' fragile hymn. This vigorous pro-Petrine stance fits in well with Rimsky's own statist views on Russian history as reflected, say, in his *Pskovitianka* of the same period.[54] But other reconstructions are certainly possible. For his 1958 re-orchestration of the opera, Shostakovich rethought the unfinished portions, ended his version of Act II with a martial fanfare instead of the "Dawn" (more appropriate, perhaps, but equally liable to a pro-Peter reading), and provided two alternative endings for the final scene. Between these two famous versions, Igor Stravinsky reconstructed an ending chorus from Musorgsky's manuscripts for the 1913 Diaghilev production that culminated with neither fanfare nor "Dawn" theme but simply with the hymn itself, which fades eerily offstage.[55] Stravinsky's solution would seem to be the one most honest to Musorgsky's intent. For *Khovanshchina* moves forward neither through the acts of individual heroes, nor through the will of massed crowds on stage, but through the otherworldly workings of fate.

Fate-based operas are common enough, of course, especially with libretti drawn from fairy tales or myth. But what is peculiar in *Khovanshchina* is the implacability of fate combined with a concreteness of historical event. Even more startling is the absence of any genuine, sustained dramatic resistance — of the sort we get in *Boris Godunov* — to what fate has decreed. Characters do not confront their destiny so much as fuse with it. The crucial concepts in the libretto are those favorite words of Marfa and Dosifei: *sud'ba* [fate] and *nevolia* [unfreedom, or "non-will"]. "In God's will lies our non-will," Dosifei consoles Marfa, and all the characters still alive by the end of the opera come around to this truth. The passage of time neither adds nor removes. This truth applies not only to matters of the spirit but also to the most insistent, passionate attachments of the flesh. In an astonishing piece of advice Dosifei says to Marfa: Do not resist your sinful love, do not censure yourself. "Endure, my dear child, love as you have always loved, and all your sufferings will pass." Even the foolish Andrei Khovansky finally ceases asking for Emma and instead sings that moving melody at the foot of the funeral pyre: "Gdye moia voliushka" [where has my dear freedom gone?].

54  See Richard Taruskin, "'The Present in the Past': Russian Opera and Russian Historiography ca. 1870," *Russian and Soviet Music: Essays for Boris Schwarz*, ed. Malcolm Hamrick Brown (Ann Arbor, Mich., 1984), 77–146, esp. 90ff.

55  See the Bessel vocal score, "Zakliuchitel'nyi khor dlia 'Khovanshchiny'" by Igor Stravinsky (St. Petersburg and Moscow, 1913). Claudio Abbado first utilized the Stravinsky ending in his 1996 Deutsche Grammophon recording.

We sense here Musorgsky's own passion and terror for human history as a powerful but ultimately blind force. In the fall of 1872, just as *Khovanshchina* was first being sketched out, Musorgsky wrote Vladimir Stasov that he was reading Darwin and in bliss: "While instructing man as to his origin, Darwin knows exactly the kind of animal he has to deal with... Without man being aware of it, he is gripped in a vise."[56]

A central message in *Khovanshchina* is man's unfreedom in history. This theme resonates variously in Musorgsky's two surviving versions of the ending scene: the uncompleted communal farewell between Dosifei and the Old Believers in the 1879 libretto, and similar choral passages, enriched with dialogue between Marfa and Andrei, in the manuscript score. In both settings lust, hate, and action are countered by profoundly passive sorrow and love. The reality of this world drops away before the eternal glory of the next. Musorgsky's inability over eight years to complete the opera perhaps attests to the difficulty of transmitting this idea of unfreedom in a format that is both dramatic and realistic. The Old Believers are the key, for they were a real historical force with an integral worldview, and yet they expected nothing from the temporal processes of this world but evil.

Such an apocalyptic, fate-based opera must of necessity transpose all positive historical reality to some other realm. The features that Emilia Frid and Galina Bakaeva note in their analyses are present in this reading too, but with a different aesthetic rationale. Action in *Khovanshchina* is indeed decentered and events "pass through one another," because man's power to control the result of his activity is profoundly restricted. If the narrative principle gives way to static lyrical digression, it is because all important personal stories have already happened and Old Believers are forever on guard to stop time. Emilia Frid links the "general idea" of these lyrical digressions vaguely with Russian patriotism, for their content is universal rather than personal. But another aspect of the lyrical interludes seems at least as significant: they are neither from nor to individuals, and they do not stimulate or expect any response. When the conservative music critic Hermann Laroche reviewed a performance of *Khovanshchina* in 1893, he

---

[56]    Musorgsky to Vladimir Stasov, 18 October 1872 (in *The Musorgsky Reader* [n. 11 above], 198). See also the review of the Metropolitan Opera production by Evan Eisenberg in *The Nation* (8 February 1986): 154–56. Eisenberg locates the central force of the opera in the hopelessness of human striving within the timelessness of the black earth of Mother Russia. The plot is confusing, he writes, "[b]ut one relation is clear: the female principle that is Marfa overpowers all the men and binds them to their fate. She is the earth they walk on, the earth that gave them birth and will take them back" (156).

faulted Musorgsky for an inability to write persuasive recitative. It was a complaint, Laroche admitted, that made him seem "more of a royalist than the king."[57]

*Khovanshchina* thus marks a somber stage in Musorgsky's own creative evolution. The libretto represents a falling-away of dialogue—not necessarily because Musorgsky's skills had deteriorated or his tastes had changed, but because the historical material provoked a cast of characters who no longer listen. If one trait links all the secular heroes in this opera (collective as well as solo), it is their tendency to be caught unawares, to wake up too late.[58] Emblematic here are the opening lines of Shaklovity's aria in Act III, sung to the *streltsy* who are dead to the world at noon: "The lair of the streltsy sleeps. Sleep on, Russian people, the enemy is not slumbering!" The Old Believers, to be sure, are eternally alert, but they can hear or desire nothing new. The opera is thus caught in an odd unfree time where those who do not oversleep merely wait until the preordained comes to pass.

There are hints of the same personal helplessness and acquiescence to fate in Pushkin's *Boris Godunov*. Musorgsky learned from Pushkin for both his historical dramas, but the lessons were different. In the 1869 and 1874 *Boris Godunov* (significantly labeled an opera, not a "people's musical drama") the title role takes on all the melodramatic guilt and self-hatred that Pushkin had deliberately laid aside in his play. All sin is concentrated in Boris's personal past, in the murder of Dmitri at Uglich. Boris attempts to atone for that sin with his death—for in the opera, fate is linked with personal action and responsibility. The individual personality remains central to the resolution of the plot. And thus both versions of the opera, while drawing on historical events and featuring historical figures, remain personal dramas in history, not dramas about history.

*Khovanshchina* is structured differently.[59] Here, much as in Pushkin's *Boris Godunov*, fate is linked with personal renunciation and impotence. Nothing anyone can do will alter events; no single character is empowered to resolve the plot. Each player merely acts his own appetite out to the end.

---

57  H. Laroche, "Musorgskii i ego 'Khovanshchina,'" *Teatral'naia gazeta* 23 (1893); cited in Rakhmanova, "100-letiiu" (see n. 1 above), 95.

58  See Sokol'sky (n. 53 above), 64–66.

59  The title itself shifts us away from the Khovanskys and into the realm of societal disorder; the suffix *-shchina* in Russian denotes troubled times associated with the excesses of the proper noun. But the action of the opera makes it quite clear that what Peter calls "Khovanshchina" or the "Khovansky mess" is not attributable to that family alone. Tsar Peter, too, is a historical figure looking for someone to blame.

All sin — and the opera is full of it — is in the present; the past is sacred, and the future (if we keep Peter's trumpets offstage) does not exist. The real ideology of the opera is stasis.

This reading suggests another level of meaning to Musorgsky's well-known lament for Russian history, written to Stasov at the beginning of the *Khovanshchina* period: "The power of the black earth will make itself manifest, when you plow to the very bottom. It is possible to plow the black earth with tools wrought of alien materials. And at the end of the 17th century they did plow Mother Russia with such tools... Paper, books, they've gone ahead — but we're still here... Public benefactors are inclined to glorify themselves and to fix their glory in documents, but the people groan, and drink to stifle their groans, and groan all the louder: still here!"[60]

The letter was written two weeks into the bicentennial celebrations marking Peter the Great's birth, launched in Petersburg at the end of May 1872.[61] The Petrine Jubilee was a confirmation of progress and historical optimism. As if in response to this affirming chorus, Musorgsky projected *Khovanshchina* as a document to which no "public benefactor" could affix his glory.

## VI

During that brief period in Soviet musicology when tsarist glorification of Peter the Great had receded and Soviet glorification of the revolutionary Russian folk had not yet become mandatory, Boris Asafiev wrote: "There is a groan that goes forth from all Musorgsky's music, and that groan stretches from the cradle to the grave."[62] But the nature of that suffering is encoded differently in *Khovanshchina* than in the other finished works of the 1870s. In both versions of *Boris*, and even more markedly in the vocal cycles *Sunless* and *Songs and Dances of Death*, private histories predominate. The dramas that unfold onstage illustrate personal loss and terror before individual

---

[60]   Musorgsky to Vladimir Stasov, 16 and 22 June 1872 (*The Musorgsky Reader*, 185–86).

[61]   For a discussion of the possible dialogue between *Khovanshchina* and this Petrine jubilee, see Sokol'sky (n. 53 above), 61–62. Sergei Soloviev's public lectures on Peter the Great, delivered at Moscow University in the spring of 1872 and widely publicized, were surely known to Musorgsky and supply another possible subtext. See S. M. Soloviev, *Publichnye chteniia o Petre Velikom* (Moscow, 1984), and esp. the interpretive afterword by L. N. Pushkarev (178–204).

[62]   B. Asafiev, *Simfonicheskie etiudy* (1922; rpt. Leningrad, 1970), 212.

death. With those works in mind, Asafiev is probably right to call Musorgsky more of a pessimistic Romantic than a realist or a populist. For the composer of those works, death "is neither a conciliatory principle nor a natural point of finalization — it is simply a senseless, unenlightened dead end."[63]

*Khovanshchina*, however, does not indulge the anguish of personal loss. The characters of this world — the *streltsy*, the Khovanskys, Golitsyn — do not engage our sympathies sufficiently for us to mourn their fall. The only sorrow we care about belongs to Marfa, and she can nevertheless end the opera on intonations of faith and ecstasy because death is for her a reunion; she has given up on earthly history altogether. Personal death is not a senseless dead end; only history is. Tragedy shifts from the individual plane to the universal, where its personal tones are muted and made less accessible.

With this move, Musorgsky emerges as a new sort of realist. He does not have the interests of the people in mind, but merely their experience. History books have gone ahead, as Musorgsky wrote Stasov; these are the books upon which historical drama must draw, but the people are *still there*. They owe the future nothing and expect nothing in return.

Musorgsky's historical stance gains special poignancy when measured against the various potential "audiences" of his opera. For educated Russians — those, that is, who wrote and read history books and believed in historical continuity — *Khovanshchina* was simply a historical opera on a period that had come to pass and that was now past. From an Old Believer point of view, however, such continuity is denied; our spectator's reality after the End is an illusion. We watch the salvation of others, their leap from the present to the Kingdom of God. Musorgsky's project, it seems, was to present an authentically apocalyptic sense of time (time before the end of time) to an audience that did not believe in it.[64] The appropriate response would indeed simulate being "gripped in a vise": everything is already over, but nothing will follow. History does not end with Divine Judgment or with any other value-producing event; it simply shuts down.

We have here, on the historical plane, the same dead-endedness that can be sensed in Musorgsky's 1875 cycle *Songs and Dances of Death*. In the first

---

[63] Asafiev, 213.

[64] For a persuasive account of changing attitudes toward time during the *Khovanshchina* era, see A. M. Panchenko, "Istoriia i vechnost' v sisteme kul'turnykh tsennostei russkogo barokko," *Trudy otdela drevnei russkoi literatury* 34 (1979): 197–98. Panchenko notes that the new historiography did not fear the Apocalypse; beginning in the seventeenth century the Final Judgment became a literary theme, an idea, and therefore distanced and allegorical. Here, we might surmise, was Musorgsky's audience, and his challenge.

three songs of that cycle, the touch of Death always ends both the life of the singer *and* the song; there is no place for survivors or witnesses. In the final song, "The Field Marshal," Death promises her victims on the battlefield that she will dance her dance over their bones, tamping the earth down so thoroughly that—contrary to the expectations of the deceased—they will never rise from the dead. That precisely is the effect of Old Believer time seriously presented to a nineteenth-century audience. From what perspective, indeed, can one tell the story of the end of time? To choose the Old Believer movement as vehicle for this bleak view of historical process was indeed a masterstroke, for the Old Belief was both in history and (from its own point of view) at the end of it.

The privileged position granted in this opera to non-communication, to stasis, perhaps even to the Apocalypse itself has intriguing implications for a poetics of opera.[65] Contrary to the spirit of Wagner—and, much later, perhaps to the spirit of Joseph Kerman as well—we seem to have in *Khovanshchina* an opera that succeeds because it is *not* drama. Individuals and events respond less to one another than to some higher temporality that renders them all powerless. And yet this operatic time and space is not mythic. The "collapse into historicity" that Wagner so lamented in German drama is thoroughly in force in Musorgsky's music-drama, which scrupulously recalls (and often reproduces) the documented historical event. This historical vision is sheathed in musical themes that recur with an almost obsessive regularity—suggesting, perhaps, that Musorgsky sought within the supremely temporal art of music some form to confirm the schismatics' faith that the passage of time no longer mattered. If his earlier operas explore the possibilities of interaction and dialogue, then *Khovanshchina*, it seems, explores the ways in which music can keep people apart. In the extremity of its final scene, it suggests how historical opera can stop history altogether.

---

[65]  These final speculations owe much to David Geppert, Gary Saul Morson, Robert William Oldani, and Richard Taruskin, who were kind enough to make numerous queries and suggestions that greatly contributed to the final shape of the text.

# 15

# TUMANOV ON MARIA OLENINA-D'ALHEIM

*The review below initially appeared in the* University of Toronto Quarterly 71, no. 1 *(Winter 2001/2002): 312–14. It commemorates one vital human link connecting Musorgsky's innovative music, especially his song repertory, with Western Europe (especially France) before the advent of Diaghilev.*

## REVIEW OF ALEXANDER TUMANOV'S
## *THE LIFE AND ARTISTRY OF MARIA OLENINA-D'ALHEIM*
## (2002)

Review of Alexander Tumanov, *The Life and Artistry of Maria Olenina-d'Alheim*. Trans. Christopher Barnes. University of Alberta Press, 2000. xix + 359 pp.

Most biographies describe history, but a rare few *collapse* it — and Tumanov's is one. The subject of this fascinating study is best approached from the end. Maria Alekseyevna Olenina, b. 1869, studied voice in St. Petersburg with Alexandra Purgold-Molas, Musorgsky's close friend and the most gifted performer of his songs. In 1963, at age 94, she was interviewed by Tumanov in Moscow. By that time Olenina-d'Alheim had outlived everyone (the best part of her life had ended in 1922, in France) and she could not remember large stretches of the 20th century. But with the reflexes of a professional singer and the capriciously functioning memory of the very, very old, she could vividly recall details of rhythm, text, and musical interpretation from the 1880s. This volume closes with a transcription, in Russian, of taped master classes on Musorgsky's vocal cycle "Nursery," conducted by Olenina-d'Alheim with two young singers in the 1960s. She was transmitting insight into performance technique that she had heard from an intimate of the composer himself. In the aural arts, where mechanisms for recording sound arrived so late and where so much is lost, this sort of continuity is thrilling.

Tumanov befriended the nonagenarian singer, uncelebrated in the capital despite her legendary services to Russian song, and was given access to her unpublished archive. His decision to stitch together a chronicle of her life out of her memoirs, correspondence, and others' reminiscences — to let her tell her own story — was a wise one, and Christopher Barnes's translation catches perfectly the naïveté and passionate stubbornness of the Russian original. The basics of her biography are as follows. Maria Olenina was born in the provinces and moved to St. Petersburg in the 1880s. Plucky, strong-willed, vision-impaired but gifted with a strong and expressive mezzo range, her extraordinary renditions of declamatory songs by composers of the Balakirev Circle won high praise from Vladimir Stasov. In 1893 she left for Paris, where she married the writer Pierre [Pyotr] d'Alheim, her Russian-French second cousin. Together they began to offer *conférences* [lecture-recitals] on Russian song and European Lieder. For the next decade the d'Alheims traveled back and forth, singing for Tolstoy at Yasnaya Polyana, stunning the Russian Symbolists Andrei Bely and Alexander Blok with their integrated programmes of music and word, collaborating with Darius Milhaud, Claude Debussy, Nadia Boulanger. But only in 1908, with the founding of *Dom Pesni* [The House of Song] in Moscow, did she command the institutional base from which to promote vocal chamber music in Russia as a sophisticated and complete art form.

Recitals, lecture series, voice coaching, publishing efforts (a monthly bulletin), and vocal competitions were undertaken on an ambitious scale. An uncompromising foe of the large hall, Olenina-d'Alheim was also wary of the virtuoso singer, who, in her view, used the song as a vehicle for self-aggrandizement, subordinating both words and context to brilliant tehnique. The singer, she taught, should be a conduit for the composer, whose genius could unfold more honestly in these modest genres than in the luxuriant, hyper-stimulated opera. Her own repertory included German, French, and English song, in addition to folk music. But Musorgsky remained at the core. That composer was hardly remembered in Russia at the time; thanks to this couple, his fame was growing in Western Europe.

In November 1918 the d'Alheims, who were French citizens, left Russia in what was part emigration, part expulsion. Pierre was slowly going insane from syphilis and died in an asylum in 1922. The widowed Marie tried to revive a "Maison du Lied" in Paris, but without success (she was impractical in organizational and financial matters and proud of it); her pro-Bolshevik sympathies and outspoken intelligentsial ways alienated her from the Parisian émigré community. Despite intervention from Maxim Gorky and Romain Rolland, attempts to return to Russia fell through. For forty years she hung on in Paris, giving the occasional recital (her last was in 1942, at age 71), supporting herself by a tiny pension and by selling leftist newspapers on the street. She never complained about her poverty. Although she joined the French Communist Party in 1945, she was not allowed to repatriate until 1959, when she was already in her 90th year. Back home, Soviet Russia's musical bureaucracy displeased her; but inquiries about a return to Paris led nowhere. She died forgotten at the age of 101.

Such documents as survive from such a free-spirited life do not easily cohere. There are large silent gaps: many of Olenina-d'Alheim's letters are undated; addresses shift and disappear; close friends (like Alfred Cortot) break off relations for decades over an obscure insult. She accumulated almost no possessions that might speak to the daily rituals of this very long life. Tumanov builds the story entirely around what she loved, and what she let drop away. Among the latter is her daughter, Marianna, born early in the marriage, whom Maria quickly considered obstreperous and shipped off to various aunts; when the girl was dying of tuberculosis as a teenager in 1910, her mother could not remain at the sanatorium because of a recital season already scheduled in Moscow. The other thing she cared very little about was money. In fact, she despised it: always in debt, Olenina-d'Alheim refused concert tours, considering them exploitative, and railed against advertising as demeaning to art. Even Balakirev, by the 1890s a grumpy and pessimistic old man, upbraided her for her self-defeating prejudice against the right of musicians to earn a living wage.

What she loved was the power of song. In the 1940s she wrote to a former student: you must possess "not only the desire, but the willpower and freedom to sacrifice your own self in favour of the composers and their creations." She never recorded her voice (of course) — but apparently a live performance by Olenina-d'Alheim was spellbinding. Not a large voice, it was absolutely at the service of the music and mood of the text, with every articulation and intonation worked out from within. That was where she lived, the only place that was ever fully in focus for her. In 1887, at her first meeting with the surviving "Mighty Handful" in Petersburg, the 18-year-old Maria Olenina from provincial Ryazan found herself in the presence of Borodin, Stasov, Cui, Tchaikovsky. "I could see no one clearly and didn't look at anyone," she recalled. "I sang ..."

# 16

# TCHAIKOVSKY'S TATIANA

---

*Among the most rewarding cultural outreach work of the past decades has been brief entries for playbills and program notes to accompany American productions of Russian opera. The entry below is a composite of two such commissions for Tchaikovsky's* Eugene Onegin: *first, the Stagebill essay for a Metropolitan Opera production in 1997; then, notes for the Houston Grand Opera in 2001.*

*The first essay, which was reprinted in* Tchaikovsky and his World, *ed. Leslie Kearney (Princeton: Princeton University Press, 1998), 216–19, was conceived under the influence of the 1995 "Tatiana wars." Reading it over after a decade, I fear that the gravitational pull of that debate might have twisted my grasp of Tchaikovsky's intent.*

---

## TCHAIKOVSKY'S TATIANA
## (1997)

### (A MET Stagebill)

Tchaikovsky's *Eugene Onegin* has often been accused of betraying its literary source — yet the charge is baffling. Operatic transposition is all about loving a text into new forms. Pushkin's novel-in-verse, finished in 1831 and hailed as a masterpiece, is hardly put in peril by the existence of a libretto illustrating its most "lyrical scenes." Tchaikovsky scrupulously preserved the poet's lines in all episodes of high emotional intensity. And unlike *The Queen of Spades*, the composer's second adaptation from Pushkin, the operatic *Onegin* remains very much Pushkin's story, the most famous Russian version of that familiar erotic plot: uncoordinated, unconsummated, yet ultimately symmetrical love.

The most common explanation for the infidelity charge is technical. Pushkin's novel, for all its familiar story, is an unprecedented, untranslatable miracle of form. A narrative of some five-and-a-half thousand lines, it is written in the intricate, 14-line "Onegin stanza," an adaptation of the sonnet with three quatrains, each differently "spun" (AbAb, CCdd, EffE), capped at the end with a rhyming couplet of self-reflexive commentary. The highly inflected syntax of Russian offered Pushkin a multitude of flexible rhymes, which he employed effortlessly (his characters all manage to chatter naturally within these elaborate constraints). Even the most fastidious and gifted translation of Pushkin's novel—and there have been several into English, most recently and brilliantly by James Falen—does not, and cannot, pace itself with the efficiency and tautness of Pushkin. This is because the Onegin stanza is both fixed and pliable: in places the rhyme groups are blurred, full stops are hopped over, the whole column of sound picks up speed—and readers find themselves disoriented, excited, and surprised each time the terminal couplet snaps the sonnet shut. In Russian, to recite *Eugene Onegin* is to treat oneself to a perpetually arousing, then consoling and relaxing, activity—in repeating 14-line segments. It has been called the closest that technical poetic form can come to inspiring in readers the temptations and unstoppable drives of love.

To touch this miracle of form, to flatten it out and then to inflate it into a libretto, could only mean a profanation—as Tchaikovsky well knew. His initial reluctance to touch the project, followed by his sudden conversion to it during the fateful year of 1877, is a staple of operatic lore. The composer was struck by Tatiana's futile letter to Onegin and by her unrequited love (surely both played a role in his own disastrous, short-lived marriage); he resolved, in a famous letter to Sergei Taneyev, to "set to music everything in *Onegin* that demands music." In keeping with Tchaikovsky's romantic gifts, this could only be a narrow extract of Pushkin's witty, abrasive, hyper-intelligent and frequently ironic text. In addition to the sentimental poet Lensky, what appealed to Tchaikovsky was pretty much all Tatiana. To understand the ambivalence and even bad conscience expressed toward this opera, however, we must look beyond technical form. Here, three aspects of Pushkin's novel are crucial.

First, with the exception of her letter in Chapter Three and her reprimand to Onegin in Chapter Eight, Pushkin's Tatiana is almost wholly silent. We know and see practically nothing about her. The garrulous, gullible narrator—himself in love with Tatiana—jealously protects her from prying eyes and from any shock that might add to the hurt he knows is already in store. He is reluctant to share her letter: seventy-nine freely-rhymed lines of unbearably frank confession, written, the narrator assures us, in French and translated for us only grudgingly. Tatiana's primary characteristic is detachment from her surroundings. She has profound feelings, but no public outlet for them. Her inner life is all fantasy, dream, or unwitnessed wandering. In an episode from Chapter Four that Tchaikovsky did not set, Tatiana has a terrifying dream: pursued through snowdrifts by a huge bear, she is ultimately entertained at table by monsters whose master is Onegin. In another unset episode, Tatiana, still smitten, visits Onegin's deserted house, seeking in his library some clue to his strange character (leafing through his books, she asks herself: "Perhaps he is a parody?"). Parody was not an option for Tchaikovsky, whose tastes in these lyrical love scenes turned toward the unmediated and pure. Pushkin's heroine reads, thinks, stores up impressions, passively waits; but except for the rash act of that one letter, she does not *act*. She is the Russians' Mona Lisa: a beckoning secret, the appeal of yet-unspent potential, of tensions in precarious balance. The very act of singing such a character would spend it and unbalance it — unless, of course, all songs for Tatiana were elegiac monologues or set pieces similar to the pastoral duet with her sister Olga that opens the opera. The operatic Tatiana begins in that mode. But Tchaikovsky, usurping the function of Pushkin's narrator with subtlety and enormous persistence, slowly reveals her inner self to us.

Second, Pushkin's novel is a lonely place. Many of its dramatic moments occur offstage or in dreams and fantasies; events are maddeningly delayed in the telling or happen to the heroes separately. We never see the initial meeting of the lovers; the letters hang there unanswered; the challenge to the duel is a private matter of terse notes, not a ballroom scandal. In Pushkin, live people often slide by one another. Obviously, any dramatization of this plot would have to bring the protagonists together. Since many of Pushkin's best lines belong to the narrator, arguably as on top of things as his creator, they must be given to someone for singing. In Act I, it is the rather-too-dim Lensky who analyzes the relationship between himself and Onegin evocatively as "wave and stone, verse and prose, ice and flame;" both men sing out their reservations about the duel while their seconds mark out paces; in the opening of Act III, Onegin sings the history of his own travels, but it is unclear why or to whose benefit. In both recitative and aria, the characters become infinitely "smarter" and more forthcoming about themselves than Pushkin's narration allows them to be.

But most disruptive to Pushkin's lonely story is the fact that in the opera's final scene, the two lovers sing their respective monologues to each other, and in the heated presence of each other. Onegin performs snatches of his earlier love letter to Tatiana (unanswered in Pushkin); Tatiana sings almost all of her reprimand to Onegin (which in the novel also goes unanswered; there, Tatiana reproaches him, rises and departs, leaving him dumbfounded on his knees). By turning these two solitary love statements into one love duet, pressure builds toward an embrace where in Pushkin there was none. Or rather, a conventional scene of "love versus duty" replaces Pushkin's much more tantalizing ambiguity.

The precise tone and overtone of Tatiana's final words to Onegin in the novel have occasioned much discussion. Olga Peters Hasty, who devoted an entire book to Pushkin's Tatiana, has suggested intriguingly that the most famous of all Russian renunciations, "*No ia drugomu otdana; / Ia budu vek emu verna*" [But I have been given to another; / I will be eternally faithful to him], also permits a literal (if only penumbral) reading along these lines: "But I have given [myself] to another" (i.e., to another person, image, perhaps of Onegin or even of her own earlier self)—and it is to that image that Tatiana now desires to be true. To bring this ideal down to the realm of mutual loving, to consummate it (at considerable risk) and enter it into real time, would most certainly destroy it. Or possibly Tatiana, an experienced married woman by the final chapter, has come to see Onegin's vices more soberly and wants none of them (this is what Tchaikovsky's orchestration suggests in his setting of this scene, with its hint of Lensky's theme recalling that unnecessary duel and death). Or perhaps she now believes the words Onegin had uttered to her in the country: that his type is simply unsuited for the bliss of love and married life. But that, too, we are not given to know in Pushkin's novel. Tatiana tells us only that she still loves Onegin and that she will be "faithful," which is to say, she will not alter her present state. Action is simply suspended—and Pushkin, abandoning his unfortunate hero as the clank of the husband's spurs is heard in the doorway, abruptly takes leave of his novel.

Such a dramatic suspension might have been possible for Musorgsky; the holy fool on stage alone at the end of *Boris Godunov* is just such an excruciatingly suspended tonality. But not for Tchaikovsky. He had chosen as his central theme Tatiana's lyric suffering, her desire, then her ultimate self-discipline—not her mystery. Pushkin, in contrast, structures his novel so that mystery is central: we do not know what Tatiana wants. In the words of the literary historian D. S. Mirsky, this "classical attitude of Pushkin, of sympathy without pity for the man and of respect without reward for the woman, has never been revived."

We thus arrive at our last point about the novelistic *Onegin*. It has to do with cultural eras. Although influenced by Romanticism, Pushkin remained a classicist—just as Tchaikovsky, for all of the realism that pressed in on him in the Age of the Russian Novel, remained a Romantic. Temperamentally an eighteenth-century aristocrat, Pushkin was not comfortable with public displays of embarrassment. He did not believe, as Dostoevsky and Tolstoy so earnestly did, that gestures of self-humiliation were proof of a person's sincerity. Such reticence was natural to a pre-Realist age, one that took decorum and social codes very seriously. To avoid public shame, after all, was one important purpose of the duel of honor, an institution that was to claim Pushkin's life (he was killed in a duel at age thirty-eight, defending his wife's honor and his own). By refusing to fall and repent, sin and tell — easy and colorful paths, full of the juice of plot — Pushkin's Tatiana is a paradigm of energy under constraint, of inspiration itself. She is the perfect neoclassical Muse.

When Tchaikovsky made Tatiana the center of his opera, he had to open her to humiliation, uncontrollable impulses, self-expression in the presence of others, the lovers' duet. Precisely in this realm are the most irrational charges of infidelity lodged against Tchaikovsky's opera, even by those who appreciate fully his genius and the glories of his music. The issue is not merely words; every libretto alters words. The blasphemy of the opera is one of psychology. It violates a personality beloved by Russians for its single act of compulsive exposure — which is then followed by silence, a commitment to privacy, a closed world that is rich but reluctant to express and define itself. For Pushkin's Tatiana is better than the rest of us: rebuffed and shamed, she does not even dream of playing out her fantasies. Paradoxically, by presenting the story from Tatiana's point of view and allowing her to struggle openly, sing back, be embraced, Tchaikovsky breaks the vessel he would most honor.

## TCHAIKOVSKY'S *EUGENE ONEGIN:*
## THE WOMEN AND THEIR WORLDS
## (2001)

(Houston Grand Opera)

As Tchaikovsky himself acknowledged, Pushkin's "novel in verse" *Eugene Onegin* (1823–31) did not lend itself to operatic treatment. Cast in intricately rhyming 14-line stanzas, it is dominated by a gossipy, intrusive narrator destined to fall out of any dramatized version of the plot. The novel is almost devoid of eye-to-eye contact, that is, potential duets. Lovers write letters, or dream, or lecture one another sternly; they do not make trysts or tenderly converse. Bad timing is the rule. Tatiana writes a letter to Onegin; he turns her down and soon after disappears. When Onegin later writes to Tatiana, she does not respond at all. In the novel's final scene, after the hero has abjectly declared his love, the heroine says no, rises, and leaves. Love in Pushkin's novel is always being aroused, nurtured, consuming the lover, but it does not give rise to reciprocated events. Can one build intense operatic confrontations out of non-events and non-meetings? This was the challenge facing Tchaikovsky when, in 1877, he turned to Pushkin's masterpiece. His response was to focus on the women.

Tchaikovsky was 37 — and during that year, two women fatefully entered his life. The first was a young student at the Conservatory named Antonina Miliukova, who wrote Tchaikovsky a letter declaring her passionate love. Not wishing to play the heartless Onegin to her helpless Tatiana, the composer not only agreed to see her but resolved to marry her. In Russian society of that time, homosexuality was condemned by the Church but tolerated if discreetly practiced; it was not uncommon for homosexual men to marry for the sake of appearances, with full understanding on the part of the wife and with no change in the husband's style of life. But Antonina apparently insisted on a "normal marriage" — which brought Tchaikovsky to the brink of nervous collapse. After three months, his wife was removed from him permanently.

The other woman in his life was far more benevolent, but equally distanced. This was Nadezhda von Meck, nine years older than Tchaikovsky, a widow who at the age of 16 had married a Russified German engineer, bore him 18 children — and who, when her husband died, discovered (perhaps not surprisingly) that she was deeply weary of men *as men*. She became infatuated with Tchaikovsky's music and offered him a stipend of 6,000 rubles annually, an arrangement that lasted for fourteen years. The one condition laid down by Madame von Meck was that she and her beneficiary never meet. In 1877, the Muse smiled on Tchaikovsky. The ill-starred wife had been banished, and the composer had befriended another woman who was willing to pay him to produce music full-time as long as he did not attempt to interact with her in any medium more intimate than written correspondence. It was the perfect Onegin-Tatiana situation as Pushkin had envisioned it: all passion was displaced on to letters, none of it happened in a present time-and-space shared by the lovers, and none of it registered on the actual body. Such were the benefits of non-consummation.

Excessive distance, however, is not dramatic. To make Pushkin's plot work on stage, the composer would have to compress and overlap the novel's private, lonely "time-space zones" so that people would *sing* to one another all those sentiments which in the novel they send off, or wait for, or suffer through in silence. Tchaikovsky desired a series of "lyrical scenes," but trust and lyric warmth were not prominent in his source. Perhaps opera could provide it, through the convention of the aria—a musical form publicly sung but privately experienced and consumed. Tatiana's Letter Scene (the first episode Tchaikovsky composed) is precisely such a trustful spontaneous outpouring. But set arias cannot be the whole of an opera; they can only be the peak moments. Singers must also cluster on stage and communicate through group dynamics. How could Pushkin's trademark atmosphere of aloneness, disjunction, and mistiming be sustained at the more "collective" moments of the opera?

Two routes presented themselves. Tchaikovsky had the resources of the orchestra, which could create tantalizing counterpoint against the words characters sing, adding a nostalgic or ironic coloration by referring back to earlier motifs and emotions. This method is used in the final scene, where Tchaikovsky forces into dialogue large segments of Pushkin's lonely, linear plot. He has the smitten Onegin *sing*, to a flesh-and-blood, physically present Tatiana, the lines that in the novel he only writes to her, and writes to her fruitlessly. Such on-the-spot singing wears down her resistance. Unlike the novelistic Onegin, the operatic hero is a stubborn fighter and a wooer. Tatiana struggles against his attractiveness. If anything keeps her true to her marriage vows, it is the persistent musical (not verbal or experiential) reminder of Lensky's death by Onegin's pistol shot, a motif that recurs only in the orchestra. In this final scene, there is no consummation—but it comes exceedingly close. Music itself dangerously thickens and complicates the emotions of the lovers, as Pushkin's lines are re-arranged, superimposed, and collapsed in time in order to create a dramatically effective scene.

There was another resource: the miracle of the libretto. It is common practice to despise the libretto as a literary form, but in fact libretti need not flatten out character nor inflate it in crude, simplistic ways. A libretto can achieve subtleties that novels cannot dream of and even spoken drama cannot do: it can portray the development of complex inner feelings in two, three, four characters *all at the same time*. In a stage play this would be cacophony, a shouting match, comic and incomprehensible; in an opera, it is simply an ensemble. Here Tchaikovsky's genius was profound. In *Eugene Onegin*, the arias—Lensky's, Tatiana's, Onegin's, Prince Gremin's—are rather straightforward; the ensembles, however, are haunting and disorienting. Characters often do not sing to each other but alongside one another, with a sort of "tubular vision," each locked in his or her own space and time. Listening in to these scenes, are we supposed to feel alone, or "together?" *Eugene Onegin*, I suggest, was a bold attempt on Tchaikovsky's part to broaden the potential of the romantic lyrical zone.

Consider only one such ensemble-cluster, the famous opening scene. It is a quartet for four female voices, organized around the four ages of women. First there is the young girl dreaming of love (Tatiana), as yet unaroused by any specific image. Then, on an upward trajectory of concrete experience, the "awakened" girl (her younger sister Olga), already engaged to be married. For the widowed mother, Madame Larina, the erotic realm is long past (in keeping with certain Romantic conventions, mothers of teen-age girls were aged like grandmothers — as if no woman produced a surviving child until she was past forty). And then, in a timeless zone of her own, comes the ancient peasant nurse Filippievna, for whom Eros presumably never existed at all, and in any case was certainly not to be remembered. The key refrain of the quartet is a famous line that Pushkin adapted from Chateaubriand: "God sends us habit from above / In place of happiness and love" [*Privychka svyshe nam dana: / Zamena schastiiu ona*]. Our life is successful to the extent that we can adjust to events beyond our control — because, as Pushkin will demonstrate, routines and habits are a very good replacement for "events," which inevitably bring pain, emotional explosion, and collapse.

A vocabulary of explosion and collapse is precisely what operas would seem to require. But Tchaikovsky, a man of impeccable taste and discretion, felt otherwise. He did not believe in the Romantic ideal of the rebellious, alienated poet. Music should not exhaust or scandalize us, but delight us. And what delights us is what we can follow easily and identify with effortlessly. Tchaikovsky was exceptionally good at musicalizing everyday experience. Thus he was attracted to the French model of the "Opèra Lyrique," which focused not on exotic adventures or supernatural events but on modest everyday *responses* to ordinary events. Tchaikovsky was a universalizer, a democrat, a crowd-pleaser — as was his beloved hero, Mozart. The best parts of the world, he insisted, were run by love that had become a habit. But how bold to attempt this everyday moral truth inside a romantic opera!

The opera's women represent this truth in its purest form. In the opening quartet, each woman sings her own words pertaining to her own phase of experience: one an extinguished past, one a nostalgic past, one a happy present, one an anxious future. (It is interesting that in an early draft of the libretto, Tchaikovsky noted down the precise ages of his characters: Tatiana is 17, Madame Larina 56, the nurse 70.) Of the four, only Tatiana moves and grows. In contrast to these richly diversified ages of women, the men's duets are aggressive and confrontational. Their behavior results in big foolish events that interrupt life's humane habits, such as the scandal at Tatiana's name day and the lethal duel that resulted from it. Although they make a show of being different, in their final duet Lensky and Onegin sing the same words. The two male leads are active, belligerent, but essentially one-dimensional. In contrast, the women in the first scene might appear passive — but collectively they have been everywhere, they absorb all of life's important events. The men are either episodic, like Prince Gremin, or else they fumble about, killing each other off.

All this is very far from the grand, consummation-oriented Italian opera, full of hysterical divas, driving appetites and melodrama, that surrounded Tchaikovsky in the 1860s and 70s. But it is rather close to Pushkin. Pushkin's story is also governed by fate and by symmetrical renunciation. But the texture is not tragic. The best life, Pushkin everywhere advises in his neoclassical spirit, is one in which there are no disruptive events; where everything happens in its right time, where you mature gracefully into your next role. "Blessed is he" who goes through life's paces in the proper order: this is one of the narrator's most insistent refrains. In the opera, the four ages of women are not spread out in a line but *stacked*, one on top of the other, singing over each other's lines. Again and again, instead of dramatic "operatic" action, we get from the women the reality of renunciation and submission to habit. Only in the final scene is temptation played out. But that resolution is not consummated; it backs off and remains at the level of two lovers' fantasies. In a way, the finale resembles the women's quartet of the opening scene: all together, but each alone. Tchaikovsky's *Eugene Onegin* is not Pushkin's, but it is among the loneliest, most self-contained and disciplined lyrical worlds ever put on stage.

# LITTLE OPERAS TO PUSHKIN'S
## *LITTLE TRAGEDIES*

---

*Turn-of-the-millennium Pushkin celebrations in Russia were ubiquitous and extra-vagant — so much so that a certain weariness set in, even in that Jubilee-loving land, before the actual day arrived. Among the abiding benefits of these gala anniversaries is an upsurge in multi-mediated cultural events that otherwise might not get a hearing. The four operas written to Pushkin's four little chamber tragedies is a case in point. The essay below, in a slightly different version, appeared in Svetlana Evdokimova, ed.,* Alexander Pushkin's Little Tragedies: The Poetics of Brevity *(Madison: University of Wisconsin Press, 2003), 265–89.*

---

## LITTLE TRAGEDIES, LITTLE OPERAS
### (2003)

In January 1999, in the Russian city of Perm on the Siberian frontier, the Pushkin Bicentennial year was set into motion with an unusual musical event. The Perm Academic Theater of Opera and Ballet premiered a project two years in the making: a cycle of five operas in three nights entitled *Operatic Pushkiniana*. It featured Musorgsky's initial (1869, chamber-sized) version of *Boris Godunov* and then, performed back to back, the four chamber operas created by four Russian composers out of Pushkin's Little Tragedies, composed at Boldino during the miraculous autumn of 1830: *The Covetous Knight, Mozart and Salieri, The Stone Guest,* and *A Feast in Time of Plague*.[1]

The Perm musicians had debated at length the unity of Pushkin's dramatic cycle. Was it a laboratory in which the poet had experimented with minimalist dramatic form? A concise encyclopedia of human passions and vices? A window into Pushkin's own anxieties circa 1830 (miserly fathers,

---

[1] For a sympathetic report of the Perm opera project by its director that includes formal and informal reviews by members of the audience, see Georgii Issakian, "Russkoe Kol'tso," *Muzykal'naia Akademiia* 2 (1999): 22–30.

professional jealousies, the pleasures of bachelor love becoming the horror of cuckoldry, the capriciousness of cholera)? Were these miniature plays meant to be "pocket metatheater," with the Baron, Don Juan, Salieri, and Walsingham each representing an eternal type — or do the heroes undergo genuine dramatic development, a moral change or moment of conversion that makes their stories more akin to the dramatized parables of didactic theater? And then there was the usual anxiety that flares up whenever Russia's most perfect poet is transposed to opera. Is it not a sort of blasphemy to dilute Pushkin's lines by adding actors and music?

One thing was clear: however one assessed the cohesiveness of Pushkin's dramatic cycle, there was no easy or ready unity among the musical works created out of its parts. The "little operas" had been composed by various hands, variously gifted, between 1869 and 1906. Each of the composers — Alexander Dargomyzhsky, Nikolai Rimsky-Korsakov, Cesar Cui, Sergei Rachmaninoff — took advantage of the remarkable verbal compression of the plays, their already "librettistic" quality, and each set Pushkin's text essentially intact, making the occasional tiny cut but neither supplementing nor rearranging the poet's words. Thus these transpositions have been spared the charge of "grossly violating Pushkin" that is routinely leveled against Musorgsky and, even more, against Tchaikovsky. Those two titans in the world of opera sinned and achieved on a grand scale. Since their source texts were not in singable (or actable) form, they were obliged to adapt and compress, producing out of Pushkin very fine, very free, and inevitably "unfaithful" full-length operas that today proudly coexist in the canon as independent creations. None of the chamber operas built off the Little Tragedies possesses the range or complex vision that governs the operatic *Boris Godunov*, *Eugene Onegin*, or *Queen of Spades*.

In fact, the problem presented by these four little musical works is an exception in the annals of nineteenth-century opera, which adapted full-length plays, novels, epics, and national legends with great inventiveness and aplomb. The plays in Pushkin's dramatic cycle required almost no reworking. The astonished librettist is confronted with that most rare thing: a source text that, as it stands, is not too long. Thus absolute fidelity to the poet's words becomes a real possibility — and another problem presents itself to the composer: what precisely should a musicalization accomplish? Why is music needed at all? Is there such a thing as over-realizing an emotional gesture or psychological moment, already pitched to perfection? The task bears some resemblance to song writing. With a miraculous confluence of talents, a perfect lyric poem can be set as a perfect song. But setting a "little drama" is not the same as setting a poem, even a very long poem or narrative ballad. In the Russian tradition, the greatest accomplishment in that genre is Musorgsky's song cycle *The Songs and Dances of Death* (1875–77), where a single voice to piano accompaniment performs both Death and its victim in four dramatic scenes depicting not just the sense of grief that follows death but the process of dying, in its own time and complete with end-point. Full-fledged dramatic episodes with more than one participant tend quickly to musical theater, however: to opera and orchestration. Thus vocal settings that strive to be faithful to a larger verbal-dramatic whole, where so much depends on dialogue and on the precise timing of encounters and scenes, are always vulnerable to that curious blend of inflation and flattening that full-scale opera knows so well. As one recent American translator of Pushkin's Little Tragedies has remarked, "each of the 'Little Tragedies' starts, so to speak, at the beginning of the fifth act, at the moment when a preexisting unstable situation is at the point of becoming a crisis, and moves swiftly and inexorably to its catastrophic climax."[2] Recast for chamber performance, these "fifth acts" come to resemble more closely a heightened dialogic fragment — the explosive end moment of recognition and catastrophe — than they do authentic drama. There is little time for musical motifs to develop, for actions to ripen, or for heroes to mature. Unsurprisingly, each little opera in its own era was welcomed as a curiosity, but received mixed reviews. It was assumed that Pushkin had written his four compact little plays in 1830 as closet drama, a privately consumed genre. To musicalize them was to take them aggressively off the printed page and on to the stage.

With the exception of Rimsky-Korsakov's *Mozart and Salieri* (and that only barely), none of the four little operas entered standard repertory. They are recalled to performance most often as an extension of Pushkin's legacy, linked to one of his jubilees, rather than recognized as musical achievements central to their composers' creative evolution. Significantly, the operas in piano-vocal score were reissued in 1999, as a Pushkin Bicentennial tribute, in a single glossy four-volume series, with brief introductory essays in Russian and English and an (uncredited) English translation of the relevant Little Tragedy at the end of each volume.[3] Cui's fragmentary effort would never otherwise have

---

2    Nancy K. Anderson, "Introduction," in Alexander Pushkin, *The Little Tragedies* (New Haven: Yale University Press, 2000), 6.

3    A. S. Pushkin, *Malen'kie tragedii. Opery russkikh kompozitorov* (Sankt-Peterburg: Kompozitor, 1999). These convenient, sturdily produced bilingual volumes are not scholarly efforts, although there are some surprising and very helpful inclusions (for example, the inter-scene "Intermezzo-fughetto" that Rimsky-Korsakov wrote for his *Mozart and Salieri* and then destroyed, but which was then discovered in a piano four-hand arrangement among his posthumous papers, is included as an Appendix to that volume).

merited so prolonged a life in such distinguished musical company. In 1999 the Perm Opera Company billed its three-night extravaganza as the "Russian Ring," but this Wagnerian promotion tactic was a considerable liberty. Any musical rationale for linking, in a single performance cycle, these four works of uncertain genre by four different composers would be slight. Could the glistening thread of Pushkin's word provide sufficient unity? In terms of musical style or technical excellence, probably not. As part of the history of nineteenth-century Russian musical adaptation of its classics (a history as dense and self-referential as its literary counterpart), very possibly so. This essay will briefly review the birth of each little opera and speculate on their collective contribution to the larger canvas of Pushkin and music.

## *Four premieres, four disappointments*

In February 1872, three years after the death of its creator, Alexander Dargomyzhsky (1813–69), *The Stone Guest* premiered in St. Petersburg's Mariinskii Theater.[4] It soon faded from repertory, making a brief revival only thirty years later in a fresh orchestration by Rimsky-Korsakov for the Pushkin Centennial. This delicate chamber work has had a curious fate. Everywhere cited as path-breaking (the first Russian "dialogue opera") and admired for its scrupulous word-for-word realization of a lyric text, the opera is nevertheless rarely performed. Without a doubt, its purely musical appeal has been obscured by the strident polemics surrounding its birth. Dargomyzhsky was a disciple of Mikhail Glinka and elder patron of the so-called Balakirev Circle of composers in St. Petersburg. This group of very young, intensely gifted "amateurs" eschewed the conservatory, with its Germanic professoriat, that had just been founded (1862) across town; instead, they trained around the keyboard, analyzing in four-hand piano reduction the latest major European compositions and experimenting with Russian variants on these genres. During the final year of his life, invalided by heart disease, Dargomyzhsky was seized with a passion for expressing "truth" in music. The values to which he pledged to be true were word-based, the intonational contours and dramatic impulse of Pushkin's speech — and the crowning work of his career, that which most perfectly honors this

---

4    The most thorough account of this opera and its significance for stage art in the 1860s remains Richard Taruskin, *Opera and Drama as Preached and Practiced in Russia* (Ann Arbor: UMI Research Press, 1981), ch. 5, "The Stone Guest and its progeny."

principle, is his *Stone Guest* (the composer died with all but a few bars complete). Dargomyzhsky was Russia's first thoroughgoing disciple of Gluck.[5] He studiously avoided the devices by which mainstream opera composers of his day subdued a vocal line and subordinated it to music: division into numbers, strict definition between aria and recitative, strophic repetition, the rounded set song, syncopation incompatible with the accent patterns of uttered speech, melisma or exaggerated pitch intervals. But unlike his fellow reformer Richard Wagner, who also sought to liberate music drama from conventional operatic structure, Dargomyzhsky did not rely on a symphonic principle to give melodic and rhythmic unity to the whole. He insisted that the orchestra serve the voice.

Dargomyzhsky did not understand voice in a naturalistic sense, however — that is, as a prosaic, expository, bluntly street-smart sound. In the mid-1860s the only member of the Circle with such radical aspirations was Modest Musorgsky, who recreated whimsical children's speech as exquisitely spontaneous melody in his song cycle *Detskaia* [The Nursery, 1868], and deliberately harsh "sung conversation" in his setting of Gogol's dramatic farce *Marriage*. Nevertheless, Musorgsky dedicated his exercise in Gogolian declamation to the older composer, a Russian pioneer in the "words first" principle. But Pushkin's graceful poetic text hardly invited the abrasive treatment that Gogol's prose summoned forth. And in any event, Dargomyzhsky's goal was more conventional. He sought a texture that was part parlando and part song, where music would enhance the expressiveness of the words but not drag the words into its own rhythmic wake, not engulf them with too much intricately patterned sound or exploit them as mere carriers for virtuoso vocal effects. With a single exception, the composer does not develop leitmotifs musically. (That exception is the Commandore's ominous "signature," five ascending and then descending degrees of the whole-tone scale, variously harmonized and embellished with the conventional horrific diminished seventh when the statue appears at the door.) Overall, leitmotifs remain mere character tags announcing the approach of a person or an idea. In Pushkin's play, Don Juan is presented equally as a man of lust and a man of poetry, in Pushkin's understanding of that sublime creative category: a person who not only pursues his own pleasures of expression, but arouses equivalent interest and appetite in others. Taking his cue from this energetic image, Dargomyzhsky presents his hero as neither farcical

---

[5]   For a brief discussion in English, see Nicholas Maloff, *Pushkin's Dramas in Russian Music* (PhD. dissertation, University of Pittsburgh, 1976), 137–39.

nor evil but as earnest, romantic, amoral, bold, a passionate and impetuous improviser who is wholly committed to realizing desire in the present. To transmit this impulse, the play is set (in Richard Taruskin's apt formulation) as "a gargantuan, kaleidoscopically varied, through-composed 'romance.'"[6] Although more of a realist than the romantics before him, Dargomyzhsky never disavowed his simple and robust gift for song.

The Balakirev Circle would become known to history as the *Moguchaia kuchka*, or "mighty handful" of nationalist composers: Milii Balakirev, Modest Musorgsky, Alexander Borodin, Nikolai Rimsky-Korsakov, and Cesar Cui. *The Stone Guest* was created literally under the eyes and ears of these "mighty-handful-ists" [*kuchkisty*], who educated themselves through musical scores and sustained themselves through charismatic personal example. They followed the ailing Dargomyzhsky's every gesture with reverence. Especially impressed was the young fortifications engineer, composer, and prolific music critic Cesar Cui, who several decades later would set *A Feast in Time of Plague*. In 1868, when the musicalization of *The Stone Guest* was not yet half finished, Cui published an essay extolling Dargomyzhsky's approach as the perfect realization of Pushkin's original.[7] It is rare, he remarked, to find a single artistic nature endowed equally with literary and musical talent. Librettists are a giftless breed and in any event (Cui argued) musicians — especially great ones — are accustomed to running roughshod over literary texts. Thus was Dargomyzhsky's experiment so extraordinary. He recognized Pushkin's play as an "ideal opera text" and was setting it "without changing a single word," guided by a passion to enhance, not engulf, the existing poetry. (Implicit in Cui's argument is a summons to rethink, perhaps even to reconcile, the ancient polemic between music and words — and to do so, one might add, in the spirit of Pushkin himself. In 1823 the poet had written to Vyazemsky that he disapproved of the latter's collaboration with Griboyedov on a comic libretto: "What has come into your head, to write an opera and subordinate the poet to the musician? Observe precedent properly!")[8] Dargomyzhsky's *Stone Guest*,

---

6    Taruskin, *Opera and Drama*, 269.

7    "Muzykal'nye zametki," slightly abridged in Ts. A. Kiui, *Izbrannye stat'i* (Leningrad: GosMuzIzdat, 1952), 143–47, hereafter cited in text. Cui's comments on *The Stone Guest* are translated in full in Taruskin, *Opera and Drama*, 298–300.

8    Pushkin to Prince Pyotr Vyazemsky, from Odessa to Moscow, 4 November 1823. Pushkin's comment about words versus music is followed by another remark on genre even more famous: "I wouldn't budge even for Rossini. As for what I'm doing, I am writing not a novel but a novel in verse — a devil of a difference!" *The Letters of Alexander Pushkin*, ed. and trans. J. Thomas Shaw (Madison: University of Wisconsin Press, 1969), 141.

Cui predicted, would become "the index by which Russian vocal composers will make corrections [in their own work] regarding accuracy of declamation and accurate transmission of the phrases of a text; this is dramatic truth, carried to its highest expression and united with intelligence, experience, knowledge of the matter and in many places [even] musical beauty."[9] There are no numbers or set pieces and no autonomous musical development; with the exception of Laura's two interpolated songs, the unfolding of the opera is identical to Pushkin's play. It was, Cui wrote, a "contemporary opera-drama without the slightest concession," and as such was a great forward-looking work.

With this first little opera, then, a principle was established that became a standard for the remaining three musical settings of Pushkin's Little Tragedies, two of which were undertaken by Dargomyzhsky's *kuchkist* friends in the twilight of their careers. This principle, common to much musical realism, is in fact a negation, the undoing of a criterion that has long distinguished spoken drama from operatic dramaturgy.[10] In contrast to staged plays, opera has traditionally insisted that the action taking place onstage (external, motivated by visible deeds, socially coherent, communicated through public recitative, responsive to the tangible world) is fundamentally separable from the inner life of the actors (which constitutes its own integral whole, answers to another logic, unfolds on its own in more private space, and is often transmitted solely through music). Thanks to this separation, musical forms can achieve independent development within the dynamic processes of operatic drama without being sensed as a distortion or a psychological untruth. A libretto is formally segmented into arias, ensembles, and recitative in order to make provision for this unfolding of purely musical structure. Judged by this traditional standard, Dargomyzhsky's *Stone Guest* — for all its musicality and inserted songs, and for all that Pushkin took the epigraph for his own play from the Da Ponte-Mozart *Don Giovanni* — can be said to contain only singing lines, not a libretto. Thus it is not an opera, and should not be judged by operatic criteria of musical structure or wholeness.

Such was the polemic, irritable and protracted, mounted by Pyotr Tchaikovsky, Ivan Turgenev, and other aesthetic conservatives of the 1870s and 1880s against Dargomyzhsky's quest for "accuracy and truth" in music. Among themselves these men ridiculed Cui's passionate defense of the *kuchkist*

---

[9]   Kiui, *Izbrannye stat'i*, 147.

[10]  I owe the initial formulation of this idea to Taruskin, *Opera and Drama*, 249–50, although he is not responsible for my extension of it here. Dargomyzhsky's "realism of dramaturgical technique and psychological penetration" permitted far more flexibility in the setting of character than did conventional operatic practice.

position. In the history of Western music, the debate is a familiar one. What is curious about its reflection on Russian soil, however, is the dual role played by Russia's greatest poet. In the crude polarization of critics during and after the Reform Era (radical anti-aesthetes such as Chernyshevsky and Pisarev against the conservative "defenders of Pushkin" — Annenkov, Druzhinin, Katkov), those parties who revered Dargomyzhsky's *Stone Guest* were musical radicals, hostile to received forms and rebels against the rule-mongering of the conservatory. But their radicalism was deployed to preserve and honor Pushkin's word, not to bury it. Their opponents in the Turgenev-Tchaikovsky camp, also worshipers of Pushkin, were not persuaded by these efforts. To them, this clarion call to "be true to the source text" was worse than misplaced fidelity; it was mistaken identity, a failure to understand fundamental rules of musical genre and the musician's role in creating a synthetic work of art. If a play or any other complex literary narrative "goes into music" without resistance and without adjustment, it could only suggest that the original was imperfect or inadequate, in need of a supplement. An "accurate" musical hybrid would not be homage to Pushkin, but quite the opposite.

Great transposed art, the conservatives reasoned, was always less timid. The literary text should work on the musician the way Pushkin's *Eugene Onegin* and *The Queen of Spades* worked on Tchaikovsky or — to borrow Leporello's formulation — the way Dona Anna's delicate shrouded heel worked on the imagination of Don Juan. For a true and original poet, one glimpse at a single part of a living whole is sufficient to trigger a creative response powerful enough to inspire a new, free work of art. Most of Don Juan's appalling erotic success in this play, and a good part of his valor in the face of death, is "improvisational" in just this inspired way, a product of his absolute trust that the needs and demands of this very minute will be satisfied, and satisfied mutually, once the spirit of the whole has been grasped. There is no prior script, no score, and thus no place for bookish fidelity or regrets. He has the perfect courage of the present. As Laura, Don Juan's female counterpart, explains this dynamic in scene 2 of Pushkin's play, all successful performance art must submit freely to inspiration in its own medium and on the spot, without relying on "words born slavishly and by rote" [*Slova lilis', kak budto ikh rozhdala / Ne pamiat' rabskaia, no serdtse*] [Words flowed out as if the heart had given birth to them, not slavish memory]. It appeared to the detractors of the operatic *Stone Guest* that Dargomyzhsky had not been free in this way. And thus, paradoxically, in his attempt to cherish Pushkin and to realize accurately the musical potential of the poet's lines, the composer stood accused of diminishing him.

In August 1898 in his St. Petersburg quarters, Rimsky-Korsakov (1844–1908) held a run-through of his just completed chamber opera, *Mozart and Salieri*. A gifted young bass from the provinces, Fyodor Chaliapin, sang both vocal parts; at the keyboard was Sergei Rachmaninoff. In November of that year, Savva Mamontov's Private Russian Opera Company premiered the work, which launched Chaliapin's spectacular career. But reception was overall lukewarm — and the composer's own voice was among the most ambivalent. With his habitual modesty and restraint, Rimsky noted in his memoirs that during the summer of 1897 he had set one scene from Pushkin's play and was pleased. "My recitatives were flowing freely, like the melodies of my latest songs," he wrote. "I had the feeling that I was entering upon a new period." In three weeks the work was done, "in the form of two operatic scenes in recitative-arioso style," which for Rimsky was new. He dedicated the opera to the memory of Dargomyzhsky. But in fact his own work is far more angular and less tuneful than his mentor's. Rimsky's sparse, arrhythmic, discontinuous orchestral texture, at times no more than chords that mimic the contours of a prior unaccompanied vocal line (usually Salieri's), recalled the experiments in musically enhanced speech undertaken by the far more radical Musorgsky. Although it approached the manner of Dargomyzhsky in his *Stone Guest*, Rimsky remarked guardedly, "the form and modulatory scheme of *Mozart and Salieri* were not quite so much of an accident."[11]

This bland reportage and cautious double-voiced tribute to his *kuchkist* past conceal a more dramatic story. Of all Pushkin's Little Tragedies, this one has most to do with music; of the four composers who set these texts, Rimsky has the creative biography most relevant to its celebrated plot of innocent genius versus professional discipline and the schoolmaster's rod. By the late 1890s, Rimsky's relationship to the Balakirev Circle of his youth had changed profoundly. The painful early stage of this weaning was compassionately described by Tchaikovsky in a letter to his patroness, Nadezhda von Meck, in December 1877: "All the new Petersburg composers are a very talented lot," he wrote,

> but they are all infected to the core with the most terrible conceit and the purely amateurish conviction that they are superior to the rest of the musical world. The sole exception recently has been Rimsky-Korsakov. Like the others, he is self-taught, but he has undergone an abrupt

---

[11]   Rimsky-Korsakov, *My Musical Life*, trans. Judah A. Joffe (New York: Vienna House / Knopf, 1972), 366–67, translation slightly adjusted.

transformation... As a very young man he fell in with a group of people who, first, assured him he was a genius, and second convinced him that there was no need to study, that schooling destroys inspiration, dries up creative power, etc. At first he believed it... [but five years ago] he discovered that the ideas preached by his circle had no sound basis, that their contempt of schooling, of classical music, their hatred of authority and precedents was nothing but ignorance. [And how much time had been wasted!] He was in despair [and asked me what to do.]... Obviously he had to study. And he began to study with such zeal that academic technique soon became indispensable to him. In a single summer he wrote an incredible number of contrapuntal exercises and sixty-four fugues... From contempt for the schools, he went over abruptly to a cult of musical technique. [His recent symphony and quartet] are crammed full of tricks but, as you so justly observe, bear the stamp of dry pedantry. At present he appears to be passing through a crisis, and it is hard to say how it will end. Either he will emerge a great master, or he will get totally bogged down in contrapuntal intricacies.[12]

In 1897, twenty-five years after that crisis summer, Rimsky (by now a great master and revered teacher) was again immersed in the study of fugues by Bach and Mozart. As he turned to Pushkin's "little tragedy" with the intention of commemorating his own past through two different paths to music, how uncannily resonant the poet's warning must have seemed.

Much attention has been given to Pushkin's self-image in this famous dichotomy. Did the poet identify with Mozart (so easy for Pushkin's infatuated readers to assume today) or, as some of the most acute Pushkinists have insisted (including Anna Akhmatova), with the nervous, neurotic, plodding craftsman Salieri? All creative work partakes of both aspects, certainly, but it is relevant to Rimsky's setting of the play to consider the nature of Salieri's envy. Two items are crucial to grasp in Salieri's opening monologue. First, Salieri is envious not of Mozart's fame — at the time, Salieri was more famous than Mozart — but of his incommensurability, his natural authoritativeness, what Salieri calls in an unguarded moment Mozart's "divinity." Salieri is sufficiently gifted as a receptor of art to know that fame and glory are worth very little, being only as trustworthy as their immediate audience. And second, Salieri is envious not so much of the man and not of the music (he

---

[12] Piotr Tchaikovsky to Nadezhda von Meck from San Remo, 24 December 1877–5 January 1978, quoted from Edward Garden and Nigel Gotteri, eds., *To My Best Friend: Correspondence between Tchaikovsky and Nadezhda von Meck 1876–1878* (Oxford: Clarendon Press, 1993), 120. Translation adjusted.

worships the music and has no problem elsewhere in his life with gratitude or discipleship). His envy rises up on behalf of the dignity of disciplined work. In Pushkin's "little tragedy," this imperative of grim and concentrated work in Salieri's mode — dry, pedantic, over-scrutinized, promising the toiler accountability and control — is foregrounded and obsessively replayed in lengthy, crabby monologues by the older man. Mozart is the briefer role, the opposite case, almost a hallucination, the spirit of pure music that analyzes itself reluctantly. In public Mozart would prefer to laugh and play.

In Rimsky-Korsakov's setting of this Little Tragedy, Mozart moves to the fore. Like Dargomyzhsky before him, Rimsky chose not to tamper with Pushkin's words (except for one seven-line cut in Salieri's second monologue).[13] He thus had two options for altering the balance between the protagonists: he could realize their two lines differently, giving Mozart a more vigorous melodic, harmonic and rhythmic profile, or he could "fill in" Pushkin's stage directions with real music, perhaps even with the real music composed by these two historical figures. Rimsky does both. It has often been noted that the two protagonists "are" their compositional styles: they sing onstage as they wrote. Salieri's part recalls *The Stone Guest* in the choppy, restricted melodic development of its recitative; although verbally passionate, it is musically quite meek and inert, taking its genres from a pre-Mozart era (for example, the species counterpoint of the opening monologue). In an intriguing variant on recitative, conventionally a "public" communicating genre, Salieri's meditations are not set as utterances — which they are not — but as thoughts, with a steady pulse and with the stress of spoken intonation unnaturally effaced, almost as if in "mental speech."[14] At no point is Salieri allowed to lose himself in song, that is, in inspiration. And when he "speaks," it is not primarily to his interlocutor onstage (to the immediately present Mozart) or even as a stage aside (to the audience), but to himself. His battle is wholly an inner one. Only two measures of the historical Salieri's actual music (his 1787 opera *Tarare*) are quoted by Rimsky — and those are sung affectionately not by him, but by Mozart.

In contrast, Mozartian music — prototypical or authentic — is abundant. When Mozart breaks in on his friend's morose monologue, he brings his

---

13    Rimsky wrote music for the entire second monologue but then omitted seven lines (following the first mention of Izora's poison) when he published the score.

14    This point is suggested by Mikhail Mishchenko in his prefatory note to the 1999 piano-vocal score of Rimsky-Korsakov's *Mozart i Salieri* (see note 3). Operatic monologue is often addressed to someone who conventionally is barred from hearing it; but Salieri addresses the impersonal future.

music with him. Throughout, Mozart's vocal line is lyrically and rhythmically rounded. The blind fiddler plays eight bars of Zerlina's aria from *Don Giovanni*; the fortepiano improvisation or "fantasia" that Mozart performs for Salieri at the keyboard is a stylization by Rimsky in the manner of Mozart's Piano Sonata in c minor. This fantasia, in two parts, contains themes that recur at appropriate psychological moments for Mozart: a limpid, lyrical section radiating harmonious good nature, followed by a dissonant ominous passage that comes to dominate in the second act as Mozart's thoughts turn darkly to the visit of the "man in black." The closer we approach the end, the more real Mozart's music becomes.

In keeping with Pushkin's stage direction and following his performance of the fantasia earlier, Mozart in his final moments sits down at the piano to play a portion of his *Requiem* for Salieri. But, as Peter Rabinowitz has pointed out, this last quotation is already performance of another sort.[15] What we hear are the opening sixteen bars of Mozart's *Requiem*, not imitated or stylized but pasted, with an overlay of piano and tiny adjustments in orchestration, directly into Rimsky's score. Since these opening measures call for the staggered entrance of a four-part chorus, those voices must resound backstage; in some productions of the opera, the *Requiem* is simply piped in. Either way, Mozart could not possibly be producing at the keyboard everything that the audience (both internal audience onstage and external audience in the hall) now hear. Salieri alone possesses sufficient musical competence to realize the majesty of the whole as it is being composed. If we in the hall hear the full-score *Requiem*, this is because we come later, with all the benefits of Mozart's fame and musical canonization. Salieri hears it through his own innate gift.

---

[15] Peter J. Rabinowitz, "Rimskii and Salieri," in *O Rus! Studia litteratia slavica in honorem Hugh McLean*, eds. Simon Karlinsky, James L. Rice, and Barry P. Scherr (Oakland CA: Berkeley Slavic Specialties, 1995), 57–68. In this contribution to his larger study of musical "listening acts," Rabinowitz draws two pairs of distinctions: between "technical" and "attributive" (or associative) listening and between primary music and imitative music (60–62). A subcategory of the imitative is "fictional music" (which imitates not some extra-musical object but other music or some other musical performance); to this category the quotation from the *Requiem* belongs. The fact that Salieri can realize its majesty from Mozart's bare-bones piano rendition onstage is indication, in Rabinowitz's opinion, of Salieri's musical superiority, both to his own contemporaries and to us, who need the aural prompt of the full score. Even if Rimsky-Korsakov the composer suspected "Salierism" in himself (and such moments are documented), then he shared with Salieri a highly gifted listener's appreciation of genius, as his handling of the *Requiem* quotation demonstrates (64). Mozart was correct to value this friend.

At this point in the opera, Rimsky-Korsakov as composer disappears, and Mozart-Salieri together become a single inspired creative unit. One sketches out a work of genius, the other perceives it in full. The historical Mozart, of course, never heard his *Requiem* at all, for he died before its premiere. Rimsky's own surrounding music pales by comparison. It is the later composer's tribute to the creators, listeners, admirers, even the fatal enviers of very great music that Mozart is more fully present during this *Requiem* — and more in possession of his own immortal legacy — than he had been as a living self. And arguably, this fully realized musical quotation within the opera (a device available only to Rimsky-Korsakov, not to Pushkin) is a more memorable episode than the melodrama of poison at the end.

The enhanced musical presence of Mozart in Rimsky-Korsakov's little opera hints at the complexity of this dialogue within the history of Russian music. As part of the musicalization of Pushkin's Little Tragedies, this second work, with its focus on Mozart, evokes that great composer's own involvement with the theme of *Don Giovanni / Don Juan / The Stone Guest*. Much as Pushkin had transfigured the literary forms bequeathed to him, so the three great operas that Mozart wrote with Lorenzo Da Ponte changed the potential of operatic genres for all of Europe. Servants no longer had to be frivolous or farcical. The classical alternation between recitative and aria could be replaced by continuous expressive musical storytelling. And musical drama at last became fully dramatic and responsive to the intricate wit of Italian speech without ceasing to be music of the genius class. Rimsky's attitude toward this legacy in the development of Russian music (and in his own evolution as a composer) could only be ambivalent. Foreign (mostly Italian) opera had reigned supreme in the Russian capitals for the previous 150 years, subsidized by the court and handsomely compensated. Only with the end of the imperial monopoly on theaters in 1883 did it become possible for wealthy private citizens (like Savva Mamontov, whose company premiered *Mozart and Salieri*) to mount Russian operas without state sponsorship or bureaucratic interference. Dargomyzhsky and the feisty band of autodidacts in the *Moguchaia kuchka* had been pioneers in "de-Italianization" during a much more difficult era. What did Rimsky owe this period of his own youth, now seen as misguided, and how does his little opera reflect that debt?

In a letter to his occasional librettist V. I. Belsky, Rimsky spoke candidly about his *Mozart and Salieri*. "This type of music (or opera) is an exclusive sort, and in most respects not a desirable one; I have little sympathy with it. I wrote this thing out of a desire to learn ... to find out how difficult it is ... [but] can it be that recitative-arioso a là *The Stone Guest* is more desirable than real, free music?"[16] One might argue that to utilize Pushkin's little text as a "learning exercise" en route to an ugly but necessary product not only mimics Musorgsky at work over *Marriage*, but is already in the pedantic spirit of Salieri. But in fact, the opera is a far more successful fusion of these two approaches to creation, and to these two personalities, than the intensely self-critical Rimsky-Korsakov allowed. The gradual usurpation of self-pity by genius and the replacement of Salieri's bitter monologues by ever purer stretches of Mozart's music (and Salieri's appreciation of it) are accompanied in the score by an increasingly dense interweaving of the two composers' motifs — and thus of their fates. Of course, Pushkin knew both realities: inspiration that is bestowed like grace and the thankless task of calculation and revision. What ultimately marks Pushkin as a Mozart in the world of poetic creators is not any childlike cheerfulness (his Mozart, after all, also suffers from insomnia and grim visions), not considerations of cosmic injustice in the distribution of talents, not details of personal behavior, but simply that Mozart's (and Pushkin's) art is great enough to transcend the costs of its genesis and the occasional inevitable complaints of its creator, whereas Salieri's is not.

In this opera, Rimsky-Korsakov — one of Russia's most indefatigable servants of music and benefactor to his more chaotic, disorganized musical friends — pays tribute to Dargomyzhsky's achievement and at the same time would transcend it. As with *The Stone Guest*, the public's appreciation was muted. Cesar Cui, the final *kuchkist* who would take on a Little Tragedy and a stern, capricious critic of the work of his own circle, was among those least impressed by his friend Rimsky's effort. In his review of the premiere in March 1899, he again praised that rare, brave librettist who bestowed equal rights on music and words. He recalled the daring of Dargomyzhsky, who in his time had resisted the temptation to modify Pushkin's text — even though the poet's *Stone Guest* "lacked several important musical elements: ensembles, choruses, and everywhere one meets ordinary rational speech, inappropriate for musical transmission."[17] But this second attempt to set

---

16    Cited in Taruskin, *Opera and Drama*, 326. Taruskin is rather negative on the success of Rimsky's opera, seeing it as a corrosion of Dargomyzhsky's more thoroughgoing, path-breaking experiment. "Rimsky cut the opera dialogue adrift from its aesthetic moorings," Taruskin writes, and then he tries to recuperate by casting "much of the music in an academically tinctured distillate of eighteenth century style...The result is a kind of superficially 'neoclassical' resurrection of the Mozartean recitative...which impoverished the genre to the point of futility." Taruskin is not persuaded that Salieri's "retrograde" music was in fact a deliberate character statement.

17    Kiui, "Moskovskaia Chastnaia Russkaia Opera," cited in Kiui, *Izbrannye stat'i*, 494–97.

one of Pushkin's Little Tragedies was, in Cui's opinion, "considerably less successful." This rebuke to Rimsky-Korsakov referred not to the "technical side" of the opera, which, given the composer's great gifts in orchestration and tone, was "almost beyond perfection;" what was deficient, according to Cui, was its "melodic recitative."[18] In his view, the dryness of the first scene was a lamentable decline from Dargomyzhsky, who had imparted musical vigor to his Don Juan from the first phrase. Apparently, Rimsky's decision to make Salieri as stiff and sterile as his music had achieved its purpose.

*A Feast in Time of Plague*, subtitled "Dramatic Scenes by A. S. Pushkin with Music by Cesar Cui," premiered in Moscow in November 1901. Fyodor Chaliapin performed in the role of the priest. It is a weak work by the weakest of the *kuchkist* composers; in addition, its source text, a fragment translated by Pushkin from John Wilson's play that features a collective protagonist, is the most diffuse and puzzling of the Little Tragedies. Yet this musical exercise too has a place in the sequence and its own lesson to impart. Cesar Cui (1835–1918) was highly regarded as a professor of military fortifications (by 1901 he had retired from state service) and as tutor in military studies to the imperial grand dukes. Although a prolific composer, he was better known for his peremptory and trenchantly self-confident music criticism, which stretched over forty years. Curiously, the militant realism and radicalism of his journalistic writings (he began propagandizing for his fellow *kuchkisty* in the early 1860s) is not reflected in his own creative work, which by general consensus is timid, mannered, elegant in its details but (with the exception of one exquisite song setting of a tiny lyric by Pushkin) easily forgettable.[19] Russian commentators kindly call Cui a "traditionalist," by which is meant a composer whose music is "heavily influenced by the high-society 'salon' culture of the nineteenth century," with "well-rounded vocal motifs" that impart a "rather static effect" to the whole.[20] Cui composed in a great variety of genres: choruses, quartets, piano music, vocal romances. Of his ten operas, seven were based on Western European literature (French and German); his three Russian-based operas draw exclusively on

---

[18] Ibid., 496, 497.

[19] That song is Cui's "Statue at Tsarskoe selo." For a thorough overview of Cui's several careers and considerable importance, see Taruskin, *Opera and Drama*, chap. 6, "'Kuchkism' in Practice: Two Operas by Cesar Cui." The two operas are *William Ratcliffe* (after Heine) and *Angelo* (after Victor Hugo). In the paragraphs that follow, I am indebted to Taruskin's summary of Cui's aesthetics.

[20] These phrases are from Mikhail Mishchenko's prefatory note to the piano-vocal score of Cui's *Pir vo vremia chumy* (1999).

the cosmopolitan Pushkin.[21] A handful of Cui's operas were familiar to the theater-going public of nineteenth-century Petersburg. But today, outside of several anthologized songs, all has slipped away with hardly a trace.

History has proved Cui more durable in his words and musical judgments than in his musical deeds. On one point, however, he was categorically consistent throughout his career, whether as composer or as music journalist. When words and music are combined in a single composition, Cui believed, each have equal rights — but the words must be written first. The opera or song composer who desires to be both emotionally moving and psychologically precise must begin with the text of a great poet. Only such highly condensed, efficient verbal material can discipline the composer, who, in the process of applying to words the richer, more flexible vocabulary of musical form, always runs the risk of dilution or vagueness of expression. It was a risk, Cui felt, to work the other way around. Since musical moods are so polyvalent, transient, and inexpressible, a well-structured musical line might call forth the most clumsy inarticulate prose or even no image at all. Least likely to emerge would be eloquent verse. Cui was not sympathetic to the familiar argument that great art songs are more safely built off second-rate poetry because (so the argument goes) only deficient poetry stands to gain rather than to lose when alien music and rhythms are added to it — even though the history of lieder writing in the Western world knows dozens of happily symbiotic examples. Little wonder that Cui's quest for the perfectly focused Russian text led him invariably to Pushkin. Unfortunately, in contrast to his fellow *kuchkist* composers, Cui was not equipped to set recitative with anything like the depth and originality that he admired in Dargomyzhsky.

Again, Tchaikovsky provides a portrait. He never understood why Cui, a miniaturist and enthusiastic devotee of light French music, should ever have associated himself with the non-aesthetic iconoclasts of the *kuchka*. All that united Cui with them, it seemed to Tchaikovsky, was dilettantism and disdain of professional schools. In the same 1878 letter to Madame von Meck in which Rimsky-Korsakov's crisis is so movingly described, Tchaikovsky wrote: "Cui is a talented amateur. His music lacks originality, but is graceful and elegant. It is too flirtatious and, as it were, too sleek, so you like it at first but then it quickly satiates...When he hits upon some pretty little idea, he fusses over it for a long time, redoes this or that, decorates it, adds all sorts of finishing touches, and all of this at very great length...Still, he

---

21  The other two are *Kavkazskii plennik* (1881) and *Kapitanskaia dochka* (1911), neither of which is in repertory.

undoubtedly has talent—and at least he has taste and flair."[22] Are grace, sleekness, and refined taste required for *A Feast in Time of Plague*? Cui in 1900 was apprehensive about the success of his *Feast* project—all the more so because he had been considering the idea for almost four decades.[23]

Cui was first attracted to the librettistic potential of Pushkin's *Feast* in 1858. Nothing came of the project at the time. Thirty years later, however, he composed "Walsingham's Hymn" (1889) and soon after "Mary's Song," the only two portions of the tragedy that are Pushkin's original poetry (that is, not a translation from Wilson's play). Both were performed in the Mariinskii Theater a decade later, in April 1899, at a Pushkin Centennial soiree. Success during that evening must have spurred Cui to wrap an opera around the two pieces. Thus in the evolution of this work we witness the reverse of Dargomyzhsky's practice with *The Stone Guest*, where the composer inserted into his musicalization two songs of his own invention that Pushkin had indicated solely in stage directions. In *Feast in Time of Plague*, the two pivotally important, nearly autonomous songs—Mary's submissive lament on the plague and Walsingham's defiant challenge to it—condense the musical virtues of the whole, and in fact preexisted that whole, by a decade.

Perhaps properly for this tableau-like and heroless play, Cui provides only two leitmotifs, both employed rather statically. The first is a boisterous "feast" theme; the second, a motif for "burying the dead." The latter is of marked interest: it is an ascending chromatic progression.[24] More common as a musical marker for dread and death, of course, is a descending scale. But Pushkin's plague-stricken, feasting Londoners resist on precisely this point: they will eventually die (of that there is no doubt), but until such time they are resolved to orient themselves upward in spirit. Beyond these two non-developing motifs and the two structurally simple songs, there is a thinness to the orchestration and a blandness to the recitative that could be seen as incongruous in so desperate an environment.

---

22  See Taruskin, *Opera and Drama*, 121, translation slightly adjusted.

23  For a good capsule history of the opera's genesis, predictably published in a Pushkin journal, see Lyle Neff, "César Cui's Opera *Feast in Time of Plague / Pir vo vremia chumy*," Prefatory note to a new English singing version of the text in *Pushkin Review / Pushkinskii vestnik* 1 (1998): 121–48.

24  The chapter on Cui's Feast in Maloff, "Pushkin's Dramas in Russian Music" (pt. 8, pp. 220–32), is valuable for bringing together what little is known about this work, its aftermath, and its feeble or ill-starred successors. The twelve-year-old Prokofiev also tried his hand at Pushkin's *Feast*, three years after Cui's premiere; in the 1930s, the émigré composer Arthur Lourié in Paris set this final little tragedy as a ballet, but the Nazi invasion pre-empted the premiere.

But paradoxically, the sweet and predictable quality of Cui's music, its static texture, lends a certain plausibility to the macabre horizon for the two central songs. Their melodies hover over the dialogic exchanges. "Mary's Song," a ballad-like composition in g minor, has a limpid, exhausted quality perfectly in keeping with its call for renunciation and the keeping of prudent distance, even (or especially) between lovers. In contrast, Walsingham's hymn resembles less a pious tribute than a crudely hewn march in syncopated rhythm, a demonic challenge,[25] with its stanzas alternating abruptly between major and minor key and ending on a high, affirmative, fortissimo command: "We'll sip the rosy maiden wine! And kiss the lips where plague may lie!" The old priest interrupts this blasphemy with his somber bass recitative in rebuke to the Master of Revels; in turn, the priest's lines evoke a choral from the feasters: "He speaks of Hell as one who knows." At this point in the opera we realize, more powerfully than is possible through the printed page, that all these various options — Mary's gentle resignation, Walsingham's defiance (demonic and increasingly unhinged), the priest's fire and brimstone — are literally on stage. Each option is being performed, each invites a response from the audience, and none can alter the final truth. The feast is then revealed for what it has in fact become, under pressure of musical realization: a singing contest, with all the rich mythological resonances of that event.

The singing contest is a cultural universal. A public competition is held in which songs are performed in the face of, and in defiance of, death. The singer would win back life, for himself or his beloved, whereas death stands mortally offended by music, that most temporal of arts, and would put an end to it forever. (The same opposition is at the base of Salieri's attempt — futile, as he knows full well — to nullify Mozart's music with something as trivial as poison.) In a paradox surely not intended by the earnest Cesar Cui, the very thinness of his operatic *Feast in Time of Plague*, its unadventurous plainness, serves to balance these two forces, music against death, and make of the contest a more terrible draw.

By generation and musical training, Sergei Rachmaninoff (1873–1943) lies outside the three composers so far considered. His *Covetous Knight* had its premiere at the Bolshoi Theater in 1906 under the composer's own direction, and its intersection with the earlier little operas is biographical and solely coincidental. In August 1898 Rachmaninoff had been the

---

25    For a reading of Walsingham's hymn as a document in Pushkin's demonology (as specific and ecstatic blasphemy), see Feliks Raskol'nikov, "'Pir vo vremia chumy' v svete problemy demonizma u Pushkina," *Pushkin Review / Pushkinskii vestnik* 3 (2000): 1–11.

pianist at a play-through of Rimsky's *Mozart and Salieri* for the benefit of Savva Mamontov, in whose Russian Private Opera he was then working as conductor. The young Chaliapin, who performed Salieri in the premiere of Rimsky, was the operatic artist whom Rachmaninoff envisaged for the all-important role of the miserly Baron in this new work. The sin examined here was greed, but the duty of fathers to sons was a vital supplementary theme. It is possible that Rachmaninoff's own father, who had squandered the family's wealth and left his newly married son struggling as a freelance professional musician, was the immediate stimulus for this opera project, just as Pushkin's own parsimonious wastrel father might well have been a pretext for the poet. In keeping with his predecessors who had composed little operas, Rachmaninoff chose to set Pushkin's text almost without change (only forty lines are omitted from the Baron's very lengthy monologue in scene 2, and two words added to the Duke). But there the similarities end. The most significant focus of difference between these two generations of musicians was their attitude toward Richard Wagner.

For members of the *Moguchaia kuchka*, a distrust of Wagner and rejection of the "symphonic principle" as the route to operatic reform was an article of faith. Again, Cesar Cui might serve as spokesman, for his position is by now a familiar one. In 1899, as part of the Pushkin Jubilee, Cui summed up four decades of polemics with his article "The Influence of Pushkin on Our Composers and on Their Vocal Style."[26] He noted that to date thirty operas had been written to Pushkin's texts, and he attributed this remarkably high number to the clarity, simplicity, and conciseness of Pushkin's language.[27] According to Cui, the appeal of Pushkin to artists working in other media yielded a double benefit: since composers were reluctant to deform such perfect verse into a routine libretto, many strove to realize Pushkin's line musically without tampering with it — and this practice, with its scrupulous attention to the poetic word, inevitably refined their own skills in musical expression. Pushkin, "our all," had again become the gold standard.

So Russians were now masters at accurate declaration and true voice setting. But Russian word-and-music dramas were different from Western European opera, Cui argued, even the most revolutionary. "In Wagner," Cui wrote, "the music does indeed illustrate the verbal text, but this illustration is located in the orchestra, to which the text hands over all major ideas; against

---

26   Cui, "Vliianie Pushkina na nashikh kompozitorov i na ikh vokal'nyi stil'," in Kiui, *Izbrannye stat'i*, 501–05.

27   Ibid., 502.

this rich background the singer might declaim properly, but he declaims non-meaningful, often content-less musical phrases. Such a system is at base false."[28] Orchestral music could amplify the verbal line but should never overwhelm it. In Cui's aesthetics, formal unity achieved by way of symphonic development was an impurity. By design or by default, large-scale Wagnerian innovations had been kept out of the first three little operas. Such was not the case with the fourth.

In the summer of 1902 Rachmaninoff, already opera conductor in Mamontov's company for several years and soon to take over at the Bolshoi, extended his European honeymoon to include a visit to Bayreuth, where he heard *Parsifal* and *The Ring*. As the themes, leitmotifs, and orchestral texture of his own subsequent opera make clear, he was powerfully influenced by this concept of music drama. Not only will gold lust be linked with Eros and death; it will destroy whole families and peoples. During two intense weeks in August 1903 Rachmaninoff created a *Covetous Knight* that was a blend of Wagnerian symphonism, the text-setting principles of his revered Tchaikovsky, and Russian mastery at declamation (Musorgsky's methods in *Boris Godunov* are especially prominent, receiving several direct quotations) — all under the aegis of mythologically heightened greed. Such a heterogeneous metaphysical texture was a harbinger of things to come. This was no longer the realist 1860s, when one argued over the relative value of Pushkin's genius versus a pair of boots. This was the symbolist era.

In obvious ways, Pushkin's *Covetous Knight* is not a grateful operatic text. There are no overtly musical episodes such as abound in Don Juan's Madrid, Mozart's Vienna, or even among the frantically feasting and singing Londoners during a plague. Female characters are wholly absent. There is only the sinuousness of gold itself, which, as the Baron's great monologue in scene 2 testifies in exhaustive detail, takes the place of everything: companionship, kindness, power, the sexual act, murder by the knife (which, like turning the key in a chest full of money, is "excitement . . . / And horror all at once"). But as with Salieri's envy, the Baron's greed is not a simple thing. What mortifies the miser about his heir, Albert, is not only that he will squander the content of the chests — wealth that the son did not earn and thus has no right to spend — but that he will remember his father as a man without passion, one who did not know "immortal longings," whose conscience never sounded, and whose "heart was all o'ergrown with moss." In this bitterness there is, of course, both miserly greed and knightly pride.

---

[28]   Ibid., 503.

Rachmaninoff attended carefully to all these aspects of Pushkin's complex hero. But both Fyodor Chaliapin, who for unknown reasons declined to sing the Baron on opening night, and Rimsky-Korsakov, whose magisterial opinion carried great weight, felt that the balance achieved was not the proper one. "The orchestra swallows almost all the artistic interest," Rimsky remarked, "and the vocal part, deprived of the orchestra, is unconvincing."[29] The overture establishes all important aspects of the conflict before any words are uttered. It introduces the three major motifs of gold (a descending chromatic figure, with a glittering tremolo effect), power (in heavy ascending lines), and a complicated, more dissonant motif of human woe; all three motifs hover continually over the Baron. The other actors in the drama are quite uni-dimensional. The drama opens on the awfulness of poverty because, in this play about the proper balance between matter (money) and spirit (honor), perversely it is poverty that ties us to matter, denies us rights to inspired movement and generosity, flattens us out. Thus Albert's character, while natively high-minded and generous, is nervous, impulsive, marked with broad melodic leaps, a man who wants to be anywhere but where he now is with the niggardly resources he now possesses. The Jewish moneylender and the Duke are portrayed, respectively, as an undulating caricature of deceitful flattery and as the Shakespearean ideal of serene, mediating justice. Everything dynamic and conflicted, musically as well as emotionally, is in those chests.

For such is the peculiar structure of Pushkin's play. Two fast-paced dueling grounds, complete with jousting and injured honor, are separated by an underground vault of static dead-weighted wealth. That vault, the site of the Baron's long and conflicted monologue, is where Rachmaninoff gives free rein to his Wagnerian "symphonism." Orchestral complexity is much less in evidence in the two flanking scenes: Albert's bargaining with the moneylender and the final confrontation between father, son, and ruler that triggers a duel and that ends, unexpectedly, with a "natural" death. In those two fast-paced dialogue scenes, Rachmaninoff muffles his sonorous orchestra, sets it whirling in repetitive patterns, and brings vocal declamation to the fore to service the swift action onstage. The exchanges between Solomon and Albert, and between Albert and the Duke, are forward-moving and in

---

29  Ossovskii, "S. V. Rakhmaninov," cited in A. Tsuker, "K kontseptsii 'Skupogo rytsaria,'" *Sovetskaia muzyka* 7 (1985): 92–97, esp. 93. Tsuker attempts to rehabilitate the opera from its traditionalist, Russian Old School detractors, claiming that although a symphonic principle is indeed at work, this "symphonism" does not manifest itself in autonomously unfolding structures but becomes a highly efficient, descriptive, psychologically astute tool tailored to individual personalities.

their own way trustworthy, for they serve coherent deeds in the social world. Each man announces his own single-minded principle and then stands by it: Albert the need to spend, Solomon the need to barter profitably, the Duke his need to reconcile his subjects justly. The Baron, however, is no longer in that pragmatic world. His is a fantasy kingdom, both burdensome and liberating, that has become completely real for him but is unreadable (of this he is certain) by anyone else. His motifs no longer communicate to others horizontally but relate only to himself. Themes drop into him, thicken, and swell up. The haunting, viscous quality of Wagnerian motivic development is perfect for this high gravitational pull of the Baron's field. And here music, which is movement incarnate, can contribute something significant to the theme of miserly accumulation.

To protect his fantasy kingdom the Baron must ensure, above all else, that nothing circulate. Albert is correct in his remark to Solomon that money, for his father, is neither a servant nor a friend but a master whom he must serve. Wealth for the Baron is reliable only when it is locked away. When it moves it threatens to speak up, take on its own tasks, become subject to someone else's market pressures, disobey. The task of standing guard over it and preventing any centrifugal outward flows of energy absorbs huge resources; indeed, for the Baron it replaces all other life. Thus the musical realization of the Baron is one cauldron of superimposed, intricately developed contradictory motifs. They are dependent upon the orchestra for their organization and subordination because they have no exit from within the Baron's own arguments. In vain does Albert request, at the end of scene 1, that his father treat him "as a son . . . and not a mouse / Begotten in a cellar." Such open-ended treatment is impossible, because that noncirculating cellar, an underground of thoroughly Dostoevskian pathology, understands only how to draw things in and cause them to stop.

In his operatic setting of this little tragedy, then, Rachmaninoff created a miniature music drama on a timelessly mythic theme with a web of orchestral language at its core: the Baron's scene 2 monologue. The composer's tribute to the time-bound, word-bound, action-bound present tense of debts and duels is parceled out to the wings, to the first and last scenes. There, in these more declamatory appendages that recall their *kuchkist* predecessors and Cui's "words-first" ideal, real dialogue is uttered, and unexpected confrontations happen. But drama, and especially tragic drama, is not only events. It can also be served by the more Wagnerian principle that musical texture, "chromatic alteration," and a constant postponement of the tonal goal are themselves forms of poetic knowledge. In Rachmaninoff's setting, Pushkin's Baron—

realized through a fusion of harmony, counterpoint, and orchestration — is, in the sense that Wagner used the term, a genuinely polyphonic hero.

## Concluding comments: the casket of gold and the feast of music

Among the debates that divided the Perm musicians while they prepared for their Pushkin Ring was the optimal sequence of the "little operas."[30] *Boris Godunov* opened the cycle, but from that point on there was no imperative to observe Pushkin's order of plays. It was eventually decided that *A Feast in Time of Plague* would usher in the tetralogy, followed by *The Stone Guest*, *The Covetous Knight*, and finally *Mozart and Salieri*. The order of the little operas became one of increasing musical excellence but also one in which national collapse gave way gradually to the spirit of music. The interpretations of all four little operas were modernist and highly stylized. (The curtain went up the first night on a huge computer monitor projected on the stage that displayed a list of writers, among whom was Pushkin. According to one eyewitness, the audience sighed. All day they had looked at screens. Could they never escape cyberspace, even on a night at the opera with their greatest poet?) As far as one can tell, all of Pushkin's cold intelligence and wit was intact in these four productions, but little of his lyricism, hope, and tenderness.

After the three-day event, members of the audience were asked to comment on the success of the cycle. The responses published in *Muzykal'naia akademiia* were overall appreciative but tended toward the pessimistic. Many referred to the topical importance of the operas for post-Soviet Russia and its recurring times of trouble. It was noted by several that Salieri washed his hands, like Pontius Pilate, after his murderous deed. An eleventh grader from Perm's Diaghilev High School, E. Tamarchenko, submitted an essay in a deeply noncarnival spirit that began: "In my view, the entire plot pivots around the idea of the feast, an idea found at the very sources of world culture…A feast presumes a special third world, one that is opposed to the highest moral values of the human being." From the feast of the plague, she notes, no one can escape. The feast of love in *The Stone Guest* is absolutely tragic. *The Covetous Knight* knows only the feast of power. *Mozart and Salieri* is a feast of creativity, but a poisoned one…

There was one published response, however, that moved against this general pessimistic grain, although still hesitantly.[31] It was evidence that

---

[30]    Isaakian, "Russkkoe 'Kol'tso'," 24. Tomarchenko's comments on the cycle are on p. 27.
[31]    N. Chernysheva, a graduate student at Perm State University, in ibid., 26–27.

even in these musicked versions, the metaphysical core of Pushkin's "little tragedies" could be turned to courage in the blink of an eye, kaleidoscopically. The author was commenting on *Mozart and Salieri*, the fact that the two protagonists in this production had been presented like parts of a single person, with their traits intermixed and dependent upon accidents of perception, envy, cowardice (Salieri was powerful and persuasive, Mozart petty and unattractive). "But they all possessed a priceless gift, the ability to create," she added, now including Pushkin in her purview. She concluded her internal dialogue on a question:

> Priceless because it cannot be paid for by anything except that utter trifle, life.
> Ars longa, vita brevis.
> A little tragedy?

This student had detected something about Pushkin's dramatic treatment of character that no transposition of his work could ever wholly efface. The more tightly compressed the Little Tragedy, the more perfectly in focus the sinner and the more we are pulled to see the conflict from all sides. Thus the sin portrayed in it remains venial, not mortal.

# 18

# PLAYBILL TO PROKOFIEV'S "WAR AND PEACE" AT THE MET

---

*This program note appeared in the February 2002 Playbill for the Metropolitan Opera / Mariinskii Theater production of Prokofiev's* War and Peace. *It was written, and read, under conditions unusual for North American cities — although reasonably familiar to the rest of the world, including Russia. The twin towers had fallen to terrorist attacks the September before. New York was still reeling from that unprecedented event; the nation was bellicose, confused, full of rumor and mourning. There is a moment in Tolstoy's novel (Book Three, Part II, ch. 17–19) where the inhabitants of Moscow are assured by their governor Rostopchin that the city was in no danger and would be defended, even though the French were advancing steadily. They prepare to flee and at the same time stubbornly refuse to alter their round of balls and entertainments. This atmosphere of denial, necessity, and relief at a dose of real life, so subtly caught by Tolstoy in* War and Peace, *was also in evidence during this spectacular Russian-American production of Prokofiev's opera at the Met in 2002.*

---

## THE ENDURANCE OF WAR, THE DECEPTIONS OF PEACE: PROKOFIEV'S OPERATIC MASTERPIECE
## (2002)

Everything about this powerful, curious opera is too large. Its 1700-page source text, its sprawling massive choruses, the number of hours required to perform it (one night or two?), the looming presence of Leo Tolstoy together with that writer's famous denunciation of opera as the most pernicious, corrupt art-form in the Western world: only a composer with the stubbornness and discipline of Tolstoy would ever take it on. Prokofiev was such a composer. He was passionately committed to opera (although plagued with bad luck in the genre). He was also committed to serving the Soviet state. In this penultimate opera, his sixth, working under crisis conditions and in increasingly ill health, Prokofiev at last succeeded in fusing his spectacular lyrical gift with patriotic spectacle.

The pace of composition was extraordinary, military-like. Writing began in August 1941. As the Nazi war machine advanced, Prokofiev, working steadily, was evacuated with his companion and librettist Mira Mendelson, first to Nalchik, then to Tbilisi, and finally to Alma-Ata in Kazakhstan. By April 1942 the eleven-scene opera was complete in piano score: in less than eight months, Tolstoy's epic novel of Russia's "First Fatherland War" (1812) had become Soviet Russia's operatic epic for her "Second Fatherland War" (1941–45). The bulk of the libretto's lines are taken straight from Tolstoy. This decision to preserve whole meandering paragraphs of Tolstoyan prose intact, without recasting the verbal material into conventional arias and recitative "filler," elicited from the official music jury the same complaint made twenty-five years earlier against Prokofiev's setting of Dostoevsky's *The Gambler*: too wordy, not enough singing, more excitement for the orchestra than for the voice. But the Stalinist arts establishment, mobilized for a terrible war, raised more substantial political objections. Are the Russian people glorious enough? Are not Tolstoy's beloved and familiar characters too trivially reduced to their erotic appetites? Where is the all-seeing Leader, predicting victory and justifying sacrifice? In three revisions submitted over the next decade — 1946, 1949, and 1952 — the loyal but harassed Prokofiev packed in ever more triumphant heroism and tuneful ensemble pieces. He added a brilliant ball in Tchaikovsky's style (thus adding dance rhythms to "Peace") as well as Glinka-style patriotic arias (thus adding inspiration to "War"). He even composed a desperately non-operatic scene of military deliberations for Kutuzov's war council ("Fili"). But during the post-war period, only "Peace" was performed, albeit to great popular acclaim. "War" never passed preliminary censorship. Prokofiev was still adjusting the opera months before his death in 1953.

Mira Mendelson and Prokofiev crafted the libretto out of Tolstoy's *War and Peace* with exeptional precision. All scenes for "Peace" are taken from Book II, Parts Three and Five. The unifying theme is Natasha Rostova's fall from innocence and the repercussions of that fall on the three men who desire her: her fiancé Prince Andrei Bolkonsky, her seducer Anatol Kuragin, and her admirer, confessor, and eventual husband, Pierre Bezukhov. At the epicenter of these events sits a famous scene that Prokofiev did *not* set: "Natasha at the Opera." In that novelistic episode, the 16-year-old Natasha — pampered, impulsive, betrothed to Prince Andrei (at a distance and with a built-in delay) but spurned by the rest of the Bolkonsky family, so badly in need of both illusion and love — attends an opera performance. Tolstoy mercilessly parodies the genre and its baleful effect on the heroine.

At first appalled by opera's crude artifice, Natasha is gradually bewitched by its brazenness, its unembarrassed grounding in deception (what Tolstoy called all social and artistic convention). Soon thereafter she falls to the corrupt, manipulative Hélène Bezukhova and her lascivious brother Anatol. Prokofiev, of course, had nothing to gain by reproducing Tolstoy's disgust at operatic convention. But he had everything to gain by showcasing the seductiveness of music. And thus, in Act I, scene iv of his second revision, he replaces the "absent center," Natasha at the Opera, with an equally intoxicating device of his own: an E-flat major waltz in compelling 3/4 time, which none of the supremely musical, resonant Rostovs are able to resist. Modulating in and out of more sinister minor keys, Hélène and Anatol keep this waltz going throughout the scene. Natasha and her father, Count Rostov, try feebly to counter with a 4/4 beat of their own but cannot sustain it; their words might resist, but they sing the waltz. For Prokofiev (unlike Tolstoy), opera is not a spectator sport; we are *in* it. Even the impeccably moral Sonya, who castigates Natasha for her profligacy and will eventually tattletale on the elopement scheme, cannot assert a successful 4/4 beat against the maddening swirl. Natasha, the spirit of music and dance, defies them all. Only the ridiculous, nearsighted, lumbering and titanic Pierre Bezukhov will preserve her, believe in her, and drive the aggressor (his cowardly brother-in-law) from Russia's ancient capital.

This same theme of seduction followed by betrayal, a fall, and a cleansing maturation is repeated in the "War" portions. But now Natasha has become all of Russia. The Frenchified salon of the Kuragins has become the French Grande Armée, carrying its "theater of war" ever closer to the Russian core. Russia is seduced, betrayed, falls. Field Marshal Kutuzov (blind in one eye, ridiculous, lumbering, titanic) will preserve her, but not without terrible losses. In the process, the wounded Andrei will die in Natasha's arms on the outskirts of burning Moscow, thus bringing together the two levels, the battlefield and the hearth. If the seductive rhythms of the waltz dominate "Peace," then the mass choral hymn, the military march (with percussion and brass fanfare), and the well-paced patriotic aria will stitch together "War." Whenever this fabric temporarily relaxes and civilian life is remembered, the waltzes briefly return.

In this opera, peace means the possibility of carnal love, and thus of love's unstoppable folly. War, in contrast, is absolutely ennobling and transcendent. We sense this truth in the maturation of Natasha (a "peace" mentality) and Prince Andrei (split between "peace" and "war"). In the first scene, both hero and heroine are equally self-absorbed. Andrei at the

Oak (his opening aria) can only think of himself, his rights to personal happiness — and even listening in later to the singing of the endearingly self-absorbed adolescent Natasha, he laments only her "indifference to his existence." By the end, Andrei on his deathbed reaches out both to her and to Russia, whose resurrection he fantasizes but will not live to see. Natasha too has been chastened by war; in the novel it sobers her caprice, transforming her impatient ecstasies into lifesaving gestures for others (persuading her family to empty their laden carts, for example, and abandon their wealth to the invading French in order to evacuate wounded soldiers). Such lyrical progressions from selfish to selfless love are still, however, conventionally operatic. The problem that audiences have today with Prokofiev's *War and Peace* is its Stalin-era pageantry and chauvinist rhetoric. Such scenes seem to defy both Tolstoy (who condemned militarism, state worship, political bombast) and musical decency. The deeply lyrical Prokofiev felt this crudeness keenly. When advised in 1947 by his close friend and patron, the Bolshoi conductor Samuel Samosud, to add more patriotic hymns (of the sort sung in classic Russian military-historical opera, by Glinka's Ivan Susanin or Borodin's Prince Igor), Prokofiev responded glumly, "I can't do that." His music for Kutuzov's major aria went through eight revisions. But one paradox of this opera is that its patriotic pageantry is in fact immensely stirring and satisfying — an indication, perhaps, of the strong link between the lyrical and the propagandistic that produced so much tremendously good film music during the Stalinist era. This aesthetic link is also in keeping with Tolstoy's musical aesthetic.

Tolstoy never approved of opera as an art form. For him, mixed-media art was by definition contaminated. But he was a fine amateur pianist and painfully susceptible to music. His celebrated condemnation of Beethoven's symphonies, of Berlioz, Liszt and Wagner was in part a protest against powerfully arousing music played to passive audiences at soirées and concert halls, where one could only sit, listen, clap. Music — as Tolstoy has the hero proclaim in his late tale "The Kreutzer Sonata" — is so powerful a stimulant that it should be controlled by the state and played only on public occasions, when arousal is necessary and leads to acts. An opera built off *War and Peace* in 1942, with Russia again under siege, was certainly one such occasion. Music is depraved only when performed in inappropriate contexts.

This bit of Tolstoyan doctrine can help us, in 2002, to swallow (perhaps even to be moved by) the bombast of the opera's Part Two, "War." Amidst its martial rhythms and pious tones, we should listen not for the triumph or bloodlust of armies on the move but for its moments of requiem and tribute to a city. Wooden Moscow, burnt to the ground in 1812, was Russia's original *gorod-geroi,* "hero-city"; Leningrad and other Soviet cities would follow in subsequent wars. Kutuzov's most inspired aria is sung in honor of "golden-domed Moscow," which the Russians could not defend but could not reconcile themselves to losing. Fix your eyes on this urban horizon. Opera communicates with us by means both external (its plot dynamics on stage) and internal (its arias and emotions), but opera is also, at peak times, a repository of the eternal. Great historical opera remains great because tragedies repeat and require commemoration. We are in such a time.

# 19

# SHOSTAKOVICH'S
# "LADY MACBETH OF MTSENSK"

---

*The excerpts below, first on Shostakovich as an adaptor of literature and then on his second opera,* Lady Macbeth of Mtsensk District, *come from a longer essay, "Shostakovich and the Russian Literary Tradition," initially published in* Shostakovich and his World, *ed. Laurel E. Fay (Princeton: Princeton University Press, 2004), 183–226. Other compositions examined in the essay, selected to display Shostakovich's remarkable versatility in musicalizing a literary source, include: the opera (or anti-opera)* The Nose *as literary montage (1928–30); his Tsvetaeva poem cycle as pure poeticity and transcendence (1973, op. 143); and "Four Verses of Captain Lebyadkin" [from Dostoevsky's* Demons], *1974, as a tribute to "bad poetry, bad prose, bad politics, bad ends."*

---

## "SHOSTAKOVICH AND THE RUSSIAN LITERARY TRADITION"
## (2004)

### *From the Introduction*

[...] In 1927, age twenty-one, Shostakovich was asked to complete a questionnaire on his relationship with the other creative arts. As regards literature Shostakovich wrote: "Above all a preference for prose literature (I don't understand poetry at all and do not value it...): *Demons, The Brothers Karamazov,* and in general Dostoevsky; together with him Saltykov-Shchedrin; and in a different category, Gogol... and then Chekhov. Tolstoy as an artist is somewhat alien (although as a theorist of art, much of what he says is convincing)."[1] As the composer grew older, poetry would rise in

---

[1]  "Anketa po psikhologii tvorcheskogo protsessa," in *Dmitrii Shostakovich v pis'makh i dokumentakh,* ed. L A. Bobykina (Moscow: Glinka State Central Museum of Musical Culture, 2000), 473–74. The specific question posed in the questionnaire (no. 4) was

his estimation, but these prosaic loves would remain. "In spite of being generally considered a symphonist," Esti Sheinberg writes in her recent excellent study of irony in Shostakovich's music, "Shostakovich seems to be rather a 'literary' composer."[2]

What this appellation "literary" might mean in the context of Shostakovich's settings of Russian texts is the subject of the present essay. His pioneering opera (if it can be called that) premiered at the Maly Opera Theatre in 1930: a musical amplification of Nikolai Gogol's deadpan surreal fantasy "The Nose." His final song cycle (if it can be called that) is a musical dramatization of some very bad, very funny poems by Captain Lebyadkin, drunken buffoon from Dostoevsky's 1872 novel *Demons*. In between those two prosaic grotesques, op. 15 and op. 146, Shostakovich set an astonishing variety of Russian literary texts to a large number of solo and choral musical genres, several of them hybrids of his own devising. Alongside pellucid song cycles on lyrics by Pushkin (1936, 1952), Aleksandr Blok (1967), and Marina Tsvetaeva (1973), he set five "Satires," far less lyrical, of the early twentieth-century poet and children's writer Sasha Chorny (1960), incidental music for Meyerhold's 1929 staging of Mayakovsky's dystopian farce *Klop* [*The Bedbug*], and contributed to the Pushkin Jubilee of 1936 a musical score for Pushkin's "Folktale about the Priest and His Workman, Blockhead," a "film-opera" realized in the form of a cartoon (1935). A full-length opera based on Nikolai Leskov's 1864 tale *Lady Macbeth of Mtsensk District* was mounted in 1934, with devastating repercussions two years later. A second musicalization of Gogol (his 1842 dramatic sketch *The Gamblers*) was started in 1942 but abandoned by the end of the year, after eight scenes had been set word for word. The composer's first choral setting, in 1921–22, was of two fables by Ivan Krylov. Of the four vocal symphonies (three of them choral), no. 13 is a monumental setting for bass and male chorus of five politically charged poems by Evgeny Yevtushenko (1962).

[...] In all his marvelous inventiveness, Shostakovich never appeared to feel the tension of words *versus* music, that is, of words crippled, enslaved, or overpowered by music. That ancient feud, which had fueled the most radically "realistic" voice-setting in the nineteenth century, is transcended in his

---

"Your attitude toward the other arts (level of professionalism, degree of interest and so on)." Unspaced ellipses in the original; ellipses with brackets in the main text indicate those points where paragraphs have been omitted from the original essay.

2 Esti Sheinberg, *Irony, Satire, Parody and the Grotesque in the Music of Shostakovich: A Theory of Musical Incongruities* (Aldershot, U.K.: Ashgate, 2000), 153.

practice by a daring and virtuosic concept of orchestral voice. Shostakovich's orchestra is not limited to commentary on events taking place onstage. While it does, of course, make use of reminiscence motifs that prompt conscience or memory in a character (as does, say, Lensky's theme in the orchestra, passing through Tatiana's frantic mind during the final scene of Tchaikovsky's *Eugene Onegin*), in Shostakovich, an instrumental line has its own autonomous tasks as well. It can reinforce the moods and memories of individual singers in their own present. It can even pre-empt and, as it were, pre-mimic a vocal declamation — as happens in Act One, scene 1 of *Lady Macbeth*, where a crude, brassy bark from the pit twice precedes the bullying father-in-law's insistence that his timid son demand an oath of fidelity from his wife. But the orchestra can also address — and undermine — the literary plot, genre, or "generation" in which these individuals are embedded. In the self-conscious Russian tradition, where the literary canon was not just known but (or so it has seemed to the more scattered, diffuse, and culturally indifferent West) known by heart, genres and generations were acutely marked.

As the third acts of both *The Nose* and *Lady Macbeth* demonstrate, Shostakovich had no scruples about supplementing the plotline of classic literary narratives with episodes drawn from other texts of the same author, period, or style. Musically he would often realize these interpolated episodes through twentieth-century genres, deployed ironically: the cancan, galop, foxtrot, silent film chase, perversely imbalanced waltz. A strong rhythmic insert of this sort serves several purposes. It could jolt the audience, defamiliarizing expectations and encouraging a fresh approach to the psychology of the nineteenth-century heroes depicted on stage. Or it could function as an internal genre parody. In the two Act 3s noted above, the relevant parodied object is the operatic convention dictating some sort of "group" (or mob) activity in the third act — usually a dance or a ballet, but why not a chase, a lineup, a riot? Such an insert could even take off on its own, animating a scene in a direction quite different from the inner life of the heroes and infecting the audience with a sense of the liberating — not only the distorting or pathological — potential of the grotesque.

This revolutionary achievement in concrete word-music-rhythm relations was noted by Boris Asafiev in an appreciative essay on *Lady Macbeth* in 1934, soon after the premiere. "Not losing sight of the word for a single moment, Shostakovich is nevertheless not distracted by externally descriptive naturalistic tendencies: he does not imitate the meaning of the words through music, he does not illustrate the word but rather symphonizes it, as if unfolding in the music the emotion not fully spoken by the words."[3] Although there are, of course, illustrative and "naturalistic" moments in Shostakovich (the infamous "pornophony" of the seduction scene in *Lady Macbeth* and the gross orchestral yawns, sneezes, and grunts in *The Nose*), Asafiev's insight is a sound one. The uttered word is both context-specific and semantically ambiguous. It communicates through inflection and intonation, and it can mean something new in each new environment. Thus its "symphonization" tends to make interpretation more — not less — difficult, intricate, and provisional. The symphonized word has nothing in common with a caption "explaining" a photograph.

In his musical dealings with Russian literature, Shostakovich had another ally during the 1920s: the cinema. It is often remarked that the young composer's tedious job as pianist for silent films, with its emphasis on the chase, the capture, the cameo love scene and other slapstick or sentimental routines, perfected his improvisatory and "storytelling" skills. It also sensitized him to the relationship between the visual and the aural in rapidly-paced movement. But the reverse is surely also true, that Shostakovich's early intimacy with silent film must have impressed upon him the many strategies (in addition to musical ones) available for undermining the tyranny of the verbal sign.

[...] The task for the new opera, then, was to reintegrate the literary word, which had been enriched as well as compromised by these media innovations. Summing up the strategies for "embodying the word" that had gained currency by the end of the first Soviet decade, Shostakovich's biographer Sofia Khentova finds four of special importance: the declamatory-conversational style of vocal parts; musical dramaturgy that imitated the framing techniques of film; a peculiar use of orchestral timbres, especially percussive; and the advent of a special dramatic hybrid, the "theatrical symphony."[4] Khentova's fourth item must be approached cautiously. Shostakovich had in mind something quite different from Meyerhold's musical theater, which had so successfully staged Gogol's *Inspector General* in 1926 by granting full artistic license to the director to alter the words, pace, and even the dramatic concept of the original. A "unified music-theatrical symphony" in Shostakovich's sense of the term presumed a rigorous fidelity to the author and to the received text (which could include its drafts or variants). It also implied a more objective

---

3   "O tvorchestve Shostakovicha i ego opere 'Ledi Makbet'" [1934], in B. Asaf'ev, *Ob opere: Izbrannye stat'i,* 2nd ed. (Leningrad: Muzyka, 1985), 310–19, esp. 314.
4   S. Khentova, *Shostakovich: Zhizn' i tvorchestvo* (Leningrad: Sovetskii kompozitor, 1985), 1:198–99.

musical structure, one where, in the composer's words, the aria-recitative distinction is replaced with an *"uninterrupted symphonic current*, although without leitmotifs."[5] [...]

## Lady Macbeth of Mtsensk District:
### *the triumph of tragedy-satire, or the confessional grotesque*

The rise and fall of Shostakovich's second opera between 1934 and 1936 is the most famous scandal to befall the musical world during the Stalinist era. The *Pravda* editorial "Muddle Instead of Music," which denounced the opera and its prodigiously popular twenty-nine-year-old composer at the end of January 1936, sent shock waves throughout the cultural establishment. That scandal is still being unraveled.[6] Here only one aspect of this well-known story is addressed: the contribution of Shostakovich's second opera to the Russian literary tradition, taking into account the genre that the composer himself assigned to it in 1932: "tragic-satirical opera."[7] One fact must be emphasized about this hybrid genre. The tragic component is concentrated almost entirely in the heroine, Katerina Izmailova. Arraigned against her are wimps, buffoons, lechers, dandies, and thugs — in a word, human material far more easily satirized than heroicized. Until the final "Siberian" scene, when intonations of tragic lament and psychological cruelty spread evenly throughout the population on stage, satire dominates the outer context of the opera, tragedy the inner landscape of the title role. Shostakovich was explicit about his sympathy for this multiple murderess. As he wrote in a 1933 essay, the author of the nineteenth-century source text, Nikolai Leskov, had demonized his

---

[5]  D. Shostakovich, "K prem'ere Nosa," *Rabochii i teatr* 24 (16 June 1929): 12.

[6]  The first book-length explication of this scandal classifies it as a "cultural revolution" motivated largely by intra-bureaucratic rivalry in the agitprop and art wings of the Party establishment, not by any particular sins on the part of Shostakovich, who was simply a convenient (because visible and accommodating) target to terrorize. See L. V. Maksimenkov, *Sumbur vmesto muzyki: Stalinskaia kul'turnaia revoliutsiia, 1936–1938* (Moscow: Iuridicheskaia kniga, 1997), esp. 73–87.

[7]  "Tragediia-satira," Shostakovich's article on his opera in progress, appeared in *Sovetskoe iskusstvo* on 16 October 1932 (excerpted in D. Shostakovich, *O vremeni i o sebe: 1926–1975* [Moscow: Sovetskii kompozitor, 1980], 31). In it the composer discusses the distinction between Leskov's story and the libretto, his warm sympathy for the heroine, his special use of the "satirical," and his departures in musical dramaturgy from *The Nose*. In English, see the discussion in Laurel E. Fay, *Shostakovich: A Life* (New York: Oxford University Press, 2000), 69.

heroine and could find no grounds on which to justify her, "but I am treating her as a complex, whole, tragic nature...as a loving woman who feels deeply and is in no way sentimental."[8] He noted with satisfaction the remark of a fellow musician at one of the rehearsals that the operatic Katerina had been cast as a Desdemona or a Juliet of Mtsensk, not as a Lady Macbeth.[9]

This lyrical purification of the title role remains the most puzzling and disputed aspect of Shostakovich's transposition. Leskov's 1864 story was also no stranger to dispute. But the original "Lady Macbeth of Mtsensk District" had startled its readers not so much for its grisly plot — the nineteenth century was raised on gothic horror stories and not easily shocked — as for its mode of narration. Its style is languid, sensuous, studded with the repetitions and rhythmic idiom of Russian folk dialect. This stylized surface is almost impenetrable. Events, no matter how horrific, are related in an objective, matter-of-fact manner, as if the narrator were a museum guide describing a gorgeous tapestry embroidered with brutal scenes. (Leskov framed his story as a "sketch for notes on a criminal court case.") There is no innerness to his Katerina, who moves as if in a trance and whose acts are depicted without emotion, as "evidence," exclusively as they appear on the outside. Why Shostakovich was attracted by this glossy, brittle tale as material for opera — a genre in which the inner life of heroines is the very stuff of arias — is a question often and inconclusively discussed.[10]

During the first decade of Soviet power, Leskov's "Lady Macbeth" was in the air. The story had enjoyed a popular revival in the 1920s: a silent film version appeared in 1927, and in 1930 a handsome edition of the tale was published with illustrations by the celebrated artist Boris Kustodiev (1878–1927). Kustodiev had close friends among contemporary writers and was passionate about music. His daughter Irina had been Mitya Shostakovich's classmate; through her, Mitya and his older sister Marusya became intimate with the entire family. Marusya even served the artist as an occasional

---

8    D. D. Shostakovich, "'Ekaterina Izmailova: Avtor ob opere," *Sovetskoe iskusstvo* (14 December 1933), as cited in *O vremeni i o sebe*, p. 35.

9    "Lady Macbeth is an energetic woman," this musician remarked after watching the rehearsal, "but it's the other way around in your opera; here is a soft, suffering woman who arouses not terror but sympathy, pity, kindly feelings." Shostakovich agreed with this assessment. D. Shostakovich, "Moe ponimanie 'Ledi Makbet,'" in *"Ledi Makbet Mtsenskogo uezda": opera D. D. Shostakovicha* (Leningrad: Gosudarstvennyi Akademicheskii Malyi Opernyi Teatr, 1934), 7.

10    On this background, see Caryl Emerson, "Back to the Future: Shostakovich's Revision of Leskov's 'Lady Macbeth of Mtsensk District,'" *Cambridge Opera Journal* 1, no. 1 (1989): 59–78.

model, and Shostakovich's first public performance of his own music, in May 1920, took place at an exhibition of Kustodiev's paintings.[11] For all his indifference to painting as an art form — in the 1927 questionnaire he calls painting a "meaningless activity," insofar as it reduces a dynamic world to stasis — Shostakovich knew Kustodiev's work well. Kustodiev's illustrations to Leskov, influenced by the *lubok* [woodcut] style of Russian folk art, were surely familiar to him. But seven years earlier, when the artist was still alive, this link to Kustodiev's visual art might have played an important *literary* role in the subsequent lyricization of "Lady Macbeth." The intermediary here is Evgeny Zamyatin, master writer of modernist and ornamental prose, minor collaborator on *The Nose* libretto, and admiring friend of Kustodiev, who illustrated several of his stories.[12]

Zamyatin was a highly distinctive prose stylist and polemicist. In 1918 he delivered his first public lecture on Neorealism, an artistic credo that attempted a dialectical synthesis of mimetic, earth-bound Critical Realism and its triumphant antithesis, otherworldly Symbolism. Neorealists believed in concrete matter and movement: energy as opposed to entropy, the efficiency of a synecdoche, sudden laughter brought about through unexpected contrast. During and after the war years, many of them were turning away from the modernized, mechanized cities "into the backwoods, the provinces, the village, the outskirts" in search of a "hut-filled, rye-filled Rus'," which they described elliptically in abrupt, compact phrases ringing with the "music of the word."[13] Much as Eisenstein would later explore visual montage in terms of temporal dynamics, so Zamyatin developed for literature a theory of prosaic meter. Its unit was the "prose foot," measured not by the distance between stressed syllables but by the distance — often devoid of explanatory verbs — between

---

[11]   Fay, *Shostakovich: A Life*, p. 13.

[12]   The Zamyatin connection was first pointed out by Andrew Wachtel in 1995, in an excellent article that also posits the tale "Rus'" as intermediary between Leskov's story and Shostakovich's opera. Since that time his thesis has been corroborated from several angles. He bears no responsibility for the somewhat different sequence of stimuli on the opera that I intuit here. See Andrew Wachtel, "The Adventures of a Leskov Story in Soviet Russia, or the Socialist Realist Opera That Wasn't," in *O RUS! Studia litteraria slavica in honorem Hugh McLean*, eds. Simon Karlinsky, James L. Rice, and Barry P. Scherr (Berkeley, CA: Berkeley Slavic Specialties, 1995), 358–68.

[13]   Evgenii Zamiatin, "Sovremennaia russkaia literatura" [1918], published in *Grani* 32 (October-December 1956): 90–101, quotes on pp. 97 and 100. *Rus'* or *Sviataia Rus'* [Holy Russia] was given currency in the nineteenth century by conservative Slavophiles; when used by twentieth-century artists it evokes images of the pre-industrial Russian countryside and its traditional peasant, merchant, and priestly cultures.

stressed words and images.[14] In his own prose Zamyatin followed these metric directives carefully. Among his exemplary Neorealist tales is the 1923 story "Rus'," which appeared as a preface, or prefatory "Word," to a small book of portraits entitled *Rus': Russkie tipy B. M. Kustodieva* [Kustodiev's Russian types].[15] Zamyatin later explained how he had come to provide this verbal "illustration" to an art book. The publishing house Akvilon had commissioned from him a review of Kustodiev's art. He wasn't in the mood to provide a conventional piece of criticism. "So I simply spread out in front of me all those Kustodievan beauties, cabbies, merchants, tavern-keepers, abbesses — and stared at them." After a few hours, an act of "artificial fertilization took place: the figures came to life, sedimenting out into a story like a supersaturated solution."[16] The plot of Zamyatin's "Rus'" is a pared-down, purified, lush but more passive version of Leskov's "Lady Macbeth of Mtsensk District."

Almost certainly, Shostakovich knew the volume *Russkie tipy*. (That very summer, Mitya and his sister had vacationed with Kustodiev at a sanitorium in Gaspra in the Crimea.) Did Zamyatin's 1923 variant on Leskov's tale impress the young composer? In an interview from 1940, Shostakovich credited not Zamyatin but Boris Asafiev for recommending to him, a decade

---

14   Zamiatin provides actual metric examples of pacing changes in his sentences, which are further conditioned by breathing patterns governed by punctuation and by the ratio of vowels to consonants. "For me it is completely clear," he writes, "that the relationship between the rhythmics of verse and the rhythmics of prose is the same as the relationship between arithmetic and integral calculus." Evgenii Zamyatin, "Zakulisy" [ca. 1929], in *Sochineniia* (Moscow: Kniga, 1988), 461–72, esp. 468. For a brief explication in English of these principles, see Milton Ehre, "Zamyatin's Aesthetics," in *Zamyatin's WE: A Collection of Critical Essays*, ed. Gary Kern (Ann Arbor, Mich.: Ardis, 1988), 130–39.

15   *Rus': Russkie tipy B. M. Kustodieva. Slovo Evg. Zamiatina* (St. Petersburg: Akvilon, 1923), 7–23. The book contains twenty-four portraits by Kustodiev, of which over half play a role in Zamyatin's story. Eleven appear to be models for the central characters (two merchants, five merchants' wives, four shop assistants/young swains); there are also prototypes for secondary figures (Marfa's aunt the abbess; the cabdrivers whose drunkenness caused the death of Marfa's parents; the trunk-maker) as well as for several cameo appearances (a pilgrim, a wanderer). Some episodes are direct narrative realizations of the pictures (Marfa in the bathhouse [no. 14]; Marfa on a walk alongside a high fence, with a male figure in the background [no. 13]; the trunk-maker Petrov reading the newspaper in the sun [no. 17]). I am grateful to my Princeton colleague Olga Peters Hasty, a specialist in Russian ornamentalist prose, for her independent suggestion that Shostakovich "might have been reading Leskov through Zamyatin's version of the tale."

16   Evgenii Zamyatin, "Vstrechi s Kustodievym" [1927], in Zamyatin, *Sochineniia*, 333–43, esp. 334. Other details of the same genesis quoted here can be found in Zamiatin's contribution to the 1930 anthology of Leningrad writers, *Kak my pishem* (Benson, VT: Chalidze Publications, 1983, repr.), 29–47, esp. 32.

earlier, Leskov's story.[17] However, the critic Mikhail Goldshtein has claimed that Shostakovich, in private conversation with him, named Zamyatin as the source for the idea of an operatic "Lady Macbeth," and that Zamyatin "even jotted down a plan for the opera."[18] Goldshtein's claim has not been confirmed. But the fact that Shostakovich did not repeat his remark — if indeed he made it — could be explained by Zamyatin's emigration in 1931, rendering impossible any positive public reference to him or his works within the Soviet Union. Let us assume that Zamyatin's Neorealist story was indeed one lens through which Leskov's nineteenth-century tale passed on its way to the twentieth-century stage, and that the young Shostakovich was alert to it. How might "Rus'" have influenced the opera?

Zamyatin's story opens on a vast coniferous forest, more the backdrop to a fantastic fairy tale than any mapped historical space. Its elements are wood, fire, water. Deep in this forest is Kustodievo, a town without vistas or prospects — for "this is not Petersburg Russia, but *Rus'*," heavy and well-anchored, its components are "alleys, dead ends, front yard gardens, fences, fences."[19] Marfa Ivanovna, a naive timid orphan, is being married off by her

---

17    See Fay, *Shostakovich: A Life*, p. 68.

18    According to Goldshtein's loosely constructed reminiscences, published in French in the 1980s, Shostakovich first discussed with Zamyatin a possible ballet adaptation of Leskov's story about the steel flea ("Levsha," the Left-handed Craftsman). But "having examined several works by Leskov, they fixed their choice on 'Lady Macbeth of Mtsensk.' In order to accommodate the needs of the stage, Zamyatin proposed that the plot be transformed and dealt with more freely. Shostakovich and Preis wrote up a libretto according to the plan that he [Zamyatin] provided. In the course of working on the opera, it was necessary to deviate from this plot. But Zamyatin's plan was preserved in its essentials... [Even though his situation was difficult and he was seeking permission to emigrate] Zamyatin found time to meet with Shostakovich. He continued to propose to him various solutions and his influence on this work is easy to discern. Shostakovich himself even played for him certain fragments of the future opera on the piano." Michael Goldstein, "Dmitri Chostakovitch et Evgueni Zamiatine," in *Autour de Zamiatine: Actes du Colloque Université de Lausanne* (juin 1987) suivi de *E. Zamiatine, Ecrits Oubliés*, ed. Leonid Heller (Lausanne: Edition L'Age d'Homme, 1989), 113–23, esp. 121. Goldshtein's intriguing testimony is flawed by the absence of precise dating and by undocumented claims elsewhere in the essay. Zamyatin's pivotal role in the opera is reaffirmed briefly in Mikhail Gol'dshtein, "Evgenii Zamiatin i muzyka," *Novoe Russkoe Slovo* (26 June 1987).

19    *Rus': Russkie tipy B. M. Kustodieva*, p. 9. The original edition of the story differs in several stylistic and plot details from later, more accessible reprints and anthologized versions. In 1923 the heroine's name is Marfa, not Daria, Ivanovna. Significantly for us, this Marfa is even more mysteriously distanced from self-serving crime. After her merchant husband Vakhrameyev dies from poisoned mushrooms, Marfa remarries. But in the 1923 original, Zamyatin does not name the new bridegroom (p. 21); in later redactions, Daria explicitly marries the Sergei figure, the "coal-black gypsy eye" (see, for example,

aunt, now an abbess. In her youth this aunt "was called Katya, Katyushenka;" now she wants her niece settled, for she "knows, remembers" the ways and temptations of the world (11). Marfa draws lots among her suitors and the rich merchant Vakhrameyev wins, a man old enough to be her father. In keeping with Zamyatin's synecdochic aesthetics, we never see all of the young heroine — only the rounded bust, white neck, downcast eyes. What we do know is that she is not some "fidgety wasp-waisted girl from *Piter* [*Piterskaia vertun'ia-osa*]" but "weighty, slow, broad, full-breasted, and as on the Volga: you turn away from the main current toward the shore, into the shadows — and look, a whirlpool" (10). Vakhrameyev shows off his young wife to his shop, visits the bathhouse with her (a direct transposition of Kustodiev's famous portrait of a nude "Russian Venus," no. 14 in *Russkie tipy*), feeds her sweets, settles back into his trade. There is no violence, no cruelty, no fancy talk, only apples ripening in the heat, buzzing insects, and the "coal-black gypsy eye" of the shop assistant, trying to catch her gaze. Vakhrameyev leaves for the fair. Marfa is alone, thirsty, idle, rustling in her silks, and when the coal-black eye invites her into the garden one warm May night ("Marfa Ivanovna!"..."Marfushka!"..."Marfushenka!"), she turns away angrily, "the silk rustling tightly across her breast." She says nothing — but goes to the garden. The next morning everything is as if "nothing had ever been" (21).

Vakhrameyev returns from the fair with gifts. Marfa is silent. Several days later he dies; the cook had mixed in some poison mushrooms with the morels. Although he departs "in a Christian fashion," still, people begin to talk — but "what won't people talk about" (21). The widowed Marfa remarries, but her new bridegroom, it turns out, was not one of Vakhrameyev's jealous rival merchants. The silence of the forest takes over. The entire event is like a stone cast into still water: circles, ripples, spreading out and fading away, "no more than faint wrinkles in the corner of eyes from a smile — and again, a smooth surface." In the expanse of *Rus'*, words are muffled by broad rivers, by massive trees, by the "copper velvet" of bell-ringing on the evening air. Characters, after coming temporarily to life, re-enter the space of portraiture, and there stasis, not movement, is the rule.

Such concentration on the visual and aural surface of things is very much in the ornamentalist and Gogolian tradition. But the effect of this texture in Zamyatin is fundamentally different from the pace and feeling of Gogol's nervous marionettes, whose non-sequiturs define the Petersburg

---

"Rus'," in Zamyatin, *Izbrannye proizvedeniia* [Moscow: Sovetskaia Rossiia, 1990], 181–89, esp. 188). Further page numbers in the text refer to the 1923 edition.

Tales. Zamyatin's objects do not collide percussively and mechanically, as do objects in "The Nose." They slumber, glide, ripen, circle round. In the capital city, energy lies on the surface and is openly spent; in the forest and the provinces, energy is bottled up, spent in private, stingy with spoken words. Natural cycles control and redeem all; human interference is quickly effaced. This "rural Neorealism" of Zamyatin's Marfa Ivanovna—her mysterious organic and lyrical depth—left a trace, I suggest, on Shostakovich's operatic Katerina Izmailova, created ten years later.

Zamyatin presents his shy, massively Kustodievan variant on Leskov's *Lady Macbeth* as an innocent creature caught in a trap. She speaks little. Rather than declare herself, she prefers to cast lots, rustle silks, or bow her head. Her mode of expression is ideally suited to the private, heartfelt genre of the aria, where inner truth is communicated to the audience in the hall, not to one's captors on stage. Far more than Leskov's callous, lascivious protagonist, Marfa Ivanovna is part of nature and moves instinctively with it. She cannot and will not abide being separated from her nature. (We can imagine Zamyatin's heroine singing the aria in scene 3 that precedes Sergei's knock at her bedroom door—"The young colt hurries toward the filly," a lament on her unnatural and unmated life—whereas Leskov's Katerina has no such sentimental resources.) Zamyatin describes Marfa Ivanovna as a "transplanted apple tree" blossoming in vain behind the merchant's high fence; when the "coal-black gypsy eye" is sent in by Vakhrameyev to treat the mistress of the house with apples and nuts, how could she be blamed for her fall (16)?[20] In the primeval Eden that is *Rus'*, emphasis is on the tree and its fruit; the human seduction scenario is fated, forgiven, and all but forgotten in advance. The underwater whirlpool follows its own laws. It is not a crime.

In his preface to the 1934 libretto, Shostakovich emphasized these new, lyrical, "natural" priorities—and in the process, he condemned his earlier practice in *The Nose*. "I have tried to make the musical language of the opera maximally simple and expressive," he wrote. "I cannot agree with those theories, which at one time were quite widespread in our country, that in the new opera the vocal line should be absent, or that this line is nothing other than conversation in which intonations should be emphasized. Opera

---

[20] This point is suggested by Alina Izrailevich in her essay "*Rus' Evgeniia Zamyatina*," *Russian Literature* XXI-III (April 1987): 233–42. In her view, Zamyatin's Neorealism expresses itself in this story as a "*lubochnyi skaz-pokaz*" (a folk story demonstration in the woodcut style), where folk sayings or wisdoms are bungled and where all human acts are justified by Nature. To this end, she argues, Zamyatin employs not cause and effect to explain events but rather the reverse: effect (that is, material result) and only then cause.

is first and foremost a vocal artwork, and singers must occupy themselves with their primary obligation — which is to sing, not to converse, declaim, or intone."[21] In his *Lady Macbeth*, this pervasive singing, melodious and rhythmically bold, would eventually encompass all emotional registers: lyrical, melancholic, lecherous, raucous. And in all genres (high-, middle-, and lowbrow) singing would be supported by an uninterrupted instrumental line and by richly orchestrated interludes between scenes. The world is thick and harmonious. It evokes our lament and awe, like the coniferous forest on which Zamyatin's "Rus'" opens, the deep pool of water on which it closes, and the lake in the forest with the huge black waves to which Katerina devotes her final aria in Shostakovich's Siberian scene. Out of this lyrical landscape will come the opera's tragedy.

It is crucial to keep in mind, however, that this fated "Kustodiev-Marfa Ivanovna" component works solely in the interests of the heroine. No other aspect of the opera partakes of it. Through Zamyatin's story, Shostakovich had a chance to cleanse his Katerina morally, to justify her (as Leskov did not) in her intoxicating physicality and intensely Russian-style unfreedom, so reminiscent of Musorgsky's tribute to silent, suffering, but mysteriously unmovable Mother Earth in his letters to Vladimir Stasov over *Khovanshchina*. Kustodiev's mysterious, Mona Lisa-like portraits are a shield that irony cannot penetrate. And such a defensive shield is necessary, because the other side of Shostakovich's hybrid "tragic-satirical" genre is a veritable battering ram of devices from his well-tested, avant-garde operatic vocabulary: an antic pace, musical caricature, and pitiless juxtapositions of lyricism with violence. Indeed, the singing fabric of *Lady Macbeth of Mtsensk* is punctuated throughout by shockingly violent scenes of graphic naturalism. High-pitched female shrieks are no longer peripheral to the plot, as was the pretzel vendor in *The Nose*, but respond to abuse taking place in front of our eyes: an authentic gang rape, and whips we both see and hear, percussive strikes that coordinate with a murder instrument being wielded on stage. No such violence is present in Zamiatin's "Rus'," nor is it the dominant note in Leskov's tapestry.

In the opera, violence is often prelude to the bluntest satire. The prolonged flogging of Sergei in scene 4, an unbearable episode, segues almost unbroken into serving up the mushrooms and from there to Katerina's faked lament over her poisoned father-in-law and the priest's little jig preceding his travestied requiem. In scene 6, the shabby peasant stumbles drunk onto the corpse of Zinovy Borisovich to the tune of a boisterous fanfare, a mood carried

---

[21] "Katerina Izmailova. Libretto" (Leningrad, 1934), in *O vremeni i o sebe*, 39.

merrily over to the policemen's chorus and its moronic interrogation of the nihilist schoolteacher in scene 7. When Boris Timofeyevich has a moment of legitimate lyrical sorrow in scene 1 (over the absence of an heir in the Izmailov house), he is allowed only a line or two of relaxed music before collapsing back into his thumping lecherous profile. His massive aria that begins scene 4 ("That's what old age means: you can't sleep") clearly parallels the heroine's "not being able to sleep" in the opening scene, but it is a parodied parallel: the father-in-law's lament quickly transforms itself into an active prowl, a sexual fantasy to be acted out on the body of his son's wife. (To the extent that Shostakovich was ethnographer to Russia's pre-revolutionary power relations, the detail is accurate: in patriarchal households, such predation was routine.) The workman Sergei also has moments of lyrical self-pity (most expansively during his initial visit, in scene 3, to Katerina's bedroom "to borrow a book"), but they occur only before consummation of their love, not after. We sense his lyricism as a mask, a seduction strategy pure and simple, and this suspicion is confirmed by his corrupt courtship of Sonyetka in the final scene. Only Katerina's lyrical outpourings, whenever they occur, are spared this sort of framing and parodic distancing. From the start, the heroine is more sinned against than sinning; her laments are introspective, needy, in touch with a deeper truth, and confessional.

This intimate juxtaposition of tragedy, violence, and satire confused some of the opera's first listeners. The composer, however, defended his hybrid of a lyrical heroine in a satirized world. In an article in *Krasnaia gazeta* a year into *Lady Macbeth*'s wildly successful run, he remarked that some musicians who had heard his opera were pleased to note that "here, finally, in Shostakovich we have depth and humanness. When I asked what this humanness consisted of, most answered me that for the first time I had begun to speak in a serious language about serious tragic events. But I cannot consider 'inhuman' my striving toward laughter. I consider laughter in music to be just as human and indispensable as lyric, tragedy, pathos, and other 'high genres.'"[22] For all the general truth of that statement, the ennobling and humanizing aspects of laughter are not much in evidence in this opera. A tragedy can always be laughed down or turned into a travesty or a burlesque, but the reverse procedure is extremely delicate: it takes real work to elevate a debased, satirized tragic-lyrical moment so that we can again put our trust in it. For this reason, one of the remarkable achievements in Shostakovich's *Lady Macbeth* is the moral insulation that the composer succeeds in wrapping around his heroine.

---

[22]   D. Shostakovich, "God posle 'Ledi Makbet,'" (14 January 1935), in *O vremeni i o sebe*, 48.

However she might act, we are never tempted to doubt the necessity of her deeds, her sincerity or pathos. Can a "tragic-satirical opera," so seamlessly combining lyricism with graphic cruelty and outright *bouffe*, be considered a variant of the grotesque? And if so, of what kind?

We recall that Esti Sheinberg distinguishes between two types of grotesque. There is the route of infinite negation, where the horrifying overpowers the ludicrous and drives the body to disfigurement or suicide. And then there is the affirmative celebratory grotesque, more like an infinite acceptance that frees the body from stereotyped judgment and makes reality itself open-ended, lyrical, and "unfinalizable." Each type comes at considerable cost — despair at one end, utopia at the other — and both types, it seems, occur in this opera. The laughter that Shostakovich values is clearly the celebratory grotesque, a utopian genre; the lyricism that he wishes us to respect (and pity) is that of infinite despair, and it accrues only to Katerina.

Sheinberg herself approaches the problem of this opera differently, through visual art. She devotes ten pages to an analysis of Shostakovich's Katerina Izmailova in the context of Kustodiev's paintings.[23] No mention is made of Zamyatin's "Rus'." Had she discussed that story, her thesis would have had to shift, for she sees in Kustodiev's ample women not a mysterious, lyric affirmation, not a stylized extension of the rotund Russian earth, its natural cycles stripped of responsibility and blame, but a more tainted ambiguity, the "unexplained charm of their devotion to their own sensuality" that "borders on the grotesque." For her, Kustodiev's famous *kupchikhi* [merchants' wives] are on a continuum with his monstrously oversized cab drivers, his gross Russian Venus in the bathhouse, and his giant "Bolshevik" (1920) striding over the city. Applying Realist rather than Neorealist criteria, Sheinberg finds Katerina's soaring vocal line wholly, tragically inappropriate to the love that the heroine feels for Sergei. "The grotesque stems not just from this incongruity but also from Katerina's total unawareness of the situation," she writes. "When balanced against the murders she commits for the sake of this love, the mixture of compassion, repulsion, mockery and admiration we feel for her is transformed into a chilling macabre grotesquerie." She senses this chill in the ostinato-like rhythms that creep into Katerina's most passionate love songs. Sheinberg's intuitions here are plausible, but could easily be subsumed by the category of the pathetic — and in any case are restricted to the insulated heroine. They do not shed light on the larger issues raised in the *Lady Macbeth* wars.

---

23    Sheinberg, *Irony*, 251–61.

What those wars involve, and their significance for the Russian literary tradition, are questions closely tied to the ambivalence of grotesque genres such as the "tragic-satirical." Shostakovich's fall from grace in 1936 was ostensibly caused by his opera's "deliberately dissonant quacking, hooting, panting, grinding, squealing" — all verbs taken from "Muddle Instead of Music" — and by the unembarrassed licentiousness of its plot. In addition, *Lady Macbeth* was accused of lacking precisely what its composer, in his 1934 preface to the libretto, had insisted was central to his reformed operatic aesthetic: "simple, accessible musical language." Yet this second opera (for all its naturalism) was so much more luxuriantly song-like than its predecessor *The Nose*, and so much more successful with its public, that these censures seem perverse. Shostakovich came to qualify as a bona fide victim of prudish, vicious Stalinism, an image polished to high sheen by Solomon Volkov in his 1979 book on the composer. This image swept the West off its feet. But a powerful dissenting voice soon made itself heard, in the person of Richard Taruskin. Between 1989 and 1997, while fully respecting Shostakovich and his genius, Taruskin laid out the case for *Lady Macbeth of Mtsensk District* being itself a Stalinist opera — or at the very least an opera that tried hard to accommodate Stalinist ideological priorities within a popular (and thus all the more dangerous) dramatic-musical language.[24] Taruskin saw grotesquerie not on the stylistic or musical plane, but on the social and moral.

Taruskin made the following case for the opera's moral depravity. Leskov had designed his Katerina to be seen as a sinner, nymphomaniac, and quadruple murderer. In recruiting this horror story as source text for the first in a planned series of operas on heroic Russian women, Shostakovich cleanses her image at its most filthy points. The suffocation of the young heir and nephew by the (then pregnant) Katerina is eliminated; in fact, that entire pregnancy, toward which Leskov's heroine was callously indifferent, disappears from the libretto. Boris Timofeyevich moves from doddering eighty-year-old to vigorous patriarch, eager to exercise a father-in-law's rights over the young wife of his wimpish middle-aged son. Katerina does agree to commit the murder of these obnoxious creatures, but by their deeds and their music these men are presented to us as soundly deserving of being dispatched; moreover, in the case of Zinovy Borisovich, it is Sergei and not

---

[24]     Taruskin's opening statement was an essay in *The New Republic* (20 March 1989): 34–40, "The Opera and the Dictator: The Peculiar Martyrdom of Dmitri Shostakovich," later reworked as *"Entr'acte:* The Lessons of Lady M.," in Richard Taruskin, *Defining Russia Musically* (Princeton: Princeton University Press, 1997), pp. 498–510.

his mistress who wields the murder weapon. As soon as is dramatically feasible, Shostakovich's Katerina has nightmarish visions of ghosts and guilt reminiscent of her Shakespearean prototype (or, closer to home, of Tsar Boris Godunov, an opera amply cited in the music). When the police come to arrest the couple at their wedding, and when Katerina realizes that it is too late to flee, she begs forgiveness of her bridegroom and holds out her hands to be bound. Sergei, however, tries to escape. The final Siberian act is a full-scale lyricization of Katerina's fate. Even in this new, more awful captivity, she trusts in love and justice—continuing to apologize to Seryozha as he takes up with other women, willing to trade her woolen stockings for a kind word. And she is betrayed. All that is ludicrous and satirical drops out of the opera. Only the tragic is left.

Taruskin correctly identifies the literary source for this cleansed, lyrical Katerina in Aleksandr Ostrovsky's famous play from 1859, *The Storm*. Its heroine Katerina Kabanova also marries into a rich and repressive merchant household, falls illicitly in love with another man, suffers a tyrannical in-law (in this case a mother-in-law), is victimized by her bigoted environment, and drowns herself. Indeed, it was against the cult of Ostrovsky's sentimental, martyred Katerina that Leskov, several years later, had constructed his chilling counter-story. In 1927, in response to that questionnaire on the creative process, Shostakovich had remarked that he "didn't much like Ostrovsky."[25] By the 1930s, however, he had come to see the usefulness of this canonically pure heroine, sacrificed to the viciousness of a mercantile world that, conveniently for Communist ideologues, had been tsarist Russia's emergent capitalist class. In effect—Taruskin argues—Shostakovich restores Ostrovsky's sentimental plot in the service of a new regime. If that regime had been musically more sophisticated and less capricious in rewarding its servants, Shostakovich's opera might have become the first in his series of Socialist Realist tributes to Russian women: long-suffering, eternally mistreated, but women with nerves of steel, capable of murdering a class enemy while remaining lyrically vulnerable, even in defeat. In Taruskin's eyes, this project qualifies as a moral grotesque.

The debate is not yet over. In 2000, in the first major post-Communist rethinking of the fidelity issues surrounding this opera, Vadim Shakhov took to task both the anti-Stalinist readings and Taruskin's counterattack—and

---

[25]   "Anketa po psikhologii...." [question no. 4], in *Dmitrii Shostakovich v pis'makh i dokumentakh*, ed. I. A. Bobykina (Moscow: Glinka State Museum of Musical Culture, 2000), 473–74.

for roughly the same reasons.[26] Shakhov notes ruefully that the West picked up this much-battered topic pretty much where the Soviet Union had left off (245). And this was unfortunate, because the status of Stalinist victim and of Stalinist collaborator or fellow traveler were equally over-politicized. Great works of art rarely benefit from being analyzed on that plane. Since Shostakovich and his co-librettist Aleksandr Preis did follow the basic shape of Leskov's plot (which, as librettos go, is a reasonably faithful transposition), and since this plot is so gruesome, most critics have been more intuitive than precise in their judgments about it, neglecting to do close, episode-by-episode comparisons of story and libretto. Shakhov provides his reader with just such a comparative chart (249–54). But he refuses to play by the usual rules in "fidelity studies," which always humiliate the derived text. He takes the *libretto* as his basic artistic text — that literary artifact, after all, is the relevant narrative under consideration — and, working backward, measures the adequacy of the original against it. Which operatic episodes are also present in the original Leskov, he asks, and which are absent? How did the two librettists, working under a performance imperative, improve on the images provided by Leskov? Which of the two stories is more effective for opera?

His findings are instructive. Even discounting the whole of Act 3 (the antics at the police station and the wedding, both absent in Leskov), the bulk of the episodes set to music can either be traced back to a line or two of Leskov's text, a mere hint at a scene, or else they have no "original" at all. The libretto certainly recalls Leskov — the setting and the characters' names are the same — but in fact, Shakhov concludes, "it is an autonomous dramatic reworking, which has not that much in common with the text or the events of [Leskov's] sketch" (254). The heroine, in Shakhov's view, is not a merchant's wife copied from a Kustodiev canvas (261); nor is she Ostrovsky's timid and accommodating Katerina; and she is not the objectified murderess of the original, whose criminal life was written up in the style of a police report. The operatic heroine is a new viable psychological construct: Leskov's story as experienced through the eyes and heart of its title character (270). Although Shakhov does not adduce this parallel, we note that Tchaikovsky accomplished a similar feat several decades earlier in his equally successful, equally controversial operatic *Eugene Onegin*. There, Pushkin's novel-in-verse

---

[26]   Vadim Shakhov, "Ledi Makbet Mtsenskogo uezda Leskova i Shostakovicha," in *Shosta-kovich mezhdu mgnoveniem i vechnost'iu*, ed. L. Kovnatskaia (St. Petersburg: Kompozitor, 2000), 243–94. Further page references in the text.

is updated and recast to resemble a novel by Turgenev, narrated (in keeping with Turgenev's own sympathies) from the perspective of its heroine, Tatyana.[27]

Shakhov's larger argument is a plea for the right of an opera transposition to coexist peacefully in its own time (and for all time) as an aesthetic whole, not lashed to some ideology and not as a derivative of some jealous "original." (After all, the Katerinas of Shostakovich and Leskov are as different from each other as both are from their Shakespearean namesake.) He has some impatient words for Western critics, whose sex-centric Freudian reflexes render them both too offended and too fascinated by Shostakovich's "naturalistic" treatment (which in any event is more in the staging than in the music or the sung text [288]) — and further blinds them to the Russian literary tradition, in which Russian women consider self-sacrifice not pathological but sweetly fulfilling (289). In his view, the "tragedy-satire" label is not a political category but an aesthetic one, part of the twentieth-century's striving to "maximally dissociate polar extremes" in performance art and thereby to enhance dramatic effect (271).

For all of Shakhov's cogent argumentation, however, there is still an element of the grotesque, of unbridgeable incongruity, at the center of this opera. I would suggest that it be sought neither in politics nor in plot *per se* but in those moments of trust that Katerina, true to her cleansed and deepened image, cannot help but extend to the outside world. The exclusive lyricization of one personality within a naturalistic musical drama is a risk-laden project. This risk is even greater if the drama is transformed, even for the stretch of a single scene, into a circus. For if everyone else is caricatured, debased, made shallow or foolish, then the lyrical heroine is without interlocutors. No one is worthy of her confessions. (The end of Act 3 is an excellent example: does it make any sense to offer yourself up honorably to the Keystone Kops?) If the repenting subject is not to sing her arias into a void, then repentance, confession, and spiritual conversion require a worthy confessor. The Old Believer Marfa in *Khovanshchina* has Dosifei, Tatiana in *Eugene Onegin* has a rapt Onegin, Natasha Rostova in *War and Peace* her loyal Pierre Bezukhov or dying Prince Andrei. But there

---

27  Boris Gasparov laid out this thesis in "Eugene Onegin in the Age of Realism," a paper delivered at the December 2000 annual conference of the American Association for the Advancement of Slavic Studies, Washington, D.C. See an expanded version in his *Five Operas and a Symphony: Word and Music in Russian Culture* (New Haven: Yale University Press, 2005), ch. 3, 62–74.

is literally no one on stage in Shostakovich's *Lady Macbeth* who can register evidence of Katerina's moral growth. In other times and cultures, of course, this recipient would be God. But in a Soviet Socialist Realist opera, such a divine interlocutor is impossible.

There is always the audience in the darkened hall, the conventional recipient of aria speech. But such an addressee, were it to represent the sole locus of seriousness, would tend to lift the heroine out of her surroundings and prevent on-stage character from becoming answerable to on-stage context. Either way, the radical aloneness of Katerina creates an odd incongruity. She is both a direct product — a victim — of her environment, not blamed for her crimes, and at the same time she is irrevocably cut off from that environment, unable to address it or anything beyond it. This situation gives rise to what we might call, building on Esti Sheinberg, the "confessional grotesque," an especially black variant of infinite negation. It is not a familiar presence on the Russian cultural horizon, traditionally rich in spiritual resolutions. But it might help explain the moral and psychological confusions inherent in this operatic masterpiece, where tragedy and satire almost cancel each other out and invite no transcendence.

Summing up this section, we might review the trajectory of this Russian "Lady Macbeth" and suggest a revised genealogy. The starting point, of course, is Shakespeare. Macbeth's wife offers a wide range of potential behaviors. Although at first she fears that "the milk of human kindness" might hinder her husband in his ambition "to catch the nearest way," once the murders are committed she comes to experience terror, guilt, and the fatal burden of responsibility. Leskov's Russian version of the plot sustains the cold-bloodedness throughout, replaces kingly politics with sexual jealousy as the primary motivation for murder, and embeds the whole in a curiously stylized police report that suppresses any "realistic" empathy with the sinful heroine. Shostakovich selected this text as the first installment of a larger, politically correct plan to portray operatically a series of courageous and energetic Russian women. There is reason to believe that he also saw in it a tale amenable to the genre requirements of more traditional opera, where the unhappy diva longs for love, sins, confesses, and sings her most moving aria on the brink of death. The composer's task in this transposition was complex. He had to reactivate the innerness and moral suffering of the title role while at the same time retaining a Russian sheen to the story, emphasizing the brutality of the enemy (mercantile) class, and imparting to Katerina Izmailova a sense of agency and moral outrage. The heroine — however her crimes are explained — could not become an agent as long as her guilt was pervasive. So the first task was to get rid of the guilt. Here Zamyatin's "Rus'" might have provided the link.

For even more than Leskov's "naturalistic" Katerina Lvovna, Zamyatin's Neorealistic Marfa Ivanovna is a folk stylization, the animation of several enigmatic portraits. Unlike Leskov's heroine, however, Marfa is justified by her context, shielded from any personal blame for her life's course, and at the end is reintegrated into the natural world that had confined her and nourished her. It remained for Shostakovich, as a Soviet composer intent upon defining a new operatic ideal, to add a didactic, proactive element to this exonerated image. He needed some intonation that would prove women stronger, smarter, and more progressive than their male captors, even as comedy and violence remain in place to draw the common viewer in. We sense these somewhat prudish, Socialist-Realist "inserts" acutely whenever they occur in the opera, for they compete, and not always persuasively, with Katerina's more conventional operatic roles as kept woman, slave of passion, repentant sinner, and martyr. (One prominent example is Katerina's incongruous moral lecture to Sergei before their hand wrestling in scene 2: "You men certainly think a lot of yourselves, don't you...And don't you know about those times when women fed the whole family, when they gave the enemy a beating in wartime?"). Thus does the Soviet-era diva sing in her own defense what the nineteenth-century literary tradition had long canonized, from Pushkin's Tatyana to the legendary Decembrists' wives up through Turgenev's heroines: that men are "superfluous," impulsive, selfish, beyond repair, while women are tenacious and indispensable. The capacious image of Lady Macbeth can accommodate itself even to this deeply Russian message.

# 20

# PRINCETON UNIVERSITY'S
## *BORIS GODUNOV*

*By 2007, Boris Godunov the Play was back — but with a difference. My earlier preoccupations with this text had been precisely that, textual; now an opportunity had arrived to perform it. The performance that resulted at Princeton University in April 2007 was like nothing Pushkin himself could have imagined in the 1820s. In part this was because the genius of Vsevolod Meyerhold and Sergei Prokofiev had been added to his own; in part it was because Pushkin, a passionate theatergoer and spectator from the hall, had no practical experience with the stage. He had read his play out loud (illicitly) to his friends, and eventually it was published in censored form. But he never benefited from the feedback of a production. Pushkin was not a "man of the theater" as Shakespeare (or even as his contemporary Alexander Shakhovskoy) had been, an intimate presence backstage who not only does theater but lives it, familiar with every production detail. In Pushkin's dramatic writing, one senses first of all the great poet sitting, listening, and looking on, not the actor or director moving around in theater space and looking out.*

*Meyerhold always maintained that Pushkin was one of Russia's greatest stage directors — whose gift, through no fault of his own, was never realized. Thus his vision had to be teased out of the page and stage direction. Only another great director could take on that task. Meyerhold's fascination with Pushkin's Boris Godunov began even before the Revolution. By 1936, when he launched his final, ill-starred attempt to stage the play, the subversive aspects of Pushkin's historical vision could no longer be contained or tolerated.*

*The challenge that this Boris project presented to our cast of undergraduate actors and musicians was unprecedented, as was the magnitude of the international response. The three excerpts below come from a retrospective forum on the project originally published in Pushkin Review / Пушкинский вестник, the USA-based annual in Pushkin Studies, vol. 10 (2007): 1–6, 32–34, and 41–45. Other sections of the forum include an antic account by the director, Tim Vasen, of his encounter with Pushkin, Meyerhold, and Russian repertory (including snippets from his diary kept during his research trip to Moscow); testimonials from each member of the acting company; two essays on visual illustrations to Pushkin's play conceived respectively as comedy and as tragedy; and a selection of color production photos. Other professional venues, such as the Prokofiev journal Three Oranges, no. 14 (November 2007, special Boris issue), published tentimonials from orchestra and Glee Club participants, alongside articles by theater scholars on Meyerhold, Prokofiev, and the debacles of 1936. In 2008, Princeton University published a commemorative picture-book of stills, and a DVD exists of the entire production.*

# EDITOR'S INTRODUCTION:
## PRINCETON'S *BORIS GODUNOV*, 1936/2007
### (2007)

On April 12, 2007, after half-a-year of intense collaboration between Music, Slavic, the programs in Theater and Dance, and the School of Architecture, the Berlind Theater at Princeton University "premiered a concept." The communications and publicity staff of the university, which prefers to work with clear-cut labels for things, initially found this idea difficult to grasp. Qualifying it as a "premiere" was the fact that the dramatic text was Pushkin's uncut, uncensored original 1825 version of *Boris Godunov* (all twenty-five scenes), rehearsed (incompletely) by Vsevolod Meyerhold, with music that Sergei Prokofiev wrote in 1936 specifically for this play but which had never been heard in its proper context. The Princeton production was still a "concept," however, and not a revival or a historical restoration — because like so much else prepared for the Pushkin Death Centennial of 1937, this musicalized play never got to opening night. It remained a partially assembled torso. This *Pushkin Review* forum hopes to capture some of the excitement of Princeton's creative-restorative project, which Simon Morrison (Professor of Music and Princeton's Prokofiev scholar) and I co-managed for much of 2006–07. For me it was the culmination of thirty years' thinking about Pushkin's play, topped by that unprecedented dream come true: seeing and hearing the whole play live, and alive, in more dimensions than Pushkin could have ever dreamed of on stage.

First, some background to the original Russian collaboration. In the spring of 1936, Meyerhold accepted a commission to produce *Boris Godunov* for the Pushkin Jubilee. He persuaded an initially reluctant Prokofiev, just repatriated to Moscow from Paris, to provide a score. Twenty-four pieces of music were eventually composed, the acting company did extensive tablework, and Meyerhold passionately — even obsessively — rehearsed half-a-dozen scenes. This was the director's third attempt to put Pushkin's drama on stage. The first was a studio workshop in set design conducted during the Civil War years 1918–19, from which a sequence of provocative sketches survive. The second was for the Vakhtangov Theater in 1924–25, from which memoirs survive. By 1936, Meyerhold's excitement was at fever pitch: at last he could provide practical evidence that "Pushkin was not only a remarkable dramatist but also a dramatist-director and the initiator of a new dramatic system."[1] But by May

---

[1]    In this same note from 1936, Meyerhold advised his company to "always start your day by reading some Pushkin, even if only two or three brief pages." See Aleksandr Gladkov,

1937 the *Boris* rehearsals had dwindled to nothing and the production was abandoned. On December 17 of that year, Kerzhentsev's article "An Alien Theater" ["Chuzhoi teatr"] appeared in *Pravda*, denouncing Meyerhold's repertory as "presenting classic plays in a crooked formalist mirror."[2] In early January 1938 the Meyerhold Theater was closed, construction on his new building near Mayakovsky Square was halted, and although the director's career temporarily stabilized and even appeared to rally, the end of the story is the familiar chronicle of the Terror consuming its greatest talent. On June 20, 1939, Meyerhold was arrested on charges of Trotskyite espionage in a spy ring with British and Japanese intelligence. After torture and forced confession (followed by a recantation of the confession), he was executed by firing squad on February 1, 1940. Prokofiev left no record of his response to this loss of his collaborator and did not refer to Meyerhold again in his diaries.

Prokofiev had accepted three large-scale, high-profile orchestral commissions for the Pushkin Jubilee: incidental music for a stage adaptation, by Sigizmund Krzhizhanovsky, of *Evgenii Onegin* for Tairov's Moscow Chamber Theater; the score for a filmed version of *The Queen of Spades*, to be directed by Mikhail Romm; and this commission for Meyerhold's staging of *Boris Godunov*. Prokofiev also composed three Pushkin Romances, and he briefly considered setting *Mozart and Salieri*. Neither the theatrical productions nor the film were ever realized, apparently for reasons unrelated to the music. Tairov, Romm, and Meyerhold were censured for creative transgressions of a more general sort during this increasingly cautious year, and these three experimental projects unraveled.

The surviving rehearsal transcripts of the abandoned *Boris* suggest that Meyerhold wanted the acting to be energetic, with overlapping scenes and minimal barriers between auditorium and stage. The play would be saturated with music, both of the "diegetic" sort (music heard inside the story space) and a more flexible "mood music" illustrating thoughts or fantasies. One of Prokofiev's major anxieties throughout his Jubilee work was how to avoid the sound of the canonized "operatic Pushkin" (Musorgsky for *Boris Godunov*, Tchaikovsky for *Evgenii Onegin*). His practice was to compose a "looser" score of discrete musical modules that could be repeated and recombined at the director's discretion. In November 1936, the composer completed a piano score that featured drunken singing, ballroom dancing (a polonaise and mazurka),

*Meyerhold Speaks, Meyerhold Rehearses*, ed. and trans. Alma Law (Amsterdam: Harwood Academic Publishers, 1997), 141.

2   "Khronika strashnykh dnei: 'Chuzhoi teatr' (17 dekabria 1937)," in Ar'ye Elkana, *Meierkhol'd* (Tel Aviv, 1991), 366–70, esp. 367.

a reverie, and an amoroso in the style of film music. These vibrant and gaudy show pieces were punctuated by two laments (one for Ksenia, another for the Holy Fool—both to Pushkin's words), a sing-along for blind beggars, three behind-the-scenes choruses, and four songs of loneliness. Russia, musically, is an *a capella* place; people hum or moan rather than sing to orchestral accompaniment. The battle music for scene 17 is a musical equivalent of the macaronic mix of three languages in Pushkin's text, a percussive clash of three differently tuned ensembles performed at incompatible tempi: one for Boris's "Asiatic" troops and one for the Pretender's Polish/"Western" forces, each interrupted by German mercenaries. In the Berlind Theater, these local brass bands were stationed in different parts of the hall.

A challenge to the collaborators was to achieve the effect of *narod bezmolvstvuet* [the people are silent] at the end, for Meyerhold was keen to attach this canonized 1830 stage direction to the full 1825 play. A hummed male chorus representing the dark, menacing rumble of the crowd was to swell throughout the final scenes "like the roar of the sea"—and then subside. In contrast to the bleakly *a capella* vocal texture of Russia (often threatening, usually lonely), musical Poland was all lyrical melody and luxurious, Hollywood-style orchestration. By May 1937, when rehearsals petered out, the score was not complete. Meyerhold had wanted Prokofiev to compose two more passages. One was for the Pretender's restless dreams (scene 6, "By the Monastery Wall. The Evil Monk," to be set as Grigory's dream on the road); the other was for the fortune-tellers who noisily besiege Boris with drums, sticks, bongos and rattles during his famous monologue in scene 8. These pieces were never composed. After the project collapsed, the composer recycled his extant *Boris* music into other works: part of the Battle music went into his opera *Semyon Kotko*, a portion of the Polish dances into his ballet *Cinderella* and the opening scene of Eisenstein's *Ivan the Terrible, Part II*, where the traitor Kurbsky is entertained at the decadent Polish court. The vocal and choral music, among the most terrifying ever composed for historical drama, fell away. These bits of recycled music took on the "programs" of the new contexts into which they entered, and their association with Pushkin's play was lost. For the purposes of our restoration, this was unfortunate. For unlike the practice of the more "biomechanical" Meyerhold of the 1920s, for whom palpable material (props, stage scenery or machinery, costumes, make-up) carried the concept, by the time *Boris* was abandoned, very few sets had been designed. There is some indication that Meyerhold was treating Prokofiev's music as a "set," that is, as a sort of aural scaffolding. The score provided the constraints, the cues for actors' expressive gestures, the pacing, and during the musicalized episodes, even a psychological transcript of the characters' inner emotions. The residue of this Centennial project consisted largely of the music and the words. The project remained in that fragmented, illusory state until 2007.

The Princeton decision to take up this "torso" and complete it was made possible by three fortuitously timed events. First was Simon Morrison's recovery of documents relating to the musical and dramatic structure of the Meyerhold production. They are scattered throughout various archival holdings in Moscow: the manuscript of the piano score and Meyerhold's detailed instructions for fitting that score into Pushkin's play in RGALI (the Russian State Archive of Literature and Art), the orchestration in the Central State Glinka Museum of Musical Culture. Since the 1984 published edition of the Prokofiev *Boris Godunov* music, by the musicologist Elizabeth Dattel', is flawed and could not have been used as the basis for a production, these archival recoveries were indispensable. Then a new acting English translation of *Boris Godunov*, by Antony Wood, appeared in 2006. (The Princeton performance was in English, with sung texts performed in Russian. But the director eventually combined several translations — including an even more recent one by James Falen — and made sure that all lines "carried" on the American stage in the comfort zone of our undergraduate actors.) Finally, a Creative and Performing Arts initiative had recently been announced by the University in the wake of a huge gift marked for that purpose, and the *Boris* venture turned out to be an excellent flagship. No one dreamed that an amateur undergraduate student production at a liberal-arts institution without a drama school (indeed, without a dramatic arts major) would catch the attention of the national, and then the world, press.

Only gradually did I learn that staging a complex piece like this at a university offered a director advantages and resources that few commercial theaters could afford today. Courses for credit could educate the participants over several months. The University Orchestra and Glee Club programmed Prokofiev's orchestral and choral music into their concert repertory for the year. The final design, evolved over five months in a graduate seminar sponsored by the School of Architecture, was thoroughly modernist, complementing Meyerhold's idea that "music was the set" by turning the stage space literally into a pluckable musical instrument, one that could be set into motion by the tremors and anxieties of the cast. It consisted of 150 movable pieces of surgical tubing (affectionately called "bungees") fastened vertically in 25-foot-long strips from floor to ceiling and fitted into five parallel tracks in the stage floor. This tubing could be stretched taut, bunched up, snapped, whacked with a rod, coiled like a noose, and swung on like a swing to express a variety of emotions and pressures externally, in keeping with Meyerhold's highly physical, gestural theater.

This generic "bungee" set, lit up in brilliant reds and blues, was supplemented with minimal standardized props (a table, throne, chairs, goblets, weapons), all looking vaguely and sinisterly industrial. The throne resembled a gallows; weapons of wood and metal spliced together a sleazy nightclub with a torture chamber. Clothing was layered. Catherine Cann, Princeton's costume designer, created a standard company outfit derived from the blocked colors and boxy shape of a Malevich figure, over which "special effects" were draped: the tsar's brocaded robe, a mourning gown for the tsarevna, a cassock for the monks, Prussian-style khaki for the tsar's commanders. Dmitry the Pretender, hailing from Poland, strutted about in an anachronistic red and blue military uniform with gold epaulettes. The orchestra, stacked in tiers at stage rear for the Polish scenes, wore pink and blue wigs. The 8-person dance troupe performed the polonaise and mazurka in muslin and silk. Every member of the company played several roles, except Dmitry: since he could pretend to anything, he could only be himself.

Among the thirteen undergraduates who made up the acting company and filled Pushkin's sixty-odd roles, a wide range of acting styles was practiced. Our choreographer, Rebecca Lazier, put the cast through Laban exercises as part of their daily rehearsal routine. But the on-stage behavior of each actor varied, from Stanislavskian-style earnestness to high stylization. This mix of styles was not inappropriate, since Meyerhold himself had long since abandoned strict biomechanical calculations in his stage work. He remained eclectic until the end. After his own theater was closed his former mentor and theoretical opponent Stanislavsky courageously appointed him director of the Stanislavsky Opera Theater, a post he held until his arrest.

Our acting company was academically credited as a seminar, meeting together once a week (in addition to hundreds of part rehearsals) for table work, background lectures, and collective physical exercises. Other courses dealing with Russian history, Pushkin's drama, and Prokofiev's music were open to all undergraduates. The University Library mounted an exhibit featuring Pushkin, Meyerhold, and Prokofiev, and a six-week course for alumni was offered on-line. Finally, the University hosted two scholarly symposia, one in English for the general public and one in Russian for our invited guests from Moscow.

Overall, we were amazed that so much *translated* in the performance. Who would have thought that "Shuisky" or "Uglich" would be words bandied about in undergraduate dorms? To be sure, the Russians in the audience had their reservations, both the émigrés and the reporting teams from Moscow (there were many of both, especially after the *New York Times* previewed the production). The non-traditional casting especially caught their eye, triggering some comments that caused our sophisticated troupe to wince in surprise. "A young negro woman in the role of the boyar Vorotynsky: that's the first thing the Russian spectator notices about Pushkin's *Comedy about Tsar Boris and Grishka Otrepiev*": thus did Channel One Moscow [*Pervyi kanal*] open its news clip on April 13. "The Patriarch here is also played by a young woman." Vladimir Rogachev, New York correspondent for *Echo of the Planet* [*Ekho planety*], wrote in his review of May 10, 2007: "Of course, to the Russian ear the 'music' of Pushkin's speech sounded quite unusual in English…It was remarkable to see the image of the chronicler Pimen and to hear the famous phrase 'One more, one final tale…' performed by an Afro-American, and to behold with one's own eyes how in the suite of the Russian tsar there appeared representatives of the African continent. In Alexander Sergeyevich's veins there flowed African blood, of course, but he too could not have imagined that his *Boris Godunov* would ever be mounted in so distant and mysterious a place as America was at that time." Overall, press coverage was positive and generous.

In the longer Russian reviews, however, one could sense some cultural territoriality. Elena Klepikova in *Russian Bazaar* [*Russkii bazar*], no. 17 (575) 26 April–2 May 2007, made special note of the fact that the bungees were originally a Russian idea. "Since Meyerhold often worked with architects," she noted, "the Princeton School of Architecture was given the job of designing the set for the production. Elastic tubing was stretched across the entire stage, from floor to ceiling. This tubing could represent trees in a forest; it could be stretched taut and then abruptly released, like bows and arrows in the battle scene. Astonishingly flexible, it could be wound around a person who at that moment was experiencing rage or despair… It's worth mentioning that even this all-important tubing was not an invention of the Americans, but taken from Meyerhold's own vast artistic workshop. Here's how Viktor Shklovsky describes the design of one of Meyerhold's early stage sets: 'The footlights were removed. The gaping expanse of the stage is stripped bare. On the stage a counter-relief with downward-hanging stretched tubing, with bent iron'…"

Off camera and out of print, one of the nicest compliments we received came from the head of the Russian television crew. He noted — part wistfully, part proudly — that "Pushkin had sold out in New Jersey." Indeed he had.

*The summary comments below, in the genre of "backstage production lore," followed the testimonials by the actors in the* Pushkin Review *forum. The final entry in that section was by Kelechi Ezie, a history major who played the Hostess as well as Tsar Boris's general Basmanov, and reads:*

Kelechi Ezie:

"The Prokofiev score made everything fall into place. It was the perfect backdrop to weave the scenes together, and it set the emotional tone for the play. It was especially effective in the final scenes. I remember one particular performance in which Erber's [Gavrila Pushkin's] microphone shorted out, and the orchestra covered most of his speech. The audience could not hear his words as he informed us, the crowd, of Dmitry's arrival in Moscow and accession to the throne. But the music carried the meaning of the words. Even for the scenes that did not have a score, the memory of the music informed my physical presence. The sound of the snare drums helped me develop a consistent, militaristic gait for Basmanov. The imposing, macabre horns helped me to pace my death, and then remain completely still as a dead body in the battle scene. The music added grace and fluidity to all of our performances."

## EDITOR'S POSTSCRIPT TO ACTORS' TESTIMONIALS
## (2007)

On stage, scenes 24 and 25 of Pushkin's play were terrifying. Prokofiev's music enabled not only Kelechi in her role as an unnamed soldier in the battle scene, but the entire Kremlin in early summer 1605 (the Godunov family at the hands of Dmitry's men), to "pace its own death." First a wordless but threatening chant-like refrain issues forth from the male chorus. This stalking rhythm is reinforced by the orchestra, rising to a roar, subsiding, then re-attacking. The stage with its bungees gorged with blood was bathed, like one huge gallows, in garish red light. The production came together as the Godunov dynasty fell apart. But there were extremely anxious moments along the way. Once resolved, these tense moments became anecdotes (in the best Russian sense): a mix of technical, cultural-historical, and personnel breakdowns that were scary at the time and then were transformed into "cast stories" and jokes that everyone loved to re-tell.

The first crisis: the orchestra and its conductor took fright at being stacked on Hollywood Squares at the back of the stage. What if the horn player lost his footing; what if the conductor, even wearing his day-glo pink wig, could not be seen around all that scaffolding? But all the players came round: the stacked squares were essential, since they doubled as a huge iconostasis in the Moscow scenes. Dmitry the Tsarevich performs a miracle on the upper tier, blazing forth during the Patriarch's tale. The final double murder took place up there in the terem as well. That murder also caused a tense moment. At one point Tim Vasen wished to substitute the Tsarevna Ksenia for Maria Godunova as second victim. She's already up there, and who in the audience has ever heard of Maria? To add that name only confuses matters at the last moment. Tim sought me out in the rehearsal hall for my approval (there was always a "cultural consultant," Simon Morrison or myself, on hand for moments like this). I was of course horrified, pointing out that there was a difference between poetic license and blasphemy. The violation — to say nothing of the murder — of Ksenia Godunova was a matter of serious historical import, and to Pushkin of serious moral import; it was not to be tampered with. The unfamiliar Maria Godunova remained in the script, her unfamiliar body sacrificed on that upper tier alongside her son.

Then there were the combat boots for Lily Cowles in her role as Holy Fool. Lily, a spectacular blonde, played both the Polish princess Marina Mniszech and the Fool. Those two parts were distant enough in the play so that the necessary character-switches could be timed in without panic. But Lily was also a soldier in the battle scenes; the entire cast was mobilized for those episodes. In Pushkin's original (1825) ordering of scenes, which was retained by us in this production, the "Nikolka" scene 18, *"Ploshchad' pered soborom v Moskve"* [Square before the Cathedral in Moscow] immediately preceded the comic-macaronic battle scene, *"Ravnina bliz Novgoroda-Severskogo"* [The Plain near Novgorod-Seversk]. The transition between scenes 18 and 19 had been pared down to fourteen seconds, and Lily was fully choreographed into the Battle that followed hard upon her exit from Red Square. There was no way she could get herself out of her rags and bungees (for her *verigi* or penitential chains, Lily wound flaccid tubing around herself, randomly whipping her torso with it before and after her lament). Nor could she pull on those high boots in time to enter with the infantry charge. Thus Tim and the costume designer hit upon the idea of sending her into Red Square to meet Tsar Boris already sheathed in those boots. I was on duty for that rehearsal, and howled stop. Holy fools had to be barefoot. Better a foot-soldier in slippers than a *iurodivyi* [holy fool] in manufactured military boots. Lily was re-choreographed later in the Battle. Thanks to the flexibility and good will of our production crew, this moment too was won for the integrity of Russian culture.

Our brief romance with beards tested integrity in another direction. Alert to the status of male facial hair in pre-Petrine Russia, for a brief span of rehearsals the cast was bearded. The beards were bushy and glossy; you couldn't see anyone's mouth. They did not add authenticity but the opposite, functioning like masks for the lower face. The Patriarch — who was convincing as she was, commanding full spiritual authority — suddenly looked like a transvestite and parody. Boris, a big blond man, resembled a little boy dressing up. Pimen's expressive face became a cartoon. The next day the

*Jess Kwong (the two tsareviches) and Philicia Saunders (Vorotynsky) after the show (photo by Denise Applewhite).*

beards came off the principals, with only the comic moments and characters thus adorned (Varlaam, the Drunken Boyars at Shuisky's House, buffoons from the public square in scene 3). We discovered that visual authenticity was a tricky business on this modernist stage.

But the biggest anxiety, as these testimonials suggest, was also the most thrilling draw: the bungee-cord set. A week before opening night, during the brief, emotional scene 16 ("*Granitsa litovskaia*" [At the Lithuanian Border]), a bungee stretched and released by Peter Schram (Kurbsky) struck Adam, the Pretender, squarely in the eye. We all held our breath; the pain was intense and the rehearsal was over for the night. It reminded us that the set was a weapon. Early in the rehearsal process, the ever-present surgical tubing had proved a constraint: ballet toe-shoes got stuck in the grooves so the choreographer had to forego the lovely idea of a dance sequence on point; the Patriarch's thumping staff wedged itself in once or twice, to the ruin of the rhythm of the scene. But this was all during rehearsal; worse was with a public. After the second night to a sold-out house, on Friday April 13, the Production Stage Manager Hannah Woodward sent around Performance Notes as usual to the cast and crew: "A good performance overall tonight with quite a few technical glitches." Glitch #4 read: "During the Battle, a bungee wrapped itself around a light and the bungee pulled the electric in such a way that we couldn't fly the Downstage Scrim in at the end of the battle. During the transition going into the Forest, Peter and Philicia saved the day and were able to free the bungee from the light so that we were able to use the Scrim for the rest of the show."

Tsar Boris had died on April 13, 1605. That bungee-noose strangling the light, we came to believe, was in honor of the 402nd anniversary of his death.

# AFTERWORD: THE FATE OF THE JUBILEE PUSHKIN ON THE STALINIST MUSICAL-DRAMATIC STAGE (2007)

Early in the *Boris Godunov* seminar, Leeore Schnairsohn (at the time a second-year graduate student in Comparative Literature) commented in one of his critiques on the openness or "eternal present" implied in Pushkin's famous final stage direction, *narod bezmolvstvuet*. He had been struck by the ambivalence, or better by the multivalence, of that silence. An aggressive prompt to cheer the new tsar had elicited no response. But perhaps that silence *was* the response: "the absence of a positive gesture leaves open the question not only of whether the people's silence is action or inaction, but also whether their gesture is fulfilled or still nascent." Schnairsohn took Belinsky's reading of Pushkin's mute closing gesture one step further, suggesting that one effect of such a sudden stoppage or bewildered silence is to "bring the audience's present moment in line with the drama's, because *bezmolvstvovat'* is precisely what the audience has been doing all along, and now suddenly it's the same silence, the same moment, on both sides of the curtain." Two cowed halls gaping at each other.

In the final moments of the Princeton production, after the successful double murder high up on the scaffolding, this radical equalization of on- and off-stage audiences was achieved by turning the glare of searchlights directly into the hall from the back of the blood-red, bungee-filled stage. It was a Meyerholdian moment—although not, of course, unique to his modernist theater. From today's perspective, our knowledge of post-1936 events in Stalinist Russia lends this indictment a meaning it could not have had in its own time. Throughout the final public-square scenes, beginning with the ominous, wordless rhythmic chanting of the male chorus and reinforced by a pulsating orchestra, horror had been growing apace with powerlessness. When Tsar Boris, already two scenes dead, reappears in company costume as a bullying Guard on the Pretender's side, history begins to blend with symbols of arbitrary, interchangeable violence. And when Lily the Holy Fool reappears as a beggar asking the imprisoned Godunov children for alms, the logic behind these twenty-five scenes of multiple casting is driven home: the Boris Tale, like all reality in Pushkin's poetic shaping of it, deals in *functions* and parallel structures as much as in human beings. People are precise and unrepeatable as themselves; they believe they are free. But their fate moves only one way and the cumulative effect of their movements will reveal a magnificent pattern. Part of the shock of Pushkin's abrupt, non-sentimental endings—Book Eight of *Evgeny Onegin* as well as the final scene of *Boris Godunov*—is that the author simply "takes his leave" once the symmetry has been realized. He walks away, with the benumbed heroes, readers, and spectators on their knees and in the spotlight. They must do something: but what?

For a long half-minute, the audience endured discomfort under that scorching light and the company remained frozen on stage (the 1830 ending). Then the play delivered its authentic, original 1825 end: rhythmic clapping on stage and an ever louder, more strident "Long Live Tsar Dmitry

Ivanovich!" In some of our performances, the audience joined in, clapping and chanting; in others, the hall continued silently to "watch." The Guard who was also Tsar Boris initiated the cheer. A total blackout put an end to it. What was the mood of that crowd in 1605, looking toward the Kremlin? Cynical and opportunistic? Manipulated and yet still naively optimistic? Genuinely optimistic that once the traitors and pretenders were purged, Russia would recover her former glory? From our present-day perspective, similarities between the texture of this power-savvy, symmetrical 1825 ending and the black comedy of 1936–37 are easy to see.

The mortality rate of the Pushkin Jubilee projects was high. Only recently, however, have the fine details of those lethal years begun to emerge. One piece fell in place during the keynote address that opened the scholarly symposium on the day of the *Boris* premiere, April 12, delivered by the Canadian-Russian scholar Leonid Maximenkov and titled "Meyerhold and his World (1929–1940)." One might have expected a tribute to the great director's innovations in the sphere of theater, cinema, and dance — but Maximenkov took those accomplishments for granted. Also routine to expect would have been commentary on Meyerhold as an angry closet dissident. This was a director, after all, who, during rehearsals of scene 10 ("Shuisky's House") had dangerously improvised on Afanasy Pushkin's speech on the tyranny of Tsar Boris. He had instructed Prokofiev to provide music for the final chorus that was "anxious, threatening," but that nevertheless delivered the message that "this undisciplined crowd would solidify, consolidate itself, and fight against its oppressors, whoever they may be."[3] Maximenkov, however, did not repeat the martyrology of Meyerhold's tragic Stalinist-era fate. He debunked that legend. Relying on hitherto unseen video footage gathered from Moscow film holdings and previously classified documents from Moscow government archives, Maximenkov, in less than an hour, re-cast fifty years of research on the most important figure in twentieth-century Soviet theater culture. In one document after another, he argued that Meyerhold, an ethnic German, perished by firing squad in 1940 not because he was a Kremlin outsider, persecuted by party hacks in the Stalinist cultural apparatus, but because he was the ultimate Kremlin insider, an intimate in the halls of power, with advance knowledge of Stalin's rapprochement with Hitler on the eve of the signing of the Molotov-Ribbentrop pact. The signing

---

[3]   Letter of Meyerhold to Prokofiev, August/September 1936, in the chapter "Meyerhold and Pushkin," in *Meyerhold at Work*, ed. Paul Schmidt (Austin: University of Texas Press, 1980), 140.

of that duplicitous pact enabled the invasion of Poland that launched the Second World War, and those who knew too much of its prehistory were on some pretext put away. With a sinking heart one realizes that such a discovery would not have surprised Pushkin.

Stalin had appointed Meyerhold a member of the All-Union Pushkin Committee, whose task it was to supervise the artistic, political, and pedagogical content of the Jubilee. Priorities for the celebration changed by the month. In December 1935, a newly-expanded Committee resolved that the focus be changed from "Pushkin, victim of tsarism" to a more optimistic message that stressed poetry, the Russian language, and a radiant future for Russian culture. Academic Pushkinists were brought in to dilute the Party bureaucrats and watchdogs. But the rising tide of arrests, international tensions, and a cautious, better-safe-than-sorry mentality registered on this Jubilee as on every other state project. By the summer of 1936, most of the creative commissions had been cancelled or had faded away, including the Prokofiev collaborations over *Boris Godunov* and *Evgeny Onegin*. The Pushkin Commission spent its time debating monuments, exhibitions, commemorative plaques, postage stamps, the size of publication runs, book distribution to schools and libraries, the renaming of streets, factories, and farms in Pushkin's honor, and even the possible transfer of Pushkin's sacred remains to Moscow.[4] Maximenkov uncovered the astonishing fact that during February 1937, the actual centennial of the duel and death when creative activity should have been at its peak, almost nothing on or by Pushkin was being performed in any Moscow theater. *Pushkin bezmolvstvuet.* Is "the gesture fulfilled, or still nascent?" This blank spot imposed an obligation on the future.

Our attempt at Princeton to acquaint twenty-first-century college students with the challenges of the collapsed Stalin-era *Boris Godunov* was one response to this obligation. But to the delight of its collaborators, Princeton's *Boris* turned out to be the beginning, not the end, of Pushkin Jubilee resuscitations. I close on a mention of one project-in-the-making, a mounting of the Pushkin-Krzhizhanovsky *Evgenii Onegin*, reunited with

---

[4] I am indebted here to Leonid Maximenkov, who shared details from his two-volume documentary study of Soviet music history in preparation (based on collections from five federal archives in Moscow). For a sample of this solely "bureaucratic" activity of the Commission, see Stephanie Sandler, "The 1937 Pushkin Jubilee as Epic Trauma," in *Epic Revisionism: Russian History and Literature as Stalinist Propaganda*, eds. Kevin M. E. Platt and David Brandenberger (Madison: University of Wisconsin Press, 2006), 196–99.

Prokofiev's music and scheduled for mid-February of 2012.[5] Although the cancelled *Onegin* and the abandoned *Boris* share certain traits (most importantly, music by Prokofiev), the collaborative *Onegin* was more thoroughly lost. Before it reached rehearsal stage at Tairov's Moscow Chamber Theater, the playscript was subject to intense criticism from the Pushkin Commission and State Repertory committees; once canceled (December 3, 1936), the project disappeared, both from domestic memory and from surveys of Soviet-era drama. Reasons for this silence are several. Tairov's *Kamernyi Teatr* has not enjoyed the fame and scholarly attention of Meyerhold's. The ethnically Polish, Ukrainian-born Russophone prosewriter-playwright who adapted Pushkin's novel-in-verse for the stage, Sigizmund Dominikovich Krzhizhanovsky (1887–1950), was only marginally visible during his life and died in obscurity. (His otherworldly stories boomed in postcommunist Russia in the mid-1990s and are now moving into European languages.) Finally, the only edition we have of Prokofiev's *Onegin* music (1973) was prepared for print by Elizaveta Dattel', a cautious and at the same time careless editor, who disapproved of Krzhizhanovsky's treatment of Pushkin and unceremoniously removed him from the credits, even though Prokofiev had written his music directly in response to this play.

True, the treatment of Pushkin's novel-in-verse was astonishing. Its psychological cohesion and boldness could only have dismayed the academic purists (among Pushkin Commission members, it appears that only Sergei Bondi and V. V. Veresaev were intrigued by it.) Krzhizhanovsky and his director Tairov wanted a real play, so their first step was to eliminate Pushkin's narrator. The participants speak for themselves, with no poet in sideburns wandering the stage and "filling in." But conversation still takes place on stage in chunks of the Onegin stanza, although (of course) spliced and cut to satisfy the time constraints of an evening's performance. There is no paraphrasing of Pushkin. There is also no singing of lines, with the exception

---

5    Thanks to the generosity of Galina Zlobina, deputy director of the Russian State Archive of Literature and Art (RGALI) in Moscow, in June 2007 I received a copy of the 1936 Krzhizhanovsky playscript, together with numerous other items in his file that clarify its creative history. Only four people had worked with the playscript since it was deposited in the archival *fond*, and the text does not appear in Krzhizhanovsky's *Sobranie sochinenii* (five volumes, 2001–11), edited by Vadim Perelmuter. My translation and annotation of Krzhizhanovsky's *Evgenii Onegin*, together with an introductory essay, appears in *Sergey Prokofiev and his World*, ed. Simon Morrison (Princeton: Princeton University Press, 2008), 60–189.

of one refrain (in French) for Onegin. Thus this adaptation, although intermittently scored for orchestra and containing singing and dance inserts, bears no resemblance to Tchaikovsky's operatic *Evgenii Onegin*. The music is still "incidental" (in Prokofiev's magnificent expansion of that genre); the feel of the verbal playtext is still "Pushkin spoken aloud." Krzhizhanovsky labeled his adaptation a "scenic projection," attending especially to the angle of lighting (the sun, moon, time of year). At times the script sounds like a film scenario, and could be realized brilliantly in that medium.

The fourteen episodes, labeled "fragments," are choreographed for the stage through impressionistic stage directions recalling Chekhov's drama (Krzhizhanovsky, a theorist of theater, left excellent essays on the stage direction as a literary form and on the art of Pushkin's epigraphs). In the adaptation, Tatyana Larina, pried free of her protective Narrator, undergoes a wondrous transformation as Krzhizhanovsky interpolates into the play other works by Pushkin: the *skazka* "O mertvoi tsarevne i o semi bogatyrekh," early Lyceum poetry, some elegiac lyrics and satiric epigrammatic verse. Folklore and superstition there is in abundance, but it is closer to the cosmic, pagan sort than to the cheerful socialist-realist worker-peasants celebrated by Maxim Gorky in the mid-1930s. All major activity happens in winter, which is for Krzhizhanovsky the most generative season of the year, linked everywhere with fidelity and unswerving fate. Tatyana's cautionary tale and inspiration is *Snegurochka* [The Snow Maiden] rather than Snow White. And most controversially, Krzhizhanovsky places at the center of his drama, taken out of Pushkin's storytelling sequence but with strict psychological logic, wedged in between the Nameday fiasco and the disaster of the Duel, the teasing terrifying account of Tatyana's Dream. This therapeutic and revelatory dream is told (at last) not by the salacious, patronizing Narrator but by the traumatized heroine herself.

Now that a decade has passed since the bicentennial of Pushkin's birth, and as more Stalin-era documents become available, Pushkinists are well rewarded by further excavations into the centennial of his death. Like the open-ended silence of that famous final stage direction, the musical, dramatic, and cinematographic riches still buried under the ruins of that year remain in the "eternal present." To release them from that captivity requires not just publicity or publication, but performance.

# 21
# "EUGENE ONEGIN"
# ON THE STALINIST STAGE

*The discovery, by Simon Morrison in 2007, of Sigizmund Krzhizhanovsky's stage adaptation of* Eugene Onegin *(1936) in the Prokofiev holdings of the Russian State Archive of Literature and Art (RGALI), Moscow, was for me a very happy accident. For over thirty years, moving Pushkin off the page and into some other form of art had been my most durable focus in the realm of Russian culture. The adaptor's name was unfamiliar — indeed, unpronounceable; the Moscow theater in which the event was to happen did not enjoy the fame of Meyerhold's or Stanislavsky's. But the boldness of the transposition (and the promise of Prokofiev's music written to it) took my breath away. Access to this archive opened up a new world. From that time dates my interest in SK's writings on drama, as well as his original comedies, stage and radio-show adaptations, prose tales, wartime libretti, feuilletons of Moscow in legend, history, and under siege, essays on theater (both as philosophy and as technical craft), and interpretations of classic English repertory, especially Shakespeare and George Bernard Shaw.*

*What follows is a sketch of Krzhizhanovsky's life and creativity. My initial publication on this author appeared in 2008: an investigation into the aborted 1936 "scenic projection" of* Onegin *(introduced at the end of the entry 20 and excerpted below). Since then, my attention has turned to a just published original work by SK: his 1937 historical farce* That Third One *[«Том третий»]. The play takes its title from the nameless third volunteer for Cleopatra's Wager (certain death for one night of love) as depicted in Pushkin's famous poem on the Egyptian queen. But there the similarities with Pushkin end. SK's travestied Cleopatra play builds on Pushkin (1828), Shakespeare (Antony and Cleopatra, 1607), and Bernard Shaw (Caesar and Cleopatra, 1898) to parody Silver-Age myths about the tyranny of female beauty and the prototypical "poet of genius" who worships it as his Muse. More illicitly, the play mocks the incompetence of a worldwide spy network and bumbling secret police that try to bring the fugitive Third to justice. Along the way and never ceasing to laugh, the play manages to mock political power of every sort: arbitrary, capricious, serving accidental good as often as accidental evil. If Pushkin's* Boris Godunov *qualifies, in my estimation, as a "tragicomedy of history," then Krzhizhanovsky's* Tot tretii *takes the corrosion of piety one step further: imperial history as tragifarce, wherever it is found — in Ancient Rome, Mussolini's Rome, or Stalin's "Third Rome," Moscow. SK's comedy was read aloud once by its author at a private gathering in 1938 (Meyerhold, already disgraced, was present that evening and liked it) but it was never performed, and published only in 2010.*

# SIGIZMUND KRZHIZHANOVSKY (1887–1950)
## BIO-BIBLIOGRAPHICAL SKETCH
### (2010)

Sigizmund Dominikovich Krzhizhanovsky [SK], Russophone writer of Polish descent, was born near Kiev and died in his adopted city Moscow, largely unpublished and unperformed. His tall thin person with pince-nez was a familiar figure in the literary salons of Kiev and, after 1922, among avant-garde circles of the capital. Over a span of fifteen years SK wrote 150 prose works — resonant, dense, as cerebral as a metaphysical poem — ranging in length from novellas to one-paragraph miniatures, often organized loosely in cycles. His hero everywhere was the *idea* [*mysl'*] trapped in the brain. This idea, the product of individualized thought responsibly confronting the phenomena of the outside world, has one task: to survive and grow potent by searching out the freest possible carrier (the person, plot, or sound) that would least obstruct or obscure it on its journey.

Parallels can thus be drawn between SK's "travelers" and the world's classic adventure and quest literature, immensely popular in the Soviet period. SK's contexts are cosmopolitan. Among his favorite themes and books were Swift's *Gulliver's Travels* (in 1933, SK helped edit Alexander Ptushko's animated film *The New Gulliver*); the fantastical German eighteenth-century adventurer and fib-master in the Russian service, Baron von Münchhausen (in the 1920s, SK wrote a novella called *The Return of Münchhausen*); and, of course, the scientific romances of H. G. Wells. His closest academic friends were the Moscow "Anglophiles," scholars and translators of Shakespeare, Dickens, Swift, Thackeray, Wells, Bernard Shaw. But SK's own style and character types owe little to the methodical half-mad British scientist, the Shavian superman, or for that matter to the French surrealists or to Kafka, about whom SK heard only late in life. The "thought" as he portrays it cannot get on a ship and sail off to exotic continents. It is land-locked, stubborn, restless — and finds itself blocked by hunger and poverty, on the border between waking and dreaming, in a tiny room. It wants to roam but everywhere it is clipped, stuck behind a wall, forced to sneak out through a fissure or chink [щель] and re-splice in a seam [шов]. Thus the "real life of the dream" must become a serious option for the thought, as it was for the imprisoned Prince Segismundo, hero of Calderón's 17th-century drama *Life is a Dream*, which SK greatly admired. The trappings of a Krzhizha-novskian dream are more cerebral than sentimental, resembling at times a scientific Wellsian thought experiment. SK's *Memories of the Future* (1929) features a recluse building a time-travel machine; in "Quadraturin" (1926), a cramped Muscovite in a communal apartment applies a magic ointment to expand Newtonian space to infinity (recalling the anti-gravity mixture Cavorite in *The First Men in the Moon*). Members of SK's *Letter-Killers' Club* (1927) meet on Saturday nights to recite tales of medieval carnival monks and ancient Roman slave-courtesans, to project bio-terrorist dystopias, and to rewrite *Hamlet* by breaking down its players into parts; their aim is to learn to live without the crutch of books — those enemies of imagination and free-ranging thought.[1] For all these pan-European resonances, however, a Russian edge of starvation, shabbiness, Bolshevik craziness and desperate lyricism separates Krzhizhanovsky from his illustrious predecessors among the intellectual circles of the bourgeois West — even their most eccentric fringe. For domestic benchmarks we should look to Evgeny Zamyatin, Mikhail Bulgakov, and Andrei Platonov.

Krzhizhanovsky was known as an excellent reader of his own work at literary evenings. The fact that his prose was orally "performed" — and by its author — with far more regularity than it was published must have reinforced SK's sensitivity to the aural, acting core of the utterance. In the 1920s, SK's long-standing interest in Kantian philosophy and dream psychology combined with revolutionary theories of time-space perception to inspire a vision of theater as an analogue for human thought and a crucial mediator between fantasies, shadows, and objects.[2] The properly-balanced sound has weight and takes up space, like a thing. The contours of a sound, when articulated fully, could almost be seen performing an action. SK had his favorite consonants, murmuring under his text in the mind's ear: the obstruent dentals (t, z, zh, ts [т, з, ж, ц]), obstruent palatals or "hushings" (shch, sh, ch [щ, ш, ч]), the hissing clusters "zr" [зр] and "st" [ст], all suggesting a force slithering along or pushing up against a surface, suddenly to break out through an explosive "k" [к] or "p" [п]. These consonants predominate in the Russian verbs that SK uses for cracking, splitting, splintering, snapping shut,

---

[1]   These SK stories all exist in English, in the mesmerizing translations of his Moscow-based translator Joanne Turnbull. See Sigizmund Krzhizhanovsky, *7 Stories* (Moscow: GLAS Publishers, vol. 39, 2006), which won the Rossica Translation Prize in 2007; SK, *Memories of the Future* (New York: New York Review Books, 2009), and SK, *The Letter Killers' Club* (New York: New York Review Books, forthcoming 2010).

[2]   For a brief (and to date the only) overview of the writer's life and works in English, see the excellent pioneering monograph by Karen Link Rosenflanz, *Hunter of Themes: The Interplay of Word and Thing in the Works of Sigizmund Kržižanovskij* (New York: Peter Lang, 2005), biography on 1–21.

clinging, hooking into, intersecting, groping by touch. The tiny slit through which we can escape into wide open space becomes a master metaphor in SK's soundscape: an eyelid, the cleft in a stage curtain concealing a world, a crack in the plaster or along the ridge of a cliff, even the precipitous flight of an idea or a word out of a public official's unhooked briefcase.

When SK arrived in Moscow from Kiev in 1922, age 34, he was without work and often without food. He found housing in a tiny, closet-like room in a former private mansion (Arbat 44/5). The letters of introduction from Kiev led nowhere; but walking the streets looking for employment in the noisy capital under NEP, he fell in love with the city. His ritual was to set out daily at 9:45 sharp, on his «блуждания по смыслам Москвы» [wanderings in search of the meanings of Moscow] to study whatever he could see, touch, and hear. Having secured a small commission to write an "ethnographic" guide to the city (and this was how he worked: a modest income-generating job would balloon into a creative project), SK eventually described these strolls in his 1925 novella "Postmark: Moscow" [«Штемпель: Москва»], as "thirteen letters to a friend in the provinces."[3] If Petersburg is the city of the pen (flexible, hard, precise, Pushkin's curlicues that reflect *thought*), then Moscow is a city of "pencil literature" [«карандашная литература», Letter 5], all smudges and scrawls; you cannot think it through but must see it. In fact, seeing is everything — for Moscow exists in her irregular, unrepeatable details. She requires her own goddess, Glyadeia the Watcher, who never sleeps; she is all eyes, all "eyelidlessly keen vision" [безвекая зоркость]. Maps and plans won't help you, SK assures his provincial friend, because Muscovites make associations not by grids but by contiguity. The city is not an ensemble like Petersburg but merely a "heap of houses big, medium, small" (the Kremlin itself is an irregular, walled-in heap). Indeed, Moscow wasn't built at all but "nested" or "hived" by instinct, as if by birds and bees, and out of equally flammable materials. Just as Petersburg is marked by its ruinous floods, so the history of Moscow is a record of her horrendous fires. And hence the paradox of Moscow space: cluttered with things, it is continually being emptied out. The city is never rebuilt soundly or with lasting materials, because everything sooner or later burns down. Thus Moscow is always full, but always empty of any definitive shape. Alleys lead nowhere. Angles don't

---

[3]  "Shtempel': Moskva" (1925), in Sigizmund Krzhizhanovskii, *Sobranie sochinenii v piati tomakh*, ed. Vadim Perel'muter (Sankt Peterburg: Symposium, 2001), 1:518–19. Henceforth these *Collected Works* (vv. 1–4, 2001–2006; v. 5, 2010, forthcoming) referred to as *SK:Ss* followed by volume number and page.

add up. Crumbling crooked fences enclose micro-villages. Walk the city, and it seems more like a dream than an urban architecture.[4]

These contrasts between Russia's ancient capital and the City on the Neva are not original with SK, of course. They recall Zamyatin, or Andrey Bely's *Petersburg* measured against his subsequent sprawling Moscow novels. But out of these images SK constructs an original spatial poetics (or better, a spatial anxiety) for many of his best phantasmagorical stories. It differs from the familiar stone-versus-wood, patriarch-versus-Mother Earth, machine-versus-organic womb, straight line-versus-circle dichotomy of the prototypical Petersburg/Moscow myth. A typical SK "Moscow story" will prominently feature a wall [стена]. A chink (or crevice, slit, fissure, crack: щель) opens up in that wall. When this slit is closed up, stitches / seams / sutures [швы] appear. The animate elements in the story—which include human beings, talking toads, hallucinations, an idea—usually wake up on the dark and cramped inner side of the wall. There it is crowded, constricted, «тесно». Consciousness must find a window, an eye or a fissure through which to burst out. But once out, it discovers that space on the other side of the wall is too broad and uncontrolled; it is not simply breathing space, not simply room to move and become real, but something «просторно», spacious as an abyss, space with no edges to it. The options here are grimly ludicrous: either be smothered with things in inner space, or dangle lost and without support in outer space. This is also the predicament of the idea caught behind the bony carapice of the brain.

Unsurprisingly, the first Russian interpretations of SK in the post-communist period tended to classify him as a Stalin-era dissident with a space phobia. His fiction risked being reduced to Aesopian social protest: the Wall as prison; waking up cramped or wanting to "grow space" in one's apartment as commentary on the Moscow housing shortage; an endless stretch of empty horizon signifying the Eurasian continent, threatening and humanless. Unhappy in his writerly invisibility SK surely was. But above all he was a philosopher. As has been argued by his subtlest

---

4    At the beginning of SK's return to public life (the early 1990s), the Tartu semiotician Vladimir Toporov, a specialist on Petersburg urban semiotics, developed out of this passive, oppressive "minus-space" an entire semiotics peculiar to Moscow. Working intensely with several stories ("Bookmark," "Stitches," "Side Branch"), Toporov extracted a theory of spatial relativity based on the walled-in experience of tiny, chaotic Moscow apartments in a sprawling, web-like, tactile metropolis. See V. N. Toporov, "'Minus-prostranstvo' Sigizmunda Krzhizhanovskogo," in *Mif. Ritual. Simvol. Obraz. Issledovaniia v oblasti mifopoeticheskogo* (Moscow: Izdatel'skaya gruppa Progress / Kul'tura, 1992), 476–574.

student in the West, Karen Rosenflanz, SK's themes were metaphysical and quite mainstream for his era. These include the capacity of wordplay and paronomasia to free up thought; the option of words behaving like things; the experiential nature of duration; and the fourth dimension as represented spatiotemporally, through a conscious human subject.[5]

Where SK added to contemporary fellow writers on these issues was in his sophisticated metaphysics of theater, developed throughout the 1920s. Most likely he developed his ideas partly in response to the well-publicized theater writings of Meyerhold, Tairov, Vyacheslav Ivanov, Maximilian Voloshin, Gustav Shpet, Nikolai Evreinov, and other modernist practitioners of the late Symbolist period. But SK was also an historian of theater for whom more distanced interlocutors were often the more direct addressees. As his own work went unpublished and unstaged, SK began to pursue his most valued ideas in the work of universally celebrated others, thereby managing to move his ideas into print attached to a canonical corpus. (In this SK bears comparison with Mikhail Bakhtin, another philosopher who turned to famous literary figures — Dostoevsky, Rabelais — to illustrate his most precious ideas; but Bakhtin had no ambitions as primary literary creator.) Devising the term "realist-experimenter" for Shakespeare's drama, SK came to see all staged art as a type of space where, across a strip of footlights, the waking state could pass into dream with almost no friction and no loss of reality.[6] Just as the brain and its roving outpost, the eye, are the locus of the real in our lived lives, so the stage is that locus within the black box of the theater. Of special fascination to SK was the potential of sudden beams of light projected on, or issuing from, a cube or square [квадрат] — the form SK frequently evokes to indicate the confinement of three-dimensional space in Euclidian geometry,[7] and a crucial organizing factor in the stage directions to his dramatized *Eugene Onegin*. SK's keen *visual* bias in all things theatrical was apparent as early as 1922–23, in his treatise "The Philosopheme of Theater." There, in a chapter titled "The Actor as the Variety and Versatility of a Person,"

---

[5]  In addition to Rosenflanz's 2005 monograph, see her path-breaking paper presented at the first SK panel at a national US Slavic conference, "Sigizmund Krzhizhanovsky and the Fourth Dimension," where she demonstrates, against the intelligentsial-dissident readings of Perelmuter and Toporov, SK's thematic incorporation of post-Kantian discoveries and hypotheses by Hermann Minkowski, Pyotr Uspensky, and Henri Bergson. Presented at the AAASS National Convention (November 20–23, 2008), Philadelphia.

[6]  "Shekspir — realist-eksperimentor..." in "Komediografiia Shekspira," in *SK:Ss* 4, 172.

[7]  In her 2008 paper, Rosenflanz discusses SK's story "Quadraturin" in connection with Bergson with the potential of cinema.

we read: "The Actor lives as long as he *is seen*: he senses the rising curtain as the huge eyelid of an eye gazing at him. Should all the spectators close their eyes at once, he would cease to exist."[8] Equipped with this vision, SK adapted works by Pushkin, Shakespeare, Swift, and G. K. Chesterton for stage and screen. He also authored hilarious works of his own for the stage (some were even given readings by theaters), rich in wordplay and philosophical allusion.

"We live as long as we are seen": the non-publication of SK's work early became a dread pattern. In 1924, the publishing house that had accepted his *Fairytales for Wunderkinder* [*Skazki dlya Vunderkindov*] folded. A screenplay, a comic drama, and several sets of stories failed to find sponsors in 1928–29. In 1933, his "Academia" edition of Shakespeare's Collected Works was canceled (it was to include his introduction and theory of Shakespearean comedy). SK's screenplay for Ptushko's first 3-D animated film, *A New Gulliver*, was set upon by hacks and finally released without his name mentioned in the credits. In 1934, his play *The Priest and the Lieutenant* [*Pop i poruchik*] was considered by several directors, praised in the Writers' Union, but mysteriously dropped. That same year, censors put a stop to a collection of his stories in press with the State Publishing House. His collection *The Unbitten Elbow* [*Neukushennyi lokot'*] was poised to appear together with another volume of tales in 1941, but the war intervened; both projects dissolved. SK's life-long companion, the theater pedagogue Anna Bovshek (1887–1971) who stored his archive in the clothes closet of her apartment, notes in her memoirs that when SK first heard confirmation, in late 1936, that *Eugene Onegin* at the Chamber Theater had also "crashed" [*postig krakh*], he was too proud to inquire why, remarking only: "Samson didn't wage battle against his windmill. He let his hair grow out — and perhaps also what lay beneath that hair: a thought."[9]

Krzhizhanovsky's invisibility was in large part due to his modernist, neoKantian (or in Soviet parlance, "idealist") aesthetics. But he was also dogged by a mix of bad luck, bad timing, personal stubbornness, and lack of

---

[8]   "Filosofema o teatre, 3. Aktyor kak raznovidnost' cheloveka," in *SK:Ss* 4, 165.

[9]   A. Bovshek, "Vospominaniya o Krzhizhanovskom: Glazami druga," in *Velikoe kul'turnoe protivostoianie: Kniga ob Anne Gavrilovne Bovshek*, ed. A. Leontiev (Moscow: Novoe literaturnoe obozrenie, 2009), 10–66, esp. 60. Subsequent page references included in the text. Bovshek's memoir is discreet, sentimental, intensely loyal; it does not help us unpack this sly allusion. Does it suggest reconciliation with fate, or resistance on some other plane? What might have been the "thought" lying beneath the hair, the secret of Samson's strength? Unlike the mad Don Quixote tilting at windmills, Samson, after he is betrayed by Delilah and shaved, blinded, and imprisoned in Gaza, lets his hair grow again and leans against the Philistines' temple (*Judges* 16:30). Its walls come crashing down, just as Samson had hoped — killing him together with thousands of the enemy.

influential patrons. In 1932, Maxim Gorky had casually assessed several of his meta-philosophical stories and found them too intellectual, "more suited to the late nineteenth century" than to the Soviet present, and unnecessary to the tasks of the working class.[10] This unfortunate verdict stuck to the author up to and beyond his death — for it was far easier and safer to read Gorky on SK than to read SK himself. When, in 1939, he was finally voted into the Soviet Writers' Union, one of his sponsors explained the embarrassing delay by noting that Comrade Krzhizhanovsky, an erudite polyglot and critic, was "very modest and impractical, unable to do anything for himself."[11] More to the point (and not mentioned during the Writers' Union hearing), he was stubborn and unwilling to revise on command, whether for censors or for well-meaning editors and collaborators. SK had always considered each of his words to be a balanced unit phonetically fused with every other unit; to edit or paraphrase would be to dissolve the structure. He was aware that this high poetic standard was a liability under Soviet conditions. In her memoirs Bovshek recalls a comment SK made to his friend Tairov, who had offered patronage during a difficult moment, to the effect that it was no use because "my worst enemy is myself: I'm that hermit in the desert who has become his own bear" (33). So SK free-lanced for a living — hiring himself out for encyclopedia entries, editorial services, translations, adaptations, and academic backup for radio shows. His closest professional friends, the Anglophone academics Mikhail Levidov (a specialist on Swift), Evgeny Lann (on Dickens) and Alexander Anikst (on Shakespeare and Shaw), helped him as they could with commissions. For six years, from 1925 to 1931, SK was a *kontrol'nyi redaktor* [head proofreader] for the Great Soviet Encyclopedia. Surely his most satisfying position, however, was as in-house stage adapter and pedagogue at the Moscow Chamber Theater, where he worked on and off from his arrival in the capital in 1922 until 1949.

During World War Two, SK tried to fit his literary gifts to Socialist Realist priorities. He turned to patriotic libretti, historical drama, and pious (although still impressionistic) sketches of Moscow under siege. He refused to be evacuated from Moscow during the war, saying that a man should not be separated from his city. To his delight, SK, who adored to travel, was briefly

---

10   See Perelmuter's outraged summary of Gorky's letter in his preface to the *Collected Works*, "Posle katastrofy," in *SK:Ss* 1, 25–31.

11   The remark was made by Vol'penshtein on 13 February 1939 at a meeting of the Dramaturgs' Section of the Union of Soviet Writers of the USSR; see "Stenogramma Rasshirennogo zasedaniia Byuro sektsii dramaturgov ot 13-ogo fevralia 1939 g. RGALI f. 631, op. 2, ed. khr. 355, p. 48.

"mobilized" on the cultural front, sent to Irkutsk, Novosibirsk, and Ulan-Ude to lecture on theater. As with other marginalized writers, SK experienced modest official success under conditions of total war. But that crisis passed, the post-war repressions began — and no collection of SK's prose ever made it through to print nor any of his original plays to opening night. Only nine stories, one stage adaptation in 1923–24, a patriotic libretto in 1942–43, and a handful of critical articles (largely on drama) saw official light of day.

Krzhizhanovsky's most productive period was the decade from 1925 to 1935, measured both by his astonishing output of original prose and by his provocative poetics for adapting others to the stage. In his (unpublished) essay "Stanza by Stanza through *Onegin*," generated in 1936 while working on his Jubilee commission for Tairov, he expressed dissatisfaction with both branches of the Pushkin industry: the subjectively ecstatic interpreters ("My Pushkin") as well as the obsessively objective biographers ("Did Pushkin smoke?").[12] To both he preferred the more creative (and in his view, more objective) method of "applied poetics" [*prikladnaia poetika*]. By this term he meant neither "slow reading" nor a scholarly enslavement to facts, but the re-realization of Pushkin in other media (stage or film) through acting, music, dancers, or mime. SK had already applied such "criticism" to G. K. Chesterton's 1908 spy novel and spoof on anarchism, *The Man Who was Thursday: a Nightmare*, which he adapted to some acclaim for the Chamber Theater in 1924, with a Constructivist set by Aleksandr Vesnin. Chesterton (who had not been consulted or even informed of the production) was scandalized. "The Bolsheviks have done a good many silly things," he wrote in 1929, "but the most strangely silly thing that ever I heard of was that they tried to turn this Anti-Anarchist romance into an Anarchist play... Probably they thought that being able to see that a policeman is funny means thinking that a policeman is futile.... they are barbarians and have not learnt how to laugh."[13] SK had redone the novel as Russia wished to see the West.

"Applied criticism" as creative performance might not appeal to all primary authors, then — nor to all censoring boards. But it was in keeping with SK's

---

[12] "Po strofam 'Onegina'" [1936], in *SK:Ss* 4, 416–17. The essay was first published in 2006.

[13] "The Man Who was Thursday," in *G. K. C. as M. C. Being a Collection of Thirty-seven Introductions* (Freeport NY: Books for Libraries Press, 1929), 202–03. For a brief and rather too ideological account of the scandal in English by a Chesterton scholar, see Lucas H. Harriman, "The Russian Betrayal of G. K. Chesterton's *The Man Who was Thursday*, *Comparative Literature* 62, no. 1 (Winter 2010): 41–54; for a more balanced and better contextualized story, see Mariia Malikova, "'Sketch po koshmaru Chestertona' i kul'turnaia situatsiia NEPa" ["'A sketch based on Chesterton's Nightmare' and the cultural situation during NEP"], *Novoe literaturnoe obozrenie*, no. 78 (2006).

theater aesthetic, which highly valued drama composed in what he called the "as-if" [как бы] mode.[14] "As-if" theater, as opposed to both Stanislavskian realism and the interactive Soviet-era mass spectacle, takes pride in its artifice and its footlights. It seeks a walled-off, heightened dream-space that can project imaginary futures, pursue verbal associations, multiply meanings on ever more minuscule terrain (a single word, a phoneme), and play out anxieties or pleasures trapped inside a text. SK's approach to another writer's "material" was thoroughly Formalist, akin to his passion for puns: he strove to activate all available co-existent potentials inside the most compact utterance. As critic and creative writer, his priorities were everywhere the same: verbal wit, rhythm, pacing, the dynamic between word and thing, the primacy of thought (*mysl'*, "life's hero") over emotion, the tight connection between the comic and cerebral. He attended like a technician to syllable counts and word breaks. And he lavished attention on the sonic envelope of individual words: homonyms, homophones, the "sound clamp" [*zvukovaia skrepa*].[15]

In Shakespeare, for example, SK distinguishes tragedy from comedy not by sad or happy moods, and not by murders at the end rather than marriages, but by the physical effects of repeated words, which hit us like weighted objects. "The task of tragedy is to work by blows directed at one and the same emotion," he writes (Kill, kill, kill, kill, kill him. [*Coriolanus*]. Never. Never. Never. Never. Never. [*King Lear*]). In contrast, comedy, with its slick exchange of insults and epithets, "sets another aim: to achieve maximally different meanings and multiple senses from similar-sounding words. Its weapon is the homonym."[16] Comedic heroes deliver blows in all directions and forever duck them, whereas tragic blows must always be final. Around such observations, SK frequently contrasts his two favorite playwrights in English, Shakespeare and Bernard Shaw. He begins a 1934 essay on Shaw by noting that Shakespearean wit relies heavily on wordplay, on the slippery one-syllable retort that flies back and forth in a verbal fencing

---

[14] In 1922–23, SK coined the triad "бытие / быт / бы" ["Being, Everyday Life, As-If"] to represent three types of theater: mystery plays and liturgy (static and undramatic); the naturalistic / illusionist stage (dynamic, but in captivity to the visual palpable world); and finally theater as projective states of consciousness. "As-if" theater believes in walls and in footlights; it "strives to reinforce all these boundaries, doubling and tripling the line that separates its world from the world, the actor from the spectator." See "Filosofema o teatre" (1923), *SK:Ss* 4, 43–88, esp. 55–56.

[15] See Rosenflanz, op. cit., ch. 2 ("*Slova*: Words"), especially "Kržižanovskij's Theoretical Stance on Wordplay" and "Wordplay in Kržižanovskij's Prose," 32–55.

[16] See the categories "Slova, veshchi, slova-veshchi, veshchi-slova i veshchie slova," in "Komediografiia Shekspira" [1930s], in *SK:Ss* 4, 213.

match, whereas Shaw "rejects this part of Shakespeare's legacy [since Shaw was] too swallowed up in the play of meanings to devote much attention to somersaulting words."[17] This belief that Shakespeare was about words in rapid, lethal, punning movement, words armed head to toe like young men on a Renaissance square, whereas Shavian comedy concerned itself with the more ponderous but bloodless exchange of ideas, is a constant in Krzhizhanovsky's criticism. In his own comedies, Krzhizhanovsky pits the rapier-like brashness of the idea-duel, central to his English predecessors and to comic scenes in Pushkin, against a dark parody of both politics and the potential helplessness of words.

Krzhizhanovsky continued to write. But as he watched his writer-acquaintances begin to be arrested he withdrew from literary society, feeling himself (in Bovshek's words) a "played-out player, a loser, ashamed of his role but at the same time not ceasing to believe in his creative gifts and the usefulness of his work" (60). In this state he began a collection of stories titled *What Men Die By* (or "become dead by," *Chem lyudi myortvy*), in bitter counterpoint to Tolstoy's 1879 parable on the power of love ("What Men Live By" [*Chem lyudi zhivy*]). And he succumbed to drink. When asked by friends what had driven him to it, Bovshek recalls him saying: "A sober relationship to reality" (61). She closes her memoir in May 1949. SK was "sitting in an armchair at the table, looking through a journal; I had settled on the couch and was reading," she recalls. "Suddenly my heart gave me a jolt, I raised my eyes, and he was sitting there with a pale, frozen, frightened face. 'What's the matter?' 'I don't understand [he said]....I can't read anything...a black raven...black raven...'" (65). A stroke affecting the visual portions of the left side of his brain had deprived him of the ability to recognize letters.[18] Bovshek devised a way to get her stunned husband to a clinic for tests. "He could write," she later noted, "but he could not read what he had written, and in general he could not read at all" (65). Page proofs of a translation of Mickiewicz lay on the table at home and he could not recognize it as a language. Bovshek ends on a poignant moment. To ascertain the extent of

---

17   "Dramaturgicheskie priemy Bernarda Shou" [1934], in *SK:Ss* 4: 473–513, esp. 503.

18   In 2010, Oliver Sacks described the effect of such stroke-induced alexia (a "special form of visual agnosia") on a creative writer, along with a history of the affliction, in "A Man of Letters. A Neurologist's Notebook," *The New Yorker* (June 28, 2010): 22–26. Apparently the subject could still write, and fluently, only he could not read what he had written. "We think of reading as a seamless and indivisible act," Sacks notes, "and as we read we attend to the meaning — and, perhaps, the beauty — of written language, unconscious of the many processes that make this possible" (23).

the brain damage, and having learned that her patient was a creative writer, the psychiatrist asked SK: do you love Pushkin? "—'I...I...[the sick man faltered]...Pushkin.' He burst helplessly into tears, sobbing like a child, holding nothing back and not ashamed of his tears. I had never seen him weep" (66). Krzhizhanovsky died in 1950.

Seven years after her husband's death, in 1957, Bovshek appealed to the Writers' Union for his official "immortalization." Such an appeal could be formally put forward on behalf of any deceased member of the Union, and would guarantee a peer inventory of the written remains. A literary commission, chaired by Aleksandr Anikst, was appointed to review all published and unpublished work. Its report a year later argued forcefully that the candidate's meager profile in print "gave absolutely no idea of the originality of his talent nor the meaning of his creative work for Soviet literature"—and thus a 1300-page, two-volume edition of his work was "absolutely indispensable."[19] The Union voted in favor. But in 1959 the project ran afoul of institutional inertia and a negative reader's report, which condemned (among much else) SK's analysis of Shakespeare's use of dreams: "How alien all this is to the highly realistic art of Shakespeare, whom this critic [SK] transforms into a decadent Symbolist!"[20] In 1968, three years before her death, Bovshek transferred the manuscripts from her closet to the Central State Archive for Literature and Art (then TsGALI, now RGALI), where they constitute fond # 2280, op. 1, containing 121 items.

In the late 1960s, almost single-handedly, the poet and critic Vadim Perelmuter began to examine these files. Twenty years later he ushered into print the first collection of SK's prose (1989), posted most of the stories on a Russian website, encouraged research into SK, and since 2001 he has been editing and annotating a five volume *Collected Works*. Volume 5 of this Russian-language edition (containing three of the ten extant dramas) was published late in 2010. SK has been translated into French and Polish; three collections of his prose exist in English. Among the early work of SK

---

[19]   See the request of Evgenii Lann, Chair of the Commission for the Literary Legacy of S. D. Krzhizhanovsky (May 31, 1958) to Sovetskii pisatel' Publishers, in "Materialy Komissii po literaturnomu naslediiu S. D. Krzhizhanovskogo (1957–59)," RGALI f. 2280, op. 1, ed. khr. 117, "V izdatel'stvo Sovetskii pisatel'," 2, 1.

[20]   See V. Zalesskii's "Otzyv o literaturovedcheskikh rabotakh S. D. Krzhizhanovskogo" (14 November 1958), in RGALI f. 2280-1-117, p. 8 of a 14-page document. Anna Bovshek wrote a polite (but ineffective) rebuttal to the charges, claiming that Sigizmund Dominikovich had never pretended to be an academic scholar of English literature but only a student of Shakespeare; "he loved him, he was studying him."

that survives in the archive is a tattered notebook of poems from 1911–18, collected under the title "Frater Vertius."[21] One poem in particular, "Kant's Skull" [«Череп Канта»], would seem to prefigure this writer's enduring images, texts, interests, and the strange alexic tragedy of his final year. In six quatrains of trochaic tetrameter, "Kant's Skull" invokes the meditations of Hamlet over Yorick's Skull in the grave-digging scene — or maybe of Vladimir Lensky over the tomb of Dmitry Larin in *Eugene Onegin* (II: xxxvii), the scene that opens SK's "scenic projection" of Pushkin's novel.[22] SK loved poetry, but considered himself a very weak poet. He confided to Anna Bovshek that his attempts at verse worked better as farcical doggerel in the spirit of Kozma Prutkov, a text to embed in his own prose or drama to comic effect, than as anything taken seriously on its own merits. But the images in this tribute to his favorite philosopher and favorite playwright are serious. They remain with him: fissures, seams, the wall of the brain, the helpless empty eyes after the thought has fled the carapice.

Here are the first two, and then the final, stanzas of Krzhizhanovsky's poem to "Kant's Skull":

| | |
|---|---|
| Из футляра костяного | Out of the bony case |
| Смертью вынут сложный мир, | A complex world was extracted by death. |
| И Ничто глядится сново | Again, Nothing gazes out |
| Сквозь просвет глазничных дыр. | Through the shining gap of the eye-holes. |
| | |
| Череп пуст: из лобных складок | The skull is empty: from out the forehead furrows, |
| Мысль ушла. Осталась быль. | A thought has departed. The true story remains. |
| Череп длинен, желт и гладок; | The skull is long, yellow, and smooth; |
| В щелях швов осела пыль. | Dust has settled in the crevices of the seams. |
| | |
| [...] | |
| | |
| Все что было — стало Былью. | Everything that was — has become true. |
| Книги полны странных слов, | Books are full of strange words. |
| Череп пуст, — и серой пылью | The skull is empty — and as grey as dust |
| Время входит в щели швов. | Time enters the crevices of the seams. |

---

21  RGALI f. 2280, op. 1, ed. khr. 23. This poem is one of several dozen published, with an introduction, by Vera Kalmykova in Sigizmund Krzhizhanovsky, *Stikhi*, in the on-line journal *Toronto Slavic Quarterly* 20 (Spring 2007).

22  I thank my colleague Michael Wachtel for informing me that a modest tradition of Skull epistles can be traced to Pushkin's era: Baratynsky's 1824 poem "Cherep" [The Skull], which is referred to in Pushkin's comic, mixed prose-and-verse "Epistle to Del'vig" [Poslanie Del'vigu] from 1827.

*This essay originally appeared in Simon Morrison, ed., Sergey Prokofiev and His World (Princeton: Princeton University Press, 2008), 60–114, as the introduction to my English free-verse translation of Krzhizhanovsky's* Eugene Onegin *(115–89). The Russian playtext translated for that volume (RGALI f. 1929, op. 1, ed. khr. 86) contained Prokofiev's marginal comments in preparation for the music, graphically reproduced in the English version. The larger essay discusses the genesis of the project with Tairov, censorship pressures, costumes (the designer did not like the playscript), and music (44 numbers composed by Prokofiev in July 1936 and tagged to scenes). SK, asked to rewrite his scenario three times, balked at making changes. By the time the project was canceled in December 1936 (in the wake of an unrelated crisis at the Chamber Theater), the score had been prepared but neither rehearsals nor staging begun. Prokofiev recycled a good part of his music into other projects, and the playscript disappeared.*

*Only the second half of this introductory essay is excerpted here, which treats themes and emphases of this 1936 Onegin transposition ("a scenic projection in 14 fragments with Prologue") as part of the history of Pushkin's novel. I have restored some details that were cut to accommodate a Prokofiev readership but might be of interest to a Russian literature specialist, while certain truisms about Pushkin and his novel are omitted. Emphasized in the excerpt below are the importance of stage directions when adapting — or "scenically projecting" — a work so heavily dependent on a Narrator; the nature of dream theater in Krzhizhanovsky's aesthetics; the three core episodes of the playscript (Nameday, Dream, Duel); the centrality of winter; and finally, how to end a love story. In what for me was a startling realization, I seem to suggest the reverse of my contentious hypothesis in "Tatiana" from 1995: that here Tatiana conjures up Onegin, and not (as in Pushkin's novel) the other way around. Perhaps in either direction the creative dynamics are the same.*

## THE KRZHIZHANOVSKY-PROKOFIEV COLLABORATION ON *EUGENE ONEGIN*, 1936 (A LESSER-KNOWN CASUALTY OF THE PUSHKIN DEATH JUBILEE) (2008)

*Krzhizhanovsky's "applied poetics": title, epigraph, stage direction*

[...] A close student of technical literary parts (titles, aphorisms, epigraphs), Krzhizhanovsky was also fascinated by the role of the stage direction [Rus. *remarka*, from the Fr. *remarque*] in the history of European theater. In his 1937 essay "The Theatrical Stage Direction (A Fragment)" he surveys its formal variety and function.[23] Shakespeare's directives, he notes, were laconic, almost mute. Such shorthand was sufficient for a playwright-director, a man of the theater who staged his own works with his own troupe. When the director's intentions are the playwright's own, transmitted directly to the company, they need not be fixed in print. As soon as the director separates from the playwright, however, more elaborate guidelines are required, and at that point the *remarka* can assume literary and narrative dimensions. These can be quite playful. In the eighteenth-century prose comedy of Denis Fonvizin, for example, a stage direction often put living people in dialogue with *things*; an object would strive to escape its imprisonment in parentheses and turn into an "almost fully-legitimate personage, perhaps still with someone else's voice but with its own thoughts" (97). And to this Krzhizhanovsky adds, as if preparing the ground for his later phantasmagorical poetics: a great deal of consciousness is trapped in what looks like a mere thing, whether "a book, or in the visual form of a telephone receiver." Pushkin, in his stage directions for *Boris Godunov* and later for the *Little Tragedies*, returned to the Shakespearean prototype (although not himself a practical man of the theater, Pushkin had absorbed the conventions of Shakespeare in print for his own dramatic work.) His focus too fell on external action: dry-eyed, laconic, a matter of verbs directing human bodies (97–98). In contrast, Chekhov, who came to playwriting after a decade of absolute mastery in the short story, introduced the "literary stage direction in its most harmonized forms" (102). Krzhizhanovsky shows in parallel columns how the opening paragraph of a Chekhov story is reproduced almost word-for-word in a typical Chekhovian *remarka* ("Ward No. 6" and *Ivanov*; "In One's Own Corner" and *The Seagull*) — with the same coordination of "props," the same precise delineation of mood, lighting, and times of day (102–03).

Unfortunately, Krzhizhanovsky does not discuss his own experience, a year before this essay appeared, of turning Pushkin's *Eugene Onegin* into a play. Stage directions were crucial to it. They function as a surrogate for the Narrator, and serve to set characters in motion, link clusters of stanzas, inform us of weather, mood, and furniture. Pushkin's own terse

---

23  "Teatral'naya remarka (Fragment)" [1937], in Sigizmund Krzhizhanovskii, *Sobranie sochinenii v piati tomakh*, ed. Vadim Perel'muter (Sankt Peterburg: Symposium, 2006), 4:89–109. Henceforth these *Collected Works* (vv. 1–4, 2001–2006; v. 5, 2010) referred to as *SK:Ss* followed by volume number and page. Subsequent references are included in the text.

"Shakespearean" *remarka* could not have been a model. Far more likely a model was the theater of Chekhov. As playwright, Krzhizhanovsky combines the impressionistic Chekhovian stage direction with an even more heightened sensitivity to the soundscape—pulsed, rhythmic, alert to the distant rattle or snapped string—appropriate to Tairov's musicalized chamber theater. In this as in so much else, Tatiana is the touchstone and ideal audience. More so than anyone else on stage, she "intently listens in" [*vslushivayetsia*] to the sounds surrounding her, diegetic as well as meta-diegetic: a drum, a knock, a creaking chair, a cricket, wind, a musical tone. Together with Prokofiev's score, the stage directions in *Eugene Onegin* function as dramatic binder. Pushkin's Narrator binds up the novel with his words; the play built off the novel, while respecting the contours of the Onegin stanza in the characters' utterances, coheres through light and rhythm.

The source, placement, and waxing or waning of light—what is illuminated or shadowed—dominate Krzhizhanovsky's *remarka*. Details of lanterns, candles, lit or dim interiors, and especially the moon permit a play of profiles versus full bodies, the shades or silhouettes of serious people versus the harshly lit, bulky, fully fleshed-out lout or buffoon. In early versions of the play, Krzhizhanovsky includes technical directions for a "projector" to cast light in rising and falling patterns across different parts of the stage.

Second in significance to lighting is pulse. Reading the stage directions as a single uninterrupted unit, skipping over the intervening dialogues, is akin to setting oneself up inside a metronome, surrounded by equipment for beating out the Onegin stanza. Acts of tapping, pacing, swaying, flapping, rocking, and chiming are fundamental to all of Krzhizhanovsky's scenes. This rhythmic priority affects the playwright's choice of props, which are scant but meticulously specified. Since Alexander Osmyorkin's surviving sketches are of costume design only, we cannot know how Krzhizhanovsky's own vision of the *mise en scène* would have been realized—or ignored.[24]

---

[24]  Alexander Osmyorkin (1892–1953), a distinguished, rather conservative illustrator of Pushkin, disliked the play from the start. According to the memoirs of his wife at the time: "Today, even after the passage of so many years, it's difficult to explain why this wonderful director [Tairov] ever resolved on such a venture. The poet's greatest creation, *Eugene Onegin*—a novel in verse—was redone into a play by the writer S. D. Krzhizhanovsky. It's simply incomprehensible how that gifted, intelligent man, a brilliant translator of Mickiewicz, agreed to do a scenic adaptation of *Onegin*." Osmyorkin was struck by this "adventurism," as he called it, but he had to admit that SK, within the dictates of his own taste, had turned Pushkin into a play. For a long time Osmyorkin pondered over whether or not to become a participant in this unlikely enterprise. But the temptation of working on *Onegin* eventually won out. "As an artist [he said], I will do everything

Physical items featured in the stage directions swing on hinges or tracks (doors, windows, drapes), oscillate back and forth from a fixed point (rocking chairs, clocks with a pendulum, treetops in a night breeze), repeat in an arc or a loop (moon and sun, dawn to dusk). Thresholds between rooms are marked, because human beings can tilt to and fro across them. As with the Narcissus-Echo myth that Onegin takes as his theme song, movement in the playscript is constant but cyclical and reversible and thus, in defiance of most romances, non-teleological. Relationships never arrive at a resting point and so can last forever. This is not, perhaps, a happy love story, but it cannot be called a tragic one. Like a swinging door, a pendulum, or the moon in the sky, the story is anchored and levered — a suspension.

So well sculpted and paced are these stage directions, they almost constitute a serialized narrative with a plot and pulse of its own. Onegin's initial rhythm is established in Fragments 2 and 4. He is bored. He seats himself in a rocking chair that seems to start swinging of its own accord; forcibly, irritably, he halts it. Such nervous frustration is a male tension in the play, characteristic of the unkindness with which men are treated in the Romantic Byronic tradition. When women are rhythmicized in this mechanical way (as is Tatiana at the end of Fragment 4, on the balcony before writing her letter, rocking in time with the breeze that sways the trees), it represents not boredom but longing. By and large, women's boredom tries to go somewhere or get out of somewhere; it is responsive and dynamic. Male boredom is existential, blocked, and thus circular, trivial, and cruel. He repeats; she spirals. Thus is the Tatiana cult delicately etched into dramatic structure.

---

just as Pushkin drew it. Let the actors wander about the stage and say whatever they are required to say — that's not my business. I already see mock-ups for all the scenes and I cannot refuse." (E. K. Gal'perina, "Predannost' Pushkinu," in *Osmyorkin: Razmyshleniia ob isskustve. Pis'ma. Kritika. Vospominaniia sovremennikov* [Moscow: Sovetskii khudozhnik, 1981], 232–39, esp. 37–38.) Judging by ten costume sketches published in 1979 (L. Olinskaya, "*Yevgenii Onegin* v iskizakh A. A. Osmyorkina," *Iskusstvo* 10 (1979): 30–37), Osmyorkin's blend of the lyrical and the satiric placed him well within the traditional, realist Stanislavsky school of design. The heroine Tatiana is ravishing, languid, resembling Pushkin's wife Natalie and the poet's own drawings of beloved women. The Nameday guests are stereotypical Gogolian caricatures: brutish face, no neck, trim potbelly tucked into white trousers, spindly legs, tiny sloping feet. There is some wonderful humor: for example, a watercolor / graphite-pencil sketch of Onegin at the duel shows the hero dressed in the hybrid style of the provinces, a visual emblem of Prokofiev's out-of-tune rural harpsichords, with a Childe-Harold cloak billowing around his shoulders and on his feet *valenki*, Russian peasant felt boots. It appears that Osmyorkin was already familiar with Prokofiev's music by the time he began work, for he produced a sketch of the Nameday Mummers, whose visit and grotesque song occur only in the playscript.

We cannot know how adaptor and composer might have collaborated in rehearsal. The interplay of rhythm, music, words, and props is closely monitored in the playscript, however. Near the end of Fragment 7, before the Mummers arrive at the Nameday, Krzhizhanovsky specified a tuning of instruments and "a dissonant conglomeration of sounds," to which Prokofiev responded in the margins: "Without music and without tuning-up." When, in Fragment 10, Tatiana visits Onegin's abandoned house and inspects his library, we are informed that the "familiar rocking chair" is now motionless and the wall clock's "ticking mechanism has fallen silent," its "pendulum hangs downward." Visual details all have weight — and if they do not move and create rhythmic inertia with this weight, they are felt as dead, even killed, things.

Thus does Krzhizhanovsky trap consciousness in a thing: a book, a clock, a piece of furniture. In Fragment 12, the first of the St. Petersburg scenes, we are given a stage direction where sounds and rhythms move freely on a continuum between objects and human beings. The ebb and flow of this exchange prefigures the hero's fate. Onegin has just kissed the hand of Princess Tatiana, which she calmly extends to him, but the rising strains of the music drown out their conversation. A dancer glides up to draw Tatiana out onto the floor. Onegin remains alone beside her empty chair. He gives its arm a push (recalling, we are told, the movement of his own rocking chair), but "the gilded *fauteuil* stands motionless on its bent little legs." Gradually the music quiets down and fades away. Tatiana does not return to her former place. The stage direction continues: "A dozen hands punctiliously move forward a chair for her in another corner of the hall." Like the military drumbeats that double for heartbeats on the Neva embankment — our earlier example of objective meta-diegetic sound — furniture can be a metaphor for life functions.

There is another and rarer type of stage direction in *Eugene Onegin* that denotes the "outdoors." Examples are the brief, wintry episode of the duel (Fragment 9) and the Neva Embankment in the early morning mist (Fragment 13). Absent here are those cinemagraphically minuscule visual details of the indoor *remarka*: dust on the spines of books, gilt on the legs of chairs. Instead, there are echoes, expanses, dreams, and fogs that project an inner psychology outward. Reality is not determined by external objects but by the responsiveness, vulnerability, porosity, and neediness of the hero. Krzhizhanovsky began experimenting with the idea of the material world as psychological projection in his "Kantian" story-parables from the early 1920s. In the "minus-Moscow" of his 1928 story "Stitches" [«Швы»], the starving, out-of-work, homeless and hallucinating narrator notes that shadows are thrown not by things but that a physical thing is "thrown" into the outside world by its shadow. Fragment 13 of *Eugene Onegin* displays a similar dynamic. We are both in, and not in, a real city. Sounds have an only approximate motivation and source. The hero at dawn hears the night watchmen calling to one another but also "the distant rattle of carriages...the flapping of wings of some gigantic bird, perhaps the splash of oars; a horn and a distant, barely perceptible song."

The starting point for such stage directions is of course Chekhov's theater, but with an important difference. Chekhov's impressionism is atmospheric, imagistic, and predominantly extra-verbal. Krzhizhanovsky tracks the deepening consciousness of his hero along the specific trajectory of Pushkin's poetic word. The rebirth of Onegin's conscience is mediated by verse: concrete bits of Pushkin's poetry spoken in the present serve to trigger his memory of other bits composed in the past.[25] When, in Fragment 13 on the Neva waterfront, carousing Lycée students return from their all-night revels tipsily singing their ode to the pleasures of wine (Prokofiev's setting of a lyric by the fifteen-year-old Pushkin, «Пирующие студенты», 1814), Onegin immediately collates the words of their boisterous song with similar words, phrases, and phonemes occurring in the novel, thereby calling up his own melancholic memories of the shameful duel in which he killed his best friend. Throughout this elaborate and largely subconscious verbal linkage, stretching over years of biographical time, one spatial image remains: Tatiana immobile at the window, gazing out. And at what? Three shadowy men drift by the parapet. In the final stage direction of this penultimate Fragment, we learn that Onegin himself does not know whether these figures are real or merely "an illusion born of the pre-morning St. Petersburg fog." That fog, too, was "thrown outward" from his agitated self.

[...]

---

[25] The dynamics of this Fragment testify to SK's sophistication as a Pushkinist. In *Eugene Onegin*, every detail of the world passes first through a literary genre, and only subsequently through concrete images and moral consciousness. The Narrator—whose role SK exquisitely appreciated, for all that he wanted him out of his play—monitors this shift of genre, moving within a single chapter (or even within a single sequence of stanzas; see chapter 1, xvii–xxi) from the celebratory diction of an eighteenth-century ode through an elegiac tone to the Romantic glitter of a fairytale to the Byronic burn-out characteristic of Onegin's view of the world, never missing a beat nor distorting a jot of the Onegin stanza. For Pushkin, the choice of a genre brings with it an entire world (first of styles, then of images and values).

## The dream and the philosopheme

In 1923–24, Krzhizhanovsky composed a series of brief tributes to the Moscow Chamber Theater. He praised its repertory as "almost always *a play about a play*, which meant that it became a theater of the highest theatricality, or more precisely — theater raised to the 'theater' degree (T$^T$)."[26] This exponential degree of theatricality was present in Tairov's 1915 production of Calderón's *Life is a Dream*, a drama that "divides Being into Waking and Dream, which simply exchange masks with one another." The exchange of masks as an interrogation of reality (and as an index of our ability, as actors, to create) lies at the heart of Krzhizhanovsky's "philosopheme of the theater," worked out in 1923 and incorporated as part of his lectures on the psychology of the stage.[27]

Krzhizhanovsky begins his discussion of this psychology with the mechanics of the eye. It is not true, he argues, that the further away an object, the blurrier it is. Only with distance and nesting (a play within a play, a dream within a dream) does any object become distinct and knowable. First-level reality — that which happens directly on the skin or presents itself directly to the eye — is indispensable, but in terms of our creativity, almost useless; only second- and third-level realities begin to teach us how to be the world. He titles the second chapter of his treatise "*Bytiie, byt, by*" [Бытие, быт, бы], a sequence literally but inadequately rendered in English as "Being, Everyday Life, As-If." In Russian, this triad of words relies for its effectiveness on the fact that it is progressively corroded from the end: letters fall away as the series approaches the ideal in art. *Bytiie*, "Being," is timeless, invisible to the eye, and thus by nature non-theatrical. Because it is unified, Being has no need for the theater, which thrives on scattered phenomena. Because it is unchanging, its reality is full and immediately present. There are no shifts to be staged and therefore nothing for actors to do. Krzhizhanovsky notes that "theater is not necessary to Being" (53). Certain theatrical genres do serve Being, such as mystery plays and the liturgy, but these are strictly contained, ornamental, non-developmental.

What then of *byt*, Being that is brought down to earth, our everyday life? As his basic unit of daily experience, Krzhizhanovsky posits the "phenomenon that plays at being a thing" (54). Whether or not our everyday world is in fact full of solid things we cannot know; Krzhizhanovsky worked constant

---

26   "Stat'i, zametki, retsentsii, opublikovannye v ezhenedel'nike *7 dney Moskovskogo Kamernogo teatra*," in *SK:Ss* 4:643, 645. This seamless "exchange of masks" is caught perfectly by Prokofiev in his marginal note preceding Fragment 8, the Dream: "Without an Interlude."

27   "Filosofema o teatre," in *SK:Ss* 4:43–88 (further references included in text).

variations on this Kantian question, and claimed it would have driven him mad, had he not ultimately chosen Shakespeare over Kant.[28] But this daily world always insists that we take it seriously. It threatens us with deprivation, obstacles, irritation, traceable causes and non-negotiable effects.[29] *Byt* is a link across and down to the material world, creating in us a veritable fetishism of groping, touching, seeing. "A person from everyday life does not believe in Being," Krzhizhanovsky writes, nor in true fantasy either; "he believes fervently in the reality of his three little rooms, in the body of his wife, in the official stamp that can be seen" (54). Everyday life jealously protects its hold on our sensuous perceptions and pretends that these perceptions are real. *Byt* is "the imaginary" [*mnimost'*] that does not want to be imaginary. For that reason it "fears the theater, which exposes [this pretension] by its very kinship with it" (54). At this point Krzhizhanovsky moves to justify theater as a moral, truth-bearing force. "Everyday life, wishing to protect itself from the danger of remembering its own imaginariness and in order to isolate and localize its own unreality, constructs among its houses a special house with the placard 'Theater' hanging on it. In doing so it naively thinks that through its windowless walls, more 'theater' will not leak out" (54–55). In his writings on Shakespeare from the 1930s, Krzhizhanovsky is more specific about this hostility: "Of course, everyday life does not react especially seriously to the intrusion of this strange, eyeless house, with a flag raised over its darkness, into its crowd of homes...By means of narrow wedges and short thrusts, theaters advanced against the decrepit timber of everyday life."[30]

---

[28]  At the end of his "Fragments on Shakespeare" (1939), SK recalls how the "German metaphysician [Kant] had overturned the objective world and taken the eraser out of his hand, a fifth-grader, and rubbed out the line between 'I' and 'non-I', between object and subject...But at that time — completely by chance — there arrived, tied up in a package and glued all over with stamps, the first volume of translated Shakespeare. My father subscribed to the series, which I didn't know. The translation, I now see, was crude and inaccurate, but I began to read the book — and suddenly I felt I had a friend who would defend me from the metaphysical delusion." In "Fragmenty o Shekspire," final segment "Shekspir i pyatiklassnik," *SK:ss* 4, 383–84.

[29]  SK partakes fully of the Russian bifurcation of "life" into two words: *zhizn'*, the generic word, and then *byt*, "everyday life as experienced," usually nuanced very negatively. *Zhizn'* implies life as it should be lived, full of spiritual ideals and hopeful striving, whereas *byt* is the "daily grind," everyday existence, full of obstacles, tedium, deceit and disillusionment. The low expectations and bad reputation that surround simply "living" — or "making a living" — in the Russian context have received much attention from literary specialists and cultural anthropologists, who conclude that it contributes to the salvational importance in that culture of art and utopian / dystopian fantasy.

[30]  "Komediografiia Shekspira" [1930s], in *SK:ss* 4, 161.

The theater of «быт» — a Russian particle suggesting a modal and conditional "as-if" state of consciousness — is the most sophisticated state of the art. If everyday life is playing with Being, then "As-if" theater plays with *byt*, reconfiguring life as it is into life as it could be, or perhaps life as we create it. It does not compete with things, but transforms and animates them. The walls of the theater remain solid. «Быт» theater does not seek to dissolve the proscenium or remove the footlights but "strives to reinforce them, doubling and tripling the line that separates world from world, actor from spectator, the struggle for existence from the struggle for non-existence" ("Filosofema" 55–56). There are obvious links between "As-if" and Symbolism as well as suggestive parallels with magical folk theater. It would have been most useful to know Prokofiev's view on this tripartite "philosopheme of the theater" from the perspective of his personal faith system, Christian Science. Much of the meta-diegetic, "as-if" texture of this *Eugene Onegin* would have come from Prokofiev's music, which permits the unimpeded flow of inside to outside to inside again with only a quiver from the solid props on stage.

With this conceptual vocabulary, we can now return to the specifics of the *Onegin* project, especially its complex use of nature mythology and dreams. One cautionary note is in order. Russian academic and artistic circles of the 1920s were well acquainted with Sigmund Freud on dream interpretation. Many Bolshevik intellectuals, most prominently Leon Trotsky, took an active interest in the psychoanalytic movement. Although this "Western" school had been banned along with many others by the early 1930s, the concepts of condensation, dramatization, displacement, inhibition, and regression had circulated for decades. But Russian twentieth-century psychology — even its unofficial, underground wings — never canonized Freud's evocative but often arbitrary constructs in this realm, and certainly not his pan-sexualization of the human psyche. Native Russian schools of developmental psychology offered spiritualized (although still tripartite) models of the self whose explanatory power proved far more fertile and better suited to their own empirical and literary experience. Pushkin himself, for all his fascination with the workings of Eros, would never have reduced it to somatic drives. Tatiana is indeed a young girl in love, but for the Poet as well as for her own essential self, she is more importantly a Muse — a symbol and goad to creativity, both her own and another's. Art is not a surrogate or sublimation of some other thing. On the contrary, those other things serve art, which (in Pushkin's view) is the life-force that endures. We may assume that Krzhizhanovsky knew and appreciated Freud, but he was a thinker beholden to no single school, and in this project it was Pushkin's priorities that he wished most to respect. He appears to have blended Russian and non-Russian views of the subconscious and fantasy in his own trademark manner.

To grasp how Krzhizhanovsky integrates "As-if" space into his theater, it might help to recall the variety of subjective inner states that can be projected on stage. Collectively they make up what we call "imagination." Simplest is mental imagery: static, realistic, a matter of concrete physical recall of an event or person in the experienced past. In the spatiotemporal realm, its metaphor is a photograph; in music, a leitmotif or recurring theme. One example would be Tatiana remembering what Onegin looks like, or vice versa — although we know from Pushkin that there is not much evidence of this in their story: they hardly glance at each other, we have no record of their first meeting (in conversation with Lensky, Onegin cannot remember which of the Larin sisters she is), and his image, for her, is largely a composite product of all the novelistic heroes she has read about and pined for. More complex than the mental image is waking fantasy. Here, images are no longer static but dynamic and sequential. They lead somewhere — usually to a forbidden place. They grow out of a glimpse, a concrete real-life stimulus. But because this stimulus is both real and open-ended, the follow-up scene that we spin out in our imagination could actually happen "as we see it." Such fantasies might be likened to watching a film and identifying with the romantic leads. In the central portion of her letter, Tatiana positions herself before Onegin in just this way, visualizing herself as a desired object. Our conscious minds and bodies can incorporate these fantasies — indeed, we can even write them out cogently to others, as Tatiana is inspired to do, although not without an immense admixture of shame.

Finally we have what Krzhizhanovsky called the "deep (or heavy or bad) dream" [*tyazholyi son*], site of our most profound desires. It too is dynamic and sequential, but it is *un*realistic and in principle non-realizable as real-life experience. Our conscious mind has no control over its shapes or behaviors. It is no longer ashamed. Its metaphor, if one can be found, is a fantasy, a fairytale projection. Fairytale logic and imagery abound in Krzhizhanovsky's playscript, most prominently in Tatiana's Dream, where, in precise replica of Pushkin's text, the heroine is pursued by a shaggy bear through a snowy forest to a hut in which monsters are tamed by the Beloved and rivals are magically, violently dispatched. When Pushkin's Narrator relates the Dream in the novel, however, he does so with the self-confidence of an outsider, as Tatiana's loving protector. He relishes its picturesque, risqué details because he enjoys digressing on her. He is also something of a voyeur. In Pushkin's novel, Tatiana — shy, unsociable, a daydreamer and reader of novels — hardly talks at all. In the play, she must be motivated to speak out this terrible, marvelous dream herself. Its events must be fused with *her* intonation. These first-person imperatives of dramatic motivation and intonation might be one reason why Krzhizhanovsky plucked the dream out of Pushkin's sequence and placed it *after* the horror of the Nameday, a liberty that outraged the Pushkin purists on the censorship boards. Had this version of *Eugene Onegin* reached the stage, and had the playwright been able to incorporate not only his verbal but also his spatial poetics into its production, Tatiana's Dream, with its astonishing music, would have been the peak of the arc, the high point of dramatic "As-if" theater. How might this dream-space have organized the episodes surrounding it? Where is space wide-open [*prostorno*] and where constricted [*tesno*]? Along what crack or fissure [*shchel'*] does the humiliated Tatiana escape from unbearable real life into the Dream, and then find her way back out again to life?

### The three central fragments: nameday, dream, duel

As presented in the play, Tatiana's Nameday party is largely the site of shame. It realizes that aspect of her letter to Onegin that we tend to underrate, so dazzled are we by its naïve honesty and outpouring of love. "Resolve my doubts," she writes to him, "either rouse my hopes / Or interrupt this heavy [bad] dream, / With a reproach, alas, so well deserved." Re-reading her letter, Tatiana "shudders from shame and fear," but she entrusts herself to Onegin and sends it all the same. Her heavy dream, as the playwright properly sees, is fully compatible with her most necessary reality (the way a light dream could not be). Without this desired thing she will not exist; she will be compelled to change completely. Krzhizhanovsky's playscript is as Tatiana-centered as Tchaikovsky's opera, but its psychology is far less sentimental. Not romantic love (with its passionate corollaries of sacrifice or satisfaction) but something more complex and durable lies at its base. This state of mind, to which Prokofiev (in a comment scribbled next to the stage direction introducing the Dream) ascribed a "tragic element" [*tragizm*], is powerful enough not only to save the heroine but also to resurrect the hero. We call this basic value "Winter," and will investigate it in connection with Tatiana's dual folkloric prototype. There, too, the porous dream-space of the central Fragments proves decisive.

Fragment 7, the Nameday, opens on a threshold. The front of the stage is dark, the sides are cluttered with furniture and trash. Only the rooms at the back are brilliantly lit and filled with polkas and waltzes. Onegin has cornered

Tatiana and is lecturing her about the need for self-control (Krzhizhanovsky had excised the Scene at the Bench and scattered Onegin's lecture across public dance-space); Tatiana clings to the doorjam trying to repress her sobs, so inappropriate in this venue. The next episode is an incarnated, Gogolian insert featuring two distasteful comic buffoons, Buyanov and Zaretsky, mentioned in Pushkin but now detached from his Narrator's fabric. The drunken, hiccupping Buyanov (his name means "Mr. Rowdy") heightens the heroine's terror.[31] For he is not just any provincial gentry, but a simulacrum of Tatiana's future in the countryside: he had proposed marriage, after all, and her mother had not opposed the match. Tatiana's choice at this point is not between Onegin's presence or absence (that is, between fulfilling her dream or fantasizing about him forever in some forested nook): her fate will be a Buyanov. This is the sinister underpinning to Prokofiev's goony, manic *tram-blyam* harpsichords. The true sound of the Russian provinces is the drunken blather of Buyanov and Zaretsky against the background of the out-of-tune polka and the "slow minuet." In her love letter to Onegin, Tatiana had remarked — again naively — that if she had not met Onegin she would, with time, have met "a soul mate" in the countryside and become "a faithful wife / And virtuous mother." This is most unlikely. In the playscript, what we see of the countryside is a landscape populated by pure Gogol, and for the shy and sociably awkward, the suitors are all grotesque. Only girls like Olga get the poets like Lensky.

Indeed, the radiant Olga emerges at every juncture during the evening as the lovely, confident hostess who has snared the only available poet in the

---

31  Buyanov, carouser and devotee of brothels, was imported by Pushkin into his novel from a famously lewd narrative poem written by his paternal uncle, the minor poet Vasily Lvovich Pushkin (1770–1830). Buyanov is hero of the racy, 154-line narrative poem *The Dangerous Neighbor* [*Opasnyi sosed*], which circulated in manuscript in 1811, was published in Russia only in 1901, but was widely known by heart. Pushkin notes the arrival of this Nameday guest in *EO* ch. 5, xxvi, 9: "My cousin, Buyanov" [Moi brat dvoyurodnyi, Buyanov], later (xliii–xliv) assigning to this "mischievous brother of mine, Buyanov" [Buyanov, bratets moy zadornyi] the task of leading the sisters Tatiana and Olga up to Onegin — where Onegin, fatefully, invites Olga to dance. In a gloss on this stanza, Vladimir Nabokov summarizes the uncle's poem: Buyanov "invites the narrator to a bawdyhouse to sample a young whore, Varyushka, who, however, turns out to be poxy, according to an older female with whom the narrator eventually retires…" (Aleksandr Pushkin, *Eugene Onegin: A Novel in Verse*, trans. Vladimir Nabokov, 2 vols. [Princeton: Princeton University Press, 1964], 2:524–26, esp. 525). Nabokov, too, is impressed that this rake is allowed to seek Tatiana's hand "and to be mentioned by the mother as a possible candidate." As Fragment 7 will suggest, what for Pushkin might have been an affectionate tribute to his uncle's mediocre poetry becomes for SK's fragile exposed Tatiana, stripped of Pushkin's protective Narrator, a far more sinister presence — and real-life option.

district, the one marriageable man who is not a buffoon. And then Onegin
starts to flirt with her, to dance with her, to embrace and touch her. How
can Olga have everything, Tatiana nothing? Twice in his marginalia for
Fragment 5 (the Letter), Prokofiev jots down: *sostoianie Tatyany* [Tatiana's
state of mind]. At the end of Fragment 7, he crosses out his initial self-
directive to compose music for "Tatiana's emotion." Instead he writes in:
"Very short." She is beyond mood music.

Olga's betrayal and flirtation, treated by Pushkin's debonair Narrator
with sympathetic condescension, propels Tatiana to her final humiliation.
In the novel we smile at Lensky and shrug off Olga because the Narrator,
too, is smiling. But in the present tense of a play, there is no distance, no
buffer between the reader and the stage. In drama we must ask: what is the
trapped heroine experiencing? Her shame and degraded desire reach a crisis
point in the final, startling event of the dramatized Nameday, an episode
not in Pushkin, which underwent at least one textual revision to increase
its grotesqueness before Prokofiev set its text to music. This is the festive
arrival and singing of the masked Yuletide Mummers.[32]

The eventual text that the Mummers sing in honor of the Nameday Girl
is both bawdy and inappropriate, a wedding ditty informing the bridegroom
how to mount his bride. It opens on a string of similes: "he's like a pole, his
head's a pestle, ears like little scissors, hands like little rakes, legs like little
forks, eyes like little holes."[33] The song bears no resemblance to Monsieur

---

[32]  The first Mummers' text that Prokofiev saw, an innocuous quatrain about rich peasants
raking up silver with a spade and promising wealth and fame to anyone who hears the
song, comes straight from Pushkin's *EO*, Ch. 5 viii: 9–12 (the song that accompanies
Tatiana's fortunetelling in the bathhouse: «Там мужики-то все богаты, / Гребут
лопатой серебро; / Кому поем, тому добро / И слава!»). But it is altogether too tame
for Tatiana's emotional state in the play. In his autograph score (RGALI f. 1929, op. 1,
ed. khr. 86, pp. 8 verso / 9 recto), Prokofiev notes after musical number 26: "Mummers:
Another text." It is unclear who initiated the change. That "other text" is a longer, more
vigorous ditty, «Сам шестом, голова пестом, Уши ножицами, руки грабельками, ноги
вилочками, глаза дырочками . . .», leading directly into the grotesquerie of the dream.

[33]  Pushkin himself had jotted this text down sometime between 1825 and 1834 in
a notebook of folksong verse. After the enumeration of body parts, the text continues:
"nightingale eyes are gazing from the tops of trees, they want porridge. The porridge was
boiled up yesterday and eaten up yesterday [repeat]; [...] the nose from bruises, that's the
matchmaker's son." Krzhizhanovsky / Prokofiev omitted the grim penultimate couplet:
"The neck is gleaming bluely / as if it had been in a noose." The text is preserved in
Pyotr Kireyevsky's archive of Pushkin folksongs. See A. D. Soimonov, "Pesni, sobrannye
pisatelyami. Novye materialy iz arkhiva P. V. Kireyevskogo," in *Literaturnoe nasledstvo*,
vol. 79 (Moscow: Institut literatury Akademii nauk SSSR, 1968), 205–06.

Triquet's ingratiating, Frenchified couplets to Tatiana in Tchaikovsky's opera. Arguably, this Mummers' text is far more devastating to the heroine, whose private fantasies have been precisely about marriage and whose shame derives from such illicit fantasies, not from the ballroom niceties and album verse where her sister feels so at home. The final stage direction of the Nameday Fragment mimics a wedding ceremony. Tatiana is brought a goblet; she bows. But before she sips, she peers across the threshold of the door into the dark room beyond. In Krzhizhanovsky's spatial vocabulary, that darkness is a fantasy-world, both punitive and wish-fulfilling, where her deepest fears and highest hopes might be successfully played out. The Nameday was unacceptable, and she must create an alternative to it. She drops the goblet — and its falling is the fissure through which Tatiana, terrified and aroused by the Mummers, can escape into the terrible, marvel-laden world of the Dream, her transition out of the Nameday humiliation into a triumph.

With this fainting and fall we are catapulted into Fragment 8. Its opening stage direction presents Tatiana at dawn, her face buried in a pillow, still in her white gown, one slipper fallen to the floor. She threw herself there in desperation the night before. The dream she has just experienced incorporated the monstrous Mummers (their masks are copied directly from Pushkin's description of Tatiana's Dream) but in this new order of events is a response to their provocation, not a prefiguring of it. Tatiana mutters "Mine. Mine. Mine. Mine" [*Moyo*, in neuter gender] — what the dream-monsters, and then Onegin, had called out to her in the hut. This phrase is not terrible, but marvelous: it is what she *wants* to hear.[34] Her Nurse tiptoes in, sees her charge asleep, then tries to leave. But Tatiana, half asleep, holds her back, for she is compelled to tell her dream. Relating it will allow her to replay elements of the shame-laden Letter Scene with her Nurse but now in something akin to folklore time, opening it up to another outcome. Was she not guilty of confessing to Onegin in her rash letter that in her

---

[34] In his essay "Onegin, Stanza by Stanza," SK compares Tatiana's Dream with Ruslan's from Pushkin's *Ruslan and Lyudmila* (1820), which lexically and structurally it closely resembles. In the folkloric realm, SK notes, dreams of this sort are heroic and enabling as well as terror-bearing ("terrifying" [*strashnoe*] and "marvelous" [*chudnoe*] are equally key for Pushkin, he notes). Although Tatiana's dream-monsters resemble the Nameday guests who are their precise model, in the Dream these monstrous images are not lewd and aggressive (like Buyanov and Zaretsky), but static, verbless, abjectly obedient to Onegin, "her savior." Plausibly and with a Freudian inflection, the Mummers' masks enable an unmasking of her own unconscious desires, a conclusion that SK does not draw but that his analysis would support ("Po strofam *Onegina*," in *SK:Ss* 4:438–40).

fantasy, she had seen him bending over her bedstead with delight and love? Had he not ridiculed that fantasy, reprimanded her, flirted with her sister? And how much better had matters turned out in the dream, where all the forest monsters — crabs mounted on spiders, horned dogs, bearded witches, a crane who was half cat — instantly obey him, fall silent before him, so he could lead her to that bench in the corner and be alone with her?

The letter that Pushkin composed for Tatiana is a tissue of Romantic-era clichés, which the Narrator presents to us indirectly and with loving irony. Deprived of the Narrator's zone, however, Krzhizhanovsky had to solve the practical dramatic problem of externalizing a dream-space event in such a way that the untalkative Tatiana has an emotionally satisfying reason to relate it. Superstitious like her author Pushkin, Tatiana never knew how to separate out her dreams. She was always on the border, looking out a window toward somewhere else. And why should this post-Nameday, "As-if" dream suffer in comparison with its wretched cousin, everyday life? At that point in her dream-narration when she glimpses Onegin at the table, Tatiana begins to speak (so a stage direction informs us) "in a completely different tone." Her experienced Nurse becomes uneasy about the unfolding story; she sees where it is leading and would like to deflect this clearly erotic narrative into something safer, a benign or distracting fairytale. But a stage direction informs us that "her reserve of images has dried up." This is odd: a nanny's reserves are always bottomless for this sort of thing. Disapprovingly, "she glances at Tania." The girl is not listening. Has she grown up? The fairytale is suddenly interrupted by the intrusion of Olga and Lensky. The dream does not end on the love fantasy, happily ever after. Lensky and Olga — the intolerably satisfied happy couple, the sister who had taken her Beloved away — enter the hut, Onegin draws his knife, strikes Lensky down, and (Tatiana confesses) "I woke up in terror, Nurse." She was surely terrified and awestruck. She was also — as the dream permits — gratified.

Onegin alone with Tatiana, leaning lovingly over her, had taken place in highly unstable space. The daytime fantasy of her Letter, transposed to a deep heavy dream, cracks open — and she is obliged to crawl back out into everyday life, where morality is imposed and punishment will be exacted. From Tatiana's snowy dream we leap directly to the blizzard of the dueling site. If Pushkin's narrator in chapter 6 expands on the details (and the injustice) of that botched duel of honor, Krzhizhanovsky is far too deeply sunk in his heroine's dual reality to shift domains entirely. Fragment 9, the Duel, is very brief, wedged in between Dream and Library, two Fragments in which we find Tatiana essentially alone. Little music was composed for the Duel, and all of it is non-developmental: a three-bar motif on page 10 of the autographed score to be "repeated as often as necessary," followed by a note to recapitulate "measures 12–20" from p. 5, which accompany the loneliest moment of Tatiana's letter scene.

The most musical stage direction of the Duel Fragment is the last, after Lensky lies dead in the snow: "Both in space and in the music, the symphony of the snowstorm [*simfoniia metelya*] grows." Blizzard symbolism is common in the folklore of the Russian north as well as in Pushkin's writings. In its folkloric guise, blizzards represent demonic or unclean forces that intervene to separate lovers. Lovers are tested in storms, and those who survive are invariably transformed. These three scenes (Nameday, Dream, and Duel) contain more of the texture of folk life and fairytale than does Pushkin's novel. As part of this rustification, Krzhizhanovsky inserts one of Pushkin's own verse fairytales directly into the playscript, recited and referred to by characters on stage. And he deploys another fairytale plot, more archaic and pagan, as a concealed subtext to the entire play. Both tales are associated with Tatiana's favorite season — winter — and relate intimately to solar, lunar, and seasonal cycles. To this cluster of symbols we now turn.

### The heart of winter

Pushkin's favorite time of year was autumn. In *Eugene Onegin,* he tilts this season toward winter. Our cue comes from the Narrator's comment about the heroine in chapter 5, iv, 1–4: "Tatiana, Russian in her heart of hearts / (Herself not knowing why) / With its cold beauty / Loved the Russian winter..." *Herself not knowing why*: this unconscious affinity between Tatiana and the darkest — and whitest — season sits at the core of the play. Krzhizhanovsky amplifies Pushkin's cue and moves as many events as possible to winter, when organic life and the sun's heat are in abeyance. Winter is the year's Night. The dead of night [*glukhaya noch'*] is a time of obstacles and revelations: Tatiana writing her love letter, or her stumbling through snowdrifts on the way to Onegin in her dream. Nothing of significance in the play happens under the unimpeded glare of high noon.

Snow, short days, and filtered, frosty winter light are means for connecting reality, daydream, and night dream. Thus liminal times and spaces are highly marked as psychological thresholds. People loiter in doorways, dance through apertures from light into dark (the dark being downstage, closest to the audience), and gaze through windows at the rising or setting moon.

The traditional concept of a dramatic scene—stirring verbal or musical closure followed by the lowering of a curtain—gives way in the Fragment to a principle akin to cinemagraphic montage: patches of action framed by a change in lighting. Overall, the temperature of the fourteen Fragments is cold. But frost and snow do not imply negativity or a drive toward death. Krzhizhanovsky is inspired by native Russian climate and geography—by the darker, waning seasons and their diurnal equivalents, the edges of the day. He even appears to have structured his dramatic action around them. Evidence for this is his four-page typescript signed "S. K." from 1936, titled *A Calendar for Onegin* [*Kalendar' Onegina*].[35]

The *Calendar* provides a glimpse into the playwright's approach to time in all its parameters: chronological, biological, cyclical, seasonal, daily, finally folkloric. In this early schema the play is still organized by scenes, of which there are eighteen. Each page contains three columns, the first labeled "Year" [*God*], the second "Time of the Year" [or season, *Vremia goda*], the third "Time of the day" [*Vremia dnia*]. The "Year" places the fictional Onegin within real Russian history, a common exercise for academic Pushkinists (Onegin was born 1796, entered society 1812, inherited his uncle's estate 1820, and so forth). The "Season" column includes such entries as "overcast December day," "January," "Winter, before Shrovetide." Times of the day contain meteorologically precise details, such as the desired slant of light: Scene 1, for example, specifies "Morning. Sun at a 30° angle to the earth." Many scenes emphasize the descent of the solar arc: "Even closer to sunset" (scene 3), "thickening twilight" (scene 4), "the lengthening twilight of a shortened autumn day" (scene 7), "that hour when both stars and candles are lit" (scene 10), "a premonition of evening" (scene 13). From this preliminary plan, it appears that Krzhizhanovsky visualized the stage set primarily in terms of light and shadow. Only the Prologue to the play, Pushkin's verse dialogue "Conversation of a Bookseller with a Poet" is exempt, perhaps as a tribute to the timelessness of literary art.[36] For "Year"

---

35  "*Kalendar' Onegina*." RGALI f. 1929, op. 3. ed. khr. 253. In her work on the 1936 *Onegin* project, N. Litvinenko discusses this document at length but attributes it to Tairov ("Nesygrannyi spektakl'," in *Rezhissyorskoe iskusstvo A. Ya. Tairova*, ed. K. L. Rudnitskii [Moscow: Vseros. teatral'noye ob-vo, 1987], 112–30, esp. 121-23), despite Perelmuter's attempts to correct her. In her later work on this production, after SK had achieved a degree of visibility in the 1990s, Litvinenko expands his role (N. Litvinenko, "Vspomnim Sigizmunda Krzhizhanovskogo—deyatelya teatra i teatral'nogo kritika," *Mnemozina* [Moscow: Éditorial URSS, 2000], 2:350–73).

36  SK's prologue has precedent in the publishing history of its source; Pushkin wrote his verse dialogue «Разговор книгопродавца с поэтом» in September 1824 and published it as a Preface to the first chapter of *Evgenii Onegin* in 1825.

we read: "All dates from all centuries crowd together on the bookshelves." And for "Season": "The twilight illumination of book-stacks [*knigokhranilishche*], which is identical at all times of the year." Of the eighteen scenes, two take place in spring, five in late summer, three in autumn, and eight in winter.

Krzhizhanovsky teased cold weather out of every possible Pushkinian detail. Consider the epigraph to Pushkin's chapter 1, which consists of one opaque line: "And one rushes to live and hastens to feel." In his essay on Pushkin's epigraphs, Krzhizhanovsky cites its source, Prince Vyazemsky's 1819 lyric "First Snow" ["Pervyi sneg"] and suggests why this wintry subtext might have won out over other candidates as the epigraphic portal to the novel (the competition included a quote by Edmund Burke and two lines from Baratynsky's influential 1816 poem, *Feasts* [*Piry*]).[37] "First Snow" is a buoyant, celebratory poem. In Vyazemsky's larger poetic context, Krzhizhanovsky notes, the need to live and feel "has an entirely different emotional filling" (393).

During the first snowfall or first serious drop in temperature, one values life more and is most receptive to sensation. In Russia, with its huge expanse and isolated hamlets, there is also a practical engineering aspect: when roads freeze over, what was an unpaved, unpassable morass of mud during intermediate seasons of thaw again becomes a swift and efficient means of travel. In Fragment 10, while visiting Onegin's library, Tatiana recites Pushkin's homage to late November. Roads open up, horses exult and sledges speed by, tossing up powdery snow. In Fragment 11 of the play, where Vyazemsky is first brought to life as a speaking character, close attention is given to the state of Russian roads, a topic of concern both to this poet and to Pushkin, his real-life friend. Vyazemsky even recites to a spellbound Moscow salon several stanzas from his own 1829 poem "The Station" ["Stantsiia"] on the potholes, bedbugs, and broken-down bridges that plague the Russian traveler, and on the utopian grid of highways that he predicts (with heavy irony) an "enlightened Russia" will eventually, in several centuries, construct. Unpaved roads are obstacle courses. But frost and crystalline snow open up lines of communication. The cold connects people and fate — whereas Spring softens the ground; the world sinks, slows down, simultaneously sprouts and decays. The dramatic *Eugene Onegin* contains few of the happy thaws or buddings that are characteristic of love stories. Everything always threatens to be "frozen out." But we cannot call this a calamity. Krzhizhanovsky associates fidelity (in friendship and in love) with the wintry season.

---

[37]   "Iskusstvo epigrafa [Pushkin]," *SK:Ss* 4, 393–94.

Beginning with Part Two (Fragment 6), the presence of late autumn and winter becomes overwhelming. Onegin, who is overall a poor reader of the seasons and a bad regulator of his own body heat, interrupts his contemplation of Tatiana's letter with a memory of beauties he had known in Petersburg, "unapproachable, / Cold, pure as winter, / Unpersuadable, unbribable, / Incomprehensible." He is touched by Tatiana's spontaneous flare-up and resolves to cool it down kindly, in brotherly fashion. At this point Lensky enters, shaking from his overcoat a "powdery-thin layer of the first dusting of snow." By Fragment 7 we are already deep into winter and its rituals; confirming the season, Krzhizhanovsky and Prokofiev add Yuletide Mummers to Tatiana's Nameday. Fragment 8, the Dream, opens on a pursuit through snowdrifts. Here ice and snow present obstacles, not a sleek smooth road, but that is required by the Dream, which must test its inhabitants as well as reveal their deepest desire. Fragment 9, the Duel, continues to test with winter at its worst, a blizzard. "The sort of weather," we read in a startling moment of subjectivity for a stage direction, "when one wants either to kill, or be killed, as soon as possible." A "symphony of the snowstorm" rises up to buttress the first stirrings of repentance in Onegin as he stands over the dead body of his friend.

In the novel, Pushkin does not specifically foreground the season of Tatiana's visit to Onegin's abandoned manor house (chapter 7). It nevertheless seems to be summer: a river flows by peacefully, beetles hum, fisherman's fires light up the twilight. The equivalent scene in the play, Fragment 10, is emphatically transposed to winter. Tatiana enters in cape and mittens; the windows of the manor are "blind, piled high with snow." Her love-smitten gesture of breathing on a cool windowpane and tracing in the mist an entwined "O" and "E" becomes more fraught in the heightened wintry context of the play (in the novel, Chapter Three, xxxvii: 9–14, she traces on the pane in late summer). The dramatic Tatiana, bundled up against the cold, first etches those initials on a hoarfrost-encrusted window in Onegin's library. About to leave, she remembers them, but frost is not mere mist from a breath. She rubs at the pane; "the frozen letters won't give way." Ice, it would appear, endures; it takes and holds the imprint of the heart. Finally a glint of the cold setting sun breaks through a thinned-out patch. Tatiana gazes out, bids farewell to her rural life, and leaves for home — her declaration of love still visibly intact on the windowpane. We next see her in Fragment 11, entering her Moscow aunt's room, bundled up against the cold and enveloped in frosty steaming air. Only after two servants proceed to "unwrap" her do the guests, Vyazemsky and an unnamed

General, realize that under that shapeless cocoon of rabbit-skin and furs, the slender contour of a girl is emerging. The General is captivated by the scene. He twirls his moustache, tugs on his uniform to straighten it, and by the next Fragment has become Tatiana's husband. This seasonal symbolism, so partial to Winter, culminates in the final Fragment 14, when the married Princess Tatiana receives an unexpected early morning visit from Onegin. To understand this scene, however, we must consider the two wintry fairytales that structure Tatiana's consciousness in the play.

The most lengthy of Krzhizhanovsky's interpolations to his *Eugene Onegin* is Pushkin's "Fairytale about the Dead Tsarevna and the Seven Knights" [«Сказка о мертвой царевне и о семи богатырях»], composed by the poet in 1833. Several familiar folktale elements feed into its plot, a variant on the Grimm Brothers' "Snowdrop" [*Schneeweisschen*] or the pan-European "Snow White." There is an evil stepmother, a magic mirror on the wall that knows which woman in the kingdom is the fairest of all, seven brothers / dwarfs, a poisoned apple, a sleeping beauty, and a kindly Sun, Moon, and Wind that help Tsarevich Yelisey find his bewitched bride. The "dead tsarevna" of the title is at first confusing, since the *tsarevna* [daughter of a tsar, the romantic heroine] falls into a bewitched trance but does not in fact die. In the pre-story, however, her mother the *tsaritsa* [wife of a tsar] dies in childbirth. It is this prior, fatal maternal segment that Krzhizhanovsky gives to the Nurse to recite to her distraught and excited young charge in Fragment 5, the Letter Scene, in hopes of distracting her from the calamitous impact of her first love.[38] (At this point in Pushkin's novel, we recall, the Nurse relates at Tatiana's bidding not a folktale but whatever pale, de-romanticized details she can remember of her own courtship and marriage.) The opening 24-line stanza of Pushkin's *skazka* contains several Tatiana-like elements attached to the fairytale bride-mother. The tsaritsa bids farewell to her tsar, who sets out on the road. She sits down at the window and stares out at the field night and day, from morning till night. Although a raging blizzard hurts her eyes, she does not lift her gaze from the white landscape. Nine months pass. The tsaritsa gives birth to a daughter at the precise moment of her husband's return. The new mother does not survive her rapture at seeing him, and dies.

---

[38] Just how much of Pushkin's Snow-White story is retold varies in different versions of the playscript. In the first revision translated in the Prokofiev volume, only the prologue is recited; a subsequent revision, however, includes a segment from the "mirror, mirror on the wall" episode, with lines about the tsaritsa's birthing and death crossed out; in that same revision, the proposed replacement ("God awards the tsaritsa a daughter") is also crossed out. RGALI f. 2579, op. 1, ed. khr. 2054, p. 15.

We are expected to know the rest of Pushkin's tale. The tsar grieves, of course, but a year passes like an empty dream [*kak son pustoi*] and he remarries. The new tsaritsa is proud, jealous, beautiful, the inevitable stepmother-witch — and her dowry includes a magic mirror. Meanwhile, the orphaned tsarevna grows up and is affianced to Prince Yelisey. Hearing from her mirror that her stepdaughter (and not herself) is now the fairest in the land, the evil stepmother sends a servant into the forest with instructions to bind the young tsarevna to a tree, where she will be gnawed to death by wolves. The tsarevna successfully entreats the servant to release her. Once freed, she wanders the forest until she comes across a hut that is home to seven knights. She enters, cleans it up, and falls asleep. When the seven brothers return, they invite her to stay with them. In rapid time, of course, all seven fall in love with her, which promises some fraternal tension. The eldest asks her openly to choose one of them. The others, he promises, "will somehow reconcile themselves to it . . . / But why are you shaking your head? / Are you refusing us? / Or are the goods not to the taste of the merchant?" The tsarevna answers that for her, all seven are equally bold and intelligent, equally her dear brothers, but that she's already affianced: "I love you all sincerely / But I'm given to another / for all time . . ." The seven brothers receive this unexpected news silently, scratch the back of their heads, apologize for having asked, quietly back out of the room, and the eight continue to live as before. The story resumes only when the evil stepmother arranges the delivery of a poisoned apple, triggering the tsarevna's death-like trance and the return of the Prince.

The body of the fairy-tale, then, produces the mandated happy ending. The maiden who is "given to another / for all time" is a transparent (pre-marital) echo of Tatiana's final words to Onegin: "But I am given to another, / And shall be true to him forever." Prince Yelisey appears, albeit only as a name, at several points in the playscript, the first time uttered by Onegin himself in ironic repartee with Lensky. But ultimately it is not the returning tsarevich Yelisey who carries the wisdom of the tale. With good reason, the Nurse in Fragment 5 delivers only the "pre-story" of the *skazka*, those nine months before the birth of the heroine. Its themes are worth noting. Immobility, patient waiting, and loyalty are fertile. If and when the absent beloved actually returns, the reward is death. The cycle of love and blossoming, if it occurs at all, belongs only to the second (female) generation. These motifs provide a clue to a deeper narrative subtext governing Krzhizhanovsky's *Eugene Onegin*.

Only in one phrase does the playwright allude to this subtext directly, although several tiny details in the initial stage directions of the final

Fragment reinforce this allusion. It would seem that Tatiana's fairytale model is not Cinderella. It is not even Prince Yelisey waking up his Sleeping Beauty. In keeping with Winter, her favorite season and the setting for all major episodes in her story, Tatiana most resembles the heroine in the Russian pagan myth "The Snow Maiden" [*Snegurochka*], a plot well-known in dramatic and operatic repertory. One of Krzhizhanovsky's favorite playwrights, Alexander Ostrovsky, wrote a folklore fantasy-play called *Snegurochka* in 1873, upon which Rimsky-Korsakov based his opera of the same name in 1881. That work was Prokofiev's favorite of all Rimsky-Korsakov's operas. A happy ending is not relevant to it. Like most cosmological parables, "The Snow Maiden" serves necessity, not personal satisfaction. Here is that myth.

Grandfather Frost and Spring the Fair have a daughter. Their marriage is a difficult one, for each spouse answers for a different season, they must be true to their respective realms, and both are protective of their child. As a young girl the Snow Maiden was always icy-cold and pure, but now that she is on the brink of womanhood, the Sun God Yarilo places in her heart the Fire of Love — which, if acted upon, threatens to melt her. Snegurochka knows this, but she is, after all, a young girl; she will be in love. By the final act, the Maiden, now engaged to the mortal Mizgir, awaits her mother at dawn. Spring rises from the lake, covered with flowers; this is her last day on earth for this yearly cycle, because Yarilo will usher in Summer. She counsels her daughter to hide in the forest shadows and conceal her love from Yarilo-Sun, who will not take kindly to it. But the impatient Mizgir rushes in and begs the Tsar's blessing on their marriage. At that moment the Sun breaks through the summer mist. When its rays fall on Snegurochka, she melts away; in despair, Mizgir throws himself into the lake. But the Sun's Holiday is not dimmed by this dual sacrifice. With Snegurochka's death, Frost loses its power over Spring and fertility returns to the earth. In this painful cosmic ritual, the breaking-through of the winter sun's rays is a turning point.

Krzhizhanovsky provides two moments of "chilly sun-rays breaking through" on Tatiana: first in Fragment 10, Onegin's Library, and then again on Princess Tatiana in Fragment 14, set (according to the *Calendar*) in a blustering, misty Petersburg April. In the first episode, Tatiana gazes out on the snowy fields. In the second, she pulls the blinds against intruding rays of the sun. The final scene of the playscript appears to be a hybrid of three texts: Pushkin's novel, and then these two interwoven fairytales. In this final confrontation of the would-be lovers, the poet's lines remain intact and its famous stanzas are recited in their entirety. Within that familiar frame, however, Princess Tatiana, smiling, recalls the first four lines of the "fairytale about Yelisey" with which she had prompted her Nurse in Fragment 5 (the tsarevna's lines: "But I'm given to another…"). After pulling the blinds, she enters into "folklore time," surrounding herself — or protecting herself — with a magic circle of keepsakes linked to her life in the country. Only in this shadowy fairytale space can she can manipulate both objects and time, turning things into rhythmic pulses and then into dreams. In the spirit of her long past girlhood, Tatiana prepares herself for the arrival of her beloved — or perhaps she conjures him up. For at just that moment Onegin himself rushes in, like Mizgir, begging her for the warmth that he knows — or needs to believe — she still feels for him, and seeking in her now the traces of that needy girl who, long ago, wrote the letter. But the Cinderella-tsarevna plot now competes with "Snegurochka," where the stakes for all parties are immeasurably higher. Support for the structural importance of this pagan folktale is found in Krzhizhanovsky's *Calendar for Onegin*, scene 17 (what will become Fragment 14 in the play, its final episode). On pp. 3–4, the following detail was entered under the column "Season": "an early northern 'Snegurochka' spring" [*rannyaya severnaya snegurochkina vesna*]. We are in the winter-spring transition that melts snow maidens.

Thus Krzhizhanovsky's *Eugene Onegin* emerges as a new fairytale about Yelisey, a new Snow White. The abandoned tsaritsa staring out the window at the snow will die upon the return of her beloved. Prince Yelisey is the Onegin who comes back but cannot claim his bride. And as Snegurochka, Tatiana is not structured to experience passionate reciprocal love in the present. She may crave it, but her wintry heart will not survive it. Her loyalty — to her husband and also to the memory of unrequited love — is essential to her, not for her happiness but for her survival. According to this economy, Tatiana will have ultimate agency to control and to remember, but not to spend.

### How to end a love story

In Pushkin's *Eugene Onegin*, the love story ends abruptly. The Narrator cuts it off. Blessed is he, we read, who can take leave of life without having drained its cup, without having read the novel to the end, who can cut off an event before it is over, "as I with my Onegin do." Tatiana and Onegin do not touch; they do not really even converse. Tchaikovsky could not endure such a deeply unoperatic denouement. In some versions and productions of his opera, the lovers actually embrace — to the intense discomfort of the Pushkin purists. Embrace or no, the end of Tchaikovsky's opera presents us with the traditional eighteenth-century choice between love and duty. True love, the realm of fairytale, lies with the smitten Onegin; duty, the realm of necessity, lies with Princess Tatiana.

In Krzhizhanovsky's play, matters are much less clear. The two are brought together — Onegin bursts in on his "former Tania" — but not as Tchaikovsky brings them together, in the shared heat of a love duet. In the play, for all that it is a palpable acted play, the gaps in pace and timing between Tatiana and Onegin are even exaggerated.[39] Unlike the final scene in Pushkin, Onegin speaks. But in reality he is reading. He immediately begins reciting to Tatiana his own letter, still unacknowledged: "I can predict everything…" But she has seen it already from within her magic circle of keepsakes, and he is too late. Their final dialogue is not a dialogue in this world. As she speaks to him, he reads to her, in a reciprocal exchange of fateful but frozen statements. Her husband the General never appears and is not a factor. Amid the furniture of her noble caste, Tatiana lives out her fairytale ending and departs, almost floats, "stepping among the flat flowers of the ottoman meadow." There is no reason to believe that the two ever make eye contact. Onegin stands silently, head bowed. On the threshold of the door he meets the Poet — he had appeared in the Prologue, and then reappeared on the misty Neva waterfront in Fragment 13 — who lets him pass and then speaks the Narrator's final words with his back to the audience and his face to the open door. Each dances out a different exit into a different dark space, where some form of art — for her a fairytale, for him a written poem — is available to them out of their dreams and memories. They are not quite fantasized figures, but facilitated by fantasy. In this variation on Pushkin's ending we see an element of Shakespeare as Krzhizhanovsky understood

---

[39]   In an essay from 1935 on endings in Shakespeare's plays, SK makes a curious observation. Comedies tend to feature the delayed, clumsy hero who arrives too late, he notes. At the last minute, however, Shakespeare will compensate the comic hero by accelerating his learning curve and allowing him to grasp the meaning of what has passed him by. A tragic hero, on the other hand, rushes ahead of his time, impatient, and events in his life speed up as they approach their denouement: swords fly, blindings proliferate, revelation piles on revelation. Shakespeare will ultimately slow his tragic hero down, permitting those who witness his death (on stage and in the audience) sufficient time to catch up with him and learn the lessons he has to share. Throughout the *Onegin* story, arguably it is the hero who has been more comic, the heroine more tragic. But neither death nor marriage consummates the plot; she ends up taking herself out of time, and he has no choice but to withdraw. As romance, the plot is "hinged" to a piece of furniture and then suspended — like the other ritualistic or cyclic rhythms so prominent in the play. See "Kontsovki shekspirovskikh p'yes," in *SK:Ss* 4:285–94, esp. 291.

his dynamic. "Shakespeare set himself the most difficult technical task," he wrote; "to force waking life to slide along with the speed of a dream, but in such a way that this hyper-real speed does not burst the bonds between real-life phenomena, does not cast them away into dream."[40] Krzhizhanovsky supplies a "Shakespearean" pacing to this phantasmagorical final encounter between Tatiana and her first love.

On the face of it, the love story is a failure. But it need not be performed in that spirit. Onegin has regained the depth and poetic inspiration that, in the Prologue, he had boasted of losing. «Зачем поэту / Тревожить сердца тяжкий сон?», he had complained bitterly to the Bookseller. «Бесплодно память мучит он» ["Why should the poet disturb the deep dream (*tyazhkii son*) of the heart? He torments memory fruitlessly…" II.129–32]. Now the hero, tormented by memory, has woken up to that deep and fruitful dream. Tatiana remains faithful to winter, her patron season. Each has become the necessary Muse for the other.

What of Prokofiev? There is no music designated for the end of this final Fragment. Perhaps the composer did not get to it, or perhaps he intended silence. But it is tempting to see, in the strange non-corporeal dance that unites and then gently separates Tatiana and Onegin, a hint of the ballet *Romeo and Juliet* as Prokofiev composed it in 1935 and hoped it would be produced. In his version of Shakespeare's story, romantic leads do not die; it is not a tragedy. Nor do they survive to marry in this world, for this world appears to fall away; it is not a comedy. Some other system of harmonies transcending both is at work, as the music of their youth returns in the pellucid score. Tatiana departs in the same unearthly way. She, like Juliet, has become a young maiden again, now that the seasons have changed. "The flowers on their spiral steel stems almost do not feel the touch of her feet." Surely Prokofiev believed that such an ending is not a Dance of Death, but of Life.

---

[40] "Komediografiia Shekspira" [1930s], concluding the subsection "Son letnei nochi i son v vechnoi nochi" [Midsummer Night's Dream and the Dream of Eternal Night], *SK:ss* 4:175–76. Krzhizhanovsky adds (174): "A dream [*snovidenie*] is the *only instance when we perceive our thoughts as if they were external facts.*"

# IN CONCLUSION

There is a fault line running through this material, I now realize, which might be addressed at the final inch in a tiny wrap-up gesture. To buttress my thesis about "Tatiana" — a recurring image in these pages — I argue that her potential as Muse is wedded firmly to the *form* of Pushkin's novel-in-verse. She is recognizably a young girl in love, of course, but her fate cannot be wept over, glorified, or moralized upon as if it belonged to the sentimental heroines who preceded her or to the vigorous, autonomous female personalities of the Realist period. Fictive persons are nurtured within chronotopes: the result not only of a chosen type of time and space but also of formal constraints. Tear them out of their native fabric and they cannot cohere.

And yet the single most insistent message arising from the body of essays collected here suggests the opposite. Themes, people, intentions, even dreams prove to be robust, flexible, endlessly transposable with all manner of new wisdom revealed in the process. Tchaikovsky, Krzhizhanovsky, and Prokofiev did not "violate" Tatiana but enhanced her, providing her with new points of view on herself from without. Pushkin's original is in no way weakened by these operations. The long answer to this paradox of fidelity and growth doubtless lies somewhere in the alchemy of Bakhtinian dialogue. But the short answer is more intuitive than theoretical, and lies at the base of most work in the humanities. The creative author or artist has an intent and strives to express it fully. This expression belongs to the artist — who will suffer keenly when it cannot be delivered in its proper form to the outside world, for any reason: censorship, inadequate performance, or the natural disasters of revolution, displacement, and decay. But fortunately, art as expression is only half the equation. There is also art as communication, and here the gifted artist is always more than the sum of a biographical fate. Someone else picks the artwork up, even if it isn't exactly what the artist intended to drop and even if the artist would have wished it otherwise. Ownership is no longer an issue. What matters now is mobilizing new talent around an aesthetically structured thing. This energy keeps an artifact in the realm of the living.

# INDEX

## A

Asaf'ev, Boris Vladimirovich: 280-82; 294 n. 53; 298-99; 344-45; 349.

Asafiev, Boris Vladimirovich (see Asaf'ev).

## B

Bach, Johann Sebastian: 88; 322.

Bakhtin, Mikhail Mikhailovich: xi; xiv; xvi-xxi; xxiii-xxvi; 1-96; 111; 133; 162; 167-72; 174-75; 192; 194; 198; 203; 205; 212-14; 219 n. 1; 225; 231; 233-34; 252; 268; 383; 416.

*Art and Answerability*: 13 n. 14; 42-52; 59 n. 9.

Carnival: xvi n. 7; xvii-xix; xxiii n. 27; xxv-xxvi; 3; 20; 29; 30-41; 43; 48; 50-51; 53-73; 85; 95; 162-87; 335; 380.

Chronotope: 41; 60; 66-67; 416.

Dialogism (dialogic): xii; xvii; xix; xxv; 3-29; 38-40; 43; 47; 51; 64; 79-80; 85; 87-90; 205 n. 10; 315; 330.

Double-voicedness: xii-xiii; 5; 7; 13; 188; 205 n. 10; 321.

Heteroglossia: 6; 88.

Monologism (monologic): 5; 9-10; 12; 16; 23-25; 29; 47; 93 n. 24; 212; 233.

Polyphony (polyphonic): xvi-xviii; 3-29; 30; 32; 39-40; 43; 63; 67 n. 18; 74; 78-79; 84-91; 203; 205; 213; 225; 227; 230-34; 335.

*Problems of Dostoevsky's Poetics*: 8; 10; 14; 17 n. 19; 40; 70 n. 22; 89 n. 20; 91 n. 23; 205 n. 10; 213-14.

*Rabelais and His World* (the Rabelais book, *Rabelais in the History of Realism*): xviii; xxvi; 30-40; 43 n. 2; 62; 63 n. 14; 70; 73; 91-92; 168; 170; 172.

*Toward a Philosophy of the Act*: 42-52.

Belinskii, Vissarion Grigorievich (see Belinsky).

Belinsky, Vissarion Grigorievich: 134; 153; 156; 169; 373.

Binyon, Timothy John: 99-108; 109-10; 112-14; 117-18; 120-21; 126-29.

Bocharov, Sergei G.: 6; 43 n. 2; 56 n. 5; 81; 99-100; 109-13; 114; 117-19; 121; 126; 129.

Brodsky, Joseph: 225-28; 234.

Byron, Lord George Gordon (Byronic): xix; 108; 111; 136; 147; 150; 152; 179; 394; 396 n. 25.

*Don Juan*: 143-44; 325.

## C

Čapek, Karel: 224-25; 228.

Chaliapin, Fyodor Ivanovich: 321; 327; 331; 333.

Chekhov, Anton Pavlovich: xiv; xx; 69; 115; 117; 120; 130; 166; 208; 226; 241; 248; 249-60; 342; 377; 392-93; 396.

"About Love": 250; 257-59.

"Anna Round the Neck": xx; 250-55; 256.

"Boring Story, A": 249.

"Bride, The": 251.

"Calamity, A": xx; 252-54; 256.

"Dama s sobačkoj" (see "Lady with the Little Dog, The").

"Duel, The": 251.

"In One's Own Corner": 392.

*Ivanov*: 392.

"Lady with a Pet Dog" (see "Lady with the Little Dog, The").

"Lady with the Little Dog, The": xx; 208 n. 14; 250; 256-57.

"Neščast'e" (see "Calamity, A").

"Nevesta" (see "Bride, The")

"O ljubvi" (see "About Love").

"Peasants": 250.

*Seagull*: 248; 392.

"Skučnaja istorija" (see "Boring Story, A").

"Ward No. 6": 250; 392.

Clayton, J. Douglas: 137-39; 149 n. 29; 155; 157; 166-67.

Conrad, Joseph: 11; 223; 228.

Cui, Cesar:  xxii; 303; 314-15; 318-19; 326-32.
  *Angelo*: 327 n. 19.
  *Feast in Time of Plague, A*:  xxii; 313; 318; 327; 329-30; 335.
  "Influence of Pushkin on Our Composers and on Their Vocal Style, The":  331.
  "Statue at Tsarskoe selo": 327 n. 19.
  *William Ratcliffe*: 327 n. 19.

### D

Dargomyzhsky, Alexander:  xxii; 162; 314; 316-21; 323; 325-29.
  *Stone Guest, The*:  xxii; 313; 316-21; 323; 326; 329; 335.
Diaghilev, Sergei Pavlovich:  276 n. 13; 295; 301.
Dolinin, Alexander A.:  159.
Dostoevsky, Fyodor Mikhailovich:  xi; xiv; xvi; xxi; 3-11; 13-22; 23-29; 36; 38; 40; 43; 58; 60; 63; 65; 67 n. 18; 69-72; 80; 82; 87-92; 134; 158; 160; 192-95; 198-99; 202-09; 211-14; 215-22; 223-34; 237; 260 n. 6; 308; 338; 342; 343; 383.
  *Brothers Karamazov, The*:  6; 7; 23 n. 29; 70; 71 n. 23; 88; 90; 134; 174; 218; 219; 220; 221; 224; 342.
  *Crime and Punishment*:  9; 16; 21; 25-27; 88; 218-20; 223 n. 1; 225; 227.
  *Demons*:  14; 16 n. 18; 19; 204; 208; 231 n. 11; 232; 342; 343.
  *Devils* (see *Demons*).
  *Idiot, The*:  9; 15; 16 n. 18; 29; 70; 207; 208; 209; 211-12; 219; 226-30; 233.
  *Notes from the House of the Dead*: 9; 14.
  *Notes from Underground*: 8-9; 16; 208; 237.
  *Possessed, The* (see *Demons*).
Dunning, Chester:  162; 184.

### E

Epstein, Mikhail:  22.
Evdokimova, Svetlana:  179; 184; 313.

### F

Fomichev, Sergei:  167; 171-72; 175.

### G

Ginzburg, Lydia.  16-18; 25; 80 n. 8.

Glinka, Mikhail Ivanovich:  264; 283 n. 33; 316; 338; 340.
Gogol, Nikolai Vasilievich:  22; 34 n. 40; 36; 69; 130; 154; 166; 206; 248; 251; 266; 272; 317; 342-43; 345; 351; 394 n. 24; 402.
  *Dead Souls*:  153.
  *Government Inspector*:  166; 248; 345.
  *Inspector General* (see *Government Inspector*).
  *Marriage*:  266; 272; 317.
  "Nose, The":  343; 352
  "Sorochintsy Fair":  266; 272.
Golenishchev-Kutuzov, Count Arseny:  267; 274 n. 11; 278; 279 n. 25.
Greenleaf, Monika:  185.
Gregg, Richard A.:  135 n. 5; 136-37; 143 n. 19; 150-51.

### H

Hasty, Olga Peters:  161; 307; 349 n. 15.
Holquist, Michael:  xi; 9 n. 9; 13 n. 14; 42; 44; 59 n. 9; 66 n. 18; 87; 198 n. 4.

### K

Karamzin, Nikolai:  xxii; 103; 121; 173; 175; 177; 183; 273.
  *History of the Russian State*:  xxii; 183 n. 29; 273.
Kiui, Cesar (See "Cesar Cui").
Krzhizhanovsky, Sigizmund:  xi-xii; xxii; xxiv-xxvi; 162; 188-91; 364; 375-77; 378-90; 391-415; 416.
  "Bookmark":  382 n. 4.
  *Calendar for Onegin, A*:  407; 412; 413.
  *Eugene Onegin*:  xxiv; 188; 364; 375-77; 378-90; 391-415.
  *Fairytales for Wunderkinder*:  384.
  *First Men in the Moon, The*:  380.
  "Fragments on Shakespeare":  398 n. 28.
  "Frater Vertius":  390.
  "Kant's Skull":  390.
  *Letter-Killers' Club*:  380.
  *Man Who Was Thursday, The:  A Nightmare*: 386.
  *Memories of the Future*:  379; 380 n. 1.
  "*Onegin*, Stanza by Stanza" (see "Stanza by Stanza through *Onegin*").
  "Postmark: Moscow":  381.

*Priest and the Lieutenant, The*: 384.
"Quadraturin": 380; 383 n. 7.
*Return of Münchhausen, The*: 379.
"Side Branch": 382 n. 4.
"Stanza by Stanza through *Onegin*": 386; 404 n. 34.
"Stitches": 382 n. 4; 395.
*That Third One*: 378.
"Theatrical Stage Direction, The (A Fragment)": 392-94.
*Unbitten Elbow, The*: 384.
*What Men Die By*: 388.
Kuchkist (see "Mighty Handful").
Kundera, Milan: 90-91 n. 22; 223-34.
*Art of the Novel, The*: 91 n. 22; 225; 232-33.
*Immortality*: 228-30.
"Jacques and His Master": 225.
*Joke, The*: 227; 230.
*Testaments Betrayed*: 90-91 n. 22; 230-31.
Kustodiev, Boris Mikhailovich: 347-53; 355; 358.

L

Leskov, Nikolai Semyonovich: xxii; 343; 346-50; 352-53; 356-61.
*Lady Macbeth of Mtsensk District*: xxii; 342-61.
"Levsha": 350 n. 18.
Lotman, Yurii Mikhailovich: 93; 113; 145 n. 24; 147 n. 26; 153 n. 35; 169-70; 174.

M

Mamontov, Savva Ivanovich: 321; 325; 331-32.
Meyerhold, Vsevolod Emilevich: xxii; xxiv; 162; 188; 238; 343; 345; 362-68; 373-76; 378; 383.
Mighty Handful: xxii; 264; 267; 284; 303; 318-19; 321; 325-28; 331; 334.
Mirsky, D. S.: 114; 206; 307.
Moguchaia Kuchka (see "Mighty Handful").
Morson, Gary Saul: 8 n. 6; 15; 23 n. 29; 39 n. 49; 62; 197; 215; 219; 258-59; 300 n. 65.
Mozart, Wolfgang Amadeus: 103; 311; 319; 322-26; 332.

Musorgsky, Modest Petrovich: xiv; xxii-xxiii; 162; 163-64; 188; 248; 263-68; 269-300; 301-02; 307; 313-15; 317-18; 321; 326; 332; 353; 364.
*Boris Godunov*: xi; xxii; 162; 163-64; 188; 248; 266; 269-75; 283; 289; 297; 307; 313-14; 332; 335; 364.
*Khovanshchina*: xxii-xxiii; 266-67; 269-300; 353; 359.
"Little Star": 266.
*Marriage*: 266; 272; 288; 317; 326.
*Songs and Dances of Death*: 278; 298; 299; 315.
*Sorichintsy Fair*: 266-67.
*Sunless*: 278; 298.

N

Nabokov, Vladimir: 129; 132; 135 n. 5; 150; 159; 207-08; 223; 228 n. 8; 402.
*Eugene Onegin* (trans.): 150 n. 31.
*Lolita*: 159.

O

Oldani, Robert: 270 n. 3, n. 4; 278 n. 22; 279 n. 25; 300 n. 65.

P

Prokofiev, Sergei Sergeievich: xi; xxii; xxiv; 162; 188; 269; 329 n. 24; 337-41; 362; 363-67; 369; 374-76; 377-91; 393-97; 399; 401-03; 409; 410 n. 38; 412; 415-16.
*Cinderella*: 365.
*Eugene Onegin*: 378-90; 391.
*Gambler, The*: 338.
*Ivan the Terrible, Part II* (dir. Eisenstein): 365.
*Romeo and Juliet*: 415.
*Semyon Kotko*: 365.
*War and Peace*: 337-41.
Pushkin, Alexander Sergeievich: xiv; xix-xx; xxii-xv; 50; 52; 80; 99-131; 132-61; 162-87; 188-91; 206; 221; 229; 238; 254; 271-75; 281-82; 284; 289294 n. 53; 297; 304-12; 313-36; 343; 358; 361; 362-77; 378-90; 391-415; 416.
*Boris Godunov*: xiv; xxii; xxiv; 104; 111; 130; 162-87; 188-91; 238; 271-72; 284; 295; 297; 362-77; 378; 392.

*Bronze Horseman, The*: 101; 187.

*Captain's Daughter, The*: 112; 177; 179.

"Conversation of a Bookseller with a Poet": 407; 415.

*Covetous Knight, The*: xxii; 313; 330; 332; 335.

"Epistle to Del'vig": 390 n. 22.

*Eugene Onegin*: xix; xxii; xxiv; 111; 132-61; 180; 187; 188; 240; 249; 304-08; 308-12; 314; 320; 344; 358; 359; 364; 373; 375-77; 378-90; 391-415.

"Fairytale about the Dead Tsarevna and the Seven Knights": 410-13.

*Feast in Time of Plague, A*: xxii; 313; 318; 327.

*Mozart and Salieri*: xxii; 313-14; 322-23; 330; 332; 335; 364.

*Poltava*: 179; 187.

"Queen of Spades, The": xx; 101; 187; 320; 364.

*Ruslan and Liudmila*: 103; 110; 187; 404 n. 34.

"Squire's Daughter, The" (see "Young Lady-Peasant, The").

"Station, The": 408.

*Stone Guest, The*: xxii; 313; 325; 326; 335.

"Young Lady-Peasant, The": 149.


R

Rachmaninoff, Sergei Vasilievich: xxii; 314; 321; 330-34.

*Covetous Knight, The*: xxii; 330; 332; 335.

Radishchev, Alexander Nikolaevich: 180.

Raskolnikov, Feliks: 100; 130-31; 330 n. 25.

Richards, I. A.: 140 n. 13; 141; 142.

Rimsky-Korsakov, Nikolai: xxii; 164; 264; 269; 270; 276-77; 279; 283; 285; 292-95; 314-15; 316; 318; 321-28; 331; 333; 412.

*Legend of the Invisible City of Kitezh and the Maiden Fevroniya, The*: 285.

*Mozart and Salieri*: 321-27.

*Pskovitianka*: 295.


S

Sandler, Stephanie: 101 n. 1; 143 n. 22; 237 n. 2; 375 n. 4.

Santayana, George: 140.

Serov, Alexander Nikolaevich: 264; 266-67.

*Rogneda*: 264.

Shakespeare, William: xi; xiv; xxv-xxvi; 37; 43 n. 2; 55 n. 4; 65; 68; 72; 89 n. 19; 102; 163-67; 169; 172; 181; 185 n. 32; 188; 189; 192; 199-202; 211; 222; 235; 240-48; 268; 333; 357; 359-60; 362; 378; 379; 383-85; 387-89; 392-93; 398; 414-15.

*All's Well that Ends Well*: 72; 245.

*Antony and Cleopatra*: 378.

*Hamlet*: 37; 163; 245; 380; 390.

*Henry V*: 245.

*Henry VIII*: 184.

*King John*: 245.

*King Lear*: 37; 163; 199-201; 243-46; 387.

*Macbeth*: 37; 163; 245; 347.

*Measure for Measure*: 72; 163; 245.

*Titus Andronicus*: 245.

Shaw, Bernard: xxv; 192; 200; 201; 244 n. 9; 378; 379; 385; 387-88.

*Caesar and Cleopatra*: 378.

Shaw, J. Thomas: 138 n. 10; 153-54; 186 n. 34; 318 n. 8.

Shklovsky, Viktor Borisovich: 135 n. 5; 233; 368.

Shostakovich, Dmitry Dmitrievich: xxii; 276; 295; 342-61.

"Four Verses of Captain Lebyadkin": 342; 343.

*Lady Macbeth of Mtsensk District*: 342-61.

*Nose, The*: 342; 343-46; 348; 352-53; 356.

"Satires": 343.

Siniavsky, Andrei Donatovich: 114; 132; 133; 165; 167.

Stasov, Vladimir Vasilievich: 163; 202; 265; 267; 270 n. 5; 271; 277; 281 n. 28; 290; 292 n. 49; 296; 298-99; 302; 303; 353.

Steiner, George: 192-214.

Surat, Irina: 100; 109-14; 117; 118; 119; 121; 126; 129.


T

Taruskin, Richard: 263; 265-68; 272; 278 n. 22; 295 n. 54; 300 n. 65; 316 n. 4; 318; 319 n. 10; 326 n. 16; 327 n. 19; 329 n. 22; 356-57.

Tchaikovsky, Peter Ilyich: xxii; 134; 288 n. 41; 303; 304-08; 308-12; 314; 319-22; 328; 332; 338; 344; 358; 364; 377; 401; 404; 413-14; 416.
   *Eugene Onegin*: 304-08; 308-12; 344; 358; 364; 377.
   *Queen of Spades, The*: 304; 314; 320.
   Tertz, Abram (see Siniavsky, Andrei Donatovich).
Todd, William Mills III: 138.
Tolstoy, Lev (Leo) Nikolaevich: xi; xiv; xxxi; 4; 6; 11; 14; 16-17; 41; 49; 70-71; 80; 100; 114; 120; 144; 153; 192-202; 205-15; 215-22; 228 n. 8; 235-39; 240-48; 249-60; 302; 308; 337-41; 342; 388.
   *Anna Karenina*: 70; 208; 219; 229; 249-60.
   "Death of Ivan Ilych": 207; 208 n. 14
   *Kreutzer Sonata, The*: 207; 211; 242 n. 5; 250; 340.
   *Power of Darkness, The*: 245-48.
   "On Religion": 258.
   *Resurrection*: 252.
   "On War": 258.
   *War and Peace*: 197; 199; 209; 245; 337-41; 359.
   *What Is Art?*: 199-200; 258.
   "What Men Live By": 388.
Tsvetaeva, Marina Ivanovna: 117; 126; 153; 342; 343.

Turgenev, Ivan Sergeyevich: xxii; 102; 120; 144; 166; 251; 257; 319-20; 359; 361.
Tynianov, Yuri Nikolaevich: 95 n. 29; 132; 153 n. 37; 160.
Tynyanov, Yuri Nikolaevich (see Tynianov, Yuri Nikolaevich).
Tyrkova-Vil'iams, Ariadna: 100; 114-29.
Tyrkova-Williams, Ariadna (see Tyrkova-Vil'iams, Ariadna).

### U
Uspensky, Boris Andreyevich: 93; 170; 174; 383 n. 5.

### V
Vinokur, Grigory Osipovich: 129-30; 172-73.
Voltaire (Francois Marie Arouet): 119; 120-21; 180; 186; 200.
Vygotsky, Lev Semyonovich: 22; 144-45.

### W
Wagner, Richard: 271; 283; 300; 316-17; 331-35; 340.
   *Parsifal*: 332.
   *Ring, The*: 332.

### Z
Zamyatin, Evgeny Ivanovich: 39; 348-53; 355; 361; 380; 382.
   "Rus'": 348-53; 355; 361.
   *We*: 39.

Lightning Source UK Ltd.
Milton Keynes UK
UKOW031935070412

190258UK00002B/3/P